DANTE AND THE
A MODERN

C000130535

Leading scholar Albert Russell Ascoli traces the metamorphosis of Dante Alighieri – minor Florentine aristocrat, political activist and exile, amateur philosopher and theologian, daring experimental poet – into Dante, author of the *Divine Comedy* and perhaps the most self-consciously "authoritative" cultural figure in the Western canon. This is the first comprehensive introduction to Dante's evolving, transformative relationship to medieval ideas of authorship and authority from the early *Vita Nuova*, through the unfinished treatises, *The Banquet* and *On Vernacular Eloquence*, to the works of his maturity, *Monarchy* and the *Divine Comedy*. Ascoli reveals how Dante anticipates modern notions of personalized, creative authorship and the phenomenon of "Renaissance self-fashioning." Unusually, the book examines Dante's career as a whole, offering an important new point of access not only to the Dantean *oeuvre*, but also to the history and theory of authorship in the larger Italian and European traditions.

ALBERT RUSSELL ASCOLI is Gladys Arata Terrill Distinguished Professor in the Department of Italian Studies at the University of California, Berkeley.

DANTE AND THE MAKING OF A MODERN AUTHOR

BY

ALBERT RUSSELL ASCOLI

CAMBRIDGE
UNIVERSITY PRESS

CAMBRIDGE UNIVERSITY PRESS

Cambridge, New York, Melbourne, Madrid, Cape Town, Singapore,
São Paulo, Delhi, Tokyo, Mexico City

Cambridge University Press
The Edinburgh Building, Cambridge CB2 8RU, UK

Published in the United States of America by Cambridge University Press, New York

www.cambridge.org
Information on this title: www.cambridge.org/9780521178440

First published 2008
First paperback edition 2010
Reprinted with corrections 2011

Printed in the United Kingdom at the University Press, Cambridge

A catalogue record for this publication is available from the British Library

ISBN 978-0-521-88236-1 Hardback
ISBN 978-0-521-17844-0 Paperback

For Barbara

Contents

Preface

When describing a big book in a short title, it seems important, as *Virgilio* instructs his pupil after the brusque hail of Farinata degli Uberti, that "le parole tue fien conte" ([you] make your words count; *Inf.* 10.39). For this reason, to adapt Mary McCarthy's renowned *mot*, each constituent part of the phrase "Dante and the Making of a Modern Author" has plural meanings, including "and," "the," "of" and "a." Let me begin with the least of these, the vowel-word, "a." The besetting temptation of single author studies, and those of Dante above all, is to turn one's object into *the* pivot around which history – literary, intellectual, and otherwise – turns. And while I would not wish to underestimate the transformative powers of the Dantean *oeuvre*, nonetheless I would also insist that, my occasional lapses into hyperbole notwithstanding, it represents neither the only way of construing modern authorship nor the only route for arriving at that complex cultural phenomenon. Rather, the ensemble of works known as "Dante" is a symptom, a case – a particular product of and participant in ongoing historical processes – neither an origin nor an end in itself.

Which brings me to the question of "modernity." There is no doubt that I am interested here in highlighting the relation between Dante and established scholarly discourses which posit a break between pre-modern and modern, not to say post-modern, modes of authorship – and of discovering how Dante may be said to anticipate – to crystallize if not to invent – traits associated with authorial modernity in the Western tradition. At the same time, however, I am deeply suspicious of the reifications and periodizations of modernity. Rather, I tend to see the "modern" as paradoxically perennial, as a vacant placeholder through which the relation of present to past is continuously construed and lived. *Modernus*, after all, comes from classical Latin, and *moderno* turns up four times in the *Commedia*. Finally, I will argue, what should concern us most is Dante's own sense of his modernity, that is, his status as a living writer faced with an *a priori* exclusion from the normative, authoritative categories of medieval *auctor*-hood, notably from the ranks of the long-dead classical *auctores* (Virgil, Aristotle, *et al.*), and from the "closed book" of the Bible to whose canonized truths neither jot nor tittle may legitimately be added.

At the center of this study, as, more or less, of the title, is the word-concept "making." The *frase fatta* calqued here suggests the process by which Dante became a, if not *the*, modern author: the use of the present participle emphasizing a mobility and a dynamism within that process. Already at this stage, however, there is an ambivalence: who, or what, made Dante into a modern "author"? His place within a complex social and discursive history? His own efforts and his consequent development over the course of a career of some thirty years of writing? Critical narratives which portray him as such, including my own? There is, however, a second sense at play in this word: that is, Dante's continuous, if evolving, understanding of his authorship as an activity of "making," at once the artisinal mastery of the *techne* of poetry (and, more broadly, the disciplines of rhetoric, philosophy, and theology) and an *imitatio* of the Divine Maker, the Author of all authors, the origin of every legitimate authority. In this sense my book strives to unpack Dante's compact definition of a poem as "fictio rethorica musicaque poita" ("a fictive invention [a made object] composed poetically with the aid of rhetoric and music"; *DVE* 2.4.2), along with his etymological derivation of "autore" [author] from *avieo* to mean a "binder of words," a maker of languages and of poems. I seek to understand him, then, as a *fabricator* of *fictions*, though in a sense not opposed, but neutral to "truth."

I will leave it to my gentle reader to perform an analogous operation on "the," "and," and "of," whose specific polysemies, in any case, follow directly from those just presented. As for the Alpha and Omega of my title, "Dante" and "Author," suffice it to say here that both have plural referents (the properness of the former name notwithstanding), and that the next seven chapters are aimed at proving just this point.

This is long book – no doubt about it – that took too long to write. Its genesis can be traced to my graduate years at Cornell in the late seventies and early eighties, although it first began to assume written form in a 1989 essay composed and published with the warm encouragement of Walter Stephens and Kevin Brownlee. In the interim, I have incurred any number of debts, direct and indirect, some of which, I fear, have been lost or deformed in the vagrant book of memory. Much of what this study has become is owed to wonderfully lucky intersections between collegiality and friendship. I cannot, for example, begin to acknowledge or to calculate the effects produced by the mentorship of Leonard Barkan and Tilde Sankovitch during my years at Northwestern. Nor can I tell fully how much the overlapping interests and intersecting passions first of Tom Stillinger and then, and now, of Ron Martinez have contributed to shaping and reshaping the ideas, and to uncovering the "facts," that drive this study. To these have been added, at crucial moments, the generosity and rigor of David Quint; the high scholarly standards and warm hospitality of Ted Cachey; the intellectual energy and collegiality of Zyg Barański; the formidable example and kind encouragements of Teo Barolini; the amicable, astute provocations of Robert Durling; the elegant, inimitable teachings of John Freccero. Among my Berkeley colleagues I owe special thanks to the intellectual comradeship of Louise George Clubb, David Hult, Timothy Hampton, Victoria Kahn, Ignacio Navarrete, Loren Partridge, Mary Ann Smart, and Randolph Starn.

If I now fall to list-making, it is not because those mentioned do not deserve to be singled out, each in her or his own way, but because, to specify the gifts received, the salutary challenges posed, the knowledge conferred (and, of course, the errors corrected and infelicities kindly overlooked) during twenty-some years would become a chapter itself. My thanks then go to Craig Berry, Howard Bloch, Lina Bolzoni, Steven Botterill, Terry Butler, James Carolan, Anthony Cassell, Gary Cestaro, Alison Cornish, Rita Copeland, Jonathan Culler, John Dagenais, Charles Till Davis, Frederick De Armas, Nancy Vine Durling, Carla Freccero, Lisa Freinkel, Disa Gambera, Susan Gaylard, Mary Gaylord, Paul Gehl, Simon Gilson, Stephen Greenblatt, Jody Greene, Steven Grossvogel, Ralph Hexter, Robert Hollander, Olivia Holmes, Amilcare Iannucci, Katherine Ibbett, Rachel Jacoff, Constance Jordan, Carol Kaske, Christopher Kleinhenz, Seth Lerer, Robert Lerner, Toby Levers, Ottfried Lieberknecht, Larry Lipking, Dennis Looney, Joe Lowenstein, Manuela Marchesini, Herbert Marks, John Marino, John Martin, Maria Luisa Meneghetti, Maria Rosa Menocal, Alastair Minnis, Mario Moroni, Gary Saul Morson, Martin Mueller, Ed Muir, John Najemy, Franca Nardelli, Annabel Patterson, Daria Perocco, Armando Petrucci, David Posner, Regina Psaki, Lisa Regan, Mary Beth Rose, Albert Rossi, Manuel Rota, Marco Ruffini, Myriam Swennen Ruthenberg, Natasha Sankovitch, Anne-Marie Sankovitch, Brenda Deen Schildgen, Cesare Segre, Phyllis Silverstein, Tom Simpson, Janet Smarr, Barbara Spackman, Paul Stasi, Ruggiero Stefanini, Justin Steinberg,

Donatella Stocchi-Perucchio, Marvin Trachtenberg, Mario Trovato, Jane Tylus, Nancy Vickers, David Wallace, Barbara Watts, Jobst Welge, Will West, Ronald Witt, Paul Wright, Michael Wyatt, Irene Zanini, and Sergio Zatti.

Over the last few years it has been my great good fortune to have worked with a series of exceptionally able research assistants. Of these I would particularly mention Jamie De Angelis, who saw the manuscript to press, and Aileen Feng, who built its index. To Kathryn (Kasey) Evans, whose keen and wise eye scanned every page of an advanced draft of this book, I owe very special thanks. I also owe a significant debt to the fine editorial and production staff of Cambridge University Press, beginning with Linda Bree, and to the two anonymous readers of the manuscript. Finally, I wish to acknowledge, belatedly, and through the hazy filter of my own lengthening career as pedagogue and pedant, a few teachers whose lessons changed me, or rather, helped me change myself, into the person who wrote this book. These include Mary Lacey, Morris Parslow, U. Milo Kauffman, Michael Mullin, Angelina Pietrangeli, Ezio Raimondi, and Thomas M. Greene. At the end of this list of i.o.u.s is its true beginning, Giuseppe Mazzotta, *incipit* and *sine quo non* of *Dante and the Making of a Modern Author*. I do not know how to thank him.

The research and writing of this book were carried out while I was employed first by Northwestern University and then by the University of California, Berkeley, both of which generously afforded me precious leave time for the project on more than one occasion. I am deeply indebted to the Newberry Library (1985–86, 1989–90) and the American Academy in Rome (2004–05) for the use of research facilities while in residence. The following grants also contributed significantly to moving the research and writing forward, however gradually: an Exxon Fellowship at the Newberry Library (1985–6); an ACLS Recent Recipient of the Ph.D. Fellowship (Spring 1986); an NEH Senior Fellowship (1989–90); a Northwestern Humanities Center Senior Fellowship (1993–94); three University of California, Berkeley Humanities Research Fellowships (Fall 1999, Fall 2001, Fall 2004) and, finally, the Paul Mellon-NEH Rome Prize at the American Academy in Rome (2004–05). Earlier versions of some of the materials incorporated into this study have appeared in print elsewhere. In particular, Chapter 2 derives from "The Vowels of Authority (Dante's *Convivio* IV.vi.3–4)," which appeared first in Kevin Brownlee and Walter Stephens (eds.), *Discourses of Authority in Medieval and Renaissance Literature*, Hanover NH: University Press of New England, 1989, pp. 23–46.

A substantial portion of Chapter 3 is revised from "'Neminem ante nos':
Historicity and Authority in the *De vulgari eloquentia*," originally pub-
lished in *Annali d'Italianistica* 8 (1991) 186–231. Finally, Chapter 6 and a
small portion of Chapter 7 revise "Palinode and History in the Oeuvre of
Dante," from Theodore Cachey (ed.), *Dante Now: Current Trends in Dante
Studies*, South Bend IN: University of Notre Dame Press, 1995, pp. 155–86.
I thank all of the original publishers for permission to reprint here.

Abbreviations of primary texts and translations

(These works are cited throughout from the following editions and with the abbreviations given in the left margin. My occasional emendations are indicated by brackets. Where no translation is indicated, translations are my own. Italics in translations, unless otherwise noted, reflect my emphasis.)

WORKS OF DANTE ALIGHIERI

CV *Convivio.* In *Opere minori*, vol. 1, part 2. Eds. Cesare Vasoli and Domenico De Robertis. Milan and Naples: Ricciardi, 1988. *The Banquet.* Trans. and introd. Christopher Ryan. Stanford, CA: Anma Libri, 1989.

DC *La Commedia secondo l'antica vulgata.* Ed. Giorgio Petrocchi. Turin: Einaudi, 1975

Inf. *Inferno.* Volume 1 of *The Divine Comedy of Dante Alighieri.* 3 vols. Ed. and trans. Robert M. Durling; comm. Robert M. Durling and Ronald L. Martinez; illus. Robert Turner. Oxford and New York: Oxford University Press, 1996.

Purg. *Purgatorio.* Volume 2 of *The Divine Comedy of Dante Alighieri*, 3 vols. Ed. and trans. Robert M. Durling; comm. Robert M. Durling and Ronald L. Martinez; illus. Robert Turner. Oxford and New York: Oxford University Press, 2003.

Par. *Paradiso.* Volume 3 of *The Divine Comedy of Dante Alighieri*, 3 vols. Ed. and trans. Robert M. Durling; comm. Robert M. Durling and Ronald L. Martinez; illus. Robert Turner. Forthcoming Oxford and New York: Oxford University Press. Consulted in manuscript.

DVE *De Vulgari Eloquentia.* Eds. Pier Vincenzo Mengaldo. In Dante Alighieri. *Opere minori*, vol. 2. Eds. Pier Vincenzo Mengaldo *et al.* Milan and Naples: Ricciardi, 1979.

De Vulgari Eloquentia. Ed. and trans. Steven Botterill. Cambridge: Cambridge University Press.

ECG *Epistola XIII* [*Epistola a Cangrande*]. Eds. Arsenio Frugoni and Giorgio Brugnoli. In Dante Alighieri. *Opere minori*, vol. 2. Eds. Pier Vincenzo Mengaldo *et al*. Milan and Naples: Ricciardi, 1979.

Ecl. "Le Egloghe." Ed. Enzo Cecchini. In Dante Alighieri. *Opere minori*, vol. 2. Eds. Pier Vincenzo Mengaldo *et al*. Milan and Naples: Ricciardi, 1979.

Philip Wicksteed and Edmund Gardner. *Dante and Giovanni del Virgilio: Including a Critical Edition of Dante's 'Ecloghae Latinae' and of the Poetic Remains of Giovanni del Virgilio*. Westminster: Constable, 1902.

Eps. *Epistole*. Arsenio Frugoni and Giorgio Brugnoli. In Dante Alighieri. *Opere minori*, vol. 2. Eds. Pier Vincenzo Mengaldo *et al*. Milan and Naples: Ricciardi, 1979.

MN *Monarchia*. Ed. Pier Giorgio Ricci. Vol. 5 in *Le opere di Dante Alighieri. Edizione nazionale a cura della Società dantesca Italiana*. Verona: Mondadori, 1965.

Monarchy. Trans. Prudence Shaw. Cambridge: Cambridge University Press, 1995.

[N.B.: references to book, chapter and paragraph are to the Ricci edition, from which the Shaw translation departs at one point. Ricci's chapter 10 of book 3 is divided by Shaw into two distinct chapters, with a break after Ricci's paragraph 17. As a consequence her chapters 12–16 in book 3 correspond to Ricci's chapters 11–15. Minor variations in chapter division appear in other editions as well.]

Q *Questio de aqua et terra*. Ed. Francesco Mazzoni. In Dante Alighieri. *Opere minori*, vol. 2. Eds. Pier Vincenzo Mengaldo *et al*. Milan and Naples: Ricciardi, 1979.

VN *Vita nova*. In Dante Alighieri. *Opere minori*, vol. 1, pt. 1. Eds. Domenico De Robertis and Gianfranco Contini. Milan and Naples: Ricciardi, 1984.

PRIMARY TEXTS CITED

Aen. Virgil. *Aeneid*. In *Eclogues. Georgics. Aeneid I–VI* and *Aeneid VII–XII*. Rev. edn. by G. P. Goold. Trans. H. Rushton

Fairclough. Volumes 63–64 of The Loeb Classical Library. Cambridge, MA: Harvard University Press, 1999–2000.

AP   Horace. "Ars poetica." In *Satires, Epistles and Ars poetica.* rev. ed. Trans. H. Rushton Fairclough. In Volume 194 of The Loeb Classical Library. Cambridge, MA: Harvard University Press, 1991. First published 1926.

CD   Aurelius Augustinus. *De civitate Dei.* Eds. Bernardus Dombart and Alphonsus Kalb. 2 vols. Volumes 47–48 of Corpus Christianorum. Series Latina. Turnholti: Brepols, 1955.

Conf.   Aurelius Augustinus. *Confessiones.* Ed. Lucas Verheijen. Volume 27 of Corpus Christianorum. Series Latina. Turnholti: Brepols, 1981.

Cons.   Manlius Severinus Boethius. *Consolatione philosophiae.* Ed. Ludovicus Bieler. Volume 94 of Corpus Christianorum. Series Latina. Turnholti: Brepols, 1957.
Boethius. *The Consolation of Philosophy.* Trans. V. E. Watts. Baltimore, MD: Penguin Books, 1969.

DDP   Dartmouth Dante Project (http://Dartmouth.Dante.edu). Director Robert Hollander.

DRM   Guido Vernani. *De Reprobationem Monarchie.* In Nevio Matteini, ed. *Il più antico oppositore politico di Dante: Guido Vernani da Rimini: Il testo critico del 'De Reprobationem Monarchie'.* Padua: CEDAM, 1958.
Guido Vernani. *The Refutation of the Monarchy.* Trans. in Anthony Cassell. *The 'Monarchia' Controversy.* Washington, D.C.: The Catholic University of America Press, 2004.

Etym.   Isidore of Seville. *Etymologiarum Sive Originum Libri XX.* 2 vols. Ed. W. M. Lindsay. Oxford: Clarendon, 1911.

MD   Uguccione da Pisa (Hugutio of Pisa). *Derivationes.* 2 vols. Ed. Enzo Cecchini. Florence: SISMEL Edizioni del Galluzzo, 2004.

Met.   Ovid. *Metamorphoses.* Trans. Frank Justus Miller. In Volumes 42–43 of The Loeb Classical Library. London: W. Heinemann, 1960–1964. First published 1915–16.

MP   Aristotle. *Metaphysics.* In *The Basic Works of Aristotle.* Ed. and trans. Richard McKeon. New York: Random House, 1941.

NE   Aristotle. *Nichomachean Ethics.* In *The Basic Works of Aristotle.* Ed. and trans. Richard McKeon. New York: Random House, 1941.

PL   *Patrilogiae Cursus Completus . . . Series Latina.* Ed. J-P. Migne. 221 vols. Paris: Garnier, 1844–64.

Pol.	Aristotle. *Politics*. In *The Basic Works of Aristotle*. Ed. and trans. Richard McKeon. New York: Random House, 1941.
RR	Guillaume de Loris and Jean de Meun. *Le Roman de la Rose*. 3 vols. Ed. Félix Lecoy. CFMA. Paris: Champion, 1965–70.
ST	Thomas Aquinas. *Summa Theologiae. Latin Text and English Translation, Introductions, Notes, Appendices, and Glossaries*. 60 vols. Cambridge: Blackfriars, 1964–1976.
Theb.	Publius Papinius Statius. *Thebaid, Books I–VII* and *Thebaid, Books VIII–XII*. Ed. and trans. D. R. Shackleton Bailey. In Volumes 207 and 498 of The Loeb Classical Library. Cambridge, MA: Harvard University Press, 2003.
Top.	Cicero. *Topica*. In *"De Inventione," "De Optimo Genere Oratorum," "Topica."* Trans. H. M. Hubbell. In the Loeb Classical Library. Cambridge, MA: Harvard University Press, 1949.

N.B., All other references in this text use the author-date system and refer to the bibliography to be found at the end of the volume. In general, series of three or fewer references without commentary are placed in parentheses within the body of the text. Longer series of references accompanied by discursive commentary are located in the footnotes.

Introduction

CHAPTER I

The author in history

Dante è un produttore di *auctoritates*. Culturalmente egli è un uomo del medio evo per il quale . . . la sentenza, il detto in cui si deposita la sapienza umana, è fonte di conoscenza non meno . . . che il ragionamento e l'esperienza diretta; salvo che, invece di limitarsi a incastonare e glossare detti memorabili . . . egli ne produce dei suoi, e conferisce lo stesso piglio legislativo a tutti i suoi enunciati.

(Contini 1965b: 76–7)

I. WHAT IS AN "*AUCTOR*"?

From the perspective of the first decade of the twenty-first century, more than seven hundred years after the fictive date in which the events recounted in the *Divina Commedia* take place, it seems obvious that no single work and no writer in the Western canon possesses more authority, in a generalized sense of widely-acknowledged cultural prestige and ideological weight, than do Dante Alighieri and the "poema sacro" ("holy poem"; *Par.* 25.1) he began not long after his exile from Florence in 1301 and finished shortly before his death at the age of fifty-six in 1321. No work is more central to the Western canon and the educational and cultural apparatus that still actively propounds it, notwithstanding numerous recent contestations; no author possesses more "cultural capital."[1] From shortly after Dante's death, and perhaps even while he was still alive, the *Commedia* was recognized as a classic, comparable to the great poems of antiquity in a way that no other vernacular work of his era was. The poem appeared in manuscript after manuscript accompanied by a rapidly growing number of learned commentaries in both Italian and Latin: a treatment no vernacular work had received previously in the Western tradition, and which – to my knowledge – no work of any kind, possibly excepting the Gospels, had ever

---

[1]   Bourdieu (e.g., 1994: 4–7 *et passim*); also Guillory 1993.

3

received within such a short time of its composition. Within fifty years, Dante's admirer and successor in the nascent vernacular tradition, Giovanni Boccaccio, was called to deliver public lectures on the poem in his and Dante's native Florence. An uninterrupted and ever expanding tradition of academic study and commentary has continued over the centuries, most thoroughly demonstrated and embodied by the vast resources of the Dartmouth Dante Project, with its compilation of seventy-three distinct Italian, English, and Latin commentaries to date.[2] Poets throughout Italy and all over Europe – for example, Boccaccio, Chaucer, and Christine de Pizan – were treating Dante as a poetic model, an *auctor* comparable to ancients such as Virgil and Ovid. Moreover, to read the *Commedia* is to know that Dante wished for this to occur and may well have hoped to be accorded authority greater than the pagan *auctores*, comparable, perhaps, to that of the fathers of the Church, or the human authors of the Bible.

Notwithstanding the apparent transparency of the question, looking at Dante's relationship with authority is a little like looking directly at the sun: despite the impression of the intensest illumination, one runs a very high risk of being blinded by what one sees, of losing track of the contingent nature and the complex causes of the object, even as one is confronted most directly by it. In other words, because Dante and the *Commedia* have "always already" possessed authority, for today's postmodern, postmillennial readers as for those who first read the poem, something very important has been lost from view. Specifically, whatever the final results may have been, it was not in any sense a given that Dante could hope to achieve authority in a late medieval culture that defined the term so as to exclude anyone like him *a priori* from laying claim to it, even as it was held up as the highest value to which a person might aspire.

What will concern us here, then, is how to historicize "authority" as a category in the conceptual repertoire of Dante's time and place, and as a word and a governing thought that figures crucially in his own understanding of himself as cultural operator and as poet.[3] To begin with, it is important

---

[2] To see the complete list, go to http://dartmouth.dante.edu and click on "index." On Trecento and Quattrocento commentaries see, *inter alia*, Barbi 1890; Mazzoni 1951, 1958, 1963, 1976–1978; Dionisotti 1965; Sandkühler 1967; Jenaro-MacLennan 1974; Vallone 1981; Barkan 1986: 163–70; Minnis *et al.* 1988 (chapter 10); Palmieri and Paolazzi 1991; Hollander 1993; Parker 1993, 1997; Barański 2001; S. Gilson 2005. Especially useful is the overview in Botterill 2005. See Baranski's cogent critique of recent scholarly use of these commentaries (2001: chapter 1), as well as Parker's apt assertion that "to read commentary is to move from a consideration of the *Divine Comedy* as a text to its use as a culture-bearing work – that is, as a social act with a variety of ramifications for successive social formations" (1997: 251). See Minnis, 2001: chapter 6, for a broad view of the emergence of vernacular commentary in Europe modeled on the Latin tradition. See also n 48.

[3] Others who have examined the categories of *auctor* and *auctoritas*, *autore* and *autorità*, in the Dantean *oeuvre* are: Mazzoni 1955; Mazzeo 1960; Nardi 1961; Dragonetti 1961b and c; Hollander 1969; Stabile

to acknowledge that medieval Latin *auctoritas* and early Italian *autorità do* overlap in significance with modern understandings of the terms. Authority was and still is a category through which an essential conjunction is posited between individual persons and impersonal sources of power and/or knowledge. To say, as Dante does, and as texts of the Middle Ages so often do, that, in a primary usage, derived from Greek *autentim* or *autentin, authority* is that quality which renders an *author* "worthy of faith and obedience" (*CV* 4.6.5), is to give an individual access to transpersonal and transhistorical "truth" – making his words worthy of *faith* – and to legitimated, and officially delimited, power – making his words worthy of *obedience*. This is not so far from what we think of today as the duly constituted authority of administrative and judicial officials or as the special credibility of certified experts, scientific and otherwise, in various fields of knowledge.

On the other hand, a world of difference separates medieval *auctoritas* from modern *authority*. There are striking differences of degree and emphasis in the way that authority is recognized and exercised: at least in theory, medieval *auctoritas* is far more rigidly hierarchical, far less subject to challenge if not exempt from it, far more liable to be asserted as grounded in an absolute order of Power and Knowledge deriving from the transcendent Deity. There are the evident differences between how the political and epistemological forms of authority are conferred: differences in the norms of political legitimation; differences between medieval science and modern, and so on. There are dramatic differences between the persons who might legitimately be eligible for or lay claim to authority. Moreover, as will appear in Chapter 2, the definition given above is only one of at least three etymologically-grounded meanings attributed to the word, not to speak of its dialectical twins, such as *actor*. Finally, in the medieval period there is a broad spectrum of cultural domains in which *authority* is a fundamental category, ranging from the poetic, through the philosophical and "scientific," to the institutional (especially the Empire and the Church), to the theological, which, in principle, subtends and comprehends all of the others, and mediates the intricate relationships, conceptual and practical, that exist among them. Both the lines that divide these distinct definitions and domains and the relations that connect them are significantly different from those now drawn.

To give one, by no means casual, example, the relationship of literary authorship to the other types of authority was generally conceived of by

1970; Mazzotta 1979; Gellrich 1985; Minnis *et al.* 1988: chapter 10 [written by David Wallace]; Minnis 1990; Stillinger 1992; Picone (e.g., 1993); Barański (e.g., 1996: 9; 1997a; 2005a); Coassin 1996; Botterill 1997; Levers 2002. My own earlier approaches to the question, here significantly revised, are in Ascoli 1989, 1991b, 1993, 1997, 2000a, 2003.

Dante and throughout the Middle Ages in a way quite alien to ours. In modern times, an *author* is a writer of texts in general and a writer of literary works in particular, and, especially in the latter case, is not an authority at all, except in the diffusely cultural-ideological sense specified above. In the Middle Ages an "author" (Latin *auctor* and *autor*; Italian *autore*) was not any old writer of literature, but was instead, and against the modern definition, a person who possessed *auctoritas*, and who might also have produced texts that were known as *auctoritates*. Thus, on the one hand, an *auctor* might not necessarily be primarily a writer at all, and, on the other, there is a restricted field of writers who qualify as *auctores*. More exactly, this dominant concept of authorship was in tension with an emerging, proto-modern usage of the word to refer to "any person who writes a book."[4] The question of how, and when, the medieval *auctor* began to look like the modern author, cogently raised by such very different contemporary scholars as Foucault (1968), Minnis (1984) and Chartier (1992), will turn out to be fundamental for thinking about Dante's concept of authorship.

Even more specifically, and as is well known, the dominant medieval idea of the *auctor*, literary and otherwise, is in sharp tension with modern concepts of individual creative personality. If authority was then, as now, a quality mediating between impersonal sources of power/knowledge and historical persons who put them into play, the stress in the earlier period, nonetheless, lay heavily on subordinating the individual to the transhistorical and impersonal, though in somewhat different ways depending upon the domain one wishes to consider. In literature, as in the various branches of philosophy, the fields most obviously relevant to Dante as writer,[5] the

---

[4] St. Bonaventure's commentary (Bonaventure 1934–64: vol. 1, chapter 12) on Peter Lombard's *Sententia* (*PL*, vol. 192, col. 519–950) distinguishes four ways in which a medieval person might participate in making a book: as *auctor*, *scriptor* (scribe; copyist), *compilator*, and *commentator* (translated in Minnis *et al.* 1988: 229). Bonaventure defines the *auctor* as the one who provides the principal materials from which a book is made. Compare Honorius of Autun's definition in *Expositio in Cantica Canticorum* – "quoque auctor libri, idest compositor" [*PL*, vol. 172, col. 348]). See also Stillinger's useful discussion of the Bonaventurian passage (1992: 1, 37–8); also Minnis 1984: 94–5.

[5] The question of the disciplinary standing of poetry is complex (see, e.g., Antonelli-Bianchini 1983; Minnis *et al.* 1988; Giunta 2002: especially 455–73; Minnis and Johnson eds. 2005), and depends to a significant extent in what context one views it. For Aquinas, writing in the name of theology poetry is "infima inter omnes doctrinas" (*ST* Ia.I., q.1, art. 9). In the school curriculum it was assigned to the first, though crucial, educational step, in the three liberal arts, grammar (Curtius 1948: 42–5 [see Chapter 3 for Dante on "gramatica"]). In the academic prologues (*accessus*) which frequently introduce the authoritative classical poets (see n 48), it is assigned to moral philosophy, aligning it with the epideictic rhetoric of praise and blame, in that it presents examples of morally-charged actions to be imitated or avoided. For the "ethical poetic" see Allen 1982; Minnis 1984: 23–7; Minnis *et al.* 1988; Carruthers 1990; Dagenais 1994; cf. Giunta 2002. The thirteenth and fourteenth centuries spawned a series of treatises on poetry, often drawing heavily on both the rhetorical works of Cicero and Pseudo-Cicero (*Rhetorica ad Herrenium*), as well as the *AP* of Horace (for Dante's debts to the

auctores consisted of a limited number of classical texts that had accrued cultural capital and with it the status of guarantors of truth and models for imitation over the centuries.[6] While authority of this kind was expressed through texts bearing the proper names of time-bound human beings – most notably for Dante, "Virgil" and "Aristotle" – the essential point was that these texts had been proven to have transcended the limitations of the inevitably fallible men who wrote them and to bear truths that exceeded the limitations of historical contingency – being valid in any time and any place. What is more, their validity was closely dependent upon the language in which they were encountered (even if they were originally written in Greek, Hebrew, or Aramaic), namely Latin, a language which is, as Dante himself says in both *Convivio* and *De Vulgari Eloquentia*, a *gramatica*, that is, shaped to resist the individual personalities and historical circumstances of its users.

On the other hand, institutional authority, whether political or ecclesiastical, *was* necessarily available to living persons, although by definition it was not conferred by individual merit or local historical circumstance, but rather transmitted from generation to generation by the transpersonal mechanisms of office and/or genealogy, an idea crystallized in Kantorowicz's formula of "the king's two bodies" (1957). Finally, there is the phenomenon of theological *auctoritas*, which in principle encompasses and determines all other forms of authority. Here, as Minnis reminds us, the paradigmatic case is that of the Bible with its dual authorship – the human "scribes" whose names are associated with individual books of the Testaments – and God, the ultimate *Auctor* not only of the Scriptures, but of its authors, and of the universe itself.[7] From this perspective, then, God is at the origin of

latter, see Chapter 3, n 4; Chapter 4, n 42; Chapter 7, nn 15, 157). These include Matthew of Vendôme, *Ars Versificatoria*; Geoffrey of Vinsauf, *Poetria Nova*; John of Garland, *Parisiana Poetria*, and so on (see Nencioni 1967). During the same period, poetry was increasingly aligned with philosophy more broadly speaking, including metaphysics (Curtius 1948: 203–13; Wetherbee 1972; Greenfield 1981; Minnis *et al.* 1988); as with theology itself (see n 48; Chapter 2, nn 67, 68, 71; Chapter 7, n 134). It was even linked at times to medicine (Olson 1982). Although Dante criticism has focused most of its attention on his alignment of poetry with philosophy (especially *CV*) and/or theology (especially the *DC*, and, if authentic, the *ECG*; see Chapter 7, n 124), in fact, Dante moves strategically among the full range of available discourses concerning poetry in the later Middle Ages (see Mazzotta 1993a: 7–12 *et passim*; also Chapter 2, nn 80, 83).

[6] On medieval notions of *auctor* and *auctoritas*, see Chenu 1927, 1950: especially 128–38; Hunt 1948; Quain 1945; Curtius 1948: especially 48–54, 57–61; Mazzeo 1960: 157–8; Stabile 1970; Minnis 1984 (especially 1–2, 10–12, 94–103, 156–8); Marenbon 1987: 9–10, 30–3, *et passim*; Minnis *et al.* 1988; Brownlee and Stephens 1989a; Stillinger 1992; Minnis and Johnson 2005.

[7] For the relation of human *auctores* to divine *Auctor*, the precedence of the latter over the former, see Augustine, *Conf.* 12.14–32, especially 18, 24–5, 30; Aquinas *ST* Ia, q.1, art. 8 (cf. Ia, q.1, art. 10, resp.). See Chenu 1950: 128, 138; Smalley 1952: 300; Minnis 1984: 36–9, 72–112, Minnis *et al.* 1988: 66–9, 75, 97, 197–200, 205, 241–2, *et passim*. See also n 52. For the topos of God as Author of both the Bible and Creation, see Chapter 2, n 87.

all human authority, whether over truth or over power, and the ultimate guarantor that it transcends the frailty of individual human beings and the contingencies of historical existence.[8]

What does this general scheme have to do with Dante Alighieri, late medieval poet, amateur philosopher, and sometime political activist, first of Florence, then from it? In the first instance, it reflects, though by no means completely or exactly, his own explicitly articulated views on what an *auctor* is and what *auctoritas* might consist of. In the entirety of Dante's canonical *oeuvre*, the Latin and Italian words for *author* and *authority* and their derivatives appear one hundred seventeen times – five more if the etymons *autentin* and *avieo* are included; one more if the *Epistle to Cangrande* is recognized as Dantean. When he uses these terms it is almost always to indicate one of the following fundamental cultural domains, in this order of frequency: (1) supreme institutional authorities, above all the temporal authority of the Emperor and the spiritual authority of the Pope; (2) canonical classical writers, especially philosophers and poets, especially *the* Philosopher, Aristotle, and Virgil; (3) poetic authorship taken in isolation; (4) God as supreme Author and Authority, and, in subordinate relationship thereto, the authority of the Bible and the Church fathers.[9] What this rough lexical scheme suggests is, first, that Dante valued *authority* as a quality with foundational applicability to the areas of experience that counted most in his culture and to him in particular, and that he returned to it at crucial moments over the course of his later career, especially in the major treatises. Second, it shows that his overt understanding of *auctoritas* was closely aligned with a typical medieval emphasis on its hierarchical and absolute nature: grounded in antiquity, legitimated institutional office, and/or

---

[8] Stillinger 1992: 20, 26–32, 74–6, *et passim*, maps the structures of textual authority onto the totalizing and hierarchical neo-platonic cosmos, the "great chain of being," as elaborated from the writings of St. Augustine and Dionysius the Areopagite and culminating in the ordered layout of the *sacra pagina* in Peter Lombard's commentary on the Psalms. While this is undoubtedly the primary conceptual framework for interpreting both textual and social orders in the Middle Ages, and while there is no doubt of its relevance to Dante (see, for example, Mazzeo 1960; Durling and Martinez 1990; cf. Schnapp 1991–92), it is not by itself sufficient to account for the complex discourse of medieval *auctoritas* in its various headings and subheadings or to explain the socio-historic forces guiding the articulation of that discourse in and around the times and places of Dante's writing. Stillinger recognizes resistances to the hierarchical-cosmological model authority both in Peter Lombard's book and in Dante's *VN* (especially 94–107).

[9] See also Stabile 1970; Ascoli 2000a. Of the one hundred twenty-three references mentioned, sixty-six are in *MN*; thirty-five in *CV*; nine in the *Eps.*, eight in *DVE*; five in the *DC*; none in other works. Of these, sixty-seven refer to institutional authorities with governing powers; thirty-seven refer to intellectual authority (primarily of classical authors); ten exclusively to poetic authorship; four to God as divine Author; two to Biblical authors; and three references are pre-definitional. (N.B., additional distinctions can and perhaps should be made; in some cases one reference indicates more than one type of authority, e.g., imperial and philosophical.)

extra-historical (i.e., divine) sponsorship. Indeed, as regards government he is one of the leading late medieval theorists of the absolute, hierarchical authority of the Emperor (see Chapter 5).

This survey shows immediately why Dante might find it difficult to attribute the role of *auctor* and the quality of *auctoritas* to himself and his works, despite his evident valorization of, and desire for, them. In his whole *oeuvre* he uses words for "authority" or "author" in relation to himself alone in only two isolated cases (*CV* 1.4.13; *Ep.* 3.2–3 [to Cino da Pistoia]), and there is only a small cluster of references in Book 2 of *De Vulgari Eloquentia* where he uses them in reference to modern poets, such as himself, as a class. Each of these exceptional cases will be discussed in due course. However, even this cursory description of what constituted *auctoritas* in the Middle Ages reveals that Dante and his works, especially the vernacular works, had limited or no access to the title and the quality he and his culture valued so highly. To the extent that a modern person *might* claim the prestigious title of *auctor*, Dante was poorly situated; he possessed none of the attributes that could help transform his own ambitions and visions into *auctoritas*: as a lay figure in a culture still dominated by clerics, a scion of a family on the fringes of the aristocracy, without the standing conferred by public office,[10] he had no claim whatsoever to institutionally derived authority.

As to literary authorship, the question is even clearer. By composing his major poetic works in the vernacular, he denied himself the intrinsic *auctoritas* of high Latin culture. More fundamentally, a modern, living individual with a distinctive personality like Dante's could not hope to claim that depersonalized *auctoritas* which belongs to the Biblical and classical *auctores*, all long dead, all part of an irretrievably distant past. Like all moderns, Dante was constitutively relegated to the role of belated *lector* of or *commentator* upon the true authors (see, e.g., Quain 1945: 225).

How, then, is one to square these two things? On the one hand are the historical circumstances, reflected throughout Dante's mature writings, which dictate that he had little or no claim to authority as it was understood in his culture. On the other is a tradition of reception that confers authority virtually without reserve, notably the vast array of commentaries that appeared almost immediately after the *Commedia* began to circulate, calling Dante an *autore* without hesitation and treating his work to much the same respectful glossing as had in the past been reserved for the Bible and the classical *auctores*. One must begin with the knowledge that, however

---

[10] Not forgetting his unfortunate two-month stint as Prior in 1301, I refer to the period of exile thereafter. For cogent reviews of Dante's involvement in Florentine politics, see Petrocchi 1983: chapters 7–9; Najemy 1993; Peters 1995; Scott 1996: 3–20, 2004: 309–36.

rigidly, ideally absolute, however much aimed at establishing a transhistor-ical, suprahistorical basis for knowledge and power, the phenomenon of *auctoritas* was a complex one in the later Middle Ages, and, in particular, was under transformative pressure from a series of intertwined histories, all of which in some way militated for a redefinition and reallocation of the quality so as to allow for the inclusion of new and different *auctores*, even moderns.

Most prominent among the historical trends in play,[11] as is well known, was the dramatic shift from a feudal culture based on hierarchy and inher-ited nobility to a commercial and monetary economy, most powerfully embodied by Dante's native Florence.[12] Along with this came the gradual opening of possibilities for lay, and even non-aristocratic, participation in a literate culture previously dominated by clergy, a trend favored not only by economic developments, but also by popularizing religious movements, especially Franciscanism in its more radical expressions. The same period saw the emergence in Italy and elsewhere of new forms of statehood and political participation: in Italy, the communes and *signorie*; in Europe more generally, the prototypes of the modern European nation-state (especially France under Philip the Fair).

In tandem with these economic, social, and political phenomena was the rapid development of the romance vernaculars – especially Occitan, Old French, Italian – into acknowledged languages of culture, capable of sustaining important literary productions. (In *Vita Nova*, chapter 25, Dante dates this from the mid-twelfth century, but in France it goes back further still.) Works in these languages increasingly modeled themselves upon and undertook to mediate high Latin philosophical–rhetorical–literary culture (Imbach 1996), whether through translations (Segre 1963b; Copeland 1991; Cornish 2000a, 2003), like Brunetto Latini's Italian Cicero, or a compendia of learning, like Jean de Meun's continuation of the *Roman de la Rose*,

[11] This digested account of political, economic, and social change draws on Davis 1957, 1984a; Tierney 1964; Waley 1969; Hyde 1973; Martines 1979; Najemy 1982, 1993; G. Holmes 1986; Imbach 1996: chapters 1–4; Durling and Martinez 1996: 3–24; Scott 1996, 2004.

[12] Dante's conflicted attitude toward proto-capitalist Florence, of which he is both product and critic, gives some indication of the dynamic complexities of the situation. On the one hand is his consistent condemnation of "la gente nuova e i subiti guadagni" (*Inf.* 16.73), that is, the new Florentine banking and mercantile class, and, on the other, the obsessive return to problems of monetary value – as in the rough equivalence established between suicide and the wasting of one's property in *Inf.* 13; as in the extension of the deadly sin of avarice to include its opposite, unrestrained generosity (prodigality) in *Inf.* 7 and *Purg.* 21; as in the elaborate metaphorics of coinage deployed throughout the *DC* (on this last, see Shoaf 1983; Ferrante 1984: chapter 6). For readings of the *DC* in terms of the economic world of late thirteenth century Florentine banking and mercantilism to which, for example, Dante's own father may have belonged in the specific capacity of usurer, see Noakes 1990, 2001, 2003; Steinberg 2007.

Latini's *Tesoretto* and *Trésor*, not to mention Dante's *Convivio*, or even the doctrinally sophisticated lyrics of Guinizelli, Cavalcanti, and, again, Dante. These developments in turn coincided with the emergence of new forms of manuscript and book culture, together with novel practices of writing and of reading, which were linked in particular to a growing legal-notarial professionalism and an increasingly literate mercantile class.[13]

Related and important changes were taking place within the domain of High Latin culture. As the work of Giuseppe Billanovich (1961), Roberto Weiss (1969) and, most recently, Ronald Witt (2000) has shown, a classicizing, secularizing humanism was taking root in the Northern Italian *signorie* from the mid-thirteenth century on, through figures such as Lovato Lovati, Albertino Mussato, not to mention Giovanni del Virgilio, with whom Dante would enter into epistolary conversation late in life (see Chapter 5, nn 7, 9; Ascoli 2009). Even in what might seem to be the best fortified bastion of the culture of philosophical and theological *auctoritas*, Scholasticism, a sea-change was under way. Both the institutions and the interpretive practices of clerical-scholastic culture had already undergone significant transformations during the twelfth century,[14] and evolved more rapidly and more radically over the course of the thirteenth. The rise of university education in the verbal arts, philosophy, and above all theology, in Paris, but also, nearer to hand in Bologna, at once reinforced and interrogated the standing of the *auctores*, as will be seen in Chapter 2, section ii.

In other words, against the basically static medieval definitions of authority and authorship, and the many deeply conservative tendencies of that culture, dynamic historical forces were at work that provided a contemporary writer of the late thirteenth and early fourteenth centuries, such as Dante, with the impetus and some of the resources to approach those categories creatively and transformatively. With this observation, we arrive at the basic project of this study: an exploration of how a culture in general, in the person of one of its most remarkable members, can engage in a distinctly conservative attempt to maintain and embody fundamental ideological categories, but still end up radically transfiguring those categories

---

[13] Overviews of the new forms of literary culture are in Antonelli and Bianchini 1983; Huot 1987; Cristaldi 1994: chapter 1 (vis-à-vis *VN*); Usher 1996; Botterill 1996b; Meneghetti 1992, 1997 (especially the remarkable bibliography: 235–66); Giunta 1998, 2002; Minnis and Johnson 2005. See also the classic studies of Auerbach (1941, 1958) and, for the Italian, Contini 1959. On manuscript and book culture, see Petrucci 1979, 1995; Ahern 1982, 1990; Antonelli and Bianchini 1983; Chartier 1992; Storey 1993; Holmes 2000; Steinberg 1999, 2007.

[14] For the importance of Chartrian Platonizing humanism, see Wetherbee 1972. For the twelfth-century Renaissance generally, see Haskins 1955; Benson and Constable 1982.

and that ideology. In the specific case of Dante, the (re-)assertion of medieval *auctoritas* paradoxically opens the way to a proto-modern notion of literary authorship, one which emerged gradually, inconsistently, between the thirteenth and the eighteenth centuries. Charting a broad set of thematic concerns and formal practices over the course of Dante's career as a writer will make possible a detailed account of the appropriation of the title of *auctor* for himself and the status of *auctoritates* for his works. It will reveal how Dante used a wide range of linguistic and conceptual resources available to him for such ends, and how he did so both implicitly and explicitly – at times with an apparent lack of any overt awareness, at others with declared intention. It will suggest, finally, just how dramatically Dante transformed the fundamental categories of the medieval culture of authority.

II. THE *AUTORE* OF THE *COMMEDIA*

> "Tu se' lo mio maestro e 'l mio autore,
> tu se' solo colui da cui io tolsi
> lo bello stilo che m'ha fatto onore"
>   (*Inf.* 1.85–87)

(You are my master and my author, you alone are he from whom I have taken the [lovely] style that has won me honor.)

In an important sense, the balance of this book constitutes a gloss on this, the best known and most prominent by far of Dante's uses of the language of *auctoritas* in his *oeuvre*, the phrase with which Dante-*personaggio* welcomes "Virgil," his spiritual guide and poetic master, onto the grand stage of the *Commedia*. For reasons that will soon appear, the most productive approach to this question is through a historically informed, rhetorically detailed reading of the prose and prosimetrum works of Dante, rather than via a frontal assault on the *Commedia* itself.[15] Nonetheless, it is hardly possible to undertake such a study without initially touching on the "sacrato poema" (consecrated poem; *Par.* 23.62). In the first place, this is because the *Commedia* provides an image of authority achieved around which the attempts of this sub-group of the *opere minori* to define and appropriate *auctoritas* organize themselves retrospectively and in the light of which

---

[15] Though not its principal aim, this book contributes to the project of reading the so-called minor works on their own terms and for their own sakes. A judicious discussion of this methodological problem is in Botterill 1996a: ix–xiii; cf. E. Gilson 1939: 83–5. See also Ascoli 1991b: 186–93, 1995; as well Chapter 6, section v. Inspiring precedents for this approach are Mengaldo's studies of *DVE* (1978a, 1979) and the work on the *rime petrose* cycle of Durling and Martinez (1990).

they must inevitably be understood – although not in the ideal teleological manner that much of the criticism, or Dante himself, would like us to believe (Barolini 1984: 29). And, in the second place, it is because, curiously, the *Commedia* constitutes by far the greatest obstacle to a truly historicized probing of these issues, by making Dante's poetic authority seem perfectly natural, or rather "naturally supernatural," and thus obscuring its complex, internally conflicted character. In other words, to arrive at the *auctoritas* he yearns for, as he will in the *Commedia*, Dante must necessarily conceal the contingent historical path that led him there. To begin to understand why and how this is so, we must look at the process by which the word *autore*, and all that it implies, is first brought into the poem, together with Virgil, the one human being of whom it is used in all the poem's one hundred cantos, including Dante himself.[16]

Anyone familiar with twentieth-century Dante criticism has an inkling of what the passage quoted above portends: an elaborate staging of Dante's relationship to Virgil, which at once betokens immense respect for the greatest of Latin poets and aims to appropriate and even to supersede Virgil's authority and that of the rest of the classical canon for Dante's language, his poem, and himself.[17] Curiously, however, the word *autore* itself, as well as the category of *autorità* (Latin *auctoritas*) on which its significance rests, has received relatively little commentary, a fact attributable primarily to Dante's success in naturalizing the concept and his relation to it. A widely accepted, and quite compelling, account of the function of this reference in the economy of the poem does exist, though it does not serve for Dante's *oeuvre* as a whole. As Robert Hollander first observed, the *Commedia's* five, carefully-positioned references to *autore* and *autorità* first evoke the classical *auctores* near the beginning of the poem, in the cited line from *Inferno* 1 and in the related encounter with the great antique poets in *Inferno* 4, especially line 113: "di grande autorità ne' loro sembianti" (with . . . great authority in their countenances). Then, near the poem's end, they refer instead to the higher authority of the human Biblical scribes (*Par.* 26.26, 47) and thence

---

[16] Alessio and Villa (1984) argue that the whole of the passage introducing Virgilio (67–87) is modeled on the *vita auctoris*, or biographical life of the *auctor*, as first laid down by Donatus in his late classical commentary on Virgil's *Aen.*, and draw as well on stylistic and other traits of the *accessus ad auctores* (n 48). Their evidence seems to me suggestive but incomplete.

[17] See especially Leo 1951; Hollander 1968, 1969, 1983a, 1983b, 1983c; Thompson 1974; Mazzotta 1979; Battaglia Ricci 1983: 154–5; Barolini 1984; Jacoff and Schnapp 1991; Iannucci 1993a. For critiques and/or modifications of this mode of understanding Dantean intertextuality vis-à-vis the classical *auctores*, see Brugnoli 1998; Shapiro 1998: especially chapter 4; 15–23; Parker 2000; Barański 2000: 10–13; Scott 2004: 178–81, 234–9. Classic resources for the Dante–Virgil relationship include: Comparetti 1872; Moore 1896: 168–97; Whitfield 1949; Nardi 1965b: 221–36. See also Chapter 5, n 15; Chapter 7, especially sections ii–iii.

to "la voce del verace *Autore*" (the voice of the truthful [or true] Author; 26.40), God, the absolute and transcendent Author of authors (Hollander 1968: 144–5; Barolini 1984: 268–9; cf. Mazzotta 1979: 256–9). Since the latter references come at the climax of Dante's successful passing of a tripartite doctrinal examination conducted by the apostles Peter, James, and John (Chapter 7, sections v–vi), and long after he had decisively supplanted his first "maestro e autore," the reader is left to infer that he now possesses an authority comparable to that of prophets and apostles, one which descends to him directly from God, and which thus removes him from the taint and contingency of historical, human authorship.

Such a *translatio auctoritatis* certainly occurs, despite the fact that Dante never overtly appropriates the title for himself, despite the historical and conceptual obstacles mentioned earlier, and despite the multiple and at times contradictory associations inherent to the word *autore*, which the classic account passes over in its exclusive focus on the poetry–theology, pagan–Christian axis of signification. So, again, what exactly does Dante-poet mean when he has Dante-pilgrim address his guide-to-be as "mio autore"? An educated, non-academic reader of the late twentieth century is likely to have one of two thoughts, or perhaps a conflation of both. In the first instance, the phrase appears to confirm the generalized modern perception of the Middle Ages as a hierarchical and authoritarian culture, one in which the "individual" was rigorously subordinated to narrow religious, political, and intellectual canons, although it might seem curious – as it often does to first-time readers of the poem – that the authority figure to whom Dante subjects himself is a pagan, rather than a Christian. In other words, it could be seen, paradoxically, as a personal expression of Dante's claim to membership in a depersonalized world. In the second instance, the phrase might suggest something very different, and apparently anachronistic, to a modern reader. If "author" is taken in its basic modern definition, the phrase means that Dante is simply calling himself a devoted reader of Virgil. From this point, and noting the augmentative sequence that leads from "teacher" to "author," we might go on to hypothesize that by virtue of this reading Dante has somehow, metaphorically, become Virgil's authorial creation, his work. In reading Virgil, he has been taught by Virgil ("tu sei lo mio maestro"), and that teaching has made him what he has now become ("e 'l mio autore").[18] This, in turn, would introduce an irony, one around which Virgil's presence in the *Commedia* continuously spirals: having "authored"

---

[18] See Stabile 1970: 455–6; Mazzotta 1979: 154–5; also Chapter 2, n 25.

Dante, Virgil himself has become a character in a book of which Dante is the author.

Anachronism? Not necessarily. For one thing, as will be seen later on, such a process can be accommodated within the medieval understanding of the intricate dialectic of *lector* and *auctor*, reading and writing. More immediately, Dante's culture had at least three, etymologically based, definitions of *auctor* to draw upon,[19] one of which – *auctor* from *augere*, "to augment or make grow" – though it does not imply original creation, does have conceptual traits in common with a modern notion of authorship:[20] Dante might not be wholly Virgil's "work" in medieval terms, but he could be attributing the mature elaboration of his poetic identity to Virgil and his poems. In fact, when it refers to the archetype of authorship, God, the "verace Autore," the word *does* have the capacity to include a wholly original and originating creativity – one to which Virgil's authorship is linked by comparison, albeit unfavorably (see Chapter 7).

Nonetheless, although Dante had access, and implicitly refers, to this meaning of *auctor* when he overtly discusses the word in the fourth book of his prosimetrum philosophical treatise, *Convivio* – the immediate predecessor of, and frequent source for, the *Commedia* – he does not use it explicitly, giving instead the other two available definitions, principally the derivation from *autentin* (4.6.5–8). *Autore* in this sense means, as noted earlier, a "persona degna di fede e obedienza" (a person worthy of faith and obedience) and Dante applies it to great philosophical and political authorities, Aristotle and the Holy Roman Emperor Frederick II, respectively. This definition has patent relevance for Dante's treatment of Virgil, since it supports a rigidly hierarchical concept of authority and is compatible with how Dante-pilgrim displays trust of and obedience to his *maestro* throughout their journey together. More specifically, Virgil, as spokesperson of classical

---

[19] For the etymological definitions of *auctor*, with examples, see Chenu 1927, 1950: especially 128–38; Stabile 1970; Minnis 1984: 10–12 *et passim*. This topic will be pursued in depth in Chapter 2. An etymology not available to Dante is that of Giambattista Vico in the *Scienza nuova*: "Quindi incomincia ancora una filosofia dell'autorità, ch'è altro principal aspetto c'ha questa Scienza, prendendo la voce 'autorità' nel primo suo significato di 'proprietà,' . . . onde restaron 'autori' detti in civil ragione romana coloro da' quali abbiamo cagion di dominio, che tanto certamente viene da *autós*, 'proprius' o 'suus ipsius,' che molti eruditi scrivono 'autor' e 'autoritas' non aspirati" (*Scienza nuova*, book 2, chapter 2, section 1), so that authority is rooted in the *properness* of the relationship between the author and his creation (Verene 1989; Mazzotta 1999: 165). Dante, however, helps put Western culture on the road toward such a concept. See sections iii and iv.

[20] Just as the medieval definition of rhetorical *inventio* is that of *finding* preexisting topoi and arguments, while modern "invention" refers to the discovery of something essentially new, so author from *augere* develops preexistent materials as against the modern, creative author. For a reflection on this idea in relation to the history of literary authorship in the nineteenth and twentieth centuries, see Said 1975: especially 83–90.

Reason if not, strictly speaking, its personification, is directly possessed of the philosophical authority sketched in *Convivio* and, as "poet of Empire" in the *Aeneid*, is indirectly yet firmly linked to authority in its political form. His service in both these capacities is made evident early and often in the *Commedia*.[21]

This, however, is not yet a sufficient gloss on the word as used in *Inferno* 1.85. Dante's other definition in *Convivio* is based on a rare Latin verb, *avieo*, meaning to "bind [tie] words together" (4.6.3–4). In this sense, he says, it refers "only to poets, who have bound their words with musical art" a definition which responds far more closely to the immediate signifying context of *Inferno* than the other, since Virgil's role as *autore* is strictly coordinated with his stylistic influence on Dante: "you alone are he from whom I have taken the [lovely] style that has won me honor" (*Inf.* 1.86–7; see Mazzotta 1979: 155–7). It is thus curious that scholarly commentaries on the *Commedia*, for example those of Singleton (1970–76: vol. 1, pt. 2), Chiavacci-Leonardi (1991, vol. 1), as well as Durling and Martinez (1996), typically cite only the first, more traditional etymology from *Convivio*.[22]

Simply substituting *avieo* for *autentin* in a gloss on the passage would, however, bring an equal number of problems. In *Convivio*, Dante creates a sharp contrast between the two types of *autore*, stressing the marginality and irrelevance of poetic authority to the basic issues of intellectual and moral–political authority addressed at this point in the treatise. Chapter 2 will explore the pertinence of this conceptual move to the internal discourse of authority in the earlier work. For now, it is enough to insist that, in *Inferno* 1, Virgil as poetic *autore* is not limited in this way, partaking in both types of *autorità*.

This, then, is one of those cases, often noted these days, though never of this particular passage, where a comparison of Dante's treatment of a given topic in *Convivio* with its transformative reuse in the *Commedia* proves

---

[21] Virgil's function as virtual personification of human reason is a commonplace, one that is particularly stressed, for example, in *Inf.* 4. His political function is already in evidence in *Inf.* 1 (e.g., 68–75, 124–9, and the Veltro prophecy, if it is indeed aimed at a secular ruler such as Henry VII or Cangrande della Scala).

[22] To judge by the *DDP* database, most commentators on line 85 over the centuries have, when not sticking to "autore" from "autentin," shared the view of the early fifteenth-century commentator Serravalle who notes dryly: "littera plana est" [*DDP*]. Only two sixteenth-century commentators and one from the twentieth century (Giambullari and Gelli [*DDP*]; Padoan [1967]) cite both definitions from *CV* as relevant. Nardi 1965b: 221–2 (cf. 1966b: 313–14) is a more recent exception who, however, reverses the usual omission and leaves "autore" from *autentin* out of his philological calculations. Picone 1993: 109–10 cites *auctor* from *avieo* as fundamental to Dante's conception of authority, but mistakenly takes it for a typical medieval definition rather than an anomaly (see Chapter 2, section ii), treating the spectrum of etymologies *en passant*. See also Minnis 1991: 36–7.

particularly interesting. On the one hand, by allusively associating Virgil with the poetic, stylistic *autore* from *avieo*, as against the philosophical or political authority, from *autentin*, Dante initiates the by now familiar process of simultaneously exalting and qualifying Virgil's mastery (see n 17). But, on the other hand, while Dante may still have the distinction between the two types of *autore* in mind in *Inferno* 1, he is also collapsing it since, as just observed, Virgil is immediately invested with the other form of authority, the one common to philosophers and emperors. Thus, the passage may also be understood in terms of another, quite familiar, Dantean strategy, as a palinodic or recantatory echoing of a passage from one of his earlier works, only to reconfigure and implicitly reject it in favor of a new, superior, position (see Chapter 6). Perhaps now, at this climactic stage of Dante's career, authorship has become broad enough simultaneously to encompass the stylistic, the philosophical, and the political dimensions. Perhaps, at least by the time the reader gets to *Paradiso* 26, it has also encompassed *theological* authority.[23]

Some preliminary conclusions can now be drawn from this investigation of the meaning of the word *autore* in *Inferno* 1. The first general point is that while the word has, more often than not, been understood either as a reflection of a stable and unvarying idea of Dante's culture (the authoritarian Middle Ages) or exclusively in terms of its function within the *Commedia* itself (Dante between Virgil as "maestro e autore" and God as "verace Autore"), the situation is much more complicated than that. The word *does* have philologically derivable roots in a medieval etymological tradition. But the tradition is plural, and, as Dante approaches it, hardly stable: he is, it will become clear in Chapter 2, drawing on all of the available meanings of the word, and is openly conditioning concepts of secular human authorship with the ideas of human authorship of the Bible and a divine Author of authors behind all of these. When these multiple meanings are brought together *sub specie aeternitatis*, from the perspective of the Otherworld, they are, paradoxically, historicized, in the sense that their meaning begins to change – an author who both "binds words with musical art" and is "worthy of faith and obedience" is different from one who does or is either of these things separately. From this perspective, the perceived anachronism of discussing Dante and his works in terms of a modern idea of originating

---

[23] As will be seen in greater detail in Chapter 7, Virgil is personally invested with theological authority, in two carefully restricted senses: (1) as the vehicle by which God – through the mediating chain of (Mary), Lucy, and Beatrice – provides guidance for Dante, he has been given special ad hoc authority (see especially *Inf.* 2.52–126); (2) as a textual site, his fourth *Eclogue* has been the means of converting the late classical poet, Statius (*Purg.* 22.62–95).

authorship may not be as captious as it first seemed. In the push of one medieval and Dantean meaning of *autore* against another, a new meaning, or meanings, begins to emerge, which anticipates, without being identical to, those current today.

In the second place, at the same time as Dante is playing with the generalized medieval discourse of authority in *Inferno* 1.85, he is also critically interrogating his own earlier treatments of the subject. The Dantean *oeuvre* is traversed by an internal history of authority, which can be traced back at least to *Vita Nova*, where the term as such is never used, but where Virgil and the classical poets are first invoked as models for contemporary vernacular poets, such as Dante (*VN* 25), and which certainly runs through *Convivio*, and other intermediate texts as well. In other words, a shifting, contingent discourse of authority punctuates Dante's life as a writer. It is one major aim of this study to reverse the typical methodological procedure of contemporary North American Dante studies, which tends to posit the teleological resolution of this discursive itinerary in the *Commedia*, and rather to chart a forward and unresolved evolution, emphasizing its tactical and adventitious character, from which the *poema sacro* itself does not remain exempt.

Toward the same end, and as a third general conclusion deriving from this preliminary examination of *Inferno* 1.85, this line can and should be read in close relation to one of the external histories mentioned above, namely that of the transition from an ecclesiastical to a lay culture. More particularly, it should be understood as a signal moment in the gradual shift from a culture in which the preeminence of Latin was unchallenged, to one in which vernaculars, the founding prototypes of national language and cultures to come, could aspire to an authority of their own, on analogy with, but historically and conceptually different from, the *gramatica* that gave rise to them.[24] The nature of the process appears in Dante's conflation of the various possible significances of *autore* in applying the term to Virgil. In *Convivio* the different meanings are marked etymologically by referring them back to distinct classical roots. In the etymological and other treatments of *auctor* and *auctoritas* by Latin writers – notably, Isidore of Seville and Hugutio of Pisa – on which Dante drew to construct his discussion in that treatise, these different senses are reflected, though not always consistently, by the presence of alternate Latin spellings with which they are correlated: *autor, auctor, actor*.[25] In the vernacular, in Italian, however, these

[24] See especially Copeland 1991; Botterill 1997; Minnis 2001: chapter 6. See also n 13 and Chapter 3.
[25] See again n 19. As Armando Petrucci has pointed out to me, because we lack autographs of any of Dante's works, arguments based on the exact spelling of these words are invalid. This might

distinctions disappear, and a single word, capable of bearing any one of the alternate meanings and even of fusing them conceptually, takes their place: *autore*.[26] In other words, the simple process of translating the word from Latin into Italian reflects, perhaps in some sense produces, a historic(al) metamorphosis.

This last point leads back to a consideration that had temporarily disappeared from view: namely, the real purpose(s) for which Dante introduces the category of *auctoritas* at the beginning of *Inferno*. Lines 85 and 86 form part of a larger unit whose aim is to define Virgil's fitness as an appropriate guide for Dante, one whose teachings are "worthy of faith and obedience" and are recognized as such by his pupil. However, as already seen, these lines in particular define Virgil as a poet who has been instrumental in shaping Dante as poet. In other words, the topic of authority is introduced in relation to Virgil so that it can then be transmitted, transferred, to Dante himself – conferring on him and his poem an *auctoritas* equal to or greater than that of the classical *auctores*, very much as suggested by Gianfranco Contini in the words that serve as epigraph to this chapter. However, and this is a crucial point, just as the process of translating Latin *auctor* into Italian *autore* transforms the concept drastically, so the *translatio* of Virgilian authority into Dantean also brings with it fundamental structural alterations that betoken a historical shifting beneath the grounds of authorship, alterations that do not map simply or exclusively onto the *trapasso* from pagan to Christian cosmos that has been the focus of most interpretation to date.

To put it bluntly then, while the issue of poetic authority in the *Commedia* has been widely, perhaps even disproportionately, explored in contemporary Dante criticism, its full significance has not been satisfactorily probed. Perhaps the single most important reason for this deficiency is that most recent scholarly discussion of authority in Dante has focused primarily on the *Commedia*, and on the intertextual relations existing between it and the works of Virgil, and other classical poets, under the general rubric of a Christian appropriation, critique, and transformation of pagan

apply in particular to *MN*, where institutional authorities are consistently designated, at least in most modern editions, as *auctores* and philosophical and other intellectual authorities as *autores* (see Chapter 5, nn 5, 20). It does not apply to the discussion of *avieo* in Chapter 2, since Dante actually spells out the word in *CV* 4.6.

26 This argument has affinities with Corti's idea that "campi di tensione" between one historical moment in a culture and another create "campi semantici mobili," that is, shifting, developing terminological meanings (1983: 38–62). Her examples focus on the *trapasso* from Latin to Italian in the Duecento and Dante of a series of key words – *magnanimità; nobiltà; felicità* – which, especially in the second case (see Chapter 2), are not unrelated to *autore*.

categories.[27] This study, instead, will track the evolution of the issue in conceptual and rhetorical terms throughout Dante's *oeuvre*, articulated in several distinct modalities. Not that such an approach is finally incompatible with reading the *Commedia*. On the contrary, in Chapter 7 this procedure will permit an examination of Dante's relationship with the character *Virgilio* in a different light, under which it can be seen as an ingenious and successful device for overcoming the formidable obstacles that stand between Dante and the canonical forms of *auctoritas*, and also as part of a continuous sequence of related stratagems undertaken in other, mostly earlier, works.

These stratagems, we will see, are what permit Dante to undertake in the *Commedia* a synthesis, perhaps unprecedented even in an age of *Summae*, among the various categories of *auctoritas* available in the later medieval period: *autore* from *augere*, *autentin*, and *avieo*; literary, political, philosophical, and theological authorship. This section began with the suggestion that this fusion was localized around Virgil and implicit in the translation effected by Dante from Latin *auctor* to Italian *autore*. It is now possible to see how, in the final analysis, it coalesces around the evolving figure of Dante-*personaggio* who comes, paradoxically, to embody the canons of impersonal authority. The pages that follow will investigate the nature – and especially the historical evolution – of this explosive fusion of the medieval *auctor* with a nascent concept of individual authorship.

My argument is now at a crucial juncture, basic to the problem of authority in Dante, and particular to its historical significance. In a fundamental sense, Dante is both traditionalist and conservative in his understanding and invocation of *auctoritas* as the highest cultural attribute.[28] Nonetheless, in his patently transgressive desire to appropriate that attribute for himself,

---

[27] In addition to the Virgil-centered criticism cited in n 19, Ovid has also drawn considerable attention: e.g., Hollander 1969: especially 202–20; Chiarenza 1980, 1983; Shoaf 1983; Barolini 1984, 1989b; Hawkins 1985; Barkan 1986: 137–70; Brownlee 1986; Sowell 1991; Jacoff and Schnapp 1991; Picone 1993, 1999, 2003a: especially 244–8, 2003b; Cioffi 1994; Clay 1999; Levenstein 2003; Scott 2004: 241–6. For representative overviews of the trend, see Iannucci 1993 a and b; Brownlee 1993; Picone 1993, 1997a, 2003: chapters 11–12.

[28] The point is not that the Dantean *oeuvre* is not innovative – which would be impossible to sustain – but rather that one should distinguish between a conservative impulse or intention and an innovative result (Ascoli 1997: 324 and n 60). A useful example is Dante's political philosophy, where the conservative impulse to the resuscitation of the Roman Empire actually appears radical in the context of contemporary papal and imperial politics (thus also Ferrante 1984: 126–7; for a "conservative" *MN*, see e.g., Ricci 1965b; 143–5; Pertile 1997b: 6, 14; for an *MN* which anticipates political modernity, see e.g., Nardi 1921c; Russo 1977). A temptation exists to see Dante as the bourgeois *arriviste* who denies his own class in favor of traditionalist, aristocratic values (as in his rediscovery of a noble crusader ancestor in *Par.* 15–17), but that would not do justice to a complex situation (also n 12).

for the vernacular, and for "modernity," he inevitably metamorphoses it into something very different from what it had been, to the point of anticipating the cult of creative authorship that is usually seen as the antithesis of medieval *auctoritas*. By fusing and thus confusing distinct categories of authority, Dante changes all of them. By seeking to localize what is by definition transhistorical and transpersonal in a historical person, himself, he changes them further. Paradoxically, as Erich Auerbach first argued more than half a century ago, it is Dante's recourse to what we might now call "creative anachronism" (Auerbach 1944, 1945; see section v and Chapter 7), i.e., his fictive self-placement outside of the dimension of time, that sets this historical process visibly in motion. The process is difficult to recognize because it is one that Dante never names in his text – a partial, contingent, *historical* process, which even the comprehensive intelligence of Dante could not understand or master, since its meaning depends on its outcome in an unknown future, of which, to quote Dante's famous misprision of Ovid, "the facts will be the Naiads" ("ma tosto fier li fatti le Naiade"; *Purg.* 33.46).[29]

In other words, the questions, the *historical* questions, raised in this study may have implications significantly beyond the limits of Dante criticism proper. In order to highlight such implications, the next three sections of this chapter will define three relevant scholarly contexts: the lively theoretical discourse on authorship and authority in Western culture that has focused so much critical energy in the last fifty years; recent studies of the historical formations of authorship and authority in the late medieval and early modern periods; and, finally, work among Dante scholars that has anticipated, inspired, and/or provoked the approach taken in this study. In each case, the aim is not simply to display the tool-kit that will be brought to bear on Dante's texts; rather it is also to show that rigorous reflection on the twinned problems of authorship and authority within the Dantean *oeuvre* bears significantly on how they may be understood in broader theoretical, historical, and/or textual terms.

III. THEORY

Three names and three texts associated with them stand out as having had key roles in stimulating and shaping the flourishing contemporary debate on authorship and authority: Hannah Arendt's "What is Authority" (1958),

---

[29] This is the structure named by De Man (1971), more recently reinscribed in political, or rather, ideological terms, for example by Zizek (1989).

Roland Barthes' "The Death of the Author" (1968), and, above all, Michel Foucault's "What is an Author?" (1968). In what follows, I will address each in turn, beginning with Arendt. Her concern is not with literary authorship at all, but with social and political "authority," which she sharply distinguishes from "power," on the grounds that the former is grounded in an originating legitimacy that the latter lacks, and is averse to the use of violence as a tool of coercion, which the other is not. Her account is historical, in that it posits the decline, even the virtual disappearance, of authority in a traditional sense during the modern era, which she roughly dates from the Reformation. She identifies two models for the constitution of authority, both of which have the effect of grounding present institutions in an originating, transpersonal, and hence legitimating source. The Roman or classical model legitimates imperial rule by recourse to a founding moment in the distant past. In the paradigmatic example, Virgil justifies Augustan Rome by locating its origins with Aeneas and the Trojan refugees. By contrast, the Christian model, that of the medieval Catholic Church, locates a transcendent origin outside of time, in God. While Arendt presents these two models as successive and alternative, from the point of view of this study, they correspond to two simultaneous, if distinctly hierarchized, moments in the medieval and Dantean treatments of *auctoritas*, namely to Virgil as "maestro e autore" and God as "verace Autore" to historical and transcendent origination.

Arendt's account is designed, first of all, to describe the passage from legitimate rule grounded in authoritative hierarchy toward a Machiavellian (read: Nazi, or Fascist, or Stalinist) modernity dominated by power politics originating in ungrounded violence, where the individual wielder of power takes center stage and no transcendent source of legitimation is available. Curiously, however, the *telos* of her essay is to discover a single, successful recapturing of the Roman model of authority, namely the American Constitution and the institutions that flow from it. In other words, despite her recognition of the relationship between authority and authoritarianism, her perspective is ultimately nostalgic – desirous of a return to the stability and continuity of political institutions with genuine authority. For her, authority is seen primarily as an alternative, not to freedom, but to unregulated, tyrannical power.

Arendt is important in this context because she defines the values that inform a culture of authority: the transpersonal, transhistorical legitimation of institutions and individuals. Her work is especially useful in relation to Dante because it makes an analogical connection between institutional authority, e.g., the Roman Empire, and literary authorship, e.g., Virgil, which implies an intrication of the two usually distinct categories. Finally, Arendt gives particularly cogent voice to the basic historical account which shapes almost all contemporary discourse on these two topics, including that of Barthes and Foucault, and which posits a dramatic shift in the nature of authority and the figure of the author a century or two *after* Dante lived and wrote. Arendt's historical scheme reveals the stakes in claiming that Dante is at once an advocate of the values of *auctoritas* and also, implicitly, their contester and transformer. On the one hand, this claim might imply that the scheme could be adjusted without essential alteration: the supposedly fundamental shift in the sixteenth century would simply be displaced back into the early fourteenth century. On the other, however, it may suggest something more radical, namely, that the persistent historiographic notion of a distinct rupture in the fabric of time is itself deeply flawed.

Roland Barthes' brief but influential essay "The Death of the Author" (Barthes 1968) can, from the point of view of this study, function heuristically as the perfect complement to Arendt. Although Barthes makes a loose association between the Author and authoritarianism, his exclusive focus in the essay is on that literary authorship which Arendt does not discuss. His historical scheme, though skeletal and undeveloped, is still typical of most such accounts, placing the "birth" of the modern Author at more or less the same point when Arendt locates the "death" of traditional authority, namely the sixteenth century, and seeing, or prophesying, our own era as the symmetrical and contrary moment of his (this normative author being normatively male) demise. Barthes depends, without substantive analysis or development, upon the traditional account of the human Author as the creative analogue of God, a figure usually understood to emerge with the rise of the humanist movement and the decline of a theocentric culture in the Renaissance (see section iv). He attributes the emergence of this authorial deity to "English empiricism, French Rationalism and the personal faith of the Reformation," omitting the more usual reference to Petrarch and Italian humanism (Barthes 1968: 142–3). For Barthes, the importance of this figure is that it has been used to authorize, delimit, and regulate textual signification, in that it locates the origins of a literary work in an integral authorial intention to which it must continually be referred back. Curiously, the very same phenomenon, namely the displacement from divine to human causality, which for Arendt means the end of *authority* grounded in authenticated origins, and the consequent unleashing of destructive individualism, for Barthes means the imposition of a regime of signification grounded in originating intentions. For Barthes, again in contrast to Arendt, the later disappearance of the Author as origin is taken to be a positive, a liberating development: one that gives free play to the infinite possibilities of textual signification, and allows the birth of a new figure, the reader, so that now "a text's unity lies not in its origin, but its destination" (148).[30]

Barthes recalls the centrality of the author's status to over a half a century of literary theoretical debate in general and offers a succinct, though profoundly reductive, version of the larger intellectual–cultural historiography that surrounds this question.[31] He is heuristically useful for two other reasons. In the first place, he introduces, outside of the Dantean context, the question of the analogy between human author and God the creator which has been so basic to the discourse of Dante criticism, and, perhaps, of Dante himself (see section v). Secondly, and more important in this context, he turns a spotlight on the intimate dialectic that binds the concept of authorship to that of readership. If it is true – and the point is not conceded here – that the reign of the individual author does not begin until the Renaissance, it might still be argued, and in fact has recently been argued, that medieval theories and practices of textuality, like those envisioned by Barthes, give ultimate control over signification to the reader. At the very least, this would point toward viewing Dante's aspirations to *auctoritas* in terms of an author-reader dialectic, particularly the struggle of the *lector* to cross transgressively into the domain of the *auctor*. Barthes' account of the author/reader dialectic is also especially useful because – despite his focus on literary textuality – it depends upon a strong analogy between the reading subject and the political subject, both seen as struggling against an oppressively hierarchical regime in pursuit of an autonomous space of freedom. The relevance of this analogy for Dante will become more evident in later chapters. Meanwhile, its larger significance is immediately apparent in considering Michel Foucault's seminal essay.

Foucault has the place of privilege both in the general discussion of these questions and in the approach taken to them here. He shares Barthes'

[30] One of many hints that Barthes is not wholly free of traditional assumptions is that the "death of the author" which liberates the reader (148) is evidently modeled on the Christian idea of God's willing sacrifice to save mankind. In a recent study focused on twentieth-century authorship, Benedetti (1999) has legitimately attacked any notion that a real "death of the author" has taken place, socio-politically speaking, in our time. She points to the many, many ways in which the cult of the authorial name remains at the center of contemporary culture.

[31] As is well-known, North American criticism and theory from the New Critics' attack on "The Intentional Fallacy" (Wimsatt and Beardsley 1946), through structuralism and post-structuralism (Derrida 1978: 226–7, cited in Grosz 1995: 9; De Man 1984; Kamuf 1988), to the New Historicism (e.g., Greenblatt 1980; Montrose 1986 a and b) and cultural/gender studies (Grosz 1995: 9–24), has consistently banished, contested, and generally problematized the author as source of textual meaning. Recently, a new "biographism," exemplified by Greenblatt 2004, has achieved prominence, although my own fascination with the problem does not extend so far. See also the theoretical-historical summary of the question in Brownlee and Stephens 1989b: 1–4.

perspective both in his desire to displace the figure of the author from the center of the culture of the book, and in his rough dating of the present era as the time in which that figure is reaching a terminus. At the same time, what interests him is not literary writing alone, but the whole domain of humanistic authorship, in which names like Freud and Marx are far more crucial than that of, say, Barthes' preferred point of reference, Mallarmé (see n 35). Moreover, he brings the question of the author openly into contact with questions of authority like those posed by Arendt, although from a very different conceptual and political perspective. In other words, he brings together the questions of authority and authorship, which are separated in Arendt and Barthes, but are tightly linked for others, including Dante.

As is well known, the emphasis in Foucault's essay is on the author not as person but "as function of discourse" with the following four specifications: "[1] the author-function is tied to the legal and institutional systems that circumscribe, determine, and articulate the realm of discourses; [2] it does not operate in a uniform manner in all discourses, at all times, and in any given culture; [3] it is not defined by the spontaneous attribution of a text to its creator, but through a series of precise and complex procedures; [4] it does not refer, purely and simply, to an actual individual insofar as it simultaneously gives rise to a variety of egos and to a series of subjective positions that individuals of any class may come to occupy" (1968: 130–1).

All of these points are pertinent to an investigation of Dante's relationship to *auctoritas*. First of all, they invite consideration of the question not exclusively or even primarily with the goal of elucidating the meaning of Dante's texts and his career: rather they strongly indicate that a critical focus of this kind falls within, and is determined by, a historically and conceptually limited paradigm of what an author is and does. In other words, they make it possible to understand the author-function called "Dante" as a symptomatic *case*, albeit a particularly ostentatious and idiosyncratic one, produced by and reflective of the late medieval "legal and institutional systems" that hedge him in. Moreover, Foucault's first, and especially second, headings support an effort to historicize the Dantean project not only in terms of subjecting it to the cultural constraints and dynamics of his time and place(s), but also of attempting to define its possibly pivotal role in the evolving construction of authorship at the dawn of a properly European and vernacular culture. In other words, Foucault provides the best theoretical justification for insisting on the mobility of the concepts in a period of fundamental social and political transformation in Europe, as for focusing on the particular efforts of Dante to reconstruct, and deconstruct, those discursive conceptions as they arrived to him.

Notwithstanding its value as theoretical call to action, however, Foucault's account renounces any "socio-historical analysis of the author as an individual" or any attempt to show "how the author was individualized in [our] culture" (115), and thus has very little to offer in the way of a tailored approach to the "case of Dante" of which, in any event, he does not speak. Moreover, the one part of his argument that touches on the medieval notion of the *auctor* is certainly misleading.[32] Many recent accounts of the Western Author that are grounded in a Foucauldian perspective pay similarly limited attention to the later Middle Ages, often insisting that a radical transformation in the institution of authorship only came about with the technological and legal developments surrounding the emergence of print culture in the proto-national world of the sixteenth and seventeenth centuries, and the pervasive "system of ownership and strict copyright rules" in the eighteenth.[33] The *case* of Dante, however, anticipates such a transformation by at least two centuries. The Foucauldian question then becomes: what other "legal and institutional systems" besides print culture and the emergent national state might have produced such a result?

More important still from the perspective of this study, Foucault's third point sponsors a detailed investigation of how the texts bearing the authorial name of "Dante" carry out "a series of precise and complex procedures" designed to appropriate for themselves the late medieval discourse of the author. And in the same way, his fourth point reinforces something any literary scholar knows, namely that the various instantiations of the Dantean "I" throughout the *oeuvre* may be traced, at least in part, to rhetorical and cultural models of individual identity beyond those texts. Nor can they be fully identified one with another: between works, and even within a single work, a variety of strategies may be mobilized around

---

[32] At one point Foucault pairs an assertion that in the Middle Ages claims to *scientific* truth were based solely on the name of the *auctor* who authorized them with the notion that in this period *literary* works were legendary and anonymous, in other words, *not* linked to a specific authorial name (125–6). The function of this opposition in his argument is to support the subsequent claim that in the modern era the two domains are reversed: the scientific domain is depersonalized, while in literature the authorial name reigns supreme. The first half of this historical chiasmus would itself demand at least qualification – but the latter half is entirely deceptive, since, as we have just seen, literary *auctores* in the Middle Ages were also "nominally" invoked. See Chartier 1992, especially 29–32, 58–9, for judicious comments on this and other aspects of Foucault's account; also Giunta 2002: 48–52.

[33] The case for the transformative effect of print has been made from a variety of perspectives. See, e.g., Eisenstein 1979; Wall 1993; Weimann 1996; Lowenstein 2002; J. Greene 2005. See Chartier 1992 (especially 32–54) for the more general question of intellectual property and the emergence of a modern "author function," which he (following Petrucci) sees as already developing in the fourteenth century with Petrarch (54–7).

the "I" to a variety of strategic purposes, none of which has a necessary, *prima facie* claim to being taken as the transparent reflection of authentic Dantean selfhood (see also section v). In other words, Foucault points out how a *rhetorical* analysis also can and should be understood as an *historical* analysis. Finally, and most crucially, he enables an understanding of Dante's treatment of authority not as the expression of an idea or cluster of ideas – that is, as a determinate intellectual content to be sought out as an end in itself – but rather as the product and producer of ideology – that is, as operating within a system which structures and disseminates ideas not for their intrinsic truth content, but as tools for the construction of a social order, and particularly for locating, and fixing, individuals within that order.[34]

Foucault's essay has to a significant extent determined the discourse on authorship in recent decades, and thus the larger significance of the Dantean *autore* may be easier to judge when placed in relation to it. At the same time, the basic principles he articulates are an important corrective to the treatment of these issues in the narrower context of Dante studies. Dante, especially the Dante of the *Commedia*, is invariably assigned, without reflective justification, the privilege of "The Author" in a Barthian and Foucauldian sense, when it is exactly such a privilege that is at stake conceptually and historically.

Nonetheless, I do not share the Foucauldian perspective fully. As just noted, his account of the medieval *auctor* is both incomplete and in part erroneous, in ways that might become a vehicle for challenging both his assumed historical perspective, and even the theory which he makes rest upon it. More to the immediate point, whatever its implications for a larger historiography of the *auctor*, the present book remains squarely focused on the Dantean *oeuvre*, and thus in some sense well within the paradigm that Foucault wishes to dispel. In other words, like any study of a single author or individual works, this one continually runs the risk of confusing – whether rhetorically or conceptually – the author–function with an embodied, psychologized writer (O. Holmes 2000: 3–4), a risk with which Foucault himself flirts.[35] Nonetheless, in taking Dante as a *case*, that is, as a complex example in dynamic relationship with a culture and a set of

---

[34] For the ideological analysis of early modern authorship, see, *inter alia*, Montrose 1986a; Weimann 1996. For an overview of the multiple ways that the word "ideology" has been used in recent scholarship, see Eagleton 1991; Zizek 1994. The definition given above follows roughly the line of Louis Althusser, conditioned by related concepts of Foucault ("discourse") and Bourdieu ("doxa").

[35] Foucault was aware of running this risk, though he claimed to have countered it. The version of the essay that appears in *Language, Memory, Counter-text*, but not in a later English version (Harari 1979), begins with a preliminary "hors-texte" that prefaced Foucault's original lecture (113–15: the first three paragraphs and part of the fourth, up to "Nevertheless . . ."). In it he asserts that in *The Order of Things*, he "employed the names of authors throughout . . . in a naive and often crude fashion" (113). The talk then goes on justifying his own invocation of authorial names, especially

historical trends, this study differs significantly from one that sets out to explain, and celebrate, Dante the author.

The aim here, then, is to negotiate the tensions between a literary–critical study of particular instances of authorship and the Foucauldian historiographical problem of the "author–function" in general. Dante, from this perspective, can be seen to exemplify or instantiate the discourse of authority in his own time, both by explicit reference to it and in a variety of indirect ways. Moreover, the historical destiny of the name "Dante" and the works to which it is attached over the intervening centuries of Western culture illustrates perfectly how a writer is turned into an Author, how a text is institutionalized and thereby converted into "cultural capital."[36] At the same time, the gap that exists between the medieval language of authority used by Dante, and Dante's status as exemplary author in the modern canon suggests something like the historical, cultural shift in the meaning of authorship on which both Barthes and Foucault insist.

Finally, and here lies a substantive difference of this study's approach from Foucault's, Dante's texts can be understood as themselves in the process of negotiating, with an evident, if by no means complete, intentionality, their relationship to past and future discourses of authority. In other words, the Dantean corpus does not simply *re-produce auctoritas* or the *Author*, but critiques these concepts, reshapes them, *produces* them in ways that cannot be *simply* reduced under the banner of "legal and institutional systems." Thus, rather than the institutional history of authorship in general, the focus of this book will be the field(s) of encounter between systemic discourses and individual writers and/or texts that are shaped by and in turn shape such discourses.[37]

The implications of this position appear when it is juxtaposed with a classic of the post-Foucauldian historiography of authorial selfhood, namely Stephen Greenblatt's *Renaissance Self-Fashioning* (1980). In Greenblatt's view, and that of many New Historicists (e.g., Montrose 1986a), the "self"

Freud and Marx, as against the fetishization of such names that he, like Barthes, explicitly rejects. In the essay's finale (131–6) he attempts to separate such figures, as he employees them, from "authors" by designating them as "initiators of discourse" (in Harari 1979: "founders of discourse"). However, it is hard to see how Marx and Freud thus used differ from Christ or Socrates or Aristotle as those names were deployed in earlier periods. It becomes even harder in light of how closely discussions of authority tie that concept to the question of origination (cf. Quint 1983).

36 On Dante's *fortuna* in the centuries since his death, see, in addition to the references given in n 2: Barbi 1890; Dionisotti 1965; Vallone 1981; McDougal 1985; Menocal 1991; Pite 1994; Pike 1997; Havely 1998; Baranski 2001; Wallace 2003; Boitani 2003; Hawkins and Jacoff 2003. See Parker 1993, 1997, for the ideological dimensions of Dante commentary. Cf. Ascoli 2003. See also section v.

37 Elsewhere I argue for recognition of the structural, unconscious forces that conspired to produce Dante and thus the *DC*, but also that such awareness is still by no means adequate to account for the extraordinary degree of express intentionality with which Dante's texts go about naming such forces and ordering their author's relationship to them (Ascoli 1993: 45–6).

like the "author" is a cultural construction or ideological fabrication, one whose autonomy is inevitably illusory and subject to transpersonal master discourses. The argument here, analogous yet in basic ways opposed to that of classic New Historicism, is that, despite the fact that in Dante's time the personified self was no doubt just as much a rhetorical effect and equally determined by the relations between individual subjects and institutions as "he" was in the sixteenth century, that rhetorical effect and those social relations constituted something distinctive, even new, in the history of Western culture. In other words, Dante's practice contributes to the opening up of a space, however provisional and tentative, for something specifically, though not irreducibly and certainly not autonomously, individual.[38] From this perspective, it is just as easy to understand social–cultural trends – such as the production of new political subjects in the communes; of new religious subjects in the rise of the popularizing Franciscan movement; of new poetic subjects with the advent of lay, mercantile, vernacular culture – as the enabling conditions of individual consciousness and distinctive personality as it is to interpret them as constituting regimes of false consciousness and full subordination to institutional agendas. In short, while Greenblatt's Renaissance "self" may be recuperated and appropriated by its culture, Dante's late medieval "self" has been constructed, dialectically, provisionally, strategically, in the interstices of cultural authority, which has not yet learned how to enfold or recuperate the vagrant "I" of an impending modernity.

Despite the suggestive power of such an account, it is, again, crucial to bear in mind that this study is limited to a single writer and to resist the tempting, generalizing claim that Dante, in fact, "made history," that is, negotiated *the decisive and definitive break* between one form of authorship and another. Dante must remain, rather, a symptom, a case, genealogically related to broader historical trends, but in no sense the direct cause of them, as idiosyncratic, that is, as *individual,* in some ways as he is archetypal or merely typical in others. This methodological caveat does not, however, prevent us from asking what form those broader trends take, or of attempting to situate Dante more exactly in relation to them.

IV. HISTORY

Foucault, Barthes, and Arendt represent a theoretical context for this study, but in each case theory is inextricably linked to specific ideas about the

---

[38] In other words, the textualized "self," and indeed the human person which generated it, is understood here as a site around and through which differences play in a distinctive, individuating way, not, obviously as an "autonomous individual" in the Burckhardtian sense.

shape of cultural history in the West. In the cases of Barthes and Foucault, these turn out to be quite traditional ideas, at least at the back end, which sit curiously at odds with the radical theoretical claims they are made to support, leaving them firmly tied to the idealist, Hegelian historiography with which, in other respects, they are at polemical odds. Most at issue here, as the example of Greenblatt was also meant to suggest, is the widely-held historiographic notion of a distinct rupture in the forms both of subjectivity and of textuality occurring between periods designated as Middle Ages and Renaissance, respectively. And, inasmuch as the author can be said to be "the subject of the text," it is unsurprising that this figure has been at the center of many of the numerous studies which have attempted to explore, to specify, to qualify, and less often, to challenge the nature and placement of such a rupture. Briefly rehearsing some of the relevant entries in this field should also help to clarify the historical location and significance of Dante's treatment of authorship. These are of two principal kinds: the more numerous and earlier established are those which write about authorship from the perspective of a supposed Renaissance modernity; more recent are those that investigate the forms and evolutions of medieval textuality.

A great deal has been written about the emergence of a new author, usually in relation to a new subjectivity, at some point between the four-teenth and the seventeenth centuries. As these dates suggest, the exact moment of said emergence varies, as does its location. Furthermore, indi-vidual formulations differ considerably depending on which author is used to exemplify the shift,[39] what themes focus the argument,[40] and whether the process is seen through the filter of a Foucauldian history of institutions and discourses or a Hegelian history of consciousness. Despite the variety of formulations, and the concomitant plurality of evaluations, however,

---

[39] Favorite candidates include Petrarch (e.g., Freccero 1975a; T. Greene 1982a and b; cf. Ascoli 1991a); Machiavelli (Pocock 1975; Skinner 1978), Luther (Weimann 1996; Dunn 1994); Montaigne (Taylor 1989); Cervantes (Lukàcs 1920; Foucault 1966; Cascardi 1992); Shakespeare (Fineman 1986). Stillinger 1992: 6–9 usefully discusses attempts – such as Fineman's – to define early modernity in terms of a new form of lyric subjectivity, along with the critique of said attempts by medievalists such as Patterson 1990 (cf. Stone 1994b). See also Latour 1993 for an interesting critique of the notion of "modernity" itself as applied to this period.

[40] These include: literary imitation of classical models (T. Greene 1982a; Quint 1983; Guillory 1983), the revival of the rhetorical tradition (Garin 1952; Kahn 1983), the secularization of culture (Burckhardt 1869; Blumenberg 1966), the emergence of "literature" as an autonomous domain (Reiss 1992; cf. Eagleton 1990; Bourdieu 1992), the Protestant Reformation (Greenblatt 1980; Weimann 1996), the advent of printing (Eisenstein 1979 [and see n 33]), the advent of global capitalism (Halpern 1991), the "civilizing process" (Elias 1939), and so on. For an interesting recent account of the "modernity" and "individualism," tangential to my interests, of the status of the body in the *DC*, see Gragnolati 2005.

the basic model remains intact, even when the focus is on the exclusion of certain groups from the dominant social formation.

Among latter-day students of the question, it is safe enough to begin with Burckhardt (1869), whose thesis of a modern, autonomous, improvisatory self emerging in a politically, ethically, and ontologically delegitimized world gives special prominence to failures in the system of political and literary *auctoritas* which in turn give rise to individual despots (thus far, Arendt), and, analogously, to a distinctively personalized creativity in arts and letters. For that matter, Stephen Greenblatt, who takes the position that self-fashioning is, in the first instance, a Foucauldian function of ideology and institutions, does not dispute the existence of a particular historical form of selfhood and of authorship characteristic of the Renaissance, and, like Burckhardt, accords special privilege to the dynamic interactions between political authorities and poetic authors (cf. Montrose 1986a).

Among the many works dedicated to the history and phenomenology of Renaissance/early modern authorship, three stand out that provide the basic parameters: Robert Durling's *The Figure of the Poet in Renaissance Epic* (1965), David Quint's *Origin and Originality in Renaissance Literature* (1983), and Robert Weimann's *Authority and Representation in Early Modern Discourse* (1996). Durling, in a justly famous chapter on Ariosto, charts the resuscitation of a classical topos, the analogy between *Deus artifex*, God the artist/author of the real, and the poet as maker of an *alter mundus*. Durling's formulation suggests a new, extreme valorization of human creativity, and a displacement of theological categories in the direction of poetic and secular ones, while, however, positing not a rupture with, but a modulation of, categories active in the Middle Ages, for example, the human *auctor*/divine *Auctor* paradigm mentioned above.[41]

By contrast, David Quint posits a rather sharper break between the two periods, asserting that "Renaissance humanism reinvented the *author*, defined by a unique individual style" which produces a "new personal voice" (Quint 1986: 1). Quint's position is fully articulated in *Origin and Originality* (1983), where he explores the tension in humanism between, on the one hand, a poetics of origin founded on imitation of ancient authoritative models, and ultimately on a connection to a transcendental source of value and meaning, and, on the other, a poetics of originality where the historicity and novelty of a modern poet's work take precedence over its derivation from authentic sources (Greene 1982a). The most typical result

---

[41] Singleton 1949 and Mazzeo 1960: chapter 4 both discuss Dantean authorship in terms of the divine analogy.

is an attempt to have both originality and origin at the same time, as for example, in Milton's novel retelling of the Biblical myth of origin and original sin in *Paradise Lost* (Quint 1983: 207–20; cf. Guillory 1993).[42] Moreover, Quint's notion that a living writer might claim to be an "initiator of discourse" – to appropriate Foucault's term for different purposes – reveals that the early modern author is at once modeled on the *Auctor* – whose capacity for originating creativity he appropriates – and radically different from Him and the culture of human *auctores* that his existence sponsors – the impersonal gives way to the personal; antiquity to the present. Quint thus places the early modern writer on a threshold between a traditionalist culture of *authority* and a Romantic concept of uniquely individual inspiration, where theological categories have been fully humanized, where – in the classic formulation of M.H. Abrams – "mirror" has become "lamp" (1953, 1971; cf. Frye 1976).[43]

One thing that most histories of authorship written from the point of view of the Renaissance and/or early modernity shared, until recently, was a notable lack of attention to the preceding historical phenomena against which the new and modern situation is being defined – in other words, they too, like Barthes and Foucault, tend to assume the most general conclusions of the most traditional studies concerning medieval textuality and authorship. An especially interesting case is Robert Weimann, whose analysis of the multi-faceted discursivity of *auctoritas* in English early modernity has several affinities with this study (though it is at once broader in scope and far more succinct). Weimann understands the novelty of authorship in the Renaissance as the product of a radically new conflictuality between distinct zones of authority – notably the personalized, "self-authorizing" discourse of Protestantism (Luther; Calvin); the increasingly ungrounded authority of the sovereign (Hobbes); the relatively wide-open world of the print-market; and, of course, the new emphasis on originality in the converging worlds of literature and theater (Nashe; Shakespeare). What is most

---

[42] Jacqueline Miller 1986 offers a formulation similar to Quint's, but dates it from Chaucer or earlier. Note that *both* aspects of this account represent a shift from the medieval position as discussed so far, since the idea of a modern writer deliberately modeling himself on an ancient suggests the possibility of a *translatio* of *auctoritas*, as in Dante's claim to have taken over Virgil's "bello stilo," which the most rigorous instantiation of the transcendent *Auctor* would seem to prohibit.

[43] For related positions, see, in addition to Durling, Frye 1957; Kermode 1967; Burke 1970; Abrams 1971. An approach analogous to Quint's is taken by Guillory 1983 who works through an inspiration/imagination dyad. The conservative pole of Guillory's opposition (poets divinely inspired from a transcendent source), like Quint's, is *already* in a tension with medieval discourse, which would have been reluctant to acknowledge the possibility of a *modern* in possession of the same *authorizing* access to divine inspiration as, say, the human scribes of the Bible. This point is illustrated by the Trecento discussions which attempt to equate poetry and theology in some way, but which, after Dante, seem scrupulously to avoid implying that poetry is divinely inspired in the same sense that Scripture is. See Chapter 7, nn 136–7, as well as n 5 above.

striking about this account is how the twin breaking points of the press and of Protestantism (the German factor, one might say) leave behind them, entirely unanalyzed, an unconflicted medieval world as absolute as Burckhardt's. Just to begin with, virtually any of the comments he makes about Luther's negotiations of the relation between secular and spiritual authority can be made with equal conviction about Dante's *Monarchia* (see Chapters 5–6), and his assertions concerning the creation of a space of individual authorial freedom may be related genealogically to Dante's self-authorizing procedures, as we will see.[44]

More recently, however, these questions have begun to be studied from the late medieval perspective of the twelfth to fourteenth centuries, with results that, though in some cases tending to support the idea of an historical rupture or transformation of categories, give a decidedly more complicated and even contradictory picture. One cluster of contemporary medievalists focuses on the radical differences between medieval culture of manuscripts and of oral performance, on the one hand, and print culture, on the other. Such scholars insist on the dramatic implications that such differences have for conceptualizing and enacting the relations between author, text, and reader(s). They begin from such fundamental earlier work as Leo Spitzer's "Note on the Poetic and the Empirical 'I' in Medieval Authors" (1946). Spitzer denies any real biographical content or creative identity to first-person poetic compositions of the Middle Ages, insisting instead on (a) the generic nature of the speaking "I" and (b) on its primary function as a locus of identification for the normative reader, the real focus of poetic meaning. Analogously, such scholars stress that even such an influential, "I"-centered work as Augustine's *Confessions* is conditioned by (a) the human writer's attribution of his identity to divine creativity rather than individual qualities (Spitzer 1946: 104) and (b) his insistence that he writes of his individual case only so that it can become a normative model for others (Spitzer 1946: 105; cf. *CV* I.2.14; Freccero 1966: 25).

The most aggressive version of this position is that of Paul Zumthor (1980), who, under the influence of Jauss and, importantly, Barthes, insists that all attempts to locate individualized creativity in poetic texts of the

---

[44] Similarly Helgerson's important study of "Self-Crowned Laureates" (1983) in early modern England, which, like the present work, focuses on the *negotiation* between unauthorized person and authorizing, impersonal system, adopts a synchronic perspective, begging the question of historical precedence as well as the Burckhardtian issue of whether medieval authorship was in some demonstrable way less personal and more systematic than its early modern counterpart. This is a paradox of much "new historical" work which, as Greenblatt recognized, in shifting his ground from "new historicism" to "cultural poetics" (1998), is often more indebted to an anthropologically inspired synchronism than to a diachronic historicism.

medieval period are anachronistic impositions.[45] Rather, he argues, in poetry of the time "no one is offering himself to be read . . . the author has completely 'depersonalized' himself in the production of his text" and, he claims, this "marks in a global way the difference between the Middle Ages and what immediately followed it" (1980: 58). Zumthor himself, however, could easily be accused of simply displacing Barthes' fantasy of unfettered readerly *écriture* back to a point just preceding the emergence of the Author-God in early modernity.

More persuasive are the rigorously historicized arguments of David Hult in *Self-Fulfilling Prophecies: Readership and Authority in the First 'Roman de la Rose'* (1986), of John Dagenais in *The Ethics of Reading in Manuscript Culture: Glossing the 'Libro de Buen Amor'* (1994), and of Mary Carruthers in *The Book of Memory* (1990). Hult carefully delimits the material features of medieval manuscript culture that tend to displace the author from the center of attention, beginning with the difference between the circulation of multiple, widely divergent manuscript versions of a given text, what Zumthor dubs *mouvance* (cf. Giunta 2002: 60–2) and the regulated, uniform copies of printed works. Also notable for him are the plural types of intervention which are likely to have contributed to the production of a medieval text, including, in Bonaventure's classic formulation: author, scribe, compiler, and/or commentator.[46] And, perhaps most fundamentally, he stresses the medieval recourse to fictionalized versions of the author in the text which, he argues, supports the Foucauldian idea of the textual determination of the author not as biographical entity but as function (see also Hult 1989). Hult takes what for Foucault is a theoretical point true for *any* of the many possible historical constructions of authorship, and gives it historical specificity in relation to the later, French, Middle Ages.

Dagenais attacks the idea of creative, personal authorship from another angle, by stressing the proactive role of medieval readers in the generating of textual significance.[47] His argument points simultaneously to rhetorical

---

[45] See, for instance, Jauss 1982: chapter 1 [1970], but also his critique of earlier versions of Zumthor's position (1979: 195–7). See also critiques of Zumthor in S. Kay 1990; O. Holmes 2000: especially 6–9; Giunta 2002: 48–62. See Stone 1994b for a "strong" reading of medieval "anonymity" as a positive alternative to Renaissance self-centered creativity (e.g., 4).

[46] See n 4 for this distinction; also Chapter 2, section ii. Even while acknowledging the historical specificity of the scheme, however, one may still ask whether there is more comparability than we usually imagine with the production of a contemporary book, say an academic study, which can be shaped, not only by the author, but also by copy editors, readers' reports, editorial boards, not to mention exigencies of the tenuring process.

[47] On the activity of reading in the Middle Ages more generally see: Allen 1982; Carruthers 1990 (especially chapter 5, discussed below); Copeland 1991; Chartier 1992: chapter 1; Lerer 1993; Petrucci 1995; Stock 1996, 2001 (on Augustine's ideas of reading and their later influence); Saenger 1997; Amtower 2000. See also the specific discussions of the medieval Latin and vernacular commentary

theory, which, as Allen (1982) demonstrated previously, gives primacy to the ethical effects of texts on their readers, and to exegetical practice, which produces a wide range of readerly glosses, from scribbled marginalia to formal commentaries on the *auctores*. The combined force of theory and practice, for Dagenais, places the production of meaning entirely in the hands of the consumer of the text. For Dagenais, authorial intention is nothing in the earlier period, while readerly intervention is everything.

Dagenais' argument at first seems to be at odds with the idea of a culture of authority, in which the *auctor* is invested with supreme prestige. This is not necessarily so, for two reasons. First, the exaltation of the *auctor* and the authoritative text has an interesting side-effect. True, moderns *are* reduced to mere commentators or compilers of the texts of the true ancient *auctores*. At the same time, because the *auctor* is treated as if transcendent, impersonal, and absolute in truth, commentators and compilers have the *de facto* license to reinterpret, even rearrange, "authoritative" texts so as to produce normative, orthodox results, which obscure the individual, historical nature of the human author and his writings.[48] The author is thus both hypostatized and banished.[49]

traditions elsewhere in this chapter, as well as Chapter 4. Giunta 1998, 2002 offers a particularly rich account of the ways in which Italian Duecento and Trecento poetry orients itself dialogically toward historically determinate readers (see also Steinberg 2007).

[48] The standard late medieval format for presenting authoritative texts was to introduce them with an academic prologue or *accessus*, which named the *auctor* and defined his *intentio*, as well as describing both the form and the content of the text, and then on each following page to present a piece of the text surrounded, literally, by commentary accumulated over several generations. The practice was originally modeled on the lives of and commentaries on the classical *auctores* (e.g., Servius and Donatus on Virgil; cf. n 16), but was adapted by Scholasticism both for commentaries on philosophical *auctores* and for the Bible itself, and then re-adapted, by Dante among others, for literature (Minnis *et al.* 1988; Minnis and Johnson 2005). On the larger history of commentary from classical times to the Renaissance, see, e.g., Goulet-Cazé 2000. On Biblical commentary, see Spicq 1944; Smalley 1952; De Lubac 1959–1965; Allen 1982; Minnis 1984; De Hamel 1984; Minnis *et al.* 1988; Carruthers 1990; Stillinger 1992 (chapter 1). Regarding commentaries on classical *auctores* both literary and philosophical, see Wetherbee 1972; Hexter 1986; Minnis *et al.* 1988; Carruthers 1990 (especially chapter 6); Copeland 1991. For the commentary tradition as it began to be applied to vernacular texts see Allen 1982; Minnis *et al.* 1988 (vii–viii, 1–11, chapters 9–10); Copeland 1991; Stillinger 1992 (chapters 2–3); Dagenais 1994. On the *accessus* specifically see Quain 1945; Hunt 1948; Curtius 1948: 48–54, 57–61; Smalley 1952; Huygens 1970; Allen 1982; Minnis 1984: 9–39; Hexter 1986; Minnis *et al.* 1988; Ascoli 1997. For the expression of these traditions in Dante's works see Mazzoni 1955; Nardi 1961; Sandkühler 1967; Trovato 1976; Battaglia Ricci 1983; Picone 1979, 1987a, 2003a; Alessio and Villa 1984; Minnis *et al.* 1988: chapters 9–10; Noakes 1988; Ascoli 1997: 323–38 and nn, also 1989, 2003; Stillinger 1992: 23–43; Parker 1993; Barański 1994b: 16–23, 2001: especially 13–17. On the application of these paradigms to the *DC* by Trecento commentators, see n 2. On the cultural functions of medieval allegoresis more generally, see Copeland 1991; Copeland and Melville 1991. See Chapter 2, section ii concerning the techniques adopted by late medieval readers for domesticating the *auctores*. See n 56 and Chapter 4 for Dantean self-commentary.

[49] This account of how the *auctor* is treated apparently reinforces the cliché of medieval anti-historicism and anti-intellectualism. While it is true that the cult of *auctores* was often constricting – it could also be enabling (cf. Chenu 1950: 83), especially in the twelfth and thirteenth centuries.

In the second place, although Dagenais does not stress this point, the reader's diminished, if not absent, responsibility to respect the intentions of a human author is decidedly replaced by an even more absolute responsibility to respect those of the ultimate *Auctor*, God. The most patent example is the often-cited section of the *Confessiones* where Augustine frees the reader of Scripture from responsibility to Moses' intentions in writing Genesis, *as long as* the resultant interpretation builds faith and charity (*Conf.* 12.14–32). The argument has also been made that Augustine's guide to Biblical interpretation, *De Doctrina Christiana*, gives the reader great freedom (Stone 1998). However, whether in the *Confessiones* or in *De Doctrina*, the Augustinian Rule of Charity gives the reader liberty to interpret freely only as long as the result is an affirmation of divine charity – i.e., only one basic interpretation is actually possible of any and every passage (1.35–36 *et passim*; see Ascoli 1999). In other words, far from a space of interpretive freedom, medieval reading is largely subject to an authoritarian regime that insists upon the endless reaffirmation of its moral and spiritual predicates.

Mary Carruthers' treatment of the relationship of the memory tradition to authorship and authority at first occupies a position very close to that of Dagenais. In a chapter entitled "Memory and the Ethics of Reading" she stresses that "medieval reading was highly active" (1990: 186) and that the activity in question was the identification and internalization of behavioral models provided by texts. And as she foregrounds the readers she effaces the author as creative individual: "one need always keep in mind that *auctores* were, first of all, texts, not people" (190). In the same place, she cites Albertus Magnus to the effect that the standard category of the *intentio auctoris* used in the academic prologues known as *accessus* (n 48) was not a version of authorial intention as it is now understood, but rather a purposiveness immanent to the text "contained in the textual signs alone" (*ibid.*). In other words, she lucidly defines one prominent aspect of the culture of *auctoritas*, while still insisting on the active participation of the text together with the reader in the generation of meaning.

In the subsequent chapter on "Memory and Authority" (189–220) she describes a structure of reciprocity binding together the activities of reading and writing. If reading is understood as an analytic of division (*divisio*),[50] writing begins as memorial re-collection of fragments of knowledge gleaned from reading leading to the synthetic composition that produces

---

[50] On *divisio* as primary mode of medieval biblical and academic reading, see Allen 1982: 127–8; Minnis 1984: 151 *et passim*; Copeland 1991: 206–20; Stillinger 1992: chapter 1. For Dante's formal and metaphysical investment in it, see Stillinger *ibid.*: chapters 2–3; Durling and Martinez 1990: 55–69 and nn. See also Chapter 4, sections i–ii and nn; Chapter 5, section iii, and nn 39–40.

new texts. Specifically, she understands the glossed medieval book, the *sacra pagina*, with text surrounded by strata of commentary (194, 215) as emblematic of a continuous process by which writing generates readings which are then turned back into writing: "Readers, in the course of familiarizing a text [by commenting on it], became its authors too" and, even more pointedly "it is commentary and imitation which make a text an 'auctor' – not the activities of its writer but its readers" (214).

Carruthers' focus on the dialectic of reading and writing will prove crucial as we proceed in defining Dante's relationship to medieval textual practices, but it is also important to note the limitations of her argument. Stillinger (1992 [see n 8]), in a comparable reading of the *sacra pagina* points to something that Carruthers "glosses over," namely that, however much commentators may define and control the meanings produced by *auctores* and may, in the process, become a kind of writers themselves, this process is predicated on (a) the identification of the textual authority with a venerable name (Virgil; Augustine; David; John); (b) the creation of a hierarchy in which, symbolically, the *auctores* are above and the *commentatores* and *lectores* are below. The combination of a text with an authoritative name and a commentary to affirm and expound its value may together *de facto* constitute medieval *auctoritas*, but that does not mean that a modern writer can easily become an *auctor*: on the contrary. Symptomatic is Carruthers' citation of Hugutio of Pisa's definition (see Chapter 2, section ii) of the *auctor* as one "worthy of imitation." In fact, the kind of imitation at issue is not that of literary modeling but rather of ethical exemplarity, as is evident in the more typical version of the definition, the one Dante deploys, where the *auctor* is "one worthy of *faith*" whose words deserve the reader's deepest trust and even, as Dante adds, "obedience." This qualification aside, Carruthers' specification of the complex interactions between reading and writing, *lector* and *auctor* anticipates the situation that Dante confronts and into which he attempts to insert himself.

In contrast to the historicist revisionism of Hult, Dagenais, and Carruthers is an older, yet still active, scholarly tradition, which seeks to discover some of the Renaissance traits of individual, creative authorship in the later Middle Ages. The trend goes back at least to Haskins' arguments in favor of a twelfth-century "Renaissance" (1955; also Benson and Constable 1982). Notable is a series of studies that relocates the emergence of the distinctive individual, so closely linked to the modern author, in the earlier period (e.g., Ullman 1966; Morris 1972; Hanning 1977; S. Kay 1990). Of particular note is Peter Dronke's *Poetic Individuality in the Middle Ages* (1970). Dronke stresses the distinctiveness of particular poetic compositions, which he sees as reflecting back on a "poet's total intention" (21), though recognizing the difficulty of recovering said intention given an extreme paucity of biographical evidence.

Dronke's argument brings into view a methodological question of genuine importance: are any of the various factors adduced by Zumthor and company – the prevalence of anonymous texts, the material conditions of manuscript culture, the theory and practice of readerly creation of meaning – sufficient to deny the validity of studying the intrinsic structures of medieval texts and of finding in them individualized, at times idiosyncratic, features that might point in the direction of complex authorial intentions, or at least of distinctive authorial psychology, conscious or not? And, for that matter, just because a writer has no name, does it mean that s/he has no "personality," no identifiable voice? However, even taking Dronke's general point – which in the case of Dante's unending first-person poetic self-reflexivity doesn't really need to be argued – its applicability to the questions surrounding authorship as a concept and as a cultural category is not certain. In one way, the question is not at all whether there are literary writers with distinctive literary styles, or who represent distinctively individual characters, in the medieval period. Rather, the most basic questions concern the general cultural standing of such writers: Who counts as an author? How is an author deemed worthy of that name to be treated?

The present reading of Dante focuses on the internal negotiations between an individual writer's production and the cultural concepts of authorship that he reproduces and confronts within his *oeuvre*. Dante is ideally suited to such an approach, because he is so often explicit about his conceptual framework, as about his understanding of its relationship to normative expectations. For this very reason, however, he is hardly typical, since the writers and texts that form the basis for the studies just mentioned tend to be very different. Thus Dagenais' study of a Spanish text is at least partly driven by the semi-anonymous status of its author; while Hult's is shaped by the unsettling phenomenon of double authorship in the case of *Roman de la Rose*.

The most formidable response to the arguments such as these – in the form of qualification rather than of refutation – comes from two different scholarly approaches that deal with similar materials and issues, but stress the places where the difference of medieval textuality (which the Zumthorians tend to see as absolute) is in the process of modulating into something like an (early) modern shape. Armando Petrucci's studies of paleography and bookmaking (e.g., Petrucci 1995), with their strong political–social component, are instructive for at least two important reasons. First, he shows that there was no single model for writing or for reading in late medieval Italy, but a variety of practices depending on social class and occupation – aristocratic or bourgeois, notarial or mercantile, etc. – as well as on place and time. Second, he shows how Italian peninsular practices of readership and authorship were evolving in ways that took them increasingly in proto-modern directions, and he especially stresses the gradual, material phenomenon of writers' control over the production and dissemination of their works (especially chapters 8–9).[51]

In more general terms, the contrast among these different materialist accounts of textuality suggests that it is not enough to talk without further qualification about historicizing a text or a discourse. There are always more ways than one to historicize – unsurprisingly, since to historicize is to specify the significance of contingency, a process which itself must necessarily be contingent (of which, more in section v). In this case, the difference is, again, between a tendentially synchronic historicism, or historical "culturalism," which attempts to define the generalizable truth of a given epoch, and a tendentially diachronic historicism which not only specifies the differences internal to a given moment but also the dynamic trends that lead it from a different past to a different future.

If Petrucci's approach provides a point of view that supplements and modifies both Hult's and Carruthers', Alastair Minnis (1984, 1991, 2001) and his collaborators (Minnis *et al.* 1988), along with Copeland (1991) do the same for Dagenais and, again, Carruthers, and the strongest historical grounding and context for this study. Minnis' 1984 study, *Medieval Theory of Authorship*, evidently takes as its focus the figure of the *auctor*, but does so through the construction of this figure via the commentaries, and particularly the prologue or *accessus* of "modern" scholarly readers with which authoritative texts were normally accompanied. In this sense, he too sees the figure of the author as generated by, and subordinate to, the reader. In this initial study of the phenomenon, he draws most of his materials from what he rightly takes to be the dominant form of the author/text/reader configuration in the later Middle Ages, and the primary model for all other types of culturally prestigious textuality, the Bible and its Scholastic *lectores*.

Minnis worked with sources very similar to those of Dagenais and Carruthers (both of whom draw on his work), but the primary vector

---

[51] On the material conditions of poetic culture in late medieval Italy, see also the critics cited in n 13. For important recent attempts to relate and/or apply an approach like Petrucci's to Dante and his milieu, see Ahern 1982, 1990, 1992, 2003; Storey 1993; O. Holmes 2000; Steinberg 1999, 2000, 2007. For the emergent phenomenon of the "author's book" in particular see Avalle 1961; Huot 1987: chapter 7; Meneghetti 1992; Storey 1993; O. Holmes 2000. Cf. Cristaldi 1994.

of his argument is antithetical to theirs. Specifically, he reveals a dramatic shift in the orientation of Biblical exegetics over the course of the thirteenth century, one that both increasingly foregrounds the figure of the (human) author as individual producer of textual meaning and, just as importantly, gives increasing priority to the literal sense of the text (which, among other things, reduces the effects of readerly allegorizing, since it stresses authorial control).[52] Minnis' book focused primarily on the question of changing perspectives on the dual authorship of the Bible, divine and human, which, however, he sees as having at least indirect implications for the understanding of literary authorship of the classical pagan *auctores* (141–2; cf. 112–17). The book concludes by arguing that there is a coordinate, consequent, development in attitudes toward contemporary writers, perhaps though not certainly modeled on the trends in Biblical exegesis as well as on commentaries of the classics, particularly Ovid. Though primarily considering the English case (i.e., Gower and Chaucer), seen as markedly different from the Italian, Minnis does hypothesize that in "Italy a clear line of development may be traced from the early glosses on profane *auctores* like Ovid, to the humanistic commentaries on 'modern authors,' like Dante" (165). He then asserts that "the Dante commentators could claim that their 'modern author' shared literary roles and forms with Scriptural authors" concluding that if "at the end of the Middle Ages, *auctores* became more like men, men became more like *auctores*" (215–16). Dante's special role in this double process is, of course, precisely what is being investigated here.

The theses of Minnis 1984 were then given extensive exemplification, with commentary, in the anthology of hermeneutical and exegetical texts collected in Minnis *et al.* 1988. While still taking Biblical commentary as normative, this volume goes much further both in illustrating the parallel phenomena of the *accessus* and *commentaria* not only to classical *auctores* such as Virgil and Ovid (in relation to whom the model of the *accessus* had first been developed before being transferred to the Bible in the twelfth century [Minnis *et al.* 1988: 6–7 *et passim*]), but also to vernacular authors, above all Dante, from the end of the thirteenth century and throughout the fourteenth century.[53]

---

[52] Minnis 1984: 5, 27, 73–118, as well as discussion and examples in Minnis *et al.* 1988: 205–6, 242, 268–9 *et passim*. Spicq 1944: especially 288; Smalley 1952: 292–308; De Lubac 1959–65: 2.2.277–9; Pepin 1970a: 82–93 all previously noted the increasing emphasis on the importance of the *sensus litteralis* in Biblical exegesis by thirteenth century scholastics, especially Aquinas. For Dante's own emphasis on the textual "letter" see Chapter 2, section v, nn 70, 79; Chapter 4, section iii, nn 68, 69; Chapter 5, section ii, n 26.

[53] See also Minnis 1990, 1991, 2001. The latter is focused specifically on how the Ovid constructed in Latin and vernacular commentaries (*Ovidius Moralizatus*; *Ovide Moralisé*) enters into the writing

To summarize: the work of Minnis, and his collaborators, can be said to relocate, and to reconfigure in a terminology and within forms surprisingly medieval, the discovery of the "modern author" usually said to occur much later on. Minnis' approach tends to reveal how utterly dependent studies of the author from an early modern perspective are on stylistic effects, and particularly on the relative, superficial, congruence of sixteenth-century modes of self-assertion with those of later European modernity. This body of scholarship makes clear that far more attention should be paid to how the languages, modes, and genres of the Middle Ages, embodied in the *accessus* and commentary traditions, however superficially different from those of modernity, nonetheless reveal concerns analogous and perhaps teleologically linked to those deployed at the present time (also Giunta 2002). The result is a set of dramatically new answers to the questions: "what is an *auctor*?" and what does "he" have to do with the literary "author"?

Finally, Rita Copeland takes an important further step, extending those of Minnis *et al.*, in exploring the *auctor/lector*, ancient/modern, Latin/vernacular dialectics with which thirteenth- and fourteenth-century European writers, including Dante were continually and variously grappling. Copeland's *Rhetoric, Hermeneutics and Translation in the Middle Ages* (1991) agrees with Dagenais and Carruthers in the sense that she stresses the "inventive" power of medieval readers over the authoritative texts they gloss, and particularly the extent to which vernacular commentaries such as the *Ovide Moralisé* appropriated a special intellectual status and a powerful control over the regulation of literary meaning. However, by focusing on the genre of translation, which hovers between interpretive readership and creative authorship, Copeland shows how medieval *lectores* are also in the process of constituting themselves as writers, potentially conferring on the texts they (re)compose in the vernacular a stature comparable to that of the Latin original. Where Dagenais sees a static, synchronic culture of ethical reading and Carruthers a stable formation of *auctores* producing *lectores* producing *auctores*, and neither differentiates significantly between Latin and vernacular textuality, Copeland, like Minnis, but from another and relevant angle, sees a dynamic period of transition from Latin to vernacular, in which readership and authorship converge and interact in the production of texts.[54]

---

of the *RR* (the *DC*'s closest thirteenth-century rival in the field of learned vernacular literature) and shapes the nascent commentary tradition applied to and by French poets of the period. For medieval Ovid commentary, see also Hexter 1986. For Dante and Ovid, see n 27; Chapter 2, sections i, v, vi; Chapter 4, nn 7, 10, 42, 58. For the *RR*, see also n 75.

[54] Minnis (1984, 2001) and Copeland (1991) show that Dante's enterprise, however special in explicitness and scope, is not so in many of its basic aims. Copeland focuses, like Minnis (1984) on the English

The Dante of *Inferno* 1.85–87 is just such a reader (of the Latin *auctor*, Virgil) turning writer (of the vernacular *Commedia*) and his consequent assumption of authoritative status is inextricable from the implicit constitution of future readers who will concede him that status, but perhaps also seek, through him, to acquire it for themselves. What is not apparent from the *Commedia*, however, is the process by which Dante moves from modern readership to the easy assumption of timeless authority. Only a double gaze, one which embraces both the culture of authority – or, perhaps better, following Carruthers, Minnis, and Copeland, the culture of the *lector/auctor* dialectic – and Dante's progressive engagement with it from at least the *Vita Nova* forward, can begin to explain the historical significance of Dante's pursuit of *auctoritas*.[55]

Earlier, the Trecento commentaries on the *Commedia* were invoked as after-the-fact evidence that Dante's campaign to achieve the status of *auctor* and/or *autore* was rewarded within a decade of the writer's death in 1321. Indeed, as chapters 9 and 10 of Minnis *et al.* (1988; also Minnis 1990) reveal, the adaptation of commentary to vernacular works is an important means for authorizing the modern vernacular writer in terms that link him to the official culture of Biblical and antique *auctoritas*. Even more cogently, and of the first importance for this study, chapter 10 (written by David Wallace), brings out briefly but powerfully the singular role of Dante's *self-commentaries* – *Vita Nova*, *Convivio*, and, perhaps, the *Epistle to Cangrande* – in this process.[56] Dante's simultaneous occupation of the roles of commenting *lector* and commented-upon *auctor* hastens along the authorizing

case, while noting the importance of the Dantean precedent (180–4). She adroitly balances the role of vernacular culture as challenge to and critique of the elitism and isolation of academic Latinity (182, 224) against its claims to be a new locus of elitist cultural authority (178; also 224–5). For other Chaucer scholars who have explored the *translatio auctoritatis*, see, for example, Jacqueline Miller 1986; the later chapters of Stillinger 1992; Lerer 1993.

[55] Auerbach 1954 and Spitzer 1955 study Dante's rhetorical constitution of the reader in direct addresses throughout the *DC*, but not in the terms discussed here. More recently, attempts have been made to define the implied readership of a number of the Dantean *opere minori* (Noakes 1990; Ahern 1992; Lansing 1992; Durling 1992; R. Kay 1992). Innumerable essays have explored the dramatic representation of reading in *Inf.* 5. From the perspective adopted here, however, Gellrich 1985: 149–54, Noakes 1988 (68–80), and Stillinger 1992: chapters 2–3 represent the most important explorations of Dante's refashioning of the author/reader dialectic.

[56] For Dante and the medieval *accessus*-commentary tradition, see n 48. The specific phenomenon of self-commentary is highly unusual, and virtually unprecedented in the vernacular prior to Dante (with the hypothetical caveat that some of the early thirteenth century *vidas* and *razos* of the troubadours may have been composed by the poets themselves [see also Chapter 4, n 18]). Sandkühler 1967: chapter 2 offers brief descriptions of Trecento self-commentaries and commentaries on vernacular authors contemporary with or subsequent to Dante's. See also Minnis 2001: chapter 6, for a survey of Trecento auto-commentary, much of it derivative from Dante, in Italy, England, and France. Notable is Francesco da Barberino's Latin auto-commentary on his vernacular poem, *Documenti d'Amore* (Minnis 1990: 35–40, 2001: 278–80; O. Holmes 2000: 20). Roush 2002 (66–7 and nn)

process by modeling it for future readers. Even more importantly, as will be seen in Chapter 4, this unprecedented conflation of formal roles that his culture had worked strenuously to keep separate, operates the same kind of dramatic redefinition of the notion of authorship, or rather of the author/reader dialectic, that the uniting of previously distinct etymologies of *auctor* implicitly does at the opening of the *Commedia*.

The scholars discussed in this chapter, especially sections i and iv, have to a large extent sketched the overlapping series of histories in relation to which the Dante of this study will be situated. While Chapter 2 in particular will offer an overview of the genealogy of *auctoritas* from classical times to the Trecento, for the most part my efforts will be directed at describing an internal evolution of the Dantean *oeuvre* whose relationship to these and other "external" histories – which it alternately mirrors and evades – will be assumed and/or inferred, but not rigorously demonstrated. Of equal importance is the fact that a number of these scholars – most notably Petrucci, Minnis, Copeland, and Wallace – preview and model the historicizing practices adopted here. In particular, I refer to the idea that historical change, even at its most radical, takes place not in the form of absolute "epistemic" rupture, but rather as the dynamic reconfiguration of words, categories, concepts within pre-established forms, for example, the complex process by which the figure of the medieval *auctor* modulates through the Dantean *autore* into that of the modern literary *author*.

From this perspective can be seen the theoretical–methodological point that most decisively separates the present study from a Foucauldian analysis of the historical situatedness of authorship. Even after foreswearing the concept of the *episteme*, Foucault's historiography tended to dwell on the

aptly refers to the unpublished Latin (auto-?) commentary of Dante's nemesis, Cecco d'Ascoli (1269–1327), on his encyclopedic *L'Acerba* (written after the *DC*, which it attacks). Commentaries on vernacular and Latin works of Dante's contemporaries are Dino del Garbo's exegesis of Guido Cavalcanti's "Donna me prega" (1999; see also Fenzi 1999a; Quaglio 1964), written sometime before 1328, Dino's death date, and at least two Latin commentaries on the Latin tragedy, *Ecerinis*, of Albertino Mussato, by Guizzardo da Bologna and Pace da Ferrara, the former perhaps to accompany the debut of the poem in 1317 (Nardi 1961: 268–9; Raimondi 1966; Minnis and Johnson 2005: 220). Specifically on Dante's deployment of the formal device of auto-commentary the *loci classici* are Jenaro–MacLennan 1960; Nardi 1961; Sandkühler 1967; cf. Pepin 1970a: 126–38. Often neglected are the cogent comments of Grayson 1963. Recent contributions, in addition to those of Noakes 1988 and Stillinger 1992 (see n 55), are Battaglia Ricci 1983: especially ii; Minnis *et al.* 1988: 373–87, 439–45; Minnis 1990; Picone 1987a, 1995c, 2003a; Ascoli 1989, 1993, 1997, 2003; Parker 1993, 1997; Barański (1994b; 1996; 2001: 13–17; 2005a). Historical–critical studies of the phenomenon of auto-commentary, beginning with Dante are Folena 1990 and Roush 2002, both of which differ substantially from the approach adopted here. *DVE*, though not formally a self-commentary, also has some claim to this designation. See Mengaldo 1978a, 1979; Botterill 1996a; as well as Chapters 2–4. For the relevance of this topic to the authenticity debate surrounding the *ECG*, see Ascoli 1997: especially 309–11, 321–3, 338 and nn; also 2000b. See also Chapter 4.

identifiability of radical differences separating distinct historical epochs.[57] This study, however, takes a different view, which might figuratively be described as "evolutionary" and "ecological" in its approach to the dynamics of historical transformation. By "evolutionary" is meant the way in which the new (the modern author) emerges in dialectical relation with the old (the medieval *auctor*), through an incomplete mutation and transformation of existing categories.[58] By "ecological" is meant the way in which the category of authorship takes on significance within an elaborate system that includes, most notably, ideas of both textuality and readership (see Chapter 4).

Foucault rightly insisted on historical differences within the category of authorship – its contingency, even instability. However, his stress on outcomes (the modern author looks profoundly different from the medieval *auctor*), leads him to lose sight of the process by which they are achieved (the interplay of continuities and ruptures by which the latter became the former), and perhaps also of some structural features that have persisted over time and in spite of change. This point also has more immediate applicability in the literary historiography of late medieval, early Renaissance Italian studies, in that it invites a reconsideration of the ways in which Dante's supposedly medieval conception of his poetic role has been used as a critical foil for the innovations of the "first modern author," Francis Petrarch.[59]

V. CRITICISM

At stake in this study is Dante's position in relation to two categories, authority and historicity, operative at both a thematic and a methodological level. In medieval terms, *auctoritas* works to transcend the limitations of the individual, and with them the contingencies of history, either by establishing the existence of timeless truths articulated in a distant, originating past, or by grounding those same truths beyond history altogether, in the

---

[57] For the "episteme" see Foucault 1966 and the partial recantation in Foucault 1970. The later Foucault works primarily through the category of genealogy as against a historiography of origin and cause. Some of my own earlier work relied extensively on a crisis model of historiography, although primarily in aid of interpreting literary representations of variously perceived crises, rather than of asserting that model as reflective of my own understanding of the dynamics of historical change (Ascoli 1987). Compare Gellrich 1985: chapter 8, especially 253; Chiampi 1981: chapter 1.

[58] Jauss 1982, chapter 1, especially 16–18, 32–7, uses the term in a related though not identical fashion. He does not deploy the category of the ecological, although his understanding of the double diachronic and synchronic character of literary history and the interplay within it of texts and their successive audiences is salient.

[59] For versions of this topos, see Freccero 1975a, T. Greene 1982a and b. Cf. Mazzotta 1993b; Ascoli 1991a, 2009.

absolute power and knowledge of the Christian Deity. Conversely, Dante's own historically contingent personhood constitutes the primary obstacle to his acquisition of that quality for himself, and dictates his protracted and varied struggles to define and appropriate it. Methodologically, then, the principal problem obstructing any attempt to understand the Dantean discourse of authority historically is that the process of constituting Dante as *auctor* in the *Commedia* necessarily has as its primary objective the transcending of the historical world and of the poet's historicity in particular. In other words, the impulse to historicize *auctoritas* runs directly up against the fact that its object is an "a-chronistic" transcendence of historical time.

This problem is reflected in Dante criticism, both sociologically and, less often, critically. On the one hand, a very influential line of criticism has described the discourse of authority in the *Commedia* as a passage from the literary *auctoritas* of Virgil to the totalizing Authorship of the transcendent Christian deity (Hollander 1968; Barolini 1984), linking it closely to the thesis that the *poema sacro* presents itself persuasively as a work of inspired prophecy, analogous to the Scriptures (see Nardi 1942b; Singleton 1954; also Chapter 2, n 88). On the other hand, the vast majority of Dante critics, whether it subscribes to this particular interpretive line or not, attributes to the author–function known as "Dante" an extraordinary cultural authority that is a positive impediment to any dynamic – ecological, evolutionary – understanding of the poet's career as subject to historical forces beyond his knowledge or control. On the one hand, the responsible, if contestable, reading of Dante as *theologus-poeta*. On the other, what Maria Rosa Menocal (1991) has called "Dante's Cult of Truth," what Robert Harrison has dismissed as Dantology (1988: ix), and what a distinguished and skeptical colleague once defined as the typical view of *dantisti* that "Dante is God."[60] In either case, however, the result is the interpretive assumption, at least heuristically, of "total coherence" in the *Commedia*, which *de facto* removes the poem from historicizing scrutiny,[61] and which does not concede the legitimacy of an analysis not fully encompassed by terms and informing principles that Dante himself provides.

In an important polemical essay, Teodolinda Barolini advocated "de-theologizing" Dante as a remedy to the defects and limitations inherent in such an attitude.[62] By "de-theologizing" Barolini did not mean reading

---

[60] The comment was made by Lawrence Lipking.

[61] See Contini 1965a: 114 on "l'illusione della cosidetta lettura totale." See also the critiques of Parker 2000: 240–1; Tambling 1992: 351.

[62] Barolini 1989a; revised in Barolini 1992: 3–20. The Italian translation of her title as "La *Commedia* senza Dio" is less reassuring. Moevs (1999, 2005), beginning from premises partly derived from

Dante apart from an historical knowledge of theological culture, much less as a writer uninterested in matters theological.[63] Her point of departure was a reaffirmation of the value of Nardi's "Dante-Profeta" (1942b), and a syncretic attempt to reconcile the Nardian thesis with Singleton's strong assertion of the theological character of Dante's project in the *Commedia* (1954). What Barolini aimed to de-theologize was the relationship of Dante criticism generally to the poet; in other words, she attacked the cult of Dante as a supremely authoritative poetic God. While insisting that the key to understanding the *Commedia* is that it makes its truth claims in all seriousness, she pointed out that critics regularly fail to distinguish between the claim to truth and truth itself (1992: 15–18; cf. Freccero 1983a: 259–60). In other words, she pointed to the widespread adoption by Dante critics of Dante's own fictional and constructed, mystified and mystifying, point of view about himself and his work.

Barolini's proposed alternative was to read the *Commedia* rhetorically and narratologically, with a sharp focus on the strategies by which Dante makes the case for himself as "truth-teller." She takes a significant step beyond the Hollander thesis, by pointing to the artistic devices with which Dante sets out to "authenticate his text" and to confer "upon himself the authority we have rarely denied him" (1992: 19) and by arguing that Dante's critics "pose their critical questions . . . within the very presuppositions of the fiction they are seeking to understand" (1992: 15). The place of history in Barolini's study, however, is less certain. It is possible to infer a historicist paradigm underlying her distinction between Dante's relation to the text and that of a modern reader. She embraces a version of the "two historicities" that Paul Zumthor has argued meet to define historicism as a condition for "reading the Middle Ages": the historicity of the modern reader, who tends to impose her or his own circumstances and interests upon a reading of the medieval text; the historicity of the medieval text itself which has its own ways and means of inscribing itself out of history and into timeless truth (Zumthor 1980: 31–4 *et passim*).

Barolini, e.g., the concept of "non-falsi errori," as it were re-theologizes Dante and attempts a heroic reconciliation of poetry and theology through a brilliant reading of the *DC*'s metaphysics. Nonetheless, his work remains within, indeed takes to an extreme limit, the paradigm critiqued here.

[63] N.B., Understanding a poem in terms of historical *information* is not the same thing as understanding the poem in terms of a historical *dynamic*. Much Dante criticism links the poet and his *oeuvre* to specific types of historical information. Rarely, however, does even the best such criticism go beyond an assertion of homologies between Dante's writings and historical circumstances – theological, philosophical, poetic, or political as may be – to investigate the dynamic processes by which materials arrived in his hands and were reshaped by him.

Bringing this point into the open, however, suggests that Barolini runs a risk equal and opposite to that she criticizes. In resisting Dante's account of himself, there is a danger that she will introduce one that is anachronistically modern. That this may be the case appears from the undifferentiated and relatively unhistoricized use that she makes of the key term "truth" which, like "author," is a word that requires both careful conceptualization and rigorous historicist contextualization (cf. Moevs 2005: 4). Moreover, by the decision to make rhetorical analysis the primary tool for implementing her critique, Barolini ensures that she will *not* differ from most of the Dante critics whose practices she condemns on a fundamental point: she takes, as they take, the elucidation of the *Commedia per se* as the *telos* of her scholarly activity.[64] When she claims that "the poem itself furnishes sufficient and incontrovertible evidence of how it wants to be read" (1992: 10; also Barański 1994b: 9–39), she has significantly narrowed the procedural gap between herself and those she criticizes.

How then can one go about historicizing Dante's relationship to authorship and authority, without at the same time betraying the details and the desires of the Dantean *oeuvre*? Again, Dante criticism, especially in English, has been quite effective in showing how the poet represents history in the *Commedia*, or rather how he orders the materials of contingency within his own theology of history. Charles Singleton, for example, long since asserted that "the poem reveals its analogy to the structure of history; and history too is God's work" (1954: 61–2). He is, however, speaking of history viewed *sub specie aeternitatis*, and thus remains within a medieval and Dantean paradigm of salvation history.[65] History in the sense of contingency and change, much less of ideological discursivity, is another matter for him, and, he supposes, for Dante: "when there is no transcendence of change . . . how can we have anything but [mere] history [i.e., contingency, flux]?" (1954: 78). In a similar vein is Jeffrey Schnapp's elegant account of the "transfiguration of history" in the light of eternity, articulated around the juxtaposition between Virgilian epic warfare and the martyrdom of Cacciaguida, the *miles Christi* (1986). In this approach, history is rigorously subordinated to an eschatological teleology ordered by God, but is also, given the mediating representation of the afterlife offered by the *Commedia*, coincident with Dante's transcendent vision.

---

[64] Some of Barolini's recent work (e.g., 2003) has adopted a New Historical perspective, by juxtaposing events Dante purportedly recounts with information available from other sources.

[65] See also Hollander 1969: 57–103. Freccero 1983a adds substance to Singleton's claim with a succinct account of how the Christian "theory of history is the foundation of Biblical allegory" (267). For an intriguing variant on this reading, see Moevs 2005.

Significantly different is the approach of Giuseppe Mazzotta whose first book, *Dante, Poet of the Desert* (1979), set out to negotiate between the extremes of Singletonian theological view of history – articulated through the Exodus typology, and especially the wandering of the Hebrews in the desert – and Erich Auerbach's view that the theological framework is not much more than an enabling device for the representation of historical reality, "the secular world." For Mazzotta, Dante's "theological interpretation of history" (1979: 4) implies "the problematic character of every individual" (5), and foregrounds the semiotic and existential problem of the human struggle for transcendence as basic to the *Commedia*'s understanding of historical experience. Summarizing his position in the first book from the vantage point of a second, *Dante's Vision*, he refers to "Dante's sense of history as the economy of redemption and as the realm of human exile" (1993a: 3). In that second book, then, he positions the *Commedia* at a nodal point in history on which converge the great, and disparate, strands of medieval thought and art, working at once within and against the totalizing, systematizing impulses of the encyclopedic tradition represented, for example, by Vincent of Beauvais' *Speculum Maius*, not to mention Aquinas' *Summae*.[66] In the event, however, Mazzotta's perspective resists the turn to history much as Barolini's does: he too remains committed to an understanding of the text's perspective, which he sees as the practice and the celebration of a poetic knowledge that stands, if not outside history as Singleton would claim, at least at its margins and boundaries. Finally, he privileges what he avers is "Dante's vision" over the histories that traverse and delimit the *Commedia* and its author.[67]

Notwithstanding this qualification, Mazzotta's work encourages a return to Auerbach as an inspiration, if not in every sense as methodological model, for the historicized reading of Dante. The present study, as hinted earlier, will argue for just such a return. Auerbach's place in North American Dante studies is peculiar. Still recognized as one of the great pioneers in the field, alongside Singleton, his primary interest in the *Commedia* as a locus of the mimetic representation of historical reality has been all but discredited.

---

[66] On Dante's relation to encyclopedism, see also Vasoli 1983, 1988a: xxviii; Di Scipio and Scaglione 1988; Shapiro 1990: 23, 35–7, 141, 170, 181–5 *et passim*; Barański 1994a; Picone 1994; cf. Ascoli 1997: 315–18 and nn.

[67] For Mazzotta 1993a, "Dante's radical claims about poetry [are that it is] nothing less than the foundation of all knowledge" (3) and in the end poetry "opposes and transcends the values and the myths of history (14)." From another angle this implies that Dante plays a crucial, even inaugurating, role in the unfolding of the concept of "poetic history" which culminates with Vico (1977: e.g., 88–92; see Mazzotta 1993a: x–xi, 1999). A less nuanced version of a Dantean "thematics of historicity" is in Franke 1996.

His account of figuralism (1944), offered in response to claims that his secularized Dante was an anachronistic creature of modern sensibilities, has been folded into the larger discourse on Dantean allegory, severing it from its original place in his argument. The question of figural allegory is not central at this point in the discussion, though it will become more so later on. Nor do I wish to defend Auerbach's claim that Dante's *style*, if not his ideology, is informed by a worldly "realism" (1929, 1945).[68] What he does have to offer in the present context, instead, is a paradigm for locating Dante and the *Commedia* within a history of literate culture and of literary artifice.

Auerbach's argument in *Mimesis* (1945) is that in combining the valorization of the individual (soul) in Christian theology generally with the structuring device afforded by a figurally ordered vision of the afterlife – each soul's punishment or reward distilling and fulfilling the essence of its historical existence – Dante is able to create concentrated, realistic representations, saturated with meaning, of human lives. This argument, initially presented in the chapter entitled "Farinata and Cavalcante" has its historical payoff only in the following chapter dedicated to Boccaccio. For Auerbach, then, the meaning of Dante's representational techniques for the history of a secularized literary realism does not appear until the *Decameron*, as it were, lifts off the eschatological framework, leaving behind only the mimetic image of human existence in this world (Ascoli 1991–92). In other words, the significance of Dante's achievement is not fully available within the *Commedia* and, presumptively, not actually present as such to its author: only *history*, as the consequential passage of time, reveals it, fulfills it.

In a series of essays, John Freccero (1983c: 95–6, 103–4, 1983a: 259–60, 1983b: 196–7) has pointed to a basic flaw in Auerbach's reading. Freccero notes that in *Inferno* 10, Auerbach's exemplary proof text, Dante systematically attacks and subverts the perspectives of those Epicureans who, like Farinata and Cavalcanti, sustain the autonomy of human history as a field of action (1983c: 103–4). Their commitment to historical temporality has led to blindness and damnation. In other words, Dante pointedly rejects secularism and its mode of representing earthly existence. One might argue, however, that Freccero's critique actually strengthens the *historical* claim of *Mimesis*, even as it discredits the Auerbachian *interpretation* of Dante's text, because it persuasively, if implicitly, suggests that Dante is as blind to the

---

[68] Dante criticism generally has missed the significance of Auerbach's claims about the mimetic *effects* of Dantean style in a rush to judgment on his flawed assertions about Dante's ethical and epistemological investments in historical reality. An exception is Barolini 1992: 14–15 *et passim*.

destiny of his own work among future readers and writers as Cavalcanti is to the destiny of his beloved son, Guido.

Furthermore, the Auerbach–Freccero *querelle* indicates a larger difficulty with what has so far appeared as a simple opposition between, on the one hand, a historicist placement of Dante in contexts that exceed and define him and his works and, on the other, a textualist preference for staying within the confines of Dante's representation and/or understanding of himself. In particular, a conflict exists between at least two different methods of historicization. Freccero's critique of Auerbach is grounded in a deep respect for the text as locus of historical knowledge. What he indicates is that, in order to make Dante a poet of historical reality, Auerbach had to ignore the historicity of medieval theology and eschatology. Singleton's account of the mapping of history onto Dante's text, Mazzotta's recourse to the medieval discourses on knowledge, Barolini's neo-Nardian recourse to the prophetic tradition, are all, to varying degrees, historicist in this sense. The point, however, is not that Auerbach was wrong and they are right. Rather, the point is that historicism, like its object(s), is inevitably plural (cf. Jauss 1982: chapter 1 [1970]). For instance, as Mazzotta's work indicates, Dante's *oeuvre* is traversed by any number of distinguishable, if not entirely distinct, late medieval discourses which are juxtaposed and re-elaborated in complicated ways (also Baranski 1996, 2000). The conflicted history of Dante criticism itself proves *prima facie* that the choice of which discourse or discourses to focus on in historicizing the poet and his works results in a wide spectrum of separately but more or less equally historicized Dantes. More to the point and to the problem at hand: to historicize Dante in *either* Auerbach's way or Freccero's is to dehistoricize him in another, that of the other.

How, then, to reverse the dominant tendency of Dante criticism, which – at least in theory – operates in accordance with the principle that "Dante knows best" – without simply effecting a different kind of exclusion, by imposing external concepts of historicity while trivializing the substance of the text? In absolute, "theological" terms, there is probably no way to escape this historiographical analogue to the Heisenberg Uncertainty Principle, this hermeneutic circle whose circumference is everywhere and whose center is nowhere. The solution, then, cannot be absolute, and, though this study will frequently employ the mode of critique, it will be in the service of an approach whose primary claim is that it produces a different and worthwhile kind of knowledge around the figure of Dante, not necessarily a better one.

This approach is implicit in the choice of a topic, authority, that brings fully into view the paradox of historicism: on the one hand, the historical formations and transformations of the cultural categories of authorship and authority; on the other, Dante's pursuit of a history-transcending role as *auctor*. From that choice follows a double itinerary: (1) a historicizing contextualization, before and, to a lesser extent, after Dante, with respect to the dominant and emergent discourses of authority; (2) a rhetorical, textualist reading of the Dantean *oeuvre* which works against the tide of traditional Dante studies insofar as these posit the *Commedia* as Alpha and Omega of their explanatory criticism. The two aspects of this method converge around the idea of an internal history of Dantean authorship, which treats the earlier works, principally *Vita Nova*, *Convivio*, and *De Vulgari Eloquentia*, as experiments in the construction of authority, whose struggles reveal a troubled and often contradictory engagement with surrounding historical discourses, and whose successes, ultimately, make possible the seamless self-authorization of the *poema sacro*.

One basic assumption, with several more specific consequences, distinguishes this approach from more typical procedures of Dante criticism. That assumption is a contrarian response to the widespread methodological imperative best articulated by Freccero: "we assume the existence of a coherent pattern and abandon our response only when our resources, or those of the poem, are exhausted" (cited in Jacoff 1986: x; cf. Freccero 1983a: 259). Freccero's commitment to the total coherence of the *Commedia* is historically grounded in his application of the model of Augustinian confession and conversion not only to the *Commedia* itself, but to Dante's *oeuvre* in its entirety, and, in the end, to the relationship of that *oeuvre* to its historical antecedents and surroundings. This model supposes the achievement, at least rhetorically, of a "perspective of the end" at once at the terminus of time, and outside of it, from which all that has gone before can be reviewed and understood (Freccero 1966: 25–7). Within the confines of the *Commedia* this comes with the final vision of Deity toward which the poem builds systematically, and in which Dante grounds the perspective that turns him into the poet, implicitly the *auctor*, who "returns" to write out his vision. Dante's earlier works are viewed then retrospectively, palinodically, as inevitable faltering steps along the way to a definitive solution (see also Chiavacci-Leonardi 1977). As concerns Dante's relationship to history, and particularly to his classical and romance literary predecessors, it means that the *Commedia* is the triumphant *telos* toward which poets from Virgil and Ovid to Arnaut

Daniel and Guido Cavalcanti have been pointing as "umbriferi prefazii" (*Par.* 30.78).[69]

While not all *dantisti* would agree with Freccero's formulation in detail, it does accurately represents how most Dante criticism operates: under a teleological model that subordinates the *opere minori* to the *Commedia* and gives this "last, best" Dante a defining, and structurally transcendent, perspective on the relationship of his works to each other and to history (e.g., Chiavacci-Leonardi 1977; see also Chapter 6). The present study, instead, assumes that total coherence is not possible – this side of the Empyrean – and that fractures and contradictions within the text are likely to be the best indicators of a less than transcendent relation to history. This is all the more true because Dante *does* pursue coherence, or at least the appearance thereof, relentlessly, and thus makes strenuous efforts to minimize disruptive moments of this kind. Furthermore, such points of fracture and contradiction are most likely to be visible in the earlier and the unfinished works, and these works should therefore be studied on their own terms for broad hints concerning Dante's evolving and often unstable relationship to the discourses of authorship and authority (see n 15). The result will be an alternate history, in which the *Commedia* may be seen as a contingent outcome of the earlier works, but not as either their unique *telos* or as the fulcrum point of interpretation from which they are to be understood.

The critical topic which most immediately offers an entrance into the problems at hand is the much-discussed question of Dante's self-representation in the *Commedia* and throughout his *oeuvre*. As Freccero (1972: 129 and n; 1973: 186 and n), and more recently, and with different emphasis, Barański (1996: 7 *et passim*), have suggested, the key modern intervention on this subject is Gianfranco Contini's, especially the funda-mental essay, "Dante come personaggio-poeta della *Commedia*" (Dante as character-poet of the *Comedy*; 1957; see also Fergusson 1953: 9–10, Noferi 1977, Battaglia Ricci 1983: 151–60). Contini's title tells most of the story: the *Commedia* offers two rhetorically distinguishable Dantes, a character whose past actions – a sequenced journey through the three realms of the afterlife – are recounted in an indefinite present, sometime after 1301, by a poet. The two usually distinct figures are united by the first-person singular

---

[69] The homologies between the internal narrative structure of the poem, the palinodic relation of the poem to earlier Dantean works, and the literary–historical relation of Dante to his precursors are made clear in Freccero 1973. On typology as the model for Dante's account of poetic history, see Mazzotta 1979: especially chapter 5. See also Barolini 1984; Picone 1987a, 1997a. See also Chapter 4, n 40; Chapter 6, nn 12, 15.

pronoun. Furthermore, as Contini and Freccero both stress, they are joined by the poem's narrative commitment not only to the *personaggio*'s spiritual *telos*, but also to the transformation of the character called "Dante" into a *poeta*, or rather, of a character who had already written a great deal of poetry into the extraordinary poet who has both the unique experience and the newly acquired tools to write the *Commedia*.

Contini's doubled "Dante" complements Singleton's well-known distinction between the two aspects of "Dante-pilgrim" namely as moral and spiritual stand-in for Everyman [sic] and as historical individual (1954: 9–13; cf. Spitzer 1955). Contini uses the distinction between universalized and particularized, personalized, "I's" to suggest how the *Commedia* negotiates between a medieval *auctoritas*, which has strong affinities to Spitzer's "poetic" as against "empirical" "I," and an individualized authorship that comparable to, if not identifiable with, a romantic or Proustian biographical author (1957: especially 38–9; cf. 1965b: 76–7, cited in the epigraph). He gives a plausibly, though in the end erroneously, historicized formulation of this distinction by adapting Francesco Mazzoni's distinction between Dante-*auctor* (writer) and Dante-*agens* (character).[70]

To date, Contini's distinction has been understood primarily in rhetorical terms as an efficacious means of describing the *Commedia*'s procedures. Thus construed, it has lent comfort to a position corollary to Singleton's dictum that "the fiction of the *Divine Comedy* is that it is not a fiction" (1954: 62), which might be restated alternately as "the fiction is that [he, Dante] is not a fiction" or as "the fiction is that it [the *Commedia*] is not [his, Dante's] fiction." These formulations then dovetail nicely with Hollander's and Barolini's previously cited interpretation of the figure of the *autore* in the poem.

According to Contini, however, this rhetorical structure was produced by and can be inscribed within two interrelated and inconclusive histories: the history of Dante's technical experiments in self-representation from his early lyrics through the *Vita Nova* and *Convivio*, up to the *Commedia* (Contini 1939), and the history of authorial first-person self-representation from at least the Occitan lyric through Proust.[71] Taking this line of argument a

---

[70] Contini 1957: 39–40; Mazzoni 1955: 178–81. I articulate the distinction as "poeta" vs. "personaggio," instead of the routine "auctor" vs. "agens" or "actor" often used in Italian criticism, because, as this study aims to show, "auctor" is a term "in play" for Dante, not an honorific to be assumed, while both "agens" and "actor" refer primarily to makers of verbal works (see also Palma di Cesnola 1995: 25–8). For "actor," see Chapter 2, sections ii, v, vi. For *agens* (taken from the *ECG*, par. 14; see also n 75), see Ascoli 1997: 336–8 and nn, as well as Chapter 2, n 24.

[71] On the models for Dantean self-representation, see Chapter 4, section ii. This study, while consistently concerned with representations of a person named "Dante" in texts which declare themselves

step further, this study argues that there is no unified and unifying Dantean "I" that informs the *oeuvre* as a whole:[72] rather, it shifts according to the narrative, figurative, and rational logics operating at a given moment and to both strategic necessities and contingencies of circumstance – from work to work, and even within individual works.[73] And yet, at the same time, it is precisely the recurrent and insistent appearance of this "I" in all its complexities and contradictions that constitutes the most overt and dramatic manifestation of the historical Dante's overwhelming will to become, as it were "authority in person."[74]

VI. ORGANIZATION

The balance of this study is divided into two sections of three chapters each. The first section considers the struggle to understand and to acquire *auctoritas* in a series of earlier works, principally *Vita Nova, Convivio,* and *De Vulgari Eloquentia.* The second turns to the mature construction and assertion of authorial stature in the two major completed works of Dante's

to be written by "Dante" will not directly engage with the generic issue of autobiography. On that topic see: Spitzer 1946; Zumthor 1973; Lipking 1981; Stock 1996; de Looze 1997; O. Holmes 2000: especially chapter 1; Bloch 2003. For Dante specifically see, *inter alia*, Freccero (numerous essays including 1959, 1966, 1973, 1975b); Guglielminetti 1977; Barolini 1984: pt. 1; Durling and Martinez 1996: 551–2, 567–8. A challenging theoretical discussion of the topic is in De Man 1984.

[72] This is not the same as Foster's distinction between "the two Dantes" (1977), which is epistemological (one Dante uses philosophical instruments of cognition, the other theological) rather than rhetorical and tends to stick to one Dante per work. Foster distinguishes between two epistemological moments in Dante's writings – his two Dantes speak, respectively, from the vantage points of reason (philosophy) and of faith (theology) – and they are relatively stable variants of the authorial self throughout the *oeuvre.* My concern, instead, is with what is in the first place a formal, not (only or always) an epistemological, division and, secondly, varies from work to work and from rhetorical situation to rhetorical situation within a given work (see especially Chapter 3, section iv; Chapter 4).

[73] See Chapter 4 for ways in which the textualized Dante is multiplied in the pre-*DC opere minori.* See also Ascoli 1997: 318–21 and nn. Stillinger 1992: 227 n 11 offers a helpful review of the various Dantes that might be distinguished within *VN*: "the protagonist(s) of the lyrics, the speaker(s) of the lyrics, the protagonist of the autobiographical prose, the implied author of the *libello,* the real historical author, and perhaps others," though he then adopts the perhaps inevitable expedient of calling them all "Dante" as will, generally speaking, also be the case here. For a related discussion of the *DC* see Battaglia Ricci 1983: 151–2.

[74] Although this study responds to the historicizing challenge of Contini, as well as of Auerbach, Contini himself typically made his points with a magisterial *auctoritas* that often omitted salient details and argumentative steps. Let me acknowledge here a provisional alignment with the Continian project, as regards not only the specific assertion of the epigraph and the implications of the poet/*personaggio* configuration, but also the embracing claim that "un costante della personalità dantesca [è] questo perpetuo sopraggiungere della riflessione tecnica accanto alla poesia, quest'associazione di concreto poetare e d'intelligenza stilistica" (1939: 4). The force of this last assertion is echoed by, among others, Grayson 1963: 41; Mengaldo 1979: 9; Battaglia Ricci 1983: 11; Barański: 1989b: 31, 1994a, 1996: *Premessa.*

later career, *Monarchia* and the *Commedia*. The study is thus designed to describe a temporal line of emergent ideas and strategies that resists the typically monolithic, *Commedia*-centered characterizations of Dantean authority: in the attention dedicated to the three earlier works for their own sake and on their own terms, in the treatment of *Monarchia* as effectively contemporary to the *Commedia* and as its equal in the representation and construction of authority, and, heuristically, in the projection of an aftermath which both registers and betrays Dante's self-creation as *auctor/*author.[75]

---

[75] I make no claim to an exhaustive review of Dante's career. This study concentrates (1) on Dante's explicit utterances concerning *auctoritas* and authorship, which occur in the prose works and *DC* (2) on the dialogue that takes shape between Italian and Latin writings, and (3) on his most innovative formal devices, including the practice of self-commentary, and the fusion of lyric, narrative, and expository modes. Dante's lyric *oeuvre* gets short shrift, except as it is incorporated and reinterpreted within the macro-textual frames of *VN*, *CV*, *DVE*, and the *DC*, and except as the criticism that has arisen around it has influenced or paralleled my thinking (e.g., Contini 1939; Nardi 1956; Boyde 1971; Barolini 1984: chapter 2, 1997, 2003, 2004; Durling and Martinez 1990; Martinez 1995b; Picone 1997b; Gorni 2001; De Robertis 2002, pt. 2; Scott 2004: 63–105). Among the authenticated Latin works I do not, with one exception, discuss the *Eps*, although the political letters in particular are undoubtedly relevant (Passerin d'Entrèves 1952: 37–41; Davis 1957: 139–46 *et passim*; Sarolli 1963: 243–4, 1966b: 64–6; Mineo 1968: 143–60; Mazzoni 1966a and b; Hollander 1969: 186–8; Pastore Stocchi 1970; Scott 1996: 42–6, 1997: 93–4, 2004: 337–47; Pertile 1997b; also Martinez n.d.). The *Q*, which overtly positions Dante in relation to the "official culture" of philosophical Scholasticism is only touched upon in passing (see Mazzoni 1957, 1962, 1979; Nardi 1959; Freccero 1961; Padoan 1966; Barański 1997b; Scott 2004: 348–50; also Chapter 2, n 27). Although Dante's last works, the two epistolary eclogues composed as part of a verse epistolary exchange with Giovanni del Virgilio, which constitute a polemical encounter with the proto-humanism fostered in the Northern Italian courts (see section i), are also omitted, I have studied them in detail elsewhere (Ascoli 2009; see also the editions with commentary in Wicksteed and Gardner 1902; Alighieri 1979b, 1980; and the critical studies of, *inter alia*, Battisti 1955–56; Reggio 1969; Martellotti 1970, 1983; Krautter 1983; Kegel–Brinkgreve 1990; Vlajcic 1995; Raffa 1996). Excluded also are two works of contested attribution, the *Fiore* and the so-called *ECG*, whose relevance to my topic, whether they are by Dante or not, is obvious. The *ECG*, which either constitutes the final installment in a trilogy of Dantean auto-commentaries (see Chapter 4) or a particularly significant moment in the reception not only of the *DC*, but also of Dante's adventures in self-authorization more generally, I have treated elsewhere (Ascoli 1997, 2000b, 2003; see also Baranski 2005b for discussion and bibliography). (N.B., as Azzetta 2003 suggests, the recent discovery of an early Trecento vernacular commentary on *DC* by Andrea Lancia with obvious debts to both the *accessus* and commentary sections of *ECG*, offers significant ammunition for supporters of authenticity.) The *Fiore*, a late Duecento Italian translation and severe abridgement of the *RR* sometimes attributed to Dante is not treated either. The possibility that a youthful Dante had engaged with the *RR* to such an extent is intriguing, to say the least. The uncertainty of attribution, however, is such that any attempt to place the work within an account of Dante's career would involve a series of precarious hypotheses amounting to a house of cards. Moreover, given that the *Fiore* tends to excise the philosophical/theological content of the *RR*, it would necessarily represent an anomaly with respect to the overall pattern this study traces (i.e., my own inclination is to see the attribution to Dante as erroneous). For further discussion see Contini 1965c, 1973; Vanossi 1979; Huot 1993; Barański and Boyde 1997; Brownlee 1997; Casciani and Kleinhenz 2000; Minnis 2001. For authorship and authority in the *RR*, see Hult 1986, 1989; Huot 1987: 99–103; Minnis 2001.

This temporalized model is, nonetheless, conditioned in two contrasting ways. First, even though only one chapter is primarily dedicated to the *Commedia*, the *poema sacro* nonetheless remains, inevitably, a focal point of the whole study, as we began to see in section ii. The *Commedia's* achievement is prepared for by the earlier works and in many ways it fulfills their incomplete aspirations, though not necessarily in ways traditionally asserted; the nature of *Monarchia's* project is understood in both comparison and contrast with it; finally, it is what, in many ways, determines both that the author–function "Dante" has an historical afterlife with a particular set of characteristics, and that the contingent process by which that author–function came into being has remained largely concealed from readerly view.

Second, despite the appearance of a linear historical direction, this itinerary is by no means straightforwardly diachronic. Throughout Dante's earlier and mature works, and on into the responses they then elicit, a powerful tension exists between various competing factors: the prestige of Latin and the novelty of the vernacular; the transcendence of an author and the immanence of a reader; a tradition of *auctoritas* and a new idea of authorship. And this is to give only a few of the possible names to the phenomenon in question. This tension takes different forms at different times and is never resolved, even in the *Commedia*, so as to allow an assertion that this, in the end, is what Dante's authority consists of, this is what it definitively means.

On the one hand, throughout the *oeuvre* we will see a Dante obsessed with relating himself to the various culturally sponsored, ideologically driven forms of authorship available to him. On the other, and at the same time, he possesses an experimental and recombinative drive to situate himself *among* multiple definitional options rather than *within* one of them in particular, and he thus emerges as an individualized and willful, proto-modern author-figure. Both of these tendencies are reflected, or, better, refracted, in the complex reception/influence of Dante's authorial self-construction in the generations that followed him.

Part i, the core of this study, does triple duty. In the first place, it continues and expands the exposition of the twinned categories of *auctor* and *auctoritas* in the late medieval context, with special reference to the encyclopedic definitions given to them by Hugutio (Uguccione) of Pisa in the *Magnae Derivationes*, Dante's avowed point of departure for his explicit reflections on the subject. Secondly, it offers more and less extended examples of how the three major early works, and one Latin epistle of the same period, both enter objectively, definitionally, into the fields of *auctoritas* and negotiate subjectively, rhetorically, the Dantean "I's" intricate relationship to the categories upon which he/it expounds.

Finally, Part 1 broadens dramatically an understanding of what is at stake in *auctoritas* for Dante. Each of the three chapters has a general focus on a single aspect of the question. Chapter 2, naturally enough, treats Dante's uses of the Latin and Italian words for authority and authorship, with major emphasis falling on the one place, chapter 6 of *Convivio* 4, where he discusses them etymologically and definitionally. Chapter 3 centers on the *questione della lingua*, namely Dante's repeated efforts, especially in *Convivio* and *De Vulgari Eloquentia* to relocate the "cultural capital" associated with Latin into the uncertain, non-prestigious realm of the vernacular. Chapter 4 then analyzes Dante's recurrent adaptation of the medieval commentary tradition, through which classical and Biblical Latin texts were at once recognized and constituted as authorities, to his own idiosyncratic practices of self-commentary.

Part 1 as a whole stresses that the Dantean discourses on authority, and the textual practices through which it is displayed and manipulated, are multiple and shifting. A study of authority in Dante that begins from the *Commedia*, as already suggested, inevitably casts the question between two absolute poles, poetry and theology, and defines a relationship at once of symmetry and of hierarchy between them. A study, like this one, which begins with the earlier works, recognizes that in the Middle Ages authority was mobilized in many different fields, and often in different modes within those fields, complicating, even thwarting, the temptations of symmetry and of hierarchical order. Just to begin with, for Dante authority can be either institutional or textual. Institutionally it can be either juridical–political or ecclesiastical. Textually it can be poetic, philosophical, and/or theological. Without promising – or even desiring! – a comprehensive synthesis, this study aims to show that notwithstanding the inevitable privilege accorded to one or the other of these fields and/or modes at a given point, Dante is constantly aware both of the need to position himself in relation to all of them, and of the rational and practical complications – at times life-threatening, at others simply confusing – that this felt need entails.

Finally, in these chapters, and throughout this study, one recurrent theme, now dominant, now subordinate, shadows, resists, and determines the Dantean discourse of authority, namely, the problem of the human will. As suggested above, a structuring tension appears at once grammatically and dramatically in the obstinate presence of the speaking "I," the pronomial projection of the author–function, which both claims and inherently contradicts the definitionally impersonal stature of *auctor*. We will return again and again to the multiple forms (e.g., first person singular; first person plural; third person singular; third person plural [in what might be called the mode of psychomachia]) that this presence takes in Dante's *oeuvre*. If Contini, Freccero, and others, have tracked this dramatized, textualized manifestation of Dante's will, however, they have not observed that it is paralleled by an objectified philosophical discourse that treats human identity – its "nobility," its faculties of understanding, above all its capacity for defining itself through willful choice.[76] Again and again, both in the *opere minori* and in the *Commedia*, invocation of and reflections on the will as the instrument of expressing and creating human personhood become the oblique yet sure site of negotiating the relationship between individual authorship and impersonal authority, bringing and binding together the separate topics considered over the course of this study.

Where Part 1 defines a "historical" stage – of struggle, development, and, often, failure – the focus of Part 2, "Authority in Person: Dante between *Monarchia* and the *Commedia*," is on the two works that most obviously represent a stage of authority achieved, or at least more successfully asserted, in Dante's career. In each case, Dante both builds upon past experience and evolves new strategies of presenting himself and his writing that place them in a relatively more harmonious relation to the medieval discourses of authorship and authority than the texts examined in Part 1. In each case Dante brings together the multiple forms and modalities of *auctoritas*, textual and institutional, in elaborate synthesis, integrating his claims to poetic, philosophical and/or theological *auctoritas* with systematic reflections on the two great institutional authorities of the historical world – Empire and Church. In each case, what makes "success" possible is the reconciliation of traditional canons of *auctoritas* with their individual instantiation in the person of Dante. As anticipated above, this reconciliation ultimately takes place on a dual track of theoretical discourse about the operations of human will and of the dramatic and/or rhetorical representation of a (willful) Dantean "I." It depends, in both cases, on the rhetorical short-circuiting of the derivation of authority over time and through subjection to institutional offices, by suggesting that Dante's oxymoronically

---

[76] Freccero's magisterial study of the "piè fermo" crux (1959) and his later elaborations of the theme (collected in Freccero 1986), make it plain how central will is not only to Christian psychology generally, but also to the experience of *Dante-personaggio* specifically. Nonetheless, the category of will as a dramatic and conceptual bridge between *personaggio* and *poeta* in the *DC* has not been sufficiently appreciated (see Chapter 7), nor, looking at the career as whole, has its relevance to the question of authority.

personal authority derives without intermediaries from the transcendent Author of authors.

If Part 2 posits Dante's mature works as a kind of typological fulfillment of his earlier career, it nonetheless deliberately resists the teleological formulation that such claims typically assume. It does this in a variety of ways. Presenting *Monarchia* and the *Commedia* as more or less contemporaneous, yet in many ways dramatically different, solutions to the rhetorical and conceptual problems confronted by the earlier works emphasizes that even here the Dantean discourse of *auctoritas* is provisional and contingent. For both works "success" is relative and partial, the product of identifiable and historicizable rhetorical and conceptual strategies. In particular, the strong affirmation of Dantean authority is still traversed in both cases by internally conflicted strategies of authorization, however well masked in comparison to the earlier works. In other words, the two ostensibly "finished" works both continue to reflect the fundamental tension between authority and personhood, remaining firmly within the grasp of historical processes that can be overcome only in contingent, imaginative terms.

Chapter 5 explores the synthesis of the various types of authority and of impersonal and personal authorship in *Monarchia*. Notwithstanding the radical elements in its political stance, *Monarchia* comes to represent the conservative pole of the Dantean quest for authority, insofar as it is his fullest and most conspicuously normative foray into the genre of the Latin philosophical *tractatus*, which both linguistically and formally mimes the canonical culture of medieval authority. *Monarchia*, seen in this perspective, perfects the language and form of *De Vulgari Eloquentia* and takes to a higher and more ambitious level *Convivio*'s claims to participate in the discourse of classical philosophy. This analysis departs significantly from the standard treatment of the treatise, which focuses on expounding its political content and situating it in the limited context of late medieval struggles for power between Church and Empire. Rather, the treatise will be read in terms of the rhetorical strategies it deploys in situating its author in relation to the temporal and spiritual authorities whose dominions he presumes to delimit. Internal contradictions will emerge which betray the "force of a desire," contaminating Dante's avowed commitment to logical argumentation. The chapter culminates with the suggestion that Dante put himself in the place of the *nuntius* or ad hoc messenger of God and that he take for himself the role of the Biblical prophet and judge, Daniel.

Chapter 6 then focuses upon one of the most powerful of the rhetorical tactics by which Dante, in both *Monarchia* and the *Commedia*, constructs his own authority, namely the palinode, a trope of recantatory allusion and citation. As we have begun to see, through the use of the palinode Dante creates an ideal, retrospective order within his *oeuvre*, reinforcing the impression that he has acquired a timeless *auctoritas*. This chapter, in certain basic respects, constitutes the polemical and methodological heart of the study. Its aim is not to demonstrate the existence of the palinode per se, since this has been done persuasively by numerous twentieth century Italian and North American critics. Rather, it is to counter the mystificatory effects which scholarship centered on the palinode has had upon our understanding of the rhetorical and historical character of Dante's career, and especially on the representations and assertions of authorship and authority within it.

Having outlined the place of the palinode both in the Dantean *oeuvre* and in Dante scholarship, emphasizing its primary function of *authorizing by de-historicizing* Dante and his works, Chapter 6 suggests that *Monarchia* offers cogent examples of the failure of the palinode to contain the traces of contingency that mark, and mar, its attempt to superimpose an ideal political order on the "secular world." It then examines symptomatic examples of textual repetition between *Monarchia* and the *Commedia*. Rather than demonstrating the recantatory mechanism, however, these instances exemplify how differences between Dantean texts do not necessarily signal a directed teleological itinerary, but often betoken the adaptation of similar materials to different rhetorical and historical occasions and needs. Not by chance, the culminating instance is that of Dante's representation of the power, but also the contingency and ultimate inadequacy, of the human will in imposing itself upon the ever-changing world of history. In other words, Chapter 6 shows how Dante alternately resists and acknowledges the forces that shape and compromise his attempts to construct himself as that impossible creature, the modern *auctor*.

Finally, Chapter 7 offers an extended consideration of Dante's *Commedia*, focused on the cantos, *Inferno* 1 and *Paradiso* 26 where the problem of the author is most explicitly posed, and on the extended sequence, *Purgatorio* 16–27, where the poet most deliberately stages his own access to authority in relation to that of the great earthly institutions of Church and Empire as well as to that of the classical poetic tradition, still represented by Virgil, of course, but now also Statius. The chapter does triple duty. First, and predictably, it provides a reading of some aspects of the *Commedia* "in the light of" the historical context(s) and methodological caveats developed in relation to Dante's major prose and prosimetrum works over the course of the first six chapters. From this angle, the *poema sacro* will figure as yet another example of Dante's long-term engagement with the figure of the *auctor* and the culture of *auctoritas*, although, inevitably, as *prima inter pares*. Secondly, the *Commedia* will serve simply as a means of verifying the significance that has been attributed to the "minor" works, because it repeats, corrects, and develops in ways both explicit and covert the issues with which they first grappled. Finally, looking beyond the "internal history" of the Dantean *oeuvre*, in whichever direction we might be reading it, this chapter will try to suggest both how the *Commedia* positions itself in relation to the past and present it knows, or thinks it knows, and the future it imagines, of the "external" history, or rather, multiple, intersecting histories, of authorship and authority in Western culture, and how we might, from our perspective, re-historicize that poem and the *oeuvre* it so deliberately subsumes.

VII: "WHAT IS AN 'OTHER'?"

No matter how often it asserts its distance from the authoritative world of the *dantisti*, this book will inevitably project a celebratory aura, in part because of the by-now ineluctable "cultural capital" attached to the name "Dante," in part because of its narrative of struggle and acquisition, and in part, of course, because I do love and acknowledge the importance, intelligence, and beauty of Dante's texts, singly and as a *corpus*. That does not mean, however, that either the *translatio auctoritatis* or the emergence of modern authorship are to be seen as intrinsically desirable events. In the first instance, they are simply inevitable – authority, with power, is always in play, in some form and passing through someone's hands – though not inevitably linked to the name of Dante. In the second, however other-directed and well intentioned, however articulated in the mode of resistance to the reigning structures of domination, Arendt's legitimating authority easily shades off into tyrannical authoritarianism. We are always other than The Author, until we become "Him."

In the last few pages of this chapter, then, it is worth asking the question: is the quest for authority, Dante's quest for authority, a righteous one? Does his achievement herald something new and valuable? Or the dawn of new regimes of social control? To begin an answer, one may consider precisely the extent to which the discourse of authority, in Dante and more generally, does depend upon positioning oneself in a relation of appropriation, and/or domination with an *other*. In the first instance Dante, at some never entirely accessible discursive outset, posits the *auctor* as the absent and/or transcendent Other whose powers he both honors and seeks to expropriate, whether this is the long-dead Virgil, the absent Emperor, or the invisible yet omnipresent God. This, of course, is to cast the Other in a substantially different light than that to which we have recently become accustomed, since rather than appearing on the margins of the social order this Other is one whose Truth and whose Law – both named in Dante by the word *ragione* – define the normal and normative "order of things": the Same, one might say, in which Dante exists and of which he is an inseparable part.[77]

Nonetheless, in setting out to define and acquire authority, and to exercise it over others, Dante casts himself as the victim of exclusionary repression and *resists* the constraints of authoritarian imposition – embodied variously as the Black Guelfs of Florence; Pope Boniface VIII; Guido Cavalcanti; Aristotle and so on. Similarly, as he modifies the meaning(s) of *auctoritas* in grappling with it, he may seem to resist and to subvert the authority of institutions (e.g., the Church), of a class (at times, the hereditary nobility, at times the "gente nuova" of the rising bourgeoisie), of "high culture" (especially, Latin as *gramatica*), of a vernacular project (e.g., Guittone D'Arezzo's or, for that matter, Cavalcanti's), while at the same time more or less successfully adapting and reallocating authority to other institutions (the Empire), to a new social order, to what will, eventually, become the highest of high Italian cultural idioms (Pietro Bembo's courtly, archaic Tuscan) and, of course, to himself.

From this latter perspective arises a temptation to impose an ennobling, anachronistic allegory (*alieniloquium*; the "other speech" so dear to medieval authors) on the Dantean project. Dante's attempts to raise the vernacular to near-parity with Latin might, for example, be compared with Whitman's or Melville's or Dickinson's or Twain's efforts to articulate an American literary language distinct from High English; or with the later, related claims of Americanists to an equal or even greater share of the glory in that anomalous North American entity, the English Department; or with the ongoing struggle to understand some form of Spanish as a second national language of the United States; or, to arbitrarily close an open sequence, the attempt to legitimate "ebonics" as the grammar of a tongue too long considered profoundly "vulgar."[78] They *might* be so compared, but I will do so only in the subjunctive and conditional modes.

A similar temptation exists, especially as regards *Convivio* and *Monarchia*, and in the light of political-military phenomena of our own time,

---

[77] For a strong (psychoanalytic) reading of the Dantean *oeuvre* in related terms, see Noferi 1977: especially 13–16, and the passage she aptly cites from *CV* 4.9.6. See also *Inf.* 26. 141 ("come altrui piacque").

[78] See, for example, Looney 2004, which is part of a larger project studying the frequent appropriations of Dante by African-American writers and filmmakers.

to foreground Dante's strong attempt to suppress the traditional understanding of political *auctoritas* as necessarily violent political expansionism, expressed in the etymology of *auctor* from *augere*, "to augment" and to replace it with an idea of imperial authority as desireless, unifying, pacifying, potentializing, and judicious: source and guarantor of perfect Justice that lets human nature achieve its rational and creative potential. One might be tempted by this vision: but, one should also probably recall that the ideology of Empire often construes domination as justice, violence as reason, conflict as peace, not to mention that Dante's dramatizations of eternal punishment in the *Commedia* have accurately been described as a "fearful art of justice" (Cassell 1984).

Finally, around the edges of Dante's Empire of Reason, scholars have, of late, arrayed a series of traditionally excluded "others" – the lower classes, women, "pagans" and heretics, Muslims, Jews, homosexuals – whom ideally, and, then, we begin to hope, in practice, might, for Dante, be admitted exceptional entrance to the typically, if ironically, exclusive *universitas* of wealthy, Catholic, male human kind.[79] We might take heart, returning to the *questione della lingua*, from the fact that Dante links the vernacular to "women and children" and to the lower-class wet-nurse at whose breast he first imbibed the knowledge of the "nobler" tongue (*DVE* 1.1.1–2). And then, of course, we might lose it, later, when that language in its perfected form turns out to be an alter-Latin, the language spoken in the precincts of power, in distinctly masculine tones (see Chapter 3). We might be encouraged by the argument in *Convivio* 4 that "nobility" is neither the hereditary property of an aristocracy nor a commodity for purchase, but rather an individual attribute, and then, again, we might begin to realize that this formulation potentially contains an even more exclusionary and anti-popular quality than those it replaces. And we might wonder if all the work that must be done in order to turn exclusionary language directed at these and other groups into something positive, does not in itself indicate that, at the very least, Dante made it possible for any reader who wanted to go on passively

---

[79] For example, after a century and more of bewildering critical attempts to refute the apparently intolerable notion that Dante could have believed that his beloved teacher, Brunetto Latini, was a homosexual, critics have begun to acknowledge that sodomy is a significant category for Dante, and even to argue that he himself felt the pull of such desire (Durling and Martinez 1996: 238–45 *et passim*; 557–60) or that his language is profoundly implicated in it (Barkan 1991: 53–66; Boswell 1994; Holsinger 1996; Cestaro 2003 a and b). On Dante's representations of women, gender and sexuality, see, for example, Ferrante 1975; Spivak 1981; Potter 1990; Jacoff 1987; Schnapp 1989a; Psaki 1996, 2004; Barolini 2000a, 2003; O. Holmes 2001 (also Chapter 2, n 14; Chapter 3 n 22; Chapter 7, n 154). On the positive aspects of his attitude toward Islam and pagan otherness, see Schildgen 2002. For the links between Islamic philosophical poetry and Dante via the mediation of Frederick II, see Menocal 1987: chapter 5; Boccassini 2003; Mallette 2005.

omitting, or positively repressing, these socially constructed "others" to do so.

To regress once more to anachronistic social allegory – "other speech" in which one discovers that others are really the same (as us) or that, to quote an ephemeral Burger King ad campaign, "different is good" – there are possible analogies to be developed between Dante's quest for authority, especially as it figures that of an emergent, lay, middle class, and the problematics explored at a certain stage in feminist discourse between the aspiration for women to achieve the same status, politically and/or literarily, as men, and the possibility that to become indistinguishable from the class of persons identified as responsible for systemic exclusions of women and many "others" is not necessarily a positive thing.[80]

To the extent, then, that there is any generalizable ideological lesson to be extracted from these reflections on Dante and authority, it is not that the process described is good or bad, productive or re-productive, liberating or oppressive. Depending on what moment in the process and its aftermath, and from the perspective of what subject or class of subjects, one cuts into it, it may be one or the other, or both: "still better, and worse." Rather, it is, again, the facts and effects of process, the relentless shifting of forms, meanings, and values that an "evolutionary"/"ecological" dynamic approach posits, which I hope to bring, however intermittently, into view, despite my own undesirable yet inevitable limitations and exclusions. Is an *autore* the Other of an *auctor*? Or yet another canonical *authority*? Does the Dantean *autore* figure and favor the struggle of others, or, omit and oppress it, and them? The questions should and will be posed: but no authoritative answers will, or should, or could, be given.

---

[80] See, for example, Cavarero and Restaino 1999 for a useful review and commentary on the difference vs. equality problem in feminist thought. For reflections on this question in relation to Dante, and Cavalcanti, see Cornish 2000a.

PART I

An author in the works: Dante before the Commedia

CHAPTER 2

Definitions: The vowels of authority

I. THE PROBLEM OF *CONVIVIO*

Dante's quest for special cultural standing, for *authority* in a general sense, began very early in his career. As will be seen better in Chapter 4, *Vita Nova*'s idiosyncratic adaptations of the Latin commentary tradition to the glossing of Dante's poetic texts aim at locating him in the structural position of the *auctor*, and this in 1293, when he was still in his twenties. The third chapter of the "libello" apparently documents a significantly earlier step in this process. By sending out the cryptic poem "A ciascun'alma presa e gentil core" to a circle of Tuscan poets, whom Dante calls the "fedeli d'amore," including his "primo amico" Guido Cavalcanti as well as Dante da Maiano and, more doubtfully, Cino da Pistoia, for interpretation, he asserts his own significance within a locally prestigious community and places his work in the authoritative position of receiving readerly commentary, albeit that of modern vernacular writers like himself.

At the same time, however, in this early work Dante scrupulously avoids using the words *autore* and *autorità*, much less their Latin equivalents. The proof case here is the chapter traditionally numbered 25.[1] As is well known, in this chapter Dante justifies the poetic practice of representing Love as a person (a "substance") when it is really an emotion experienced by persons ("an accident [i.e., occurrence, happening] in a substance"), by recourse to a brief history of lyric poetry in the vernacular (Occitan and Italian), and a comparison of the practices of modern "dicitori d'amore" with those of the classical "poete" (Virgil, Lucan, Horace, Homer, Ovid). The "poete" regularly use the poetic figure of prosopopeia (personification) and other

---

[1] I accept both the retitling of the work by Gorni (1995, 1996) and the critique of Michele Barbi's arbitrary division of the work into forty-two chapters by Gorni (*ibid.*) and Cervigni and Vasta (1995: 19–28), anticipated by Marti 1965, 1991. Following the latter (20), I will continue to use the traditional chapter numberings for reference, though not for interpretive purposes, since these are still found in most editions.

tropes that distort the literal truth, and Dante asserts he and other "dicitori" have the right to do the same.

In other words, Dante insists that his activity is comparable, at least in one respect, to that of the classical *auctores*. As has been widely observed (e.g., Barolini 1984: 188–9; Iannucci 1993b; Picone 1997a), it is no accident that these same five *auctores* will then reappear in *Inferno* 4 identified explicitly as such (Virgil already introduced as Dante's "maestro e autore," and the classical crowd generally having "grande autorità ne' loro sembianti" [having great authority in their visages; 4.113]), or that Dante will then be made a full partner in their community ("sesto tra cotanto senno" [sixth among such wisdom; 4.102]). But it is also no accident that in this earlier context they are, just like the modern vernacular versifiers, called "poeti," of whom a subset is specified as "dicitori d'amore," not "autori."[2] In addition, he scrupulously limits the activities of modern "dicitori" to the subject of love between men and women, a topic represented in only one of the five classical examples[3] – that of Ovid (Picone 1993 and 1997a) – and restricts their audience to the (culturally secondary) class of women, who are unable to read Latin and thus can only be addressed in the vernacular. Although arguments from omission are notoriously untrustworthy, I would still hazard that Dante knew the classical poets were entitled to be called "autori" and that he avoided doing so because it would have made prematurely explicit his own aspirations to that title, which, as we shall see, are nonetheless implied throughout the *libello*.

Whatever the reason for avoiding the language of authority in *Vita Nova*, Dante's practice has significantly changed by the time he came to compose the three documents – his two major unfinished treatises, *Convivio* and *De Vulgari Eloquentia*, and the infrequently studied *Epistle* 3 to the poet-jurist Cino da Pistoia – in which such language appears for the first time in his career and where he first explicitly sets out to situate himself in relation to the traditional definitions of *auctor* and *auctoritas*.

All three of these texts belong to the years immediately following Dante's exile from Florence in 1301, the radically traumatic event to which he returns

---

[2] The topic of *auctoritas* in *VN* has been extensively treated by Picone in a series of essays beginning in 1977, to which I owe a considerable debt (see Chapter 4, sections i–ii, especially nn 9–10). Nonetheless, to call the "io" of *VN* "auctor" as a settled fact (e.g. 2003: 230) is to miss a constituent dynamic that informs Dante's career from the *libello* through the "poema sacro." *Poeta* is also a loaded term for Dante. De Robertis 1970: 185; Tateo 1970b: 65–8; Barolini 1984: 270n rightly assert that its transfer in *VN* 25 from the classical poets to the vernacular writers already points at Dante's ambitions for his language and himself. For its use in *CV*, see section v; for *DVE*, section vi and Chapter 3, section iv. For the *DC*, see Chapter 7, section vi and nn 148–150.

[3] On chapter 25, see Chapter 4, section ii: for the classical examples see n 42; for *prosopopeia*, see n 50 (also nn 14, 42, 64, 88 of this chapter).

over and over in the great poem and elsewhere. During this period Dante distanced himself not only from those who had orchestrated the failure of his valiant attempts to mediate local factional disputes (namely, the Florentine "Black" Guelfs, with the encouragement of Pope Boniface VIII and the military intervention of a French prince, Charles of Anjou), but also from his fellow exiles of the "White Party." At the same time he shifted the focus of his activities from the local politics of Florence to a global, or at least peninsular, activity as cosmopolitan man of culture. During this period as well, his intellectual and poetic activities evidently underwent a sort of "growth spurt": not so much in the technical skills of versification, which were already highly developed, but in the reflective examination of the moral and philosophical dimension of his poetics, and the conscious attempt to integrate it not only with other important elements of vernacular literature, but also with those of the master discourses of classical and Christian Latin philosophical and theological culture.[4]

In the second book of *Convivio* Dante says that soon after the trauma of Beatrice's death (1290), and well before his exile, he had undertaken some formative readings, notably Cicero's *De Amicitia* and Boethius's *De Consolatione Philosophiae* (2.12.1–4), which then led him to seek out Lady Philosophy "là dove ella era, cioè ne le scuole de li religiosi e a le disputazioni de li filosofanti" (there where she [was], that is, to the schools of the religious and the disputations of the philosophizers; 2.12.7).[5] The traces of those readings, he says, appeared in the pre-exilic *Vita Nova*, "as if in a dream" (2.12.4),[6] but in the post-exilic *Convivio* they have been translated into the foundations of a discursive, philosophical prose, which in turn serves as showcase for a newly consolidated philosophical and theological culture. Here, for example, Dante first explicitly acknowledges the influence, at once intellectual and stylistic, of Augustine's first person spiritual autobiography, the *Confessions*. As Ulrich Leo has shown, he seems also to have undertaken a major rereading of Virgil's *Aeneid* (1951; see also n 76 and Chapter 5, n 5), most likely between the completion of books 1–3 and the writing of book 4. Most prominently, of course, he returns again and again in *Convivio* to the Latinized Aristotle and his thirteenth-century commentators. As to the latter, he was ranging freely

---

[4] Ascoli 1993; Botterill 1996a: xvi. For Dante's education, begin with Davis 1965, 1967; Petrocchi 1983; Witt 2000: 213–24. See also the helpful summary in Cristaldi 1994: chapter 1; also nn 7 and 27 below and Chapter 5, section i, and n 7.

[5] See De Robertis 1988: 205–10 nn.

[6] For example, De Robertis 1961: 18–19; Durling and Martinez 1990; and Martinez 1998 make cases for Boethian influence on *VN*, but see Chapter 4, especially n 20. On Dante's relationship to Boethius in general, see Tateo 1970a; on *CV* specifically, see Guglielminetti 1977; De Bonfils-Templer 1983.

through contemporary scholastic philosophy and theology, including such mainstream thinkers as Aquinas, Bonaventure, and Albertus Magnus, but also, most likely, evidently heterodox authors such as Siger of Brabant and, perhaps, the speculative grammarians whose most prominent representative was another Boethius, this one from "Dacia," i.e., Denmark (Corti 1981; Alessio 1984; Shapiro 1990; Imbach 1996; see also Chapter 3). This experience may possibly have been stimulated by a post-1302 sojourn in Bologna, the most important university center in Europe outside of Paris, as well as the originating point of the philosophically sophisticated poetry of Guido Guinizelli.[7] It was certainly favored by exposure to the "proto-humanistic" Latinity of the Northern Italian courts (see again Chapter 1, section i).

This phenomenon was no doubt a response to the unwanted leisure of his "new life," but was also stimulated by the pressures of radically novel circumstances and the need to recalculate his own standing in a world that looked very different from the one in which he had been raised: that is, the world of mercantile and banking Florence, itself "heterodox" with respect to a normative "medieval" social-cultural circumstance. The most complete and dramatic expression of this experience of philosophical study colored by exile, as well as by far the most detailed treatment of poetic authority in any of Dante's works, is to be found in *Convivio*, and it is there that I will begin my discussion of his explicit engagement with the language and culture of medieval authority.[8] *Convivio*, like *Vita Nova*, is a structured mixture of prose and poetry, written entirely in Italian, and was composed, to give the widest possible range, between 1302 and 1308,[9] before Dante had begun to work on the *Commedia*. It was left unfinished, as was the Latin treatise *De Vulgari Eloquentia*, composed at approximately the same time (see Chapter 3, section i).[10] For our purposes, the work as

---

[7] See *Dante e Bologna* 1967; Vasino *et al.* 1970. For the special place of Bologna in the linguistic argument of *DVE* and in the verse epistolary exchange between Giovanni del Virgilio and Dante, see, respectively, Chapter 3 and Ascoli 2009.

[8] The philosophical contents of *CV* will receive short shrift here, except where they bear on the problem of *auctoritas*, as does the discourse on "nobilità" in book 4. Useful introductions to the treatise are Barbi 1964; Simonelli 1970; Fenzi 1986; Vasoli 1988a; Scott 2004: 107–42. In addition to the essays cited on specific points below, see also Pietrobono 1938; Pézard 1940, 1967; Nardi 1960a; Corti 1983; Shapiro 1986; Trovato 1990 a and b; Dronke 1997. Excepting Pézard 1940, none of the above addresses my topic substantively.

[9] See Corti 1983: 142–4 and Vasoli 1988a: xiv–xv for succinct reviews of the evidence. The dating scheme applies to the prose commentary, not necessarily to the *canzoni*.

[10] The manuscript tradition of *CV* is notoriously corrupt and consequently modern editions must often resort to speculative emendations and interpolations. For the checkered history of the text,

it has come down to us can be divided into three sections. The first, book 1, entirely in prose and divided into thirteen chapters, seeks to define and justify the project that the rest of the work will undertake, namely the divulgation of philosophical knowledge in the vernacular for the majority of men, who are too lazy or, better, too occupied with "cura familiare e civile" (family and civic responsibilities; 1.1.4 and 13) to undertake the necessary study in Latin,[11] proceeding via prose explications of a series of *canzoni* written by Dante himself. The second section includes books 2 and 3, each of which begins with a *canzone* and then goes on to give first a literal and then an allegorical prose exposition of its contents. The two books form a unit in that together they afford a preliminary description of Dante's "innamoramento" with Lady Philosophy as well as defining and praising "her": they are presented as reflecting the biographical *sine qua non* for the transfer of knowledge to others that will take place in the balance of the treatise. From this perspective, the last section is constituted by book 4, which has the same basic "prosimetrum" form as the second and third books, except that the commentary is, unexpectedly, entirely "literal," because the philosophical content of the *canzone* is explicit. The remaining eleven books – each to have been composed of a *canzone* plus commentary – were projected but never completed, and would likely have treated the eleven active moral virtues as defined by Aristotle.[12]

see Vasoli 1988a: lxxx–lxxxix. De Robertis' editorial interpolations are indicated with brackets. The readings offered here do not rely substantively on these editorial interventions.

[11] See Chapter 1, n 55 for Dantean readership in general. For a splendid interpretation of the intended readership of *CV* and projected moral effects thereon, see Fenzi 1986: 14–23 *et passim*. For a darker and in the end more convincing account of Dante's projected relation to his audience not only in *DVE* and the *rime petrose*, but also *CV*, see Durling 1992. See also Copeland 1991: 181–2; Lansing 1992. For Dante in the larger European context, see Auerbach 1958: especially 295–321. Note the slightly different definition given in 1.9.5 (see also 2.1.3 and n 74 below), which both anticipates the theme of nobility in book 4 (Fenzi 1986: 16–17) and adds *women* to the group of potential readers, at once recalling the theme of female readership in *VN* and highlighting the expansion of horizons in the interim. For Dante's readership in *VN*, see Chapter 4, section ii and n 13. As will appear, *CV* breaks off before fully entering into its stated educative mission. Moreover, it did not circulate widely in the Trecento and cannot be assumed to have reached its intended audience(s) (Vasoli 1988a: lxxx–lxxxii; Pertile 1993; cf. Chapter 6, n 7). The treatise's primary reader, then, is Dante himself, who, as discussed in Chapters 1 and 6, obsessively rereads and rewrites materials from it in other works, not only the *DC* but also *DVE, MN*, and, if authentic, *ECG*. See also n 94 and Chapter 3, nn 8, 12, 43 on the similar status of *DVE*.

[12] Aristotle, *NE* II.vii.1107a, 28–1108b, 10. Explicit references suggest book 14 would have treated Justice (1.12.12; 4.27.11; cf. 2.1.4); book 15, the last, Liberality (1.8.18; cf. 3.15.18); book 7, perhaps, Temperance (4.26.8). All three are among the eleven virtues listed in 4.17.4–6. Barbi 1964: xli; Simonelli 1970; Vasoli 1988a: xii–xiii are skeptical about this hypothesis. Fenzi 1986: 12–14 balances it with other possibilities. Trovato 1976: 14 and Corti 1983: especially 98–109 accept it, as do I. See also Scott 2004: 138–9. My view is that books 1–3 are preliminary, while book 4 defines *nobilità* as the seed

Both in form and in content *Convivio* presents itself as the obvious successor to *Vita Nova*, the product of an evolution in Dante's thinking and writing:

E se ne la presente opera . . . più virilmente si trattasse che ne la *Vita Nuova*, non intendo però a quella . . . derogare . . . veggendo sì come ragionevolmente quella fervida e passionata, questa temperata e virile esser conviene. Ché altro si conviene e dire e operare ad una etade che sono sconci e biasimevoli ad altra . . . E io in quella dinanzi, a l'entrata de la mia gioventude parlai, e in questa dipoi, quella già trapassata. (1.1.16–17)[13]

(. . . if in the present work . . . the subject matter is treated in a more [virile] fashion than in *Vita Nova*, this does not mean that I intend to disparage that earlier work . . . [seeing] how reasonable it is that the earlier work should be fervent and passionate, and this one temperate and [virile]. For what is required of us in our speaking and acting varies from one stage of life to another, because certain ways of behaving that are appropriate and laudable at one stage rank as demeaning and blameworthy at another. In that earlier work my voice is that of someone just entering into his [youthful adulthood]; in this later one it is that of someone [who has gone through that stage].)

As already seen, *Convivio* engages overtly and systematically with the Latin philosophical tradition – Cicero, Boethius and, above all, *the* Philosopher, Aristotle, who appears in the very first sentence of the work. Dante aims to demonstrate that his poetry after *Vita Nova* was and is no longer limited to the topic of passionate heterosexual love as asserted in the earlier work. While the poems of that earlier work had represented the love for an exceptional human woman literally, the later *canzoni* conceal and personify

---

of all the virtues (4.16.10), especially the eleven moral virtues, which are also particularly apt for Dante's chosen audience. One of Dante's significant thirteenth-century sources/analogues for *CV* – Egidio Romano [sometimes Egidio Colonna; in English: Giles of Rome], *De Regimine Principum* uses a comparable list of the Aristotelian virtues as a structural principle (1967: especially book 1, part 2), differing only in that he also includes *prudentia*, which Dante excludes on the grounds that Aristotle calls it an intellectual rather than an ethical virtue (4.17.8 [in fact, it is both: Kahn 1983]). Egidio is cited at 4.24.9 in company with Cicero and Virgil. Dante puts ethics before metaphysics as the object of philosophical contemplation in 2.14 (E. Gilson 1939: 104–12; Imbach 1996: 137–8; Scott 2004: 122–3, 133–4; also Ascoli 1997: 332, 335–6 and nn 81, 88; cf. Nardi 1940b: 211–21). A reason often educed for discarding the proposal is the difficulty in matching all eleven virtues with extant *canzoni*; but this assumes that the *canzoni* to be treated had already been written when the commentary was begun. Though there is some warrant to make this inference in book 1 (e.g., 1.1.14, 18; 1.2.16; 1.3.2), it is not conclusive. The difficulty disappears if the *canzoni* are "the past" not with respect to a "present of writing," but rather to the "present of reading," or the conjectural "present of writing concluded" in relation to which most works of this kind orient themselves syntactically. For the organization of *CV*, see also Chapter 4, sections iii–iv.

[13] This autobiographical passage points proleptically to the impersonal discourse on the forms of nobility appropriate to the four ages of man in 4.23–28.

love for wisdom (Filo-Sophia) in the allegorical guise of love for a woman (2.12.6 *et passim*),[14] as the prose commentary will make explicit.

Despite maintaining, up to a certain point, the pose of merely expounding on writings of classical authorities, Dante makes new and ambitious claims in *Convivio* – both within the context of his own career, and in that of late medieval vernacular writing more generally – for himself as writer, for poetry as vehicle of philosophical wisdom, and for the vernacular's capacity to treat topics generally reserved for Latin. It is no wonder, then, that as Dante's work enters more overtly into contact with classical poetic and especially philosophical culture he should feel the necessity to grapple explicitly with the defining category of *auctoritas*.

In what were probably Dante's first uses ever of the words *autoritade* and *autore*, *Convivio* contains two important passages that raise this topic directly, and make startlingly obvious its relevance to Dante himself. The first comes near the very beginning of book 1, as the writing "I" sets out to justify his divulgative project by purifying it of various "macule" or imperfections. In particular, he notes that:

Conviemmi che con più alto stilo dea, ne la presente opera, un poco di gravezza, per la quale paia di maggiore autoritade (1.4.13)

(It is only right that by adopting a loftier style I should endow this present work [distinguished from earlier writings of his] with a certain gravity in order to lend it more authority)

We will return to the larger context from which this passage is taken in due course. For now it is enough to observe that even in this relativized form ("maggiore") it is unusual for a vernacular writer to speak of his own authority, all the more so because Dante typically avoids using this word in reference to himself (Chapter 1, section i, and n 9).[15]

The second passage comes in the sixth chapter of the fourth book as part of a long digression in which Dante confronts the problem that his definition of the concept of "gentilezza" (nobility) in the *canzone* being commented upon, "Le dolci rime d'amor, ch'i' solia," seemingly contradicts the authority not only of the Emperor Frederick II, but also of Aristotle, who has been Dante's principal classical authority from the very first sentence

---

[14] For the personification of wisdom, as Filosofia or Sapienza, in *CV*, see especially Corti 1983: 74–8 *et passim*; Nardi 1921a: 157–9, 163–4 and 1921c: 266, 1960a; Armour 1979: 9–13; Vasoli 1988b. See also Trovato 1990a: 249–50, 1994; Carugati 1994; O. Holmes 2001, 2007; Boccassini 2003; Moevs 2005: 82–5; and nn 86, 88 below. See Newman 1995 for the personified figure of *Sophia* in the Middle Ages. Chapter 6, section i and n 2 for a partial rehearsal of the Beatrice vs. "donna gentile" controversy.

[15] The exceptions are discussed in section vi below. See also n 46 for one of the many examples of Dante's *indirect, associative* application of these words to himself.

of the treatise (1.1.1). At this juncture, Dante gives the two etymologically grounded definitions of *autore* discussed briefly in Chapter 1, sections i and ii. The principal and operative definition is the following:

L'altro principio, onde "autore" discende, sì come testimonia Uguiccione nel principio de le sue *Derivazioni*, è uno vocabulo greco che dice "autentin," che tanto vale in latino quanto "degno di fede e d'obedienza." E così "autore," quinci derivato, si prende per ogni persona degna d'essere creduta e obedita. E da questo viene questo vocabulo del quale al presente si tratta, cioè "autoritade"; per che si può vedere che "autoritade" vale tanto quanto "atto degno di fede e d'obedienza." [Onde, avvegna che Aristotle sia dignissimo di fede e d'obedienza,] manifesto è che le sue parole sono somma e altissima autoritade. (4.6.5)

(As Uguccione indicates at the beginning of his *Derivations*, the other source from which "author" is derived is the Greek word *autentin*, which is equivalent to the Latin meaning "worthy of [faith and obedience]." As thus derived, "author" refers to every person worthy of being trusted [i.e., worthy of faith] and [of being] obeyed. From this comes the word with which we are concerned, "authority." It is clear then that "authority" means the same as "an act worthy of [faith and obedience]." [Whence, given that Aristotle is most worthy of faith and obedience, it is] clear that his words are of the greatest and most revered authority.)

This is, as we will see, a standard definition, though it is significant both because of the priority given to the person, since *autoritade* derives from *autore* and not the reverse, and because of the possibility that Dante might be guilty of proposing a definition of nobility which is neither faithful nor obedient to the relevant Aristotelian *auctoritas* (4.8.4–5).

What most complicates an understanding of this passage is that it is preceded by a digression in which Dante presents an alternative definition of the word *autore*, whose relevance to the context and to Dante in particular is explicitly denied but, as asserted in Chapter 1, implicitly great:

Questo vocabulo, cioè "autore," sanza quella terza lettera C, può discendere da due principii: l'uno si è d'uno verbo molto lasciato da l'uso in gramatica, che significa tanto quanto "legare parole," cioè "auieo." E chi ben guarda lui, ne la sua prima voce apertamente vedrà che elli stesso lo dimostra, che solo di legame di parole è fatto, cioè di sole cinque vocali, che sono anima e legame d'ogni parola, e composto d'esse per modo volubile, a figurare imagine di legame. Ché, cominciando da l'A, ne l'U quindi si rivolve, e viene diritto per I ne l'E, quindi si rivolve e torna ne l'O; sì che veramente imagina questa figura: A, E, I, O, U, la quale è figura di legame. E in quanto "autore" viene e discende da questo verbo, si prende solo per li poeti, che con l'arte musaica le loro parole hanno legate: e di questa significazione al presente non s'intende. (4.6.3–4)

(This word, namely "autore," can descend from one of two sources. One is a verb no longer much used in grammar [i.e., Latin], namely "auieo" which means as much as "to bind words." And whoever looks carefully at it in its first person singular form will see that it openly demonstrates this meaning, because it is made up only of the bonds of words, that is, only of the five vowels, that are the soul and bond of every word, and composed of them in a mobile form that figures the image of a bond. Thus: beginning with "A" it then turns back to "U," then proceeding directly through "I" to "E," and then goes backward, returning to "O": so that truly it images this figure: A, E, I, O, U, which is the figure of a bond. And inasmuch as "autore" derives from this verb, it is taken to refer to the poets alone, who with musical art have bound together their words: and with this meaning we are not concerned at present. [author's translation])

This passage is curious for several reasons, as will soon appear. For the moment is enough to ask why exactly it is that Dante says he is not concerned with poetic authorship, specifically distinguishing it from philosophical *autorità*, when the declared goal of *Convivio* is to show that Dante's poems have philosophical content.

Taken together, the three passages just quoted make plain Dante's interest in and engagement with the categories of *auctor* and *auctoritas*, and show that both implicitly and explicitly his concern in *Convivio* is to situate himself in relation to those categories and to deal with the multiple problems that such a move creates for him and his works. More specifically, chapter 6 of book 4 indicates Dante's most immediate point of entry into the long medieval definitional tradition that sustains these categories: namely the *Derivationes* of Hugutio of Pisa (Uguccione da Pisa). Before returning to detailed analyses of these passages, then, I will now turn to a review of that tradition in general, as well as of Hugutio's text in particular.

II. "AUTHOR" AND "AUTHORITY" IN MEDIEVAL DISCOURSE

The concept of *auctoritas* is usually traced back by its historians to a *locus classicus* in Cicero's *Topica* (19.73–20.78), where it is discussed at length as that quality in a juridical witness, the *auctor*, which inspires faith, that is, trust, in his testimony (cf. Chenu 1950: 130; Stabile 1970: 456):

For our present purpose we define testimony [*testimonium*] as everything that is brought in from some external circumstance in order to win [faith, or belief, or trust; *ad faciendam fidem*]. Now it is not every sort of person who is worth consideration as a witness. To win [faith], authority [*auctoritas*] is sought; but authority [*auctoritatem*] is given by one's nature or by circumstances [*tempus*]. Authority [*auctoritas*] from one's nature or character depends largely on virtue [*in virtute*]; in circumstances there are many things which lend authority, such as talent, wealth, age, good luck, skill, experience, necessity, and even at times a concurrence of fortuitous events. For it is a common belief that the talented, the wealthy, and those whose characters have been tested by a long life, are worthy of credence. This may not be correct, but the opinion of the common people [or "vulgar herd"] can hardly be changed, and both those who make judicial decisions and those who pass moral judgments steer their course by that [*ad eamque omnia dirigunt et qui iudicant et qui existimant*]. (*Top.* 19.73)

For Cicero, authority of this kind is a matter of persuasive appearance rather than of truthful essence; a matter of politics, law, and rhetoric, rather than of philosophy and theology.[16] Most importantly, since it refers to the rhetorical force and/or credibility of a legal witness's testimony it depends directly on individual character and contingent circumstances – in other words, it is a personal and historical quality.

In the Christian era, however, Jerome applied the term to the Bible as verbal witness of God's work in history (Curtius 1948: 464). As an obvious consequence, medieval concepts of *auctoritas* shift away from the rhetorical notion of authority as the persuasive *appearance* of truth toward the theological idea of an original, essential, and transcendent Truth and Power behind appearances, from which all circumscribed human authority, textual and institutional, ultimately derives.[17] The personal and historical become the impersonal and transhistorical. In the Holy Trinity, the Father's absolute Power is linked to the Son's absolute Wisdom by the Holy Spirit's perfect Love (cf. *CV* 2.5.8): God is thus the *Auctor* of *auctores* because what He knows is what He willed into existence, which is everything. His authority is complete because He is subject and object and copula of every sentence in His own Book of Creation (Curtius 1948: 319–26; see n 87).

The fundamental problem with defining *auctoritas* in these terms was how to understand and to identify plausibly its transmission from a perfect God to imperfect humanity. Thus most of the discourse about it focused on its nature and operation among human beings. As an immediate corollary, Chenu points out, the most obvious path of derivation for human authority is in the theological–ecclesiastical field (1950: 128; cf. Minnis 1984: 114), as illustrated in this passage from Dante's own *Monarchia*, which specifically traces out the descent of divine *auctoritas* through the Scriptures to the Fathers and the Church, down to the Decretals:

It must be borne in mind that some scriptures [writings] preceded the church [Ecclesiam], others coincided with the founding of the church, and others followed it. Before the church are the Old and New Testaments, which "he hath commanded

---

[16] Cf. *Top.* 20.78: "In homine virtutis opinio valet plurimum [ad fidem faciendam]." Throughout, Cicero is more concerned with the rhetorical effectiveness of a witness (*auctor*) than with veracity.

[17] See *MN* 3.15.15; *CV* 4.9.3; Aquinas, *ST*, Ia, q.33, art. 5, ad.1. See also Stabile 1970: 458. For the dual authorship of the Bible, see Chapter 1, n 7.

forever," as the Prophet says . . . Contemporaneous with the church are those venerated principal councils at which Christ was present, as no believer doubts, since we know that he said to the disciples as he was about to ascend to heaven: "Lo, I am with you always, even to the end of the world," as Matthew bears witness. There are also the writings of the doctors of the church [scripture doctorum], of Augustine and others; anyone who doubts that they were helped by the Holy Spirit has either entirely failed to see their fruits or, if he has seen them, has not tasted them. Then after the church come the traditions called "Decretals," which, while certainly to be revered on account of their apostolic authority [que quidem etsi auctoritate apostolica sunt venerande], yet must take second place to the fundamental scriptures, given that Christ reproached the priests for doing the opposite . . . Now if the traditions of the church come after the church, as has been shown, it must be the case that the church does not derive its authority from the traditions, but that the traditions derive their authority from the church [necesse est ut non Ecclesie a traditionibus, sed ab Ecclesia traditionibus accedat auctoritas]. (3.3.11–16)[18]

The passage suggests that while *auctoritas* was seen as transhistorical and transpersonal in its divine origins, its extension through human history was specifically conditioned by time: antiquity if not identical with authority was virtually always a *conditio sine qua non* of it. Thus, in general, as Minnis remarks, "it would seem that the only good *auctor* was a dead one" (1984: 12), and long dead, at that. At the same time, the possibility always remained open that the transcendent God, as present today as He had been at any moment in the history of the world, could intervene to infuse his authority into a suitable human receptacle.

Needless to say, as one moved away from the strictly theological domain, the problem of linking human authority to a divine original became increasingly complicated. Compensatory explanations were often deployed to overcome these difficulties. For instance, the alleged Donation of Constantine was often construed as putting imperial rulers under papal and, ultimately, divine supervision.[19] Just so, as will be seen further on, Aquinas and others carefully positioned the philosophical reasoning of Aristotle in a relation of support and subordination to theological revelation. Inevitably, however, such explanations were also liable to Christian critique and demystification. Theological attempts to valorize and even to appropriate the political could be countered, authoritatively, by an Augustinian insistence on the radical separation of the glorious City of God from the irredeemable

---

[18] On this passage, see De Lubac 1959–1965: 2.2.319–20; Cassell 2001: 8–9, 2004: 85–7 and nn; and, especially, Stillinger 1992: 31–2. For its polemical weight within the economy of *MN* 3, see Chapter 5, especially section ii.

[19] Tierney 1964: 1–5, 21–22, *et passim*. For the Donation, see Chapter 5, n 47.

City of Man (see Tierney 1964: 7–13, *passim*). Neo-Aristotelian theologians were faced with neo-Pauline attacks on the blindness and madness of pagan philosophy.[20] The list of conceptual and historical dilemmas could be multiplied. What becomes apparent is that the problem of the authority of origin which can, in theory, be resolved by a single act of Christian faith, soon dissolves into a far less soluble series of cruxes regarding the derivation and mediation of divine and transcendent authority by human agents.

Notwithstanding these conceptual difficulties, and their even more pronounced historical correlatives, over the more than millennial course of what is still usually called the Middle Ages, the definitions of *auctor* and *auctoritas* were refined and expanded, both to cover their use in a range of distinct cultural areas and to set them in dialectical relationship to other cultural figures and other types of experience. During this period, "authority" became a fundamental concept for defining the status of intellectual and professional discourses (whether theological, philosophical, scientific, or poetic) and institutional (whether secular or sacred). The *auctores* who possessed and exercised it were treated as privileged cultural figures. They were hypostatized in names and epithets (e.g., Aristotle; The Philosopher), which figured – impersonated – Truth, rather than designating contingent identities. As seen in Chapter 1, "authority" in this sense refers to the legitimized or legitimizing truth-value or power or both accorded, at least in theory, to a text or an office-holder, both referred to as *auctoritates*. Thus Aristotle, as well as Plato, Homer, Virgil and other classical figures is an *auctor*, whose texts may be cited as *auctoritates*, carrying superior credibility. Thus, *a fortiori*, the Scriptures, and the Church fathers, command the obedient attention of their readers. Thus, in the institutional domain, the Pope and the Holy Roman Emperor are said to wield supreme authority intrinsic to their respective offices. Again, Dante uses the terms in all of these various ways, with well over half of the total number of references in his *oeuvre* concentrated in *Monarchia* and dedicated to institutional authority (see Chapter 1, n 9; Chapter 5, section ii and n 21).

Into this pervasive "culture of authority" numerous typologies, distinctions, and qualifications were introduced. The most fundamental

---

[20] E.g., I Corinthians 1:18–22. In the thirteenth century such attacks were often launched by the radical Franciscans, with whom Dante had some affinities (see, e.g., Davis 1980; Mazzotta 1993a; Havely 2004; cf. Suitner 1999, Vettori 2004 for recent readings of the earlier Duecento Franciscan poet, Jacopone da Todi). In the fourteenth and early fifteenth centuries, the Christian humanism of Petrarch and others directly opposed the Pauline-Augustinian problem of the fallen will to scholastic rationalism. For the Petrarchan critique of Dante on such grounds, see Lerner 1986; Ascoli 1991a (see also Chapter 5, nn 4, 27). Cf. Nardi 1940c.

distinction, as already noted, was that between God as transcendent Author of authors, and the human authorities which derived from him. This distinction, again, appears most fully formed in the special case of Scripture which is understood to be the product not only of several human authors, to whom differing degrees of "faith and obedience" are due, but also, and ultimately, of a single divine Author whose encompassing intentions unite and/or supersede those of the "scribes of God" through whom He speaks. As we have seen, Dante drew on both the general and particular versions of this distinction in his uses of the words *autore* and *autorità* in *Inferno* 1 and 4, and again in *Paradiso* 26.

Much of the work of definition in the Middle Ages was done through etymological analyses of the key words *auctor* and *auctoritas*, which produced a limited range of competing etymologies. The field, as M.D. Chenu (1927; 1950) first demonstrated, was dominated by two competing etymological definitions, sometimes distinguished according to spelling, sometimes not. As noted in Chapter 1, these were (1) *auctor* from *augere*, "to augment or make grow," referring to the one who is at once the originator of and the authenticating witness to an act, especially an act of composition; and (2) *au[c]tor* from Greek *autentin*, defined as "one worthy of faith and imitation" (reflected, with a difference, in Dante's second definition).[21]

A maximum of differentiation within the *auctor/autor* complex is reached in the early thirteenth-century *Derivationes* of Hugutio of Pisa, which Dante cites as his source, as his *auctoritas* in fact, for the discussion of *autorità* in *Convivio* 4.6. In addition to being an encyclopedist, Hugutio was probably a bishop of Ferrara and leading scholar of canon law, one of Dante's predecessors in the struggle to keep Church and Empire separate.[22] In the *Derivationes*, Hugutio gives not two but three distinct etymologies, and variant spellings, of *auctor* to cover three distinct areas in which authority is exercised:

Augeo–es . . . to amplify, to augment. Whence *auctor*, i.e., augmentor, and it must be written with a "u" and a "c." When, however, it signifies *autentin*, that is, authority proper, . . . it must be written without the "c," as in "this and that *autor*," and it derives from *autentin*. There is also found a certain defective verb, namely, *avieo –es*, i.e., *ligo –as*. And thence comes *autor* [MS. variant: *auitor*], i.e. binder,

[21] The distinction is commonplace; see, e.g., Isidore *Etym.* 9.3.16, 9.4.34, 10.1.2; Guillielmus Brito 1975: 1.75. See again Chapter 1, n 19.

[22] For Dante's indebtedness to the *MD*, see Toynbee 1902: 97–114; Schizzerotto 1976. For the bishop–scholar's political views in the context of the medieval debate, see Tierney 1964: 116–26; Cassell 2004: especially 13–17 and nn, 305 nn 123–5. For Hugutio's biography, including the ongoing debate over whether or not the encyclopedist and the canon lawyer were the same person, see Schizzerotto 1976; Cecchini 2004. See also Chapter 5, nn 20, 46.

likewise . . . without the "c." Following the first meaning, rulers [emperors] are properly called *auctores* from the augmentation of the public domain. Following the second meaning, philosophers and the inventors of the arts [*inventores artium*] such as Plato, Aristotle, and Priscian and others of great authority have to be called *autores*. And following the third meaning, Virgil and Lucan and other poets must be called *avitores*, because they bind their verses with feet and with meter [*ligaverunt carmina sua pedibus et metris*]. And from *autor*, which means *autentin*, is derived this *autoritas*, i.e., a lesson worthy of imitation [*sententia digna imitatione*] as well as *autenticus* . . . and *autorizabilis* . . . a man is *autenticus* or *autorizabilis*, whose authority has to be believed [*autoritatis cui credi deberet*]. We also say *autenticus*, that is "noble" [*autenticus, id est nobilis*] and *autorizo* . . . in the same sense, that is, "I affirm; I make authentic [I authenticate]" . . . And from *autenticus* comes *autentica*, that is, a certain legal book thus called because in it are contained authenticated sayings. Also, from *augeo* comes *Augustus*, namely any Roman emperor, from the expansion of empire [*ab augendo imperium*]. (*MD*: II.A.1–4, 11; translation mine.)

Hugutio's tripartite definition draws on traditional etymologies. However, he also innovates, first of all by imposing a rationalizing specification and division into three distinct types: the political *auctor*, the academic *autor* (especially the philosopher, but also those who discovered the liberal arts that compose the medieval curriculum – like Priscian the grammarian par excellence), and, the poetic *autor* [or: *avitor*]. Of special importance to Dante is Hugutio's creation, apparently original with him, of a separate heading for the poetic *autores* [or *auitores*].[23] We shall see shortly how Dante's subsequent discussion in *Convivio* 4 then both draws on and transforms all three types of authority treated by Hugutio, despite the apparent disappearance of the *auctor* from *augere*.

---

[23] The strict limitation of *auctor* from *augere* to *imperatores* involves a conflation of two traditional etymological entries. Isidore of Seville gives a general etymology of "auctor ab augendo" (*Etym.* 10.1.2), but also derives "Augustus" as imperial name specifically from *augere* (9.3.16: "augerent rem publicam amplificando"). In a separate passage, Isidore, following Varro (*De Lingua Latina* 7.36) also applies "vieo" to the poet as "vates," i.e., as divinely inspired prophet, but does not make the link to "auieo" and "auctor/autor" (8.7.3: "Vates a vi mentis appellatos . . . vel a viendis carminibus, id est flectendis"). Dante, significantly, uses "vates" only twice in his *oeuvre* (in *MN* 2.3.12 of Virgil; in *Ecl.* 1, responding to Giovanni de Virgilio's salutation of him by that name), although in 4.6.3–5 he may have in mind Hugutio's entry for "vieo," which follows Isidore's closely, but does makes the connection to the *autor* from *avieo*: "Vieo -es, -evi vietum, idest vincire, ligare . . . Et hic et hec vates –tis, sacerdos: quandoque sic dicitur poeta, quandoque propheta divinus, et dicebantur vates poete, quia metra ligarent pedibus et sillabis et verba modis connecterent, et etiam per furorem divini eodem erant nomine, quia ipsi quoque plura versibus efferebant; vel vates a vi mentis dicti sunt vel a video, quia futura videbant . . . Item vieo componitur avieo . . . idest alligare, valde ligare; unde hic et hec autor, idest ligator, sed hoc in principio huius operis distinximus" (*MD*: II.U.25.1–2, 4). The etymology of "augere" is the first in the whole of the *MD*, placed out of the alphabetical sequence that Hugutio follows closely throughout his work, perhaps reflecting concern for his own *auctoritas* (see also Prologus.8: "Si quis querat huius operis quis autor, dicendum est quia Deus; si querat huius operis quis fuerit instrumentum, respondendum est quia patria pisanus, nomine Uguitio").

Even as the *auctor* underwent this internal process of distinction, the term was also defined in relation, and sometimes opposition to adjacent concepts and categories. Chenu (1927; 1950: 129–30) notes an important traditional opposition between the *auctor* as guarantor of a text's truth, and the *actor* (from "agere," "to do, to make") who is the artisanal maker of a given object, but who confers no special status on it. Dante never explicitly make this distinction, unless one counts the *agens* of the *Epistle to Cangrande*,[24] but alludes to it in important ways, as will be seen beginning in section vi.

Important also is Bonaventure's distinction between the *auctor* and other, less prestigious producers of texts: the *scriptor*, who physically produces a manuscript; the *compilator*, who assembles the texts of others into a new manuscript; the *commentator*, who creates his own text in explicating the text of an *auctor*, usually classical or biblical (see again Chapter 1, nn 4 and 47). This typology further emphasizes the temporal dimension of authority – the sharp separation between, on the one hand, an authoritative past of writers which signifies illumination and order and, on the other, the reverential modern culture of readers which assembles, physically produces, and "consumes" texts deriving from that past: then, the *auctor*; now, the *scriptor*, *compilator*, and *commentator*. The particular importance of these distinctions for Dante will become more apparent in Chapter 4. Similarly, we may note that the infallible *auctor* is sometimes set off against the learned but fallible *magister* (hence, perhaps, Virgilio as ambiguously both "maestro e autore").[25] Finally, as Aquinas states lucidly, *auctoritas* as an epistemological category is to be seen in complicated relation to two other potential, and potentially competing, modes of reaching truth: reason and experience (*ST* Ia, q.1, art. 8; see n 32).

From this brief summary it is apparent that the field of cultural *auctoritas* in the later Middle Ages was both complex and historically mobile. Indeed, the more amply and sharply this field was articulated, the more of the kinds of problems noted above arose within it: the more work had to be done to justify and to recuperate the value of ideal *auctoritas* as it was put into practice both textually and institutionally; the more various aspects of it

---

[24] For the *ECG*, see Chapter 1, n 75. As for the *agens* heading (par. 14), as noted in Chapter 1, n 70, I disagree with the widely-adopted Mazzoni thesis that the term refers primarily to the *DC*'s first-person singular dramatic protagonist rather than, like *actor*, the maker of a book, though of course in Dante's case, especially in the *DC*, poet and *personaggio* are inextricably intertwined. See also sections v–vi.

[25] For the distinction between the *magistralia* and the *autentica*, see Chenu 1950: 20, 136–7. Stabile 1970: 455–6 and Mazzotta 1979: 154–5 note its applicability to the paired terms in *Inf.* 1.87. See also Chapter 7, n 1.

seemed to be undergoing dramatic transformations of one kind or another. A key example is the renegotiation of the relationship between the divine and the human authors of the Bible over the course of the thirteenth and fourteenth centuries, with new prominence being given to the latter (Chapter 1, especially nn 7 and 61). Moreover, at least as early as the twelfth-century *Sic et Non* of Peter Abelard theologians had been confronting the problem that in many cases prestigious human *auctores* held diametrically opposed positions on any given question, and had begun to devise rationalizing techniques for determining the prevailing *auctoritas* on a case-by-case basis, thus moving significantly in the direction of a relativization of authority.[26]

Playing a crucial role, naturally, was the rise of the universities – in Paris, of course, but also nearer to Dante's hand, Bologna – as a focal point both for propagating and for testing *auctoritas*. From the exploration of divergences among *auctores* developed the genre of the written *quaestio*, and subsequently the university exercise of the public *disputatio* on an assigned topic. In these venues, typically, apparently conflicting authorities were tested against one another with the ostensible aim of reconciliation, while at the same time giving the "modern" scholar or student a clear opportunity for self-assertion in carrying out an interpretation of and adjudication among them.[27] Thus, even as the *lectio* of *auctores* formed the centerpiece of the school curriculum, university culture could present a challenge to the traditional notion of *auctoritas* as conveying timeless, impersonal truth.[28]

---

[26] On Scholastic practices for resolving differences between conflicting *auctoritates*, see Curtius 1948: 53; Chenu 1950: 139–45; Panofsky 1957: 65–70; Wetherbee 1972: 38–40; Marenbon 1987: 13–14, 29–31; Minnis *et al.* 1987: 87–100. These techniques did not always prevent recourse to more drastic measures, for example, warfare or the active repression of "heretical" texts and thinkers, such as Abelard himself and, later, Siger of Brabant and Boethius of Dacia. Minnis 1984: 59–63 correlates this phenomenon with Abelard's humanization of the *auctores*, including Church fathers. As the passage from *MN* quoted earlier illustrates, temporal priority is usually taken as a defining attribute for establishing an effective hierarchy of authorities. At the same time, in the specific case of Biblical authorship, divine authority takes precedence over human and historical *auctoritates* no matter how venerable (see n 32 below).

[27] On the *quaestio*, see Smalley 1952: 66–82; Marenbon 1987: 10–14, 27–34. On the *disputatio*, see Smalley: 209–13; Marenbon: 19–20. Over the course of his career, Dante increasingly adopts the posture and the tools of these intellectual forms, culminating in *MN* 3 (e.g., Scott 2004: 157; see Chapter 5, especially n 36) and the *Q*, inspired by an academic discussion in Mantua and then delivered publicly in Verona in 1320 (see Chapter 1, n 75). In the *DC*, Dante's education at the successive hands of Virgilio, Beatrice, and St. Bernard, with a pause for an examination over the theological virtues at the hands of Saints Peter, James, and John (see Chapter 7, section v), frequently mirrors school practices. The applicability of a variant of the *quaestio* model in *CV* 4 is discussed below, especially n 48. Despite attempts to prove that Dante studied formally at the universities of either Paris (almost certainly not) or Bologna (unlikely, although he likely had contact at various points with members of the Scholastic community there), he should be seen as a knowledgeable outsider.

[28] On the *lectio*, see Smalley 1952: 196–209; Marenbon 1987: 16–19.

Especially significant in the present context is the cultural project of the neo-Aristotelian Scholastics, especially Albertus Magnus and Thomas Aquinas, which had dominated the intellectual landscape in the century preceding Dante, and whose influence is pervasive and increasing in his works from at least as early as the *Vita Nova*. On the one hand, Scholastics on the whole continued to treat the Scriptures, the fathers of the Church, and selected classical writers as worthy of special "faith and obedience," typically adopting the stance of the commenting *lector* when confronting *auctores* of all kinds (e.g., Smalley 1952). On the other hand, by systematically revisiting and reinterpreting the canonical dicta of the Fathers, the Scholastics in some sense relativized their authority, and staked a claim for "modernity," even to the point that one could seriously entertain the question of whether "Magister Thomas" was himself to be considered an *auctor*.[29]

The unprecedented privilege accorded by Scholastics to the newly translated Aristotle, who quickly became *the* classical *auctoritas* (Chenu 1950), in one sense took the culture of *auctoritas* to its highest point. But it also revealed that *auctoritas* was historical and relative: the canon of *auctores* could and did change through the critical agency of moderns. By emphasizing the analytical power of reason, Scholasticism made, at least implicitly, a case for the independent power of the human intellect to approach truth without reliance on *auctoritates*,[30] but also for opening up the *auctores* even further to critical scrutiny, even Aristotle himself (Bianchi 1994).[31] Aquinas illustrates this contradictory attitude clearly. In one section of the chapter from the *Summa Theologiae* referred to above, he states that argument from human authority is the weakest kind, specifically inferior to rational proof, while then insisting on the absolute preeminence of scriptural authority over reason (cf. Chenu 1950: 138; Stabile 1970: 459).[32]

---

[29] Chenu 1925 documents a late fourteenth-century debate among Parisian theologians on the question of whether "maître Thomas est-il une autorité?" Even at that very late date, however, the official answer was "no." Nonetheless, the posing of the question is itself significant.

[30] Curtius 1948: 53, cf. 57, 483; Chenu 1950: especially 64–5. Dante's drive to rationalize his choices and beliefs using neo-Aristotelian logical arguments seems, at times, to lead him into largely uncharted conceptual realms, precisely because he insists that logic takes precedence over ideas received through traditional *auctoritates*. See, for example, the discussion of his treatment of vernacular in *CV* I (Chapter 3, section i).

[31] On the question of individual reason vs. impersonal authority, the doctrine of the "possible intellect" was one available means of foregrounding human reason without conceding special authority to any individual person (see Chapter 5, section iii, and especially nn 12, 27, 50; Chapter 6, section ii).

[32] Aquinas posits the following concerning rational argument (his own and others) about revealed Truth: "Praeterea, si sit argumentativa, aut argumentatur ex auctoritate, aut ex ratione. Si ex auctoritate, non videtur hoc congruere eius dignitati: nam locus ab auctoritate est infirmissimus, secundum Boetium. Si etiam ex ratione, hoc non congruit eius fini: quia secundum Gregorium in *Homilia*, 'fides non habet meritum, ubi humana ratio praebet experimentum.' Ergo sacra doctrina non est

Such conceptual problems with establishing and prioritizing authorities were often juxtaposed with historical events and trends that either dramatized the limitations of the ideal "culture of authority" or ignored them altogether. Most obvious were the repeated, and at times quite violent, jurisdictional clashes among institutions – notably, for Dante, the papacy and the empire under Frederick II and Henry VII – that raise serious questions about the scope and legitimacy of both parties' *auctoritas*, and in particular about their relationship to the divine source of authority (Tierney 1964). One thinks as well of the challenge to the institutional authority of the Church by the personalized and sometimes radical spirituality of Francis of Assisi and the order that arose under his name. Furthermore, in the domain of literary authorship the cult of classical *auctores* had not prevented the emergence of a flourishing vernacular literary tradition from the eleventh through the thirteenth centuries (see Chapter 1, section i, especially n 13; Chapter 4, section ii).

I began with a straightforward opposition between Cicero's classical concept of the *auctor* in personal and contingent terms and a medieval Christian *auctoritas* which is rooted in the transpersonal and transhistorical Truth and Power of the triune God, and which grows stronger the further it recedes into dim antiquity, conferring a quasi-divine transcendence in which the speaking or governing person disappears and a timeless truth or power takes

argumentativa." His reply to the objection is even more instructive: "argumentari ex auctoritate est maxime proprium huius doctrinae: eo quod principia huius doctrinae per revelationem habentur, et sic oportet quod credatur auctoritati eorum quibus revelatio facta est. Nec hoc derogat dignitati huius doctrinae: nam licet locus ab auctoritate quae fundatur super ratione humana, sit infirmissimus; locus tamen ab auctoritate quae fundatur super revelatione divina, est efficacissimus. Utitur tamen sacra doctrina etiam ratione humana: non quidem ad probandum fidem, quia per hoc tolleretur meritum fidei; sed ad manifestandum aliqua alia quae traduntur in hac doctrina. Cum enim gratia non tollat naturam, sed perficiat, oportet quod naturalis ratio subserviat fidei; sicut et naturalis inclinatio voluntatis obsequitur caritati. Unde et Apostolus dicit (2 Corinthians 10:5): 'in captivitatem redigentes omnem intellectum in obsequium Christi.' Et inde est quod etiam auctoritatibus philosophorum sacra doctrina utitur, ubi per rationem naturalem veritatem cognoscere potuerunt; sicut Paulus (Acts 17:28), inducit verbum Arati, dicens: 'sicut et quidam poetarum vestrorum dixerunt, genus Dei sumus.' Sed tamen sacra doctrina huiusmodi auctoritatibus utitur quasi extraneis argumentis, et probabilibus. Auctoritatibus autem canonicae Scripturae utitur proprie, ex necessitate argumentando. Auctoritatibus autem aliorum doctorum ecclesiae, quasi arguendo ex propriis, sed probabiliter. Inititur enim fides nostra revelationi Apostolis et Prophetis factae, qui canonicos libros scipserunt: non autem revelationi si qua fuit aliis doctoribus facta. Unde dicit Augustinus, in epistola ad Hieronymum (19.1.3): 'Solis eis Scripturarum libris qui canonici appellantur, didici hunc honorem deferre, ut nullum auctorem eorum in scribendo erasse aliquid firmissime credam. Alios autem ita lego, ut, quantalibet sanctitate doctrinaque praepolleant, non ideo verum putem, quod ipsi ita senserunt vel scripserunt'" (*ST* Ia, q.1, art. 8, obj. 2 and resp.). See Chenu 1950: 54–65, 138; E. Gilson 1938. Stock 1996: 6–7 and nn (see also 180, 212) succinctly presents the earlier, Augustinian view that all in all authority takes precedence over reason. While Aquinas's discussion is more refined, both, unsurprisingly, put the authority of Scriptures above other modes of knowledge. Compare *CV* 4.3.10, cited below, and *MN* 1.5, 2.1.

the stage (Curtius 1948: 51–2). This scheme, however, has been significantly complicated as I have sketched, and only sketched, the complex discursive field(s) through which authorship and authority were defined in the later Middle Ages and the dynamic histories which traverse and transform those categories over time. At this point, in other words, the Ciceronian problem of rhetorical appearance and political interest reemerges *de facto* and historically in every serious attempt to reduce the origin of authority back to God's power and truth.

Dante was keenly aware of the complexity and dynamism of the situation. Virtually all of the definitions, distinctions, and oppositions listed above figure in some important way in his various treatments of the question, as we have begun to see. Thus in considering his treatment of authority and authorship in *Convivio* and elsewhere, we must simultaneously adopt two perspectives. First, we must acknowledge Dante's in-principle adherence to the ideal of transpersonal and transhistorical *auctoritas*. Second, we must recognize that in contingent and historical terms he explicitly faces the problems that haunt that ideal, and most specifically the difficulty of legitimating human authority by deriving it from a transcendent origin. He faces this issue in two, continuously interpenetrating forms: in an objectifying definitional attempt to understand what "authority" is in the abstract and how it is embodied in the world; and in exploring his own "subjective" relation to the category, in what ways he is excluded from it, in what ways he might appropriate it for himself, his poetry, and his beloved vernacular.

III. DANTE'S "*MAGGIORE AUTORITADE*" (*CV* I.4.13)

The ground has now been laid for returning to the passages in books 1 and 4 of *Convivio* where Dante introduces the topic of authority, in relation both to his own position within the treatise and to several of the medieval discourses on authority just considered, especially that of Hugutio. The first book is almost entirely given over to justifying Dante's ambitious vernacular foray into a domain, classical philosophy,[33] usually reserved for the classical "Latin" *auctores*. This book reveals both the scope of his ambitions – if not to join the *auctores*, at least to enter into dialogue with them – and his keen awareness of the barriers that stand between him and that role: on the one hand, his use of an "inferior" language; on the other, his own status as modern, "personalized" individual. Book 4 then explicitly addresses his

---

[33] See Fenzi 1986; Imbach 1996: especially chapter 5. Dante accentuates *CV*'s novelty, and the need to justify it, by overlooking precursors such as Brunetto Latini, Jean de Meun, and Cavalcanti (especially "Donna me prega").

apparent willingness to challenge the *auctoritas* of two imposing figures, representing two of the three types of authority delimited by Hugutio, namely, *the* Philosopher, and a Holy Roman Emperor, and implicitly puts those modes of authority into relation with the third, that of the poet as "binder of words." Behind a screen of impersonal, "definitional," reflection, Dante at once affirms the traditional validity of *auctoritas* as a mode of knowledge and being, delimits it in such a way as to partially efface the difference between ancient *auctores* and modern commentators on them, and, implicitly, attributes to himself a comprehensive mode of authority that begins with the poetic but then moves out to encompass all three of Hugutio's types – philosophical, political, as well as poetic – under a fourth category, the theological.

Book I opens, as we have seen, by setting itself apart from Dante's earlier career, especially as represented by *Vita Nova*, and by moving into an area – that of serious philosophical speculation – from which he had earlier, at least explicitly, excluded himself and the vernacular. From the first, however, *Convivio* also puts in jeopardy its own, and its author's, ability to carry out such a project. The whole of the first book is a confession of his apparent lack of *autorità*, offering a disconcerting mixture of disclaimers that he seeks it together with more and less obvious attempts to appropriate it.

The very first words of the treatise are: "Sì come dice lo Filosofo nel principio de la Prima Filosofia, tutti li uomini naturalmente desiderano di sapere" (As the Philosopher says at the beginning of the *Metaphysics*, all men naturally desire to know; 1.1.1). This phrase does multiple duty. On the one hand, it boldly defines a new area of discourse for the vernacular, and puts it in relationship to a new area of classical culture; on the other, it seemingly places Dante in the role of a modern and pious *commentator* on classical authorities: the name and words of Aristotle are so often invoked throughout the four books that Dante at times appears as a third-degree *compilator*, rather than even a *commentator*, much less *auctor*.[34] Most crucially, the thought for which Aristotle is cited as authority follows the Scholastic valuation of reason as the common property of all humanity and as a mode of knowledge superior to temporal *auctoritas*. In other words, implicitly it levels the playing field between ancients and moderns, between Latin and vernacular, between Aristotle and Dante. Dante's stated

---

[34] Busnelli and Vandelli 1964, note to *CV* 4.6, reports that Aristotle is cited more than fifty times throughout the work. Maria Corti has much higher figures and gives a specific breakdown for books 2–4 (1983: 130–1). Compare the two explicit references in *VN* (25.2, 41.6). For a review of the wide variety of the other certain and possible philosophical and theological *auctoritates* cited in *CV*, see De Matteis 1970: 373–4; Vasoli 1988a: lxiv–lxxx. See also n 60.

aim of communicating philosophical truths to those who have not studied the Latin authors themselves actually implies that the differences between "high" and "low" cultures are contingent rather than absolute, and that the gap can be bridged.

Similarly ambivalent is the use of the titular metaphor of intellectual edification. Within the text, Dante refers to himself as one who does not sit at the feasting table of the philosophers, but rather "a' piedi di coloro che seggiono ricolgo da quello che da loro cade" (at the feet of those that are seated, I gather some of what they let fall; 1.1.10). At the same time, by assigning the work as a whole the title of "Banquet" he puts himself not only back at the table, but at its head. When in his description of the intellectual food offered as "pan degli angeli" (bread of angels; 1.1.7; cf. 1.1.7–13) and as "quel pane orzato del qual si satolleranno migliaia" (that fine barley bread on which the thousands will amply satisfy their hunger; 1.13.13), he implicitly compares his feast not to Plato's classical *Symposium*, but rather to the divine food provided by the Christian God, and specifically to Christ's miracle of the loaves and fishes.[35]

The bulk of book I is dedicated to an exculpatory "purging" of three "*macule*" (stains), two "accidental" (contingent) and one "substantial" (essential) from Dante's text. Each of the "*macule*" in its different way brings into view both an obstacle to Dante's assumption of a newly authoritative position and a strategy for overcoming that obstacle. They are as follows: (1) that Dante speaks continually about himself in the course of the treatise, despite the classical rhetoricians' prohibition of self-reference, as introducing a distorting element of subjectivity that takes credibility away from one's discourse (1.2); (2) that Dante uses an elevated style – the same style which is designed to acquire "maggiore autoritade" for him – in the commentary on his philosophical *canzoni*, when his audience is composed of humble people who will have difficulty in understanding it (1.3–4; cf. Stabile 1970: 459); (3) that Dante writes his commentary in Italian, which is essentially inferior to Latin as a vehicle for communicating complex philosophical concepts (1.6–13). All three sections point in important ways to the primary authorizing device of *Convivio*, namely Dante's decision to treat his own vernacular *canzoni* as worthy of commentary, thus placing them, implicitly, in the formal position of *auctoritates* and himself in that of *auctor*.[36] At the same time, however, none of them addresses this issue

---

[35] John 6: 5–13. The passage is traditionally allegorized as the dispensing of divine wisdom. On the Christological analogy, see Ransom 1977.

[36] See also Minnis 1990: 28–34; Stillinger 1992: 38–42, cf. 109–16.

directly. Indeed, by framing Dante's problems in the text in other ways, they tend to "naturalize" his boldest self-authorizing stratagem.

Only in Chapter 4 (especially section iii), however, will I turn directly to the question of "self-commentary" as a strategic mode of self-authorization, which Dante both reveals and conceals in book 1. Similarly, I will defer until Chapter 3 consideration of the problem of authorizing Italian as a vehicle of cultural discourse both in *Convivio* and in *De Vulgari Eloquentia*. For now, instead, I want to focus on the primary fact – preliminary to either of the previous two considerations, as to any study of Dantean authority – that all three of the "*macule*," but especially the first two, foreground Dante as contingent, historical person: simultaneously presenting "personhood" as the primary obstacle to "authority" and strategically aiming to overcome that obstacle.

The first "*macula*," as we have seen, is explicitly concerned with the possible problems inherent in a rhetoric as heavily dependent on self-reference as Dante's.[37] This concern is specifically marked as a dramatic shift from *Vita Nova*, whose pervasively self-absorbed "I" feels no need to explain himself, with one notable exception, which will be considered in Chapter 4. As also noted earlier, the reason given for referring to himself in a context where it "pare non licito" (seems improper; 1.2.2) is that Dante needs to show that his *canzoni* are no longer merely records of a subjection to the amorous "passione" of youth, but instead constitute the covert, allegorical, account of a love not for another human being, but for a personified "Lady Philosophy" (1.2.15–16). In other words, he must speak "personally" and "subjectively" in order to show, paradoxically, that his poetry concerns not individual passion but the detached love of transpersonal Truth.

Dante's exposition of the problem reveals that what concerns him is the loss of an authority that grammatical impersonality and objectivity confer. When one speaks of oneself, he says, it is always either to praise or to blame. But self-praise is self-defeating because it always implies that one is not well thought of, that one needs overtly to defend one's reputation. As such it actually amounts to self-blame in the ears of listeners (1.2.7). On the

---

[37] Curtius (1948: 515–18; also Giunta 2002: 48–53) has shown that the later Middle Ages did not so thoroughly discourage self-reference and self-naming as Dante, and scholars like Zumthor (1972: especially 64–9, 172–4), suggest, however apt the prohibition may seem in a culture of ancient authoritative names and self-effacing modern commentators. It is not easy to recuperate this form of self-reference under Spitzer's idea of the "poetic" as against the "empirical" "I" (Spitzer 1946; see Chapter 1, section iv), since it is so specifically directed at Dante's distinctive biography. The point, here as with the issue of "vulgarization" of philosophy (see n 33), is that whether or not there are historical precedents in the Middle Ages for a self-oriented authorship, Dante himself goes to considerable trouble to call attention to problems with this mode.

other hand, open self-blame is even worse because it simply reveals that one recognizes one's own failings without willing a real change in them (1.2.5–6). Above all, Dante says, we are simply in no position to refer accurately and objectively to ourselves since "non è uomo che sia di sé vero e giusto misuratore, tanto la propria caritate ne 'nganna" (no one of us is capable of measuring his own worth truly and justly, so much does self-love deceive us; 1.2.8). Note that he simultaneously gives a justification for an impersonal form of authorship, and specifies that the reasons for such impersonality are rhetorical, that is, that they are concerned with the contingent production of effects in an audience, and thus Ciceronian in the sense noted earlier.

The justification for violating the taboo against self-reference is even more instructive. Dante argues that it may after all be permissible to speak of oneself for either of two reasons: (1) if, like Boethius in the *Consolation*, one thereby escapes danger of "infamia" (1.2.13), or (2) if, like Augustine in the *Confessions*, one thereby benefits others by setting a positive model for imitation (1.2.14).[38] The Augustinian model corresponds to the basic ethical–political project of *Convivio*, that is, the instruction in higher philosophical truths, the "bread of angels," of the members of a vernacular culture, for whom Dante, whose own culture had been primarily vernacular, will be a model to imitate as well as a "maestro." The Boethian model of self-justification by self-reference, which is the one that concerns Dante specifically at this juncture, defines a second and parallel project that, as noted, dominates the first book and then continues unabated, though less apparent, through the next three books as well.[39] The most obvious function of this citation of two classical cases is to give authoritatively ancient precedents for personalized authorship, and, previewing the treatment of Virgil in the *Commedia*, to put Dante implicitly on an equal footing with recognized *auctores*. By citing the less directly relevant case of Augustine alongside that of Boethius, Dante also manages to imply that the apparently self-interested recourse to self-reference is ultimately other-directed.[40] In other words, the two types of self-reference have an ideal point of convergence: Dante's (personalized) authority will make him a good teacher of others.

---

[38] The usual source given is Brunetto Latini (De Robertis 1988: 14–15 n). Lollini 2001 cites Aquinas, *ST* IIa.IIae, q.109, art. 1.

[39] On Boethius as Dante's primary model in *CV* for self-representation, see Guglielminetti 1977: 74–5, 97–9; see again n 6. Freccero 1986 stresses Augustine as Dante's model here and in the *DC*.

[40] See *CV* 3.1.5, 4.8.3, for references to the basis of other-love in self-love. Lerer 1985, especially 203–36, discusses the *Cons.* in terms of the construction of Boethian *auctoritas* via references to poetic and philosophical *auctores*.

The second "*macula*" at first seems to be very different, although the issue is still rhetorical, and it again arises as a by-product of an attempt to remedy a defect of the apparently amorous *canzoni*:

[L]o mio scritto, che quasi comento dir si può, è ordinato a levare lo difetto de le canzoni sopra dette, ed esso per sé fia forse in parte alcuna un poco duro. La qual durezza, per fuggir maggior difetto, non per ignoranza, è qui pensata. (1.3.2)

([T]his work, which can [perhaps] be described as a commentary, is designed to supply what is lacking in the *canzoni* under discussion, and yet may itself perhaps be somewhat difficult to understand in certain parts. This difficulty is quite intentional here, arising not from inadvertence but from a desire to avoid an even greater deficiency.)

This greater defect, for which "maggior autoritade" conferred by stylistic difficulty is then said to be the sovereign cure, is immediately revealed to be a product of Dante's personal historical circumstances, and, even more specifically, an effect of his personal presence on the way his writings are received:

Poi che fu piacere de li cittadini de la bellissima e famossissima figlia di Roma, Fiorenza, di gittarmi fuori del suo dolce seno – nel quale nato e nutrito fui in fino al colmo de la mia vita, e nel quale, con buona pace di quella, desidero con tutto lo cuore di riposare l'animo stancato e terminare lo tempo che m'è dato – per le parti quasi tutte a le quali questa lingua si stende, peregrino, quasi mendicando, sono andato, mostrando contra mia voglia la piaga de la fortuna, che suole ingiustamente al piagato molte volte essere imputata. Veramente io sono stato legno senza vela e sanza governo, portato a diversi porti e foci e liti dal vento secco che vapora la dolorosa povertade. (1.3.4–5)

(From the time when the citizens of Rome's most beautiful and famous daughter, Florence, saw fit to cast me away from her sweet bosom, where I was born and nourished until [the mid-point of my life], and where, with her gracious consent, I desire with all my heart to rest my weary mind and complete my allotted span – I have made my way through almost all the regions to which this language extends, [a pilgrim and stranger], reduced almost to beggary, and showing against my will the wound inflicted by fortune, which is very often imputed unjustly to the one afflicted. I have indeed been a ship lacking sail and [without helmsman], carried to various ports and rivers' mouths and shores by the parching wind raised by painful poverty.)

In other words, Dante is even more like Boethius than initially appeared. His banishment from Florence in 1301 makes him a virtual *döppelganger* of the late classical philosopher who "sotto pretesto di consolazione escusasse la perpetuale infamia del suo essilio" (sought, under the pretext of finding consolation, to excuse the everlasting [infamy] of his exile; 1.2.13) – that is, his fall from the favor of Theodoric, barbarian king of Rome, his metamorphosis from political and judicial authority into condemned prisoner.[41]

It then turns out, at least by implication, that the difficulty of Dante's "comento" is a necessary depersonalizing counterpoint to the equally necessary foray into self-representation. He states that the primary reason for his *loss* of authority is that, in the course of his wanderings after banishment from Florence in 1301:

[S]ono apparito a li occhi a molti che forse chè per alcuna fama in altra forma m'aveano imaginato, nel conspetto de' quali non solamente mia persona inviliò, ma di minor pregio si fece ogni opera, sì già fatta, come quella che fosse a fare. (1.3.5–6)

([M]any have seen me in person who perhaps entertained a different image of me in virtue of a certain reputation I enjoyed, so that in their eyes not only do I myself [become vile], but all my works, those still to be produced no less than those already completed, are cheapened.)

In other words, Dante's personal presence contrasts with the disembodied fame that circulated with and around his texts, undercutting their, and his, prestige.

The powerful, and pathetic, effect of personal presence is said to have three causes. The first two belong to those who perceive Dante: (1) most are too ready to judge by external appearance alone (1.4.3–5); while (2) others have their judgments distorted by envy (1.4.6–8). The last cause is in Dante himself, and any human being (any writer) – since no mortal person is without defect or stain:

La terza [cagione] si è l'umana impuritade, la quale si prende da la parte di colui ch'è giudicato e non è sanza familiaritade e conversazione alcuna. Ad evidenza di questa, è da sapere che l'uomo è da più parti maculato e, come dice Agustino, "nullo è sanza macula." . . . [L]e quali cose [that is various types of "macule"] la fama non porta seco ma la presenza, e discuoprele per sua conversazione. E queste macule alcuna ombra gittano sopra la chiarezza della bontade, sì che la fanno parere men chiara e men valente. E questo è quello per che ciascuno profeta è meno onorato ne la sua patria . . . Per che manifestamente si vede che per impuritade, sanza la quale non è alcuno, la presenza ristringe lo bene e lo male in ciascuno più che 'l vero non vuole. (1.4.9–12)

(Human imperfection is the third cause. This is a feature of the person who is judged, and is not revealed unless people have some familiarity and personal

---

[41] See also 2.12.2. In *Inf.* 13, Dante dramatizes the fate of Pier delle Vigne, whom Frederick II first entrusted with high office, then imprisoned. Pier's case, as he recounts it, recalls Boethius's treatment by Theodoric and parallels Dante's situation (13.52–78); for a harsh judgment of Pier's "special pleading" within the economy of infernal justice see Stephany 1982; Cassell 1984: 32–56. Dante converts Boethius's imprisonment into exile, strengthening the parallel that will emerge in *CV* 1.3.

acquaintance with him [i.e., without him being present]. To make this point clear, it should be explained that a man can be [stained] in many ways, and, as Augustine says, "[no one is without stain]" . . . It is one's presence, not one's reputation, that brings such matters to light, for they emerge in the course of becoming personally acquainted. These [stains] cast a certain shadow over a person's luminous goodness, and make it shine less clearly and brightly. That is why every prophet receives less honor in his own country. . . It is, then, perfectly clear that imperfection, from which no one is free, in [every] case causes a person's presence to diminish, more than truth warrants, the good and evil he has done.)

The human stain which appears inevitably in Dante when he presents himself reminds us that he is trying to purge this and other stains ("*macule*" – the word is the same) from his work by these self-justifications (1.2.1–2). In other words, his own stained, sinful nature detracts from the authority that his works, by themselves, deserve to acquire.

Over the course of these three preliminary chapters (1.2–4), Dante specifically locates a crisis of authority around the questions of self-representation (in his work) and of self-presentation (to the Italian courts where he passes his exile). The ostensible aim of the chapters is to re-acquire *fama*, and authority, by confronting explicitly the dangers that threaten it. He must take the risk of re-presenting himself in words, thus diminishing any claim he might have to *auctoritas*, because his reputation has already been tainted by misinterpretations of his poetry. He must resort to an elevated rhetoric that partially compromises his divulgative mission because his "stained" human presence had compromised it even further. Most crucially, authority lost through *self-presentation* must be recovered by *self-representation*. Impersonality is coincident with authority, but Dante's route to authority cannot fail to reveal his stained personality and his contingent circumstances. He at once sets up *auctoritas* in its traditional form as the goal to which he aspires, and reveals that he cannot hope to obtain it without a detour through its antithesis – a detour that is likely to transform it beyond recognition, to give it a human face.[42]

If these passages can be read as expressive of Dante's desire to conform to the medieval model of authorship, they can equally well be seen as a radical critique and reconfiguration of that model. In them, Dante brings together, around his own vocation as writer, the opposed concepts of vulgar *fama*, opinion based on mere appearance and dangerous passions, and of

---

[42] I.e., Dante comes to function as a *prosopopeia* of authority (see also n 88). On the issue of person-ification in Dante as it pertains to the question at hand, see Chapter 4, especially section ii, and n 50. For another reading of Dante's first-person presence in *CV*, see Guglielminetti 1977: 78–80.

autoritade, the impersonal and transcendent name that inspires faith and guarantees truth (cf. Allen 1982: 257). In his extended account of how both evil and good *fama* work, the biased report of either friend or enemy gives rise to a series of exaggerations which gain force as they recede in time and space from the person whose name is repeated (1.3.6–11). This could well be taken as a subversive genetic account of the creation of *auctoritas* itself, which grows with antiquity. At the same time, a personalized version of authorship does not seem to be a viable alternative. Dante's subsequent discussion of the operations of *fama* and *infamia* in relation to the effects of personal presence suggests that these are just as deceptive as those created by distorting distance. In other words, neither the objectifying work of time nor the immediacy of personal presence guarantees the value of a text, its worthiness of "faith and obedience." In theory, then, no way remains to guarantee that a person, an author, will be taken for what he really is – no grounds either for establishing authority on traditional, impersonal grounds or for creating a new and personalized concept of authorization.

Rather than constituting an insuperable impasse, however, Dante's confrontation with the "macule" of his text – which are figuratively conflated with his own, quintessentially human, "macule" – is just the opening gambit in an ongoing process of self-authorization that continues into the discussion of a third and more substantial stain: that of the use of Italian as a vehicle for learned commentary instead of Latin. Again, this issue will be considered in greater depth in Chapter 3. The principal charge against the "volgare" is that while "lo latino è perpetuo e non corruttibile, . . . lo volgare è non stabile e corruttibile" (Latin has a permanent form and is not subject to change . . . the vernacular is unstable and is subject to change; 1.5.7). The vernacular changes with both time and place: it is subject to history, living and dying in a way that mimes the cyclical course of individual human lives. In other words, the flawed, individualized character of the vernacular is analogous to the flawed, individualized character of Dante as he presents himself in the Italian courts.

The connection between Dante and the "volgare" becomes explicit, and explicitly personal, near the end of his lengthy justification for using it in spite of its historical variability. The point is first made in an abstract argument, whose impersonal form belies its intimately "individual" account of the relationship between the vernacular and its users. Citing the authority not only of Aristotle but also of Cicero, Dante says that his great love for the vernacular, which makes him desire to promote its welfare, is the result of "prossimitade":

Tanto è la cosa più prossima quanto, di tutte le cose del suo genere, altrui è più unita: onde di tutti li uomini lo figlio è più prossimo al padre . . . di tutta la terra è più prossima quella dove l'uomo tiene se medesimo, però che è ad esso più unita. E così lo volgare è più prossimo quanto è più unito, che uno e solo è prima ne la mente che alcuno altro, e che non solamente per sé è unito, ma per accidente, in quanto è congiunto con le più prossime persone, sì come con li parenti e con li propri cittadini e con la propria gente. È questo è lo volgare proprio; lo quale è non prossimo, ma massimamente prossimo a ciascuno. Per che, se la prossimitade è seme d'amistà, come detto è di sopra, manifesto è ch'ella è de le cagioni stata de l'amore ch'io porto a la mia loquela, che è a me prossima più che l'altre. (1.12.4–6)

(Of all the members of any given class of things, [that] one is closer to a person the more fully it is united to him; so, for instance, of all men a son is closer to his father [than to any other human being] . . . of all the countries of the earth the one which is closest to a person is the one in which he himself resides, since it is most united to him. Similarly, that vernacular is closest to a person which is the one most fully united to him, [since by itself and all alone it is first among all languages in the mind, to which it is united not only in itself, but by circumstance, in the sense that it is also conjoined with the persons who are] closest to him, such as his relatives, his own fellow citizens, and his own race. I am of course speaking of each person's own vernacular, which is not simply close to him, but close in a most intimate way. Granted, then, what was said above, that closeness is a seed of friendship, it is clear that closeness must be counted one of the causes of the love I bear for my own vernacular, which is nearer to me than any other.)

What begins as a metonymical argument from proximity (one loves the vernacular because one uses it), shades at its climax into a metaphorical argument of quasi-identity (one loves the vernacular because it is specific and "proper" to oneself, virtually identical, in fact). In other words, Dante and the vernacular coincide, and they do so because they are both contingently shaped individuals: as Dante is distinct from all other people, "his speech" is distinct from all others by virtue of being the product of a specific time and place. What had been the vernacular's fatal flaw, what prevented it from any claim to intellectual authority, has now become its specific virtue as the vehicle for Dantean authorship.[43]

---

[43] Significantly, in the passage immediately following this one, where Dante goes on to discuss why "bontade" as well as "prossimitade" makes him love his vernacular, he enters into a digression on the virtue of justice in which he recalls his earlier excursus on why an author may speak of himself to be exonerated from unjust accusations: "Li quali [tradimento etc.] sono tanto inumani peccati, che ad iscusare sé de l'infamia di quelli, si concede da lunga usanza che uomo parli di sé, come detto è di sopra, e possa dire sé essere fedele e leale" (1.12.11). In addition to anticipating the role of *fede* as the quality inspired by the *autore*, this passage also fuels the comparison between Dante and Pier delle Vigne (n 41), who insists repeatedly on his *fede* to *Fede*-rigo (*Inf.* 13.74–5, also 13.61; see Stephany 1982).

This personalization of the vernacular is given a much more vivid and "embodied" form in the next chapter, when Dante assigns to it responsibility for his very existence as well as for his introduction to the intellectual world of Latin (cf. Cestaro 1991b: 64–5):

Con ciò sia cosa che due perfezioni abbia l'uomo, una prima e una seconda – la prima lo fa essere, la seconda lo fa essere buono – se la propria loquela m'è stata cagione de l'una e de l'altra, grandissimo beneficio da lei ho ricevuto . . . Questo mio volgare fu congiungitore de li miei generanti, che con esso parlavano . . . per che manifesto è lui essere concorso a la mia generazione. Ancora, questo mio volgare fu introduttore di me ne la via di scienza, che è l'ultima perfezione, in quanto con esso io entrai ne lo latino e con esso mi fu mostrato. (1.13.3–5; see Cestaro 1991b: 64–5)

(The fact is that a human being has two perfections: . . . the first makes him *be*, the second makes him *be good*, and if my own speech was the cause of both in me, then I have received the greatest benefit from it . . . This my vernacular was the uniter of my parents [those who generated me], because they spoke using it . . . Clearly then it participated in my generation. Furthermore, this my vernacular introduced me into the ways of knowledge, which is the final perfection, inasmuch as with it I entered into the knowledge of Latin, which was expounded to me using it. [author's translation])

If the vernacular has been responsible for making Dante what he is, he will in turn make *it* into what *it* desires to become:

Ciascuna cosa studia naturalmente a la sua conservazione . . .; onde, se lo volgare per sé studiare potesse, studierebbe a quella; e quella sarebbe, acconciare sé a più stabilitade, e più stabilitade non si potrebbe avere che in legar sé con numero e con rime. E questo medesimo studio è stato mio . . . (1.13.6–7)

(Everything naturally pursues its own perpetuation . . . [T]hus, if the vernacular were able to pursue its own ends, it would pursue that one, and it would consist in preparing itself for greater stability, and greater stability could not be obtained than by binding itself with numbers [meter] and with rhymes. And this same pursuit has been my own . . . [author's translation])

This final gesture of reciprocity seals identification between Dante and the vernacular, which is increasingly, specifically, and personally his. Yet it also does more: it implies a reversal of the conceptual field, which turns both Dante and the vernacular back in the direction of that quality, transhistorical and hence transpersonal stability, which is a *conditio sine qua non* of authority. Dante will take the contingent and provisional essence of his personal language and impose the permanent, depersonalizing ordering of poetic meter and rhyme upon it.

A further implication may then be teased out of the final, ambiguous line: "this same pursuit has been my own." The obvious sense is that he, like the vernacular, has pursued *its* stability and permanence. It may also, however, be read as meaning that, like the vernacular, and every other created thing, he has pursued *his own* permanence. This reading would be forced, were it not that, in terms of the discourse of self-authorization we have been tracking, the permanence of the vernacular in which Dante composes his poetry is exactly what would guarantee *his* permanence – his survival over time, beyond his own contingent yet inevitable death, into the impersonal stature of the *auctor*, hypostatized in the words that originated with him.

Until the end of book 1, then, Dante continues to oscillate between two discursive poles. On the one hand, he distances himself from the traditional culture of *auctoritas*, represented by impersonal absence of the authorial self, and by the timeless permanence of Latin. On the other he pursues such *auctoritas* for himself actively, in the turn to a higher and more difficult style of discourse, and in the project of conferring on the vernacular, *his* vernacular, the same transcendent stability as Latin, and in doing so guaranteeing his own survival. Throughout this analysis of book 1, we have seen that Dante himself points to the obvious slippage between the respectful pursuit of classical *auctoritas* and the embracing of a new, personal and vernacular, mode of authorship.[44] On the one hand is the overt and continuing submission to the authority of Aristotle. On the other is the claim that his work and its language are radically new, departing, with reason, "da quello che per li altri è stato servato lungamente" ([from that which has long been observed by others]; 1.10.1), that the banquet he prepares is "luce nuova, sole nuovo" (a new light, a new sun; 1.13.12), which will rise as its precursor (Aristotle? Latin?) is setting.[45]

Nevertheless, if the Dantean "I" who presents himself in *Convivio* is aware of such a tension, he is not in full control of it. The wild swings between "new" and "old," personal and impersonal, modes of authorship, as well as between Dante's self-proclaimed lack of authority and his large claims upon it, can be measured in the space between the opening image

[44] Quint's model (1983) of a simultaneous pursuit of "origin" and "originality" seems apt to this configuration.

[45] See Fenzi 1986: 14–15, 19–25 for valuable analysis of these chapters. Grayson anticipates the notion of an oblique, rhetorical rather than rational, process by which authority is transferred from *gramatica* to *volgare*, particularly in noting that the qualities assigned to Latin in 1.5.7 (*virtù* and *bellezza*), return in 1.10.12, now in possession of Italian (especially 1965: 19). See also Guglielminetti 1977: 82–7; Barański 1986a: 47–9, 52–4 and nn; Vasoli 1988a: xix–xxi; Scott 1995: 33–5, 2004: 109–12. More typical of the dismissive attitude toward 1.5–13, which even Grayson shares at times (18), is Nardi 1921b: 180.

of a dog-like collector of the crumbs of others and the closing parallel, mentioned earlier, between Dante's intellectual banquet for his readers and Christ's multiplication of the loaves. It is, then, in relation to this intense, yet incomplete and unresolved, staging of the drama of self-authorization that Dante's efforts in book 4, and especially chapter 6, to define the nature of the *auctor* and his *auctoritas*, and to situate them vis-à-vis himself and his text, can best be understood.

IV. "*AUTORE*" FROM "*AUTENTIN*"

The two books that follow the introduction continue to be concerned with constructing an authority-conferring ethical-intellectual history of the authorial self, even as they also begin the process of providing philosophical knowledge for their "vulgar" readers (cf. Fenzi 1986: 27–8). As already observed, book 2 offers an account of how Dante was won to the love of Lady Philosophy after the death of "quella gloriosa Beatrice" (2.12.1–9; cf. 2.15.1).[46] Book 3 then describes the nobility of Dante's new beloved (cf. 2.15.3), who ennobles the human nature of her lovers, including Dante, by leading it to the perfection of its highest faculty, reason. In each case, the lesson offered to the reader is doubled by an account of the author's own experience, the history of his ascent toward the position from which he looks back and offers his own knowledge as a guide to others.

In book 4 this autobiographical troping seems to have ended, although he does offer an account, to which Chapter 4 will return, of the circumstances of the poem's production. It is as if Dante had now achieved the authority necessary for writing *Convivio* itself. Specifically, the canzone, "Le dolci rime d'amor ch'i' solia," is by its author named "Contra-li-erranti mia" after Aquinas's *Summa Contra Gentiles*, because it assumes a privileged position of philosophical insight to dispel the errors of willful ignorance about the nature of true nobility (4.canzone.141 and 4.30.2–3). The new "impersonality" of book 4 is, however, only apparent. What Dante personally has at stake is precisely the nobility and authority that allows him to write book 4, though we can only discover this by carefully examining the implicit parallels between his central topic, nobility, and the preliminary discussion of his relationship to the *auctoritas* of Frederick II and of

---

[46] In 2.12.5, Dante refers to the "vocabuli d'autori e di scienze e di libri" that he found in Cicero and Boethius, and that led him to understand how Philosophy, "che era donna di questi autori," was a most noble thing. When he then presents "her" as his Lady (2.12.8–9 *et passim*), he puts himself in the place of the "autori."

Aristotle, including the two definitions of the word itself already cited on a number of occasions.

The ostensible purpose of the definitional excursus is *not* that of attributing special *auctoritas* to Dante himself. Rather, it is explicitly aimed at showing his respect for traditional canons of authority, and for two *auctores* in particular, the Emperor Frederick II (4.4–5), and *the* Philosopher, Aristotle, who is also *the* authority of *Convivio* (4.6). In this scenario Dante continues to position himself, as he did at the outset, as modern commentator on classical thought. At the same time, however, he presents the contents of the book as an original product of his own reflections on the philosophical question at hand: "grande e alta opera sia per le mani al presente e da li autori poco cercata" (an important and difficult task is being undertaken here, and one in which established authors have taken little interest; 4.3.3).[47] Moreover, echoing Aquinas's hierarchy of arguments, he claims that his proofs will rely, not on human authority, but on "la vertude de la veritate, che ogni autoritade convince" ([the power of] truth, which is superior to every authority; 4.3.10; see also 4.24.9; cf. n 32). And, finally, he invokes the *auctores* not, as so often throughout the treatise, as the source of his ideas (i.e., Foucauldian "initiators of discourse"), but rather as potentially opposed to him.[48] In other words, he reaffirms his loyal membership in a culture of authority at the very point when he seems on the verge of breaking out of it. However, the complications do not end there.

[47] This line of argument is not original with Dante, however. Significantly, a closely comparable version is in Boethius, *Cons.* 3.3–4. For the discourses of nobility available in the early Trecento, see Corti 1959, 1983: especially 53–6; Consoli 1973; De Robertis 1988: pp. 527–29 nn, 543 n; Trovato 1990 a and b. Nor is the theoretical opposition as widespread as he indicates. In practical socio-political terms, however, the feudal order to which the mercantile republicanism of Dante's native Florence presented a stern challenge, contradicted it flatly. The political climate in Florence around 1300 conditioned Dante in at least two ways: allowing him to conceive easily of relative political-intellectual independence from authorities; but also instilling in him an urgent sense of the need for hierarchical authority to restore lost order (Nardi 1965a: 50–1; Simonelli 1966: 56–8, 1970; Consoli 1973: 58; Corti 1983: 38–56). See also nn 52–53.

[48] As a number of commentators (including Nardi 1960a: 15, 1965a: 48–9; Segre 1963a; Grayson 1963: 51 *et passim*; Simonelli 1970; Corti 1983: 123–45; Vasoli 1988a: xvii) have observed, in book 4 Dante is following closely both the language and the procedures of Scholastic argumentation, especially those of the *quaestio*: for example, in dedicating the first half of the book, or rather, thirteen chapters thereof, to refuting erroneous positions, and the second half, fourteen more, to proving and illustrating his own thesis (4.30.1). Dante's lengthy treatment of the topic resembles Marenbon's description of fourteenth-century developments of the form in the direction of greater liberty for the airing of one's own views (1987: 31–3). At the same time, a typical feature of the *quaestio* in its earlier stages is to set out apparent contradictions between two *auctoritates* and then to demonstrate an actual harmony between them (Marenbon 1987: 29–31). Stabile 1970: 459 sees this in book 4. If so, however, it is only present in the apparent contradiction between Dante, on the one hand, and Aristotle and Frederick, on the other, with the implication that Dante has tacitly assumed the structural role of *auctor*. For the *quaestio* in general, see n 27.

Dante's primary definition, as we have seen, is that *autore* comes from *autentin* and refers to one "worthy of faith and obedience." The etymology is standard throughout the Middle Ages, and not only in the work, Hugutio's, cited as his source. The mention of Hugutio, however, is apt: first because it points toward the source of the other definition explicitly given in *Convivio* 4.6 (from *avieo*), and second because it invites consideration of why Dante makes only a fleeting allusion to what was Hugutio's first definition, the political *auctor* from *augere*, and whether or not Dante too approaches the question of authority not through a bipartite but rather a tripartite division according to fields. It does not take long to realize that Dante has, for all intents and purposes, folded the political *auctor* and the philosophical *autor* of the *Derivationes* into the single definition in Italian of the *autore* from *autentin*. One of the two authorities invoked, Aristotle, is explicitly given as an example of the *philosophi* who are called *autores* by Hugutio. The other, however, is not a philosopher at all – despite the importance of his court as a cultural center, and his own dabbling in poetry and other forms of authorship, including a treatise on falconry – but is rather a Roman emperor, who, as a class, Hugutio defines as belonging under the rubric of *auctor* from *augere*.[49] A linguistic trace of this definitional fusion comes with Dante's change from Hugutio's definition of the *autor* from *autentin* as one who is worthy of "faith and *imitation*" to his own "faith and *obedience*," a formula rarely if ever attested in the Middle Ages (E. Gilson 1939: 144). The point, of course, is that "obedienza" suggests indirectly the relationship of subject to ruler, all the more so given the preceding definition of the imperial office: "E così chi a questo officio è posto è chiamato Imperadore, però che di tutti li comandamenti elli è comandatore, e quello che esso dice a tutti

---

[49] Dante does allude, by negation, to Hugutio's first definition, specifying that the two definitions he will offer are "senza quella terza lettera 'C.'" Since he does this just after claiming to have already spoken about imperial authority, one might infer that he has assumed the definition with the letter "C" in the chapters that treated the Empire, even though, since he is writing in Italian rather than Latin, all five references (4.3.10, 4.7 [2], 4.8, 5.15; see also 4.6.17, 6.18, 7.1, 9.1) are to imperial "autoritade," without any "c" (see Chapter 1, section ii, and n 26). *Sed contra*, one might with equal reason infer that he is pointing out that he has *not* explicitly adduced this definition, nor will he thereafter. That 4.6 begins with a construction in which the one word "autoritade" is used in reference to both Emperor and Philosopher ("l'altezza della imperiale autoritade e de la filosofica"; 1) suggests a single concept distributed over the two fields. Moreover, the conception of Empire articulated in the two preceding chapters does not square well with the etymology of *auctor* from *augere*. Since Dante already believes that the Roman empire is universal, and its mission not that of conquest but rather of bringing justice, liberty, and peace to the world, the notion of "augmentation" does not seem apt – not to mention that he goes to some lengths to defend the Empire from (Augustinian) accusations of violent expansionist imperialism (*CV* 4.4.8–12; *MN* 2.1 *et passim*; see Chapter 5, n 35). Stabile 1970: 457 assumes that the "imperial autoritade" in book 4 refers to the "auctor" from "augere." See also n 23; Chapter 1, n 25; Chapter 5, n 20.

è legge, e *per tutti dee essere obedito* e ogni altro comandamento da quello di costui prendere vigore e *autoritade*" ([thus] whoever is appointed to this office is called Emperor, since he governs all [governance], his word is law for all, and must be obeyed by all, and all other government must draw its force and authority from his; 4.4.7).

Having yoked the two types of authority distinguished by Hugutio under a single term, Dante then immediately proceeds to distinguish sharply between them, reintroducing a separation that he has just effaced. Before he ever gets to the point of trotting out the etymological definition, Dante spends three chapters (4.3–5) attempting to prove his submission to "la imperiale maiestade e autoritade" ([imperial majesty and authority]; 4.4.7) and to show that imperial authority was legitimately conferred on the Roman Empire and its ruler by God (see also *MN* 2 and Chapter 5, section iii, below). He nonetheless reserves the right to disagree with the Emperor's philosophical views because, he argues, his authority extends only over the human will and the field of human actions subject to law:

[A] perfezione de l'umana vita la imperiale autoritade fu trovata, e . . . ella è regolatrice e rettrice di tutte le nostre operazioni, giustamente; ché per tanto oltre quanto le nostre operazioni si stendono la maiestade imperiale ha giurisdizione, e fuori di quelli termini non si sciampa. Ma sì come ciascuna arte e ufficio da lo imperiale è a certi termini limitato, così questo da Dio a certo termine è finito. (4.9.1–2)[50]

([I]mperial authority was established [for the purpose of perfecting human life]; it rightly regulates and oversees all of our activities, for the area covered by the term "our activities" is precisely coextensive with the area over which the imperial majesty has jurisdiction, whose extension reaches only to the boundaries of that area. But just as every other human art and [office] is confined within definite boundaries by the imperial office, so the imperial office itself is limited within a boundary set by God.)

And furthermore:

Dire si può de lo Imperadore, volendo lo suo officio figurare con una imagine, che elli sia lo cavalcatore de la umana volontade. (4.9.10)

([O]ne may describe the emperor in figurative language as the rider of the human will.)

---

[50] This passage suggests another reason why Dante might put imperial authority under the heading of *autor* from *autentin*, namely to stress that imperial rule is an *art*, that of administering justice (for Hugutio the *autores* include all the *inventores artium*). See especially 4.9.9–10: "A questa [la ragione scritta (i.e., the law)] scrivere, mostrare e comandare, è questo officiale posto di cui si parla, cioè lo Imperadore, al quale tanto quanto le nostre operazioni proprie, che dette sono, si stendono, siamo subietti; e più oltre no. Per questa ragione, *in ciascuna arte* e in ciascuno mestiere *li artefici* e li discenti sono, ed esser deono, subietti al prencipe e al maestro di quelle, in quelli mestieri ed *in quella arte*; e fuori di quello la subiezione pere, però che pere lo principato."

Similarly, just as Frederick, *qua* Emperor, has dominion over human will, Aristotle, inasmuch as he personifies philosophical authority, is "maestro e duca de la ragione umana" ([teacher] and leader of human reason; 4.6.8). Between them, they divide up the two faculties that define human experience within the order of nature, and each is subject to the authority of the other in his particular field and dependent upon the other as far as the proper exercise of his own authority is concerned (E. Gilson 1939: 141–2; cf. Stabile 1970: 458; also n 88 below):

L'autoritade del filosofo sommo . . . non repugna a la imperiale autoritade; ma quella sanza questa è pericolosa, e questa sanza quella è quasi debile, non per sé, ma per la disordinanza della gente; sì che l'una con l'altra congiunta utilissime e pienissime sono d'ogni vigore. (4.6.17)

([T]he authority of the greatest philosopher . . . does not in any way detract from that of the emperor; rather the latter authority without the former is dangerous, and the former without the latter is rendered weak, not because of anything intrinsic to it, but because people tend to act irrationally. So when these two operate in unison each is at its most beneficial and carries its fullest weight.)

Having made this distinction, Dante is then ready to insist that he does not presume against either type of authority:

Con tutta reverenza e a lo Principe e al Filosofo portando . . . mostrerò come . . . né contra l'imperiale maiestade, né contra lo Filosofo si ragiona inreverentemente. (4.8.4)

(I, who fully respect both the Prince and the Philosopher, . . . shall make it quite clear that [I do not reason irreverently] about either the imperial majesty or the Philosopher.)

He then proceeds to a lengthy proof of how his discussion of *nobilitas* respects the authority of both, apparent disagreements notwithstanding.

At this point, the outlines of a Dantean strategy for simultaneously respecting authority and circumventing it have become apparent. Over half a century ago, Etienne Gilson pointed to a curious feature of Dante's attitude toward authorities in a number of different fields or institutions – notably the political, the philosophical, and the ecclesiastical – which he dubbed the *aporia dantesca* (1939: 156; see also 140, 147–8, 188; cf. Vasoli 1979).[51] What Gilson remarked upon is a consistent doubleness in Dante's treatment of the nature and scope of human authority. On the one hand, Dante desires to make an individual absolutely authoritative within his own domain, and yet, on the other, he defines the limits of that domain, beyond

---

[51] Gilson does not discuss poetic authority, since his primary focus is on *MN*, where this question is not explicitly raised.

which this individual possesses no special authority. Gilson was thinking primarily about the attempt in *Monarchia* to free imperial rule from any subordination, in temporal matters, to the papacy, whose field was to be exclusively spiritual (see also Chapters 5–6). As just seen, *Convivio* book 4 offers a related and equally clear example. The *aporia dantesca*, the little gap between the Emperor's and the Philosopher's domains is, presumably, the place where Dante's own nascent authority subsists. What Gilson did not remark upon, and what will concern us shortly, is the issue of how that second definition, of poetic *auctoritas* from *avieo*, pertains to the respective authorities of Emperor and Philosopher, and to that of Dante himself.

First, however, one especially thorny question raised by the last quotation needs to be considered, namely the relation between nobility, which is the principal topic of this book – and which Dante seeks to find in himself as well – and the theme of authority. The plan of book 4 is, first, to refute a complex of erroneous, though generally held, definitions of human nobility, and then to offer a counter-definition, which is the true one.[52] The errors Dante wants to erase are encapsulated in a phrase attributed by him to Emperor Frederick II – that nobility consists in "antica ricchezza e belli costumi" ([ancient] wealth and pleasing manners; 4.canzone.21–24; 4.3.6), with the added implication that nobility is derived genealogically, by birth. From this authoritative account, according to Dante, stems the ignorant "vulgar" opinion that wealth and high birth equal nobility (4.3.7; 4.14–15). Finally, Aristotle himself is brought into the question, not because of an errant definition of nobility, but because he says, or rather, Aquinas says he says (Aquinas 1934: bk. 7, lect.13, n.1509), that something which is believed by many cannot be entirely false. The Philosopher thus seems to lend his *autorità* to the truth of this or any other popular belief or opinion (4.3.98).

In opposition to Frederick, Dante offers a definition of nobility as an entirely individual or personal attribute, one that is the ground or root out of which all the active virtues grow, the heaven in which the starry virtues shine (4.18.5, 19.1–8).[53] Since he defines virtue as an "elective habit,"

---

[52] General discussions of *nobilitas* in book 4 are in Corti 1959; Simonelli 1966; Consoli 1973; Fenzi 1986: especially 29–36, 47–51; Vasoli 1988a: xxxviii–lii; Trovato 1990b. Fenzi stresses the nexus between book 4 and the questions of linguistic nobility in book 1 and of the "nobilitade" of Lady Philosophy in books 2–3 (e.g., 30, 39–42, *et passim*; also Minnis *et al.* 1988: 381).

[53] Despite a citation of Guinizelli's "Al cor gentil" (4.20.7), *CV* revises the Guinizellian concept of "gentilezza"/"nobiltà" as simultaneous with the loving heart deployed in *VN* (especially chapters 19–20). In *CV* it is love of wisdom, rather than of woman, which ennobles, echoing *Cons.* 3.3. The last paragraph of the last extant chapter of the treatise, 4.30.6, reiterates that nobility and philosophy are inseparable.

nobility becomes the basis for a series of continuing free and autonomous acts of will, which are not conditioned by personal possessions, ancestry, or standing in society (4.17.1–2, 7–8; 20.5). Moreover, *nobiltà* is a combination of the disposition of an individual body/soul complex with God's direct gift to that individual (4.20–21). Finally, in chapter 16 (par. 6), Dante carefully rejects one of Hugutio's etymological definitions, where he derives "nobilis" from "notabilis" that is, "well known," in favor of a second the innocuous "non vilis," not vile or ignoble (*MD* II.N.57.15; cf. *Etym.* 10.184) – to ensure that nobility is not dependent upon *fama* or opinion, but is rather an intrinsic quality. And with this last affirmation we begin to see an implicit connection forming between the "impersonal" argumentation of book 4 and the very personal account of Dante's own subjection to the vagaries of *fama* related in book 1.

To begin with, a straightforward analogy may be drawn between the "objective" philosophical discussion of *nobiltà*, on the one hand, and, on the other, Dante's struggle to acquire an *autorità* that is not dependent on its genealogy or antiquity, its impersonality, its general reputation, its acceptance and promulgation by authoritative institutions – but is rather *individual*. In other words, Dante's thesis concerning nobility gives a principled – philosophical, theoretical – basis to the unsystematic, and deeply ambivalent, emphasis on a newly personalized and individualized authorship in book 1.

Significantly, the terms of Dante's discussion of *nobiltà* bear a striking resemblance to those of Cicero's consideration of the nature of juridical *auctoritas* quoted earlier (*Top.* 19.73). Cicero there gives two sources for *auctoritas*: the individual *natura* of a witness, but also contingent circumstances, including wealth and other attributes conferred by Fortune. The intrinsic quality that confers authority on an individual for Cicero is his personal *virtus*, which corresponds to Dante's own account. On the other hand, the Roman orator's account of authority derived from temporal circumstance is closely analogous to "Frederick's" as Dante represents it, and he concludes his discussion by an affirmation that *auctoritas* ultimately depends on "vulgi opinio" which parallels the thought Dante initially attributes to Aristotle. In other words, the traditional terms in which *auctoritas* was understood systematically parallel those applied to *nobilitas* in book 4 and might well predispose both Dante and his readers to see the connection between them.

Confirmation of the interconnections between the problem of *auctoritas* and that of *nobilitas* comes, again, from Hugutio. Even if Dante does not quote it, he could hardly have overlooked that point in Hugutio's discussion of the etymologies of *au[c]tor* that directly equates *autenticus*, the adjectival companion of *autor* from *autentin*, with *nobilis*, an equation which, we can now affirm, subtends the explicit concerns of book 4. Dante makes the link overtly, and shows its relevance to him personally, at the point when he asserts the need to prove his respect for the two great authorities: "in questo trattato ... di nobilitade trattando, me nobile e non villano deggio mostrare" ([in this treatise, which treats of nobility, I must show myself noble and not base]; 4.8.5). In fact, as noted above, much of the "impersonal" discourse on nobility later in book 4 – for example the chapters dedicated to the four ages of human life – reflects back on the key elements of Dante's autobiography with which he was explicitly concerned throughout book 1 and in part in books 2 and 3 as well (see, for example, n 13).

There is still, however, a problem, because when he says he wants to show himself noble it is not explicitly in the sense of demonstrating intellectual autonomy. Rather, as we have seen, Dante is engaged in proving his "faith and obedience" toward Frederick and Aristotle – and he makes no open and direct claim that he himself possesses the authority he defines and describes (E. Gilson 1939: 146).[54] If we look more closely at the way in which he goes about proving his respect for the two *auctores*, nonetheless, it will be clear how this superficial subservience and self-effacement is aimed at establishing independence from them.

As noted earlier, the treatment of Frederick is relatively straightforward – an attempt both to honor one kind of authority and to delimit it.[55] Dante can freely and flatly contradict the Emperor, because his authority simply does not include intellectual truth. By contrast, the treatment of Aristotle's authority is not even apparently simple, since it does not directly concern nobility at all, but rather the Philosopher's claim for the veracity of popular opinion. This is a crucial matter, because we have already seen that, in *Convivio*, opinion or *fama*, that is, unfounded belief, is both the inimical antithesis and enemy of authority, and its parodic double, insofar as both are versions of *fede*, faith or trust, in a name. Thus Dante deliberately entertains the notion that Aristotle authoritatively sets forth a view that

[54] Earlier in the same chapter, however, Dante makes the expression of due reverence depend upon true self-knowledge: "arroganza e dissoluzione è sé medesimo non conoscere, ché [sé medesimo conoscere] principio è ed è la misura d'ogni reverenza. ... [M]ostrerò come ... né contra l'imperiale maiestade né contra lo Filosofo si ragiona inreverentemente" (4.8.3–4). In other words, his professed respect for impersonal authority becomes the occasion for affirmation of a self-reflective, personal wisdom.

[55] For historical background on Frederick, see Kantorowicz 1931; Tierney 1964; Van Cleve 1972; Abulafia 1988; Mallette 2005: chapter 3. For Dante's treatments of, and indebtedness to, Frederick see Vallone 1965; Dragonetti 1989; Pertile 1994; and especially Boccassini 2003. See also nn 41, 43. The importance of Frederick for Dante will be further explored in Chapters 3 and 6.

undercuts hierarchical authority, subjecting truth to whatever the greatest number of people happen to think at the present moment. Dante's solution to the problem is equivocal – he simply says that Aristotle must have meant opinion based on rational understanding rather than on deceptive sensory appearances (4.8.8; see De Robertis 1988: 609–11 nn). Chenu has suggested that the redefinition of key terms is a typical tactical device of the Scholastics for conserving *auctoritas* when it becomes problematic (1950: 140–1; see also n 26 and Stabile 1970: 459), just as Dante conserves Frederick's authority by circumscribing it. On the other hand, it might suggest how *auctores* become whatever their interpreters want them to be – how the culture of authority is really a culture of readership (see Chapter 1, section iv).

The matter does not end at this rather uncertain point. It gets even more complicated, but also clearer, if we recognize something rather startling: that the opinion attributed to Frederick, and then to the vulgar herd, according to which nobility comes from ancient wealth and good manners, ultimately derives not from Frederick at all, but rather from the *Politics* of Aristotle (8.1294a.20–22).[56] In *Monarchia*, written several years later, Dante actually quotes this passage openly (2.3.3–4), a fact I will return to later.[57] This point has not gone unnoticed by commentators, but it is usually assumed – with a view to protecting Dante's reputation for candor, one supposes – that he remained ignorant of the Aristotelian source until well after writing *Convivio* 4. By contrast, I am persuaded that he knew the passage when he wrote *Convivio*, either from William of Moerbeke's Latin translation or from Aquinas's *Expositio* of the *Politics*.[58] He explicitly cites an *auctoritas* from

[56] In William of Moerbeke's Latin translation this passage reads: "Quoniam autem tria sunt, quae altercantur de aequalitate politiae, libertas, divitiae, virtus (quartum enim quod vocant ingenuitatem assequitur duobus: ingenuitas enim est virtus et divitiae antiquae)" (Aquinas 1951: 211, text 470). Dante probably did read it through the filter of Aquinas's commentary, where Moerbeke's "ingenuitas" is reinterpreted as "nobilitas" (Aquinas 1951: 213, comm. 613), since the version in *MN* reads "Est enim nobilitas virtus et divitie antique, iuxta Philosophum in Politicis." No persuasive source linking these words to Frederick has been found, and in fact a poem attributed to him says very much the opposite (De Robertis 1988: 544n). However, the point is not that Frederick did not say it, but that Aristotle *did*, and that Dante probably knew he did. On the other hand, see the recent effort of Boccassini 2003 to demonstrate that *CV* engages with Frederick's *De arte venandi* (e.g. 395–6, but *passim*). See also Cassell 2004: 67–9.

[57] As will be seen in Chapter 6, section ii (especially n 21), in *MN*, Dante is talking about the conservation of institutional authority through genealogical descent, where family and "ricchezza" are crucial. In *CV*, he avoids any serious problematization of the relation between individual and institutional authorities, thus marginalizing a central question of medieval politics (on which, see Kantorowicz 1957).

[58] Gilbert 1928 (606–13) argues Dante did not know the *Pol.* in either version at this point. Nardi (1930a: 299); Passerin d'Entrèves (1952: 34–5); De Robertis (1988: 545 n, 554 n) largely support this view. Berti 1973: 585–6 argues persuasively that he did.

the *Politics* in his discussion of the need for there to be a single Monarch governing the entire world (4.4.5), although it can and has been argued that the reference is second hand, perhaps from Aquinas (De Robertis 1988: 554n). The hypothesis also gets strong support from the fact, to my knowledge not previously noted in the scholarship, that the same section of the *Politics* containing the notion that nobility comes from wealth and virtue also presents a version of the thought that Dante *does* attribute to Aristotle: "In all of these [aristocracy, oligarchy, democracy] there of course exists the right of the majority, and whatever seems good to those who share in government rules" (*Pol.* 4.8.1294a.11–15).[59]

By attributing Aristotle's idea to Frederick, however, Dante compasses at least two important strategic ends. In the first place, as already seen, he structures a dyad of complementary and rival authorities – philosopher and king – allowing him to find an intermediate place in which to assert his own views against theirs without, apparently, showing himself irreverent toward either. In the process, he demonstrates that, at least in this initial phase of his struggle with the concept and the problem of *auctoritas*, he conceives of it most explicitly not in terms either of poetry or theology, the domains to which contemporary *dantisti* continually turn, but rather of politics and ethics. In other words, he engages broadly and inventively with multiple aspects of the "culture of authority" at once, using the specific categories through which that culture defines and defends itself. In fact, as will soon appear, he will continue to engage both critically and synthetically with authority in its institutional *and* epistemological forms, in its theoretical *and* its pragmatic aspects throughout the remainder of his career. On the other hand, in *Convivio* he is already carefully positioning a specifically poetic authorship, the *autore* from *avieo*, in relation to authority both as knowledge and as power.

In the second place, and of more immediately obvious personal consequence, the stratagem of confronting Aristotle behind the screen of Frederick allowed Dante to have it both ways with the authority of "The Philosopher." He could both draw upon it, appropriating it to himself as humble mediator, and attack it obliquely, opening the way for his own redefinition

---

59 Moerbeke's translation reads: "Haec autem, quodcumque videatur pluribus, in omnibus existit, etenim in oligarchia et aristocratia, et in democratia, quodcumque videatur maiori parti participiantur politia, hoc est dominans"; while Aquinas's commentary paraphrases: "Melius enim iudicant plures quam pauci vel unus: item plures sunt potentiores quam pauci vel unus: et ideo quod videtur pluribus melius videtur, propter potentiam ipsorum observatur et habet vigorem" (Aquinas 1951: 211, text 468; 213, text 610).

of an autonomous and personal *autorità*.[60] Moreover, by attributing to Frederick/Aristotle an idea, namely the inevitable authority of the "vulgi opinio" (the opinion of the masses) over "qui iudicant et qui existimant" (those who judge and those who deliberate; *Top.* 19.73), which could have been even more easily attributed to Cicero, Dante manages to keep the question of both *auctoritas* and *nobilitas* in the domain of ideal rationality and out of the realm of rhetoricity and contingency where individual *virtus* and historical circumstance blur inevitably together, revealing the precariousness of Dante's own position, his subjection *qua* modern, personal *autore* to the vagaries of public opinion.

Implicitly, he goes even further, to create a sort of chiasmus in which individual nobility becomes the only stable grounds for true authority, while the illustrious names of classical *auctores* are drained of value. By creating a structural parallel between the conception of nobility as genealogically derived and the received concepts of *auctoritas* grounded in antiquity, the latter might then be attacked on the same grounds as the former, as a mere name assigned by popular opinion. If time does not confer nobility (4.14–15), why should it bring authority? Carried to its logical and explicit conclusion, which it is not in this text, such a line of argument reveals that every *autore* is in the same position as the Dante of the first book – an historical and fallible ("stained") person, a Ciceronian "witness" who

---

[60] For Aristotle in Dante begin with Moore 1896: 92–156, 334–431; the studies of Nardi (e.g., 1942, 1944, 1960a, 1966a, 1967); Boyde 1993: 3–10 *et passim*; also Cogan 1999. Opinions about the depth or nature of Dante's attachment to Aristotle vary, with discussion focusing on such subtopics as whose Aristotle he prefers (Aquinas's as many have assumed, or Albertus's [on the latter see Nardi 1956: 28–9, also 1922, 1923; Vasoli 1979, 1988a: lxxv–lxxvi; Trovato 1990 b]; Siger's? [Imbach 1996]); which translations he made use of (Corti 1983: 94–7); and why Virgil rather than Aristotle serves as the spokesman of classical authority in the *DC*. See also n 34; as well as Chapters 5–6 on the issue of Dante's supposed radical Aristotelianism (i.e., Averroism). Rarer are attempts, like Peterman 1973, to make an "unfiltered" comparison between a Dantean text (in this case *MN*) and an Aristotelian one (the *Pol.*). For Aristotle's pervasive presence in *CV*, see again n 34. Barański 1994b, 1997b offers useful caveats about the complex meanings gathered around the name "Aristotle" in the later Middle Ages. In *CV* there is only one explicit disagreement with "The Philosopher," though on a key point of astronomy: "Aristotile credette, seguitando solamente l'antica grossezza de li astrologi, che fossero pure otto cieli, de li quali lo estremo, e che contenesse tutto, fosse quello dove le stelle fisse sono, cioè la spera ottava; e che di fuori da esso non fosse altro alcuno. Ancora credette che lo cielo del Sole fosse immediato con quello de la Luna, cioè secondo a noi. E questa sua sentenza così erronea può vedere chi vuole nel secondo De Celo et Mundo, ch'è nel secondo de' libri naturali. Veramente elli di ciò si scusa nel duodecimo de la Metafisica, dove mostra bene sé avere seguito pur l'altrui sentenza là dove d'astrologia li convenne parlare" (2.3.3–4; see E. Gilson 1939: 155). Notably, and reinforcing the points made about the self-critical nature of neo-Aristotelian *auctoritas* in section ii, Dante indicts Aristotle for having followed without question prior authorities and attributes a palinodic correction to the "maestro di color che sanno" (cf. Chapter 6).

must prove and/or construct his authority from the ground up[61] – if not a latter-day prophet who receives it directly from God.[62]

V. "*AUTORE*" FROM "*AVIEO*"

At this point we are finally ready to consider the function of the secondary definition of the poetic *autore* from *avieo* as "binder of words" with meter and rhyme.[63] As noted in the first section, the inclusion of this definition is curious, and that in several respects. The first curiosity is why it is present at all, given that Dante explicitly says it is not relevant to his concerns in book 4. The second is why, given its declared irrelevance, as a digression within what is already marked as a digression, it is accorded such promi-nence. It is, after all, placed first, before the definition that Dante says *does* concern him at this juncture, and it significantly elaborates on Hugutio, adding especially the explanatory point that *avieo* is a word composed exclusively of the five vowels ("v" in medieval Latin being interchangeable with "u").

One might simply argue that the passage is included as an "effect of authority," to show that Dante knows whereof he speaks as concerns the discursive field into which he is about to enter. A third curiosity, however,

---

[61] Lollini 2001: 40–54 *et passim* places Dante in a history of "witness," stressing the "individualization" and personal construction of testimony in *CV* and, especially, *Par.*, as an anticipation of Petrarchan modernity, without, however, referring to Cicero or the word-concept "autore."

[62] Dante distinguishes between the "natural" and the "theological" causes of nobility, with an odd, potentially unorthodox, equivocation. Just *before* turning from the "natural" disposition of body and soul to a "theological" infusion from above, he attributes to an unspecified "alcuni di tale oppinione" the idea that a perfect natural disposition to receive nobility would result in another man-God, a second Christ (4.21.10). The failure to cite an *auctor* for this notion, with the recourse to unspecified "oppinione," make this claim particularly suspicious and interesting. Dante revisits and corrects this idea in *Par.* 13.49–87 by specifying that in his *own* opinion there will never be another such (*pace* Moevs 2005: 83–4). Nardi 1921a: 151–2 shows an analogue for this idea in Albertus Magnus, *De somno et vigilia* 3.1.6. In 1942b: 289–91, he relates this to Dante's special prophetic mission (cf. De Robertis 1988: 770–1 n). In 1960a: 81–2 he links it to Avicenna and the Averroists. See the discussion of related passages by Nardi 1930b: 119–23; Durling and Martinez 1990: 246–7, 434 n167. Compare the quest of nature to create a perfect man in Alan of Lille, *Anticlaudianus*.

[63] This etymology has been all but forgotten by commentators of the *DC*, although Nardi 1965b: 221–2 and Mazzotta 1979: 256–9 are exceptions (see Chapter 1, section ii), and is typically ignored by readers of *CV*. For the etymology, see Stabile 1970; Mengaldo 1970a. For interpretations, see Dragonetti 1961b, 1961c: 53–4; Pézard 1967: 237–60; and Lombardi 2000, who also elaborates on the thematics of linguistic binding in *Par.* Guerri 1907: 68 and n 29 cites John of Garland, *Compendium Gramaticae*, to explain the vocalic names of God in *Par.* 26: "*a* est littera sonora et agilis et levis, sicut ignis est elementum leve – *e* [convenit] cum aere, unde obusam habet figuram – *o* convenientam cum aqua que fluctilis est – *u* ultimo sedet in numero, sicut terra infimum elementum est et fixum suo pondere" and "*i* gracilius sonat in medio, tamquamque cathena aurea vel glutens, elementa ligare videtur." The vowels here figure the four natural elements plus the principle that binds them together, suggesting not so much a direct source as an indication that the vowels were regularly used to designate an "elemental" compositional structure. See also Chapter 7, section v.

should dispel any attempt to minimize its importance: namely, that at the very moment that Dante is dismissing poetic authority as different from and irrelevant to philosophical authority, he is in the midst of composing a work whose overarching purpose is to prove that his *canzoni*, his mature poems, have a philosophical content, and, at least in the case of "le dolci rime d'amore," that this content is important, original, and controversial.

The last point notwithstanding, I have had very little to say so far about the poetic texts around which *Convivio* is constructed, and about the role that poetry per se has in Dante's struggles with the culture of *auctoritas* throughout the treatise. This is because, rather surprisingly, Dante barely confronts the issue, focusing instead on the prose commentary that makes up the bulk of the work. Notably, the three *macule* which Dante sets out to purify in book 1 are all qualities specifically said to inhere to the prose: the recourse to self-reference, the difficult style adopted in the quest for "maggior autoritade," and even the problem of writing in the vernacular. At the same time, however, the prose commentary is said to be subordinated to the poetry, as servant to master (1.5.7–9, 7.1–2). In addition, as we will see better in Chapter 4 (section iii), the *macule* infecting the prose actually arise as effects of the poetry and of the unique project of self-commentary that binds prose and poetry together. The message is consistently ambivalent: the importance and problematicity of poetry, specifically Dante's vernacular poetry, is assumed from the outset, but at the same time its status has been touched on only *en passant* and obliquely.

Nonetheless, from the beginning of the treatise a tension is created between poetry and philosophy, which tends to degrade the former in favor of the latter (see also Pinto 1994: especially 152). The structuring movement from *canzoni* to commentary, ostensibly intended to both defend and illuminate Dante's poetry, has a double effect on our perception of the status of poetry in the new project. The poetry, understood to be the conduit of intellectual, philosophical, truth, is the origin and destination of the treatise, but it also exists in a marginal and dependent state with respect to the prose. Dante repeatedly stresses that without prosaic philosophical commentary the poems' content is unintelligible – a point that is made explicitly in "Voi ch'intendendo il terzo cielo movete," the *canzone* commented upon in book 2. The *canzone* says of itself that its goodness (*bontade*), that is, its true meaning, can only be understood by the angelic Intelligences of the Third Heaven (2.canzone.1–3, 53–55; see also 2.12.8), while, as the poetic "I" says in the *congedo*, human listeners remain at the level of purely "aesthetic" delight in artistic beauty

(2.canzone.61).[64] From this split between surface form and hidden content, we are led directly to the famous, and famously controversial, passage at the beginning of book 2, which defines the allegory used by poets in general as "verità nascosa sotto bella menzogna" (truth hidden under a beautiful lie; 2.1.3; see also 1.1.15 and 18; 1.2.17; 2.12.8–10). Clearly, this is a definition that trivializes the poetic surface per se at the same time that it claims for its content the status of philosophy.

This passage – surprisingly, given the scholarly uses to which it has most often been put[65] – is not aimed in the first instance at accounting for the active signifying mechanisms by which the poetry leads the reader to hidden moral treasures, but rather describes the interpretive procedures, literal followed by allegorical exegesis, that will be adopted in the prose commentary. Before trotting out the first "course" of his banquet, Dante says "voglio mostrare come mangiare si dee" (I wish to explain how it should be eaten; 2.1.1). By this, he immediately reveals, he means that:

questa sposizione conviene essere litterale e allegorica. E a ciò dare a intendere, si vuol sapere che le scritture si possono intendere e deonsi esponere massimamente per quattro sensi (2.1.2)

([T]his commentary should be literal and allegorical. To indicate what this means, it should be explained that texts can be interpreted, and must therefore be elucidated, principally in four senses)

---

[64] The commentary glosses the lines as follows: "dico al presente che la bontade e la bellezza di ciascuno sermone sono intra loro partite e diverse; ché *la bontade è ne la sentenza*, e *la bellezza è ne l'ornamento de le parole*; e l'una e l'altra è con diletto, avvegna che *la bontade* sia massimamente dilettosa. Onde con ciò sia cosa che *la bontade di questa canzone fosse malagevole a sentire . . . e la bellezza fosse agevole a vedere*, parvemi mestiero a la canzone che per li altri *si ponesse più mente a la bellezza che a la bontade . . .* Dico adunque: Io credo, canzone, che radi sono, cioè pochi, quelli che intendano te bene . . . Ora appresso ammonisco lei e dico: Se per avventura incontra che tu vadi là dove persone siano che dubitare ti paiano ne la tua ragione, non ti smarrire, ma dì loro: *Poi che non vedete la mia bontade, ponete mente almeno la mia bellezza*" (2.11.4–5, 7–8). See also 2.11.9, cited in n 81. For the related question of *prosopopeia*, see nn 3, 14, 42, 88; Chapter 4, especially n 50. For the *bontade/bellezza* opposition in *CV*, see Pézard 1940: chapter 7; Grayson 1963: 49–57 *et passim*.

[65] Despite the corrupt state of the manuscript tradition and the need to make use of interpolations at crucial junctures, the passage has been used to support the notion that Dante distinguishes between an "allegory of the poets," the mode used here, and an "allegory of theologians," the mode used in the *Commedia* and described in par. 7 of the *ECG* (see Singleton 1954: especially 1–17, 84–98; Hollander 1969: 29–40, 1976) or to refute that claim (e.g., Green 1957; Scott 1973, 1990b, 1995: 36–9), a question which does not concern me here (but see Ascoli 1997: 315–16 and nn; also Ascoli 2010). Perhaps the most balanced accounts are those of Pepin 1970: 60–9; Minnis *et al.* 1988: 382–5. Other notable readers of the passage are De Lubac 1959–65: 2.2.319–26; Chiarenza 1980; Corti 1983: 80–2; D'Andrea 1987; De Robertis 1988: 108–16 nn; Freccero 1993; Pinto 1994: 144–57; Barański 1999; Ferrucci 2002. For an excellent overview of allegory in Dante which is relatively abstemious in regards to the various intoxicating polemics that swirl around it, see Martinez 2000.

Twice he uses the word "intendere" in the sense of readerly comprehension and twice he uses "esponere"/"esposizione" in the sense of interpretive glossing:[66] chapter 2.1 is going to tell us how to read Dante's poem by following Dante's reading of that poem.[67] In this way too, the secondariness of poetry and its dependence on philosophical commentary is reinforced.

On the other hand, of course, the chapter also gives strong hints of a very different kind. By coupling the ambiguous reference to how *teologi* "take" or interpret the first allegorical sense with Biblical examples (the Transfiguration of Christ and the exodus of the Hebrews out of Egypt) of the second and third allegorical senses, Dante creates an ill-defined analogy, at once offered and denied, between his poetry and the Bible, which may in fact be extended beyond a mode of interpretation to a mode of signification.[68] In particular, the example of the fourth sense, anagogy, overtly invokes the categories of scriptural allegory:

[66] Pepin 1999: 52 and n 2 notes the frequency with which Dante calls his commentary a "sposizione" in *CV*, observing that *expositio* is the typical word used of theological commentaries on the books of the Bible (67). On "intenzione," see also Chapter 4, n 37.

[67] Here I follow Pepin 1970: especially 11; Scott 1990b: especially 34, although I would not go as far as Scott in arguing that both 2.1 and *ECG*, par. 7 refer exclusively to a practice of reading (*allegoresis*) rather than to a practice of writing (*allegory*). Rather, it seems to me that Dante is equivocating, in part to avoid making too overt his claims for the power of his poetry and especially possible parallels with Scripture. In *the* pivotal phrase for the critical debate, Dante says, concerning the first allegorical sense that "[v]eramente li teologi questo senso prendono altrimenti che li poeti; ma ... mia intenzione è qui lo modo de li poeti seguitare" (2.1.4). The phrase is equivocal between reading and writing, since "prendono" could mean either "make use of" or "interpret" and "teologi" could mean either human authors of the Bible or scholars who study "theology" (although Dante's other references to "teologia" in *CV* point to the latter [2.13.8, 14.19–20]). There is no such equivocation with "poeti," however: they are writers, not interpreters. Later, in 2.12.8, Dante–commentator specifically refers to his poetic intention of concealing the true "sentenza" of his *canzone*: "io, sentendomi levare dal pensiero del primo amore a la virtù di questo, quasi maravigliandomi apersi la bocca nel parlare de la proposta canzone, mostrando la mia condizione *sotto figura d'altre cose*: però che de la donna di cu' io m'innamorava non era degna rima di volgare alcuna palesemente po[e]tare; né li uditori erano tanto bene disposti, che avessero sì leggiere le [non] fittizie parole apprese; né sarebbe data loro *fede a la sentenza vera, come a la fittizia*, però che di vero si credea del tutto che disposto fosse a quello amore, che non si credea di questo." In other words, his allegorical reading follows directly from his poetic intention. For the "allegory"/"allegoresis" distinction see Whitman 1987: 10–11 *et passim*; Copeland and Melville 1991; as well as Chapter 4.

[68] Dante's adaptation of the fourfold scheme of Biblical exegesis to the purposes of "fictive" poetry in *CV* 2.1 is idiosyncratic, and I will address it elsewhere in greater detail (Ascoli 2010). See especially Nardi: 1944a: 55–61; Chydenius 1958: 44–7; De Lubac 1959–1965: 2.2.319–26; Hollander 1969: especially 39; Pepin 1970: especially 68–9, 1999; Corti 1983: 80–2; D'Andrea 1987. The most obvious incongruity is that 2.1 illustrates each of the three allegorical *sensus* with a different text rather than expounding the meaning of a single text according to each of the four senses, as most Biblical commentaries and the *ECG* do. For other, earlier examples of overlaps between allegoresis of poetry with that of Scriptures, see De Lubac 1959–1965: 2.2. 208–14; Charity 1966: 211–12; Huygens 1970: 64, 69; Scott 1973: 573; Ascoli 1997: 316 and nn 32–3. For the claim that these examples do not constitute a real precedent for Dante, see Hollander 1976: 92–4 *et passim*; Minnis *et al.* 1988: 386.

Lo quarto senso si chiama anagogico, cioè sovrasenso; e questo è quando spiritual-
mente si spone una scrittura, la quale ancora [sia vera] eziandio nel senso litterale,
per le cose significate significa de le superne cose de l'eternal gloria: sì come vedere
si può in quello canto del Profeta che dice che, ne l'uscita del popolo d'Israel
d'Egitto, Giudea è fatta santa e libera./Che avvegna essere vera secondo la lettera
sia manifesto, non meno è vero quello che spiritualmente s'intende, cioè che ne
l'uscita de l'anima dal peccato, essa sia fatta santa e libera in sua potestate./E in
dimostrar questo, sempre lo litterale dee andare innanzi, sì come quello ne la cui
sentenza li altri sono inchiusi, sanza lo quale sarebbe impossibile ed inrazionale
intendere a li altri, e massimamente a lo allegorico. (2.1.6–8)

(The fourth sense is called "anagogy," that is, transcending the senses [or: "highest
sense"]: this is brought out when a work [or: "scriptural passage"] is expounded with
regard to its spiritual meaning; even though the work is true in a literal sense [by
the things signified it signifies supernal things of eternal glory]. One can see this,
for instance in that song of the Prophet [David] which says that, [in the exodus of
the people of Israel from Egypt], Judah [is] made holy and free./For although what
is said there is clearly true in a literal sense, the spiritual meaning of these words
is no less true, namely that [in the exodus of the soul] from sin, it is made holy
and free [according to its capacity]./To establish this sense, the literal sense must
always be accorded primacy, as the one in whose meaning all others are contained,
and without which it would be impossible and irrational to attend to the other
senses, especially the allegorical [i.e., the first, Christological, allegorical sense])

Here not only is the letter Biblical, but the anagogic reading of it is typical
of the exegetical tradition. Even more to the point, the locution "per le
cose significate significa de le superne cose" points directly at the divine
allegoria in factis by which God signifies his meanings not only through
the words of the Bible but also via real historical events, in stark opposition
to the beautiful lies of the poet's variety of *allegoria in verbis* (Pepin 1999:
57).[69] This in turn leads Dante to assert that the "letter" always precedes
and determines the meaning of the allegory, a position which at first seems
to apply only to the fourth sense of Biblical signification, but then morphs,

---

[69] The term was first used by Augustine (*De Trinitate* 15.9.15) and given its most commonly cited
formulation by Aquinas, *ST* Ia, q. I, art. 10, resp., who states that while humans signify with signs
alone (*allegoria in verbis*), God can signify through signs *and* the *things* they signify (*allegoria in
factis*). This distinction has been widely described in the study of late medieval scriptural exegesis
(De Lubac 1959–64: 2.2.140; Minnis 1984: 73 *et passim*; Minnis *et al.* 1988 [with examples]: 72–3,
203–6) and often put to use in the debate surrounding Dantean allegory (Hollander 1969: 16–21;
Giannantonio 1969; Pepin 1970: 47, 69–72; Eco 1985: 233–4; Freccero 1993; Pinto 1994: 137–44).
In Ascoli 1997: n 77, I took a skeptical view of its relevance to either *CV* 2.1 or the *ECG*: I have,
however, been persuaded otherwise by Pepin 1999. The notion of *allegoria in factis* is closely tied
to the idea that God's creation in its historical unfolding is his first Book the Bible his second; it
thus represents the point of intersection between *allegory, figuralism,* and *typology* (Auerbach 1944;
Singleton 1949: 38–42; Mazzeo 1960: 175–80; Chydenius 1958; Charity 1966; Freccero 1983a, 1993).
For the topos, see n 87.

without transition or justification, into a description of his own practice in the commentary of *Convivio* (2.1.8–15; cf. Chapter 4, n 69).[70]

Even more revealing of how 2.1 indirectly promotes Dante's poetry while directly subordinating it to the commentary is the extraordinary example illustrating the first allegorical sense – what Biblical exegetes called allegory proper: "quod credas"[71] – hidden behind the *bella menzogna* of his verse:

> questo è quello che si nasconde sotto 'l manto di queste favole . . .: come quando dice Ovidio che Orfeo facea con la cetera mansuete le fiere, e li arbori e le pietre a sé muovere; che vuol dire che lo savio uomo con lo strumento de la sua voce fa[r]ia mansuescere e umiliare li crudeli cuori, e fa[r]ia muovere a la sua volontade coloro che non hanno vita di scienza e d'arte: e coloro che non hanno vita ragionevole alcuna sono quasi come pietre. (2.1.3)

> (This is the sense concealed under the [mantle] of these fables . . . An example of this is Ovid's saying that Orpheus with his lyre made the wild beasts tame, and moved stones and trees to follow him; what this signifies is that the wise man, with the instrument of his voice, can tame and soften cruel hearts, and make those whose lives are devoid of knowledge and culture act according to his wishes. [And t]hose whose lives are devoid of all reason are aptly described as stones.)

What would ordinarily, in the run-of-the-mill allegories produced according to the interpretive practices developed by the medieval "ethical poetics" (see Chapter 1, n 5), provide a moral lesson for the reader to discover and apply to "himself," is instead a figuration of the Orphic poet who composes persuasive, indeed, compelling, verse.[72] That is, the "moral" applies ostentatiously to Dante as poet rather than to Dante as commentator, much

---

[70] For the crucial importance of the "letter" for Biblical exegetes of the Duecento, and its correlation with the emergent importance of human authorship and intentionality, see Chapter 1, especially n 52. For further exploration of its significance in 2.1 and throughout *CV*, see Chapter 4, section iii and nn 68, 69; for its place in *MN*, see Chapter 5, section ii, n 26.

[71] With the phrase, "[v]eramente li teologi questo senso prendono altrimenti che li poeti" (see again n 67), Dante specifically invites his readers to recall how theological exegetes *do* take this sense, which always refers either to the Christ event or to the history of the Church. In this case, since Orpheus was often given Christological interpretation in the Biblical commentaries on Ovid and the other classical works (e.g., Virgil, *Georgics* 4) where he appears (Sarolli 1966b: 31–2; Friedman 1970; cf. Scott 1995: 36), it is presumably the former that Dante stresses, and it is the possibility that Orpheus, poetry, and he, Dante, have been substituted for Christ that he both implies and denies. Finally, through the next example, that of the Transfiguration, which *is* Christological in the letter, although oddly adapted to a "moral" allegory worthy of Machiavelli ("a le secretissime cose noi dovemo avere poca compagnia" [2.1.5]), Dante calls further attention to the fact that the superimposing of the fourfold Biblical scheme on the twofold poetic scheme is forced.

[72] In his later discussion of the liberal art of "music," Dante makes it clear that he uses the term, in keeping with the broad classical and medieval idea of "armonia," to refer both to "parole armonizzate" (words harmonized [in verse]) and to "canti" (songs) proper, a point also implied by his reference to the "arte musaica" of the poets in 4.6.4 (cf. 1.7.14–15). For the classical and medieval conceptions of "harmony," see Spitzer 1963. For Dante, see, e.g., Shapiro 1990: 36–8, 207 n 63; Durling and Martinez 1990: 18, 30–1, 337 n 554; Mazzotta 1993a: 21 and n 15, 233–4 and nn. The description

less to his readers, and it calls attention to the dual seductive (literal) and educative (allegorical) powers of his poetry,[73] and the ways in which the former works in the service of the latter.[74] It is, in the felicitous phrase of Martinez (2000: 31–2), a Dantean "allegory of allegory," slyly celebrating the verses, and their versifier, who had apparently been left in the shadows, anticipating the similarly oblique workings of the etymology of *autor* from *avieo* now being considered.

Notwithstanding the mixed messages conveyed by 2.1, however, the overwhelming impression that Dante explicitly creates throughout the *trattato* is that without the aid of a philosophizing prose, and without the claim that the value of the verse lies in its subordination of those attributes that constitute it as poetry (i.e., figurative language and other forms of verbal ornamentation; rhyme and meter) to a content taken from the higher disciplines of ethics and metaphysics, these *canzoni* would appear indistinguishable from the passionate outpourings of *Vita Nova*. This is partly an effect of the vernacular poet's sense of inferiority when writing in a language that has no established claim to intellectual seriousness. But there is more to it. The most notable classical poetic *auctores*, Ovid and Virgil, are rarely cited in the first three books of *Convivio* – the reference to the Ovidian Orpheus is a rule-testing exception – ceding pride of place to Cicero, Boethius, and, of course, Aristotle. In other words, it is not just *vernacular* poetry that is treated as a problem, but *poetry* in general as a mode of discourse.

Convivio, then, echoes the traditionally problematic relationship of poetry to other types of culturally authoritative discourses, and in particular its long-standing battle against the claims first of philosophy and then of theology to epistemological superiority. Plato notoriously linked his attempt to unite power and knowledge, king and philosopher, with the condemnation of poetry and the exile of the poet from his ideal

---

of how "music" in this generalized sense affects its hearers also further illuminates the Orpheus reference and aligns his art with the seductive *bellezze* attributed to "Voi che intendendo" and other poems: "la Musica trae a sé li spiriti umani, che quasi sono principalmente vapori del cuore, sì che quasi cessano da ogni operazione: sì è l'anima intera, quando l'ode, e la virtù di tutti quasi corre a lo spirito sensibile che riceve lo suono" (2.13.24). Cf. n 80; Chapter 1, n 5.

73 See Pézard 1940: 15–26; Sarolli 1966b: 29–33; Hollander 1976: 119–20 and nn; Padoan 1973; Scott 1995: 36–8; and especially Barański 1999 for readings of the example of Orpheus. Cf. De Bonfils-Templer 1983, whose discussion of the myth of Orpheus in *CV* does not touch on 2.1. Also Rossi 1985 on Orpheus and Aristeus in the *DC*.

74 Compare as well the discussion of Dante's intended audience above (n 11). His account here is decidedly less sympathetic than in the more explicit references. Chapter 4 will explore in greater depth the mechanisms by which Dante apotropaically wards off misreading by becoming the interpreter of his own works.

Republic.[75] Dante's era had its own highly developed version of the Platonic critique, notably that of Aquinas, and its understanding of a primary connection between poetry and grammar, the most elementary of the liberal arts (see nn 80 and 83). And here Dante too juxtaposes a fantasy of the complementarity, though specifically not the identity, of political and intellectual authorities (again, Frederick and Aristotle) with the marginalization of the poetic *autore*.

This trend toward the effacement of poetry per se in favor of philosophical truth reaches its climax, but also a turning point, in the canzone, "le dolci rime d'amor," that opens book 4.[76] From its first stanza, the poem is an explicit rejection of poetic delight in favor of a philosophical style "aspr'e sottile" (4.canzone.14), that recalls the "durezza" of the prose style said to be aimed at acquiring "maggiore autoritade" for Dante. It is thus set in palinodic opposition to the *canzoni* of books 2 and 3, whose pleasurably erotic surfaces have successfully concealed their hidden depths from most readers.[77] As Dante incorporates the language of philosophy into the

---

[75] *Republic* 2.376e–3.403b, 10.595a–608b. The argument is not that Dante knew these texts directly, which he did not, but that he is dealing with the same basic configuration of authorities. He *was* familiar with the neo-platonic, Christian attacks against poetry as worthless fiction – represented by Augustine (*Conf.* 1.16–18; 3.2) and Aquinas himself (*ST* Ia, q.1, art. 9; see also Chapter 1, n 5). On the Dantean "defense of poetry" against this tradition, see Chapter 7, nn 136–37. On the late medieval defense of poetry in general, see Chapter 1, nn 5, 43.

[76] It has been argued that book 4 represents a new phase in Dante's thought with respect to the previous two books. In particular, Maria Corti, building on philosophical arguments first raised by Nardi (1960a: especially 14–15, 75–83; cf. 1930a: 298) and formal issues raised by Segre 1963a, also Vasoli 1988a: xvi–xvii, argues that the reference to a crisis in Dante's relationship with Lady Philosophy (4.1.8) betokens a turn to a new philosophical model, deriving from the avant-garde Aristotelians at work in Paris and Bologna (1983: 123–45; cf. n 48). She correlates this shift with increasing recourse to Scripture that anticipates the *DC* and with a reconciliation between rational and theological argumentation (83–4, 130–1, *et passim*; also Trovato 1990b). She does not address Leo's point (1951) that the number of literary *auctoritates* cited also increased dramatically in book 4 (for a blending of the two, see Scott 1995: 48–50, 2004: 135–6). For another reading of the crisis in the relationship with Philosophy, see Ferrucci 2001: 68–74, 2003: 93–5. My arguments here and in the next two chapters tend both to support the idea that something radical has happened and to establish a dialectical continuity with the rest of the treatise. In particular, as will be seen in Chapter 3, section i, the discussion of the vernacular in book 1 culminates implicitly yet surely with the etymology of *auctor* from *avieo*. Corti does not entertain the idea advanced in n 12 that the discourse on "nobiltà" in book 4 is a structural pivot, preparing the treatise to carry out its primary mission of defining the eleven moral virtues. Nor does she recall at this juncture the relationship between the foregrounding of the "literal" sense of poetry in *CV* 2.1 – which she insisted upon earlier (80–2) – and the turn to a "literal" poetics in book 4 (see Chapter 4, section iii). The differences between us are attributable to Corti's lack of interest in the problem of *autorità* in book 4. For a different account of the "unity" of the extant books of *CV*, see Fenzi 1986: 46 *et passim*. For the intersection of this issue with the relative dating of *CV* and *DVE*, see Chapter 3, n 8. For the significance of the specific philosophical question that precipitates the crisis (4.1.8), see Chapter 4, n 37.

[77] In addition to the examples from book 2 given above (especially n 64), see.1.14 (cited in Chapter 4, section iii) and 1.1.16.

letter of the *canzone*, he also frees the poetic text from utter dependence upon an explanatory philosophical prose.[78] He explicitly claims that no allegorical commentary is necessary at all in this case – a literal gloss is all that is required, albeit a very long one, proportional to the difficulty and importance of the concept treated. In other words, Dante has tacitly but surely abandoned the "allegory according to the poets," and with it the poetics that underpin *Convivio* as a whole (4.1.10–11).[79] This bald attempt to convert poetry directly into philosophy, or, perhaps better, to absorb philosophy within poetic discourse, is then hammered home by the name he gives the canzone, *Contra-li-erranti mia*, which, as noted, reflects his aspiration to follow in Aquinas's footsteps. Curiously, however, at this point the classical poetic *auctores* – Statius, Ovid, Lucan, and above all Virgil – finally make an appearance in force (Leo 1951; Hollander 1968, 1969; Picone 1997a: 59–60). In other words, the turn to a literally philosophical poetry is accompanied by a reduction of the hegemony of philosophical *autori* like Aristotle, and Aquinas, in favor of poets, not only the ancients, but Dante as well.

Into this charged context Dante inserts his discourse on authority, and especially the opposition between the two etymologies of *autore*. In one sense, the dismissal of the poetic *autore* from *avieo* in favor of the philosophical *autore* from *autentin* is perfectly in keeping with the preference for philosophical content over poetic delight that led Dante to the composition of a *canzone* that boasts of having sacrificed delight to the literal presentation of philosophical truth. Nonetheless, it seems strangely out of step with the resulting work in which the letter/allegory, poetic surface/philosophical depth split is healed, where poetry and philosophy are ostensibly one.

Thus, the first definition of *autore*, far from being a digressive excrescence, constitutes a conceptual crux that goes to the heart of Dante's project in *Convivio*, and especially his attempt to assert that poetry is a mode of knowledge consonant with philosophy. So again we ask: what is it doing here, and how does it function? The answer, unsurprisingly, is complex. On the one hand, as noted, Dante attempts to maintain the fiction that he is not aspiring to the status of an *auctor* himself, and thus to focus on the

---

[78] Grayson 1963: 53–4 also foregrounds the shift to the literal sense in "le dolci rime d'amor," but reads it as a reduction of the poetry to the level of the prose, the real protagonist of the *trattato* (55; see also 39–40). On this issue, however, see Chapter 4, section iii.

[79] Dronke 1997: 54, 58–9 objects that Dante still uses allegory in *CV* 4, e.g., in passages on the three Marys (4.22.14) and on Cato and Marcia (4.12.13–16). True enough, but this is beside the point since: (a) Dante's assertion that he has abandoned allegory is significant in and of itself; and (b) unlike the two preceding *canzoni* "Le dolci rime" is literally about a philosophical subject, and the allegories in question are part of the exegesis of the *canzone*'s literal sense.

prose is to stress his subordinate role as *commentator*, a role appropriate to a belated modern writer. From this perspective, to call attention to himself *qua* writer of poetry would be to invite more direct comparison between himself and the classical *auctores*, philosophical *and* poetic, and to risk (justified!) accusations of ambition and presumption.

Thus, from one perspective, the attempt radically to distinguish poetic authority as "binding of words" from the authority which commands *fede e obedienza* might be interpreted as part of Dante's attempt to minimize his otherwise audacious claims for "Le dolci rime d'amor," to stress that he is not *really* interested in setting himself up as a critic of Frederick's elitist political and social theory or as the demystifier of Aristotle's privileged role as philosophical *auctor*. The separation of the poetic author from the others is perhaps sufficient proof of this, along with the corollary implication that the poet has no *prima facie* claim to "faith and obedience" from his readers. Inasmuch as the definition implies that the poet's authority derives from expertise in the art of creating verse through an "arte musaica" which binds together available elements of language, it merges conceptually with Chenu's *actor*, the lesser counter-part of the *auctor*, whose artisanal *making* brings with it no special access to truth or power at all.

In another sense, as with the example of Orpheus in 2.1, the tacit claims of the definition for poetic authority, and by extension for Dante, seem to be quite extravagant. Even as the text cordons off the poet from other authorities, it equates the poetic art with the very constitution and perfection of language, which is built out of the constituent sounds represented by letters and bound together by the vowels. Moreover, and even more importantly, it points toward an intimate connection that binds the form of language to the meanings it bears within it. The "vowels of authority" contained in *avieo* are the formal glue that holds language together.[80] At the same time, they imitate, etymologically and even pictographically, the

---

[80] On this point, see Chapter 3, section i. Compare the discussions of *DVE* 2.1.1 in section vi and of *Par.* 26 in Chapter 7, section v. As the means of "constructing" language, the "arte musaica" of the poet may also be said to constitute the degree zero of the discipline of grammar. Grammar and music, further combined with rhetoric, produce the beautiful poetic surface, as exemplified by "Voi che intendendo": "la sua [i.e., of the *canzone*] bellezza, ch'è grande sì per construzione, la quale si pertiene a li *gramatici*, sì per l'ordine del sermone, che si pertiene a li *rettorici*, sì per lo numero de le sue parti, che si pertiene a li *musici*" (2.11.9; see also 2.11.7–8, cited in n 64). "Musici" include those who produce both "le parole armonizzate e . . . li canti" (2.13.23; see also n 72). This etymology partially anticipates the composite definition of poetry in *DVE* as "fictio rethorica musicaque poita" (2.4.2), in which, Shapiro 1990: 36 argues, Dante combines grammar, music, and rhetoric (see also Schiaffini 1958; Mazzotta 1993a: 21), and where "fictio" clearly refers to (rhetorical) "making" rather than "feigning" (cf. Papparelli 1960 and the discussion of "actor" and "faber" in section vi; *pace* Grayson 1963: 40 and n). This multiplication of disciplinary affiliations in both *CV* and *DVE* is typical of Dante's "encyclopedic" tendencies (see again Chapter 1, n 66), and compatible with the

meaning of the word that they form.[81] That is, the word *avieo* acts out
the linguistic binding that is made possible by its constituent vowels and
that it, as a word, is meant to signify.[82] Put otherwise, even as it apparently
sets poetry off as a separate, and inferior, field of discourse, this definition

specific ties articulated between *CV* and rhetoric, not just in the case of the *canzone* addressed to the
heaven of Venus, which Dante associates with rhetoric (2.13.13–14), but also to the larger project of
an "ethical poetic," itself intimately tied to the project of epideictic rhetoric (see also Shapiro 1986;
Mazzotta 1986; cf. Nencioni 1967). The three disciplines (grammar implied in the study of *canzoni*)
actually appeared together in book 3, in subordinate relationship to Philosophy understood as the
encyclopedic totality of disciplinary understandings: "Onde non si dee dicere vero filosofo alcuno
che, per alcuno diletto, con la sapienza in alcuna sua parte sia amico; *sì come sono molti che si dilettano
in intendere canzoni ed istudiare in quelle, e che si dilettano studiare in Rettorica o in Musica,* e l'altre
scienze fuggono e abbandonano, che sono tutte membra di sapienza" (3.11.9). See also Chapter 4,
section iii.

[81] It is important to understand what is meant and what is *not* meant by the use of etymology here.
On the definitional use of etymologies, real and spurious, in the Middle Ages, see Curtius 1948:
495–500; Bloch 1983. Bloch (45–9) points to the multiple medieval understanding of signification –
ranging from the extremes of prelapsarian Adamic naming as the natural adequation of sign to thing,
on the one hand, and, on the other, the grammarian's awareness of the sheer conventionality of
language shaped by humans to their own purposes. He further argues for the evolution of a middle
position according to which names are specifically constructed by their users to image, imitate or
represent the things they designate, and it is this position that comes closest to Dante's. In *VN* (13.4),
Dante famously articulates the principal on which etymological understanding is based: "nomina
sunt consequentia rerum." This is often taken to suggest an essential participation of the signifier
in the thing signified. Nardi 1921b: 173–8, however, rightly called attention to Dante's immediately
preceding gloss on this phrase ("con ciò sia cosa che li nomi sèguitino le nominate cose") and its
primary origin in Justinian's *Institutiones* and the legal tradition, to show that "consequentia" does
not imply a link in essence of word to thing, but rather a linguistic *convenientia* or decorous imitation
of the qualities of the thing referred to (see also Colish 1983: 167; Shapiro 1990: 140, 157–9, 170; for
an attempted refutation, see Pagliaro 1962: 239–46; cf. Corti 1981: 70–4; Noakes 1990). Thus words
are "consequences" in the sense that they "follow after" things, rather than proceeding uniquely and
directly from them. This would seem to be the point made at *CV* 3.11.1 ("la diffinizione è quella
ragione che 'l nome significa") just prior to the etymological parsing of "Filo-Sofia." See also n 82.

[82] *Autore* from *autentin* is also defined etymologically, and there are numerous other examples in *CV*,
most notably *Filo-Sofia* (3.11). In those cases, however, the relationship between word and referent is
conceptually driven (*autentin* means "worthy of faith and obedience," and thus appropriately gives
rise to *autore*). *Avieo*, not only means "to bind," which is conceptually appropriate for the poet who
"binds words," but its form prior to conceptualization illustrates the concept it will signify. One
might object that the illustration is analogical, insofar as the vowels bind together language in general,
while the poet binds together a very specific subcategory of language. But in Dante's case, poetry
will prove to be the model for prose and the vehicle for stabilizing by "grammatizing" the Italian
vernacular (Chapter 3). In relation to the question posed in the previous note, we should understand
that the definition of *avieo* imagines the poetic author manipulating the vowels, and other formal
features of language, to create a stable link between sound and sense – which is the exact opposite
of the notion of a "divine language" in which there exists an *a priori* and natural identity of word
and thing. However, because the thing signified by these basic constitutive elements of language is
language itself, there is a sense in which this particular etymology *does* realize a utopian reciprocity
between signifier and signified, and thus why it lends itself perfectly to the "divine analogy" (God's
Word as the origin and telos of all created things) which will now be considered. For related
considerations, see Lombardi 2000. The issue of divine vs. human language, and particularly the
topos of the perfection of "Adamic" speech, will be further explored in relation to *DVE* (especially
1.6) in Chapter 3 (especially nn 4, 17, 57, 59) and to the *DC* (especially *Par.* 26.124–38) in Chapter 7.

makes poetry into the ground of all verbal discourse,[83] and attributes to it the power to generate the totality of meanings through language. From this perspective, far from being inferior to the authority of the Philosopher and the Emperor, the poet's, rooted in language itself, is the constitutive ground out of which theirs arises, just as, Dante will later say, nobility is the ground out of which the separate virtues arise. In these terms, the rationale behind Dante's assumption of the role of one who can best define the relationship between intellectual and political authorities, their simultaneous dominion over, subjection to, and dependence upon one another, becomes quite clear.[84]

There is, finally, an implication of something even more grandiose behind this seemingly innocuous, if eccentric, definition. I suspect that Dante's focus on vowels is ultimately related to their deliberate omission from the Tetragrammaton, the Hebrew representation of the unutterable name of the unrepresentable God. For Aquinas, in his crucial and lengthy consideration of the names of God, the Tetragrammaton is the most proper of all human designations of Deity, because it paradoxically expresses His incommunicability.[85] Thus, to make the poet "master of the vowels" is to make him a theologian, indeed, more than Aquinas's theologian, and certainly more than any classical philosopher limited to the resources of human reason alone, since he then seems uniquely capable of "filling in the blanks" in our knowledge and representation of God.

Such an implication would seem to be at odds with the distinction made in book 2, chapter 1, between poetic and theological modes of interpretation

---

[83] The *avieo / autentin* opposition may also be taken to reflect the two fields to which poetry is most often allied in the Middle Ages: "grammar," or the teaching of the constitutive elements of language (Curtius 1948: 42–5; Cestaro 2003a: especially chapter 1 and nn; see also Mazzotta 1993a: chapter 1 *et passim*), and moral philosophy (e.g., Allen 1982). See also Chapter 1, n 5. See Grayson 1965: 11–12 for the attempt to keep "poetry" and "grammar" distinct, at least in *DVE*. Given that Dante uses *gramatica* primarily to refer to the regulation and stability of Latin (in *CV* 1 and *DVE*), he clearly gives immense weight to what is often seen as "merely" preliminary.

[84] Here is the larger passage, an excerpt of which was analyzed in the previous section. Note the immediate historical applicability that Dante gives to his "theoretical" claims: "[È] manifesto lo principale intento, cioè che l'autoritade del filosofo sommo di cui s'intende sia piena di tutto vigore. E non repugna a la imperiale autoritade; ma quella sanza questa è pericolosa, e questa sanza quella è quasi debile, non per sé, ma per la disordinanza de la gente: sì che l'una con l'altra congiunta utilissime e pienissime sono d'ogni vigore. E però si scrive in quello di Sapienza: 'Amate lo lume de la sapienza, voi tutti che siete dinanzi a' populi,' cioè a dire: congiungiari la filosofica autoritade con la imperiale, a bene e perfettamente reggere. Oh miseri che al presente reggete! e oh miserissimi che retti siete! ché nulla filosofica autoritade si congiunge con li vostri reggimenti né per propio studio né per consiglio . . . Ponetevi mente, nemici di Dio, a' fianchi, voi che le verghe de' reggimenti d'Italia prese avete – e dico a voi, Carlo e Federigo regi, e a voi altri principi e tiranni –; e guardate chi a lato vi siede per consiglio . . ." (4.6.17–20).

[85] See Aquinas, *ST* Ia, q.13, art. 9, resp. and art. 11, ad 1. For more recent reworkings of this problem, see Rimbaud, "Voyelles," and Joyce, *Ulysses* (the latter discussed in Rabaté 1985: especially 67–72).

(and, secondarily, of signification). However, in addition to the confusions internal to 2.1 explored above, the overt premise of the earlier chapter was abandoned at the beginning of book 4 when the claim was made that "Le dolci rime d'amor" contains its meaning in the letter. Thus the *canzone* commented upon in book 4 no longer fits the earlier definition of poetry as "verità nascosa sotto bella menzogna," and to this extent resembles the scriptural texts interpreted by theologians, at least insofar as the "letter" is itself taken to be true.[86]

Indirect confirmation of this possibility, with implications for understanding the function of *Convivio* in preparing the way toward the *Commedia*, can be found by returning to the depiction of God as "verace autore" in *Paradiso* 26.40, foregrounded by Barolini and Hollander in their discussions of authorship and authority in the *Commedia* (see Chapter 1, section ii; Chapter 7, sections i, v). As Mazzotta (1979: 258–9) has observed, the combination of this passage with the proximate reference to the deity as "Alfa e O . . . di quanta scrittura,/mi legge Amor" (26.17–18) not only anticipates the later vision of God as a transcendent poet whose creation is "legato con amore in un volume" (bound with love in one volume; 33.86),[87] but also hearkens back to the poetic vowels of authority in *Convivio* (cf. Dragonetti 1961b: 91). Mazzotta, following the letter of *Convivio* 4.6, claims that while the poetic *autore* is abandoned in the earlier work in favor of the *autore* from *autentin*, in the *Commedia* this echo works to "seal, as it were, by the authority and power of the Logos the poet's words" (1979: 259). I would argue, however, that the analogy between poet and God as

---

[86] With this partial elision of the gap between poetry and theology (begun in 2.1; see especially n 67), it becomes hard to sustain the common distinction between *CV* as rationalist philosophical text and the theological, faith-based perspective of the *DC*. Versions of this opposition are to be found in Pietrobono 1932, 1938; Freccero 1973; Hollander 1975a, 1990; Corti 1981. Nardi, who sees this opposition operating between *MN* and the *DC*, argues for a conflation of classical *Filosofia* with Biblical *Sapienza* in *CV* (1921a: 157–64; Vasoli 1988b; cf. n 14 above). For alternative perspectives, see also E. Gilson 1939: 87–92 *et passim*, Foster 1977, Scott 1990a: especially 259–61, Pertile 1993, Trovato 1994, Barański 1995: 17–20, Dronke 1997, Moevs 1999: 84 n 75. For book 4 as much more "theological" than the rest of *CV*, see n 76. There is already in the earlier books, especially book 3, a strange oscillation between proto-humanistic exaltations of human rationality (1.1.1, 3.2.14–15, 3.3.5–12, 3.8.1–2, 4.19.6–7, 4.20.3) and a strong sense of the epistemological and expressive limitations of human minds and words (e.g., 3.canzone, 3.3.13–15, 3.4.1–4, 3.8.14–17). On ineffability in *CV*, see De Bonfils-Templer 1990. The crucial point is that human knowledge, unlike the pure intellection of angels, is always mediated by images derived from sensory experience by the fantasy and stored in the memory (3.4.9–11). For the same question in the *DC*, see Mazzotta 1979: 260–8 *et passim*. On this opposition as prime mover of the Dantean "palinode," with a critique thereof, see Chapter 6, section i.

[87] For the topos see Curtius 1948: 319–26, as well as Spitzer 1937: 103–7; Singleton 1949: 38–42. For its relationship to the allegorical–typological tradition, see De Lubac 1959–1965: 2.2.173–8; Pepin 1970: especially 26. For Dante's use of the image, see also Singleton 1949, 1954; Ahern 1982; Gellrich 1985. Again, see n 69 concerning the *allegoria in factis*.

creators is present by implication in *Convivio* (see also Chapter 4, n 37). We have had hints of this aspiration as early as book 1. When Dante speaks of the debilitating effects of personal presence, we recall, he says, disingenuously, "e questo è quello per che ciascuno profeta è meno onorato ne la sua patria" ([T]hat is why every prophet receives less honor in his own country; 1.4.11), thus assigning himself the role of divinely inspired prophet. Moreover, we earlier observed him comparing his "Banquet" to the miraculous feast prepared by Christ.

With the addition of a theological dimension to a typology of authority that already included philosopher, emperor, and poet, we can now get a more complete picture of how Dante imagines the field of authority as a totality, and how he locates both poetry and himself within it. The situation can be illustrated, reductively yet usefully, with a diagram:

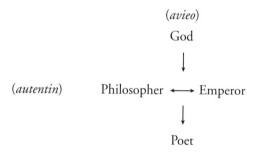

While the poet's place is the lowest in this scheme, it is also transformed by the possibility of a direct relationship, whether of analogical creativity or inspiring authorization with God, which gives him a claim to a totalizing vision, capable of subsuming those human authorities who are ostensibly above him in the world. This, then, is what allows Dante to operate, within the space of the "aporia dantesca" defined above, as an "authority on authorities," without too obviously claiming the role of *auctor* as his own. In exploiting the potential of this quasi-prophetic model of a writing grounded outside of history in the absolute authority of Deity, Dante is able, and not only in *CV*, to effect a conceptual and rhetorical reconciliation between the fundamentally opposed demands of modern, personal, contingent authorship and of traditional, depersonalized, *auctoritas*.[88]

---

[88] For Dante as prophet and/or "Scriba Dei" in general, see: Nardi 1942b; Singleton 1954; Mineo 1968; Sarolli 1971; Hollander 1976; Mazzotta 1979; Battaglia Ricci 1983, 1988; Dronke 1986; Hawkins 1988; Gorni 1990: 109–31; Barolini 1992, chapter 1; Benfell 1995, 1997; Palma di Cesnola 1995; Pertile 1998; Barański 2000: especially chapters 4, 6, 7; Scott 2004: 295–7, 302–5; Moevs 2005. See also

VI. "*LA SUA PRIMA VOCE*"

Convivio implicitly transforms its writing "I" into a proto-Renaissance poet-God, or at least into a "scriba Dei," like the one who will assert himself in the *Commedia*. However, we should still bear in mind that Dante carefully avoids making these implications explicit, and that if in attempting to decide what model of authorship he has arrived at over the course of the treatise, the two more obvious choices are: (1) authority on philosophical questions, on analogy with Aristotle who has functioned as a less personalized version of Virgil in the *Commedia*; and (2) a workman-like "binder of words" and crafter of poetry, who has particular affinities with the medieval *actor*.

The latter two are the figures that re-emerge, respectively, in explicit references to authorship and authority by Dante in two other texts written during this early phase of his post-exilic career: a letter directed to his fellow poet and exile, Cino da Pistoia, and the second great treatise of this period, *De Vulgari Eloquentia*. The *Epistle*, conventionally numbered three in modern editions (Alighieri 1979a), and perhaps dating from 1305–1306, accompanies a sonnet ("Io sono stato con amore insieme") sent in answer to Cino's query, also articulated in a sonnet ("Dante, quando per caso"), concerning the question of "utrum de passione in passionem possit anima transformari" (whether the soul may be transformed from one passion into another; par. 2). As Mengaldo (1979: 9) observes, *Epistle* 3 is yet

---

Chapter 1, section vi; Chapter 5, section vi and nn 15, 54, 56, 58; Chapter 7, section iv–vi, especially nn 86, 107, 113, 114, 147. In the chapter immediately preceding the excursus on *autore*, Dante gives an interesting preview of his scribal persona: "io nel comminciamento di questo capitolo posso parlare con la bocca di Salomone, che in persona de la Sapienza dice ne li suoi Proverbi (8:6): 'Udite: però che di grandi cose io debbo parlare'" (4.5.2), The choice of Solomon is wise indeed, since he is the Old Testament author most closely associated with Wisdom itself, and as such stands at the boundary between rational understanding and the mysteries of supra-rational understanding (where Dante places himself in 4.5.1). Moreover, as a king who "embraces" wisdom, he is especially appropriate in the context defining the reciprocal roles of emperor and philosopher (see also the citation of Sapienza in 4.6.18–20; noted by Boccassini 2003: 426). The reference triply marks the distance traversed by the Dantean "io" since *CV* I.I.I. First, his voice now coincides with that of an *auctor*. Second, that *auctor* himself is speaking with the impersonal voice of the Biblical version of Sophia, divine *Sapientia*. Thus Dante not only moves beyond his role as servant to the master discourse of classical philosophy, he also implies that he is now not just a lover of Lady Philosophy, but can, at least rhetorically, speak in her name and voice (cf. *VN* 24.5, where Beatrice is identified with Love Himself). Finally, he makes explicit that the Wisdom he loves and transmits is superior to that of the pagan *auctores*, given its Biblical pedigree (he thus anticipates his relationship to *Virgilio* and the other pagans "of great authority" in the *DC*). For Solomon in *CV* and the *Filosofia–Wisdom* equation, see also Boccassini 2003: 415 and n 436–8. For Dante and Solomon more generally, see E. Gilson 1939: chapter 4, part 3; Sarolli 1963 and 1973a; Cornish 1999. On Dante and the Wisdom tradition, see also O. Holmes 2008. For the Song of Songs in particular, see Pertile 1998; Nasti 1998. For *prosopopeia*, nn 3, 14, 42, 64; Chapter 4, n 50.

another example of Dantean auto-exegesis in the mode of self-commentary, although, I would add, undoubtedly the least studied. Ironically, and no doubt deliberately, the topic addressed is precisely that changeability in relation to love objects against which Dante spends books 2 and 3 of the *trattato* defending himself. Even more ironically, the answer he gives, anticipating Francesca in *Inferno* 5 (see Chapter 4, n 52, Chapter 7, nn 17, 28), is that free will has no power against Love, and that one must allow oneself to be spurred in whatever new direction Eros chooses.[89]

To our specific concerns, Dante explicitly points out that in soliciting his opinion on a question of this type Cino is inviting him to assume the role of an *auctor*:

Quod quamvis ex ore tuo iustius prodire debuerat, nichilominus me illius auctorem facere voluisti, ut in declaratione rei nimium dubitate titulum mei nominis ampliares (1)

(Although this [answer] would more justly come from your mouth, nonetheless you wished that I should be the author of it, so that by thus making me expound a question full of uncertainties you would increase the renown of my name)

There is little doubt, especially after the prose summary in the *Epistle* of the contents of the response ostensibly reserved to the sonnet, that the *auctor* in this case is the one derived from *autentin*, or, at the same time, that Dante is now explicitly conflating this type of *auctoritas* with that of the poet who speaks – as in the *canzoni* of books 2 and 3 of *Convivio*, though not 4 – through allegorical figures (inspired by Calliope, Muse of epic poetry and, perhaps more to the point here, especially given that the poem glossed is a sonnet, mother of *Orpheus*):

Redditur, ecce, sermo Calliopeus inferius, quo sententialiter canitur, quanquam transumptive more poetico signetur intentum, amorem huius posse torpescere . . . (2)

(Here below is Calliopean speech [the sonnet], in which is sung the significance of how love can wither away . . . albeit its meaning is signified figuratively in the poetic manner)

This is the single case in all Dante's *oeuvre* where he directly applies the appellation *auctor* to himself alone, and indeed one might be tempted to see it as letting down one's guard when communicating, not to a general

---

[89] Dante responds to Cino's sonnet, "Dante, quando per caso s'abbandona"; two later sonnets directed to Cino ("Degno fa voi trovare ogni tesoro" and, especially, "Io mi credea del tutto esser partito") instead reprove him for his amorous inconstancy (Barolini 1998b: 47 and n).

readership, like that proposed for and by *Convivio*, but to an especially intimate friend. In these few sentences, Dante manages to provide a complex, nuanced, and still deeply equivocal account of his relationship to the culture of *auctoritas*. For example, even as he applies the term *auctor* to himself, he displaces the desire to confer this title from himself onto the generosity of his friend Cino, whom he also says would be equally capable of responding to the question posed.[90]

Cino's supposed solicitousness for bolstering his friend's reputation harks back to the beginning of *Convivio*, and the pathetic description of the degrading effect that Dante's exile had on his *fama*. The point is explicitly prepared by Dante's usual designation of himself as "Florentinus exul inmeritus" in the letter's heading, and, reinforced, indirectly but surely, by the locution "titulum mei nominis," which echoes Ovid speaking of himself in his poem of exile, the *Tristia* ("tituli/mihi nominis"; 1.1.53–4).[91] In other words, the epistle, like the opening of the far better known treatise, brings together personal fragility and misfortune with impersonal authority in a way that puts them in precarious balance.

What then follows in *Epistle* 3 is of equal interest, as Dante provides three more explicit, complicating references to the principle of *auctoritas* and to the figure of the *auctor*. The first of these seems to continue the displacement from impersonality to personality, drawing on an easily recognizable vocabulary from the medieval discourse of authority. In beginning his exposition of the problem, Dante pairs an argument from authority with one from reason, and seemingly subordinates both to the experience of the individual (thus bringing together all three of the traditional modes of knowledge discussed in section ii):

Et fides huius, quanquam sit ab experientia persuasum, ratione potest et auctoritate muniri (3)

(And *belief* [faith] that this is so, although we are persuaded to it by *experience*, can be reinforced by *reason* and by *authority*)

---

[90] Critical discussion of *Ep.* 3 is rare and brief (see, however, Pastore Stocchi 1970: 707–8; Ferrucci 2001: 69–70 and n 8, who calls attention to Cecco d'Ascoli's attack on Dante's position here [*L'Acerba*, 3.1]; also Scott 2004: 338–9, cf. 94–5). Cino appears again as Dante's *döppelganger* in *DVE*; see Chapters 3–4, as well as Shapiro 1990: 32–3, 206 n 58, for more on this topic. For the relevance of Cino's juridical studies to Dante's *MN*, see Chapter 5, n 23.

[91] Noted in Alghieri 1979a (533) by Frugoni and Brugnoli. The complete passage in Ovid (1993) is: "donec eram sospes, tituli tangebar amore/quarendique mihi nominis ardor erat." Note the relevance to the question of the impeachment of Dante's name – his *fama* – by exile, raised in *CV* I, and to the association in *Ep.* 3 between *auctoritas* and *fama*. On Dante and the Ovid of the *Tristia* in the *DC* only, see Smarr 1991; Picone 2003b.

The balance of the *Epistle* is then dedicated first to a brief rational exposition of the question and then to the citation of a series of three *auctoritates*:

Auctoritatem vero Nasoni, quarto *De Rerum Transformatione*, que directe atque ad litteram propositum respicit, superest ut intueare: scilicet ubi tradit *autor* equidem in fabula trium sororum . . . Sub hoc frater carissime, ad prudentiam, qua contra Rhamnusie spicula sis patiens, te exhortor. Perlege, deprecor, *Fortuitorum Remedia*, que ab inclitissimo phylosophorum Seneca, nobis velut a patre filiis ministrantur, et illud de memoria sana tua non defluat: "Si de mundo fuissetis, mundus quod suum erat deligeret."

(It remains to consider the *authority* of Ovid in the fourth book of the *Metamorphoses*, which directly and literally concerns this argument, namely where the *author* speaks of the fable of three sisters . . . On this score, dear brother, I urge you to prudence and to endure the arrows of Nemesis. Read attentively, I pray you, the *Remedies of Fortune* which are offered by that most famous of philosophers, Seneca, to us like a father to sons; and do not let slip from your mind these words: "If you had been of the world, the world would love its own.")

In placing the argument from authority last, Dante at once respects its conceptual secondariness, and at the same time gives it "the final word." More importantly, the series of citations is designed to put Dante in the company of traditional *auctores*, and, less obviously, but surely, to establish a hierarchical order and relationship among distinct types of *auctoritates*.

Citing Ovid as his first *auctoritas*, Dante makes explicit the allusive link to the classical poet that the phrase "titulum mei nominis" had earlier introduced. Ovid here represents a bridge linking the moderns (Cino and Dante) to classical poetic authority, in the same way that Virgil does in *Convivio* 4 and then in the *Commedia*, and as Ovid himself had in *Convivio* 2.1.3 and in *Vita Nova* 25.[92] Similarly, in the earlier reference he furnished a biographical parallel with Dante – in his exile and role as political scapegoat – analogous to that established with Boethius in *Convivio* 1. The choice of Ovid is particularly apt because he is in many ways the closest of the classical poets to the subject matter that Dante in *Vita Nova* had identified as the specific province of vernacular "dicitori in rima," here obviously exemplified by Cino and Dante himself, namely love. The *Metamorphoses* are then especially suited to the subject of the mutability of earthly love, as the *Tristia* are to the mutability of earthly fortunes.

Ovid, however, is only the first in an ascending sequence of *auctores*. Next comes a reference to the authority of the philosopher Seneca, to whom Dante, like much of the Middle Ages, attributed the writing of a book

[92] For Dante and Ovid, see again Chapter 1, n 27.

on overcoming the vagaries of fortune, in the tradition of Roman stoicism as of Boethius's *Consolation*. Finally, there is an unattributed but easily recognizable quotation from the Gospel of John: "Si de mundo fuissetis, mundus quod suum erat deligeret" (If you had been of the world, the world would love its own; 15:19). This passage, abstracted from John's account of Jesus' discourse to the disciples after the Last Supper, takes up the theme of resisting the assault of earthly things ("mundum") now in the name of a higher, other-worldly Truth, and it continues with the observation that because the disciples have been chosen by Jesus, they will be hated by the *mundum*, continuing the theme of the effects of "exile" from the *Tristia* allusion.

Dante first cites the authority of a profane classical *auctor*, moving thence to a philosopher, and thus figuring by other means the conflation of poetic and philosophical discourses that the *Epistle* and its accompanying poem perform, which in turn follows the prosimetrum model established in *Convivio*. The final citation then moves beyond both poetry and philosophy to the authority of the Bible and of a human *Scriba Dei*, John, who in this passage is directly quoting the words of Christ, the God made flesh. In other words, the *Epistle*, like chapter 6 of *Convivio*, book 4, not only connects poetic and philosophical authority but hints at their subsumption under the highest form of human authority, Biblical authorship, which derives directly from the divine Author of authors.

Finally, the *Epistle* connects all three authorities back to Dante – both as a reading subject whose case is mirrored in the textual *auctoritates* and as himself the *auctor* of authoritative poetic-philosophical-theological texts. This point will be clearer if we recognize that the second and third *auctoritates* are not aimed directly at the question raised by Cino. Rather, they turn from the general issue of the mutability of love in the human subject to the need for Cino himself to resist external changes – presumably his exile from Pistoia along with others of the "White party." As this summary account suggests, the two questions mirror one another – Cino, like Dante, has been the victim of a change in the "affections" of a beloved home city. The implication is that the real issue is not whether human beings can change love objects – as Dante says at the outset, experience makes it plain that they can and do all the time – rather it is how to find permanence beyond the changes of the world, grounded in a higher and unalterable love – a Johanine *caritas* rather than Ovidian desire, or Senecan suppression of emotion.[93] This, then, provides a theoretical underpinning

---

[93] It is possible that in the passage from Ovid to John Dante is playing on a biographical connection between the two, namely that both passed their later years in exile on a small island (Ovid on Tomis;

for Dante's salutational claim wishing a permanent, charitable "ardor" for his friend (per tempora diuturna salutem et perpetue caritatis ardorem [health for many years and the ardor of perpetual love; 3.title]), which is in implicit opposition to the love he analyzes in the letter and poem.

What makes this configuration especially apt for the present discussion is the specific way in which it sutures together Dante as personalized subject of exile and victim of earthly change and "disinnamoramento" with Dante as "impersonal" authority on the subject of love mutable and immutable, through the mediating figure of Cino da Pistoia. As we have seen, Dante conceives of Cino having asked him this question as a remedy for his exilic misfortunes, as a way of giving him the stabilizing, impersonal stature of an authority (it is not too great a stretch to say that what makes Dante an authority on violent change is that he has been subjected to it so often). He then turns his authoritative discourse on change back into a remedy for Cino's misadventures, which strikingly mirror his own. Cino, then, is doubly Dante's *döppelganger* – as poetic authority on love and as exilic subject – and he figures the paradoxical conflation of these two distinct entities under the "title" of a single name. Or to put it another way: Dante grounds his impersonal, immutable authority in the personal experience of exile and change, for which such authority is also potentially the remedy.

Cino's relationship to Dante, and its relevance to Dante's construction of his own authority, is, as we will see in the next chapter, a crucial feature of *De Vulgari Eloquentia*. Here instead, I want to focus briefly on the second book of *De Vulgari*, where the poetic *autore* from *avieo* resurfaces, not on the margins but at the center of Dante's discourse, evidently used in the limited technical sense with which we began discussing that etymology in *Convivio*. In this book Dante narrows his focus down from vernacular as language in general (to be discussed in Chapter 3) to the specific problem of poetic style. In chapter 1 he justifies what will be an exclusive focus on poetry by arguing that while the illustrious vernacular can be used in prose and poetry alike, prose authors ("prosaycantes") receive knowledge of it from the poets ("avientibus," from *avieo* [compare Dragonetti 1961b: 53–4]) and not the reverse, giving the poets primacy (2.1.1).[94] In chapter 8 he calls the one who writes a *canzone* "autor" without further etymological specification, though in terms that make clear its affinity to the poet as

John on Patmos). If one recalls Seneca's misfortunes at Nero's hands, all three *auctores* pre-figure Dante's unhappy circumstances.

[94] On Dante's shifting place in the rhetorical *querelles* between prose and poetry, see Mengaldo 1978a: 49–5; see also n 78 . On the hypothesis that the projected but unwritten book 3 of *DVE* would have been dedicated to prose, see Rajna 1921: 85–6; Mengaldo 1970b: 403–4, 1979: 142 n 1; Corti 1993: 82–4. See also Chapters 3–4.

"binder of words," particularly through a strong metaphorics of formal ligature that opens and closes the chapter.[95] Indeed, the *autor* (from *avieo*) here shades over into the domain of the *faber*, or maker, and thus resembles increasingly the *actor*, from *agere* "to do, to make." The *canzone* is said to be "fabricatur ab autore suam" (created by [its] author; 2.8.4, cf. 5), and is specifically defined as "fabricatio verborum harmonizata" (a harmonized fabrication of words; 2.8.5).[96] Dante goes on to insist specifically that the poem is the property of the one who makes it, rather than of its performers ("nunquam dicimus 'Hec est cantio Petri' eo quod ipsam proferat, sed eo quod fabricaverit illam" [we never say: 'that's Peter's song' when referring to something Peter has performed, but only to something he has [created]; 2.8.4).[97] In other words, the definition of poetic author as "binder of words" is here stripped at least temporarily of any overtones of transcendence such as those we found implicit in *Convivio* or of any special proximity to the authorial "truth-teller" from *autentin*, and instead points toward the poet as individual artisan with possessive rights over the work he has produced.[98]

Between them, these texts split Dantean poetic authority in two, following *Convivio's* radical division of poetry into an artful verbal surface and a hidden philosophical content. They do, however, share one even more

---

95 See 2.8.1–2 and 2.8.9: "Preparatis fustibus torquibusque ad *fascem*, nunc *fasciandi* tempus incumbit. Sed quia cuiuslibet operis cognitio precedere debet operationem, velut signum ante ammissionem sagipte vel iaculi, primo et principaliter qui sit iste *fascis quem fasciare* intendimus videamus" and "Satis etiam patere videtur quid intelligimus cum cantionem vocamus, et per consequens quid sit ille *fascis* quem *ligare* molimur." Compare 1.11.4; 2.3.2; 2.4.6; and *CV* 1.13.6–7; 4.6.3–4. See also Shapiro 1990: 171–2.

96 Compare *CV* 4.30.2, where Dante defines himself, with his usual ambivalence as "buono fabricatore," or rather as "seguitatore di quello," in the *congedo* to "Le dolci rime d'amor."

97 Note the intriguing distinction between active and passive authorship (and in an immediately preceding passage, between active and passive readership: "lectio passio vel actus legendi" [2.8.3]), which may have implications for the author/reader dialectic discussed in Chapter 1, section iv, to be taken up again in Chapter 4. See also Dragonetti 1961b: 73; Noferi 1977: 15–25 *et passim*; Ascoli 1991b: 215–16 and n 43; Chapter 4, n 34; cf. Stone 1994b: 50–1. Shapiro 1990: 167–9 translates the terms *actio* and *passio* as "action" and "passion" and assimilates them to the terminology of the speculative grammarians. In the process, it seems to me, she misses Dante's key point about individual authorial ownership of the verbal products actively generated rather than "passively" rehearsed. The parallel distinction in kinds of reading, which probably refers, on the one hand, to the active *lectio* of Scholastic interpretation (n 28) and on the other to the "passive" experience of texts by non-academic and/or student readers, offers a large hint about Dante's assumption of the role of "active" reader of his own text and others in the auto-commentaries of *VN, CV, Ep.* 3, and, in a sense, *DVE* as well.

98 In book 1 of *DVE*, God is twice referred to as "Faber" or Maker (1.5.1, 1.7.5), so one might infer an implicit analogy is being created here (see Curtius 1948: 544–6 on the topos of "God as Maker"; see Boyde 1981: chapter 8 for the ramifications of the topos in Dante). As will be seen in Chapter 3, however, within the economy of the treatise this would also imply a resemblance between the would-be poet-God and the presumptuous builders of the Tower of Babel. See also *CV* 4.9.6 for a careful distinction, not specifically aimed at poetry, between human and divine making.

basic feature, namely the willingness to attribute authority specifically to Dante, and to foreground an apparently successful compromise between individual personality and medieval canons of impersonal authorship. This, then, may be the most important acquisition of the elaborate and seemingly painful struggle for and with authority that Dante undergoes in this phase of his career and acts out at length in *Convivio*.

In closing, then, let me return once more to the key passage on the poetic author from *Convivio* 4.6. I have stressed the tension inherent to this passage, which, while bearing centrally on Dante's own standing as poet, and as aspirant to authorship, maintains a posture of rigorously detached objectivity, and sustains the fiction that it has no immediate relevance to Dante or to his project in *Convivio*. Nonetheless, hidden in plain sight at the conceptual center of the passage is a straightforward reference to the possibility of an individual and personal authorship that is in some sense compatible with the medieval culture of impersonal *auctoritas*. In this sense too, the etymology of *autore* from *avieo* is a fitting climax to the struggles toward personal authorship dramatized in book 1. The point is, as Dante specifically notes, that the root word in question, *avieo*, is the first person singular, present, form ("la sua prima voce") of a Latin verb. It is not an infinitive with unspecified subject meaning simply "to bind" or "to author by binding"; instead it means "I bind, I author": I, Dante, author.

CHAPTER 3

Language: "Neminem ante nos"

I. VERNACULAR AUTHORSHIP BETWEEN CONVIVIO AND DE VULGARI ELOQUENTIA

If Dante's definitional approach to *autorità* in *Convivio* has gone virtually unexamined in the scholarship, his choice of the vernacular over Latin has not. It is widely recognized, in no small measure because Dante insists on it, that his sense of himself as author-on-the-make is intimately bound up with the problematic status of the nascent Italian language as a vehicle for serious intellectual and moral discourse, its patently inferior status with respect to the normative language of high culture in the Middle Ages.

This issue is already on the table in *Vita Nova*. For instance, it is visible in the interpolation of Latin tags at various strategic points throughout the text.[1] It is a central feature of chapter 25, where the vernacular "dicitori d'amore" are both distinguished from and compared to those classical *poeti* — four of five writing in Latin — whom Dante dares to present as their counterparts in the deployment of figurative language.[2] On the other hand, no overt defense of the use of Italian as against Latin is made, except in the negative sense of limiting vernacular poetry to the subject of the love for a woman, and of defining women as a crucial segment of the work's intended audience.

In *Convivio* the situation has changed (cf. Grayson 1963: 46). Nine of the twelve chapters in book 1 that are dedicated to purging the stains that compromise Dante's authority are focused on the use of Italian in the prose

---

[1] Barański 1986a: 63–5 notes twenty-one distinct uses of Latin in *VN* which he sees as prose adaptations of *barbarolexis*, a device to heighten the stylistic level and hence the authority of vernacular poems. He also recalls Dante's specific declaration that his *intendimento*, and Cavalcanti's, was that the *libello* be written in *volgare*, not Latin (chapter 30, par. 2–3). Cf. Spitzer 1937; Singleton 1946. See also Chapter 4, section ii, especially nn 29, 31, 38, 42.

[2] For the "language question" in *VN*, see Grayson 1963: especially 41–5, 1965: 16–17; Picone 1979: 18–25; Tavoni 1984; Brownlee 1984: 602–3; Barański 1986a: 63–5; Mazzaro 1981: especially 85–6; Noakes 1990. For links between chapter 25 and *DVE*, see Luzzi 1998: 175–6.

commentary – and this defect is said to be "substantial," that is, integral to the essence of the text, whereas the other two are merely "accidental."[3] As we also saw when discussing the final chapters of book 1, Dante insists on the intimate connection, verging on identity, between the language responsible for his very existence and his own personal vocation as author.

The comparative treatment of Italian and Latin in book 1 closely mirrors the humble hierarchical relationship that Dante initially defines between himself and Aristotle, and intermittently reinforces over the course of the treatise as a whole. On the one hand, he explicitly posits the hierarchical superiority of Latin as a vehicle for knowledge. The vernacular is constantly changing with time and location: there are many different vernaculars – each place has its own – and the vernacular changes significantly in as few as fifty years, and within one thousand years has become virtually unintelligible to those who first used it (1.5.9).[4] Latin *gramatica*, on the other hand, is governed by unchanging rules and remains exactly the same over time (1.5.7). Its exemption from the forces of history makes it the privileged vehicle of philosophical truths, which are unalterable in their essence. On the other hand, he is prepared to defend his own use of Italian at great length: because of its unique suitability as a vehicle of commentary on vernacular poetry (see Chapter 4); because it can reach the specific

---

[3] Curiously criticism focused on *CV*'s treatment of language is sparse, and what there is tends to subordinate it to *DVE* (see nn 4, 8). For exceptions see Chapter 2, n 45.

[4] That Dante's *auctoritas* for part of this assertion is Horace (*AP* 60–2, 70–2), which refers to the Roman poet's own language, hints at a relativization of the authority of *gramatica*. A second suggestion to similar effect is in *CV* 2.13.9–10: "Dico che 'l cielo de la Luna con la Gramatica si somiglia, . . . [per] la variazione de la sua luminositade, che ora luce da uno lato, e ora luce da un altro, secondo che lo sole la vede. E . . . la Gramatica . . . luce or di qua or di là, in tanto quanto certi vocabuli, certe declinazioni, certe construzioni sono in uso che già non furono, e molte già furono che ancor saranno: sì come dice Orazio nel principio de la Poetria, quando dice: 'Molti vocabuli rinasceranno che già caddero'" (cf. 2.14.10; cited in Mazzocco 1993: 131). The connection with the earlier passage is evident, not because of the word *gramatica*, which does not refer directly to Latin in *CV* 1 (the equation Latin = [a] grammar could be inferred from 1.11.14 and 12.4, but is explicit only at 3.2.18 and 4.5.3), but because of the citation of the Horatian passage alluded to previously. What to do, however, with the linking of *gramatica* to instability rather than to its opposite, as in *DVE*? Critics who have noticed the passage (Grayson 1965: 7–8; De Robertis 1988: 224n; Shapiro 1990: 18, 189; Mazzocco 1993: 176), usually associate it with the radically historical position on language adopted in *Par.* 26, and, less often but fruitfully, with the Heaven of the Moon (Cestaro 1991b: 56–8), particularly Beatrice's correction of Dante's earlier interpretation of lunar spots (Nardi 1917, 1965a: 76–7; Mazzeo 1960: 180; Mazzotta 1993a: especially 46–7; Lombardi 2000; cf. Chapter 6, n 29). Except Lombardi, no one has come to grips with its anomalous place in *CV*'s discourse on language. The simplest solution would be to say that here *gramatica* refers not to Latin specifically, or to the prescriptive teaching of languages, but rather, as does Cestaro 1991b, to the contingency of fallen language in general, against which Latin, and now Italian "bound together with rhythm and rhyme" oppose themselves, anticipating *DVE* (1.9.1). On the multiple meanings of *gramatica* for Dante, see n 20. Dante returns to the Horatian thought in *DVE* 1.9.7, as well as *Par.* 26.124–6, 137–8 (Chapter 7, section v and n 157).

audience of Italian speakers the treatise is aimed at better than Latin; and, as seen earlier, because of his own love of and relationship to it.

For all the explicitness of this treatment, however, there is one way in which *Convivio*'s treatment of the vernacular fails to go beyond the studied reticence of *Vita Nova*. Specifically, the defense of the use of Italian is directed exclusively toward the prose commentary, while the bearing of the "language question" on Dante's claim for high philosophical content in his vernacular *canzoni* is not directly examined. The importance of this omission cannot be overestimated. As noted in Chapter 2 (section v, cf. n 94), prose commentary is constitutively subordinated to poetic *auctoritates* (*CV* 1.5.7–9, 7.1–2; see also Chapter 4, section iii, and n 66). In other words, Dante uses this discussion to acknowledge the relative lack of authority of his Italian prose, without ever fully admitting that the same limitations apply to his poetry, the mode upon which, in the end, he stakes his claim to the role of *autore*.

Or rather, just as Dante's explicit subordination of himself to Aristotle is accompanied by a counter-discourse in which he tacitly assumes the authority to challenge the greatest classical thinker, so book 1 initiates a counter-discourse that aims to appropriate for Italian the same status, the same formal permanence and conceptual power, as Latin. Consider the following passage viewed from another angle in Chapter 2:

Every being naturally seeks to preserve its own existence; if, then, the vernacular were itself able to seek a goal, this is what it would seek; this would in practice consist of equipping itself with greater stability, and this it could attain only *by binding itself together with [numbers, i.e., meter] and rhyme*. It is this very goal for which I have striven [più stabilitade non si potrebbe avere *che in legarsé con numero e con rime. E questo medesimo studio è stato mio*] (1.13.6)

Though the connection is not made explicit, Dante's zealous pursuit of a stability that will perpetuate *his* vernacular evidently aims to appropriate for it the same qualities to which he has previously attributed the greater nobility of Latin *gramatica*, and to which he had allusively linked vernacular prose (1.10; cf. Chapter 2, nn 46 and 82; Chapter 4, section iii).

Just how central this project is to *Convivio* can be seen by returning to the definition of *autore* from *avieo*:

This word, namely "autore," can descend from one of two sources. One is a verb no longer much used in grammar [i.e., Latin], namely "auieo" which means as much as "to bind words" ["*legare parole*"]. And whoever looks carefully at it in its first person singular form [*ne la sua prima voce*] will see that it openly demonstrates this meaning, because it is made up only of the bonds of words [*solo di legame di parole è fatto*], that is, only of the five vowels, that are the soul and bond [*legame*] of every word, and composed of them in a mobile form that figures the image of a bond [*a figurare imagine di legame*]. Thus: beginning with "A" it then turns back to "U," then proceeding directly through "I" to "E," and then goes backward, returning to "O": so that truly it images this figure: A, E, I, O, U, which is the figure of a bond [*figura di legame*]. And inasmuch as "autore" derives from this verb, it is taken to refer to the poets alone, who with musical art [*arte musaica*] have bound together [*legate*] their words . . . (4.6.3–4)

Once the direct recall of the language of 1.13 is recognized, the point could not be plainer: the definition with which Dante claims "not to be concerned" both reflects on him in general terms as first-person singular author of poetry and is also the culmination of the project of building, by binding, a vernacular language capable of rivaling Latin (see Lombardi 2000). As seen in Chapter 2, the overt confirmation of this comes at the beginning of book 4, with the appearance of a literally philosophical poem, "Le dolci rime d'amore ch'io solia."

What *Convivio* does obliquely, as a defensive digression subordinate to its primary mission of divulgative education, and without ever *explicitly* claiming that the vernacular might aspire to the authoritative status of a *gramatica* in its own right, or that his own poetry might be the vehicle for acquiring such status for Italian, *De Vulgari Eloquentia* does overtly and as its central concern. It daringly reverses the hierarchy between grammars and vernaculars in general, claiming as its constituent premise that the vernacular is nobler than "grammar" (1.1.4). Book 1 having identified the "illustrious vernacular" best suited to literary pursuits, the second book, a veritable *ars poetica vulgaris*, sets out to demonstrate that this language may be deployed in the highest of the classical styles, the "tragic,"[5] and that it is capable of sustaining a "poetry of rectitude" whose mission is moral instruction (2.4.4–8; cf. 2.2.5–9).[6] Most crucially, in its

[5] See Mengaldo 1978a: 87–91 for the much-debated relationship between the *vulgare illustre* and the tragic style (see also nn 43, 49). The invocation of the three styles of classical Latin, linking the vernacular *canzoni* with the highest of these, is the point in *DVE* where Dante is most obviously propping his language and his poetry on classical authority (Barański 1986a: 56–7, 69–76; cf. 1991a and b) and most closely paralleling *VN* 25 and *CV*'s invocation of Aristotle *et al.* See n 7 on Dante's "sources and analogues" for the treatise. As a discussion of the *convenientia* of the "tragic" style to its three proper subject matters will show (sect. iv), Dante uses this "classicizing" gesture to foreground his own talents (cf. 2.6.7 and n 55). Battaglia Ricci 1983 and Barański 1986a focus on the disparity between the preeminence of the "high style" in *DVE* and the turn to a mixed, "comic" style or "sermo humilis" (Auerbach 1941) in the *DC*. For a review of the arguments over both the three styles and the title of the *DC*, with reference to *DVE* and the *ECG* see Ascoli 1997: 325–9 and nn 28–9, 64, 66–9, 71. See also Chapter 4, nn 19, 72 and 77.

[6] On the "poetry of rectitude," see Colish 1983 and discussion below. This locution shows that that the problem of language for Dante is first of all ethical (Barański 1989a). See also Chapter 2, n 12.

discussions first of vernacular language and then of vernacular poetry, *De Vulgari* consistently offers as its principal example the poetry of Dante himself.

After *Convivio*'s tortuous rhetorical maneuvering to demonstrate Dante's adherence to normative canons of *auctoritas*, and to subordinate both itself and him to the *autorità* of Aristotle and of Latin, *De Vulgari Eloquentia* seemingly embraces and elaborates the new language and mode of vernacular, modern, authorship at which the other treatise only hints. Where *Convivio* opens with a self-effacing gesture of submission, "sí come dice lo Filosofo . . ." (as the Philosopher says; 1.1.1), *De Vulgari* immediately asserts Dante's autonomous originality and modernity: "neminem ante nos de vulgaris eloquentiae doctrinam quicquam invenimus tractasse" (since we find that no one before us has treated the doctrine of eloquence in the vernacular; 1.1.1). Moreover, its subject is one for which there are no applicable authorities: "inquirere intendamus de hiis in quibus nullius autoritate fulcimur" (we propose to investigate a subject in which authority can give us no support; 1.9.1).[7]

Put thus, *De Vulgari Eloquentia* seems to represent a step forward in the Dantean discourse on authority, a natural sequel to *Convivio*, as the latter suggests in referring to "un libello ch'io intendo fare, Dio concedente, di Volgare Eloquentia" (a book that I intend to make, God allowing it, on Vernacular Eloquence; 1.5.10).[8] Nonetheless, the relationship between the

---

[7] Dante's claim to novelty here is largely justified, as the scholarship has often acknowledged. This does not mean, however, that *DVE* lacks a genealogy; rather, its recombinative eclecticism is unusually high given the medieval propensity for rehearsing authoritative models. The point is made by Corti 1993, who notes Dante's use of the technical term "compilando" to describe his practice in *DVE* (1.1.1; cf. Chapter 1, n 4; Chapter 2, section ii). Crucial is the meaning the two claims have as explicitations of Dante's evolving relationship to the culture of *auctoritas*. Note the parallel claim of novelty in his treatment of nobility in *CV* 4, which, however, is: (a) less objectively warranted (Chapter 2, n 47) and (b) accompanied by an elaborate defensive effort. See also *MN* 1.1 (cf. Chapter 5, section i and nn 12–13). On *DVE*'s classical, Biblical-patristic, and late medieval, vernacular and Latin, sources and precedents see D'Ovidio 1876: 69; Weiss 1942; Ewert 1940; Di Capua 1945; Pagliaro 1962: 222–3; Mengaldo 1970b: 411–13, 1978a: 44–8, 1979: 10–14; Corti 1981, 1993; Alessio 1984, 1995; Dronke 1986; Poe 1984; Shapiro 1990; Cestaro 2003a: especially chapters 1–2. Botterill 1996a: xvii notes the treatise reflects Dante's typical fusion of genres and modes of discourse ("commentary; poetics; rhetoric; speculative grammar"; cf. Chapter 2, n 80). Shapiro, building on Mengaldo (1979: 13), Corti 1981 and others, argues that the treatise's most distinctive feature is the transformation of the grammatical study of language (Priscian *et al.*) and the rhetorical study of poetry (Geoffrey of Vinsauf and co.) by turning them toward a philosophical investigation of causes, forms, and essences (e.g. Shapiro 1990: 44–5, 137). Mengaldo (especially 1970b: 411–12; 1978a: 33–6, 39; 1979: 11–13) anticipates a number of my concerns with the specific problem of *auctoritas* in the treatise, especially in regard to the complex treatment of the ancients (cf. n 55). See also Barański 1989a: 115–19; Shapiro 1990: 6–7, 14, 21–2, 26, 42–5, 133, 143–4.

[8] The pairing of *CV* and *DVE* is traditional. See especially Grayson 1965; Vinay 1959; Nardi 1960a: 20–36; Mengaldo 1970b, 1978a, 1979; as well as D'Ovidio 1876; Ewert 1940; Weiss 1942; Cambon 1966;

two is more complicated than it first appears, just as the seemingly straightforward celebration of vernacular authorship conceals complexities. Both of these points can be heuristically illustrated with reference to an apparent (and well-known) contradiction between the two treatises, which returns to the paradox at the heart of the self-authorization project. As we have seen, *Convivio* explicitly designates Latin as superior to the vernacular, but implicitly contradicts this by being composed entirely in Italian. *De Vulgari Eloquentia*, composed entirely in Latin, explicitly designates the vernacular in general as superior to *gramatica*. A shift in one direction at the level of content is then followed by another, diametrically opposed shift at the level of form. This recourse to Latin as a vehicle for defending the vernacular might imply that Dante does not here feel the compunction against putting *gramatica* "in the service" of Italian that he felt in *Convivio* (Durling 1992: 30; see Chapter 4). More obviously, it suggests that he is not so very confident in the superior nobility of the vernacular, since he props it up against the authority of the very kind of language he says is inferior to it![9]

For these reasons, it is difficult to make any definitive statement about the order of composition, and this chapter will therefore proceed only on the uncontested assumptions that: (a) *Convivio* and *De Vulgari Eloquentia* are roughly contemporaneous, belonging to the period of early exile (ca. 1302–1308),[10] and (b) both precede the *Commedia*.[11] On this basis, two general observations can be made about them as a pair. First, their concerns, especially that of establishing the authority of vernacular culture and of Dante himself as its representative, overlap to a great extent. Secondly,

---

Fenzi 1986: 25–7. Despite the chronological implications of the *CV* passage, no substantial agreement exists about the order of composition. In fact, the primary tendency is to assume overlapping times of composition. Vinay (1959: 239) argues that *CV* I precedes, while *CV* 4 follows, *DVE*, an argument taken up by some who assert a rupture between *CV* 1–3 and *CV* 4 (Chapter 2, n 76). See also Grayson's revision of Vinay's position (1965: 19–24), as well as Corti 1983: 142–5, Fenzi 1986: 11. I read *CV* 4 as a logical consequence of book 1, without precluding a possible hiatus. For the dating of *DVE* see Mengaldo 1970b: 401–2.

[9] Mengaldo 1978a: 62–4, 1979: 6–9; cf. Marigo 1948: cxx–cxxi; Shapiro 1990: 148–9; Alessio 1995: 60.

[10] On exile as historical motive for and thematic concern of *DVE*, see Mengaldo 1978a: 58–9; Shapiro 1990: *et passim*; Cestaro 1991b: especially 58–64; Menocal 1994: 92–106. For the connection between exile and language in the Christian, especially Augustinian, tradition, see Ferguson 1975; for exile's shaping role in Dante's poetics generally, see Mazzotta 1979, 1984; for its place in *DVE*, Shapiro and Cestaro. Shapiro's intermittently brilliant reading of the treatise is marred by a number of misleading imprecisions (see, e.g., nn 50, 51, 57). Cestaro's treatment is more compatible with mine. See also n 42.

[11] *DVE* was even less well known than *CV* in the '300 and even the '400, reappearing only in the early '500 through the efforts of Giangiorgio Trissino (Mengaldo 1978a: 22–6; Corti 1993: 81; Botterill 1996a: xv–xvi). The treatise is mentioned by Giovanni Villani (in the first redaction of his *Cronica nuova* 10.136 (2002: 532 n 12) and Boccaccio in his *Vita di Dante* (1974: 489, par. 200; 530, par. 138), though misdated by both. Cf. Chapter 2, n 11.

given their proximity in time and their affinities in agenda, they show a disconcerting propensity for qualifying and even contradicting one another.[12] Moreover, both their shared concerns and their conceptual differences are best understood not in terms of the evolution of an integral and coherent intellectual position or definitive vernacular poetics, but rather as elements in a complex of rhetorical strategies designed to appropriate and transform traditional medieval *auctoritas* for Dante, his language, and his poetry.

II. VERNACULAR AND GRAMMAR

In *Convivio* the problem of constructing authority pivots explicitly and anxiously around three related questions: authorial personality and self-representation; the inferior status of the Italian language; the marginal situation of poetry as a discourse vis-à-vis other fields of cultural discourse – principally philosophy, but also politics and, allusively, theology. In *De Vulgari Eloquentia*, by contrast, the search to acquire cultural legitimacy for vernacular language in general and for the illustrious Italian vernacular in particular is *the* central concern from the beginning of the treatise, taking apparent precedence over the other two, which are no longer openly thematized as obstacles to authority. As to the matter of the vernacular itself, as just seen, *De Vulgari Eloquentia* initially appears to be much farther down the road to full Dantean self-authorization than its companion.

Dante's status as author of the treatise is not brought openly into question in *De Vulgari Eloquentia*, nor is his "personhood" overtly seen to be subversive of his authority. The humble apologist of *Convivio* is replaced by a self-confident voice of reason, which stands at a dispassionate distance from its subject. In the Italian treatise, Dante's contingent standing as an exile is immediately presented as a positive obstacle that must be overcome to write the treatise. In *De Vulgari Eloquentia* his exile is mentioned only after five chapters, and then only to assert that it allows him to judge matters concerning dialects with impersonal reason. In other words, here exile

---

[12] Mengaldo 1970b (especially 412), 1978a (especially 60–76), 1979 (6–7), gives the best account of the potential contradictions between the two, as also within *DVE* itself (see n 19). See also D'Ovidio 1876: 75–9; Nardi 1921b: 181–4; Contini 1957: 37–8; Stefano Rizzo 1969: 72–3; Pagani 1982: especially 154, 249–51; Shapiro 1990: 187–90; Cestaro 1991b: 64–6; Alessio 1995. See n 56 for the special case of *nobiltà/nobilitas*. Attempts have been made to deny these conflicts: e.g., Marigo 1948: 57; Nardi 1921b: especially 173, 182–4; Weiss 1942: 160; Ewert 1940: 356; Stefano Rizzo 1969: 78; Scaglione 1988: 31; Mazzocco 1993: chapter 8, especially 151–2. These are of two basic kinds: (1) synchronic (there is no conceptual contradiction after all); (2) diachronic (changes can be accounted for by a narrative of logical evolution over time). Nardi 1921b: 178–84 and the critics cited on this point in n 8 are the best examples of the second. On the prevalence of contradictions among and within Dante's works, see Chapter 6.

is a source of authority, not an impediment to it (although, as will appear, subsequent references have a different effect). Where in *Convivio* the question of self-reference is addressed apologetically, in *De Vulgari Eloquentia*, the speaker begins his discourse without hesitation and continues without exception in an "imperial," or at least authoritative, first person plural ("neminem ante *nos*"). Furthermore, he introduces "himself," albeit in an indirect third person singular form, as the prime exemplar of his discourse. This "other Dante" is, until very late in the treatise, designated not by name but in the third person singular as the "amicus" of Cino da Pistoia (1.10.2, 17.3; 2.2.8 [2], 5.4, 6.6; cf. 1.13.4; see also Barolini 1984: 89, 125).[13] Finally, all this is accomplished without either thematizing the need for justificatory commentary on his poetic works or problematizing the relation of the prose to the poetry it discusses,[14] both of which are central features of *Convivio* book 1.

I will suggest, in due course, that these issues, central to *Convivio*, return, subtly and implicitly, but no less surely, in *De Vulgari Eloquentia*. I will show, in particular, that while the relationship between two Dantes – one a prose expositor, one a poet – may not be explicitly thematized here, nonetheless the formal division between the two is of the greatest significance for understanding Dantean authorship here as elsewhere. I will begin, however, where *De Vulgari Eloquentia* itself begins, with the apparently unequivocal and self-evident triumph of vernacular over *gramatica*, which reverses not only *Convivio*, but also the official culture of the day.

In the event, the *gramatica* / *volgare* opposition is only the opening gambit in a much more elaborate strategy. Dante acknowledges the inadequacies, even the constituent sinfulness, of most vernaculars, recuperates the values usually associated with *gramatica*, and eventually develops the concept of one particular Italian vernacular, the *vulgare illustre*, which is really a hybrid of the qualities initially divided between vernacular and grammar. Thus, book 1 is structured by movement from this opening opposition toward the definition and qualification of the *vulgare illustre*. It follows an argument that is alternately "historical" and "rational," diachronic and synchronic, in its treatment of language (cf. Mengaldo 1978a: 29; Corti 1981: 62).

Criticism of *De Vulgari Eloquentia* has consistently returned to the problem of how the beginning of the first book should be related to its ending. There are two basic positions: one that emphasizes the empirical historicity of the *vulgare illustre* and one that stresses its rational ideality. The first

---

[13] On Cino and Dante, see again Chapter 2, section vi, and n 90.

[14] The relation of prose to poetry comes up, but only as regards the Italian vernacular that is the treatise's subject, not the language of the treatise itself. See Chapter 2, section vi and n 94.

position argues for direct continuity between the vernacular in general and the *vulgare illustre*, claiming that the latter is in the same oppositional relation to grammar as the former.[15] This conclusion is obtained, primarily, by stressing the historical actuality of the *vulgare illustre*, which, in addition to being the transcendent *langue* from which the individual *parole* of each regional dialect is derived, has its own empirical existence. Dante identifies it as the once and future language of a central Italian court, like that of Frederick II in Sicily, where he claims it was spoken (1.12.3–5). He argues that it is the current language of the *curia* in exile, the group of "doctores illustres" (illustrious men of learning; 1.19.1) now dispersed throughout the peninsula, but linked by "gratioso lumine rationis" (the gracious light of reason; 1.18.5).[16]

The second position posits the *vulgare illustre* as itself a form of *gramatica*, an ideal language of regulated art.[17] According to this account, Dante deliberately abandons the inductive and empirical search for the elusive "panther" (1.16.1), or illustrious Italian vernacular, only to assert its existence on ideally rational grounds. The *vulgare illustre* is defined as the "simplicissima signa" ([most fundamental signs]), against which all empirical uses of the *lingua di sì* are to be judged. By comparing it to the law (*lex*) and to "virtue as we understand it in general" (virtutem . . . ut generaliter illam intelligamus), and by defining it as the rule by which all linguistic acts of Italians can be "weighed and measured" (*simplicissima signa . . . quibus latine actiones ponderantur et mensurantur*), Dante treats it as an abstract standard for judging cases rather than as itself a "case," that is as

[15] The first advocate of this position is Nardi 1921b: especially 182–4, 189; also Vinay 1959, Grayson 1965. Of special interest is Pagani 1982, who reviews the interlocking debates surrounding *DVE* and reasserts Nardi's thesis (especially 193–252). Mazzocco 1993: 128 takes the extreme position that "the illustrious vernacular means the reacquisition of the Italian idiom in its first developmental stage," which he calls "proto-Italian" (138–9, 141). In my view, he confuses temporal priority with ontological priority.

[16] See Mazzocco 1993: 136–8 for an account of the ideal situation imagined by Dante in 1.16–18. Although his position generally falls into the camp described in the previous note (140), he denies any real contradiction between the "vulgare," *illustre* or not, and *gramatica* (245 n 27). See also n 51.

[17] Marigo 1948: especially lxii–lxxvi; Dragonetti 1961b: especially 29–35, 45–52. For Corti 1981, 1993: chapter 4, whose work takes this thesis to its highest point, the *vulgare illustre* combines the naturalness of post-Babelic vernacular with the universality of regulated grammars to recapture the natural and universal quality of prelapsarian language, the product of "grammar" understood as an innate human faculty of language building (especially 59–60, 76; see also Stefano Rizzo 1969: 84–6). This position should be distinguished from the unfounded thesis of Stone 1994b (5). See Pagani 1982 for a useful, if polemical, review of the criticism on this point. An alternate position, which splits the difference between Marigo 1948 and Nardi 1921b, is in Pagliaro 1962, for whom the *vulgare illustre* is a non-ideal, historical entity, as Nardi asserts, but also a "grammar" that derives from the multiple vernaculars of Italian as Latin once did from its own unspecified vernacular (227–8). See also Vinay 1959: 247–8.

an empirically extant language (1.16.3). In conclusion, by comparing the *vulgare illustre* to the One from which the many derive, to the White which contains all colors within itself (16.2), and finally to the "simplicissima substantiarum" (simplest of substances), that is, to God vis-à-vis his creation (16.5), the "nos" who writes pushes this illustrious vernacular, figuratively if not rationally, beyond abstraction to transcendence.[18]

What supporters of *both* positions tend to reaffirm, however, is the need to find a logical continuity from one end of the book to the other, which defines in fairly schematic terms "what Dante thinks." Until recently, only Pier Vincenzo Mengaldo, who is responsible for the best critical edition and annotations of the treatise, had argued that the *De Vulgari Eloquentia* is shot through with "contraddizioni teoriche" (Mengaldo 1978a: 11; cf. 1970b and 1979) which are not susceptible to logical conciliation, and which can be held responsible for the contrasting interpretations of the work's structure (5; see also Vinay 1959: 272–3).[19] I take the further step of suggesting that those contradictions do have a logic, but that it is the logic not of a "truth," not of a coherent idea about language, but of a desire: Dante's impossible desire to reconcile historicity with ideality, and to appropriate for his vernacular the authority of Latin *gramatica*. In other words, at one point or another Dante does make arguments in favor of both

---

[18] Marigo 1948: lxxvii–lxxv; Mengaldo 1970b: 412; Shapiro 1990: 30, 32; *et al.* For the opposition, see Pagliaro 1962: 239–44, Mazzocco 1993. Mazzocco (especially 111–2, 126–9, 141–9) focuses on aspects of the initial description of the *simplicisissma signa* that bring the *vulgare illustre* closer to earthly realities, dismissing the analogy with God as limited and without metaphysical dimensions. As will appear, I disagree, believing that 1.16 deliberately hovers between the two possibilities. For further discussion of the *simplicisissma signa*, see Shapiro 1990: 147, 159–61.

[19] Subsequently, a number of critics, including myself (Ascoli 1991b), have both put the conflicts and contradictions in the foreground and pursued explanations which do not aim to "save the appearances." Battaglia Ricci 1983: pt. 1 and Barański 1986a (especially 55–63, 66–8) have stressed the dynamic, partial, experimental, and ultimately failed, place of *DVE* in the evolution of Dante's relationship to "plurilingualism" (the term derives from Contini 1964; see also Cambon 1966). Shapiro explores what is sometimes the tension between and sometimes the pacific coexistence of two projects corresponding to two different notions of *gramatica*: the practical rhetorical–poetic handbook (the tradition of *DVE* as "rhetorica Dantis") and a philosophical exploration of the nature of human language in general (e.g., 1990: 44–5, 133, 179). Cestaro (1991a; cf. 2003a: especially 52, 55–6) also argues that *DVE* is marked by two contrasting voices, one that of grammar (regulated, disciplined, masculine-patriarchal, corresponding to *both* types of *gramatica* discussed by Shapiro), the other as that of "poetry" (fluid, open, feminine). Finally, Mazzotta 1993a: 20–4 sees "poetry" in *DVE* as a comprehensive mode of knowledge by which Dante brings together aesthetics and epistemology, and at once fuses and critiques the usually disciplinary boundaries of the traditional liberal arts. The latter three play on the controversial, composite definition of poetry as "fictio rethorica musicaque poita" (2.4.2) discussed in Chapter 2, n 80. See also n 49. From a methodological point of view, however, the clearest difference of my approach from those of the latter three critics is the attempt: (1) to describe the treatise's dynamic, sequential deployment of carefully articulated rhetorical strategies; (2) to do this within the larger perspective of Dante's "quest for authority" (also in Chapter 2, section vi; Chapter 4, section iv).

positions – and the key to reading *De Vulgari Eloquentia* is to understand how he negotiates between them and to probe the motives that drive him to do so.

At the beginning of the treatise, vernacular in general is opposed to grammar on the following grounds: (1) the former is common to all people, while the latter is available only to a few populations and to few people within them; (2) the former is imbibed "sine omnia regula" (without any rules) at the breast of one's wet-nurse, while the latter is "regulated" and "artificial"; (3) the former is the language first used by humankind (i.e., the language of Adam and Eve was a vernacular), while the latter was apparently first invented much later, as a way of arresting the effects of the Babelic *confusio* (confusion of tongues; 1.1.2–5; cf. 1.9.11). In addition, at the level of image, Dante associates the vernacular with a "feminine" and childish innocence and fecundity – it is the language of "mulieres et parvuli" (women and little ones) and of the "nutricem" (wet-nurse) – as against the "maleness" of Latin (1.1.1–2; cf. Hollander 1975a: especially 120–3; Schnapp 1988; Cestaro 1991b, 1997, 2003a; Cornish 2000a). He thus deploys the terms of the gendered opposition of languages described by Walter Ong (1971), while apparently reversing the value system that usually governs it.

Much of what happens subsequently in the treatise creates logical confusion between the initially opposed terms, especially by shifting around their qualifying attributes and images, while nonetheless leaving in place the rhetorical priority assigned to vernacular. This confusion is greater because, after the initial opposition, Dante never returns to a systematic contrast between *vulgare* and *gramatica* in rigorous, philosophical terms (cf. Vinay 1959: 250). Nor does he ever explicitly attempt to reconcile or synthesize them. I do not believe, in fact, that the basic terms, *vulgare* and *gramatica*, are ever used again in exactly the same way as they are at the beginning – to signify the general classes of empirically extant vernacular and grammatical languages, rather than individual empirical instances of grammar or vernacular, on the one hand, or, perhaps, the mind's potentiality to generate such languages, on the other.[20] The one formal definition

[20] Cestaro (1991b: 53) distinguishes four senses in which *gramatica* can be understood in the Middle Ages, but then suggests no one of these can account for Dante's uses of the word. Lombardi (2000) distinguishes three primary meanings. More generally, as Ewert (1940) observed long ago (discussing the term "eloquentia"), "Dante uses his terms loosely, without attributing to each [one] . . . a meaning capable of being formulated in a single definition" (362). Cf. Mengaldo 1978a: 74; Scaglione 1988. As we will now see, much recent *DVE* criticism has debated whether the treatise plays upon the distinction between grammar as a practical liberal art and the philosophical study of language by "speculative grammarians" of the late thirteenth century (see n 21). See also n 4. See Chapter 2, nn 80, 83, for grammar in relation to the other curriculum *artes*.

of the term, "gramatica nichil aliud est quam quedam inalterabilis locutionis ydemptitas diversibus temporibus atque locis" (grammar is nothing less than a certain immutable identity of language in different times and places; 1.9.11), does not cover all of the specific uses and is seemingly contradicted by *Convivio* 2.13.9–10 (see n 4). In a sense, the criticism has been hyperconscious of the definitional problem, since interpretations almost always begin and end with a redefinition of the terms so as to support one position or the other, as we have already begun to see.[21] However, this does not recognize the lack of a systematic definition of terms as significant in itself, given Dante's obvious desire to assimilate his Latin prose to the exhaustive philosophical explications of Scholasticism, and thence to infer his deliberate concealment of insuperable contradictions in the argument.

The treatise does consistently invite attempts to look beyond the nominal continuity between *vulgare* and *vulgare illustre*. The search for the "illustrious vernacular" is carried out over the last half of book 1, with a review of the fourteen regional dialects of Italy. These are rated against one another, from the depths of Florentine and Roman to the heights of Bolognese, and are then judged, as a class, to be inferior to the true *vulgare illustre*, which is the language not of one region or city, but of all Italy (1.10.15). By itself, the reader's discovery that Dante thinks of most vernaculars as anything but *nobilior* constitutes a significant qualification on his opening assertion. Moreover, he makes it clear that this universal language of all Italians (1.16.3–6) is, like *gramatica*, actually used only by an elite few, namely that "*curia* in exile" mentioned previously (1.18.5). As Dante defines it, the *vulgare illustre*, however natural its origins, is well on its way to becoming a language of art and/or artifice. In book 1 this appears mostly in the use of

---

[21] As Pagani 1982 shows, the debate centers on two related controversies: (1) the opposition between vernacular and "grammar" and (2) the definition of the *vulgare illustre* vis-à-vis the first two categories The most important moment in the controversy, has been the series of attempts (by Marigo 1948; Dragonetti 1961b; Corti 1981, 1993: chapter 4; Shapiro 1990) to show that after 1.1 the definition of *gramatica* changes radically, referring to the "speculative grammar" of the *modistae* (Boethius of Dacia *et al.*) and the counter-balancing efforts to show it doesn't (Nardi 1921b: 183–4; Vinay 1959; Grayson 1965: 19–20; Mengaldo 1979: 79–80 nn; Pagani 1982). See Alessio 1984 for a judicious review of the evidence in favor of Dante's exposure to the theoretical grammarians. Shapiro (1990: 135) attempts to save the appearances by referring to "the movable meanings of *grammatica* [sic] as Latin, or systematic grammar, or both at once," the latter option covering five of six appearances of the word (also 149–51 and n, 164). She suggests convincingly that in the philosophical texts of Boethius of Dacia and his fellows grammar as philosophy of language props itself against the empirical grammar of Latin (1990: 146–7); that the *modistae* do not together represent a single, coherent point of view (1990: 176); and that Dante adapts their categories to his own purposes. Lombardi (2000) denies that Dante ever uses *gramatica* to signify the general faculty for language production, but puts his linguistic writings into a productive relationship with the idea of *syntax* developed by the *modistae*. Finally, Cestaro (2003a: chapters 1–2) convincingly places Dante in relation to another relevant tradition, the iconography of Lady Grammar personified.

examples from self-conscious poets, who may or may not be imitating the rules of grammar in constructing their language, and from the connection to an intellectual elite. Book 2, then, explicitly offers the formalization of a highly regulated art (especially 2.3–4 and 9–11), which deliberately imitates Latin *gramatica* (1.10.1, 2; 2.4.3 and 9–11, 6.7; cf. 2.8.6–7, 11.12; see Mengaldo 1978a: 36, 71–5; but cf. n 55).

Finally, while Dante scrupulously avoids reusing the key terms of the opening opposition in his definition of the *vulgare illustre*, especially *naturalis* and *artificialis*, as if to leave the logical relationship between the two moments as obscure as possible, his marked use of gendered imagery in characterizing the panther shows that a reversal has taken place. The *vulgare illustre* is said throughout to be the language, not of family, females, and infancy, but rather of the "patria," the fatherland. Early on he mocks the citizens of the generically provincial Petramala who think that their "maternam locutionem" (mother tongue) is the most delightful in the world (1.6.2). Later, after highlighting the gendered character of language by criticizing two regional vernaculars for making women sound like men and vice-versa (1.14.2–5), Dante specifically celebrates the one Romagnolo he knows who has turned "a materno ad curiale vulgare" (from his mother tongue . . . [to] a vernacular worthy of the court; 1.14.7). In other words, he specifically rejects the "female" quality of the vernacular which he earlier valued. It comes as no surprise later on that he designates the *vulgare illustre* as patriarchal "paterfamilias" (1.18.1), or that the selection of words suitable for use in the highest, tragic, style of the *vulgare illustre* involves the rejection of "puerilia" and "muliebra" and the acceptance of "virilia" (2.7.2).[22]

The logical result of these displacements would be to move the *vulgare illustre* from the camp of vernacular in general into that of *gramatica*, as some critics have tried to argue. But since Dante does not work the question out logically, but rather rhetorically, that is, implicitly and imaginatively, in the service of other ends, the effect is simply additive. As already suggested (n 17), the *vulgare illustre* keeps the qualities of Edenic naturalness and universality with which it began, while adding those of a rational and exclusive

---

[22] On this passage, see also Cestaro 1991b: 71–2. The implications for more developed readings of *DVE* and other Dantean works in terms of the "cultural construction of gender" are obvious, as, again, Cestaro (1991b; 1997; 2003a) has demonstrated. In this connection note also the rejection of Eve as originator of language on grounds of her femaleness (1.2.6, 4.2) and the insistence that Adam, who does found human speech, is "vir sine matre, vir sine lacte" (1.6.1) (Cestaro 1991b: 58–9, 74–6; cf. n 57). For discussions of gendered language in the *DC* see Noferi 1982–3: 68–70, 84–8; Jacoff 1987: 172–3; Schnapp 1988; and, especially, Cestaro 2003a. See also Cornish 2000a. Ferguson 2003 (especially 87–8, 125–9) places Dante near the historical beginnings of a gendered discourse concerning "national" vernaculars in early modern Europe.

artfulness. The reason for this apparently disingenuous procedure can be found in the chapters that lead from *vulgare* vs. *gramatica* to *vulgare illustre*: specifically in Dante's obvious desire to further legitimate the vernacular by placing it within the economy of salvation history, especially two founding linguistic events recorded in *Genesis* – the invention of language in Eden and the dispersal of that original tongue into multiple languages at the Babelic *confusio* (nn 32 and 34)

Dante's reflections on the history of language are prefaced by a consideration of human speech in the abstract, particularly its role in communicating ideas by sensory means between individuals who would otherwise be entirely isolated from one another, constituting each, as it were, "sua propria specie" ([a species unto oneself]; 1.3.1). Against this dispersive, antisocial tendency built into human nature, Dante imagines God as having created "certam formam locutionis" (a certain form of language; 1.6.4) at the same moment that Adam was brought into being, which in turn gave rise to the invention of human communication, in the exchange between the first man and his Maker (cf. Chapter 7, n 121). However, Dante depicts the subsequent history of human language as one of linguistic fragmentation and isolation. The pivotal and emblematic event in this process is the Babelic *confusio*, which produces the shift from a single (vernacular) language common to all (Hebrew, again) to an ever-increasing dispersal and variety of tongues (1.8–9).[23]

Dante specifically presents Babel as a surrogate of the Fall of humankind and the loss of Paradise. It comes as the culmination of a series of three instances of human presumption and degradation: the Fall itself, the Flood, and now the building of the Tower. It is explicitly tied to the transgressive pride of Eve, itself a linguistic sin, as Dante specifies, because based upon her conversations with the serpent (1.7.3–4; cf. 4.2), and to the exile of humankind from the original "patria," Eden (1.7.2). Most important, for my purposes, it is described as being the fruit of sinful human *nature* ("O semper natura nostra prona peccatis!" [O human nature, always inclined towards sin; 1.7.2]), and the attempt of humanity "arte sua non solum superare naturam sed etiam ipsum naturantem, qui Deus est" (to outdo in skill [art] not only nature but the source of its own nature, who is

---

[23] For the Babel story in the Middle Ages, see Borst 1957–63; Copeland 1991: 213–18. Critics who have discussed its importance in *DVE* include: D'Ovidio 1931; Dragonetti 1961: especially 36–8; Corti 1978 (but see n 34); Barański 1989a: 106–8, cf. 119–25; Shapiro 1990: 9–10 *et passim*; Cestaro 1991b: especially 58–63; Mazzotta 1993a: 20; Mazzocco 1993: especially 159–65; Steinberg 1999: chapter 5; Lombardi 2000. My own contribution consists in placing 1.7.4–8 in the rhetorical, conceptual, and "libidinal" economy of the treatise as a whole, as well as in specific points raised in nn 52, 60.

God; 1.7.4). Babel thus adds a key dimension to the art/nature opposition that at once clarifies and complicates its application in the case of the *vulgare* and *gramatica*. On the one hand, the asserted superiority of natural vernacular to artificial grammar finds an implicit grounding in this traditional critique of Nimrod's aspiration to raise human art to cosmic heights. On the other hand, postlapsarian nature itself is presented as an equivocal category and, in particular, *human* nature is shown to be irremediably corrupted.

That corruption, it will soon appear, plays itself out in the history of language consequent to the tertiary fall of Babel. Moreover, while these post-Babelic effects are not specifically assigned to "our sinful nature," they *are* attributed to the fact that humanity is "instabilissimum et variabilissimum animal" (a highly unstable and variable animal; 1.9.6), a characterization that any medieval Christian would have seen as dating from the Fall. A *de facto* reversal of the opening claims has thus taken place – the vernacular continues to be "natural," but now it is the corrupt nature of the postlapsarian world, while its universality is maintained only in the deeply ironic form of a universal linguistic dispersal.

At this point *gramatica* reenters the picture in a very different guise:

Hinc [the variations in human language across time and space] moti sunt inventores gramatice facultatis: que quidem gramatica nichil aliud est quam quedam inalterabilis locutionis ydemptitas diversibus temporibus atque locis. (1.9.11)

(This was the point from which the inventors of the [faculty] of grammar began; for their *gramatica* is nothing less than a certain immutable identity of language [speech] in different times and places.)

The affirmation of grammar's, that is, Latin's, power to arrest the Babelic dispersal, taken with two subsequent references that serve to transfer the prestige of grammar to the Italian vernacular and its authors,[24] implies a second way to see the application of artifice to language: not just as another sign of Babelic presumption, but also as a necessary *reparatio* against the

---

[24] These are found in 10.1.1 and 2. The sense of both passages is disputed both as to the actual meaning of *gramatica* and as to the relationship, genetic or otherwise, subsisting between "Latin" and "Italian" (see nn 29–30; cf. nn 15, 17, 20, 21). In favor of the derivation of the Romance vernaculars from Latin is Paratore 1968; *sed contra*: Mazzocco 1993: 173–6. On the typical medieval view of the (non-genetic) relationship between the two tongues see Silvia Rizzo 1990: 7–9 and nn. More generally on the question of whether the *vulgare* of "sì" derives from Latin *gramatica* or whether *gramatica* is itself derived from a *vulgare* not unlike Italian, see D'Ovidio 1876: 84; Pagliaro 1962: 227–8; Vinay 1959: 243–55; Grayson 1965: especially 10–12; Mengaldo 1978a: 70–1; Pagani 1982: e.g., 104; Tavoni 1984; Alessio 1995. One thing is clear: that Dante continues to see the two terms, vernacular and grammar, and the two tongues, Italian and Latin, in close relationship to one another, as he trades on the cultural prestige of Latin to bolster his case for the illustrious vernacular.

corrupting effects of fallen nature and of the fallen human will. This argument is not made explicit in *De Vulgari Eloquentia*, although, as will be suggested in Chapter 7, section iii, it can be inferred from Marco Lombardo's analogous discussion of free will in *Purgatorio* 16. In that canto, which addresses a basic point of Christian doctrine, Dante has Marco assert the necessity of placing imperial and ecclesiastical authorities over the fallen will which can no longer be trusted to choose the good "naturally."

De Vulgari Eloquentia thus opens onto a vertiginous dialectic of supplementation, according to which, on the one hand, "nature" is the only answer to the presumption of Nimrod's art, and, on the other, "art" is the only corrective to postlapsarian nature (Derrida 1967: 141–69; cf. Ascoli 1987: 196 and n). In the face of this particular *contraddizione teorica*,[25] Dante turns to the image of a *vulgare illustre* that, like *gramatica*, partially reverses the Babelic dispersal, but also, imperceptibly and illogically, blends together nature and art in one language (cf. Di Capua 1945: 39; Corti 1981: 59–61; especially Dragonetti 1961b: 31–5). By inventing a transcendent and synchronic origin for the Italian vernaculars in the ideality of a quasi-divine "simplicissima substantiarum," Dante tacitly displaces their historical, diachronic original, the "ydioma tripharium" (tripartite language; 1.8.2: cf. 8.5)[26] out of the flow of history, only to reinstate it later, as we shall see, through the language of the *curia* in exile and through his own poetry.

It should now be evident that the first critical position outlined above, which sees the *vulgare illustre* as the logical and/or historical product of the original definition of vernacular in general, cannot be maintained. Nor can the second, which assimilates the *vulgare illustre* to *gramatica*, unless *gramatica* is redefined in such a way as to logically accommodate art and nature, historicity and transcendence. It is this latter feat, however, that Corti claimed to have achieved in her influential study, *Dante a un nuovo crocevia* (1981; see also 1993), which aims to give historical and textual substance to an argument first advanced by Rajna (1921) and Marigo (1948), later developed by Dragonetti (1961b; cf. Pagani 1982: 39–86).

In brief, the argument runs that, in addition to the intertwined meanings of *gramatica* as any empirical rule-governed speech (cf. 1.1.3) and as one such in particular, i.e., Latin, Dante introduces a third and for him more

---

[25] Mengaldo 1978a: 74, 77, notes the ambiguity in Dante's use of the term *ars* both positively and negatively. Cf. Vinay 1959: 247–8; Grayson 1965: 20. See also n 29; Chapter 2, n 50.

[26] Mengaldo 1979: 71–2 n 5 observes a slide in Dante's use of this term – first it refers to a tongue that ramified into Northern European, Southern European, and Greek (1.8.2); then the one that ramifies into the vernaculars of "oc," "oil," and "sì" (1.8.5; 9.2).

decisive sense, taken from the speculative grammars of radical Aristotelians such as Siger of Brabant and, especially, Boethius of Dacia.[27] "Grammar" in this sense refers not to a language, or to a positive set of rules for language use, but instead to the natural and innate human faculty for the creation of languages. For Corti, it is this structuring potentiality, rather than a specific language, that Dante says was "co-created" with Adam, and subsequently rediscovered by the "inventores gramatice facultatis" (inventors of the faculty [art] of grammar; 1.9.11 [Corti 1981: especially 38–9, 60, 76 and 1993: 100–2; Shapiro 1990: especially 149–50]). This potentiality provides the key to generating an ideal language, at once transcendent *langue* and immanent *parole*, that fuses the universality and naturalness of vernacular with the immutability and order of "grammar" in the first sense, that of a specific language. It thus permits the revival of the qualities inherent to Adam's prelapsarian, pre-Babelic language (Dragonetti 1961b; Hollander 1975a: 120; Corti 1981: especially 46–56, and 1993: 107–12; Brownlee 1984: 601; Shapiro 1990: especially 27–9). The language in question, of course, is the *vulgare illustre*.

Nonetheless, important problems dog Corti's discovery of a subterranean logic of speculative grammar that bridges the gap between vernacular and *gramatica* as Dante initially defines them.[28] For example, each of her three most important examples of what she believes to be technical language taken from the *modistae*, namely the phrases "inventores gramatice facultate,"[29]

---

[27] Marigo 1948: lvii–lxii; Dragonetti 1961b: 40–1; Corti 1981: especially chapter 2 and 1993: chapter 4; Shapiro 1990. Shapiro (especially 136–49) gives a useful, digested description of the philosophical approach to grammar as articulated by Boethius of Dacia and company, along with ample citations of the scholarship on speculative grammar to that date (begin with Bursill-Hall 1971). She also presents terms she believes Dante shares with the *modistae* (149–69), not always persuasively. Cf. Cestaro 2003a: especially 12–13; Lombardi 2000.

[28] Pagani 1982: 253–73; see also Scaglione 1988: 33–6; Mazzotta 1993a: 20. The principal problems are that: (1) Dante never, in *DVE* or elsewhere, makes explicit the distinction that Corti finds implied throughout the treatise; (2) in *DVE gramatica* refers unequivocally to Latin or "regular" languages generally on a number of occasions (1.1.3; 1.11.7; 2.7.6), while all proof texts for the presence of "speculative grammar" can also be interpreted coherently if the other reading is adopted (1.9.11; 10.1, 2; cf. 1.6.4, 7); (3) even assuming that the "radical Aristotelians" are Dante's "source" she does not take into account that Dante might use their terminology in a new way (as instead do Alessio 1984; Shapiro 1990; Lombardi 2000). See also nn 21, 29–32, 34, 56.

[29] Corti argues that the "inventores gramatice facultatis" of 1.9.11 are the philosophical originators of language in general (whose "grammar" is that of natural vernaculars as well as languages of art), while the "gramatice positores" of 1.10.1 are those who explicitly codify the rules of this or that particular "grammar" (1981: 37–8, 1993: 100–2, developing Marigo 1948: lxi n 2; see also Alessio 1984: 86–7; Shapiro 1990: 28–9, 162–4; compare the critique of Grayson 1965: 5). However, Dante does not place the *inventores* and the *positores* in a logical opposition, but rather leaves them in ambiguous proximity where they could also be understood as synonyms (cf. Vinay 1959: 252–4). Moreover, he later uses the term *inventores* (i.e., "omnes cantionum inventores"; 2.13.6), so that those referred to are not the discoverers of *langue* (the form of *cantio* in general), but the producers of *parole* (authors

"gramatice que communis est,"[30] and "certam formam locutionem"[31] are arguably easier to interpret if one assumes that the "gramatica" or "locutio" in question refers to an historical extent form of speech (Latin or, in the last case, Hebrew). The biggest obstacle to her thesis, however, is that it virtually ignores an element centrally present in Dante's treatise which is at odds with the theories of the speculative grammarians and which would make the identification of the *vulgare illustre* with Adamic speech not only logically impossible, but also a clear instance of idolatrous pride: the Fall and its linguistic repetition in the Babelic *confusio*.[32] The intrusion of history, and specifically of those events that determine the nature of postlapsarian historicity – the contingency and corruption of both the

of individual *canzoni*). The form of "invenire" used in close proximity to the contested reference ("quicquid redactum est sive inventum ad vulgare prosaycum"; 10.1.2) also designates makers of extant objects, as do the other uses of the verb in *DVE* (especially 2.9.2; cf. 1.11.4). A possible middle usage of the word *inventores* available to Dante, though not used in his etymological discussion of *autorità*, is Hugutio's definition of the *autores* from *autentin* as "inventores artium," i.e., as those who founded, or discovered, intellectual arts. Dante does seem to echo Hugutio's phrasing at *CV* 4.8.7: "secondo lo cercamento e *la invenzione che ha fatto l'umana ragione con l'altre sue arti*, lo diametro del corpo del sole è cinque volte quanto quello de la terra . . ." [cf. 4.11.7]), thus pointing to *inventio* as "artistic" *praxis* rather than as *theoria*. That the equation *inventores/auctores* was a medieval topos is documented by Silvia Rizzo 1990: 8–9, with the further implication that what the *auctores* "invented" were specific *gramatice*, like Latin, rather than a general philosophy of language (cf. 12 n 15). On the force of "arte" see also n 25; Chapter 2, n 50; poetry defined as "arte musaica" in *CV* 4.6.4 (Chapter 2, n 80); *DVE* 2.9.2, which states that a single stanza contains the "whole art" of the *canzone*.

30　Corti interprets the "gramatice que communis est" in 1.10.2 as the capacity for creating language common to all humans, rather than as a shared etymological relationship, genetic or not (see n 24), of all three Romance languages to Latin grammar (also Shapiro 1990: 162–3). The passage is as easily interpreted in one way as another, and thus the former interpretation depends heavily on how convincing her reading of "inventores gramatice facultatis" is (see n 29; cf. Corti 1981: 61–3; Shapiro 1990: 28 and n 54, 146–9, 162–4).

31　The "certam formam locutionem" (1.6.4) given by God to Adam can be seen as either the abstract power to invent languages (Corti 1981: 47, 1993: 88–91; Shapiro 1990: 162–4), or a specific language, i.e., Hebrew (Mengaldo 1970b: 404; Mazzocco 1993: 160; Imbach 1996: 207). By then singling out Hebrew as the "language of grace" (1.6.7) and by omitting any reference to the naming of animals (which might evince Adam's "invention" of language; cf. n 57), Dante points to the latter alternative. Only 1.6.7 ("fuit ergo hebraicum ydioma illud quod primi loquentis labia fabricarunt") offers strong evidence for the first (Corti 1981: 49–50). Cf. Ewert 1940: 359.

32　Shapiro 1990: 162–3 does not see this problem. For her, the Babelic fall compromises only empirical instances of language and not the faculty for generating them. In fact, she implies, Babel is the source of one of the basic premises of the *modistae*, namely the arbitrariness of human signification. But this explanation leaves open the question of what effect the Fall and/or Babel may have had on said language-making faculty (as it did on both the will and the intellect, through which such a faculty surely operates; see section iii). Could it be that the fallen version of a shared human capacity for inventing linguistic structures leads to the Babelic multiplication of languages rather than to the unifying, anti-Babelic phenomenon of a *vulgare illustre*? Or at least that this capacity lends itself neutrally to either multiplication or unification? In the terms of Dante's text, one of the latter two options must be the case. Thus Shapiro's defense of Corti actually undermines the critic's most important claims about what a modistic idea of grammar might be doing in *DVE*. (N.B., at 179 she adopts a seemingly different position.)

human mind and its linguistic products – disrupts the proto-structuralist ideal of a transcendent *langue* that generates immanent *parole*.[33] As Dante knew very well, and Corti too for that matter, the historicizing of language at the Fall and at Babel is what makes it impossible to recover any truly "natural and universal" *forma locutionis* without passing through the fallen *parole* of historical languages and specific individuals,[34] in this case, as we shall see, of one individual's language.

In the end, Corti's structuralist and/or Averroist reading of the *vulgare illustre* does find partial justification in Dante's claim that this language is not immanently present in any of Italy's myriad municipal dialects but is instead the transcendent template upon which all Italian dialects are modeled. Her reading, and even more Dragonetti's (1961b: especially 44–6; cf. Marigo 1948: lxxv) and Shapiro's (1990), are in tune with the ideal, trans-historical imagery that envelopes the "cardinal, courtly, curial, illustrious vernacular."[35] On the other hand, it is said to have had an historical existence in an Italian imperial court (that of Frederick II [1.12.3–5]) and to sustain the continuing present possibility of one (1.18.2–3; cf. Pagani 1982: 246–7). This possibility, though not realized now, is also not purely ideal: instead it exists but only, as it were, in exile, on a pilgrimage, among the lowly and throughout the Italian peninsula (also Shapiro 1990: especially 194):

[N]ostrum illustre velut acola perigrinatur et in humilibus hospitatem asilis, cum aula vacemus (1.18.3).

([O]ur illustrious vernacular wanders around like a homeless stranger finding hospitality in humbler homes – because we have no court.)

---

[33] Corti 1981 does not explicitly invoke the Saussurian model, but her description of the relationship between the language-producing faculty and the empirical instances of language makes it obvious. Moreover, she argues that the radical Aristotelian, or Averroist, notion of language runs parallel to, and is a consequence of, the opposition between impersonal "possible intellect" and the practical exercise of intelligence by individuals (cf. 48, 66). Ironically, Corti's account derives from Bruno Nardi's reading of Dantean Averroism (see Chapters 5 [especially n 27] and 6), although Nardi himself (1921b) saw the *vulgare illustre* as a radically historical language.

[34] Although Corti 1978 is aware of the novelty of Dante's representation of Babel (see nn 23, 39), in her 1981 account of its place in the treatise she first skips over it as a formal bow to a theocentric culture (40–1, 46). Critics are divided over how committed Dante is in *DVE* to the theology implied by his references to Eden and Babel. For example, Pagani (1982: chapter 4) and Shapiro (e.g., 1990: 15, 24 [but cf. 159 and see again n 32]) share Corti's dismissive stance; while Mengaldo 1978a: 61, 1979: especially 5, thinks theological concerns are preeminent. The Babel typology is also a stumbling block for Nardi's claim that the *vulgare illustre* is a sheerly historical, political entity – as can be seen in Pagani's efforts to discredit Mengaldo's anti-Nardian position. In other words, the "negative theology" of Babel prevents conceiving of the *vulgare illustre* either in sheerly contingent and historical or in purely rational and ideal terms.

[35] As noted earlier, in its non-local unity, it is compared to God as "simplicissima substantiarum" (16.5). Furthermore, Dante figures it as a "panther," an animal glossed in the bestiaries as a figure of Christ (cf. 1.16.1 and Mengaldo 1979: 126–7 n; Smarr 1986: 112–15 and nn), the ubiquity of whose perfumed breath, "ubique et necubi" (1.16.1), mirrors a defining quality of the transcendent God. On the importance of hunting symbolism in *DVE*, see Boccassini 2003: 339–40.

In its exile, the *vulgare illustre* echoes and repeats the primal exile which, as Dante recalls earlier in *De Vulgari Eloquentia*, is the essential experience of postlapsarian existence, and which the Babelic dispersal itself repeated ("exulabas a patria" [you . . . live in exile from . . . your homeland; 1.7.2; cf. 1.7.3–4]).

What then to do if neither a historicist nor an idealist accounting of the *vulgare illustre* can successfully reduce its complexities and its contradictions, and if no logical path can be found to square it with the initial opposition of *vulgare* to *gramatica*? The answer, again, is that the movement of *De Vulgari Eloquentia* follows its attempt to reconcile the contingent necessities of historical reality, that is, of a burgeoning vernacular culture in early Trecento Italy, with culturally mandated definitions of poetic *auctoritas* as impersonal, ancient, and non-vernacular (i.e., Latin), in order to satisfy Dante's desire for an oxymoronically personal authority. Its elisions, contradictions, and ambiguities are thus products of a complex rhetorical strategy that must collapse the opposition between vernacular and grammar, Dante and the Latin *auctores*, without admitting that it is doing so and thereby discrediting itself. The value of Corti's work is to have identified the desire for a language whose authority transcends historicity, and with it individuality – but what it omits is the recognition that, in the terms of *De Vulgari Eloquentia*, as in those of *Convivio*, such a transcendence can be imagined, and even rhetorically asserted, but it can never truly be achieved.

III. INDIVIDUALITY AND UNIVERSALITY

Having tried to confront the problem of the *vulgare illustre*, as it were, from inside the logical and detached perspective of the analytical prose *nos*, it is worth asking some more probing questions about what the other Dante, the "friend of Cino," has at stake *qua* individual vernacular author and how those stakes make themselves felt in the rhetorical unfolding of *De Vulgari Eloquentia*. The problem is, however, that this treatise is as careful to avoid bringing Dante's status *qua* poet within the confines of its explicit, rationalizing, meditations as book 1 of *Convivio* was, while it is far *less* open than the other work in confronting other dubious aspects of his vernacular authorship. Still, just as book 4's apparently objective and impersonal philosophical meditations on *auctoritas* and *nobilitas* prove to have a crucial bearing on Dante himself, so here the abstract opposition of universality vs. individuality, which plays a key role in the definition and defense of the vernacular language, gradually opens onto the problematic situation of

Dante as individual author and of the language which is finally proper to him alone.[36]

Book I of *Convivio* stresses the personal, familial, and individual quality of Dante's attachment to the otherwise inferior vernacular, to the point of implying some identification between the two, which is in keeping with its earlier exploration of the problematics of authorial self-representation. Here, both the *vulgare* in general and the *vulgare illustre* in particular are remarkable for possessing a universality that is specified as the opposite of individuality. The *vulgare* in general is presented as the tongue which "totus orbis ipsa perfruitur" ([is employed by] the whole world; 1.1.4) as against the "locutio secundaria" (secondary speech) in which "ad habitum vero huius pauci perveniunt" (few . . . achieve complete fluency; 1.1.3). The only elements of "familiarity" in this redefinition of the vernacular are the references to its origins in the imitation of one's "nutricem" (1.1.2) and to its use even by "parvuli et mulieres" (1.1.1). And because these characteristics are assumed to be common to all human beings, and are not specifically connected to Dante himself, they too simply serve to emphasize the vernacular's universality.

The *vulgare illustre* gathers the individual dialects of the Italian peninsula into a single language, the many into the one:

Que quidem nobilissima sunt earum que latinorum sunt actiones, hec nullius civitatis Ytalie propria sunt, et in omnibus communia sunt. (16.4)

([T]he most noble actions among those performed by Italians are proper to no one Italian city, but are common to them all.)

This idea that it is a universal ("common to all") not an individual ("proper to none") language is repeatedly stressed (cf. 1.16. 4 and 6; 18.2), culminating in the assertion that it is to be found "ubique et necubi," like God, everywhere and nowhere (1.16.2).[37]

As with the vernacular/grammar relationship, a key to understanding the dialectic of individuality and universality is Dante's retelling of the Babel

---

[36] See Corti 1981: especially 56–70, on what is at stake for Dante in this opposition. See also Cestaro 1991b: especially 59–65, 69–70. Luzzi 1998 uses the term "individuality" in an extratextual, potentially anachronistic, sense, while placing *DVE* in a line of creative autobiography stretching from *VN* to *Purg.* 30–31. Mengaldo earlier emphasized the "autobiographical" and "auto-exegetical" aspects of the treatise (e.g., 1970b: 407, 1978a: 12–13, 1979: 3).

[37] The structural relationship between the "universal" *vulgare illustre* and the multiplicity of regional, municipal, district, familial and personal vernaculars closely resembles the dialectic of "procession and return" from the Creating One to the created many, and back again, that characterizes the Christianized neo-Platonism of Dante (Durling and Martinez 1990: especially 15–19; also Mazzeo 1960). While the structure translated into the linguistic domain may have an orthodox analogue and precedent, however, for the reasons offered here, Dante is not able to present it overtly.

story (cf. Corti 1981: 56). The pertinence of Babel to the thematics of individuality and universality in language is evident. Like Eve in her abusive colloquy with the serpent, which led to the definitive act of corrupted and corrupting will, Nimrod personally embodies the presumption of humanity asserting autonomy from, even superiority to, its creator (1.4.2–3, 6.4, 7.3–4). The radically isolating individualism of such willful disobedience is then expressed in the "confusion of tongues," which in its logical extreme leads to a chaotic one person–one language equation which *De Vulgari Eloquentia* only implies, but which explicitly appears in Dante's depiction of Nimrod in *Inferno* 31.77–81:

> [Q]uesti è Nembrotto per lo cui mal coto
> pur un linguaggio nel mondo non s'usa.
>   Lascianlo stare e non parliamo a voto;
> ché cosí è a ciascun linguaggio
> come 'l suo ad altrui, ch'a nullo è noto.

(That is Nimrod, because of whose evil thought the world no longer speaks one language. Let us leave him alone and not waste speech, for to him every language is like his to others, unknown.)[38]

In the version of the story told in *De Vulgari Eloquentia*, Nimrod's proud individualism is also the focal point, but the punishment stops short of its logical conclusion. Instead Dante offers an innovative account of the punishment by professional groups that worked on the Tower:[39]

Solis etenim in uno convenientibus actu eadem loquela remansit: puta cunctis architectoribus una, cunctis saxa volventibus una . . . et sic de singulis operantibus accidit. Quot quot autem exercitii varietates tendebant ad opus, tot tot ydiomatibus tunc genus humanum disiungitur; et quanto excellentius exercebant, tanto rudius nunc barbariusque locuntur. (1.7.7)

(Only among those who were engaged in a particular activity did their language remain unchanged; so, for instance, there was one for all the architects, one for all the carriers of stones . . . and so on for all the different operations. As many as were the types of work involved in the enterprise, so many were the languages by

---

[38] Among critics who have signaled the Babel–Nimrod link between *DVE* and *Inf.* 31 are Dragonetti 1961b: 24–6; Cambon 1966: 39–40; Dronke 1986: 38; Shoaf 1988: 158–60; cf. Barański 1989a: 119–24; Benfell 1992; Imbach 1996: 210–13; Lombardi 2000. See Hollander (1975a: especially 118–21), Yowell 1986; Barański 1989a: 106–12; Lombardi 2000 for other echoes of *DVE* and Babel in *Inf.* Mazzotta 2001 shows a contrastive echoing of *DVE*'s review of municipal vernaculars through the matching up of sins of fraud with specific cities in lower Hell.

[39] Cf. D'Ovidio 1931; Pagliaro 1962: 224–5; Stefano Rizzo 1969: 70, 84; Mengaldo 1979: 61–2 n 5; Shapiro 1990: 9–10, 192–3; Durling 1992: 30–2.

which the human race was fragmented; and the more skill required for the type of work, the more rudimentary and barbaric the language they now spoke.)

Just which "guild" spoke the language that became Italian is not mentioned, although the text later gives a subtle hint at a solution to the crux (n 52). Similarly, it will become clearer further along just why Dante does not explicitly arrive at the ultimate Babelic equation of one person to one language here, even though as sole head of the project, Nimrod would have no fellows in his speech.

Throughout the text, in any case, Dante stresses that the tertiary Fall of Babel creates a historical situation where the *dispersio* and variety of dialects approach as a limit a condition of radical individuality and incommunicability. Every little town, each Petramala, thinks its "proprium vulgare" is the best way of speaking (1.6.2). The post-Babelic world houses an ever-widening series of divisions and subdivisions of languages and dialects – from the three European language groups, to the three southern European languages, to the fourteen regional dialects of "sì" – culminating in the thousands of sub-vernaculars of the Italian peninsula, where even citizens of a single city may speak radically different tongues (1.9.4–5) and where each family may have its own vernacular (1.19.3).

The problematic linking of language and individual will in the treatise does not only come from the traditional doctrinal associations of the Fall with the corruption of the will and of Babel with the Fall. The role of the will both in shaping and corrupting language is taken as an explicit focus throughout the treatise and first of all in the philosophical definition given to language near its beginning. Dante explains why human beings alone among God's creatures need to use language:

[H]omo non nature instinctu, sed ratione moveatur, et ipsa ratio vel circa discretionem vel circa iudicium vel circa electionem diversificetur in singulis, adeo ut fere quilibet sua propria specie videatur gaudere. (1.3.1)

([H]uman beings are moved not by their natural instinct, but by reason, and . . . that reason takes diverse forms in individuals, according to their capacity for discrimination, judgment, and choice, to the point where it appears that almost everyone enjoys the existence of [a species unto himself])

The hybrid nature of humans, as corporeal and sensual creatures who are also rational, makes them so different from one another ("in singulis") in their judgments and choices that without a common vehicle of communication the gap between them will be such that each individual becomes, as noted earlier, like a distinct species. That vehicle is the linguistic sign, whose composite character, at once rational and sensible, matches humanity's dual nature – translating intellectual concepts into a sensual medium from which they can be retranslated by another person (1.3.1).

Thus, language is a necessary remedy for the limits of individual human reason. And based on the three aspects of rational activity specified (*discretio, iudicium, electio*), what makes language particularly necessary is the human characteristic of choice guided by knowledge – the arbitrariness of human individuality which is the *sine qua non* of our free will ("arbitrium").[40] In addition, language itself is subject to the rational will: "in quantum aliquid significare videtur ad placitum" ([inasmuch as something is signified at the pleasure of the speaker]; 1.3.3), that is, by the choice, or even the whim, of the one who uses it (Nardi 1921b: 174–5 and 186–7; Pagliaro 1962: 223–4; Stefano Rizzo 1969: 84; Shapiro 1990: 158–9). Language is for Dante, as many critics have noticed over the years, fundamentally a social phenomenon, whose primary task is to transcend the arbitrariness of the free exercise of individual will and reason unchecked by community.[41] Moreover, and this point is crucial for understanding the limits of Dante's claims to stand objectively outside his subject, the use of language binds reason to the will and to the world of corporeal contingency, and thus continuously subjects it to individuality and historicity (cf. Pagliaro 1962: especially 219).

Dante's description of the post-Babelic linguistic situation returns to the problem of the individual will, assigning it explicit responsibility for the *confusio*. Dante traces out the fate of a post-Babelic language. From its pre-Fall unity ("unum . . . a principio confusionis" [this language was once unitary, at the time of the primal confusion; 1.9.2]) it was "a nostra beneplacito reparata" after Babel ([repaired according to our will]; 1.9.6), and subsequently divided into many tongues which "per locorum temporumque distantias variari opportet" (must vary according to distances of space and time; 1.9.6–7). Responsibility for the dispersal is assigned to humankind, that "most unstable, most changeable animal" (1.9.6), and specifically to the changes in "mores et habitus" (manners and customs) born of "humanis beneplacitis" ([human will]; 1.9.10). Here too human "beneplacitus," or assertion of will, is responsible both for (re)constituting language and for subjecting it to individual whims.

---

[40] On *arbitrium* in *DVE*, see D'Ovidio 1876: 83; and especially Nardi 1921b: 186–7. On the importance of *discretio*, i.e., the discriminating action of the rational will, see Di Capua 1945: 53–80; Dragonetti 1961b: 65. For relevant definitions of *discrezione*, see *CV* 1.11.3–4, 4.8.1; and for *elezione* as the basis of ethical virtue, see 4.17–18. On the general problem of the mediation between reason and will through the closely related categories of *iudicium* (*giudizio*) and *arbitrium*, see Kahn 1983. For additional considerations on the problem of the will and of judgment in Dante, see Chapters 5–7.

[41] Cf. Di Capua 1945: especially 35–9; Dragonetti 1961b: 13–14; Pagliaro 1962; Corti 1978: 251–6.

At this juncture, Dante makes his claim that the regulated, unvarying language of grammar was invented specifically to ward off the harm done by the will ("arbitrio") of individuals:

Adinvenerunt ergo illam ne, propter variationem sermonis *arbitrio singularium fluitantis*, vel nullo modo vel saltim imperfecte antiquorum actingeremus *autoritates* et gesta. (1.9.11)

(So those who devised this language did so lest, through changes in language dependent on the arbitrary judgment of individuals, we should become either unable, or, at best, only partially able, to enter into contact with the deeds and authoritative writings [*autoritates*] of the ancients . . .)

In light of all that has been said about the nature of *auctoritas*, it is not surprising that this impersonal language, free from the arbitrary judgment of willful individuals, should be the chosen vehicle for gaining access to the ancient *auctoritates*.

By now it is clear why Dante presents his discourse on the vernacular as disinterestedly and impersonally as possible and avoids the impression that the language he is discussing could be in any sense a product of his own efforts or identifiable with his poetic *oeuvre*: why, in other words, he omits the apologetics of *Convivio* 1 from this treatise. In Dante's own terms, language which is the product of individual will, the "property" of a personal author, risks duplicating the uncommunicative isolation which punished the presumption of those who built Babel. Thus, if he is to assert himself as author, it is only through the oblique device of making himself, in objectified, third-person form, into the humble exemplar and representative of a language that is radically impersonal. If he does not take the vernacular on this detour outside of history and personality on the way to reappropriating it as his own personal and historical instrument, readers might suspect that rather than Dante being authorized by the illustrious vernacular, the illustrious vernacular is itself the creature of Dante's writing.

We have seen that Dante's main effort in defining the universal "panther" is to stress its transcendence and thus to remove it from the flow of post-Babelic history. We can now see that this also exempts it from concomitant subjection to the *arbitrium* of individuals. Even when he does restore it to a qualified historical existence, it becomes the language of the *aula* (royal court) of the *rex* (king), who is the personification of the impersonal body politic (Kantorowicz 1957), and thus speaks not for himself but for his *regnum*, and of the elite *curia* that ideally surrounds him. Far from remaining subject to the willful vagaries of those who deploy it, the *vulgare illustre* is given the power (*magisterium*) to shape and teach the wills of those who read and hear it (1.17.4), and it thus has an authority analogous to that of the Emperor ("cavalcatore della volontà umana") as defined in *Convivio* book 4 (4.9.4–10). Even the fact that, in the current absence of a regal *aula*, it is identified primarily with the *curia* in exile, dispersed throughout Italy, and is exemplified by two individuals who would presumably be members of that body, Cino da Pistoia and by his "friend," Dante (1.10.2, 17.3; cf. 13.4), does not necessarily fatally compromise its transhistorical character, since these individuals might still be relegated to the status of secondary examples, of immanent *paroles* deriving from transcendent *langue*.

It would be a different matter, however, if the stain of historical contingency and willful individuality were already embedded in the ostensibly rational and transcendent definition of the *vulgare illustre* as "simplicissima substantiarum." That this is so appears in the pathetic image of the illustrious vernacular as pilgrim wandering homeless throughout the Italian peninsula, dependent for asylum on the kindness of strangers (1.18.3; cited above). In addition to the generic recall of both the Fall and the Babelic dispersal as exilic experiences, the more immediate function of the image is to echo the historical fact of Dante's own exile, explicitly mentioned in the preceding chapter:

Quantum vero suos familiares glorioso efficiat, nos ipsi novimus, qui huius dulcedine glorie nostrum exilium postergamus. (1.17.6)

(And I myself [nos] have known how greatly it [the illustrious vernacular] increases the glory of those who serve it, I who, for the sake of that glory's sweetness, [pay no attention to my exile].)

This passage in turn harks back to the earlier reference to the "objectifying" effects of exile on Dante's judgment:

Nos autem, cui mundus est patria velut piscibus equor, quanquam Sarnum biberimus ante dentes et Florentiam adeo diligamus ut, qui dileximus, exilium patiamur iniuste, rationi magi quam sensui spatulas nostri iudicii podiamus. (1.6.3)

(To me [nos], however, the whole world is a homeland, like the sea to fish – though I drank from the Arno before cutting my teeth, and love Florence so much that, because I loved her, I suffer exile unjustly – and I will weigh the balance of my judgment more with reason than with sentiment)

In other words, if the *vulgare illustre* is, on the one hand, figuratively equated with God, the Author of authors, on the other it is indirectly identified with an individual human writer, Dante himself,[42] just as in *Convivio* 1.13.

---

[42] For identifications of the *vulgare illustre* as Dante's personal language, see, e.g., Di Capua 1945: 47; Mengaldo, especially 1978a: 91–2. Shapiro 1990: 194 made a similar point. Opponents include Ewert 1940: 363; Mazzocco 1993: 245 n 27. Despite suggestive hints in Mengaldo and Shapiro's elegant summary, none of these critics has explored the rhetorical process by which the identification is

Clearly, this identification serves the same function of obliquely authorizing Dante as did the apparently impersonal etymology of the poetic *autore* as "binder of words" in *Convivio* 4.6.3–4. Again it betrays a fear that the claim can only be made imaginatively, that it would not stand up to direct rational scrutiny. Dante had, after all, first grounded his authority to speak rationally and dispassionately about the vernacular on the fact of his exile, which separates him from all local attachments and prejudices (1.6.3). Perhaps more than any other cultural figure of his time, the exiled, errant Dante was in a position to have experienced and appreciated the full variety of local dialects and thus to have effected the syncretic selection of the best from each by which he says one arrives at knowledge of the illustrious vernacular. But in this imaginative identification, Dante is not simply an exemplary, even privileged, historical knower and user of the *vulgare illustre*: he *is* the illustrious vernacular; he oxymoronically *personifies* its authority and nobility, even as he sets out to define that authority in transpersonal terms.

Indeed, Dante goes even farther, because as just noted the identification with the "simplicissima substantiarum" is also an analogical identification with the "Most High," or perhaps, better, with the Son of the Most High, wandering in exile through the world, doomed to suffer unjustly because of his love for humanity. If human history after Babel renders corrupt any identification between individual and language, then Dante will look *beyond* history for a theological and transcendent authority with which to infuse himself and his language. Thus, just as in *Convivio*, and with equal obliquity, Dante tries to prop his personal, unauthorized mission of "binding together" Italian into an authoritative language upon God as Word, as "Alpha e O" that binds the universe together with love in a single volume, emerging as a living linguistic oxymoron: "Italian personified."

At the same time, this condition of exile shared by author and language, along with the tacit equivalence between a language and a single person, points not toward prelapsarian Eden, but toward Babel, that monument to the perversity of individual will, the starting point of the exilic dispersion and wandering of humans and their languages. The first reference to Dante's

effected or its implications. See, however, Cestaro 1991b: 59–64 for a comparable account of the interactions between "personal," "linguistic," and "universal" histories, around the key symbolic elements of Eden, Babel, and exile. The element which for him is the master trope behind all these versions of "exile" and the primary determinant of "personality" and "individuality" is the loss of primal contact with a nurturing maternal body, a reading which I find appealing, but which remains extrinsic to my concerns here. This argument parallels the discussion of nobility, *autorità*, and their oblique applicability to Dante personally in *CV* (Chapter 2, especially sections iv–v and nn 13, 47, 52, 56, 57, 62).

exile, for all its positive implications, nonetheless also immediately precedes the reference to the exile of humanity from Eden (1.7.2, quoted above), which in turn introduces the story of Babel and with it the *confusio*, that is, the radical historicity and individuality of language.

Dante's philosophical, rational argument (1.9.1, 16.1) in support of the impersonal power and prestige of the *vulgare illustre* is countered implicitly by his rhetorical situation as author of the treatise and as exemplary vernacular poet (the "friend of Cino"), as well as by an imaginative counter-logic that subtends his reasoning. That self-effacing rhetorical strategy, that imaginative logic, is, however, a response to an impossible predicament: radically conflicting desires for a language that (1) transcends history and individual personality and (2) confers upon the historical person, Dante, his identity as a truly "Italian" poet who speaks, even in exile, with the political and intellectual authority of the *aula* and the *curia* behind him. At worst, in book 1 of *De Vulgari Eloquentia*, Dante is in danger of seeming to be a sort of Nimrod who equates himself and his works with Deity.[43] At best, his relation to the *vulgare illustre* is deeply ambivalent: suspended between ideality and historicity, between Eden, where Adam's language (Hebrew) is at once his own and humankind's generally, and Babel, where Nimrod became a language and a species unto himself.

IV. THE POET'S LANGUAGE

This, however, is not the end of the story. Having focused, with Dante, on the question of language in general in book 1, we now need to consider the specific place of poetry in the authorizing process undertaken throughout the incomplete *De Vulgari Eloquentia*. Does poetry figure, as it does in *Convivio*, as the paradigm and paragon of all language use, indeed, as the *ars* by which the irregular, unstable *vulgare* can be made to resemble regular, permanent *gramatica*? Or is it here, as some have argued, a special and not necessarily generalizable subset of language in general (cf. n 49)? At the close

---

[43] Shapiro 1990: 34, 179 implies this in passing. See 2.4.9–11, signaled by Durling 1992: 32, which refers to the "tragic style" to which Dante hints the "vulgare illustre" and he as "poet of rectitude" are best suited. The passage creates a double comparison – between Dante and Aeneas descending into the netherworld and between Dante and Virgil as author of the *Aeneid*. It then goes on to attack the hubris of *others* who aspire – presumptuously, babelically – to what he tranquilly assigns to himself: the imitation of the eagle soaring up to the stars (indeed, he may himself be the eagle they seek to imitate; cf. *Purg.* 9.19–24). Although Dante does not use *constructio* to describe Babel, 2.4.9–11 does come at the beginning of a series of references to the "building" of the *stantium*, in which forms of that word appear repeatedly. Note also that in the dual references to an infernal descent and a heavenly ascent, the structure of the *DC* is proleptically anticipated. For Virgil and the *Aen.* in *DVE*, see also Shapiro 1990: 10–13; Luzzi 1998: 166–7 and nn.

of the first book, Dante sets aside as complete the project of defining the illustrious, and hence authoritative, Italian vernacular. There the illustrious vernacular is defined not only as the language of the *curia* in exile, but also and more specifically as that which "usi sunt doctores illustres qui lingua vulgari poetati sunt in Ytalia" (is used by the illustrious men of learning who have composed poetry in Italy; 1.19.1). This then prepares the move in book 2 to a detailed and practical study of the employment of the "illustrious vernacular" – its proper uses, users, materials, and audience – and thence – in projected future books – to other, lesser forms of the "lingua di sì" (1.19.2–3).[44]

At the beginning of book 2, Dante declares that the *vulgare illustre* is a language equally suited to prose and to verse, but, as seen in Chapter 2 (section vi and n 94), he gives the poets, called "avientibus" from *avieo*, pride of place. In the event he narrows his topic even further, concentrating on one form only, albeit the most exalted one, of the illustrious vernacular: the high, or tragic, poetic style, along with the subjects – war, love, virtue – and the verse form – *cantio*, or *canzone* – most suitable to it. As Mengaldo (1978a: 15) has observed, *De Vulgari Eloquentia*, in this aspect, can be taken with *Convivio* as a single, elaborate meditation on and defense of the *canzone* as poetic form, one then abandoned with the invention of *terza rima* for the *Commedia*. Needless to say, however, the foci of the two works in this regard are very different. In *Convivio*, at least overtly, the binding formalism of the poet is posited and given thematic prominence without specification, and the emphasis falls instead on looking beneath the poetic surface, or, in the case of "le dolci rime d'amore," directly at it, to discover a philosophical content. By contrast, in *De Vulgari Eloquentia* book 2, the decorous intersection of form with meaning (*convenientia*) foregrounds the issue of style and entails no complicating reflections on the relation between literal and allegorical senses (2.2–4). Thus the bulk of book 2 (chapters 3–14) is concentrated on describing the formal attributes (construction, vocabulary, verse forms, and so on) of the poetic surface.[45]

---

[44] At the end of book 1, Dante states his "encyclopedic" intention to cover the whole gamut of vernacular forms, from the highest to that proper to "one single family" (1.19.2–3). At 2.4.7 he projects the treatment of the "middle" style in a fourth book, and, it appears, the humble style as well. As noted in Chapter 2, n 94, scholars have speculated that book 3 would have focused on prose in the *vulgare illustre*. For how book 2 might have been completed, see Rajna 1921: 79; Mengaldo 1970b: 403, 1979: 26–7. Most critics assume that four books were all that Dante planned, but this remains conjectural. For summaries of the question, see Mengaldo 1970b: 403–4, 1979: 5; Corti 1993: 82–4; Botterill 1996a.

[45] See Shapiro 1990: 180–1 for a similar contrasting of the two works. I agree that, in some sense, syntax in *DVE* is "semanticized" (190, 192, 194). On the latter point, see Lombardi 2000, developing Freccero 1983a.

The question remains as to whether or not *De Vulgari Eloquentia* shares *Convivio*'s anxious sense of poetry as a problematic mode of discourse and the felt need to appropriate a special, compensatory, authority for poets and their works. Here too at first the answer seems to be a resounding no, perhaps even more so than in book 1. In book 1 the status of poetry vis-à-vis language is not directly considered until the very end, but poets are privileged in exemplifying the *vulgare illustre* throughout. In particular, the constant allusions to Cino and "his friend" give Dante and what would come to be known as "dolce stil nuovo" poetry a leading role in defining the illustrious vernacular. In 1.10.2 Cino and friend are specifically identified with the "vulgares eloquentes" (eloquent writers in the vernacular) who "dulcius subtiliusque poetati vulgariter sunt" (who have written vernacular poetry more sweetly and subtly); in 1.17.3, they are again indicated as those who show "magistratu quidem sublimatum [vulgare illustre]" (it [the illustrious vernacular] is sublime in learning). They are, in short, the most visible representatives of the *curia* in exile and of the "doctores illustres" who have written poetry in Italian.

The most troublesome feature of book 1 is the identification between an individual person and the illustrious vernacular. Strikingly, in book 2 this is not only assumed without comment as concerns the relation of individual poet to the vernacular poetry he writes, but has also become a positive virtue to be celebrated. In book 2, the agency of individual will *is* once more a central concern, but is presented so as to suggest that all the linguistic anxiety of book 1 has been dissipated, and the conflicts inherent in the definition of the *vulgare illustre* are left behind in turning to poetry, to the tragic style, and to the *cantio*.

This key point can be illustrated by turning to the apparently peripheral issue of rhetorical *decorum*. As Mengaldo has shown, Dante's definition of the decorum essential to poetry constitutes a sharp departure from the usage of the *poetriae* and the rhetorical tradition (1978a: 57–9). As against the usual insistence on the adequation of style to subject matter (to which, however, we will return in a moment),[46] Dante calls for a different type of decorous *convenientia*:

---

[46] For the importance of decorum in the more usual sense in *DVE* 2, see Battaglia Ricci 1983: especially 19; Botterill 1996a: xxv. For decorum and the related question of "adequation" in the *DC*, see Battaglia Ricci 1983: 26–7 *et passim*; Shoaf 1988; Mazzotta 1993a: especially 79–90; as well as the related discussion of the word "disconvenevole" in *CV* 1.5–13 by Lombardi 2000. Di Capua 1945: especially 56–63 notes an overlap between *decorum* as a stylistic and "aesthetic" category and *discretio* as a moral and intellectual one. Cf. n 40.

Exigit ergo istud [vulgare illustre] sibi consimiles viros, quemadmodum alii nostri mores et habitus; exigit enim magnificentia magna potentes, purpura viros nobiles; sic et hoc excellentes ingenio et scientia querit, et alios aspernatur, ut per inferiora patebit. Nam quicquid nobis convenit, *vel gratia generis, vel speciei, vel individui convenit,* ut sentire, ridere, militare. Sed hoc non convenit nobis gratia generis, qui etiam brutis conveniret; nec gratia speciei, qui cunctis hominibus esset conveniens, de quo nulla questio est – nemo enim montaninis rusticana tractantibus hoc dicet esse conveniens – *convenit ergo individui gratia. Sed nichil individuo convenit nisi per proprias dignitates, puta mercari, militare ac regere.* (2.1.5–7)

(The illustrious vernacular requires that those who use it have true affinity with it, as is the case with our customs and [fashions]: so magnificence requires those capable of great deeds, and purple calls for noble men; and, in the same way, the illustrious vernacular demands writers of outstanding intelligence and knowledge and spurns all others, as will become clear below. For whatever is suited to us is so because we belong to a genus, or a species, or because we are who we are [because of our individual natures]: this is true, for instance, of our having sense–perceptions, or laughing, or [making war]. But the illustrious vernacular is not suited to us because we belong to a genus – otherwise it would also be suited to brute beasts; nor because we belong to a species – otherwise it would be suited to every human being (for no one would suggest that it is appropriate for mountain-dwellers discussing country matters); so it must be suited to us as individuals. But nothing suits an individual except in respect of the particular qualities he possesses, as in the case of carrying on a trade, or [making war], or governing.)

Rather than a correspondence between words and subject matter, Dante insists upon the intersection of the "optimum vulgare" with the moral and intellectual character of the individual poet who uses it. Here, the prose *nos* openly desires the intersection of individual personality and poetic language (cf. Mengaldo 1978a: 90; Steinberg 1999: chapter 4), where, by contrast, in book I his effort was to establish a language ideally free from the "arbitrium singularium."

Just as striking is the subsequent passage in which Dante, now treating stylistic decorum in the more traditional sense of correspondence between form and content, defines the three subjects of the high, tragic style as corresponding to the three souls that are in human beings (2.2.6). This second form of decorum is related to the first, since in both cases style is required to conform to the qualities of the composite human soul, although the emphasis shifts from the empirical person to the ideal individual. The greatest of the three is the rational soul, whose concern is the *honestum*, and whose equivalent poetic subject matter is therefore *virtus*:

Quare hec tria, salus videlicet, venus et virtus, apparent esse illa magnalia que sint maxime pertractanda hoc ea que maxime sunt ad ista, ut armorum probitas, amoris accensio et directio voluntatis. Circa que sola, si bene recolimus, illustres viros invenimus vulgariter poetasse, scilicet Cynum Pistoriensem amorem, amicum eius rectitudinem. (2.2.7)

(So these three things [self-preservation], love, and virtue, appear to be those most important subjects that are to be treated in the loftiest style; or at least this is true of the themes most closely associated with them, prowess in arms, ardor in love, and [direction of the] will. On these themes alone, if I [*nos*] remember rightly, we find that illustrious individuals have written poetry in the vernacular: . . . Cino da Pistoia on love, his friend on [direction of the will].)

Now the noblest subject of the noblest poetic style becomes the proper direction of the will, and the example par excellence of one who has written such poetry is none other than "the friend of Cino," who, we infer from the earlier passage, must be a person of sufficient personal luster to match the greatness of the *vulgare illustre* and to exemplify the "direction of the will" his poetry will effect.

In other words, not only does Dante theorize the intersection of an individual poet's personality with an exalted "poetry of rectitude" whose task it is to direct the individual wills of others, he makes it obvious that he is that poet, and that the highest form of poetry is his alone, no longer shared even with the previously ubiquitous Cino. As if to mark Dante's "coming out," the subsequent treatment of the *cantio* – the most excellent form of the most excellent style in the most excellent language – makes Dante himself the principal exemplar of it. At the same time, and of the utmost significance, the prose "nos" begins to refer to himself in an entirely new way:

Dicimus ergo quod cantio, in quantum per superexcellentiam dicitur, ut et nos querimus, est equalium stantiarum sine responsorio ad unam sententiam tragica coniugatio, ut nos ostendimus cum dicimus: "Donne che avete intelletto d'amore." (2.8.8)

(So I [*nos*] say that the *canzone*, in so far as it is so called for its pre-eminence, which is what we [*nos*] too are seeking, is a connected series of equal stanzas in the tragic style, without a refrain, and focused on a single theme, as I [*nos*] showed when I [*nos*] wrote: "Donne che avete intelletto d'amore.")

Dante-poet is no longer separated off from the prose *nos* who composes the treatise – he too is a first person (plural) presence, openly acknowledging his proprietary relationship to the best form of the best vernacular.[47]

---

[47] For additional discussion of this phenomenon, first treated in Ascoli 1991b, 1993, see Chapter 4, section iv. Compare Stone 1994b: 43–4; Luzzi 1998: 172–3. While Mengaldo 1978a: 108–10, 1979: 17 does not note the grammatical shift, he does observe a corresponding phenomenon, the

The key to understanding why these remarkable shifts take place – why Dante's personal authority emerges now, even as the value of individual will is recuperated – is to see that this, from chapter 8 forward, is the part of the treatise where Dante's prosaic subject matter most closely coincides with his poetic talents – when he is not talking about language in general, or the *vulgare illustre* more particularly, or even about the range of poetic styles, but only about a single, privileged form, the *cantio*, a form in which he has specialized, particularly in his maturity.

Here too, remarkably yet by no means coincidentally, the treatise first explicitly thematizes the problem of *autoritate* and of the poetic *autore*, notably in a passage that occurs in close proximity to the densest cluster of Dante's new first person self-references (2.10–11):

> Vide ergo, lector, quanta *licentia* data sit cantiones poetantibus, et considera cuius rei causa tam largam *arbitrium* usus sibi asciverit; et si recto calle ratio te duxerit, videbis *autoritatis dignitate sola* quod dicimus esse concessum. (2.10.5)

> ([See therefore, reader, what license should be given to those who compose poetic *canzoni*, and consider for what cause such a large degree of will is ascribed to them by custom, and if reason leads you upon the right path, you will see that that which we have said is conceded by the dignity of authority alone.])

Arbitrium and *autoritate*, *licentia* and *ratio*, now peacefully coexist, if only in the poetic act of composing the *cantio* as poetic form (cf. Durling and Martinez 1990: 24–5 and n 60). At this point too comes the cluster of references to the *auctor* of the *cantio* cited at the end of the preceding chapter which constitutes the closest thing to a direct application of that title by Dante to himself in one of his major works, precisely because he has just proposed himself as *the* exemplar of the tragic style and the "poetry of rectitude" that are the form and matter of the *canzone*.

There is a catch, however. As first suggested in Chapter 2, section iv, this open approach to *auctoritas* is made only when Dante has restricted the term to its most limited sense. As against book 4 of *Convivio* – where Dante as *autore* is implicitly compared to and made the peer of two great worldly authorities, Aristotle and the Emperor Frederick, and is even put in analogical relationship with God the creator – here the *auctor* or "binder of words" is presented as a craftsman, a maker or "faber," who verges on the circumscribed role of the *actor* from *agere*.

---

abandonment late in book 2 of Cino as Dante's constant verbal companion for Guido Cavalcanti (2.12.3, 8; cf. 1.13.3; 2.6.6). On the dismissive treatment of Cavalcanti in *DVE*, see Barolini 1984: 124–6.

The basic point at issue here is that the success of book 2 in the overt representation of Dante's individual *auctoritas* is predicated upon the resigned acceptance of a larger failure in book 1: a failure to achieve the same appropriation of political, philosophical, and, allusively and by analogy, theological authority aimed at in *Convivio* 4. This failure is determined by Dante's tortuous confrontation in the first book with his own, his language's, and his country's irremediable historicity.[48] Recognition of failure may reduce the *vulgare illustre* from the legitimate vehicle of political power and philosophical truth to the language of a single class of persons, the poets, and, indeed, to a unique individual poet, Dante. Nonetheless, it simultaneously frees Dante-poet to assert openly a limited personal authority as historical *avitor* or *actor*.

The long-standing debate in Italian criticism over whether the treatise is truly concerned with the social-political reality of Italian language or "merely" with a poetic style proper to a small group of writers,[49] not only reflects the shift in focus from book 1 to book 2, but also points to a genuine ambivalence in book 1's treatment of the relationship between the *vulgare illustre* and the poetic examples thereof. Poets and poetry do

---

[48] For another account of book 2 as retreat from politics into matters of poetic style, see Barański 1986a: 62, 67.

[49] Two traditional critical *querelles* explore the question: (1) what is the nature of the *vulgare illustre* itself? Is it a socio-political reality or does it exist only in the poetic examples to which Dante consistently returns?; (2) what is the relation of book 1 to book 2: is the "tragic" or high poetic style the equivalent of the *vulgare illustre*, or is it simply one instance of how the *vulgare illustre* can be deployed poetically? The two issues are closely related, since book 1 is obviously "linguistic" and broadly socio-political in focus, while book 2 is just as obviously rhetorical and poetic. Among the originators of the view that the *vulgare illustre* is "merely" a poetic style, are D'Ovidio 1876: 106 and Rajna 1921: 78–80, taking up Alessandro Manzoni (1868; see Luzzi 1998: 601; Pagliaro 1962: 215–16). See the related comments of Grayson 1965: 11–15; Alessio 1995. Those for whom the *vulgare illustre* is, instead, not a style but a socially and historically verifiable language are Nardi 1921b; Pagliaro 1962: especially 219–21; Cambon 1966: 37; Dionisotti 1967: 35–6; Pagani 1982; Barański 1986a; Steinberg 1999, 2007. The most helpful critics are those who have seen that the *vulgare illustre* is both, or at least alternately, a language and a poetic style (cf. Ewert 1940: 360–2; Vinay 1959: especially 272; Mengaldo 1978a: especially 81–7, 1979: 4; Battaglia Ricci 1983: 13). See also Mazzotta 1993a: 19–24 for a reformulation of "poetry" that accounts for most of what the criticism has typically divided up between "language" and "poetic style." And see Chapter 7, section vi, for the upshot of this intersection in *Par.* As for the question of the relationship between book 1 and book 2, most critics have tended either to assume a fundamental discontinuity (D'Ovidio 1876: 109; Vinay 1959: 263–74) or simply to ignore book 2 altogether (as Pagani 1982 does, because it distracts from her political reading of *DVE*). Cf. Marigo 1948: lviii. For book 2 see Mengaldo 1970b: 404–5, 1978a: especially 87–92, 1979, but also Dragonetti 1961b, whose discussion of the *cantio* (52–77, especially 72–7) is the most suggestive, if not fully credible, attempt to link the linguistics of book 1 to the poetics of book 2 and to suggest the centrality of the *canzone* to Dante's thinking about language and art. See also Botterill 1996a: xxiv–xxv; Scott 2004: 47–55 *et passim*. In an important reading of book 2, Durling and Martinez 1990: especially 19–32, argue that the treatment of the *cantio* constitutes a major step in Dante's development of a "poetics of the microcosm," which will lead to the *DC*. See also Chapter 2, nn 96, 98.

play an important yet poorly defined role in book 1's construction of an
ideal vernacular language, preparing the focus on poetry in book 2, as well
as in the assertion that it is the privileged form of language, superior to
prose. At the same time, the actual definition of the *vulgare illustre* over
the space of three dense chapters (1.16–18) attempts to appropriate for it,
and for Dante, an authority that is evidently far greater than the "merely"
poetic.

In chapter 16, as shown earlier, Dante confers upon the panther, by
analogy, the theological status of creative Logos, then displaces that the-
ological authority by an implicit associative chain onto himself. In the
two subsequent chapters the defining qualities of the illustrious vernacular,
"illustre, cardinale, aulicum, et curiale" (illustrious, cardinal, courtly, and
curial; 1.16.6) embody that authority in the realm of history, further broad-
ening Dante's claims for it. The first of these chapters, 17, is dedicated
exclusively to explaining the suitability of the principal adjective "illus-
tre," which anticipates all of the qualities exfoliated in the three adjectives
treated together in the following chapter. The applicability of *illustre* to the
panther is revealed in a series of steps that may at first seem logical in a
philosophical sense, but are actually dictated by a figurative logic of dis-
placement by analogy. By *illustre*, he says, we mean something "illuminans
et illuminatum prefulgens" (that gives off light [and] reflects the light that
it receives from elsewhere; 1.17.2). This image of light is then transferred to
"viros illustres" (illustrious [or illuminated] men) of two kinds: those who
"potestate illuminati alios et iustitia et karitate illuminant" (enlightened by
power, they [illuminate others through] justice and charity; 1.17.2); those
who "excellenter magistrati, excellenter magistrent" (excellently taught . . .
teach most excellently; 1.17.2). These two forms of illustriousness are then
exemplified, or, better, personified, by Numa Pompilius (second king of
Rome) and Seneca (the philosopher), showing that Dante sees *illustre* as
enfolding both power and knowledge, kingship and philosophy. On anal-
ogy with its application to famous men, then, the *vulgare illustre* is said to
be "sublimatum . . . magistratu et potestate" (sublime in [instruction] and
[in] power; 1.17.2; cf. 17.3).

Here, then, is a curious structural affinity with *Convivio* 4, where Dante
tacitly situates the authority of (his) poetry between, yet also outside and
above, the paired and complementary authorities of Frederick II and Aris-
totle. In *De Vulgari Eloquentia* too this negotiation occurs indirectly, now
in the form of an analogy. Moreover, once the parallel has been estab-
lished, *magisterium* and *potestas* come to mean something rather different
in reference to language than they do when applied to illustrious men.

By linguistic "magistracy" Dante means the ability to transform the rough words and constructions of Italian dialects into poetic performances as perfect as the *canzoni* of Cino and friend (1.17.3), rather than overt philosophical instruction. By *potestas* he means the rhetorical (as against judicial or military) power to sway the will of the hearer "ut nolentem volentem et volentem nolentem faciat" (so as to make the unwilling willing, and the willing unwilling; 1.17.4), though in this its possessor resembles not only the Emperor as defined in *Convivio* (4.9.4–10), but also Orpheus as poet-figure (2.1.3).

By the end of book 1, Dante has appropriated for the *vulgare illustre* and for himself both *magisterium* and *potestas*, although a certain violence has been done to the sense of the words and although the appropriation is only and obviously rhetorical. As if to stress the latter point, he concludes chapter 17 with a backhanded reminder that although he and other poets lack the *potestas* of kings, they may rival their lords in fame:

Quod autem honore sublimet in promptu est. Nonne domestici sui reges marchiones, comites et magnates quoslibet fama vincunt? (1.17.5)

(That it [the illustrious vernacular] raises to honor is readily apparent. Does not the fame of its devotees exceed that of any king, marquis, count or warlord?)

The ironic import of this passage is then immediately revealed as Dante notes (in the passage cited earlier: 1.17.6) that the fame he himself has earned in this way is a consolation for his exile (cf. Chapter 2, section iii).

In chapter 18, the stakes become clearer and higher. The first adjective treated is "cardinale," which refers to the pivotal and transcendent role of the *vulgare illustre* vis-à-vis the municipal vernaculars, its presumed status as the language not of one region or group but of all Italy and Italians (1.18.1). The next two adjectives, "aulicum" and "curiale," specify that this universality is not simply stylistic, but also political and rational. Through the exegesis of these qualifiers, Dante attempts to transform the figurative analogy that links the *vulgare illustre* to political power and to philosophical knowledge into a substantive historical reality. The *vulgare illustre* would be the language of the *aula*, or regal court, which "regni comunis est domus et omnium regni partium gubernatrix augusta" (the court is the shared home of the entire kingdom, and [of] the [august] governor of every part of it; 1.18.2). In addition, it would be the language of the *curia*, defined through the quality of *curialitas* as "librata regula eorum que peragenda sunt" ([well-balanced rules concerning those things which have to be done]; 18.4), but also referring to an administrative court surrounding and supporting the king and the *aula*. The primary functions of this *curia*, in Dante's terms, would be to supply the knowledge needed for rule and to participate in administering the power deriving from that rule.[50]

To summarize: in book 1 Dante tries to define a language that is at once Italy's, the prince's, the *curia*'s, the poets', and his own, guided by the desire to impose political order and cultural coherence upon the "geographical expression" of Italy, where disorder and incoherence currently reign supreme.[51] This he would accomplish through a projection of his personal sense of identity and the formal perfection of the *canzone* onto the domain of political-social history through the vehicle of the *vulgare illustre*. Nonetheless, by the end of book 1, the dream of a language knitting together all of Italy ("cardinale") through the power of a *Princeps* joined to the wisdom of a *curia* founded on justice and reason patently breaks down in the face of intractable historical facts. As already noted from another perspective, Dante feels obliged to acknowledge that the *vulgare illustre* wanders in exile for lack of a regal *aula* (18.3) and that the *curia*, likewise dispersed throughout Italy, is bound together only by the "gratioso lumine

---

[50] For "aula" and "curia," see Marigo 1948: lxxix–lxxxiii; Di Capua 1945: 49–51; Mengaldo 1970b: 414; Colish 1983: 178–9; Mazzocco 1993: 133–8, 149–53, 245 n 27. The present discussion depends on a series of structural inferences to align the "aula"/"curia" pairing as first presented with the "Numa"/"Seneca," "potestas"/"magisterium," dyads of *DVE* 1.16. Under normal circumstances, the *curia*'s functions would include counseling the *Princeps* (ideally portrayed in the reciprocal relationship of emperor and philosopher of *CV* 4.6.17.20), as well as carrying out administrative-bureaucratic duties and judicial responsibilities on his behalf. (Incidentally, this regal *curia* should not be confused with administrative court of the papacy [*pace* Di Capua 1945: 50; Shapiro 1990: 4, 16], or for that matter with the imperial court [*pace* Passerin d'Entrèves 1952: 97; Shapiro 1990: 32]), although in the latter case Dante himself is largely to blame [see n 51]). In short, Dante understands *aula* and *curia* as ideally inseparable, although historical circumstances that deprived Italy of its regal *aula* have also forced the scattered *curia* in exile back onto the disempowered resources of reason alone. This would explain why Dante is so careful to distinguish the two adjectives (for an objection, see Mazzocco 1993: 245 n 27, responding to a version of this note in Ascoli 1991b: 219 n 46). I also take this opportunity to acknowledge the learned, challenging, and very helpful comments of Robert Lerner on Ascoli 1991b.

[51] Dante is not clear about what kind of political structure and figure he is talking about here, although it *is* evident that the *vulgare illustre* should not be referred to as an "imperial" tongue (as in Shapiro 1990: 5, 8, 12 [cf. 31–2; the point is finally clarified somewhat at 177]), since there is no indication at all that Dante foresees or desires its use outside of the Italian peninsula. The court is to be Italian, but Dante does not openly break with the notion of a transnational state under the aegis of an Emperor, the sovereign of choice in *CV* 4 and in *MN* (cf. Passerin d'Entrèves 1952: 19–20; Scott 1996: 30–4). What permits the equivocation is that his historical example is Frederick II, who, unusually, fit both descriptions. (For the special place of Frederick in Dante's *oeuvre*, see also Chapters 2 and 6). *Pace* Vinay (1959: 256–8; critiqued by Grayson 1965: 26; Mengaldo 1978a: 66), there is no necessary evolution in Dante's linguistic thinking tied to the equation of Latin with the Empire – although the *vulgare illustre* is undoubtedly meant to serve political purposes. Dante simply ignores the question in both *CV* 4 and the *DC*, for the rhetorically astute reason that he wants both to legitimate Italian as a distinct, geographically based, language and to revive the Empire, without foregrounding the potential conflict between national language and transnational monarchy. For the problematic political status of "Italy" in Dante, see also Davis 1984b. For Dante's understanding of the politicized vernacular as a forerunner of early modern uses of language in nation-building, see Ferguson 2003.

rationis" (gracious light of reason; 18.5). Given the opening definition of language as the indispensable bridge between isolated rational subjectivities, however, the latter assertion is tautological: the rationality of the *curia* legitimizes the *vulgare illustre*, but use of the *vulgare illustre* is what defines the *curia* as rational. With this in mind, we receive the news in the next and final chapter of the book that the "doctores illustres" (illustrious [men of learning]) who compose the *curia* in exile are simply those who have written poetry in Italian (1.19.1). Even as it is being given definition, then, the *vulgare illustre* slides from theological transcendence, to the immanence of human knowledge and power, to the formal marginality of poetic style.[52] And the force of this collapse is all the greater when contrasted with the comparable passages in *Convivio* 4.6, where Dante never confronts directly the possibility that the necessary symbiosis between philosopher (structural equivalent of the *curia*) and the emperor (again Frederick) could fail.

The turn in book 2 to the language of poetry, and of one poet in particular, thus constitutes a further acknowledgement that the ambitious political project of book 1 is doomed to unsuccess, at least until a new strategy can be devised for encompassing it. The open affirmation of the personalized authorship of poetic making is marked from within by a persisting sense of exclusion from the world of society and politics. Most prominently, in chapter 6 of book 2 a seemingly innocuous series of Latin prose examples of *constructio* conceals a continuing preoccupation with the unruliness of history, and the inability of even "poets of rectitude" to put it right. The chapter begins with an allusion to the most famous classical model for the intersection of philosophical and political authority – "Aristotiles phylosophatus tempore Alexandri" (Aristotle philosophized in Alexander's time; 2.6.2) – one that is most apt to the ideal intersection of *aula* and *curia*, but which also emphasizes their unhappy disjunction in Dante's monarchless-Italy.

Dante goes on to give a list of examples illustrating degrees of *stylistic* "urbanitas,"[53] from least to greatest, which at the same time implicitly offers a grim picture of contemporary life in the peninsula:

Sed non minoris difficultatis accedit discretio priusquam quam querimus actingamus, videlicet urbanitate plenissimam. Sunt enim gradus constructionum quamplures: videlicet insipidus, qui est rudium, ut "Petrus amat multum dominam Bertam"; est et pure sapidus, qui est rigidorum scolarium vel magistrorum, ut

---

[52] In this way, I speculate, Dante may give an indirect answer to the question of which guild, which professional group at Babel, first gave rise to the *lingua tripharium* and thence to Italian: he and his fellow poets apparently speak a language that no one else can hear, or at least understand. See Luzzi 1998: 166–7 for a related interpretation.

[53] *Urbanitas* refers etymologically to the *urbs*, and so points to the attempt of poetic style to adequate its representations to a social-political world.

"Piget me cunctis pietate maiorem, quicunque in exilio tabescentes patriam tantum sompniando revisunt"; est et sapidus et venustus, qui est quorundam superficientenus rethoricam aurientium, ut "Laudabilis discretio marchionis Estensis, et sua magnificentia preparata, cunctis illum facit esse dilectum"; est et sapidus et venustus etiam et excelsus, qui est dictatorum illustrium, ut "Eiecta maxima parte florum de sinu tuo, Florentia, nequicquam Trinacrium Totila secundus adivit." Hunc gradum constructionis excellentissimum nominamus, et hic est quem querimus cum suprema venemur, ut dictum est. (2.6.4–5)

(But a distinction no less tricky than this must be made before we can find what we seek, which is the construction with the highest possible degree of urbanity. For there are many degrees of construction. There is the flavorless, for example, which is typical of the uncultured: "Peter loves Miss Bertha a lot." There is one that is flavored and no more, typical of pedantic students and teachers: "I am stricken with sorrow more than most, for whomever drags out his life in exile, revisiting his native land only in dreams." There is the one that is graceful as well as flavored, which is found among those who have made a superficial study of rhetoric: "The laudable discretion of the Marquis of Este, and his widely displayed generosity, make him beloved of all." And there is the flavored one that is graceful and also striking, and this is typical of the illustrious writers: "The greater part of your flowers, o Florence, having been snatched from your breast, the second Totila advanced in vain towards Trinacria." This is the degree of construction that I call most excellent, and this is what we are looking for when we hunt the best.)

The third example recalls the violence of Italy's ignorant and bestial rulers through the drippingly ironic reference to the dreaded Marquis of Este, Azzo VIII. The fourth is a bitter evocation of Florence's subjugation by the barbaric invader of Italy, that "new Totila," Charles of Valois.

Most movingly, into this "detached" presentation of a hierarchy of styles Dante inscribes, for the last time in the treatise, the pain and impotence of his own exile, precipitated by Charles's invasion. The "flowers snatched from [Florence's] breast" in the final example obliquely refer to the White "fuorusciti," including Dante, while the empathetic first-person evocation of exiles who often revisit their "patria" in dreams unmistakably recalls Dante's earlier references to his own circumstances in both this treatise and *Convivio*. The pathos of the latter image belies the earlier, hopeful, claim that "I [*nos*] who, for the sake of that glory's sweetness, [pay no attention to my exile]" (1.17.6; cited above).[54] The obvious inference is that the retreat into questions of poetic style, and the reduction of authorial ambitions to those of the poetic craftsman, is the only tenable position in a historical

---

[54] Mengaldo 1979: 181–3 nn reviews both the stylistic traits and topical content of the examples. Others who have commented on the content are: Dragonetti 1961b: 67; Scaglione 1988: 30. Cestaro's (1991b: 61–4) reading of the phrases is similar to mine. Cf. Shapiro 1990: 153–5, 171–2.

situation where Dante and his language no longer hold out any hopes of successfully mediating between knowledge and power.

This dramatic lowering of expectations accounts for why *De Vulgari Eloquentia* book 1 struggles so hard to keep individuality in general, and the first person Dante in particular, from being openly identified with the *vulgare illustre*, while in book 2 Dante comfortably assumes a personalized authority as vernacular poet. It also helps explain the shift in attitudes toward poetic authority from *Convivio* to *De Vulgari Eloquentia* 2: the former explicitly dismissing the poetic *autore* as irrelevant to its concerns while betraying a deep anxiety about the status of poetry; the latter equally explicit in its untroubled assertion of poetic authorship. In the final section of this chapter I will further probe the curious mix of "contraddizione" and complementarity around the question of poetic authorship in the two treatises.

V. THE AUTHOR'S LANGUAGE IN HISTORY

In *Convivio*, Dante lays the groundwork for the assignment of nobility, and implicitly authority, based on personal worth, but he does so in the impersonal, self-effacing terms of Scholastic discourse. At the same time, he positions a vernacular poetic *autore* outside the grasp of the traditional political and intellectual authorities, whose vocalic powers suggest a teasing analogy with the Tetragrammaton and a possible theological authorization from beyond the confines of history. *Convivio*, however, never moves beyond implication and indirection to assert its new personal *and* transcendent, poetic *and* theological, authority, and never renounces the project of allegorically "vulgarizing" ethical philosophy in verse, even though it has far exceeded that mandate by the beginning of book 4. Nor does it ever explicitly instantiate a form of writing at once personal and authoritative.

De Vulgari Eloquentia, rather than being more successful in legitimating Dante, his language, and his art than *Convivio*, is in some sense less so, because it risks a great deal more, and more openly exposes the risks it takes. By confronting directly the problem of conferring nobility and thence authority on vernacular language, Dante deprives himself of the possibility of passing himself off again as a humble disciple of the ancient authorities,[55]

---

[55] Mengaldo (1978a: 36; 1979: 11–12) rightly calls attention to the following passage, where Dante posits the authority of vernacular poetry in relation to that of the ancients in a very different way from either *VN* 25, or *CV*: "Nec mireris, lector, de tot reductis autoribus ad memoriam: non enim hanc quam supremam vocamus constructionem nisi per huiusmodi exempla possumus indicare. Et fortassis utilissimum foret ad illam habituandam regulatos vidisse poetas, Virgilium videlicet,

and must face up to both the magnitude of the claims he wants to make for himself and his poetry and the formidable conceptual and historical obstacles to realizing them. Here too he tries to escape the historicity and personality that compromise authority by figuratively conferring a transhistorical and theological status on the *vulgare illustre*. But the analogy with God who is everywhere and nowhere will not hold in the face of the brutal historical realities of a decentered Italy and the inevitable identification of the *vulgare illustre* with the exiled "friend of Cino." A retreat into the contingency of a purely, even "merely," poetic authorship follows. What *De Vulgari Eloquentia* does do that *Convivio* seemingly cannot, however, is to bridge the distance between the author of the Latin treatise and the vernacular poet who is, finally, his own principal subject, though only by foregoing, however temporarily, any claim to authority more than poetic.

The two texts thus operate as the hermaphroditic halves of an original intention that is unable as yet to become whole. *Convivio* completes the rhetorical appropriation of an impersonal philosophical authority, while laying the hidden theoretical foundations for a vernacular poetics of literal truth. In *De Vulgari Eloquentia*, by contrast, rhetorical self-assertion picks up where theory leaves off, or breaks down, acknowledging and affirming the newly personalized *autorità* of an individual vernacular poet.

The situation can be summed up by returning to the apparent dispute between *Convivio* and *De Vulgari Eloquentia* concerning what constitutes the *nobilitas* of a language – naturalness (i.e., the *vulgare*) or stability (i.e., Latin). The shift, as many critics have observed (e.g., Corti 1993: 78), can be accounted for by recognizing that Dante uses his key terms in distinctly different ways in the two contexts.[56] This shift in usage, however, is itself a strong indicator of the contingency and historicity of human rationality:

Ovidium Metamorfoseos, Statium atque Lucanum . . ." (2.6.7; see also Picone 1997a: 58–9). It is notable both that the vernacular versifiers are referred to as "autoribus," while the classical writers are called "poetas" (Stoffi-Muhlethaler 1986: 104), and that the ancients, while held up as examples, are simply meant to bolster the primary point made with reference to the moderns. See also Shapiro 1990 (especially 143–4). For recent readings of *DVE* in terms of constructing a literary history, see Menocal 1994: chapter 2; Luzzi 1998; Steinberg 1999, 2007. For Dante's self-placement within literary histories of his own construction, see, for example, Mazzotta 1979 (chapter 5) on the *DC* and Barolini 1984, on both the *DC* (throughout) and *DVE* (91–100, 124–6, 185–6, 287–97). On the significance of the title *poeta* as against *au[c]tor*, see Chapter 2, n 3; Chapter 7, section vi, especially nn 148–150. On the term *poeta* in *DVE* specifically see Schiaffini 1958; Picone 1979: 10–14.

[56] In *CV* Latin is said to be more noble at 1.5.7, 14 (see section i). For the different usages of *nobilitas* see D'Ovidio 1876: 77–8; Ewert 1940; Vinay 1959: 257; Nardi 1960: 20–36; Grayson 1965: 19–24; Mengaldo 1978a: 62; Copeland 1991: 180–1. See also n 42. Cf. nn 12, 19, 20 on the general shiftiness, at times self-contradictory, of Dante's technical vocabulary.

not only in its subjection to the "sensible sign," but also in its variability according to circumstance. What Dante seems to know – and his career-long propensity for self-contradiction in matters philosophical bears this out – is that the terminology of rational philosophy is itself historical and contingent, subject to the will of the individual speaker and the specific circumstances of time and place, like all language after the Fall from Eden and the confusion of Babel. What a word like *nobilitas* means depends on what context it is applied in: if what we are talking about is naturalness, the vernacular is nobler; if we focus on ability to resist change, then grammar is superior. The ideal would be to have a language that was at once natural and unchanging, like Eden itself, but that place is lost forever, as a historical possibility, and humanity now wanders in exile, divided in language as in all other things. It finally doesn't matter where one starts, with nature or with immutability, the turn will always be in the direction of the other quality, in an attempt to recover what *cannot* be recovered. Language remains suspended between earth and heaven, historical contingency and transcendent permanence.

One might then argue that even this paradox can be recuperated into a coherent, redemptive Christian typology of salvation history. After all, if Babel is the figure of the fallen historicity of the human city and its human language, it is also the antitype of that which exceeds and redeems humanity and its history: the Logos, the City of God. Thus, remarkably, by putting contemporary Italy and its languages under the sign of Babel, Dante brings them within the illuminating confines of scriptural authority. Nonetheless, as shown earlier, this version of the Babel story is marked by the traces of historical fact and exigency that separate it from the Biblical original and reveal it to be a product of the contingent needs of Dante's treatise and a reflection of contemporary Italian history. Dante authorizes his discourse by deriving it from the book of God; but at the same time he is the author of a decidedly human *fictio*, capable of rewriting the Bible itself.[57]

Specifically, Dante seems to have developed the non-Biblical account of the Babelic *confusio* expressed guild by guild in order to give logical

---

[57] Stefano Rizzo 1969: 79, then Castaldo 1982, make this point using the example of Dante's misrepresentation of the first attribution of human speech in Genesis (1.4) – both in erroneously asserting that the Bible has Eve utter the first words and in omitting mention of Adam's naming of the animals (Nardi 1921b: 190–1; Dragonetti 1961b: 13–14; Cestaro 1991b: 75–6; *pace* Shapiro 1990: 9 [but see also 24]). The omission of this latter passage provides suggestive negative evidence against Corti's and Dragonetti's thesis (cf. section ii, especially n 29). See again n 22 for the gendered implications of these passages. Barański 1989a: especially 93–106 explores implications of Dante's rewriting of Genesis in *DVE*.

substance and rhetorical direction to the narrative of the dispersal of languages. His need to make a historiographical bridge between the Biblical account of Babel and the linguistic realities of his own time requires that the post-Babelic world be confused but not too confused. Languages need to be divided, but they still must work, and to work they must be usable by communities. The logical consequence of the Biblical Babel story in languages spoken by one and only one person, would have brought human speech to a historically determinable halt. Dante's historical linguistics, by contrast, requires an expansion and iteration of Babel throughout history, so that, as noted above, the Babelic languages themselves are subdivided, and subdivided again, until every quarter, every street, every family may have its own language, which is unintelligible to others. As D'Ovidio (1931), Corti (1978) and now Steinberg (1999, 2007) have shown, this account is unmistakably informed by the Florentine social and class system that Dante so often and so powerfully condemns, but that nonetheless permeates his thought (see, e.g., Chapter 1, n 12). In this sense too, if *De Vulgari Eloquentia*'s retelling of Babel is part of a Christian and specifically Dantean theory and theology of history, it also marks Dante as part of a historical narrative that is not so easily closed or theorized, one that he himself could not possibly have written or perhaps even understood.

The degree to which this ambiguous historicity pervades *De Vulgari Eloquentia* can be appreciated by considering the representation of Nimrod and Babel in *Inferno* 31, where it *is* overcome, or at least masked rhetorically. Of special note are the different results obtained by Dante in the two texts as he tries to bring the contemporary Italian historical scene into the typological framework of Babelic temporality. In canto 31, Dante and Virgil enter the circle of the traitors, which at first appears to the bewildered pilgrim as a walled city punctuated by a series of great watch towers. This city within the city of Dis is, however, an optical illusion, since the towers are not towers at all, but giants, traditional emblems of mortal pride and resistance to divine order. It is thus particularly apt that one of these towering giants is Nimrod, architect of Babel (cf. Pézard 1958; Kleinhenz 1974).

Like so much of the *Commedia*, this canto brings together classical and Biblical narratives, assimilating the war of the Titans on Olympus to the account of the Babelic challenge to God's supremacy. The syncretism goes further still, bringing contemporary Italy allusively into the picture, as Dante compares one of the giants, Anteus, "figlio della terra" (son of the earth), to the Garisenda, the great Bolognese feudal tower which still stands today, reaffirming at the close of the canto the giant/tower equation and confusion with which he opened it.[58] Throughout lower Hell, as is well known, Dante systematically links the historical cities of central, communal Italy to classical and Christian typologies of the city *in malo* – human or demonic, Thebes or Dis, as may be – under the sign of the Augustinian "city of man." Thus it is unsurprising to find Bologna and its towers used in this way, especially because of the association of towers with the rampant factionalism that Dante saw as a basic evil of his own and other Italian cities (Dronke 1981: 36–7; Corti 1978: especially 250; Ferrante 1984; Bruni 2003).

In the *Commedia*, the Bologna-Babel connection is carefully articulated within a powerful "theo-logic" that brings Dante's Italy into the typological economy of salvation history, from the secure perspective of eschatology. From the perspective of Hell, the radical historicity of language, the *confusio*, constitutes the despised Other of the transcendent Logos.[59] Anticipating *Inferno* 31, *De Vulgari Eloquentia* book 1 also establishes a special relation between Babel and the contemporary reality of Italian cities – the "municipal" culture that Dante repeatedly condemns – and here too Bologna occupies a pivotal place. In the first instance, it is just one part of a larger display of Italian cities and their dialects that form the historical aftermath of the Babelic confusion.[60] However, Bologna is singled out in ways that no other city is, not even Dante's natal Florence. It is, for example, specifically offered as the modern, historical, double and consequence of Babel, since each quarter, each street, has its own individual idiom (1.9.4). Thus, on the one hand, it enters the typological scheme of fallen historicity. On the other hand, when Dante undertakes to sift through the various dialects, Bolognese alone among all the other municipal tongues comes in for praise, since it combines elements from both sides of the peninsula into a more-than-municipal tongue, tacitly reversing the process of

---

[58] On the recurrent importance of Bologna for Dante, in the *Inf.* particularly, see the essays in *Dante e Bologna* (1967), especially Raimondi 1967. For the importance of Bologna in Dante's late, Latin verse epistolary exchange with Giovanni del Virgilio, see Ascoli 2009. On the Garisenda in particular, see also Dante's youthful sonnet "Non mi poria già mai far ammenda" (ca. 1287).

[59] In *Par.*, especially in the exchange with Adam concerning the first language (26.80–129), mutability becomes simply the condition of human speech *tout court*, including the *poema sacro*. In their meeting, Adamo alludes to Nimrod and Babel, and silently corrects *DVE*'s singling out of Hebrew as the first language. On the shift from *DVE* to *Par.* 26, see Rajna 1921b: 81; Nardi 1921: 191–5; Ewert 1940: 359; Dragonetti 1961: 38–9; Cambon 1966; Stefano Rizzo 1969; Casagrande 1976: especially 363; Mengaldo 1978a: 68–9, 1979: 10; T. Greene 1982a: 4–8; Brownlee 1984: 600–1 and nn; Dronke 1986: 49; Barański 1986a: 76–7, 1989a: 113–14; Mazzotta 1993a: 49–51, 191–2; Mazzocco 1993: 159–79; Imbach 1996: 208–10; Alessio 1995; Cestaro 2003a: 58–60, 163–5; Lombardi 2000. For more on *Par.* 26, see Chapter 7, section v.

[60] For critics who have studied the connections between *DVE* and *Inf.* 31, see n 38. To my knowledge, however, no one has seen, much less interpreted, the parallel uses of Bologna in the two texts before.

confusio by reuniting dispersed elements, turning multiplicity back toward unity (1.15.2–7). In its syncretism the vernacular of Bologna anticipates the *vulgare illustre* itself, although the simple fact of localized existence disqualifies it from being equated with that transcendent tongue. Bologna, in other words, represents the range of linguistic possibilities within the historical city, but in this text, unlike the *Commedia*, it is at once inside and outside the typological schematics of Babel – in other words, it flaunts an ambiguous historicity. No wonder that its presence in the treatise has been taken to be historical in the most literal sense: as a possible scene of Dante's early exile and the treatise's composition, and as the contingent conduit of a transcendent theory of language.[61]

The power and the limit of Dante's rhetorical strategy in *De Vulgari Eloquentia* is that it consistently adapts rational absolutes and theological categories to contingent circumstances, or, rather, to the basic circumstance of contingency itself. As Chapter 1 began to suggest, this continues to be the case even in the *Commedia*. There, however, it is transformed by the apparently simple expedient of adding what both treatises point to allusively as the *sine qua non* for going beyond their failures: a direct theological authorization that removes Dante, his language, and his poetic art from the *macule* of historicity and of personality, or, perhaps more accurately, that wholeheartedly accepts those stains, while grounding them in the authority of the divine Author himself.[62]

---

[61] Cf. D'Ovidio 1876: 64, 102–4; Corti 1981: 17–31, 1993: 78–80; Davis 1984b: 9; Shapiro 1990: 138; Scott 2004: 43, 56–7. Mengaldo 1970b: 402, 1978a: 22. Vasino *et al.* 1970, questions the likelihood of the post-exilic visit, while acknowledging the probability of an earlier sojourn.

[62] On the *trapasso* from *DVE* to the *DC*, see Nardi 1921b: especially 191–5; Vinay 1959: 274; Mengaldo: 1970b, 1978a; Ferrucci 1971; Iannucci 1973; Battaglia Ricci 1983: pt. 1; Hollander 1983; Colish 1983: 182–3; Barolini 1984: 214 *et passim*; Brownlee 1984; Barański 1986a, 1991b; Lombardi 2000. See also nn 32, 52.

CHAPTER 4

Auto-commentary: Dividing Dante

I. "*FO DUE PARTI DI ME*"

The two preceding chapters provide a distinct perspective on Dante's pursuit of authority, considering, respectively, his relationship to the definitional tradition of the words *auctor* and *auctoritas*, and his struggle to renegotiate the hierarchy that attributes cultural authority to Latin and denies it to the vernacular. Both topics point toward a basic tension between the quest for an impersonal, traditional and/or transcendent *auctoritas* and the emergence of a personalized, modern and/or contingent authorship: a tension that tends to be linked to textual appearances of a Dantean "I," *io* or *nos*, as may be. Both topics thus direct attention to the pervasive question of Dante's propensity for self-reference and auto-exegesis,[1] and especially to his particular preference for forms in which he plays dual, even multiple, rhetorical roles, permitting an oscillation between impersonal object and personal subject of discourse.[2] This chapter will consider how the *forms* of self-representation and self-interpretation adopted by Dante offer perhaps the most penetrating means of entry into such questions. In particular, a series of formal experiments, beginning with the pre-exilic *Vita Nova* and continuing through *De Vulgari Eloquentia* and, especially, *Convivio*, negotiate the immense distance between the relatively conventional, and thus impersonal, "I" of the early lyrics and the distinctively individual – internally differentiated – *poeta-personaggio* of the *Commedia*.[3]

---

[1] Literature on Dantean auto-exegesis broadly construed is extensive. Begin with Contini (qtd. in Chapter 1, n 74). See also Sarolli 1966b; Noferi 1977, 1982–3; Mazzotta 1979; Iannucci 1981; Battaglia Ricci 1983; Barolini 1984; Baranski 1994b, 2005a. On the related issue of autobiography, see Chapter 1, n 71. This chapter focuses on the formal structure of self-commentary, for which, see Chapter 1, n 56; n 5 below.

[2] Noferi 1977: 26 speaks of "la soggettivazione dell'oggettività e l'oggettivazione della soggettività" in the *DC* and before – a formula also applicable to the structure of self-commentary.

[3] On the generic "I" of medieval lyric and its applicability to Dante, see again Chapter 1, section iv; as applied to *VN* see Mazzaro 1981: 102–3; cf. Stillinger 1992: especially chapter 1. Study of the evolution

Anyone familiar with the Dantean *oeuvre* knows that in his prose, and even in some poetry (e.g., "Le dolci rime d'amor ch'i'solia"), Dante frequently adopts an objectifying analytical mode indebted to Scholastic rationalism, and that he does so even when speaking about himself. More specifically, in an idiosyncratic evolution of Scholastic *divisio*,[4] Dante formally splits himself in two: there is one "Dante" who analyzes, another "Dante" who is analyzed, and these often correspond to an interpreting reader and an interpreted writer (cf. Chapter 1, n 72). For example, near the end of the last chapter we saw that *De Vulgari Eloquentia*, which in some respects follows the model of a Scholastic *tractatus*, divides Dante into a first-person plural prose author and a third-person singular poet, the *amicus* of Cino da Pistoia, whose works exemplify points made by the prose "nos."

The most spectacular version of this phenomenon, however, is Dante's adaptation of the widespread medieval practice of academic glossing into distinctive, and virtually unprecedented, forms of auto-exegetical self-commentary,[5] incorporated into hybrid texts combining poetry with prose. Dante's use of prosimetrum self-commentary follows a relatively straight-forward developmental path, moving ever closer to Latin, Scholastic models and thus toward the reproduction of normative canons of cultural *auctoritas*. It begins in the highly idiosyncratic prosimetrum form of *Vita Nova*, proceeds through the more standard text/commentary combination of *Convivio*, and culminates in a text, the so-called "Epistle to Cangrande," that may or may not have been written by Dante, but in any case deliberately fulfills the self-exegetical paradigm inaugurated by him.[6]

Before turning to a close analysis of the specific forms that self-commentary takes in Dante's two major prosimetrum works, let me

---

of the "io" through the *rime* might add significantly to the story told here (Ch. 1, n 75; see also n 54 below). Exemplary is Durling and Martinez 1990 on the "moment" of the *rime petrose* in itself and in relation to Dante's *corpus* more generally. A polemical review of the critical tradition relating the earlier poetry to *VN* is in Barolini 2004.

[4] On *divisio*, see Chapter 1, n 50. For analytical *divisio* in *MN* 2, see Chapter 5, section iii and nn 39–40. For *CV*, see section iii.

[5] On the medieval commentary tradition and its relevance to Dante, see Chapter 1, section iv, as well as nn 2, 48, 50. For the rare examples of commentary, in Latin or vernacular, on texts contemporary with or coming soon after Dante, and for the formal device of self-commentary, begin with Minnis *et al.*, 373–87, 440–5 and Minnis and Johnson 2005; see again Chapter 1, n 56. Roush's sharp distinction between self-commentary and commentary by others (2002) apt to her purposes is antithetical to mine.

[6] The *ECG* differs from the other two texts both in being composed in Latin and in departing from the prosimetrum model – it is a "hybrid" only in the sense that it reproduces, in Latin translation, verses from the poetic text, the *Par.*, on which it comments. In both senses, it has moved closer to the high culture template of academic commentary. See Ascoli 1997, 2000b.

adumbrate the significance of the device for understanding Dantean self-authorization. Much as with the use of Virgil as guide in the *Commedia* (Chapter 1, section ii; Chapter 7, sections i–ii), the initial decision to adopt the mode of self-commentary in *Vita Nova* and then *Convivio* has dramatic implications, apart from the specifics of implementation. As discussed in Chapter 1 (especially section iv), in the later Middle Ages commentary is normatively written in Latin and reserved for texts with established cultural *auctoritas*: the classical poets (e.g., the *Ovidius Moralizatus*) and philosophers (Scholastic commentaries on Aristotle); the Bible as a whole (the *Glossa Ordinaria*) and its separate books (e.g., commentaries on the Psalms). The relationship established between (modern) commenting reader and (ancient) commented text is hierarchical; it implicitly or explicitly places both figures within a cosmic order by which impersonal Truth descends from God through his chosen instruments into the world of history.[7] Thus, for Dante to treat vernacular poetic texts by a modern writer (himself) as worthy of commentary is, *de facto*, to elevate them to the status of *auctoritates*, and himself to that of *auctor*. To divide himself between the roles of commenting *lector* and commented-upon *auctor*, furthermore, is to appropriate for both "Dantes" the impersonality that traditionally accompanies this relationship. In this sense, his use of the device follows the same conservative impulse to reproduce the traditional norms of the culture of authority at play in *Convivio* in the positing of Aristotle as the type of philosophical authority and of Latin as the model for linguistic prestige.

On the other hand, an exploration of the complex, compromised, forms that self-commentary takes first in *Vita Nova* and then *Convivio*, will show that this device embodies the paradoxical tension between Dante's traditionalism and his radical experimentalism. If self-commentary mimes the canons of Latin authority, it also implicitly contests them by displacing them into the vernacular. If, at one level, it reproduces the hierarchy of *lector* and *auctor*, at another it breaks that hierarchy down, by revealing that a single person, however carefully divided up in temporal and formal terms, can occupy the roles of both reader *and* writer (cf. Mazzaro 1981: 80).[8] In

---

[7] See Chapter 1, n 8. While this model works best for the Bible, and may be more or less explicitly present in other venues of commentary, such as glosses on the works of Virgil or Ovid (cf. n 10; Chapter 1, n 53), underlying assumptions are similar.

[8] On the *auctor/lector* dialectic in Dante, contemporary theory and the later Middle Ages, see Chapter 1, sections ii–iv and nn 47–48, 55–56. Boccaccio's copy of *VN* excludes the *divisioni* from the text proper, treating them as marginalia (D'Andrea 1982: 14–17; Noakes 1988: 80–7; Stillinger 1992: 57–9). Boccaccio's own adventure in self-annotation, the *Teseida*, takes the "conservative" tack of marginal annotations (Hollander 1977; Noakes 1988: 87–97; Carruthers 1990: 218; Schnapp 1991–2; Stillinger 1992: 3–18 *et passim*; Roush 2002: chapter 2).

short, Dante's adoption of the formal device of auto-commentary provides
the best illustration of how the pursuit of traditional *auctoritas* leads him
to take on traits of a new and different kind of author, one distinguished
by his close affiliation with a new and different idea of readership.

II. VITA NOVA

So far, the interpretive *scoglio* that is Dante's *Vita Nova* has played only a
minimal role in this study, with the excuse that this first of Dante's fully
authenticated works to step beyond the generic confines of the lyric form
does not make use of the language of *auctoritas* at all, and touches only
briefly, if consequentially, on the problem of legitimizing the vernacular.
Initially, the *libello*'s main concern seems to be that of locating Dante in
relation not to the culture of *auctoritas*, but rather to that of the flourishing
contemporary Tuscan literary scene, the lyric community "fathered" by
the Bolognese Guido Guinizelli and led by Dante's *primo amico*, Guido
Cavalcanti (cf. De Robertis 1961: especially 17–18). However, once attention
is focused on the device of auto-commentary, the relevance of this "little
book" becomes obvious, since it is the first, and in many ways the most
complex, of Dante's forays into that mode. In brief, *Vita Nova* represents
an early, if not necessarily the first, step in Dante's efforts to confer greater
seriousness on himself and the vernacular by moving them in the direction
of the themes and forms of high classical and/or Latin culture.[9]

At the same time, however, when compared to the texts previously con-
sidered, *Vita Nova* shows only a minimal *explicit* awareness of the larger
cultural consequences of its radical formal experiment in self-representation
(cf. Grayson 1963: 46; Tateo 1970b: 56). Some clarification on this point is
needed. Needless to say, Dante *is* eminently self-reflective in this text: he is
concerned with the evolution of his own emotions and of his poetic style,
as well as the relation of his poetry to its immediate vernacular precur-
sors. Nonetheless, intense self-consciousness in these areas only makes the
absence of meta-critical reflection on the project of the book as a whole – and
especially on its unique brand of auto-commentary – all the more notice-
able. My working hypothesis is that this lack of reflection, whether deliber-
ate or unconscious, is crucial in enabling Dante to take a first dramatic step

---

[9] De Robertis 1984: 3: "È tra i caratteri più significativi [della *VN*] . . . la prepotente forza di autoaffer-
mazione che la percorre da capo a fondo, la vocazione, per così dire, di autorità, in cui è compresa e
riassunta la stessa vocazione poetica." The relation of the form of *VN* to the constitution of Dantean
poetic authority is explored by Picone: e.g., 1979, 1987a, 2003a; Harrison 1988: 54–65; Menocal 1991:
chapter 1; Stillinger 1992: 44–117; Cristaldi 1994; O. Holmes 2000: chapter 6; Roush 2002.

down the road to *auctoritas* – since neither he nor his readers are forced to confront the scope of his transgression.

This section will examine *Vita Nova* in some detail, following two general lines of inquiry – roughly speaking "formal" and "thematic"– into the implications of its auto-exegetical enterprise. First, drawing on the research of several scholars,[10] it will show how this remarkable work eclectically adapts available models, both Latin and vernacular, to create a modified prosimetrum structure that evokes without reproducing the normative models of commentary on authoritative texts. This will be followed by a consideration of how the text both thematizes and dramatizes the relation between reading and writing, and how that relation evolves over the course of the *libello*, both toward a more normative commentary model (*CV*) and toward a redefinition of the author/reader dyad (*DC*). We need to begin, however, with a brief description of the text and its place in Dante's career.

Vita Nova was written in the first half of the 1290s when Dante was in his late twenties, and it constitutes a kind of retrospective summing up, as well as a palinodic reframing and reinterpretation, of his earlier career as vernacular love lyricist.[11] The book is a formal hybrid, surrounding a series of poetic lyrics in Italian – mostly sonnets, but also a few longer compositions, especially the multi-stanzaic *canzone* – with explanatory and explicatory prose, also in Italian. The poems recount individual moments related to Dante's experience of love for Beatrice, and they themselves are presented as artifacts of the past, contents of the "libro della memoria" that are being transcribed. They are accompanied by prose, which belongs to the "present" of the book's composition. The prose itself is subdivided into *ragioni* (present, selective narration of the past in which the poems were composed), and *divisioni* (products of the present that analyze the poems

---

[10] Jenaro–MacLennan 1960; De Robertis 1970: especially 177–238; D'Andrea 1982; Noakes 1988: chapter 3; Botterill 1994; Gorni 1996: xxxix–xli; Picone 1977 a and b, 1979, 1987a, 1995c, 2003a: 237–48. Picone's insistence on Ovid's *Remedia amoris*, with medieval commentaries, as Dante's principal model remains, without specific formal examples, sheerly thematic (e.g., 1993; 1997a: 56–8; 2003: 244–8). Stillinger 1992 reviews several historical models that have been adduced for the form of *VN* (54 and nn). I am indebted both to his list of models and to his account of the carefully structured syncretism of Dante's form. Cristaldi 1994 offers a relatively undigested but extensive compendium of Duecento literary and cultural phenomenon in relation to which *VN* may be situated.

[11] *VN* is typically seen as subject to palinodic revisitation by later texts (notably *CV* and *DC*; see Chapter 6, nn 2, 5, 7, 9), but is also a proving ground where Dante develops this textual instrument, perhaps influenced by Guittone d'Arezzo (see nn 16–17; Chapter 6, n 8). On the palinodic structure of *VN*, see Barolini 1984: 15; Noakes 1988: especially 70; Harrison 1988: especially 149–51; as well as Singleton 1949: especially chapter 3; De Robertis 1961: 8; Moleta 1978; also Chapter 6, section i. A related issue is the re-writing of some of the poems to conform to the narrative needs of the *libello* (De Robertis 1961: 13–14).

synchronically, as timeless objects).[12] Although the poems, as against the prose, exist in only one form, the two types of prose offer two different approaches to them – one "diachronic," one "synchronic" – and so they too can be viewed in a double light.

The narrative *ragioni* and analytical *divisioni* have quite distinct functions. The *ragioni* provide a narrative of the events in Dante's earlier love life that gave rise to the poems, and often detail both the process of composing the poems themselves and their reception by various readers.[13] In other words, they simultaneously narrate Dante's emotional history and his development as a poet. Sometimes the narrated events are identical with those described in the poems, but often the prose goes beyond the poetry, and sometimes there are significant differences between their accounts (cf. Stillinger 1992: 48; Picone 2003a: 252–3). The prose deliberately creates a chronological and narrative relation between the individual poems that could not easily be deduced from the poems themselves.[14]

The prose in its second, analytical, guise makes formal divisions of most of the poems, breaking them down descriptively into sub-units based on content. For much of the treatise the poems are preceded by narrative and followed by the divisions. After the death of Beatrice (chapter 28) the divisions are relocated so that they still follow the narrative, but precede the poems they analyze (chapter 31, par. 2–7; cf. D'Andrea 1982: 35–6; Vickers 1989; Stillinger 1992: 73, 104–7; Botterill 1994: 71–2). From time to time, particularly later in the *libello*, Dante omits division without comment (chapter 27), or asserts that no division is required (chapters 14, 26, 35, 36, 39, 40; Botterill 1994: 73–6). Despite the variety of poems, and in a number of cases their thematic and stylistic novelty and/or accomplishments, it is widely agreed that, as Domenico De Robertis put it, "è la prosa il fatto nuovo di questo libro" (1961: 6, see also chapter 1; cf. Singleton 1949: chapter 2; Vallone 1963) – the prose, and the unique manner in which the prose is combined with the poetry, is the hallmark of *Vita Nova*.[15] From this

---

[12] On the structure of *VN*, especially the prose *ragioni* and *divisioni*, see Rajna 1902; Singleton 1949: especially 29–54; Jenaro-MacLennan 1960; De Robertis 1970: especially 177–238; Vallone 1963; Picone 1977 a and b, 1979, 1987a, 2003a; Moleta 1978; Mazzaro 1981: chapters 3–4; D'Andrea 1982; Noakes 1988, chapter 3; Harrison 1988: 62–6; Durling and Martinez 1990: 55–69 and nn 7, 15, 18–19; Stillinger 1992: 44–117; Menocal 1991; Barolini 1994; Botterill 1994; Cristaldi 1994; Martinez 1998; Roush 2002: chapter 1. For the *divisioni*, see the handy schematics in Gorni 1996: 281–6; also D'Andrea 1982: 20–1.

[13] On the gamut of readers interpellated by *VN*, see Antonelli and Bianchini 1983: 204–5; Ahern 1990, 1992; Noakes 1988: chapter 3; cf. Ascoli 2003; on the projected readership of *CV*, see Chapter 2, n 11; see also Chapter 1, n 55.

[14] On *VN*'s narrative structure, see Singleton 1949: 8, 24; Guglielminetti 1977; Harrison 1988; Stillinger 1992; Pinto 1994; Cristaldi 1994; also n 82.

[15] The same caveat applies here as to *CV* (see n 66), namely that the prose, even as it transforms the sense of the individual poems it surrounds (n 11), is ultimately at the service of Dante-as-poet in a

perspective, *Vita Nova* may well be the single most innovative text Dante ever composed – with the possible exception of the *Commedia* itself – and it has certainly proved the most opaque to critical deciphering.

By innovation, I must stress, is not meant *ex novo* originality. Rather, the uniqueness of the *libello* is borne of reproducing while also reconfiguring what was already available, of bringing together multiple sources from widely disparate areas of cultural discourse. In other words, the structural hybrid described earlier is in turn the result of a sort of literary-historical composite, which draws upon precedents from two different linguistic traditions and several genres from within those traditions, but which is not identical to any of its models. Thus, while numerous past efforts at understanding the form of *Vita Nova* have sought to identify a single dominant, if not exclusive, source for it, this chapter will argue instead that its composite form is drawn from an equally composite repertory of sources – and that this eclecticism is the sign of a conscious effort by Dante to locate himself strategically within the range of possibilities available in the cultural field of authorship.

The first tradition he draws on, evidently, is that of the "vernacular," which includes Old French and troubadoric Occitan, as well as the developing Italian tradition. The poems, though aspiring to specific differences in content from their predecessors, nonetheless come directly out of the lyric vernacular tradition as it evolved over the thirteenth century, a point made explicit on a number of occasions, prominently in chapters 3 and 25. Moreover, as much recent scholarship has stressed, there are also several precedents for the collection of multiple poems, often (sub-)grouped as the works of a single writer, in one manuscript.[16] Cases such as those of Guiraut Riquier and Guittone d'Arezzo may even provide examples of a single-poet collection and are arranged according to coherent narrative and thematic principals, probably by their own authors (Poe 1984: chapter 5: Huot 1987: 330–7; O. Holmes 2000: chapter 1).[17] On the other hand, no convincing vernacular precedents exist for *Vita Nova* as a book of mixed prose and poetry composed by a single author.

---

larger sense, a point evidenced here in discussions of chapters 25 and 42. For the "poetics" of *VN*, see especially Tateo 1970b, 1971; Mazzotta 1983; Harrison 1988; Menocal 1991. See also n 12.

[16] These collections actively participate in canon formation, with attendant emphasis on individual authorship, in ways that anticipate Dante's strong literary historical and anthologizing tendencies. See, e.g., Antonelli and Bianchini 1983: 186–9; Petrucci 1995; Meneghetti 1992; Storey 1993; Steinberg 1999, 2000, 2007. See also Picone 1987a, 2003a. For *VN* as lyric anthology, O. Holmes 2000: chapter 6; Picone 1995c, 2003a: chapter 11.

[17] On Guittone in particular, see Moleta 1978; Antonelli and Bianchini 1983: 200–1; Barolini 1984: 100–12 *et passim*, 1997; Storey 1993; Picone 1995 a and b; Antonelli 1995; O. Holmes 2000: chapter 3; Borra 2000; Steinberg 1999, 2007; Scott 2004: 103–4. On the late medieval "author's book," see Chapter 1, n 51.

The narrative portions of the prose combine elements of two Occitan genres that comment upon lyrics, namely the so-called *vidas* and *razos* of the early thirteenth century, which, respectively, give thumbnail sketches of the lives of poets and short accounts of the circumstances of composition of certain poems.[18] There are even a few cases that might be said to anticipate the hybrid and extended format of *Vita Nova*. On the one hand, at times these prose commentaries accompany manuscript collections of poems; on the other, they occasionally incorporate poems and fragments of poetry. Some manuscript collections of *razos*, and especially those on Bertran de Born and Peire Vidal, anticipate the sort of macronarrative generated by the sequence of poems and prose in *Vita Nova* (Poe 1984). Nonetheless, neither genre ever approaches the elaborateness of *Vita Nova*, falling far short both of its wealth of biographical detail and of the length and continuity of its narrative, not to mention providing no precedent at all for either the technical language or the procedures of its *divisioni* (Poe 1984: 90). Nor to my knowledge do they ever take the form of first-person auto-commentary (cf. Jenaro MacLennan 1960: Poe 1984).

As for possible Latin models, once again, precedents come from a number of different domains and genres of writing. In general, vernacular models predominate for the poetry, with one important exception: the acknowledgment in chapter 25 of a group of classical poets – Homer, Virgil, Horace, Lucan, and Ovid – whose use of *prosopopeia*, personification, is given as a justificatory precedent for the employment of this trope by Dante and other vernacular "dicitori d'amore."[19] In general, however, Latin exemplars are more evident in relation to the two kinds of prose.

Specifically, for the narrative *ragioni*, various Latin precedents have been cited. Augustine's *Confessions* is tempting, not only because of the later,

---

[18] For the *vidas* and *razos*, see Avalle 1961: 129–34; Marshall 1972; Poe 1984; Egan 1985; Huot 1987; Burgwinkle 1990; Meneghetti 1992: especially chapters 5–6; O. Holmes 2000: especially chapter 1; cf. Stone 1994b: 8–9. For their pertinence to Dante and *VN*, see Rajna 1890; Singleton 1949: 51–2 and n; Jenaro MacLennan 1960; Zumthor 1973; Picone 1979: especially 33–9, 1987a, 1995c, 2003a: 242–4; Mazzaro 1981: especially 87–8; Poe: 88–92; Shapiro 1990: 99–112; Meneghetti 1992: 212; Dronke 1994: 107; Pinto 1994: 98–9.

[19] Chapter 25 is key to my argument. See n 41 for relevant criticism. Alessio 1995: 58–9 points out that *prosopopeia* is a trope specific to the high or tragic style according to the Latin rhetorical tradition and that its linkage here to *Amore*, a topic equally traditionally confined to the low or comic style, is an implicit challenge to the separation installed between classical *poete* and vernacular *dicitori* (and to the hierarchy of styles itself – see n 72; Chapter 3). See also Martinez 1998: 4 and n. Another bridge to high Latin culture is constituted if, as D'Andrea argues (1982: 24–5, 38–9), chapter 25 follows the model of a scholastic *quaestio* (ch. 2, nn 27, 48), an association reinforced by the presence of one of two references to Aristotle in the *libello* (par. 2; the other is in chapter 41, par. 6; cf. Chapter 2, n 34 and Paolazzi 1994: 91–2). Paolazzi 1998 also argues for the influence of Horace's *AP* on chapter 25 (127–37). For more on *prosopopeia*, see n 50.

apt reference in *Convivio*, but also because it offers a comparably detailed view of the autobiographical subject's life (cf. Guglielminetti 1977; Mazzaro 1981: 32–7 *et passim*). The Augustinian conversion story provides a broad analogue for the various "turning points" dramatized in *Vita Nova*: e.g., the shift to the new "stilo" of praise (*VN* 26.4; also 18–19); the traumatic changes surrounding Beatrice's death; the reversion to Beatrice *in morte* after flirtation with a *donna gentile*. On the other hand, the *Confessions* offer no precedent for the formal hybridity of the work, or for the analytics of the *divisioni*. Even more tempting is Boethius' *Consolation of Philosophy*, also invoked in *Convivio*, because it combines an "autobiographical" writing with a hybrid mix of poetry and prose. Notably, however, in the *Consolation* the poems function to rehearse the prose and to reflect critically on it (in *CV*'s terms, they are its "servant"), whereas in both *Vita Nova* and *Convivio* the relationship goes in the opposite direction. From a normative late medieval standpoint, the Boethian text cannot be said to fit the description of self-commentary at all.[20]

Michelangelo Picone has suggested that, in addition to the *vidas* and *razos*, the part of the Latin academic prologue, or *accessus ad auctores*, known as the *vita auctoris* might constitute a generic precedent (1979; 1987a), and this would also constitute a further link to the commentary tradition, to which the *accessus* was closely linked. However, just as with the Occitan prefaces, there is little specific comparability even between the *vitae auctoris*, which tend toward sketchy impersonality, and *Vita Nova*, while none of the other traditional headings of the *accessus* are recognizably treated as such.[21] On the other hand, the combination of *accessus* prologues with literary texts – notably those of the four Latin authors mentioned in chapter 25 – that are often also accompanied by formal descriptive and or analytical commentaries, does look more like *Vita Nova* formally speaking than most of

[20] Stillinger 1992: 41–2 argues that the "prosimetrum" form *stricte dictu*, as practiced, for example, by Boethius in the *Cons.* and by the *De Nuptiis Philologiae et Mercurii* of Martianus Capellus should be distinguished from the text-commentary combination, even when both parts are authored by a single person, because the latter posits a hierarchical relation between the two parts and a temporal separation in their composition which the former does not. See Jenaro-MacLennan 1960: 84–5 (following Zingarelli); Mazzaro 1981: especially 27–32; De Robertis 1984: 13. *Pace* Roush 2002: 15–17. This point further limits the usefulness of the *Cons.* as a *formal* model for either of the Dantean works (even as an "anti-modello" as Picone argues [2003a: 238–41]). D'Andrea's suggestion that Dante may have seen an edition of the *Cons.* with appended commentary is suggestive, but does not address the self-commentary issue (1982: 26–9; see also Chapter 2, nn 6, 39). On medieval commentaries of the *Cons.*, see Minnis *et al.* 1988: *et passim*. Interestingly, Boethius also authored a treatise on *divisio* which "divides division" (cf. D'Andrea 1982: 19). On the longer history of the mixed prose/verse form, see Dronke 1994.

[21] For the *accessus* form generally and in Dante, see also Chapter 1, nn 16, 48; also n 59 below.

the alternatives, since they include three distinct elements that correspond, *grosso modo*, to the three elements of the *libello*.

This model suggests two important points. First, *Vita Nova* establishes a formal relationship with an almost exclusively Latin tradition of surrounding the *auctoritates* produced by *auctores* with an elaborate critical apparatus, assimilating itself and Dante to that tradition.[22] To this degree, it may *also* follow on the *vidas* and *razos*, which can be thought of as aiming to appropriate by imitating the culture of Latin *auctoritas*, and specifically the *accessus* (Meneghetti 1992: 209–44; cf. Marshall 1972: especially lxxxi, xciii; see again n 18). On the other hand, Dante has not attempted to mirror the *accessus* and commentary tradition faithfully, neither referring to it specifically – as he does in *Convivio* – or imitating it closely – as the "Epistle to Cangrande" will (Ascoli 1997).

The feature of *Vita Nova* most easily accounted for through Latin sources is the analytical *divisioni*,[23] which of the three elements of the *libello* is the one that until recently has aroused by far the least critical interest. Here precedents in both style and content are to be found among the philosophical prose of Scholasticism, as Pio Rajna suggested over a century ago (1902; also D'Andrea 1982: 20–4 *et passim*). Most suggestively, as Stillinger points out (1992: especially 57–65), there is a special affinity with the *divisiones* included in Latin commentaries on the Bible, especially those on the *Psalms*, which were known in the Middle Ages to be poems, though the Vulgate renders them in prose. The "Sacra Pagina" literally surrounds a kind of poetry with multiple types of commentary (De Hamel 1984: chapter 2), especially with *divisioni* similar to Dante's, making it a compelling model for *Vita Nova*. In the *divisioni* Dante comes closest to treating his works *as if* they were the products of an *auctor* – and, as the precedent of commentary on the Psalms suggests, seems to be headed toward the analogy between himself and the human authors of the Bible that becomes so prominent in the *Commedia*.[24]

---

[22] For *VN*'s closest competitors as commentaries on "modern" authors see Chapter 1, n 56. De Robertis (1970: 208–25) argues that Dante draws on Brunetto Latini's *divisio* in his *Rettorica*. I accept D'Andrea's critique of this argument (1982: especially 18–20), although Latini does anticipate the rapprochement of modern reader and ancient author through the figure of the "sponitore" and may well have influenced Dante. As I have argued elsewhere (1997; 2003), *VN* establishes, with *CV*, and possibly the *ECG*, a paradigm that enabled the proliferation of commentaries on the *DC* in the '300 (see Chapter 1, n 2). As Parker puts it: "Dante commentary begins with Dante himself" (1993: 27).

[23] Which is not to deny that Dante puts his particular stamp on the procedure, as Durling and Martinez 1990: chapter 1 and Stillinger 1992: 94–100 have shown: see Chapter 5, nn 39–40.

[24] Because of this chapter's focus, discussions of sources which are thematic and allusive rather than structural are mostly omitted: e.g. Branca 1967 (saints' lives); Nolan 1970 (Revelation); O. Holmes 2000: chapter 6 (Gospel of John). More cogent are examinations, like Stillinger's, of *VN*'s links to

This rapid survey establishes several key points. First, in *Vita Nova* Dante makes eclectic, synthetic use of formal models, including both vernacular and Latin, suggesting an *ad hoc* appropriation for the purposes of an individual literary project, rather than a programmatic attempt to elevate Italian in relation to *gramatica*. At the same time, although neither the prose nor the prose/poetry hybrid can be accounted for through any single source in either Latin or the romance vernaculars, the use of prose commentary on poetry points directly toward a high-cultural practice of Latin that signals the prestige of *auctores*, literary and otherwise. It thus suggests, implicitly, a parallel between Dante's vernacular lyrics and canonical Latin texts, both secular and sacred. Third and finally, the single most striking feature of *Vita Nova* is also the least easily accounted for, namely the combination of first-person self-reference with the use of commentary forms. No vernacular precedent exists for auto-commentary of this kind. Nor is the situation much better in Latin, where the two most obvious candidates, Boethius' *Consolation* and Augustine's *Confessions* do not participate in the commentary tradition in and of themselves.[25]

In *Vita Nova*, Dante adapts a notable formal feature of Latin scholastic culture to the vernacular, namely commentary, but in his adaptation changes it radically, by introducing a first-person commentator identical with, though temporally successive to, a first-person author. Reviewing the deployment of formal models leads to a consideration of how the pursuit of authority is staged over the course of *Vita Nova*, and particularly of how it dramatizes the respective roles of reader and of author. The basic issues are delineated in the first three chapters, which together constitute an introductory unit that describes the genesis of the book and lays out its basic formal and thematic patterns.[26] Here, the prose "io" of *Vita Nova* describes the writing of the text as both resulting from and producing acts of reading, beginning with the very first lines:

In quella parte del *libro* della mia memoria dinanzi a la quale poco si potrebbe *leggere*, si trova una *rubrica* la quale dice 'Incipit *Vita nova.*' Sotto la quale rubrica io trovo *scritte le parole* le quali è mio *intendimento d'assemplare* in questo libello; e se non tutte, almeno la loro *sentenzia*. (1.1)

the combined text-commentary of individual Biblical books, e.g., Nasti 1998 (Song of Songs) and especially Martinez 1998 (Lamentations). See also Chapter 2, n 88; Chapter 5, section iv, nn 56, 58; Chapter 7, section v, especially nn 86, 107, 113, 115, 119, 147.

[25] Curtius (1948: 221) does offer one eleventh-century example of a Latin author who introduces his own work using an *accessus* format.

[26] Gorni gathers these materials in one chapter (Alighieri 1996). He places the last paragraph of the traditional chapter 3, which recounts the responses of the sonnet's readers, in his chapter 2. For reasons that will become apparent, this may not have been the right decision.

(In that part of the book of my memory before which there is little to read is a chapter heading that says 'Incipit *Vita Nova*.' Under that heading I find written the words that it is my intention to copy out in this little volume; and if not all of them, at least their basic meaning.)[27]

These two sentences display at least four features relevant to this discussion: (1) *Vita Nova* presents itself, to use Bonaventure's categories, as a scribe's or compiler's transcription of another book of the same name;[28] (2) the originary book on which the "libello" is based is apparently written in Latin and follows high culture models of rubrication ("Incipit *Vita Nova*");[29] (3) in choosing this figure to describe his book, the "io" who writes tacitly turns himself into a text to be glossed and studied, effecting the conflation of person and book which, as with the "Virgil" of the *Commedia*, is a defining trait of *auctoritas*; (4) the separation between Dante as authoritative text to be glossed and Dante as transcriber, compiler, and commentator on that text is the separation between past and present, again echoing the traditional structure of *auctoritas*.[30]

Chapter 2, which describes Dante's first sight of Beatrice at age nine and his consequent *innamoramento*, continues the textual metaphor:

E però che soprastare a le passioni e atti di tanta giovetudine pare alcuno parlare fabuloso, mi partirò da esse; e trapassando molte cose le quali si potrebbero trarre de l'essemplo onde nascono queste, verrò a quelle parole le quali sono scritte ne la mia memoria sotto maggiori paragrafi. (2.10)

(And because dwelling on the passions and the acts of one so youthful may seem to some to speak fantastically, I will leave them behind, and passing over many things which could be drawn from the text from which these arise, I will come to those words which are written in my memory under greater headings.)

Dante the scribe becomes a judicious *compilator*, using the formal model of the book to ward off the danger that his account will be seen as the fictive

---

[27] For the continued use of the standard chapter numbers for reference, see Chapter 2, n 1.

[28] See Chapter 1, n 4. For the figure of the "scribe" see, e.g., De Hamel 1984: chapter 3. For considerations of the prose "io" of *VN* in terms of these categories, see, first of all, Singleton 1949: chapter 2; also Huot 1987: especially 335; Stillinger 1992; Cristaldi 1994: 102–3; O. Holmes 2000: chapter 6; Picone 1995c: 164; 2003a: 225–6, 246; Levers 2002: 10–14 (cf. Chapter 1, n 73). See also Noferi 1982–3: 58–60. On the *"book of memory,"* see Curtius 1948: chapter 16; Yates 1966; Carruthers 1990; Bolzoni 1995. For Dante, see again Singleton 1949: chapter 2; also Spitzer 1937: 103–7; Tateo 1970b: 73–5; Guglielminetti 1977; Mazzotta 1983.

[29] *Vita Nova* is ambiguous on multiple levels: it can refer to the title of the book, or to Dante's biography, and then either to his chronological age ("the young life"; e.g. Gorni 2001: 133–6) or to his psychological-spiritual existence ("the new, miraculous life"; De Robertis 1961: 16, 117–20, 1984: 27–8n; Picone 1987a: 64–5). It may also be taken as either Italian or Latin.

[30] On Dante's Virgil, see Chapter 1, section ii; Chapter 7, especially sections i–iii. On the temporal structure of *auctoritas*, see again Chapter 2, section ii, especially the citation from *MN* 3.3.11–16, and Minnis 1984: 13.

ravings, the "parlare fabuloso," of an imaginative youth. A similarly objec-
tifying, analytical and "authorizing," function is served by the rhetorical
gesture of dividing his psychological self into three distinct "spiriti" (cf.
Stillinger 1992: 80–2; Paolazzi 1994: 63–4), each of which comments *in
Latin* on the experience of seeing Beatrice and of Dante's consequent sub-
jugation to the Lord of Love.

The message of this chapter is decidedly double as concerns the status of
the treatise and its author. The Dantean subject, already divided up between
past and present, is further sub-divided as to its past experience, and all three
parts (which themselves can be divided: as the "spirito sensitivo" includes
the "spirito visivo" and others) are then subjected hierarchically to Love
(cf. Durling and Martinez 1990: 407 n 66). They all speak in Latin – in
keeping with the initial implication that the book of memory is written
in that language – and thus align Dante with the higher culture. At the
same time, Dante introduces a quotation from the greatest of the classical
poets, Homer, which is given in Italian.[31] In other words, this chapter tacitly
anticipates the *Commedia*'s strategy of lifting Dante up to the level of the
auctores while bringing them down to his own.

Chapter 3 introduces what quickly becomes the systematic double focus
of the book on Dante's experience of Beatrice (in the form of a visionary
dream of her) and on the production and reception of poetry in relation
to that experience. It also models the characteristic tripartite form of the
libello: narrative *ragione*, followed by poem, followed by analytical *divisione*,
followed by a return to the *ragione*. It thus adds "commentator" to the
"io's" list of readerly occupations. And it parallels the psychological *divisio*
of chapter 2 with a splitting of the text. Despite the elaborate procedure,
however, Dante offers no justification for either the double focus of the
narrative or the tripartite form: both are introduced without explanation
(cf. Botterill 1994: 66).

The narrative of a dream vision confirms the hierarchy described in
chapter 2: Dante as loving subject is in thrall to both Beatrice and *Amore*.
It also continues the recourse to Latin, although the two citations – "Ego
dominus tuus" and "Vide cor tuum" – are now assigned to the lover's Lord
and not to him directly. The subsequent account of the production of a
poem reporting the vision, however, shifts the book's focus dramatically. In
the first place, it complicates the textual metaphor. Having been told that
Vita Nova is a book that records the contents of memory figured as a book,

---

[31] For the use of Latin in *VN*, see also Chapter 3, n 1. On this passage, cf. De Robertis 1961: 29; Spitzer
1937: 107–9. On Homer in *VN*, see also n 42.

we now learn that the book of memory not only records biographical events, but also copies out poetic texts produced by and recording those events: texts within the text now transcribed in yet another text (cf. Singleton 1949: 28–9, 53). Furthermore, the implicit quest to be integrated into the ranks of the classical *auctores* leaves off almost before it has begun, as the narrator recounts the story of a much earlier stage in his development.[32] Dante tells not only of composing "A ciascun'alma presa," but also of sending it out for interpretation by a community of contemporary readers – specifically to the poets he calls the "fedeli d'amore," including Guido Cavalcanti, his "first friend" (3.14).[33]

The focus of this part of the *ragione* then is doubly on interpretive reading and on writing. In sending the poem to the *fedeli d'amore* Dante asserts his credentials as a vernacular poet, a "trovatore" who has already learned, "l'arte del dire parole per rima" (the art of saying words through rhyme; 3.9). This is not the first poem he wrote, but it is the one with which he chose to make a public debut. Through it, Dante demonstrates that he has a readership concerned with understanding the meaning of his poetry: he is a poet not only because he writes in verse, but also because others treat him as one by reading him both "passively and actively."[34] That readership, furthermore, is composed of the community of vernacular writers into which he hopes to be assimilated.

Given the normatively hierarchical relation between medieval readers and writers, the scene suggests that the newest writer, "l'ultimo arrivato," is submitting himself humbly to the "giudizio" of his betters, although he *is* careful to point out first that they are not his teachers, since he learned this art on his own ("per me medesimo"; 3.9). At the same time, however, he also turns the tables on them, submitting them to him as their superior, by converting them from writers into readers. Crucially, he also insists that as readers they are unsuccessful: no one, not even Guido, ultimately decodes

---

[32] See also Chapter 2, section ii. Note that the poem, written earlier, omits the Latin. In other words, chapter 3 works on two levels: the present of the *libello* where Dante engages classical culture, and a past where he remains within the sphere of the vernacular.

[33] Readings of chapter 3 tend to focus on the dream vision and the poetic interpretations of it (e.g., Singleton 1949: 13–14; Mazzotta 1983; Harrison 1988: 17–28; Noakes 1990: 49–52; Stillinger 1992: 46–51; Pinto 1994: 47–50; Stone 1994a; cf. Menocal 1991: 38–46), but rarely probe the significance of sending the poem around for interpretation to the *fedeli d'amore*. Exceptions are De Robertis 1961: 38–43; Picone 1979: 30–1; Ahern 1992; Fenzi 1999b: 9–14. On the key motif of friendship in *VN* and elsewhere in the Dantean *oeuvre*, begin with Gorni 2001: 133–48; cf. Mazzotta 1983; Ascoli 1997: 319. On Cavalcanti in *VN*, see nn 35, 39, 44.

[34] Compare *DVE*, 2.8.3: "lectio passio vel actus legendi" (Ch. 2, n 98). The passage is particularly relevant to the present discussion of the interpenetrating roles of author (singer) and reader. See also n 8.

the poem correctly, even though its meaning is *now*, at the moment when he composes the prose *ragione* of *Vita Nova* 3, clear even to "li più semplici" (the simplest minds; 3.15).

Chapter 3, then, at once evokes the traditional medieval writer/reader relationship and anticipates a dramatic reconfiguration of it. On the one hand, Dante has visibly divided himself up between his past activities as a poet and his present occupation as transcriber of the contents of the book of memory and commentator on the poetry it contains. He has traded shamelessly on the distinction in defining his relationship to the *fedeli d'amore* and to Guido. On the other hand, he is also on the way to collapsing the distinction between the activities, or at least to locating them simultaneously in a single individual. One might say that the poem itself is already given in the form of a transcription of the originating vision – that is, it is a reading in the text of Dante's psyche. More cogently, the *fedeli d'amore* are at once poets, if not *auctores*, and their "readings" return to Dante in the form of poems they have written. In addition, even as Dante divides and sub-divides himself textually, he is taking no pains to conceal that the author of the poems and the *scriptor/compilator/commentator* of them are one person, though they remain separated in time (cf. Moleta 1978: 369–78). Finally, to complicate matters, an implicit question is raised about Dante's status as interpreter of his own experiences, as well as of the poems in which they are recorded. If "lo verace giudicio del detto sogno non fue veduto allora per alcuno" (the true meaning of said dream was not seen then by anyone), one might infer that Dante too was unable to decipher it (cf. Stone 1994a: 135–6).

Vita Nova then goes on not only to recount Dante's experience of Beatrice, and Love's dominion, but also to narrate significant shifts in both his understanding of the nature of Love and his approach to writing poems about it. Notably, chapters 24 and 25 return to the visionary experience of Love and to the enterprise of vernacular poetry in a way that both completes and goes beyond the problematics opened in chapter 3.[35] As often observed, chapter 24 occupies a privileged narrative and thematic place vis-à-vis the vision of Love in chapter 2 – designating an illuminating shift in Dante's perspective from traditional erotic Love to Love as a transcendent principle

---

[35] For a succinct review of Love's evolving appearances in *VN* and the shift in the relation of Dante-commentator to "Him," see Tateo 1970b: 58–61. The *locus classicus* is Singleton 1949: chapter 3; cf. De Robertis 1961: chapter 3. A reading of chapters 24–25 as inextricably connected to each other and to the poetic project shared with Cavalcanti is in Marti 1991, who rightly insists that the formal separation between chapters derives from Barbi's editorial fiat (500–1; cf. Chapter 2, n 1). Picone 1979: chapter 2 also pairs 3 with 24 and 25. See also nn 39, 44 below.

that is similar to Beatrice, perhaps even equivalent to the Christian God.[36] In fact, this chapter and the next one also complete the process of placing Dante at the head of the class of vernacular poets, ready to move beyond to something greater. At the same time they operate a parallel, upward shift – of conversion or internal palinode – in the relation between reading and writing. In them, Dante both trades on the traditional *auctor/lector* dichotomy and points the way beyond it to a more modern concept of an author who is also a reader, and whose understanding of his own text (*intendimento*) is thus identical to his original intention (*intendimento*) in composing it. In so doing he implicitly comes to resemble his creator, the Author of authors, whose understanding (*intellectum*) is simultaneous with his perfectly realized creative intentions (*intentionem*) (Nardi 1938: 198–9).[37]

Chapter 24 undoubtedly constitutes a high water mark in the ongoing narrative of Dante's development as a vernacular love poet. Following soon after the conversion to a new "stilo," that of praise (26.4, also 18–19; see Chapter 7, section v, especially nn 113, 120, 122, 125), this chapter recounts a new "imaginazione" or vision of Love, who says to Dante: "Pensa di benedicere lo dì che io ti presi, però che tu lo devi fare" (think of blessing the day that I took you, since you must do it; 24.2). In direct contrast to the scene of Dante standing by as anguished witness to the devouring of his own heart, this chapter depicts him as he experiences a rapturous pleasure: "parea avere lo cuore sì lieto, che me non parea che fosse lo mio cuore, per la sua nuova condizione" (it seemed to me that my heart was so glad that it seemed not to be my heart, on account of its new condition; *ibid.*).

---

[36] Singleton 1949: especially 55–77, 90–2, 112–14; Picone 1979: chapter 2; Durling and Martinez 1990: 392–3 n 50; Potter 1990: especially 75–6; Shapiro 1998: 114–5; Fenzi 1999b: 23–5; Durling 2001: 307–12, 2003; cf. Picone 1979; Harrison 1988: 10–11, 50–5; Gorni 1990: 28–31, 45–50; Martinez 2000: 28.

[37] For the related allegory/allegoresis equivocation in *CV* 2.1, see Chapter 2, nn 66–67 (also Pinto 1994: 120, 151–7). On *intendimento* in *VN*, see Durling and Martinez 1990: 64–5; Pinto 1994: especially 120; also Ahern 1990: 29; Cristaldi 1994: 102–3; Barolini 1998b: 38 and n 23 (who notes that "intenzione" in *VN* also refers to desire). For *intentio* in *MN*, see Cassell 2004: 295 n 11, 310 n 103; also Smalley 1952: 306–7; Chapter 5, n 26. See also overviews in Gregory 1971; Marenbon 1987: 139–43. On the *accessus* category of *intentio auctoris*, see Chapter 1, section iv. For different accounts of how the Dante of the *DC* points toward modern or postmodern ideas of reading see Gellrich 1985; Noakes 1988: chapters 2–3; Stone 1994a; Franke 1996; as well as the Auerbach (1954)–Spitzer (1955) *querelle* on Dante's addresses to the reader. See also the telegraphic, anachronistic, but suggestive pages of Spivak 1981 (54–5). Finally, the theological doctrine of the coincidence of "authorial" intention and intellectual understanding in God adduced by Nardi in the passage cited above comes in his gloss on *CV* 4.1.8, where Dante describes the crisis of his relations with Philosophy over the question of whether "la materia prima de li elementi era da Dio intesa," which led to his "digression" on the topic of nobility in *CV* 4 (1938; cf. De Robertis 1988: 529–31 nn). From the perspective of my Chapter 2, this apparently abandoned topic dovetails with the problem of the author from *avieo*, which concerns the poet's god-like shaping of the "materia prima" of language, the vowels (see again Chapter 2, section v, especially n 82).

Immediately after this vision, a "gentile donna" appears to Dante, followed by Beatrice herself:

E poco dopo queste parole, che lo cuore mi disse con la lingua d'Amore, io vidi venire verso me una gentile donna . . . che fue già molto donna di questo primo mio amico. E lo nome di questa donna era Giovanna, salvo che per la sua bieltade . . . imposto l'era nome Primavera, e così era chiamata. E appresso lei, guardando, vidi venire la mirabile Beatrice . . . e parve che Amore mi parlasse nel cuore, e dicesse: "Quella prima è nominata Primavera solo per questa venuta d'oggi; ché io mossi lo imponitore del nome a chiamarla così Primavera, cioè 'prima verrà' lo die che Beatrice si mostrerrà dopo la imaginazione del suo fedele. E se anche vogli considerare lo primo nome suo, tanto è quanto dire 'prima verrà,' però che lo suo nome Giovanna è da quello Giovanni lo quale precedette la verace luce, dicendo: 'Ego vox clamantis in deserto; parate viam Domini.'" Ed anche mi parve che mi dicesse, dopo queste parole: "E chi volesse sottilmente considerare, quella Beatrice chiamerebbe Amore, per molta somiglianza che ha meco." (24.3–5)

(And soon after my heart said these words to me in the tongue of Love, I saw coming toward me the noble lady of this my first friend. And the name of this lady was Giovanna, although on account of her beauty she had been given the name Primavera [springtime], and thus she was called. And beside her, as I looked, I saw coming the miraculous Beatrice . . . and it seemed that Love spoke to me in my heart and said "this first one is called Primavera only because of her coming today, on account of which I moved the one who imposed that name to do so: that is, she will 'come before' on the day that Beatrice will display herself following the vision of her faithful one. And if you wish also to consider her first, given name, Giovanna, it comes from that John who preceded the true light, saying 'I am a voice crying in the wilderness; prepare the way of the Lord'. And it also seemed to me that afterward he said these words: "And whoever wished to consider with subtlety would understand that Beatrice should be called Love, on account of the great resemblance that she bears to me.")

Not only is Dante's emotional experience of Love different, but Love himself has changed in significant ways. First, the god speaks Italian, rather than Latin, a point that might suggest the elevation of the former language, but also implies a relative de-classification or at least a reconfiguration of Love himself.[38] On this score, it is important that Love, while still figured as a character external to Dante, does not appear visually, but only as a voice, and that his autonomy is doubly compromised, first by the claim that it

---

[38] *Pace* Singleton 1946. Note the use of Latin in the passage, but only as a quotation from the Bible, which becomes the new point of comparison for Dante's writings, just before he brings the four Latin *poete* on stage. As Scott 2004: 8 points out, Love speaks in Italian for the first time in 12.4. On chapter 12, see nn 54, 80 below.

is really Dante's heart that speaks "con lingua d'amore" and then by the assertion that Beatrice is entitled to use the god's name.

The most striking aspect of the passage is the analogy between Giovanna and Beatrice, on the one hand, and, John the Baptist and Christ on the other. As the magisterial reading of Singleton 1949 (chapter 3) suggests, the comparison, and the chapter as a whole, displaces the near-blasphemy of a *religio Amoris* (cf. Lewis 1936: especially chapter 1) permeating the troubadoric and early Italian tradition, into a claim that Beatrice is a *figura Christi*, and can thus be called Love just as God himself is *caritas*, or spiritual love (1 John 4: 8). Apart from the implication for Dante's spiritual autobiography, the analogy also designates a new stage in his development as a vernacular poet. Instead of being one among many poetic *fedeli d'amore*, Dante is now cast as the *fedele* of Beatrice-Amore, and he is left with only one companion-poet, namely Cavalcanti.[39]

Moreover, Dante establishes an invidious hierarchy that concedes mere temporal primacy to Cavalcanti and his lady, while giving superiority of essence to his own beloved, his works, and himself (see nn 35 and 36). As Giovanna (who "*prima* verrà") is to Beatrice, so Guido ("*primo* amico") is to him: a prophetic precursor showing the way toward the typological fulfillment of the vernacular in its true "redeemer."[40] This move is emphasized as Dante points out that he omits some of his vision from the poem, which he writes to Guido alone ("tacendomi certe parole le quali pareano da tacere" [keeping quiet about certain words that I thought worth keeping quiet about; 24.6]). The part omitted, in fact, is the placement of Giovanna in Beatrice's service, and thus the implied subordination of Guido to Dante (Fenzi 1999b: 24–5; cf. Marti 1991: 488–94). The process of moving Dante

---

[39] The prevailing thesis is that chapter 24, usually in tandem with chapter 25, constitutes an implied "overgoing" of Guido that belies the continuing rhetoric of friendship. On the Cavalcanti–Dante relationship in *VN* see, among many, De Robertis 1961 (32–43, 71–85 *et passim*), 1970 (231–8, 269), 1973, 1986; Nardi 1962; Contini 1968; Picone 1979: 30–2, 64–72; Lipking 1981: 28–9; Mazzotta 1983; Barolini 1984: especially 136–9, 1998b; Harrison 1988: chapter 4; Hainsworth 1988; Gorni 1990; Marti 1991; Cristaldi 1994: 184–203; Pinto 1994: 45–55, 119–22; Paolazzi 1998: 134–7 *et passim*; Fenzi 1999b: 23–9; Durling 2001: 307–12, 2003; Ardizzone 2002: 41–6 *et passim*; Martinez 2003b. The situation is complicated by the increasingly popular thesis that "Donna me prega" did not precede *VN* as traditionally assumed (e.g., De Robertis 1984: 172n [but now see 1986: 31n]; Mazzotta 1986: 60–3; Menocal 1991: 42–3 and n; Paolazzi 1994: 55), but rather Cavalcanti's *canzone* responds to the provocations of the *libello* (Tanturli 1993; Malato 1997). See the favorable summary of Fenzi 1999b: 30–5 and the cogent critique of Barolini 1998b: 60–3. Though influenced by Harrison, Fenzi and Durling, I believe that the Cavalcanti question has overshadowed important aspects of chapter 25. See n 44.

[40] See De Robertis 1961: 47; Barolini: 1984: 138–9; Picone 1987a, 2003a: 232; Marti 1991: 197–8; O. Holmes 2000: 137. On poetic typology in the *DC*, see Chapter 1, n 69; Chapter 6: section i and nn 12, 15; Chapter 7, section ii.

from *ultimo arrivato* to top spot among the *trovatori* and *fedeli* is complete, and the open recourse to a Biblical, prophetic language shows the way to a very different conception of Dantean authorship.

It is no coincidence that the following chapter (25) constitutes a meta-literary digression, in which, for the only time in *Vita Nova*, Dante reflects overtly on the status of his poetic enterprise, placing it in relation to the nascent vernacular tradition, which is in turn directly compared to the classical literature written by *poete*, that is by the figures more usually known as *auctores*.[41] Even here, however, the ancient/modern question is brought in as an ostensible sidebar to another, apparently separate issue, namely that of Dante's repeated personification of Love as a human being who talks and walks and laughs, although Love is not – as he puts it, again using ostentatiously Scholastic terminology – a "substance," either physical or spiritual, but rather an "accident in substance," i.e., an event taking place within the mind and body of a human being. This question follows logically from the reappearance of Love in the preceding chapter (see n 35), where Dante hedges his bets by variously qualifying the personification of Love who had earlier appeared in the guise of feudal lord, in the vein of Capellanus and the troubadours (i.e., of chapter 3; cf. De Robertis 1961: chapter 3).

In order to justify this apparently abusive linguistic usage, or so he claims, the Dantean narrator introduces a brief history of love poetry in the Western tradition:

A cotale cosa dichiarire ... prima è da intendere che anticamente non erano dicitori d'amore in lingua volgare, anzi erano dicitori d'amore certi poete in lingua latina; tra noi, dico, avvegna forse che tra altra gente addivenisse, e addivegna ancora, sí come in Grecia, non volgari ma litterati poete queste cose trattavano. E non è molto numero d'anni passati, che apparíro prima questi poete volgari; ché dire per rima in volgare tanto è quanto dire per versi in latino, secondo alcuna proporzione. E segno che sia picciolo tempo, è che se volemo cercare in lingua d'oco e in quella di sì, noi non troviamo cose dette anzi lo presente tempo per cento e cinquanta anni. E la cagione per che alquanti grossi ebbero fama di sapere dire, è che quasi

---

[41] On chapter 25, see Lewis 1936: 47–8; Singleton 1949 (especially 29–30, 48–50, 57–8, 74–6), 1954: 67–73; De Robertis 1961: 150–1, 1970: 185, 231–8, 1973, 1984: 171–8 nn, 1986; Grayson 1963: 42–6, 1965: 16–17, 1972b: 64–6; Tateo 1970b; Hollander 1974: 20–1; Picone, 1979: especially 18–26, 1987a, 1997a: 54–8, 2003a: chapters 11–13 *et passim*; Lipking 1981: 24, 28; Spivak 1981: 52–5; Mazzotta 1983: 8–10, 1986: 62–3, 1993a: 19; Tavoni 1984; Brownlee 1984; Barański 1986a: 51–2; D'Andrea 1987: 74–5; Harrison 1988: 54–68; Paolazzi 1994: 54–7, 1998: 127–37 *et passim*; Cristaldi 1994: especially 70–2, 104–5; Gorni 1995: 179–81; Fenzi 1999b: 25–9; Martinez 2000: 28; Roush 2002: 34–6. Pinto 1994: chapter 5 sees here an anticipation of *CV*'s poetry/philosophy struggle (Chapter 2, section v). See also nn 35, 36; Chapter 3, n 2. For the term *poeta* in the Dantean *oeuvre*, see Chapter 2, n 2; Chapter 7, sections iv, vi and nn 148–150; for *VN*, see especially De Robertis 1970: 185–6; Picone 1979: chapter 1.

fuoro li primi che dissero in lingua di sì. E lo primo che cominciò a dire sì come poeta volgare, si mosse però che volle fare intendere le sue parole a donna, a la quale era malagevole d'intendere li versi latini. E questo è contra coloro che rimano sopra altra matera che amorosa, con ciò sia cosa che cotale modo di parlare fosse dal principio trovato per dire d'amore. (25.3–5)

(To clarify this matter . . . I shall begin by saying that, in ancient times there were no speakers of love writing in the vernacular, the only speakers of love were certain poets in the Latin tongue; among us [and this probably happened in other nations as it also happened in Greece] it was not vernacular but learned poets who wrote about these things. And not many years have passed since these vernacular poets first appeared, [I call them poets too] because to speak with rhyme in the vernacular is the same as to compose [metered] verses in Latin, analogically speaking. And proof that it is but a short time is that if we look at the Occitan and Italian literatures, we shall not find any poems written more than 150 years before the present time [i.e., mid-twelfth century]. And the reason that a number of crude writers acquired the reputation of knowing how to speak [of love] was that they were almost the first that spoke [wrote] in the Italian language. And the first one that began to speak as a vernacular poet was moved to do so because he wished to make his words understood to a woman, for whom it was very difficult to comprehend Latin verses. And this is said against those who rhyme concerning other than amorous matters, on account of the fact that such a way of speaking was first found in order to speak of love.)

Dante then justifies his use of the trope of personification on the grounds that the ancient "poete" also used it. And at this point he gives the examples from the five classical *auctores* –Virgil, Lucan, Horace, Homer, and Ovid – only one of whom, Ovid, is strictly speaking a poet of love.[42]

The rhetorical effect of this poetic history is twofold. In the first place, it establishes a line of continuity between past and present, between the authoritative antiquity of the Greeks and Romans and the "vulgar," and at times crude, innovations of the "dicitori d'amore" in Italian and Occitan. A certain license to fictionalize and to portray figuratively belongs to the

---

[42] The specific examples offered deserve scrutiny. It is doubly significant that the Ovid example comes last – not only emphasizing the priority of other "higher" types of discourse, but also opening a further passageway between Dante and the classics (Picone, e.g., 1993, 1997a; cf. n 10). But it is also noteworthy: (a) that Virgil comes first and actually furnishes three separate examples (cf. Brownlee 1984: 603); (b) that Horace's example is both his own and a citation of Homer, suggesting a model for literary historical succession (Greek to Latin, Latin to vernacular); and (c) that the Homer–Horace example is an invocation of the poetic Muse who, given the question of *prosopopeia* addressed, may be understood as a projection of the poet's own abilities, with possible relevance to Dante and his "book of memory" (cf. Picone 2003a: 240–1). Compare *Inf.* 2.7–9, where the Muses and Dante's poetic memory blend into one. For Horace as a primary source for Dante in chapter 25, see Paolazzi 1998: 127–37. For Dante and Horace more generally, see Paolazzi 1998: chapters 1–3, as well as Barański 1999; also Chapter 7, nn 15, 157. For Dante and Ovid in general, see Chapter 1, n 27. For Dante's use of Ovid in *Ep. 3*, see Chapter 2, section vi.

vulgar poets because it first belonged to the ancients. Moreover, the poets from whom he cites examples are, as we have seen, the greatest of the poetic *auctores*. This is a first major step down a road that will make Dante a companion and presumptive equal ("sesto tra cotanto senno" [sixth among so much wisdom]; *Inf.* 4.102) in the gathering of these same five poets in Limbo.[43]

At the same time, Dante tells his story so as to maintain a sharp distinction between ancients and moderns, Latin and vernacular, limiting to a single point of contact the similarities between them. As discussed earlier, the vernacular is said to be a legitimate alternative to Latin poetry only in the case where one wishes to speak to women, who were not usually educated, and its subject matter is limited to love (presumptively the love of heterosexual men). In other words, the chapter follows what becomes the typical Dantean oscillation between an ambitious rapprochement of ancient and modern, and a humble, or at least mock humble, deference to the great *auctores* and *auctoritates* (e.g., *Inf.* 2.32).

One indication that, while humility prevails in the explicit rhetoric of the chapter, its underlying aspirations are much greater, appears if one presses a little harder on the claim that the vernacular is limited to the topic of love. In the first place, this claim is overtly associated with the contemptible "grossi" (crude ones) who inaugurated the tradition. More important, however, is the implicit contrast between "Love" as presented in chapter 25, where "he" seems to be much the same erotic taskmaster as when he first appeared in chapters 2 and 3, and "Love" as "he" appeared, only to be reconfigured, in chapter 24. There, as just seen, Love is no longer just an "accident in a substance," but rather is potentially identical with a substance – namely Beatrice, who is herself a "figura Christi." If this is so, then Dante's claim that modern *dicitori in rima* are restricted to figurative representations of Love is a red herring, at least in his own case, since Love has just been redefined to include the divine Love responsible for the creation of all things.[44] *That*

[43] See, among many discussions of the link between *VN* 25 and *Inf.* 4, Barolini 1984: 188–9; Brownlee 1984: 602–5; Iannucci 1993b; Picone 1997a.

[44] Deriving from Durling and Martinez 1990 (341 n 12, 392–3 n 50; see also Durling 2001: 307–12, 2003; Fenzi 1999b: 23–9) this reading develops and corrects Singleton (1949: 75–6; see again n 36). From this perspective, the question of Love's identity (ch. 24) and the problem of Love personified (ch. 25) are tied not only to each other but also to Cavalcanti's own definitional approach to Amore in "Donna me prega," (especially via the term "sostanza"; ll. 1–2). For prosopopeia as "the" trope in Cavalcanti's poetry, see, e.g., Harrison 1988: especially 77–81. Against earlier claims that the *quaestio* of chapter 25 does homage to Guido (especially De Robertis 1961: 231; Contini 1968), the Durling and Martinez thesis sees a coordinated attack on him both in chapter 24 and in the disingenuous representation of Love's nature in chapter 25. While assenting to both propositions, I do not think they exhaust the purpose of the *quaestio*. The personification of Love, endemic to the lyric tradition,

Love, as *De Vulgari Eloquentia* would later put it, is no "accident," but the "the simplest of *substances*" (1.16.5). In other words, limiting poetry to the representation of Love in *this* sense is no limitation at all, since it is the informing principle of all things, human and divine: even the *trapasso* from love of a human woman to love of philosophical wisdom in *Convivio* is less ambitious!

Thus far, a reading of chapters 24 and 25 has tracked the traditional critical preoccupation with Dante's interest in appropriating classical and/or Biblical *auctoritas*. There is, however, a strong hint in chapter 25 that Dante's idea of authorship is linked to his other identity as reader, and thence to the hybrid structure of the work itself. This linkage then threatens to transform the concept of *auctoritas* as such beyond recognition. Dante asserts, and then emphatically repeats his assertion, that for his justification of the use of personification to hold for modern *dicitori in rima* they should be able to demonstrate that they know exactly what they are doing:

> . . . se alcuna figura o colore rettorico è conceduto a li poete, conceduto è a li rimatori. Dunque, se noi vedemo che li poete hanno parlato a le cose inanimate, sì come avessero senso e ragione, e fattele parlare insieme; e non solo cose vere, ma cose non vere . . . degno è lo dicitore per rima di fare lo somigliante, ma non sanza ragione alcuna, ma con ragione la quale poi sia possibile d'aprire per prosa. (25.8)

(If any rhetorical figure or trope is conceded to the classical poets, it is also conceded to the vernacular rhymers. Hence, if we see that the classical poets have spoken to inanimate things as if they had feeling and intelligence, and made them converse together; and [they have] not only [spoken] to real things but to fictive ones . . . the vernacular speaker in rhyme is worthy of doing something similar, but not without any good reason – rather with a reason that can be expounded openly in prose.)

At chapter's end he reiterates:

> E acciò che non ne pigli alcuna baldanza persona grossa, dico che né li poete parlavano così sanza ragione, né quelli che rimano deono parlare così non avendo alcuno ragionamento in loro di quello che dicono; però che grande vergogna sarebbe a colui che rimasse cose sotto vesta di figura o di colore rettorico, e poscia, domandato, non sapesse denudare le sue parole da cotale vesta, in guisa che avessero verace intendimento. (25.10)

cannot be laid at Cavalcanti's door alone. Rather, as the rest of chapter 25 makes plain, it (also) points to the use of figurative language in poetry generally, ancient and "modern" alike, and facilitates Dante's passage out of the company of the "fedeli d'amore" and into that of the classical *poete* (see also n 47).

(And so that no crude person may become overbold because of this, I say that the [classical] poets did not speak in this way without reason, and that the vernacular rhymers should not speak thus if they cannot give a rational account of what they say. For it would be a great shame to one who, rhyming of matters under the cloak of figurative language or rhetorical colors, did not when asked know how to strip his words of said cloak so that they could be truly understood.)

To obtain the same license to figurative expression as the ancients, the modern vernacular poet should be able to prove he understands what he has said by explaining it, that is, by translating its figures into the rational and open language of prose.[45]

Put another way, in these two passages Dante says that a modern poet worthy of the name must be able to demonstrate authoritative control over the informing intention of that work (cf. Harrison 1988: 64–5); he must be able to interpret it.[46] For an informed reader of our own times this statement seems intuitively obvious, and perhaps for that reason has rarely been given much consideration by Dante critics. From the perspective of a medieval culture in which the significance of the utterance of *auctores* was taken for granted, and its exposition entrusted to modern *lectores* and *commentatores* who often appear to deform original intentions beyond recognition, it is unusual, to say the least. Moreover, taken in the larger context of *Vita Nova* the implications of this imperative to self-explanation are many and extraordinary.

To begin with, this seeming digression justifies the hybrid, prosimetrum form of *Vita Nova* as a whole: all of the narrative *ragioni* and the analytical *divisioni* serve, among other things, to create the impression – accurate or not – that Dante-poet knows exactly what he is doing.[47] Confirmation of this point comes in the analogous, now explicit, explanation given of the

[45] On "aprire" in *VN* see Singleton 1949: 47–8 and n; Jenaro-MacLennan 1960; Grayson 1963: 42–3; Tateo 1970b; Picone 1979: 24–5; Botterill 1994. "Aprire" is also used in this exegetical sense in 14.13 and 19.22. See Stillinger 1992 on the equation Beatrice–poetry, and the implied homology between interpretive and sexual unveiling. Compare also the complex metaphorics of opening and covering, with both sexual and textual implications, in the *canzone* "Doglia mi reca" (Barolini 2000: 77–86; and see n 65). For *aprire* in *CV*, see n 67.

[46] Durling 2001: 311 rightly notes that *stricte dictu* Dante does not require explanation but only the potential to do so. However, in criticizing the unnamed "persona grossa" – often identified with Guittone – for an inability to "open" their work, Dante virtually obliges himself to offer proof of his contrary practice. In addition, the phrase "poscia domandato" highlights the fact that the "io" of *VN* repeatedly assumes the role of a hypothetical questioner – a worthy reader – in order to guarantee that potentiality becomes actuality. Thus chapter 25 begins "[p]otrebbe qui dubitare persona degna da dichiararle onne dubitazione, e dubitare si potrebbe . . ." (1); to which the balance of the chapter then responds "a cotale cosa dichiarire . . ." (3); cf. 12.17, cited above.

[47] A lucid statement is in De Robertis 1984: 176n. See also Singleton 1949: especially 47–50; Jenaro MacLennan 1960: 87; De Robertis 1970: 231–2; Tateo 1970b: 68–75; Picone 1979: 22, 1997a: 56; Pinto 1994: 118–19; Marchesi 2003: 65–8; cf. Baranski 1997a: 9–10. By contrast, Harrison (1988:

need for allegorical prose commentary on the *canzoni* in *Convivio* (cf. V. Russo 1994: 14):

> Intendo anche mostrare la vera sentenza di quelle [le canzoni] che alcuno vedere non si può s'io non la conto, perché è nascosa sotto figura d'allegoria: e questo non solamente darà diletto buono a udire, ma sottile ammaestramento e a così parlare e a così intendere l'altrui scritture. (1.2.17)

(I intend as well to show the true meaning of those [the *canzoni* to be commented upon] which may not be seen by some unless I recount it, because it is hidden under the figure of allegory: and this [exposition] will not only give good pleasure when heard, but also subtle teaching, both in how to speak [i.e., to write poetry in this way] and how to understand the writings of others.)

This passage, which imagines the possibility of teaching its readers *both* to "speak" poetry of their own ("a così parlare") and to interpret the poetry of others ("a così intendere"), makes clear the underlying assumption that while formally divided, reading and writing can and should coexist in a

---

57, 62), seconded by Roush (2002: 34–6), argues that this "theoretical" moment is at odds with Dante's practice throughout the *libello*. Durling and Martinez 1990 assert that he does not explain his (misleading) personification of Love despite asserting he could do so (341 n 12; see also Durling 2001, 2003). The explanation offered is no doubt problematic as concerns the new ontology of Love implied by the prose of chapter 24. However, Dante does something simpler, namely explain that, *qua* poet, he intentionally uses poetic tropes to represent psychic events and higher spiritual realities (see also Tateo 1970b: 63; Mazzotta 1983; Pinto 1994: chapter 5), and that he does so based on the precedent of the ancient poets. In this sense, then, the *quaestio* "explains itself." Even assuming that the equation "Deus caritas est" (1 John 4:8) is the basic text behind chapter 24, nonetheless, any name of God – including Amor/Caritas – is necessarily inadequate, improper, and thus figurative (cf. Durling 2001: 310–11nn; see also n 51; Chapter 7, section v), just as, more overtly, the nominal connection of Beatrice with Amore is figurative – a similitude, not a rationally proven identity. Perhaps most importantly, the Durling and Martinez reading assumes that the explanatory power invoked by Dante refers to *VN* as a whole; instead, as *commentator*, the "io" of *VN* proposes to explain its *poetry*, a point reinforced by the exclusive focus on poetic activity in chapter 25 (cf. Singleton 1949: 29–30, 35, 48). And "Io mi sentì svegliar" does not suggest the same evolution of Amore as the prose (cf. De Robertis 1981: 97–100). None of these readings accounts adequately for the sequential rapprochement of Dante to the "fedeli d'amore," to Cavalcanti, and to the classical *poete*. None explains the forceful repetition of the (to my knowledge unprecedented) call for moderns to be able to "explain themselves," nor deals with the evident homology between chapter 25 and the otherwise unexplained deployment of *ragioni* and *divisioni* throughout. None explores chapter 25's evident affinity to Dante's rapidly growing obsession with self-justification and auto-exegesis (e.g., *CV* and *DVE*), nor the fact that such justification and exegesis more often create an effect of transparency than realizing the thing itself. In this sense, *VN* 25 anticipates the tension in *CV* between allegorically "opening" poetry for a large vernacular public (thus Jenaro–MacLennan 1960: 87 and with due qualification Tateo 1970b: 71–2) and the use of "difficult" prose to assert authority (Chapter 2, section iii): there, and here, Dante with equal seriousness claims to be revealing his intentions and conceals critical elements thereof. In any case, even if one assumes a "good faith" effort on Dante's part to explain himself, it is important to remember that the activity of self-glossing is necessarily a *mise-en-abyme*, in the sense that interpretations of poems which constitute part of the larger prosimetrum text themselves require interpretations, which themselves require interpretations, and so on (cf. Derrida 1974).

single individual who participates in a community of similarly diversified individuals.

If these passages offer a synchronic justification for the structure of *Vita Nova tout court*, they also mark a major diachronic, narrative-thematic development of the relation between reading and writing over its formulation in chapter 3. In presenting himself (along with Guido Cavalcanti) as capable of such self-interpretation, and illustrating it by his exegesis of *Amore*, Dante not only proves himself superior to the other *fedeli d'amore*, including Guido, who failed to see the meaning of the dream recounted in "A ciascun'alma presa," but also leaves behind his own apparent mystification about its significance, which pivoted around the nature and actions of the personified Lord of Love.

Finally, it is important to remember that, although the impetus to self-exegesis is directed at making moderns the equals of classical poets, it also distinguishes sharply between the two groups. To belabor the obvious, ancient poets did not themselves offer prose rationales for their poetic discourse – on the one hand, they did not have to do so, since their *auctoritas* guaranteed the worthiness of their works, and, on the other, they could not do so, short of returning from the grave. Rather, exposés of grammatical and rhetorical technique and of subject matter were typically supplied in *accessus* and commentaries written by later *lectores*. The modern writer, by contrast, does not have the privilege of having his good intentions assumed or the significance of his poetic *auctoritates* taken for granted by worshipful readers.[48] Instead, he must be able to prove that he deserves such authority by demonstrating that his poems can be "opened" and an underlying intelligence and significance can thereby be revealed – an authorial intention can be recovered by an astute reader. He must show that he is not only able to write poetry, but also to read and comment upon it, thereby proving his deliberate artistic control. Even as Dante assimilates modern poets, such as himself, to the classical *auctores*, he silently transforms the medieval notion of the *auctor*, whose meanings are revealed by the commentary of modern *lectores*, to a proto-modern idea of the *author*, whose conscious intentions govern the meaning of his own work, quite apart from the readings of others.[49]

---

[48] Cf. Picone 1997a: 56. I refer to an ideological position implied by and rhetorically deployed in the argument of chapter 25. As observed earlier, especially Chapter 2, section ii, the positions of classical *auctores* were increasingly up for debate in practice.

[49] See Pinto 1994: 109–22 for a parallel argument concerning the "modernity" of Dante's conception of literature and literary culture in chapter 25.

As far as the internal economy of *Vita Nova* is concerned, this implicit
conflation of author and reader – the author as reader of his own work,
the reader as reproducer of originating authorial intentions – implicitly
accounts for the textual split between poetry and commentary. At the same
time, it can also anticipate the abolition of any such split, when the artificial,
analytical, division of the self into multiple parts will be done away with,
and these "two Dantes" coalesce again into one. Such coalescence does not
take place in chapter 25, however, and the composite form of the text goes
unchallenged until the very end of the *libello*, as will be seen in the final
section of this chapter.

There is another way in which chapter 25 anticipates a fusion of Dante's
various roles, and it lies in the apparently marginal and arbitrary conundrum
which is the pretext for the narrator's reflections on vernacular versification:
the possibly deceptive use of the trope of personification in chapter 24
and elsewhere earlier in the treatise. The problem with personification, or
prosopopeia, is that it represents "an accident in a substance," treating an
emotional experience as if it were a living individual.[50] From a Christian
point of view this trope is the driving mechanism behind much of pagan
religion, which reifies its desires in the form of deities – in other words,
prosopopeia, if its figurative nature is not understood, is the instrument of
idolatry.[51]

Another problem, of more direct concern here, is that use of personifi-
cation results, paradoxically, in the fragmentation and consequent "deper-
sonalization" of the human subject: the individual subject is dispersed into
its attributes, each of which is given the features of a distinct person. This
is the process at work in Dante's description of the three spirits, all parts of

---

[50] See Boyde 1971: 269–79 for Dante's innovative use of the rhetorical trope of *prosopopeia*, particularly
in the poems of *VN* and *CV*. Boyde calls attention to personification's proximity to, and often simul-
taneity with, other figures of speech, especially *apostrophe, sermocinatio* (the dramatic attribution of
speech to another person; see also Martinez 1997: 52 *et passim*; as well as Steinberg 1999 and Giunta
2002: chapters 1–2 on the dialogic and *tenzone* mode of poetry in the Duecento), not to mention
allegory, and to the special, self-reflexive cases of addresses to a reader or readers (see Spitzer 1955;
cf. Chapter 1, n 55). On Dante's linkage of *prosopopeia* with the device of the "congedo," see n 54.
CV re-proposes the question of *prosopopeia* at greater length. Notable is the following passage: "ed
è una figura questa, quando a le cose inanimate si parla, che si chiama da li rettorici prosopopeia, e
usanla molto spesso li poeti" (3.9.1–2; see also 2.11.1–7, 3.10.6–7). For personification in chapter 25
and elsewhere in *VN*, see Mazzotta 1986: 62–5; Noferi 1977: 28, 1982–3: 77; Martinez 1998, 2000.
For the classical and medieval tradition of personifying love, begin with Lewis 1936: chapter 3. For
the problem of self-representation and *prosopopeia* more generally, see De Man 1984; for apostrophe,
see Culler 1981: chapter 7. See also nn 19, 42, 51, 52, 54, 57; Chapter 2, nn 3, 14, 42, 64, 88; Chapter
7, sections ii, v, and nn 10, 28.

[51] Cf. Durling 2001: 308–11. As Mazzotta observes (1993a: 47–8), this is also the substance of Dante's
discussion of the allegorical truth behind Plato's doctrine of ensouled stars in *Par.* 4: 40–8.

his own indivisible human soul, in chapter 2. This is the process by which he seems to have deceived himself into thinking that he was the helpless pawn of an external force known as *Amore* in chapter 3.[52] It is also the process that will later lead him to say, in a more self-conscious vein, that in a certain sonnet "I make two parts of myself" (38.5).[53] Finally, this process allows him to divide himself among the various textual roles distributed across the three different forms of discourse combined in *Vita Nova*: *scriptor, compilator, commentator*, and, implicitly, *auctor*. By pointing toward the non-essential, fictive, quality of this trope in chapter 25, then, he gives the reader, and himself, an indirect push toward a concept of an underlying unity of the reading and writing selves. Not only is "Amor" – the "Amor" of chapter 3 and much of the early part of *Vita Nova* – a mystified projection of individual subjectivity, so too is the multiplication of writing and reading "Dantes."[54]

III. CONVIVIO

Chapter 25 of *Vita Nova* displays the writer's intense desire, bound up with his quest for poetic legitimacy and *autorità*, to assert his intentional control

---

[52] See also Durling and Martinez 1990 for this issue in the *rime petrose* (179–85). The problem resurfaces in the *DC*, now attributed to Francesca da Rimini, who blames *Amore* for her sin as if "he" were an external agent constraining her, rather than an "accident" internal to her and to Paolo (*Inf.* 5.100–106). On *Inf.* 5, see Barolini 1998b: especially 46. For the multiple meanings of Love in late medieval discourse, especially the lyric tradition, see De Robertis 1961: especially chapter 3; Nardi 1942c; Gorni 1990: 50–71. See also n 50; Chapter 7, nn 17, 28.

[53] For readings of Dante's "self-division" in *VN* see Noferi 1982–3: especially 66–7; Poe 1984: 92; and especially Stillinger 1992: 74, 79–84, 103–7.

[54] Dante anticipates chapter 25 in chapter 12 by calling attention to the arbitrariness of personification in the *ballata* "Ballata, i' voi che tu ritrovi Amore": "potrebbe uomo opporre contra me e dire che non sapesse a cui fosse lo mio parlare in seconda persona però che la ballata non è altro che queste parole ched io parlo: e però dico che questo dubbio io lo intendo solvere e dichiarare in questo libello in parte ancora più dubbiosa [i.e., chapter 25]; e allora intenda qui chi qui dubita, o che volesse opporre in questo modo" (12.17). The *ragione* of chapter 12 recounted a complex dream vision of Love personified, confirming its status as relay between chapters 3 and 24. "Ballata, i' voi" is the limit case of a rhetorical device conventionally confined to a final stanza, the *congedo*, where the poet addresses his personified poem directly. *CV* 2.11 connects the use of the *congedo in* "Voi che intendendo" to the (allegorical) split between the "bellezza" of the *canzone*'s poetic decoration and the "bontade" of the *sentenza* concealed within (see Chapter 2, n 64). When the subject of *prosopopeia* comes up explicitly in 3.9 (see citation in n 50), it is again in conjunction with a poem (the "ballatteta," "Voi che savete ragionar d'Amore") where he speaks in direct address to his own composition. In 3.10 he then comments on the *congedo* addressed to "Amor che nella mente mi ragiona" (87–90), now naming the trope in question, whereby "le parole sono a una persona e la 'ntenzione a un'altra," as *dissimulatio*. The relationship between the internally self-reflexive structure of the *congedo* and Dante's auto-exegetical drive deserves more attention than I can give it here (cf. n 3). On the structural relationship between 12 and 25, see Tateo 1970b: 57–8; Moleta 1978: 384–5; also Singleton 1945.

over the significance of his texts by providing anticipatory/internal readings of them (Ascoli 2003; Marchesi 2003). This textual phenomenon would be move fully realized in *Convivio* and *De vulgari Eloquentia*, not to mention *Monarchia* and the *Commedia*. In *Convivio* this desire is unequivocally tied to the composite structure of *canzoni* followed by prose that reveals their significance (1.2.17; quoted above). The shared structural feature – that is, the division of Dante into an author of poems and a reader who comments on those poems – constitutes the closest link between *Convivio* and the *libello* (cf. Jenaro-MacLennan 1960). Within the text-commentary complex, there are further particular points of comparison. *Vita Nova* sharply distinguishes between its biographical *ragioni* and its exegetical *divisioni*. In *Convivio*, biographical materials are also often preliminary to the commentary proper. This is certainly the case in book 1 which is preliminary to the work as a whole and is intermittently concerned with Dante's biographical relation to it, as well as to the language in which it is written. It is also found near the beginning of all three later books (2.2.1–5, 3.1.1–12, and 4.1.1–11). As Guglielminetti (1977) points out, however, there are far fewer biographical specifics in *Convivio* than in *Vita Nova*, but, at the same time, a "thinking 'I'" is much more present in the commentary proper (e.g., 3.9.15–16). As for *divisioni*, the commentaries in books 2–4 each begin with a distinction of the *canzoni* into its major parts according to the scheme of the *divisio textus* (2.2.7–9; 3.1.13; 4.2.1–2), whose function Dante explicitly announces once and for all at 2.2.6. Subdivisions of these parts are then given at the appropriate moments in each book,[55] while the commentary, especially the literal commentary, proceeds to discuss the lines of the *canzone* in order. What the *Convivio* commentary does that *Vita Nova* does not, of course, is to gloss the key words and concepts of the poetic text, often at great length, in ways that assimilate it to the Latin encyclopedic tradition (Vasoli 1983; cf. Chapter 1, n 66), as well as its vernacular imitators, such as Brunetto Latini.

In other words, once the basic commonalities of form between the two works have been registered, what becomes most noticeable are the many differences between them, especially the normalization and explicitation in the later treatise of implicit features of the earlier text (Minnis *et al.* 1988: 375–8; Stillinger 1992: especially 63–4, 109–16). As we have already seen, *Convivio* has moved much closer to the authoritative textuality of

---

[55] 2.7.1–3; 2.10.1–2; 3.2.1; 3.5.1–2; 3.7.1–2; 3.9.1–3; 3.11.1; 4.3.1–5; 4.10.2–3; 4.14.1–2; 4.16.2–3; 4.19.1–2; 4.23.1–2; 4.30.1.

Latin culture, both in matter *and* in form.[56] Moreover, the relegation of the vernacular to the subject of erotic love in poems directed primarily at women, only implicitly contested in the *libello*, is abandoned with ostentatious embarrassment in favor of a claim of an elevated love of *Sophia*, the female personification of wisdom, which is represented so it can be shared with a wide vernacular audience, primarily composed of men.[57] The very notion that the *canzoni* might be about love in *Vita Nova's* sense is now presented as one of the stains to be purged from the intellectual bread of Dante's banquet.

Specifically, in book 2, chapter 1, Dante aligns his poetry with an established tradition that attributed metaphysical and especially ethical knowledge to the classical poets, *primi inter pares*, Virgil and Ovid. This tradition is reflected in the standard *accessus* topic which places poetry within moral philosophy and which stands behind the notion of an "allegory according to the poets," of truth hidden "beneath a beautiful lie." Dante emphasizes this dimension in his reading of the story of Orpheus as an "allegory of allegory," that is an allegory of ethical education through poetry (see Chapter 2, section v and nn 71–73). Indeed, allegorical *accessus* to and commentaries on the Latin classics, themselves written in Latin, were a primary vehicle by which this tradition was given substance.[58]

Despite the relative infrequency of references to the poetic *auctores* in books 1 through 3 (Chapter 2, especially n 76), Dante does insert himself into this interpretive line. In book 4, for example, he reads the *Aeneid* as an allegorical recounting of the second stage (*gioventù*) of human development (4.26.7–15).[59] Much earlier he had made it clear that this is the formal

---

[56] See, e.g., Chapter 2, n 48. On Dante's Duecento precursors in the *translatio studii* from Latin to Italian, see Chapter 1, nn 13, 24, 54; Chapter 2, n 33.

[57] On *Sophia*, see Chapter 2, nn 14, 88. Note the ironic symmetry with *VN* 25: there Dante says he wants to show that Love is not a real person but a personification of his own desire; here he wants to prove that he is not in love with a real woman, but rather with a *prosopopeia* of the wisdom he desires for himself (see n 50). See Spivak 1981: 54–5 for the extreme, but not unfounded, claim that "Beatrice" in *VN* is reduced to a trope mediating between the male subject and the patriarchal divinity. For *prosopopeia* in *CV*, see nn 50, 54. On the intended audience of *CV*, see Chapter 2, nn 11, 74.

[58] These include the late classical works of Servius, Fulgentius, and others; also twelfth- and thirteenth-century commentaries such as Bernardus Sylvestris on the *Aeneid* and the *Ovidius Moralizatus* (see Allen 1982; Minnis 1990, 2001; Minnis *et al.* 1988: especially chapters 1, 2, 4, 8; Minnis and Johnson 2005: especially chapters 5, 6, 14). See again Chapter 1, n 48.

[59] This allegorization, like that of Orpheus, is self-reflexive, connecting, as Dante observes, to the initial distinction between the work of his youth, *VN*, and that of his maturity, *CV* itself (1.1.17). See also Chapter 2, n 13.

model for writing a series of commentaries on his own *canzoni*. In book 1 he claims that while Latin has often been used for purposes of commentary, the vernacular never [sic] has:

[D]arà lo volgare dono non dimandato, che non l'avrebbe dato lo latino: però che darà sé medesimo per comento, che mai non fu domandato da persona; e questo non si può dire de lo latino, che per comento e per chiose a molte scritture è già stato domandato, sì come ne' loro principii si può vedere apertamente in molte. (1.9.10)

([T]he vernacular will give an unasked-for gift [in commenting upon these *canzoni*], which Latin would not have given: since it will give itself in the form of commentary, which no one ever asked for; and this cannot be said of Latin, which has already been requested to comment upon and gloss many writings [or "scriptures"], as can be seen clearly at the beginnings of many of them.)[60]

In other words, he simultaneously aligns himself with the tradition of Latin commentary but also stresses the specialness, even uniqueness, of his adaptation of it (Jenaro-MacLennan 1960: 92–3). And that specialness consists not only in the use of vernacular, but also in presenting himself, in different aspects, as writer both of poetic allegories and of interpreting allegoresis (cf. Pepin 1970: 131–2).

Returning then to a comparison between the two prosimetrum works: in *Convivio* the hybrid, radically innovative form of *Vita Nova* has been discarded in favor of a text/commentary arrangement that more closely resembles the typical Scholastic presentation of classical *auctoritates* and exegetical glosses. Of course, it still has some unusual features – a peculiar variant of the *accessus* form (n 60) and the very fact that it is a self-exegesis – separating it from the standard commentary format (Stillinger 1992: 39; cf. Roush 2002: chapter 2).

---

[60] The last phrase refers specifically to the genre of *accessus* (see above, section ii, Chapter 1, nn 16, 48). For *CV* 1 as an *accessus*, see Trovato 1976, also Minnis 1990: 30. I am not convinced, though the argument works better here than it does for *VN*. Like an *accessus* book 1 occupies a liminal position and contains elements (e.g., explanation of the *titulus*, description of the structure and content of the work, information about the author) proper to it. On the other hand, it falls well outside the narrow range of forms in which *accessus* traditionally appear and is far longer than customary (see especially Huygens 1970; Minnis *et al.* 1988: especially chapters 1–3). Moreover, its function is primarily "apologetic" and defensive, which the descriptive *accessus* is not, some exception made for justifications of the study of pagan authors. Finally, to the extent *CV* 1 makes use of *accessus* categories, these are more concerned with the *commentary* than with the work *commented upon* (cf. Minnis 1990: 30). At this point, the traits it shares with the *accessus* become interesting, since they aim to cope with the problems created when *auctor* and *commentator* are one and the same (cf. Roush 2002: 40–1). To complete the picture, one would need to consider the *accessus* portion of the so-called *ECG* (par. 5–16), which follows a normative *accessus* pattern much more closely than *CV*, though by no means exactly (see Chapter 1, n 75).

Another striking feature of the treatise in comparison to *Vita Nova* is that even as Dante presents his *canzoni* and his auto-commentaries in terms that assimilate them both to Latin *auctores* and *commentatores* and to normative high cultural models of textual signification, to that very same degree his text becomes more overtly aware of that assimilation, more conscious of a need to justify its transgressive ambitions. In particular, he sets out deliberately to confront and to rationalize the complex of innovations involved in a modern vernacular poet producing a work of this kind. To this issue he directs the passage just cited. By turns, as illustrated in Chapters 2 and 3 of this study, he addresses issues – of self-reference, the use of commentary, the status of the vernacular, the figure of the *auctor* himself – that are raised, but only fugitively or implicitly, by *Vita Nova*. In other words, *auctoritas* has now, in *Convivio*, become an explicit, even anxious, concern.

Nonetheless, some crucial assumptions are still left unexamined. In part for the reasons discussed in Chapter 2 (section v), Dante is curiously skittish about discussing the status of the poems. He is especially reticent about why, exactly, they deserve the unique attention that his prose commentary will give them. He never directly addresses the question of self-commentary – the most unique and most scandalous feature of this work as of *Vita Nova* – in any comprehensive way. On the other hand, each of the three problems, or "stains," that he does address in book 1, together with the crucial passage on allegory at the beginning of book 2, ultimately arise from the project of self-commentary by a modern author on vernacular poetry (see Chapter 2, section ii).

Dante begins his apologies in book 1 by addressing two apparently distinct "stains," which turn out to be fundamentally connected:

Nel cominciamento di ciascuno bene ordinato convivio sogliono gli sergenti prendere lo pane apposito, e quello purgare da ogni macula. Per che io, che ne la presente scrittura tengo luogo di quelli, da due macule mondare intendo primieramente questa esposizione, che per pane si conta nel mio corredo. L'una è che parlare alcuno di sé pare non licito; l'altra è, che parlare in esponendo troppo forte pare non ragionevole. (1.2.1–2)

(At the beginning of every properly arranged banquet it is customary for the servants to take the bread set out and purify it of any blemishes. Since I play their role with respect to the present writing [i.e., qua commentator he is the servant to the "master texts" of philosophical *canzoni*], my first concern regarding this exposition – which has the place of bread in what I am providing – is to clear it of two blemishes. One is that it seems improper for anyone to speak about himself; the other is that it seems unreasonable to speak too profoundly when giving an exposition.)

In regard to the first stain, he goes on to cite the taboo according to which "the established canons of rhetoric forbid anyone to speak of himself except for some compelling reason" (1.2.3; cf. Chapter 2, n 38). As to the second, he elaborates that:

> . . . lo mio scritto, che quasi comento dir si può, è ordinato a levar lo difetto delle canzoni sopra dette, ed esso per sé fia forse in parte alcuna un poco duro. La qual durezza, per fuggir maggior difetto, non per ignoranza, è qui pensata. (1.3.2–3)

> (. . . this work, which can be described as a commentary, is designed to supply what is lacking in the *canzoni* under discussion, and yet may itself perhaps be somewhat difficult to understand in certain parts. This difficulty is quite intentional here, arising not from inadvertence but from a desire to avoid an even greater [defect].)

That "greater defect," as already seen, is the lack of respect, of *autoritade*, that his personal circumstance as dispossessed exile has brought upon him.

In both cases the central, yet partially obfuscated, issue is what it means to be writing a philosophically ambitious commentary on one's own poetry. Dante's need to explain why he is talking about himself, entirely absent from the self-absorbed *Vita Nova*, does not apply to the first-person lyric voice of the poetic *canzoni* per se: nothing could be more rhetorically conventional than that voice (see n 3). Rather it pertains to the exposition and justification of the poetic self in a prose commentary. This is evident from Dante's definition of his role in the treatise as *sergente*, or medieval "waitperson," which, as we will soon see, anticipates the later distinction made between the poetry as master and prose commentary as servant (1.5.7–9; 1.7.1–2).

Dante begins his discussion of the second objection by calling attention to the prose's generic status as commentary ("parlare in *esponendo* troppo forte pare non ragionevole"; cf. Pepin 1999: 52 and n 2). He then highlights the belief that personal presence has created a problem for the prose commentary, requiring special measures to preserve his and the treatise's authority (1.3.4–5; see Chapter 2, section iii). A conflation of the issues treated separately in the two objections reveals a circular dilemma: Dante needs to write a difficult commentary to confer authority on himself and his work (1.4.13), while, at the same time, writing such a commentary in the first-person singular present tense has the opposite effect, removing the *fede* that defines the power of the *auctor* over his readers. Evidently the problem of self-commentary is a textual extension of the difficulties created by the personality and individuality of Dante in both *Convivio* and *De Vulgari Eloquentia*. Partly to avoid confronting the insoluble dilemma produced by the configuration of self-commentary, and thus to bracket the oxymoronic figure of the personalized *auctor*, Dante splits his problem into two ostensibly separate questions about the prose commentary, one concerning its recourse to self-reference, the other the style it deploys.

In all likelihood, Dante focuses attention primarily on the commentary because it is the genre into which, as a modern, he is entitled to enter. Focusing on the verse would raise the issue of whether this modern, vernacular poetry deserves to become the object of commentary or is really able to claim profound philosophical content for itself. Nonetheless, the problems Dante identifies with the commentary arise on account of the poetry. He needs to use the first-person mode for self-justification because people have read the poems incorrectly, that is literally, and have found in them evidence both of carnal desire and of amorous infidelity – rather than properly and allegorically, as expressing love of Wisdom personified. Moreover, a discrepancy between Dante's fallible personal presence, on the one hand, and, on the other, the (poetic) works that had generated the disembodied fame which preceded him forces him to write in a difficult style, ill-suited to its stated mission.

After dealing obliquely with the general issue of self-commentary in chapters 2 through 4, for the remaining nine chapters of book 1 Dante shifts the focus onto the "substantial" *macula* of writing the treatise in Italian rather than in the usual Latin. Here again, however, his attention is apparently directed to the question of writing a prose *commentary* in Italian (as in 1.9.10, qtd. above), while he carefully avoids the issue of what makes his vernacular *poetry* a worthy master for servile commentary. This strategy is evident from the first major argument he offers, which is, as discussed in Chapter 3, based on the ontological inferiority of changeable Italian with respect to perpetual, incorruptible Latin (1.5.7–9; cf. 1.7.14–15).

The question is articulated in terms of an analogy with the hierarchical political-social order of the feudal Middle Ages:

[C]olui che è ordinato all'altrui servigio dee avere quelle disposizioni che sono a quello fine ordinato, sì come subiezione, conoscenza e obedienza, sanza le quale è ciascuno disordinato a ben servire . . . se elli non è . . . [obediente], non serve mai se non a suo senno e a suo volere, che è più servigio d'amico che di servo. Dunque a fuggire questa disordinazione, conviene che questo comento, che è fatto invece di servo a le 'nfrascritte canzoni, essere subietto a quelle in ciascuna sua ordinazione, ed essere conoscente del bisogno del suo signore e a lui obediente. Le quali disposizioni tutte li mancavano, se latino e non volgare fosse stato, poi che le canzoni sono volgari. (1.5.5–7)

([A]nyone who is ordered to someone's service must possess those dispositions which are ordered to that end, namely subjection, close knowledge and obedience; without these, he is ill-suited to perform good service . . . if he . . . is not obedient . . ., he will only serve as he thinks right and as he wishes, which is rather the service of a friend, than of a servant. To avoid any such inversion of the proper order, therefore, this commentary, which is meant to act as a servant to the *canzoni* given below, must be subject to them in every respect, must closely know their master's needs, and must be obedient to him. Since the *canzoni* are written in the vernacular, the commentary would lack these dispositions entirely if it were written in Latin and not in the vernacular.)

The master–servant metaphor assumes, without argument, a hierarchically superior place for the poetry with respect to the prose commentary, and, indeed, inserts it into a position of seigniorial superiority analogous to that assigned initially to the writings of the classical philosophers (1.1). At the same time, however, the passage reveals indirectly why no rationale for treating vernacular poetry in this way can plausibly be offered. In arguing for the necessity of using vernacular prose in the commentary – because Latin is the nobler language and cannot be put in the position of commenting on its inferior (*vulgare*) without a dramatic confusion of hierarchy[61] – he indirectly points to the fact that his appropriation of the "text/commentary" model is itself a usurpation and potential disruptive transformation of the medieval "culture of authority." This argument clearly constitutes a more highly developed version of the mixture of deference to and emulation of the Latin "culture of authority" found in *Vita Nova* 25.

This essentially negative argument in favor of a vernacular prose commentary is followed by a second and more positive justification. The claim is that, in using *volgare* for the commentary, Dante is demonstrating his own generosity (1.8–13). He concludes this section with the striking conceit that a gift given unasked is better than one given on demand and then avers, in the passage quoted earlier, that "Latin has already been asked to comment upon and to gloss many writings," while the vernacular has never ever been asked to serve in such a capacity before (1.9.10–11; cf. 1.10.1). That is, he contrasts the traditional use of Latin in commentary (presumably on Latin texts, given what has just been said), with the absolute novelty of his own use of vernacular for this purpose. No mention is now made at all of the (vernacular, poetic) objects of the commentary, or of the equal rarity, and greater presumption, of treating them as worthy of the same.

---

[61] For the servant/master metaphor see also Grayson 1963: 41, 43, 47–51; Copeland 1991: 184; Stillinger 1992: 26 and n 9. Compare the "servo"/"signore" word-play in "Doglia mi reca" (25, 39, 41–3, 48, 64–6, 68, 88, 98, 158).

To highlight both the innovation and the need to justify it so extensively he begins the following section with the following warning:

[V]uole essere evidente ragione che partire faccia l'uomo da quello che per li altri è stato servato lungamente, sì come di comentare con latino. E però vuole essere manifesta la ragione, che delle nuove cose lo fine non è certo; acciò che la esperienza non è mai avuta onde le cose usate e servate sono e nel processo e nel fine commisurate. Però si mosse la Ragione a comandare che l'uomo avesse diligente riguardo ad entrare nel nuovo cammino, dicendo che "ne lo statuire le nuove cose evidente ragione dee essere quella che partire ne faccia da quello che lungamente è usato." Non si maravigli dunque alcuno se lunga è la digressione de la mia scusa, ma, sì come necessaria, la sua lunghezza paziente sostenga. (1.10.1–4)

([O]nly a cogent reason will justify setting aside what has long served others well, as has the use of Latin in composing commentaries. This requires a clearly justifiable reason, because new ways of acting have no guarantee of success, since in their case that experience is completely lacking which has proven the worth of what has been tried and found useful. That is why the Law takes pains to command men to think carefully before setting out on a new path, where it says that "in establishing new [things], clear reason must be advanced for making us depart from what has long been [the custom]." No one should be surprised, then, if the digression in which I justify my action is long; he should recognize that its length is unavoidable, and should patiently bear this.)

This passage can be seen as among the most explicit acknowledgments by Dante of his systematic mixture of conscious innovation with attempted respect for traditions, to the point of equating them with the Law (*Ragione*) itself. It can also be seen as echoing and reinforcing the "imperative of explanation" articulated in *Vita Nova* 25. Nonetheless, it too omits any hint of that which is really most innovative in *Convivio*: the embedding of vernacular poetry in a structure of self-commentary.

Only in the last section of book 1 – once the use of Italian is taken for granted, rhetorically speaking – does Dante almost imperceptibly shift focus from commentary to poetry, and from his role as *commentator* to his vocation as poet and, potentially, as *auctor*. Even here, however, the treatment of the poetry is, with one shining exception, oblique, and the question of self-commentary remains untouched. In these final four chapters, as seen in Chapter 3, he justifies the use of Italian for the prose commentary on the basis of his natural love of the language. To begin with, he suggests that he has made manifest the overlooked virtues of his "friend," the vernacular:

[Q]uesta grandezza do io a questo amico, in quanto quello elli di *bontade* avea in podere e *occulto*, io lo fo avere in atto e *palese* ne la sua propria operazione, che è *manifestare* conceputa sentenza. (1.10.9)

(This greatness I give to this friend, in that what it possessed potentially and in a hidden way, I cause it to possess actually and [openly] in its proper activity, which is to express the thoughts conceived in [the] mind.)

No doubt that Dante still refers here to the prose commentary, as well as to his own remarkable abilities in actualizing its expressive potential, its power to translate complex thought into words.[62]

At the same time, however, he indirectly recalls that the prose's function as initially defined had been to make open and accessible meaning that was hidden, not immediately in a mind (his mind), but rather in the poems conceived earlier by that same mind. Here again is how he puts it in the first chapter of the treatise:

La vivanda di questo convivio sarà di quattordici maniere ordinata, cioè quattordici canzoni sì d'amor come di vertù materiate, le quali sanza lo presente pane aveano *d'alcuna oscuritade ombra*, sì che a molti loro *bellezza* più che loro *bontade* era in grado. (1.1.14; cf. 1.2.17)

(The food for this banquet will be served as fourteen courses, that is, as fourteen *canzoni* treating of both love and virtue. When the bread [that is, the prose] provided here was lacking, these *canzoni* were veiled in a certain obscurity, so that many drew pleasure from their beauty rather than from their goodness.)

The later passage echoes and displaces the terms of the earlier one: where the function of the prose was to reveal the *bontade* hidden beneath the *bellezza* of Dante's *canzoni*, now Dante's function in relation to his "friend" the Italian *volgare* is to reveal its hidden *bontade* by actualizing the potential of vernacular prose for opening up "conceputa sentenza." The homology between Dante's relation to the *volgare* and the prose's to the poetry is not simply a structural parallel, however, since the *sentenza* expressed in the prose has already been defined as being the hidden *bontade* of the poetry, which in turn is the product of Dante's creative mind. In other words, what declares itself to be a celebration of the prose is also a reminder that the prose serves the poetry, whose hidden virtue and knowledge it explicates, just as the prose *ragioni* and *divisioni* of *Vita Nova* are meant to show that Dante knew what he was up to in the poems.

---

[62] The circular, even narcissistic, quality of this passage increases when Dante looks back on it two chapters later: "E noi vedemo che in ciascuna cosa di sermone lo bene manifestare del concetto sì è più amato e commendato: dunque è questa la prima sua bontade. E con ciò sia cosa che questa sia nel nostro volgare, sì come manifestato è di sopra in altro capitolo, manifesto è ched ella è de le cagioni stata de l'amore ch'io porto ad esso; poi che, sì come detto è, la bontade è cagione d'amore generativa" (1.12.13). In effect, he says, he loves the vernacular because of its "bontade," a "bontade" for whose "actualization" he had just taken credit. And what is that "bontade"? The ability to express Dante's own thoughts ("conceputa sentenza") clearly and beautifully.

To judge by the quoted passage from 1.10.9, the return of the "repressed" poetry is apparently incomplete, since the quality of *bellezza* earlier paired with and in some sense opposed to *bontade* is absent.[63] The climactic passage of chapter 10, however, brings *bellezza* back into the picture and with it the first explicit reference to the poetry in some time, though now cast in a curiously negative light:

[P]er questo comento la grande *bontade* del volgare di sì [si vedrà]; però che si vedrà la sua vertù, sì com'è per esso altissimi e novissimi concetti convenevolmente, sufficientemente e acconciamente, quasi come per esso latino, *manifestare*; [la quale non si potea bene manifestare] *ne le cose rimate*, per le accidentali *adornezze* che quivi sono connesse, cioè *la rima e lo ri[ti]mo e lo numero regolato*: sì come non si può bene *manifestare* la *bellezza d'una donna*, quando li *adornamenti* de l'azzimare e de le vestimenta la fanno più ammirare che essa medesima./Onde chi vuole ben giudicare *d'una donna*, guardi quella quando solo sua naturale *bellezza* si sta con lei, da tutto accidentale *adornamento* discompagnata: sì come sarà *questo comento*, nel quale si vedrà l'agevolezza de le sue sillabe, le proprietadi de le sue co[stru]zioni e le soavi orazioni che di lui si fanno; le quali chi bene agguarderà, vedrà essere piene di dolcissima e d'amabilissima *bellezza*. (1.10.12–13)

([T]hrough this commentary people will be led to recognize the [great] goodness of the Italian vernacular: they will see the power it has as it expresses the most sublime and [newest; strangest] ideas aptly, fully, and attractively. This power cannot be displayed well in [rhymed works], because of the incidental embellishments belonging to [these], namely rhyme and rhythm [and regulated meter], just as the beauty of a woman cannot be displayed well when the embellishments of her finery and her clothes, rather than she herself, draws people's admiration. So whoever wishes best to appreciate a woman should see her when she is graced by her natural beauty, unadorned by any incidental embellishment. Such is how this commentary will appear, in which will be seen the smoothness of the syllables of this language, [the propriety of its constructions], and the [sweet orations] fashioned from it, which will be recognized, by anyone who pays them careful attention, to be full of the sweetest and loveliest beauty.)

Once again the focus is on the prose, whose capacity to reveal the *bontade* of the *volgare* is much greater than "cose rimate," rhymed things, which are like women who conceal their true beauties beneath extrinsic adornments. These reified "cose rimate" seem very far away from the *canzoni* which were initially presented as the principal nourishment to be consumed in

---

[63] Dante does not gloss the relationship of "bellezza" and "bontade" in speech until 2.11.4 (cited in Chapter 2, n 64; also nn 72, 80). The uses of the two words in book 1 follow this scheme, which equates beauty with form and goodness with content, closely, but there is some slippage, for reasons that will appear shortly (cf. Chapter 2, n 45).

the intellectual banquet of the treatise.[64] As if to add insult to injury, Dante even removes the one quality most obviously associated with the poems-as-women, their verbal beauty, and reassigns it at simile's end to the prose. In short, the poetry is brought temporarily back into view, but not as the hermetic bearer of profound philosophical truth, or even as the aesthetic pinnacle of vernacular writing; rather, it seems – for the moment – only to serve as a foil for the prose, which possesses both more *bontade* and more *bellezza* (specifically, grammatical and rhetorical *bellezza*) than its supposed "master."

There is still more to say about this passage, however. The reason is that the figuration of poetry as a beautiful, if overdressed, woman – especially when taken with Dante's governing assertion in this chapter of his *love for* his native tongue – deliberately echoes the opening of the treatise and anticipates important developments to come. Specifically, the figure of poetry as *bella donna* evokes Dante's initial discussions both of the *content* and of the *form* of the *canzoni* (cf. Pézard 1940: chapter 7). As to the content, the problem with the poem – which as just argued first calls forth the prosaic commentary – is that, taken literally, it seems to refer to and to represent Dante's love for, and praise of, a beautiful woman, a "donna gentile" with whom he fell in love after Beatrice's death. As Dante asserts from the beginning of the treatise, however, his new *donna* is not an object of wayward erotic desire, but rather a figure signifying precisely a "conceputa sentenza." Better still, "she" is the very capacity for loving and thence conceiving truths, namely *Filosofia*, whose *bellezza*, as books 2 and 3 will demonstrate in great detail, is at one with her *bontade*. The *canzoni*, as just seen, treat "both love and virtue" (1.1.12), with the "matter" of love linked to an open, apparent beauty and that of *vertù* to a concealed moral-intellectual goodness, that is, to Lady Philosophy. Thus, a primary function of the image in 1.10.12–13 is to remind the reader that whatever *bontade* and *bellezza* the *comento* may possess derives from and is in the service of the wisdom conveyed by Dante's poetry.

Turning then to the *form* of the poetry, the figure of a *bella donna* takes on yet another association, one even more apt to the context of chapter 10 and the problem at hand, namely that of the poetry itself personified as female object of desire. This is implicit in Dante's original reference to the fact that "to many [the *canzoni*'s] beauty was more pleasing than their goodness." It becomes explicit a book later, in Dante's gloss on the literal

---

[64] This may well be the point where Dante comes closest to embracing the trivializing assessment of poetry with which he struggles throughout the treatise (see Chapter 2, section v).

sense of his address, through the device of the *congedo*, to the *canzone* "Voi che intendendo." Here the objectifying personification of his own words, to which he called particular attention in *Vita Nova* 12 (see again n 54), is given the further twist of including a moment when the poet imagines telling his poem how to speak to her, definitely *her*, uncomprehending audience:

> Ora appresso [in the *congedo*] ammonisco lei e dico: Se per avventura incontra che tu vadi là dove persone siano che dubitare ti paiano ne la tua ragione, non ti smarrire, ma dì loro: "*Poi che non vedete la mia bontade, ponete mente almeno la mia bellezza.*"/Che non voglio in ciò altro dire . . . se non: O uomini, che vedere non potete la *sentenza* di questa canzone, non la rifiutate però; ma ponete mente la sua *bellezza*, ch'è grande *sì per construzione* . . . *sì per l'ordine del sermone* . . . *sì per lo numero de le sue parti* . . . Le quali cose in essa si possono *belle* vedere, per chi ben guarda. (2.11.8–9)

> (I go on immediately to admonish her [the poem], saying: if you chance to come into the company of people who seem to you perplexed as to your [philosophical] meaning, do not lose heart, but say to them: since you cannot see my goodness, at least recognize my beauty. What I wish to say here . . . is simply this: O [men] who cannot grasp the [sense] of this *canzone*, do not for that reason spurn it: rather, recognize the great beauty it has, in its [syntactical construction, . . . in the order of its speech], and in the rhythmical [metrical] form of its parts. . . . These features in her can be appreciated as beautiful by every attentive observer.)

It is no accident that the beauties he attributes to "her" are grammatical (*construzione*), rhetorical (*l'ordine del sermone*), and "musical" in the broad sense (*lo numero de le sue parti*) and closely parallel the beauties attributed to the prose ("constructions"; "sweet orations") in 1.10 (see Chapter 2, nn 72 and 80). In other words, the declared love for prose personified as a "male" *amico* in 1.10 becomes figuratively and conceptually entangled with Dante's emerging personification of poetry as a female beloved.[65]

Despite these strong intimations, it is only at the very end of book 1 that poetry briefly, yet decisively, emerges at the true center of Dante's discourse on the vernacular. Chapters 11 and 12 continue to set forth proofs of how and why Dante loves the vernacular, without either stressing that he is speaking primarily of the prose or offering particularly strong hints about the status of the poetry, though there are some indications to support both possibilities. In the thirteenth and final chapter, however, Dante makes the crucial claim, considered for different reasons in each of the two previous chapters, that he has sought to give permanence to "his" vernacular, and thus, implicitly, to make it the equal of Latin by "binding [it]

---

[65] See Stillinger 1992: especially 50–1 for an identification of Dante-as-lover with the prose of *VN* and Beatrice with the poetry.

together through rhythm and rhyme" (1.13.6). In this last, best proof of love for the vernacular, poetry emerges unequivocally as the focus of his attention, though even now not in the capacity of object of prose (self-) commentary.[66] In 1.10 rhyme and rhythm were specifically, if disingenuously, dismissed as extraneous adornments; here they have become instead the means by which the vulgar tongue can be given a permanent essence, an enduring life, comparable to that of Latin – potentially overcoming the rigid hierarchy announced in 1.5.

Having spent the better part of book 1 in keeping poetry – ostensibly the main course of this intellectual banquet – well out of view while lavishing attention on the prose, at this critical point Dante suddenly brings it back into the picture. As he does so, he again makes visible the dual roles that he plays in the treatise: as the "sergente" who composed the servile (though expressive!) prose commentary, but also as the poet who binds together the vernacular with his rhyme and rhythm. It seems reasonable to infer that Dante's success in the latter undertaking is what has made his poetry a worthy, authoritative, object of commentary in *Convivio*, just as it is what entitles him – in principle, and tacitly – to the title of *autore* from *avieo*.

With poetry finally emerging from behind the protective screen of commenting prose, one might think Dante would begin to address directly the intertwined issues of presenting verse in the *vulgare* as worthy of commentary and of the coincidence of *commentator* and *auctor* in the innovative mode of auto-exegesis. However, the last lines of book 1 apparently turn back to the prose alone, even as they offer yet another equivocation:

Così rivolgendo li occhi a dietro, e raccogliendo le ragioni prenotate, puotesi vedere questo pane, col quale si deono mangiare le infrascritte canzoni, essere sufficientemente purgato da le macule, e da l'essere di biado; per che tempo è d'intendere a ministrare le vivande./Questo sarà quello pane orzato del quale si satolleranno migliaia, e a me ne soperchieranno le sporte piene. Questo sarà luce nuova, sole nuovo, lo quale surgerà là dove l'usato tramonterà, e darà lume a coloro che sono in tenebre e in oscuritate, per lo usato sole che a loro non luce. (1.13.11–12)

(So if one casts one's eye back over what has been said, and gathers together [the reasons which have been noted down], it is clear that this bread, which must be

---

[66] Grayson argues that the prose is *the* protagonist of *CV* (1963; cf. Chapter 2, n 79). Indeed, the prose is not only quantitatively preponderant, but also qualitatively constitutive, radically expanding the meaning of the previously composed *canzoni*. Still, the explicit *telos* of *CV* is to reveal the poetry's hidden content, while an implicit goal is to establish the poetic *autore* as maker not just of single poems, but of an entire language. For *VN*, see n 15.

eaten together with the following *canzoni*, is satisfactorily purged of its [stains] and of any blame attaching to its being made from [fodder (i.e., Italian)]. It is, then, time to set about serving the various courses. This commentary will be that fine barley bread on which thousands will amply satisfy their hunger, while for me there will be basketfuls left over to enjoy. This will be a new light, a new sun which will rise to take the place of the old sun which is setting, and give light to those now lost in darkness because for them the old sun sheds no light.)

In 1.13.11, the *pane* is, as it has been from the beginning, the prose, and we are now reminded specifically that its purpose is to accompany the *real* intellectual food of the banquet, namely the *canzoni*. In 1.13.12, however, the *pane* becomes the miraculous bread which feeds the hungry thousands (of vernacular speakers without access to Latin) and the "new light, new sun" which will replace the setting orb of Latin. Is the *pane* of 1.13.12 the same as that of 1.13.11? It must be, to judge both by the elementary canons of syntax and the explicit declarations of 1.10. To judge, instead, by Dante's stated desire to remake the vernacular in the "image and likeness" of Latin through the binding instrument of poetic verse, it must now have come to signify prose *and* poetry, poetry even more than prose.

Why does Dante at once assert and obscure the powers of poetry? Why does he blur and reaffirm the formal markers between commenting prose and commented *canzoni*? The main reason can be inferred from 1.10.12–13 (cited above), where Dante *commentator* explicitly claims that the "accidental" ornamentation of vernacular poems obscures their ability to communicate complex and sublime ideas comparable to those expressed in Latin. In Chapter 2, this notion was discussed in terms of the discursive status of poetry – vis-à-vis not "prose" in general, but philosophy as a mode of understanding. However, it also accounts very well for the hybrid configuration of the treatise as poetic text followed by prose commentary.

To rehearse the essential point: from the very beginning of *Convivio* the reader is told that the closed, "bound," and ornamented poetic text possesses a hidden meaning concealed within its closed, "bound" and ornamented exterior, but that said meaning can only be revealed, "opened," by the explanatory readings offered in the *comento*.[67] This last point is made, to adduce one of several possible examples in the passage cited earlier, to illustrate the proximity of the rationale for *Convivio*'s structure to that given in chapter 25 for *Vita Nova*'s:

---

[67] For the metaphor of "opening" as interpretation in *CV*, see Grayson 1963: 47, 53. Cf. Mazzotta 1979: 225–6 and n on the related use of "aprire" in *Purg.* 22. For *VN*, see n 47.

I intend as well to show the true meaning of those [the *canzoni* to be commented upon] which may not be seen by some unless I recount it, because it is hidden under the figure of allegory: and this [exposition] will not only give good pleasure when heard, but also subtle teaching, both in how to speak [i.e., to write poetry in this way] and how to understand the writings of others. (1.2.17)

This is substantially the same point made in the treatment of allegory and/or allegoresis at the beginning of book 2:

Dico che, sì come nel primo capitolo [i.e., 1.1.15 and 18; also 1.2.17], questa sposizione conviene essere litterale e allegorica. E a ciò dare a intendere, si vuol sapere che le scritture si possono intendere e deonsi esponere massimamente per quattro sensi. L'uno si chiama litterale, [. . . l'altro si chiama allegorico,] e questo è quello che si nasconde sotto 'l manto di queste favole [dei poeti], ed è una veritade nascosa sotto bella menzogna. (2.1.2–3)

(I say, as I did earlier in chapter 1 [of book 1], that this exposition should be both literal and allegorical. And so that this may be understood, you must know that writings may be understood and must be expounded primarily according to four senses. One is called the literal [sense], the other [which can be subdivided into three], is called the allegorical, and this is that which hides beneath the cloak of these [poetic] fables, and it is a truth hidden beneath a beautiful lie.)

What can be added to the earlier analysis of this passage (Chapter 2, section v, especially nn 65–74) is that it contains a relatively faithful version of the standard medieval *auctor*/*lector* dialectic. A privileged text, the poetic *auctoritas*, guarantees that a profound meaning exists and that it bears such meaning within itself, but without the intervention of the commenting reader that meaning will never be revealed. The poetic *auctoritas* remains mute and insignificant without its "servant" commentary. In other words, only through the fiction of the separation of commentary from poetry can the *auctoritas* of the former gain credence: no wonder then if Dante hesitates to lower the formal barrier between the two modes.

Once this point has been established, however, the distinction becomes increasingly tenuous: Dante *auctor* and Dante *commentator* grow closer together: the commenting prose begins to look like it might be capable of expressing "conceputa sentenza" all on its own, while the poetry turns out to be the key to the construction of a language capable of rivaling the intellectual authority of classical Latin in the present day. At the same time, as the two "Dantes" and the two modes of discourse associated with them converge, the differences of this writer and this text from the traditional "culture of authority" become increasingly apparent. In the terms of the unfolding of *Convivio* itself, this phenomenon is expressed in the gradual displacement of allegory (which can only be "opened" through commentary) in favor of the letter (the substance of the poetry *qua* poetry).[68] In 2.1, as became apparent in Chapter 2, Dante stresses the indispensable role of the letter, not merely as "bella menzogna" composed of extrinsic ornaments, but as the *sine qua non* for arriving at the underlying significance of the text (2.1.8–15).[69] The first two books of commentary follow this model: first a literal exposition, then an allegorical interpretation, although in both the literal exposition takes up the greater part of Dante's attention (in book 2, the letter gets ten chapters [2.2–11; 2.1 is a preliminary definition of the double expository procedure Dante will then follow], the allegory four [12–15]; in book 3, the letter again gets ten, the allegory five).

The real transformation, however, occurs only with book 4, just as, and not coincidentally, Dante directly addresses the paired issues of his relationship to authority and of nobility as an individual quality. As we have seen, the third *canzone*, "Le dolci rime d'amore ch'i'solia," presents itself, even in its opening line, as a palinodic departure from an earlier "poetry of love," presumably including the previous two *canzoni*, taken at the letter (Chapter 2, section v, especially nn 76 and 78). One aspect of this change of poetics is that the need for an *allegorical* exposition of the text has dropped away entirely:

E cominciai una canzone nel cui principio dissi: "Le dolci rime d'amor ch'i'solia." Nel quale io intendo riducer la gente in diritta via sopra la propia conoscenza de la verace nobilitade; sì come per la conoscenza del suo testo, a la esposizione de la quale ora s'intende, vedere si potrà. E però che in questa canzone s'intese a rimedio così necessario, non era buono sotto alcuna figura parlare, ma convennesi per via tostana questa medicina, acciò che fosse tostana la sanitade, [dare]; la quale corrotta, e a così laida morte sí correa. Non sarà dunque mestiere ne la esposizione di costei alcuna allegoria aprire, ma solamente la sentenza secondo la lettera ragionare. (4.1.9–11)

(I began a *canzone* in whose beginning I said "the sweet rhymes of love that I used to [pursue in my thoughts]." By means of which *canzone* I intend to lead people back onto the straight way concerning the proper understanding of true nobility, as one may see from an understanding of the text, to the exposition of which I now turn my intentions. And because this *canzone* was conceived as an urgently

---

[68] For the increasing importance of the literal sense in Biblical exegesis of the Duecento, see Chapter 1, n 52. Corti 1983: 80–1 argues that Dante's emphasis on the letter here follows a passage from book 6 of Hugh of St. Victor's Didiscalion. Among critics who have called attention to the role of the "literal sense" in *CV* I are Pepin 1970: 53–7, 71–4, 82–93; Chiarenza, 1980: 84–5. See also Chapter 2, section v and nn 70, 78, 79. When the *ECG*, so often cited to prove Dante's commitment to the fourfold scheme of Biblical allegory, comes to comment on the text of *Par.*, it eschews the allegorical sense(s) for an exclusively literal "expositio," which "nichil aliud est quam forme operis manifestatio" (17, 42–3; cf. 19, 52).

[69] Surprisingly, over half of the chapter, which stands at the center of debates over Dantean allegorizing, is dedicated to the primacy of the literal sense (2.1.8–15).

necessary remedy [for vulgar errors about the nature of nobility], it was not good to speak under any figure, but this medicine had to be delivered by the quickest way, so that health could be restored quickly, since when it remains corrupted, one races toward an ugly death. It will not therefore be necessary to open up any allegory in expounding [this *canzone*], but only to reason about its meaning [*sentenza*] according to the letter.)

This passage does *not* mean that Dante intends to do away with commentary; on the contrary, the prose of book 4 contains as many chapters (thirty) as the other two put together. However, as the distinction between allegory (the hidden sense revealed by reading) and letter (the sense given explicitly by the text itself) disappears, so does the original basis for Dante's distinction between *auctor* and *commentator*, since, as we have seen, the need for the prose was initially predicated on its ability to say what the poetry could not. To put things in the terms of *Vita Nova*: where prose commentary was once necessary to reveal the author's intention, or at least to show that he understood what he had done, now the poetry is self-explanatory, revealing its intentions literally. From this perspective it seems no accident at all that Dante's next great poetic project, the *Commedia*, abandons the prosimetrum mode, and lets the poetry speak for itself. It is, then, finally, to the vexed question of the relation of *Convivio*, as well as *De Vulgari Eloquentia* and *Vita Nova*, to the *sacrato poema* that this chapter turns in closing.

IV. FROM DANTE DIVIDED TO THE *POETA-PERSONAGGIO*

At the outset, this study posed the question: how did Dante arrive at the strategy of self-legitimation that enabled him to write the "seamlessly" authorized text of the vernacular *Commedia*, not to mention the ambitious political treatise, the Latin *Monarchia*? What role did the earlier, "minor," works play in bringing him to that point? The second part of this study will probe these issues extensively. In particular, it will reject the usual practice of reading backwards "palinodically" from the *Commedia*, understood teleologically as the necessary and natural, or rather supernatural, outcome of Dante's career. Instead it will follow a chronological progression in which the earlier works are seen as places where strategies of self-representation are being developed, and where the naturalized mechanisms of the *Commedia* can be more easily seen and understood, because they not yet have been perfected.[70]

---

[70] For the concept of "naturalization," originally developed by Barthes especially 1957, see Culler 1975: 134–60.

As will be seen, especially in Chapters 6 and 7, one of the most effective instruments deployed in the *Commedia* is that of removing the poem and its poet from the historical flow, creating an effect of temporal distortion that disrupts the ordinary order leading from a prior to a successive work, so that the latter seems to be the cause of the former, rather than the other way around. This perspectival distortion has only been reinforced by the fact that both *Convivio* and *De Vulgari Eloquentia* remained unfinished: *Convivio* having only four of a projected fifteen books; *De Vulgari Eloquentia* only one, plus a large fraction of a second, out of a probable four. For this reason, critics often assume that the two works were abandoned because they represented false paths discarded in favor of the true enterprise of the *Commedia*. *Vita Nova*, open-ended if technically complete (Harrison 1988: 130), lends itself similarly to the teleological model, given that it concludes with what sounds suspiciously like a prophecy of a (the) masterwork to come.

Typically, scholars posit a radical shift in epistemological perspective and in poetic-linguistic practice, amounting to a veritable conversion, which opens a gaping abyss between the treatises and the *poema sacro*. For example, the *trapasso* from *Convivio* to *Commedia* is said to entail a shift from a philosophical perspective, of human reason reflecting from within and upon the order of nature, to a theological one, of human reason subordinated to divine revelation.[71] Instead, in moving from *De Vulgari Eloquentia* to the *Commedia*, the transformation is typically seen as formal and linguistic, namely in the abandonment of the idea of importing a high tragic style from Latin rhetoric and poetics into the vernacular and the concomitant turn to the mixed "comic" style.[72] The *Commedia*, moreover, abruptly gives over the joint attempt of the treatises to define the *canzone* as the noblest vernacular form (see Chapter 3, section iv), capable of delivering moral and intellectual content comparable to that of the classics, in favor of the radically innovative mode of *terza rima*. This poetic form, among other things, adds an entirely new narrative capability to vernacular verse, in addition to embodying the link between human author and "verace autore" in its Trinitarian structure.[73]

The present chapter points toward yet another significant shift in Dante's practice in the *Commedia*, namely that he abandons the composite mode of

---

[71] See Chapter 2, nn 75, 86 and especially Chapter 6.

[72] For the tragic style in *DVE*, see Chapter 3, n 5, as well as section iv and nn. On the stylistic practice of the *DC*, begin with Auerbach 1941 on Dante and the Augustinian *sermo humilis* and Contini 1964 on Dante's "plurilingualism." On the shift between *DVE* and the *DC*, see Chapter 3, n 62. See also n 19.

[73] On *terza rima* see especially Freccero 1983a; Durling and Martinez 1996: 20–3.

self-commentary that had characterized his two most ambitious "literary" works and that had found modified expression as well in his treatise on language and poetry. This shift, *a fortiori*, entails the disappearance of any overt structural (prose vs. poetry; cf. Grayson 1963: 56–7) and/or grammatical (first vs. third-person) distinctions and divisions between plural textual selves. True, the Dante of the *Commedia* is still a *poeta-personaggio*, whose two aspects can be distinguished temporally: even though the *personaggio* is already a poet – as he reminds the reader periodically, beginning in *Inferno* 1 – only over the course of the poem does he become the writer capable of narrating this journey in the first-person singular (see Chapter 1, section v and Chapter 7, section i). Here, however, the different aspects of Dante, as of Augustine in the *Confessions*, are integrally connected to one another.[74] The rest of this section, then, will attempt to show how, rather than merely rejected or superseded alternatives, the earlier works constitute the condition of possibility for the self-representational strategies of the *Commedia*.

Once again, *Convivio* is the place to start. When Dante invokes Augustine and Boethius as models for self-representation near the beginning of book 1, he implicitly defines two distinct projects that the treatise will carry out: (1) an "Augustinian" program of ethical education of others to "virtute e canoscenza," which will involve expounding the eleven moral virtues described by Aristotle and (2) a "Boethian" program of self-justification and authorization. There is no doubt that the first of these projects remains incomplete. As noted in Chapter 2, sections i and iv, books 2 and 3 are preliminary in that they simply describe Dante's personal circumstances (his turn to Philosophy) which led him to undertake the writing of the treatise. Book 4's topic, nobility, initially described as a digression (4.1.8–9), turns out to be the ground out of which all the active virtues grow (4.18.5; 19.1–10 *passim*). In other words, book 4 ends where *Convivio* proper, that is the "Augustinian" exposition of the eleven virtues rooted in nobility, would have begun (see Chapter 2, especially n 12).

On the other hand, as far as the "Boethian" goal of self-authorization is concerned, a "pro-spective" reading has suggested that it is effectively complete by the end of book 4, and that what has been achieved thereby is a concept of authorship sufficient for the composition of the *Commedia*. This is true in that Dante's definition of nobility can be understood as serving to confer that quality on himself, creating a model of autonomous

---

[74] Singleton's distinction (1954: 9–13) between Dante as individual and Dante as Everyman is a different matter, since, rather than referring to a formal separation of one Dante from another, he posits the simultaneous presence of two aspects or functions in a single character. See again Chapter 1, section v.

personhood and individual agency that frees him from social and historical restraints that seem to bar him from authority. It is true in that he has found a way past his apparent subordination to the great political and philosophical authorities. It is true in that he has been able to confer on the vernacular the poetic and intellectual authority comparable to that of Latin. It is true in that he has discovered a means, however oblique and allusive, to ground his own "merely" poetic authorship in the absolute authority of the Creator-God (especially through the analogy of poet and Deity implicit in the etymology of *autore* from *avieo*).

Finally, it is also and most importantly true in that he has arrived at a poetic mode which is no longer bound by the limitations of the "allegory of poets" and which thus allows him to speak directly of the most difficult topics, without the necessary interposition of exegetical prose to reveal otherwise hidden intentions. If this great leap forward in "le dolci rime d'amore ch'i'solia" does not yet aspire to the sort of textual status which requires analysis according to the theological understanding of allegory, it has, at least, gone so far in that direction as to give the letter of the text an absolute primacy in the revelation of authorial intentions. Thus, *Convivio* is a "self-consuming artifact," to adapt Stanley Fish's now venerable term (1972). The "Boethian" project of self-authorization proves so successful that the prosimetrum form of text and commentary through which it has been carried out, and the consequent splitting of Dante himself between the roles of writer and of reader, is, by the end of book 4, no longer necessary: *Convivio* itself is obsolete (cf. Scott 1995).[75] What remains is a sketch for the "undivided," and "finished," author of the *Commedia*.

Moreover, variants of this same dynamic process can be detected in both of the other works considered at length in the two preceding chapters. As Chapter 3 argues, the unfinishedness of *De Vulgari Eloquentia* can be understood in much the same way as that of *Convivio*.[76] In the former, a failure to carry out the promise of treating with encyclopedic thoroughness the potential range of expressive forms in the vernacular is coupled with provisional "success" in defining Dante as master of the illustrious vernacular and of its highest poetic achievement, the "poetry of rectitude" embodied in the "tragic" *canzone*.[77] Furthermore, the completion of the first project dictates

---

[75] Hence, perhaps, its limited circulation, as that of *DVE* (Chapter 2, n 12; Chapter 3, n 11).

[76] Welliver (1981: 13–16) conjectures that the incompleteness of the treatise is only apparent, and in fact reflects a fully realized authorial intention. I believe instead that an unstable conflict of authorial motives runs throughout the treatise.

[77] For attempts to reconstruct the original plan of *DVE*, see Chapter 2, n 94; Chapter 3, n 42. I follow Mengaldo 1970b: 408, 1978a: 91–2, 1979: 4 who situates the treatise between: (1) a projected "encyclopedia" of language and style and (2) a personalized poetics which posits Dante's unique suitability to the "poetry of rectitude," written in the *vulgare illustre* and the tragic style.

the renunciation of the second. Dante's self-identification as the poet of the illustrious, tragic *cantio* would only be diluted by moving through the range of Italian vernacular experiences (Mengaldo 1978a: 91–2). To put it another way, to assert one's personal identification with the illustrious, tragic *canzone* is to lose the impersonal authority over the encyclopedic totality of linguistic experience. In the end *De Vulgari Eloquentia*, like *Convivio*, contains only those parts of the initially projected whole that directly bear on Dante's personal experience as vernacular poet – what is omitted is everything else that was to be included for the didactic benefit of *others*.

The text/commentary division cannot be mapped exactly from *Convivio* onto *De Vulgari Eloquentia*. As a *tractatus* rather than a prosimetrum work, it is generically exempt from this device. Moreover, by virtue of being written in Latin, it possesses the authority of that language intrinsically, and thus does not need to indulge in the defensive gestures of *Convivio* book 1. However, as was clearly established in the two preceding chapters, *De Vulgari Eloquentia* does deploy a rhetorical separation between the Dante who writes the treatise (the prose "nos") and the Dante whose poetry is used as a recurrent and privileged example first of the vernacular and then of the *cantio*, and who is consistently referred to, throughout the first book and well into the second, in the third-person singular and periphrastically, as the *amicus* of Cino da Pistoia.[78]

As also seen, however, the way in which this second personage is referred to changes dramatically at a key point in the second book. I cite, once more, the critical passage:

So I say [dicimus] that the *canzone*, in so far as it is so called for its pre-eminence, which is what I too am seeking [querimus], is a connected series of equal stanzas in the tragic style, without a refrain, and focused on a single theme, as I showed [ostendimus] when I wrote [dicimus]: "Donne che avete intelletto d'amore." (2.8.8)

The repetition of the first-person plural *dicimus* at either end of the phrase emphasizes how the split between the prosaic, grammarian, Dante, who writes the treatise in Latin and the poetic Dante who, as synecdochic representative of the vernacular tradition, is its subject, has been rhetorically bridged by a shared personal pronoun, whose pluralness is now magisterial, rather than schizophrenic. Dante will cite himself seven more times in *De Vulgari Eloquentia*, each time using the "nos," just as in all prior references he had used the third-person singular (2.10.2; 2.11.5, 7, 8; 2.12.3; 2.13.2, 13).

---

[78] The device enacts an ambivalence similar to that surrounding self-representation in *CV* and reflects the same rhetorical taboo against self-reference invoked there. See Chapter 2, section iii; Ascoli 1997: 327 and n 56.

Never again will he appear in the company of his "friend" Cino, who last appears in a long list of *canzoni* writers at the end of 2.6. The previous chapter stressed that this explicit "reunion" of the two Dantes is coordinated with the valorization of individual (creative) will and the identification of vernacular writers, like Dante, as *auctores*. To this can be added that such a reintegration previews the constitution of an undivided Dante in the *Commedia*, even more explicitly and exactly than in *Convivio*, where the intersection of Dante *auctor* and Dante *commentator* is only potential.

Finally, *Vita Nova* too provides at least the hint of a similar closing integration of its various Dantes. The case is curious. On the one hand, this work predates the authorizing processes undertaken in the course of *Convivio* and *De Vulgari Eloquentia* by about ten years and thus would hardly seem to have reached a point where this step was possible. On the other hand, not only is the work formally complete in itself, but it also ends with the prediction of a newer and greater work to come about Beatrice *sub specie aeternitatis*, and in both respects seems to go beyond the later treatises, and thus to be much closer to the *Commedia*.[79]

However one conceives of the relation between the *libello* and the treatises, *Vita Nova* undoubtedly anticipates the movement of the later works toward closing the gap between the present of an analytical reader and the past of an analyzed writer (cf. Moleta 1978; Menocal 1991: especially 37). A reading of *Vita Nova* 3 showed that Dante casts the *fedeli d'amore* as simultaneously occupying the position of readers and writers. At the more advanced stage represented by chapters 24 and 25 Dante implicitly justifies the function of his readerly commentary as an erstwhile poet's demonstration that he knew what he was doing. From this later perspective, commentary aims to reproduce the poet's intention at the point of composition, bridging the temporal gap between Dante reader and Dante author, in sharp distinction from the situation in chapter 3 when no one, including Dante himself, seemed to know what the dream recounted in "ciascun'alma presa" meant until long after the poem was written.

Vita Nova 41 and 42 return to the situation of a (dream?) vision recounted in poetry that has accompanied each of the previous moments of particular reflection on the relation between reading and writing.[80] These chapters mark a further development in a number of ways. In the first place, the last

---

[79] To the point that it has been argued that chapter 42 was added after the *DC* had been conceived (see Chapter 6, nn 5, 7).

[80] In addition to chapters 3 and 24, see also chapter 12 (n 54) and compare chapters 9, 23, 39. On the question of the modality of seeing (dream; "imaginazione"; "fantasia"; "visione"), consult Singleton 1949: 15–17; Hollander 1974: 13–18 and nn; D'Andrea 1987: 74; Mazzaro 1981: 32.

poem recorded, "Oltre la spera che più larga gira," was evidently composed near the time in which *Vita Nova* itself was written, since the vision of which it speaks is the last psychic event recorded in the text and determines the state of mind in which the author of the *libello* presently finds himself, that is, studiously preparing to say something new and different about Beatrice. In other words, the gap between the "book of memory" and the "little book" itself has narrowed, along with the distance between Dante-poet and the one who writes *ragioni* and *divisioni*.

In the second place, a curious reversal takes place in the relation between vision and poem. In the earlier examples, a vision occurs and is then recorded in verse, followed by attempts to report and interpret verse and vision. In this case, however, the poem seemingly precedes, or at least is simultaneous with, the vision: "Appresso questo sonetto apparve a me una mirabile visione" (soon after [the writing of] this sonnet a miraculous vision appeared to me; 42.1). The odd sequencing suggests, at the very least, a scrambling of the temporal separation between Dante as loving subject and Dante as the poet who records and interprets the experiences of that subject. At the most it hints that the loving subject is now the product of the poetry, rather than the reverse.[81]

More immediately comprehensible from the perspective I have been developing here, and more to its purposes, is the effect that Dante says this vision had on him:

[N]e la quale io vidi cose che mi fecero proporre di non dire più di questa benedetta infino a tanto che io potesse più degnamente trattare di lei. (42.1)

([I]n it [that vision] I saw things that made me propose to say no more about this blessed woman, until I should be able to treat of her more worthily.)

The point is that poetry is no longer confined to the past, but is projected into a future when Dante will have learned better how to speak of her (embracing for a moment the developmental fantasy, one might imagine that *Convivio* and *De Vulgari Eloquentia* are what will teach him to "to treat of her more worthily"). Moreover, the person speaking in the prose asserts that he was, is, and will be a poet, a claim that is then reinforced by the further promise to "dicer di lei quello che non fue mai detto d'alcuna" (say of her that which has never been said of any woman; 42.2–3). The past,

---

[81] See Marti 1965: 669, for examples. He does not signal the anomaly, however. Noteworthy is 13.1: "Appresso di questa soprascritta visione, avendo già detto le parole che Amore m'avea imposte a dire . . ." (referring to the usual vision-poem sequencing). Compare also 9.8, 16.1, 20.1–2, 22.12, 23.1, 24.1, 27.1.

and the book of memory in which it is recorded, have become prologue: the reader will turn author again, as the temporal gap between them vanishes.[82]

All three of Dante's major "earlier" works approach the question of the poet's authority, each adopting its own distinctive rhetorical and conceptual strategies in so doing. All these efforts at self-authorization culminate with a rapprochement, formal and/or conceptual between prose and poetry, between Dante-*lector* and Dante-*auctor*. Finally, I would argue, this trend implies a latent and growing desire to produce a text that is complete in itself, and which integrates the elements that are divided among the various Dantes and among the various types of writing associated with those fractional selves (cf. Grayson 1963: 55–61). Notably, where *Vita Nova* separates its text into lyric (poems), narrative (*ragioni*), and analytical (*divisioni*), the *Commedia* includes within its verse the lyric topic of Dante's love for Beatrice, an autobiographical narrative, and a series of philosophical and theological expositions.[83] Most of all, the *Commedia* begins where the others end as far as the project of authorial self-representation: with an integrated *poeta-personaggio* who remains undivided grammatically, conceptually, and formally. My claim is that this feature of the *sacrato poema* is made possible, though not fatally determined, by the earlier works, even as it represents itself as effecting their supercession.

What, then, are the historical implications of this passage from unfinished and divided authorship to a (re)integrated authorial self who now speaks unequivocally *in propria persona*? Unsurprisingly, the concept of authorship dramatized in the *Commedia* points simultaneously in two opposite directions, historically speaking. On the one hand, the form of auto-commentary can be abandoned now because Dante feels he has obtained sufficient *auctoritas*, traditionally defined, so that he no longer needs to go to the potentially pathetic extreme of himself providing commentary of which no one else considers him to be worthy. From now on – and the historical fortunes of the *Commedia* bear this out – others will take care of supplying the commentary (Chapter 1, n 2, cf. Pepin 1970: 127–30): Dante will be an *auctor*; they will be the *lectores*. In other words, the traditional medieval model is simply reproduced.

---

[82] For the narrative temporality of chapter 42, see Moleta 1978: 386–7; Harrison 1988: 128–57. Hollander makes the point that only here is the present tense used of Beatrice (1974: 19–30). On the temporality of the *libello* generally, see Singleton 1949 (especially 8, 25–35, 114–15); De Robertis 1961 (e.g., 11); Moleta 1978; Noferi 1982–3; Mazzotta 1983; Picone 1987a: 67–8; Noakes 1988: 77–80, 1990; Stillinger 1992: 81–4, 114–15; Barolini 1994; Cristaldi 1994; Pinto 1994: chapter 4; Cervigni and Vasta 1995: 28–44; and the excellent essay of Levers 2002.

[83] On the *DC*'s internalized "self-glossing," see Wlassics 1975; Noakes 1988: 80; Mineo 2000.

To reach this point, Dante has had to transform the basic medieval notion of authorship beyond easy recognition. He has had to move it from Latin into Italian. He has, in the course of this translation, reduced the range of Latin words and concepts designating authorship (*auctor*; *autor*; *avitor*; even *actor*) under the umbrella of a single Italian word, *autore*, where he can maneuver freely among the possibilities, as we saw him doing in *Inferno* 1.85–7. He has had to make historically present, and endow with individual personality, an authorial figure whose qualities are usually derived instead from his antiquity and/or transcendence, and from his access to impersonal truth.

He has, in the final analysis, insisted that the *auctor* and the *lector*, the writer and the reader, are not hierarchically distinct, but one and the same, and, as a consequence, that the author must know and control the meaning of his texts.[84] For all its many affinities with most traditional beliefs and practices of medieval Christianity, what sets the *Commedia* apart is that this poem was written by an author who believed himself to be in full and conscious control of his own meaning, and that he has produced a poem which insists that it can "explain itself."[85] In this sense, with the *Commedia*, Barthes' dead, modern, author is born (cf. Minnis 1991: 51).

[84] In Dante, then, two apparently opposed late medieval tendencies – the new prominence of the human author (Minnis 1984) and the emergence of the "exegete as *auctor*" (Copeland 1991: 125, also 158) – converge as complementary aspects of a larger phenomenon.

[85] Dante's claim to be in control of his meanings does not guarantee either that his self-interpretation is always complete and/or trustworthy, or that empirical readers have always understood and/or followed his intentions (see n 47; Ascoli 2003).

PART 2

Authority in person: Dante between Monarchia *and the* Commedia

CHAPTER 5

"No judgment among equals": Dividing authority in Dante's Monarchia

I. *MONARCHIA* AFTER *CONVIVIO* AND *DE VULGARI ELOQUENTIA*

At the close of the previous chapter, the stage was set for an examination of the *Commedia* as a logically, if not necessarily or exclusively, entailed outcome of the exercises in authority-building conducted in all three of Dante's major early works, and particularly *Convivio* and *De Vulgari Eloquentia*. There is, however, another important text that deserves consideration as an example of the next, "mature" or "finished," stage in Dante's career, namely the Latin treatise entitled *Monarchia*. *Monarchia*, no less than the *Commedia*, can be read as fulfilling some part of the aspirations to *auctoritas* articulated in the abandoned treatises. Such a reading, I believe, gives insight into aspects of the Dantean project that cannot be seen, or are at least very difficult to see, in the "poema sacro." In particular, the treatise helps make clear how the individual, poetic and/or theological authority with which Dante is usually associated is inextricably linked to problems of "official," institutional *auctoritas*.

While the most problematic aspects of Dantean authorship have receded from view in *Monarchia*, this treatise as much as the earlier two can be read in terms of elaborate rhetorical strategies by which Dante both defines and delimits the authority of others and stakes his own claim to undertake such a definitional enterprise authoritatively. The first problem to address, then, is how to relate *Monarchia* to Dantean authorship and authority as defined in the earlier works. Until recently, the treatise had been notoriously difficult to locate, both chronologically and conceptually, within Dante's career. Now, however, while *Monarchia*'s relationship to the *Commedia* remains significantly contested, at least as to its doctrinal emphases,[1] there

---

[1] Debates over the treatise have largely focused on two interrelated questions. First, what is the meaning of Dante's use of the Aristotelian category of the "possible intellect" in book 1 (3.6 and 8; 4.1)? Does attributing the term to Averroes mean that he embraces heretical doctrines ascribed to the

is little remaining doubt that it assumed final form well after the three works examined in the previous section of this study, overlapping with the composition of the last canticle of the *Commedia*.[2] On the whole it

Arab philosopher and/or his Duecento Scholastic followers, or can it be reconciled with Christian orthodoxy? Second, what is the exact nature of the separation Dante installs between the "two ends" of man – earthly and celestial, rational and theological – and thence between Church and Empire in book 3 (15.3–10)? Is it absolute, and, if so, why does he add a final phrase suggesting that the Emperor is "in some sense" (*quoddamodo*) subject to the Pope, owing "reverence" to him as a first-born son to a father (3.15.17–18)? Depending on the answers given (see n 27), Dante may appear to be a proto-modern advocate of secular government and the separation of Church and State, the inventor of an "Averroist politics" (Nardi, e.g., 1960a; Passerin d'Entrèves 1952; Imbach 1996); as a relatively orthodox thinker for whom reason complements faith, as the Empire complements the Church (Maccarrone 1955; Vasoli 1988a; Scott 1996; Cassell 2004); or as some complex, original compromise between these positions (Gilson 1939; Vinay 1962). These issues are complicated by attempts to demonstrate either continuity or discontinuity between *MN* and the *CV* (taken to be prior) and between *MN* and the *DC* (either subsequent or roughly contemporary). Versions of the evolutionary hypothesis are Ercole 1927–1928; Nardi, e.g., 1921c, 1930a, 1940b, 1960a; Passerin d'Entrèves 1952; Chiavacci-Leonardi 1977; cf. Ricci 1966. Versions of the consistency hypothesis are Maccarrone 1955; Scott 1996; Cassell 2004. The latter concern is closely tied to the dating controversy (n 2) and is addressed in Chapter 6. Generally speaking, critics on all sides assume the internal coherence of *MN* (intermittent exception made for 3.15) and treat its argumentative procedures only as they bear on establishing an overall meaning for the treatise. This study is concerned instead with slippages and inconsistencies within the treatise's rhetorical structures and the ideas it propounds.

[2] Hypotheses concerning *MN*'s date of composition range from shortly before Dante's exile through the late 'teens. Given the lack of topical references or other clear internal evidence – with one obvious exception – the basis for dating has typically been hypothetical correlation either with important biographical-historical events, or with supposed developmental patterns in Dante's thought, or both. In the former category, Dante's traumatic experience of the interference of Boniface VIII and Charles of Valois in the affairs of Florence (1301–2) and Clement VII's displacement of the papal see from Rome to Avignon (1308) are significant precursor events, perhaps leading to Dante's first articulation of the divine mission of Empire in *CV* 4.3–5. However, most often advanced as precipitating the writing of *MN* are the descent of Emperor Henry VII into Italy (1311–1313; [Vinay 1950, 1962; Passerin d'Entrèves 1952: 42–3; Maccarrone 1955: 137–40; Davis 1957: 263–9; Mazzoni 1966a: lxiii–lxv]) and various events connected to the imperial vicariate of Dante's sometime patron Cangrande della Scala, in the years from 1315 to 1318 (e.g., Ricci 1966; R. Kay 1998: xx–xxxvi; Cassell 2004: 21–2 and nn *et passim*). In the latter category, the most aggressively stated position is that of Nardi (1921a: 133–8, 1921c: 273–5, 1930a: 297–310, 1960a: chapter 2; 1979: "Introduzione"), who placed the treatise between *CV* and the *DC*, ca. 1308. In order for supporters of this early date to make a case, they had to claim that the specific reference in *MN* 1.12.6 to Dante's treatment of free will in *Par.* 5.19–24 ("sicut in Paradiso *Comedie* dixi") is a later editorial interpolation, given the general agreement that the last canticle of the *DC* was not composed until late in the second decade of the fourteenth century. See the "softer" version of Nardi's ideal sequencing in Chiavacci-Leonardi 1977: 181–3. Recent scholarship, beginning with Ricci (1965a, 1971: 1000–2) and culminating in P. Shaw (1981, 2005), has demolished this claim. See the succinct reviews in Scott 1990a: 270–2 and nn (also 1997: 95–7, 2004: 143–4); Cassell 2004: 3 and n 1. See Mazzoni 1966a, Petrocchi 1983, Scott 1996: 3–59 (also 2004: 309–36) for Dante's reactions to the principal political–institutional developments of his time. The current state of affairs leaves room for a speculative suggestion that the *Par.* reference was inserted by Dante after the rest of the treatise was completed, or that the treatise was composed over a period of years, with the *Par.* reference coming late in the process. Still, to treat *MN* as contemporary with or even subsequent to the *DC* now seems unproblematic, though this does not necessarily mean the two texts are in fundamental agreement. For the relationship of *MN* and *CV*, see n 3. For the relationship of *MN* and the *DC*, see Chapter 6, section iii, especially n 31; also nn 27, 42, 47, 51 below.

has been considered separately from those works, although scholars, and first of all Bruno Nardi, have located it in a relation of development and transformation to the philosophical and political concerns of *Convivio*.[3] It has rarely, if ever, been analyzed from the literary-rhetorical point of view, much less in terms of Dante's pursuit of personal authority.[4]

At first glance, there is ample justification for the latter omission. In the three earlier texts, Dante is primarily concerned with establishing his credentials as an individual, primarily poetic and vernacular, author who aspires to produce works comparable to ancient poetic *auctores* in style and to ancient philosophical authors in content. On several counts, *Monarchia* constitutes a departure: (1) as a work in Latin; (2) as a work exclusively in philosophical prose unconcerned with poetry, except as a source of standard *auctoritates* to illustrate argumentative points;[5] (3) as a work in which the author makes far fewer first-person appearances than is his wont. On the face of it, *Monarchia* is overtly concerned not with the authority of any individual poet or philosopher, but with a very different type of institutional *auctoritas*, which is apparently derived and exercised in very different ways.

Each of these features can still be seen as an extension or development of some features of the prior works, though at the expense of others. *Monarchia*'s use of Latin aligns it, of course, with the Latin political epistles (see nn 8, 56 below, also Chapter 1, n 75). More important for these purposes, however, is its comparability with *De Vulgari Eloquentia*, Dante's initial foray into the prestigious venue of the Scholastic prose *tractatus*. Beginning with the fact that it actually completes the intellectual task it proposed to carry out, *Monarchia* is a far more "normative" and ambitious

---

[3] For the relationship between *CV*, especially 4.3–5, and *MN* see Nardi 1921c: 260–2, 1930a: 281–4, 1960a: 34–6: chapter 2; 1965a: 51–2; Passerin d'Entrèves 1952: 17–18, 34–7; Vasoli 1979; Took 1990: 150, 156; Scott 1990a: 269, 1995, 2004: 129–31. See also nn 1, 5, 12, 17, 22, 27, 29, 35, 41; Chapter 6, section ii. Though Nardi's polemical dating of the two treatises is discredited, his analysis of their respective perspectives remains fundamental.

[4] Because *MN* is not a literary work or a work about literature, it has been read primarily for "content," rather than in terms of rhetorical practice. P. Shaw 1995: xxxiv–xxxvi is an exception, though brief. Because most Dante scholars separate the questions of political–institutional authority primarily addressed in *MN* from those of poetic authority it has not been featured in discussions of Dantean authorship (see nn 5, 8).

[5] Classical poets, especially Virgil *are* deployed as *auctoritates* in book 2 (cf. Passerin d'Entrèves 1952: 45–6; Scott 1996: 151–2; P. Shaw 1995: xx–xxiv), but only in the sense of bearing witness to the truth of a given claim (e.g., 2.4.5), that is, as authors from *autentin*. They are thus indistinguishable from philosophical and historical *auctores*, (especially Aristotle [1.5.2; 1.5.3] and Cicero [2.5.7]). For Virgil's role in the formation of Dante's imperial politics, beginning in *CV* 4 and continuing into *MN*, see Leo 1951; Davis 1957: 100–38; Passerin d'Entrèves 1952: especially 29–30; Nardi 1930a: 302–3, 1960a: 101–2 *et passim*, 1966a: 51, 62–3, 1965b: 221–36, especially 229–31; Hollander 1968; Mazzotta 1979: especially chapter 4; Scott 1996: 38–40, 64–5. See also Chapter 1, n 17; Chapter 2, especially n 75; Chapter 7, sections ii–iii.

example of the genre. Notably, where *De Vulgari Eloquentia* focuses on a topic, vernacular eloquence, that is at the least marginal to, at the most radically contestatory of, high Latin culture, *Monarchia* takes as its subject the two institutions that sit at the top of its rigorously hierarchical order, i.e., the Holy Roman Empire and the Roman Catholic Church. In the process he enters into a long-standing theological-political debate.[6] More generally speaking, the treatise fulfills Dante's early drive toward Latinity, especially as articulated in the use of Latin models and tags in *Vita Nova* and the express emphasis on the nobility of Latin, and on Latin authors – including, *de facto*, Aristotle – as the locus of wisdom to be appropriated in *Convivio* I.

In the first instance, then, the dramatic entrance of *Monarchia* into the world of high medieval culture and politics both distinguishes it from the *Commedia* and makes it interesting as a window onto Dante's self-construction as a specifically Latin *auctor*. At first this assertion may not seem entirely convincing. Even if *Monarchia* is taken on its own terms – as a Latin *tractatus* in the Scholastic mode concerned with a central late-medieval question of political theory – it does not necessarily have a *prima facie* claim to historical importance in the emergence of a prestigious modern authorship. From the point of view of late medieval Latinity it is not, stylistically, on the cutting edge. As Ronald Witt has argued, a proto-humanistic culture of lay Latinity flourished in Northern centers like Padova far more than in Florence where Dante was first educated. Witt makes the strong claim that it was Dante's "northern exposure" in the years of exile, especially his contacts and friendships in Verona, Padova, and Bologna, which led him increasingly to use Latin and to engage more fully with classical culture.[7] In the more traditional scholarly terms through which these

---

6   A classic review, with documents, of the controversy from the eleventh to the fourteenth centuries is Tierney 1964. See also Maccarrone 1951, 1952, 1954; Tierney 1972; M. Miller 2005. For Dante's place in and debts to the debate, see Nardi 1921c, 1930a, 1960a: chapters 2–3, 1979; Vinay 1950, 1962; Maccarrone 1950, 1951, 1955; Davis 1957; Ricci 1965b, 1973; also Ferrante 1984: 13–38 and nn; Botterill 1992; Scott 1996: 21–7; Cassell 2004: prolegomena, chapter 1. Fenzi 2004: especially 88–102 is unusual in viewing the treatise through the lens of the anti-imperial discourse of the French monarchy and in calling attention to how *MN* is shaped in response to the problem of France, without ever speaking overtly of it (as Dante does repeatedly in the *DC*: see Chapter 7, sections iii–iv).

7   Witt 2000: especially 214–23, as well as Billanovich 1961, 1994; Weiss 1969; Ascoli 2009. See also Chapter 1, section ii and Chapter 2, section i (especially n 4) on Dante's cultural context and intellectual development. Though Witt's work is fundamental, I believe he overstates the absence of substantive engagement with the classics in Dante's earlier works. Brunetto Latini's classicism should be given its due (see, e.g., Nencioni 1967; Davis 1967), as should early influences of the Bolognese intellectual context (mediated as well through Cavalcanti). Citations in *VN* both of the classical poets (especially chapter 25; see Chapter 4, nn 42–43) and of Aristotle (chs. 25 and 41; see Chapter 4, especially n 19) are non-trivial. Durling and Martinez 1990 make a strong case for a philosophically informed

matters have been considered, Dante's Latin *oeuvre* was almost immediately eclipsed by a humanist movement that took Petrarch, and secondarily Boccaccio, as its model and inspiration. Petrarch himself notoriously relegated Dante to the debased world of vernacular culture, although it is arguable that he knew better (Ascoli 2009). In addition, from the point of view of its content, *Monarchia*'s attempt to reassert the universality of the Roman Empire seems quixotic now, and may have seemed so even at the time, given the emergence of the French state as the pivotal player in Europe (at least from the Italian perspective), and the repeated failures of various Emperors, beginning with Frederick II, either to take their "Roman" mission literally or to press what claims they did make successfully.[8]

Nevertheless, when *Monarchia* is viewed in terms of the internal history of Dante's career, and particularly of its place as successor to the two earlier treatises, a different picture emerges. To begin with, despite the achievement of the *Commedia*, Dante's later, post-exilic, career in large measure marks a turn to Latinity,[9] as well as an increasingly direct claim to be *not only* a poet with philosophical and theological interests, *but also* a philosopher properly speaking.[10] Dante's extant Latin production dates entirely from the time of his exile, including the twelve authenticated prose epistles, *De Vulgari Eloquentia*, the late scholarly treatise *Questio de Aqua et Terra*, the two Latin epistolary eclogues addressed to Giovanni del Virgilio, and *Monarchia* itself.

The turn to Latinity, and to direct (and risky!) engagement with the dominant Latin theological, philosophical, and political culture, can be seen as the fruit of what I earlier called Dante's "growth spurt," that is, of his systematic, if still idiosyncratic, indoctrination into that culture in the years following his exile. This development was probably favored by

VN. On Dante's Latin style, see Brugnoli 1965; Paratore 1968; Dronke 1986; Silvia Rizzo 1990. For proto-humanist and humanist evaluations of his Latin, see e.g., Aurigemma 1965. See also Ascoli 2009. For the Latin/vernacular opposition in his works, see again Chapter 3.

[8] For Dante's view of Frederick II, see Chapter 1, n 79; Chapter 2, especially sections iii–iv and n 55; Chapter 3, especially n 51; Chapter 6, especially section ii. For the historical Henry VII see especially Bowsky 1960; for Henry in relation to Dante, see Davis 1957: chapter 2; Mazzoni 1966a; Scott 1996: 40–9. Dante's principal references to Henry are in the political *Eps.* (5, 6, 7, 11; see again Chapter 1, n 75) and *Par.* 30. For his criticisms of Rudolfo, Adolfo, and Alberto, see *CV* 4.3.6; *Purg.* 6.76–126 (cf. Scott 1996: especially 103–6, 123–4). In fact, Petrarch followed Dante in the attempt to resuscitate the Empire (e.g., letters directed to Charles IV in the *Familiares*) and in a critique of papal abuses of wealth and power (e.g. *Liber Sine Nomine*).

[9] Not to discount a certain ambivalence, notably expressed in the *tour-de-force* Latin verse epistle rejecting Giovanni del Virgilio's suggestion that he should abandon the vernacular for a major Latin poetic project (see Chapter 1, n 75; Ascoli 2009).

[10] In the *Q*, Dante makes this claim explicit, referring to himself both at the beginning and the end of the treatise as "the least of the philosophers," a formula whose adjectival modesty masks its substantive hubris. See Barański 1997b for a different interpretation. See also Chapter 1, n 75; Chapter 2, n 27.

more expedient and material concerns than the sheer, natural love of wisdom proposed at the beginning of *Convivio*. In the years of his exile he supported himself by working for a series of noble patrons, including the Malaspina family of Lunigiana, and of course Cangrande della Scala in Verona and the Polenta family of Ravenna, in contexts where his skills as Latin secretary and polemicist may well have been of as much or more value than his fame as a vernacular writer. At the same time, his political perspective was broadened to pan-Italian, indeed to pan-European, dimensions as he sought to understand and to counter the forces that had turned him into "exul inmeritus" and citizen of the world. To intervene with any hope of effectiveness in a situation that included, variously, the Papacy, the French monarchy, and the Holy Roman Empire, Latin was the only option available to Dante. Of the several Latin works produced in this period and under these circumstances, *Monarchia* is by far the most ambitious and, together with a few of the epistles (especially 5–7, 11), the most significant politically.

From the perspective of this study, all of this can be seen as an extension of the pursuit in *Convivio* and *De Vulgari Eloquentia* of an authorial standing and a textual authority comparable to that of classical Latinity and/or its Scholastic propagators. In other words, *Monarchia* might be read as the realization of the most culturally "conservative" pole of Dante's earlier engagement with the culture of authority, the work in which he comes to look and sound most like one of the Scholastic *doctores*.[11] The other pole, of course, is the appropriation of such authority for vernacular poetry, culminating with the *Commedia*. If in *Convivio* Dante takes the dramatic and culturally eccentric step of comparing a vernacular *canzone*, "Le dolci rime d'amore ch'i' solia," to Aquinas' *Summa Contra Gentiles*, with *Monarchia* he writes a prose Latin treatise that more obviously and less obtrusively mirrors the dominant philosophical-theological discourses of the day.

As this last point suggests, the turn away from poetry and toward philosophical prose is also one natural outcome of the earlier treatises as well. As we have seen earlier, both *Convivio* and *De Vulgari Eloquentia* explicitly subordinate prose to poetry, respectively as servant to master and as imitator to imitated. But both are also primarily prose works and their prose is the vehicle that links Dante most closely to the authoritative Latin tradition – by content in *Convivio* and by style and argumentation alike in *De Vulgari*

---

[11] By this I do not necessarily mean conceptually or politically conservative; see again Chapter 1, n 28; also n 27 below.

Eloquentia. In particular, *Monarchia* takes to one logical extreme the priv-
ileging of philosophy as mode of discourse throughout *Convivio*, and the
proposal of Aristotle as the paradigmatic *autore*. In this view, rather than
adopting the tortuous expedient of teasing hidden philosophical content
out of poetry, Dante now speaks directly, and with far greater authority, in
the voice of a prose philosopher.

The point is illustrated in the passage that opens the treatise:

Omnium hominum quos ad amorem veritatis natura superior impressit hoc
maxime interesse videtur: ut, quemadmodum de labore antiquorum ditati sunt,
ita et ipsi posteris prolaborent, quatenus ab eis posteritas habeat quo ditetur. Longe
nanque ab offitio se esse non dubitet qui, publicis documentis imbutus, ad rem
publicam aliquid afferre non curat; non enim est lignum, quod secus decursus
aquarum fructificat in tempore suo, sed potius perniciosa vorago semper ingurgi-
tans et nunquam ingurgitata refundens. Hec igitur sepe mecum recogitans, ne de
infossi talenti culpa quandoque redarguar, publice utilitati non modo turgescere
quinymo fructificare desidero, et intemptatas ab aliis ostendere vertitates. Nam
quem fructum ille qui theorema quoddam Euclidis iterum demonstraret? Qui ab
Aristotile felicitatem ostensam reostendere conaretur? . . . Nullum quippe, sed
fastidium potius illa superfluitas tediosa prestaret. Cumque, inter alias veritates
occultas et utiles, temporalis Monarchie notitia utilissima sit et maxime latens et,
propter non se habere inmediate ad lucrum, ab omnibus intemptata, in proposito
est hanc de suis enucleare latibulis, tum ut utiliter mundo pervigilem, tum etiam
ut palmam tanti bravii primus in meam gloriam adipiscar. (1.1.1–5)

(For all men whom the Higher Nature has endowed with a love of truth, this above
all seems to be a matter of concern, that just as they have been enriched by the
efforts of their forebears, so they too may work for future generations, in order
that posterity may be enriched by their efforts. For the man who is steeped in the
teachings which form our common heritage, yet has no interest in contributing
something to the community, is failing in his duty: let him be in no doubt of that;
for he is not a "tree planted by the rivers of water, that bringeth forth his fruit
in due season," but rather a destructive whirlpool which forever swallows things
down and never gives back what it has swallowed. Thinking often about these
things, lest some day I be accused of burying my talent, I wish not just to put
forth buds but to bear fruit for the benefit of all, and to reveal truths that have
not been attempted by others. For what fruit would a man bear who proved once
again a theorem of Euclid's? Or who sought once again the nature of happiness,
which has already been shown by Aristotle? [. . .] None at all; indeed, the tiresome
pointlessness of the exercise would arouse distaste. Now since among other truths
which are hidden and useful, a knowledge of temporal monarchy is both extremely
useful and most inaccessible, and since no one has attempted to elucidate it [on
account of its not leading directly to material gain], I propose to draw it forth from
where it lies hidden, so that my wakeful nights may be of benefit to the world, and
so that I may be the first to win for my own glory the honor of so great a prize.)

The treatise opens with a variation on the same Aristotelian topos of the natural human love of wisdom, i.e., "philo-Sophia" in its etymological meaning, as does *Convivio*, forming an immediate connection between the two.[12] Now, however, there is no attribution to an *auctor*: Dante presents the thought as his own. Moreover, when Aristotle *is* introduced a little later on he is used only to provide an example of a topic – human happiness – that Dante is *not* interested in addressing, on the grounds that it *has* previously been treated. In other words, as against the earlier treatise, he here establishes the function of the ancients (i.e., the *auctores*) as a template for his aspirations: by teaching posterity as he himself was taught, he will not merely translate authoritative discourses, but, rather, realize his own intellectual ambitions. This passage, then, is a virtual palinode, a "recantation" of the modest stance toward philosophy adopted at the beginning of *Convivio* (cf. E. Gilson 1939: 162; Nardi 1979: 282–4 nn). At the same time, it is equally a logical extension both of the value assigned to philosophy in the earlier work and of the implicit rivalry between Dante and the ancients established there, especially in book 4.

Most striking is the insistence on the absolute novelty of Dante's subject. Just as in *De Vulgari Eloquentia* the Dantean "nos" insists that "no one before us" (1.1.1; cf. 1.9.1) has treated the subject of the vernacular, here he twice repeats (shifting to the first-person *singular*), that his topic is "intemptata" by anyone else.[13] Moreover, that subject is an extraordinarily ambitious one. The first book declares that the telos of the Monarch is to create the conditions of possibility for realizing fully the natural desire of humanity as a whole for knowledge. In other words, Dante's subject is the *conditio sine qua non* of philosophy itself as the highest expression of properly human identity in this life. The apparently casual reference to Aristotle's position on human happiness actually betrays the even greater reach of Dante's topic, since his arguments eventually come to subsume and perhaps to supersede the Philosopher's position on this subject, in his argument concerning the "two ends" of man in 3.15.[14]

---

12 Though the allusion both to Aristotle and to *CV* 1.1.1 is evident, the passage refers not to the universal thirst for truth of human beings but to a specific subset of men whom God has endowed with a love of truth (Cassell 2004: 50; *pace* R. Kay 1998: 2 n) – the first book, however, will come to focus on the "possible intellect" of human kind as a whole (see below, especially nn 27, 50).

13 There is considerable agreement that *MN* is unprecedented in its effort to define the nature and function of universal empire (see e.g., Nardi 1921c: 144–55; E. Gilson 1939: 164; Ricci 1965b: 138–9), though filiated both with the political philosophy of the Scholastics, especially Aquinas, *De Regimine Principum*, and his continuer, Ptolemy of Lucca, and with the polemical debates surrounding the relationship of ecclesiastical and temporal power (see again n 6).

14 The first end, a temporal happiness achieved by rational understanding of natural truth follows Aristotle, while the second, spiritual beatitude achieved by a faithful transcendence of reason in the

In short, *Monarchia* aims to realize the "unfinished" ambitions both of *Convivio* (entering, now on equal terms, into the realm of the classical philosophical *auctores*), and of *De Vulgari Eloquentia* (bringing to completion an ambitious treatise written in Latin). Furthermore, these successes go far toward explaining another of the apparent differences of *Monarchia* from the earlier treatises: the new, and significantly reduced, place of the first-person author. The first chapter of *Monarchia* does call attention to Dante's role in composing the treatise, and the first chapters of the next two books – it will soon appear – do the same. Nevertheless, they do not perform the same extensive apologetic or definitional function as the first book and the first part of the fourth do in *Convivio*, much less use Dante himself (the friend of Cino) as a primary example of the points being made. Dante simply posits that he has wisdom to offer, and an appropriate language and formal vehicle to offer it in, and goes on from there. One might even be tempted so far as to claim that, having spent the earlier treatises in the acquisition of authority, though at the cost of leaving their avowed subject matter incompletely explored, in *Monarchia* Dante exercises such authority unproblematically, concentrating his full attention on the topic at hand.

Predictably enough, however, Dante is more concerned with defining or acquiring authority in this context than at first appears. The question to be considered, then, is how, and why, his strategies for self-authorization have changed. One obvious point is that Dante now generally respects the rhetorical taboo against self-representation so ostentatiously violated in *Convivio*. He does so for the same reason that he omits virtually all reference to the present historical realities at which the treatise's abstract consideration of imperial and papal authority is directed. He does so to escape the appearance of interested partisanship that his own historical circumstances – traceable directly to papal malfeasance – inevitably suggest.[15] Similarly, he avoids a series of complications to his arguments that reference to the recent history of the Empire would bring, starting with Frederick II's conflicts with the papacy in the early part of the century, continuing with the *de iure* vacancy of the imperial seat for some sixty years between Frederick and

---

experience of divine truth, obviously goes beyond the Philosopher (3.15.7–10; but already in 1.12.6). For Aristotle on happiness and Dante's relationship to him, see Lerner 1986. For the debate over the "duos fines," see n 27, as well as nn 1, 46, 48.

[15] Lack of personal reference is also characteristic of the genre in which Dante writes. However, on the one hand, this restriction had not kept *CV* and *DVE* from intense self-referentiality and, on the other, compared with normative exemplars, *MN* does give more than usual attention to the "ego" of the writer (section iv). The point, then, is what the treatise looks like, relatively speaking, within Dante's evolving practice.

Henry VII, and concluding with Henry's unhappy adventures in Italy.[16] In other words, the high historical stakes of the treatise – nothing less than the government of the whole world as Dante knew it – paradoxically require that historical specifics be avoided as much as possible, so that a position which might appear to be driven contingently and situationally will instead seem to be grounded in a universal truth that transcends individual time, place, and person (Cassell 2004: 24; cf. Chiavacci-Leonardi 1977: 176).

This consideration leads back to the last of the apparent differences that separate *Monarchia* from *De Vulgari Eloquentia* and, especially, *Convivio*: while it is concerned with questions of authority, the authority in question is of another kind and is treated in terms distinct from those of the earlier works. Specifically, it is concerned with defining the exercise of legal power through transpersonal institutions, rather than with treating either the poetic or even the philosophical authority that accrues to an individual name. This issue comes close to the heart of the matter that is treated here and will thus require additional discussion.

Chapters 2 and 3 showed that, while focusing on poetic, philosophical, and, implicitly, theological authority, both *De Vulgari Eloquentia* and *Convivio* are intermittently concerned with another form of authority, the political. In book 4 of *Convivio*, the authority of the Emperor, personified by Frederick II, appears primarily so that Dante can preclude its claims to special mastery of intellectual questions, in which it must acknowledge a subordinate role to the Philosopher, not to mention Dante's philosophical *canzone*. Chapters 3 through 5 of *Convivio* 4, however, do make a succinct case for the divinely sponsored authority of the Roman Empire over matters temporal, anticipating many of the arguments to be treated in *Monarchia* (see again note 3). Then in book 1 of *De Vulgari Eloquentia* the imperial court of Frederick appears as the scene in which an illustrious, poetic Italian first emerges, and, implicitly, as a model for the utopian Italian curia which would now be the proper locale of the *vulgare illustre*, if only it had an empirical existence.

In both of these cases, politics are subordinate to other matters of greater immediate concern: respectively the philosophical discourse on nobility (*CV* 4) and the linguistic discourse on the historical existence of a *vulgare illustre*. In both cases too, Dante stresses that political *auctoritas* depends

---

[16] See Chapter 6, section ii, especially n 26 for the omission of Frederick. One might add the intense controversy surrounding the election of Ludwig of Bavaria to the imperial throne in 1314 – the split among the electors – the refusal of John XXII to recognize Ludwig. The assertion (Scott 1996: 54–5; Cassell 2003: 3, 23 and n) of an obvious if indirect allusion to the controversy, however, is not especially convincing (see again n 2).

upon the wisdom provided by poets and philosophers and that, conversely, poetic-philosophical *auctores* need the ear and the protection of legitimate political authorities if they are to make their wisdom count and avoid the harsh fate of exilic wandering. In these treatises, then, the focus remains resolutely individual, begging significant questions regarding the fundamentally "institutional" nature of imperial authority.

In *Monarchia* the emphasis shifts in two interrelated ways: institutional *auctoritas* is *the* focal topic, to the apparent exclusion of the individualized authority of philosophers, much less poets; and such authority is seen in primarily collective, rather than personalized, terms. (The question of individual will does, however, return in significant ways, as will be seen.) Concerning the first point, the treatise systematically asserts the absolute political dominion of the Roman Empire and its legitimate Emperor over life in this world, and their privileged relationship to the domain of autonomous human nature – the realm of the practical intellect. In this sense *Monarchia* is simply an elaboration of the defense of the Empire's divine mission in *Convivio* 4.4–5 and of the subsequent claim that the Emperor serves as "cavalcatore della volontà umana." But while the telos of universal monarchy is that of creating the condition of possibility for philosophy to flourish, thus foregrounding the dependence of philosophers on the Emperor, the reverse move is here omitted – no attempt is made to establish the Emperor's dependence on the Philosopher, which was instead the polemical vector of the discussion in *Convivio*.[17] One reason for this omission (another will emerge shortly) is that, in order to assert the definitive supremacy of the Empire in the temporal realm, Dante has to juxtapose its authority to that of another institution, the Papacy, supreme in matters of the spirit. Thus, *de facto*, the Emperor/Philosopher pairing has been replaced by the Emperor/Papacy dyad, with a consequent shift in the nature of the discourse on authority. The poet, as already observed, has vanished entirely.

With this first shift comes the second. The nature of poetic and philosophical authority requires a sometimes agonizingly complicated

---

[17] E. Gilson 1939: 146, 188–91, 195–200 (see especially the diagram on p. 200) brings together the emperor/philosopher pairing of *CV* with the Emperor/Pope pairing of *MN* to produce a coherent tripartite scheme of three distinct yet mutually reinforcing authorities (see also Vasoli 1979: 31–2, 34; cf. Nardi 1965a: 52; Vinay 1962: 60). In doing so he glosses over the absence of the pope from the discussion of *CV* 4.4–6 (Nardi 1930a: 279–84) and of the philosopher per se from *MN*. (N.B., at the end of the treatise Dante twice refers to the "phylosophica documenta" [3.15.8, 11] and once to the "phylosophos" [3.15.9] that guide the Emperor – these passages do not, however, probe the relation between the three authorities in question; in addition, they imply a *four*-term analogy: "phylosophica documenta" are to the Emperor as "Holy Scripture" is to the Pontiff (see also section iii and Chapter 7, section iii, especially n 67).

negotiation of the relation between the individual *auctor* and the imper-
sonal *auctoritas* that his words are said to possess. By contrast, even as the
key problem of legitimating and depersonalizing an individual person to
generate a locus for the exercise of authority remains constant in the case
of institutional authorities, the means through which such authority is
acquired and perpetuated are, at least in theory, much better defined and
regulated than they are in the case of poetry and philosophy. Notably, it is
relatively easier to articulate how, in the institutional domain, a transcen-
dent and impersonal principle can be embodied by a historically limited
individual, and how that principle can be passed down over time despite
the inevitable intervention of human mortality.

The essential concept is that encapsulated in the title of Kantorowicz's
classic study, *The King's Two Bodies* (1957). On this side is the figurative
"body politic," which incorporates all human individuals within a larger
structure that reproduces itself regardless of the fate of any individual per-
son. The "head" of this corporate entity, the Emperor, is by definition
immortal, exercising continuous dominion according to the legally, and
ultimately divinely, determined coordinates of his office. On the other side
is the individual person who for a certain time fills the imperial office: not,
however, by his own merits or for his own benefit, but rather as temporary
"vicar" or place-holder of something greater than himself. Thus it is that
when any particular emperor dies, the Empire and its Emperor live on.

On this basis, two more provisional conclusions emerge concerning the
evolution of Dante's concern with *auctoritas* between *Convivio* and *Monar-
chia*. On the one hand, *Monarchia's* treatment of its subject builds upon
both an explicit, if digressive, concern of the earlier treatise (the nature of
imperial authority and the mission of the Roman Empire) and a principal
rhetorical-conceptual device (the pairing off of two distinct authorities who
complement and qualify each other's area of competence). On the other
hand, in contrast with *Convivio*, where that subject and that device are used
in the service of a discourse about individual nobility and as an oblique
reflector on the Dante's personal authorial status, *Monarchia* foregrounds
the institutional question, and puts the issue of individual and personalized
authority distinctly in the background.

II. *AUCTORITAS* IN *MONARCHIA*

To confirm that *Monarchia* shifts the terms of the discussion of *auctori-
tas* toward an impersonal consideration of institutions, but also to show
that it creates a decisive link between institutional and "epistemological"

authorities, including but not limited to the philosopher,[18] I will now turn to the explicit appearances of the "vocabulary of authority" (i.e., forms of the key words *auctoritas, auctor*, and *auctorizare*), again using *Convivio* as a benchmark.[19]

The first thing to observe is that this treatise at no point gives any substantive definition of *auctoritas*, etymological or otherwise, or even a hint that it is simply following the definition(s) offered in *Convivio*. A review of the evidence might support an inference that the concept of *auctoritas* being used throughout and in relation both to those who wield political authority and those write about it is an expanded version of *autor* from *autentin*, that is authority understood as that which legally or otherwise constrains the "[epistemological] faith and [behavioral] obedience" of those legitimately subject to it. Dante is not, however, drawing on either of the other two available etymological possibilities, since the poetic *autore* from *avieo* never shows his face at all (see also n 6), and since the (political) *auctor* from *augere*, if he makes any appearance, does so only in one conceptually marginal place (*pace* Cassell 2004: 99 and n 187).[20] On the other hand, it is useful to recall that already in *Convivio* Dante was at some pains to avoid linking the primary definition, from *autentin*, directly

---

[18] I use the term "epistemological authorities" to designate those who claim or to whom is assigned masterful knowledge of some subject, because this type of authority expands beyond the rational-philosophical horizon to include supra-rational theological and Biblical authorities based in faith, "the evidence of things unseen."

[19] A key debate in medieval political theory concerns the relationship between *potestas* and *auctoritas*, sometimes but not always used to distinguish between imperial power and papal authority (see Tierney 1964: 10–11 for the range of meanings assigned to the two terms). In *MN*, however, the word *potestas* appears only seven times and never in opposition with the much more frequent *auctoritas* (see n 21). This poses an additional problem for Maccarrone's reliance on the theory of "potestas indirecta" to describe the Monarch/Pope relationship in 3.15 (1954; cf. Nardi 1960a: chapter 3).

[20] Despite the focus on Empire, no strong case can be made that Dante now resorts to Hugutio's political *auctor* from *augere*; rather, as argued in Chapter 2 (especially n 49), he apparently uses *autentin* as an umbrella category for both epistemological and institutional authorities, based on his understanding of how closely the two areas interact. *MN* does contain the one explicit use in all of Dante's *oeuvre* of the word *auctor* in a way that *must* be referred back to *augere*: "Dardanus yliace primus pater urbis et auctor" (2.3.11). However, it is used (a) in passing and not as an integral part of Dante's argument; (b) only once in this way; (c) in quoting Virgil (*Aen.* 8.134). N.B. as seen in Chapter 2, section ii, Hugutio distinguishes between *auctor* from *augere*, spelled with a "c" and *autor* from *autentim*, spelled without a "c," a difference Dante alludes to fleetingly at *CV* 4.6.3. The Ricci edition of *Monarchia* (Alighieri 1965), i.e., the basis for the text cited here, uses the spelling with "c" for institutional authority and the spelling without for epistemological "authors." As Nardi 1979: 306–7 n points out, however, the spellings are not consistently used in the manuscript tradition, and result from Ricci's explicit editorial decision (Ricci 1965a: 123–4; probably following Chenu 1927). Reproductions of the principal manuscripts are now easily viewed in electronic form for comparison (P. Shaw 2005). The lack of an autograph makes it impossible to know what, if any, system Dante originally employed for this text. See also Chapter 1, n 25.

to the legal-governmental functions of the Emperor. The overall effect of the lack of concern to offer a formal definition is to place *Monarchia* well within the confines of normative medieval *doxa*, both in the sense that (as in so many other features of the treatise) Dante simply assumes his rightful mastery over a basic "high cultural" discourse, and in the sense that by far the most problematic portion of *Convivio*'s definitional passage, the one that challenged conventional categories most directly, as well as personalizing Dante's relationship to the question, has simply vanished (i.e., again, the *autore* from *avieo*).

The second, complementary, point to be made is that while *Monarchia* does not take the trouble to define *auctoritas*, it contains by far the largest number of uses of that word and its relatives of any work in the Dantean *oeuvre*: sixty-six references over the course of the treatise. Of these, an overwhelming majority (some fifty-four) refer directly or indirectly to the institutional *auctoritas* of the Emperor and/or of the Pope, with most of these coming in book 3,[21] where the specific question posed and answered by Dante is

[U]trum *auctoritas* Monarche romani, qui de iure Monarcha mundi est . . . , inmediate a Deo dependeat an ab aliquo Dei vicario vel ministro, quem Petri successorem intelligo. (3.1.5; cf. 1.2.3)

([W]hether the authority of the Roman Monarch, who is the monarch of the world by right . . . derives directly from God or else from some vicar or minister of God, by which I mean Peter's successor [the Pope].)

As already noted, in pairing off the Emperor with the Pope as potentially competing authorities in a given domain, *Monarchia* echoes *Convivio*'s negotiations between the Emperor and Philosopher, arguing for a similarly complementary relationship between them.[22] The Emperor is still restricted to governance of life in this world, although the claim made is now aggressively positive, as against the restrictive function of the discussion in *Convivio*. The papacy is then assigned authority over matters concerning the life to come. In order to ground this separation of the two great institutional authorities, Dante expands the concept first seen in *Convivio* that God imposes "certo termine" to every art (4.9.2), and thus to every human authority, by suggesting that institutional authority in general always has its

---

[21] For the distribution of these words in Dante's *oeuvre*, see Chapter 1, section i, and n 9: over half (66 of 123) appear in *MN*: five times in book 1; ten times in book 2; and *fifty-one* times in book 3.

[22] Dante stops short of giving the Emperor direct authority over the Pope in temporal matters as instead he does vis-à-vis the Philosopher (*CV* 4.6.17).

origins, direct or indirect, in God, who is the "fon[s] universalis auctoritatis" (origin of universal authority; 3.15.15).[23]

While institutional authority is at the very center of *Monarchia*, there *is* a second type of authority referred to in the treatise, one which does bring us back both to the discussion of Aristotle's claim on "faith and obedience" in the intellectual realm and to the issue of the status of any discourse, including, implicitly, Dante's, which takes on the task of deliberating about the nature of institutions. As previously seen, the status of the philosopher, and especially his relationship to the Emperor, are no longer an explicit subject for Dante; nonetheless, the authority of philosophers, and others, whose works either support or oppose Dante's views on the Monarch, *is* evoked and discussed. The number of uses of *auctoritas* in this sense are relatively few, but they are strategically located, and of evident importance.

In the first book, which remains almost entirely within the rational domain that belongs to philosophy, this deliberation takes the form of a standard Scholastic balancing between invoking philosophical *auctoritates* and the power of rational demonstration:

Itaque prima questio sit: utrum ad bene esse mundi Monarchia temporalis necessaria sit. Hoc equidem, *nulla vi rationis vel auctoritatis obstante*, potissimis et patentissimis argumentis ostendi potest, quorum primum *ab autoritate Phylosophi assumatur* de suis *Politicis*. Asserit enim ibi *venerabilis eius autoritas* quod, quando aliqua plura ordinantur ad unum oportet unum eorum regulare seu regere, alia vero regulari seu regi; quod quidem *non solum gloriosum nomen autoris facit esse credendum, sed ratio inductiva*. (1.5.2–3)

(So the first question is this: is temporal monarchy necessary for the well-being of the world? That it is necessary can be shown with powerful and persuasive arguments, and *neither reason nor authority provides any strong counter-argument.* The first of these arguments may be taken from the *authority of Aristotle* in his *Politics*. Now *this revered authority* states in that work that when a number of things are ordered to a single end, one of them must guide or direct, and the others be guided or directed; and it is not only *the author's illustrious name* which requires us to believe this, but *inductive reasoning as well.*)

This passage is in keeping with the balancing act already performed, although more visibly and uncomfortably, in *Convivio* 4 (cf. 4.3.10: "la vertude de la veritade che ogni autoritade convince"), and promotes Dante's

---

[23] The idea is not radical: e.g., Aquinas, *ST* Ia q. 33 art. 4 ad.1: "fontalitas et auctoritas nihil aliud significat in divinis quam principium originis." More controversial is the claim that the Emperor's authority derives "sine ullo medio" from God, though this too has substantial precedents. Maccarrone 1955: 124–5 (also 135–6, 138) finds it in Justinian's prologue to *Novella* 6, i.e., in the fundamental code of Roman law, the *Corpus Iuris Civilis*, and thence in the work of Dante's friend Cino da Pistoia, the Ghibelline master of jurisprudence

assumption in *Monarchia* 1 of a discursive rationality that places him on a par with Aristotle and other *auctores*. It is also typical of Scholastic discussions of the relation between reason and authority, and thus reinforces the "normative" quality of the treatise.

By the beginning of book 2, however, the restriction of Dante's discourse to human reason and the authority of classical (pagan) *auctores* proves insufficient to his purposes, and reason is now juxtaposed with a different form of epistemological authority, taking the further step upon which Aquinas had also insisted (see Chapter 2, section ii and n 33):

Veritas autem questionis patere potest *non solum lumine rationis humane, sed etiam radio divine auctoritatis*; que duo cum simul ad unum concurrunt, celum et terram simul assentire necesse est. Igitur fiducie prenotate innixus *et testimonio rationis et auctoritatis* perfretus, ad secundam questionem dirimendam ingredior. (2.1.7–8)

(The truth of the matter can be revealed *not only by the light of human reason, but also by the radiance of divine authority*;[24] when these two are in agreement heaven and earth must of necessity both give their assent. Relying therefore on the faith [in God's assistance] of which I spoke earlier [1.1.6] and trusting in *the testimony of reason and [divine] authority*, I proceed to resolve the second question.)

From a pairing of (philosophical) authority and reason in which reason clearly has the upper hand, Dante shifts to the pairing of reason and divine authority, in which the latter is the more significant. The question then becomes how *auctoritas* of this second and more crucial kind is made accessible to humanity, in other words, how it is transmitted from its transcendent source into the world of history.

At this point we can begin to see that the problem of "epistemological" authority (whether based in reason or in faith) bears a striking structural resemblance to the problem of institutional authority concerning which it deliberates. If the definition of institutional authority comes to rest on the problem of origination and mediation (cf. 3.1.5, cited above), so does that of the epistemological *auctor*, rational or supra-rational as may be. The latter point is demonstrated most fully in the passage from book 3, cited at length in Chapter 2 (section ii; see also n 18), where Dante sketches a temporalized hierarchy of authorities on the question of the nature of the Church and its authority over life in this world (3.3.11–16). In this account, authority (concerning the Church) descends over time from the Scriptures through the Councils and the Fathers (*doctores*) and finally to the Decretalists, whose belated and derivative status gives them virtually

---

[24] Note the pairing of human "ratio" with divine "radio."

no authority at all, at least as regards the question that Dante is addressing. Thus, Dante's treatment of both institutional and epistemological authority is informed by the standard medieval preoccupation with establishing the lines of derivation and mediation by which legitimate authority is conferred, and, at the same, with determining a relativized hierarchy of temporal authorities, so that judgments can be made as to who has final authority in a given area and over a given question.

Interestingly, the two passages just mentioned seem at first to differ as to the path by which authority is normally derived. The question of where the Monarch's authority comes from highlights its eventual, whether immediate or relayed, dependence on God, who stands beyond history but intervenes in it at any moment He chooses. Moreover, Dante's own answer to this question makes plain his belief that institutional authority is conferred directly by God without historical intermediary:

... auctoritas temporalis Monarche sine ullo medio in ipsum de Fonte universalis auctoritatis descendit. (3.15.15)

(... the authority of the temporal Monarch flows down to him without any intermediary from the fount of universal authority [i.e., God].)

The tracing out of the descending authority of Scripture, Councils and patristic *doctores*, and Decretalists, however, follows a historical line and seems to imply a necessary element of historical antiquity in the constitution of authority.

The exclusion of the divine *Auctor* from the process in 3.3 is, however, tactical and rhetorical, and does not express Dante's basic understanding of the matter. The very next chapter foregrounds the issue of scriptural authority – as part of a refutation of the Decretalists' attempts to appropriate it to shore up their own – thus reinserting divine agency into the picture. First Dante quotes Augustine's *De Doctrina Christiana* (1.37) to the effect that "titubabit fides si Divinarum Scripturam vaccillat *autoritas*" (faith will waiver if the *authority* of Holy Scriptures is shaken; 3.4.9–10). Then he denounces misinterpretation of Scriptures as betraying not only the meanings intended by their many human authors, but the (authorial and authoritative) intentions of God himself:

O summum facinus, etiamsi contingat in sompniis, ecterni Spiritus intentione abuti! Non enim peccatur in Moysen, non in David, non in Iob, non in Matheum, non in Paulum, sed in Spiritum Sanctum qui loquitur in illis. Nam quanquam scribe divini eloquii multi sint, unicus tamen dictator est Deus, qui beneplacitum suum nobis per multorum calamos explicare dignatus est. (3.4.11)

(O supreme wickedness, even if it should happen in dreams, to abuse the intention of the eternal Spirit! For this is not a sin against Moses, nor against David, nor Job, nor Matthew, nor Paul, but against the Holy Spirit who speaks through them. For although there are many [scribes of] the divine word, it is God alone who dictates, deigning to reveal his pleasure to us through the pens of many.)

Notwithstanding a subsequent reference to the intention of Moses in Genesis 1:16 (3.4.16), Dante is following the established, Augustinian, interpretation of the relationship of human and divine authorship of the Bible, according to which God is *Auctor* dictating to a human *scribe* or *scriptor*, as he had earlier with reference to David (3.1.4).[25] At the same time he is apparently (but only apparently) setting aside the prominent role that Minnis sees being assigned to the human authors of the Bible in the thirteenth and fourteenth centuries.[26]

It is now possible to give a preliminary overview of Dante's overt treatment of *auctoritas* in *Monarchia* and to specify its most substantive differences from the earlier works. In the first place, Dante demonstrates a sophisticated and at the same time normative understanding (at least as sophisticated and certainly more "normative" than in *Convivio*) of the category, and of the issues and problems that surround the culture of authority in the Middle Ages. In particular he addresses: (1) the "vertical" problem of the possible sources of authority – historical antiquity and/or transcendent inspiration; (2) the "horizontal" problem of the relationship between different types of authority. The latter issue can be further subdivided. On the one hand it involves specifying the relationship of different institutional authorities to each other (Papacy and Empire). On the other it involves understanding the relationship of epistemological authorities (whether those asserting truth based in faith or those asserting truth based in reason) with institutional authorities: the former defining the function of the latter, the latter operating in such a way as to promote the dissemination of the truths produced by the former.

Modifying the diagram given in Chapter 2 accordingly, the result is the following:

---

[25] The image of the human scribe taking divine dictation parallels *Purg.* 24.52–4, on which see Chapter 7, sections ii and v, especially n 27. Cf. nn 54, 58 below.

[26] See Chapter 1, nn 7, 52; Chapter 2, section ii and nn 17, 26, 70; Chapter 4, nn 68, 69. Smalley 1952: 306–7, though not concerned with Dante's exegesis of his own authorial intention, argues that in *MN* 3.4.13, 16 (cf. 3.5.1. 6.1, 7.1–2, 8.1–2) he follows Aquinas's practice of valorizing the literal *sensus* of Scripture, where the human author's intention is expressed, in his critique of the Decretalists' allegorical reading of the "two great lights" of Genesis 1:16 with arguments concerning Moses' intentions. See also Maccarrone 1952: 36; Pepin 1970a: 57–9; Cassell 2004: 324 n 323. On the "two lights" in *MN* in relation to Dante's use of the imagery elsewhere, particularly *Purg.* 16.106–12, see Chapter 6, section ii, and n 32.

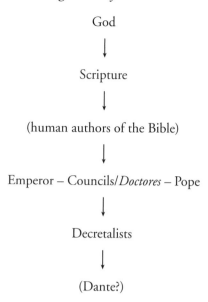

God

↓

Scripture

↓

(human authors of the Bible)

↓

Emperor – Councils/*Doctores* – Pope

↓

Decretalists

↓

(Dante?)

To confirm a point already made: those who are most obviously absent from *this* version of the hierarchical scheme are not only the poets as a class, but also Dante as an individual person. It is easy enough see where he would be placed according to his own criteria, however: simply in virtue of being human he is subordinate to the Emperor in matters temporal and the Pope in matters spiritual (see again 3.15). Furthermore, by virtue of his historical belatedness, along with his lack of any official status, he should be at the end of the epistemological chain that descends from God down through the Decretalists. In other words he *should* have even less authority in such matters than these last, who, he says, have no authority at all.

One simple way of accounting for this omission is to claim that Dante wanted to avoid drawing attention to his entirely subordinate position. This may well be, but it is substantially at odds with the obsessive consideration he gives to his personal standing in all of the other major works, with the "progress" made in those works toward self-authorization, and with the confidently "authoritative" voice he assumes in defining both institutional and epistemological authorities throughout *Monarchia*. Rather, *Monarchia*, in addition to and indeed by means of its primary mission of defining institutional authorities, carries out an elaborate negotiation that both affirms and renders problematic Dante's own position as author of the treatise, and in the end simultaneously ratifies the scheme just delineated, and posits Dante as a solitary and clamorous exception to it.

III. THE MONARCH'S AUTHORITY: CONFLICT AND JUDGMENT

Before confronting the question of Dantean authority directly, it will be necessary to show in greater detail the nature of the Monarch's authority, the terms and strategies which Dante employs to establish it, and, above all, the evolving rhetorical-conceptual dynamic of the treatise. As seen, Dante's initially stated purpose in *Monarchia* is to define the nature and affirm the necessity of universal temporal empire, using the tools of natural human reason. In book 1 he sets out to prove logically that the fulfillment of human nature requires a condition of universal peace, which in turn depends on the existence of a single Monarch able to resolve all disputes and conflicts that obstruct such a peace. In book 2, now supplementing reason with another type of authority, he goes on to argue that this ideal monarchy was and is embodied historically by the Roman Empire, and to prove in particular that Rome obtained universal dominion "legitimately," justly, and by the divine will rather than, as at first appears, by the illegitimate imposition of violent force (cf. *CV* 4.4.8–13). In book 3, he attempts to show that absolute imperial authority is not superseded by papal authority, but also does not usurp its higher, spiritual dominion. Rather, he asserts that each is supreme within its own, specialized area of competence. Though each book tackles a different question, together they further a sequential argument that leads from an abstract affirmation of Empire to a historical specification of its existence, to the issue most relevant to its contemporary incarnation, or lack thereof – the ongoing struggle between Popes and Emperors for secular dominion. As will now be seen, a set of basic terms and argumentative strategies links each book to the others, but also highlights some fundamental conflicts and contradictions between them that, in turn, implicitly bear on Dante's position as author of the treatise.

Throughout *Monarchia*, the problem of imperial authority is explored via the paired categories of judgment and legitimation. The situation as Dante delineates it is paradoxical: imperial authority is that which confers the power to judge legitimately in a given jurisdiction (the substance of book 1) – but authority itself must be judged legitimate in order to be exercised (the topic of book 2). This paradox, in turn, is subtended by another, even more telling: the importance of judgment (*iudicium*) is that it resolves conflict (*litigium*), but the question of *who* shall be considered the legitimate judge always passes first through a deciding conflict, often violent, always tainted by a suspicion of illegitimacy. Inevitably, the attempt to establish that the Emperor is the supreme judge placed legitimately over the entire human race leads both the ideal of world monarchy and Dante's argument concerning it back into the very same illegitimately "litigious" domain from which the Emperor is meant to rescue them.

Dante's basic argument in book 1 is as follows. For the human race to fulfill collectively its natural intellectual potential, absolute justice, and the peace it brings with it, must reign throughout the whole world. Only in this way can the "possible intellect" (1.3.6, 8; 4.1) – the unique distinguishing feature of humanity in the hierarchy of creation – fulfill its destiny (see especially 1.4.2–5).[27] The primary function of political authority in the treatise is thus the judicial, and hence legitimate, non-conflictual, resolution of *litigium* or conflict: "Et ubicunque potest esse litigium, ibi debet esse iudicium" (Now wherever there can be conflict there must be judgment; 1.10.).[28]

For human justice to be put into effect universally, however, there must be a single supreme authority, the Emperor, who has ultimate competence and legitimacy in every case because he stands outside the infinite "litigii" that afflict humanity (E. Gilson 1939: 174–8). Unity is the absence of conflict,

---

[27] Using the *auctoritas* of Averroes to support this idea (1.3.9) has led numerous readers of *MN*, beginning with Guido Vernani (*DRM* book 1, par. 33–44), to accuse Dante of heterodoxy, possibly influenced by Siger of Brabant and Boethius of Dacia. Lerner argues intriguingly that Petrarch was implicitly critical of Dante on related grounds (1986). For a brief introduction to Averroes, see Ivry 1998. On Scholasticism and Averroism, see E. Gilson 1938: 54–63; Nardi 1965a: 3–37; Marenbon 1987: 69–74; Imbach 1996: 74–9. For an overview of Averroes in Dante, see Vasoli 1970. In modern Dante criticism the case for some form of Dantean Averroism has been made, in relation not only to *MN* but also *CV* and *DVE*, by Nardi 1921c: 247–50, 1930a: 302–8, as well as 1940b, 1960a: 66–120 *et passim*, 1965a; Vinay 1962: 27–35; Corti 1981, 1983. Imbach 1996: 141–8 claims this position had not been abandoned in the *DC*. For discussions of the "possible intellect" in *MN* 1 which stress its heterodox elements, see Nardi: 1921c: 229–44, 1921a: 142–61, 1940b: 232–4, 1979: 295–303 nn; Passerin d'Entrèves 1952: 48–51; Vinay 1962: 27–35, 1950: 22–7 nn; Imbach 1996: 180–5. E. Gilson 1939 (126, 167–72, 188–91 *et passim*) sees Dante's use of the term as differing significantly from Averroes', insisting that *MN* cannot be considered an Averroistic text (212–24), since it puts concepts derived from Averroes' to work in the service of Dante's very different purposes (N.B., Nardi himself is clear that Dante does not entertain the extreme "Averroistic" positions of the "mortality of the soul" and of a thorough-going "double truth"). In this vein, see also Vasoli 1979: 30–5; R. Kay 1998: 18–21 nn; Cassell 2004: 52–60 and nn, 345 n 26; Scott 2004: 134–5, 145–7 and nn. The doctrine of the *duos fines* of mankind and the "two beatitudes" associated with those ends (3.15.7; see also nn 1, 14, 46, 48) has been similarly interpreted as aligning Dante with a radical separation between reason and faith, philosophical and theological knowledges. Variants on this reading are in Nardi (e.g. 1921a: 162–72; 1940b: 235–42; 1960a: 83–116, 272–313; 1965a: 70–1); Passerin d'Entrèves 1952: 52–9, 107–9; Foster 1977: 240–3; Lerner 1986; Imbach 1996: 147–8; cf. Vinay 1950: 281–2 nn, 1962: 32–5; Chiavacci-Leonardi 1977: 152–7. Against it are Maccarrone 1955: 112–41; Vasoli 1979: 30–7, 1988b; Trovato 1988; R. Kay 1998: 308–25 nn; Scott 2004: 162–5; Cassell 2004: 104–7. Judicious intermediate discussions are in E. Gilson 1939: 162–3 n, 191–201, 212–24; Vinay 1962: especially 50–75. On Guido Cavalcanti's supposed Averroism and Dante's critical relationship to it, see Nardi 1940a; Corti 1983; Ardizzone 2002 (cf. Chapter 4, section ii above). On Averroes and Averroism, see also nn 49, 50; Chapter 2, nn 31, 62; Chapter 3, n 33; Chapter 6, section ii, especially n 28.

[28] For analogous arguments in both imperial and hierocratic publicists, and for the force of the word "litigium," see Vinay 1950: 50–1 n.

while multiplicity, and its special case, duality, invariably mean the presence of conflict, conceptual and metaphysical, but also corporeal.[29] If there are multiple authorities with competing competence there will be no way to judge between them if the need arises and so a "third" and higher judge is required if conflict is to be avoided:

Inter omnes duos principes, quorum alter alteri minime subiectus est, potest esse *litigium* . . . ergo inter tales oportet esse *iudicium*. Et cum alter de altero cognoscere non possit ex quo alter alteri non subditur – nam *par in parem non habet imperium* – oportet esse tertium iurisdictionis amplioris qui ambitu sui iuris ambobus principetur. (1.10.2–4)

(There is always the possibility of *conflict* between two rulers where one is not subject to the [other]; such *conflict* may come about . . . therefore there must be *judgment* between them. And since neither can [comprehend] the other – since neither is [subject to the other] and *an equal has no [dominion] over an equal* – there must be a third party of wider jurisdiction who rules over both of them by right.)

At the highest level must be the Monarch who has no peer with whom conflict could possibly arise (1.10.4–5).[30]

As an obvious, but not obviously realizable, corollary, the supreme authority who occupies this unique, unjudgeable office must be one who will never require judging himself. To establish that this improbable situation could actually exist, Dante is forced to make a very peculiar argument:

Iustitie maxime contrariatur cupiditas, ut innuit Aristoteles . . . Remota cupiditate omnino, nichil iustitie restat adversum; unde sententia Phylosophi est ut que lege determinari possunt nullo modo iudici relinquantur. Et hoc metu cupiditatis fieri oportet, de facili mentes hominum detorquentis. Ubi ergo non est quod possit optari, inpossibile est ibi cupiditatem esse: destructis enim obiectis, passiones esse non possunt. Sed Monarcha non habet quod possit optare: sua nanque iurisdictio terminatur Occeano solum. (1.11.11–12; cf. 13.7 and *CV* 4.4.3–4)[31]

(The thing most contrary to justice is greed [cupidity], as Aristotle states . . . When greed [cupidity] is eliminated nothing remains which is opposed to justice; hence [the Philosopher's] opinion that those things which can be resolved by law should in no way be left to the judge's discretion. And it is fear of greed [cupidity] that makes this necessary, for greed [cupidity] easily leads men's minds astray.

---

[29] See 1.14.2: "sequitur non solum melius esse fieri per unum, si fieri potest, quam fieri per plura, sed quod fieri per unum est bonum, per plura simpliciter malum." See also *MN* 1.10.6, 15.1–4; *CV* 4.4.5.

[30] For juridical sources of the standard phrase "par in parem non habet imperium," see Vinay 1950: 52n; R. Kay 1998: 47 n.

[31] See Nardi 1979: 337–9 nn on Dante's "forced" reading of the *NE* (5.2.1129.a 32–b 10). Also Vinay 1950: 62 n.

But where there is nothing to be coveted, it is impossible for greed [cupidity] to exist, for emotions cannot exist where their objects have been destroyed. But there is nothing the monarch *could* covet, for his jurisdiction is bounded only by the ocean.)[32]

Since the Emperor rules everything and lacks nothing, he must necessarily be absolutely free of the cupidinous desire (unstated: the desire for power) which besets the rest of humankind and which is the root cause of those conflicts ("litigii") that imperial justice must resolve.

To anyone conversant with the Christian, and especially the Pauline-Augustinian, theory of will and desire, Dante's claim that the Emperor is *necessarily* without desire *in malo* (i.e., *cupiditas*) seems suspicious. From this standard Christian perspective, desire is based in the ontological insufficiency of the human creature (rather than in the external nature of the objects whose possession is sought), and may never be fulfilled except in the presence of the ultimate object of all desires, God. Consider, for example, Dante's own expression of the idea in this well-known passage from book 4 of *Convivio*:

L'anima nostra, incontanente che nel nuovo e mai fatto cammino di questa vita entra, dirizza li occhi al termine del suo sommo bene, e però, qualunque cosa vede che paia in sé avere alcuno bene, crede che sia esso. E perché la sua conoscenza prima è imperfetta, per non essere esperta né dottrinata, piccioli beni le paiono grandi, e però da quelli comincia prima desiderare. Onde vedemo li parvuli desiderare massimamente un pomo; e poi, più procedendo, desiderare un augellino; e poi, più oltre, desiderare un bel vestimento; e poi lo cavallo, e poi una donna; e poi ricchezza non grande, poi grande, e poi più. E questo incontra perché in nulla di queste cose truova quella che va cercando, e credela trovare più oltre. Per che vedere si può che l'uno desiderabile sta dinanzi a l'altro a li occhi de la nostra anima per modo quasi piramidale, che 'l minimo li cuopre prima tutti, ed è quasi punta de l'ultimo desiderabile, che è Dio, quasi base di tutti. Sì che, quanto da la punta ver la base più si procede, maggiori appariscono li desiderabili; e questa è la ragione per che, acquistando, li desiderii umani si fanno più ampii. (4.12.15–18; cf. *Purg.* 16.85–93; 17.91–105)[33]

---

[32] P. Shaw translates *cupiditas* as "greed," but Dante is referring primarily to the "greed" for dominion, and explicitly evokes the Augustinian opposition between *cupiditas* and *caritas*, where *cupiditas* refers to human desire *in malo* in all of its infinite, and infinitely perverse, shapes (1.11.13–14). Similarly, the *lupa* of *Inf.* 1 can be taken to refer specifically to the sin of avarice, but is also the root of *all* evils ("radix . . . malorum est cupiditas," Timothy: 6:10). See also Chapter 7, section iii.

[33] On this passage, see Barolini 2000b: 95–8. Nardi 1979: 339–40 nn cites the earlier part of the same chapter to make a similar point about *MN* 1.11.11–12. Vernani (*DRM* book 1, par. 44–46) criticizes Dante's assumption that any man other than Christ can achieve the perfection he attributes to the Emperor, though not in connection with this passage (Scott 1997: 95–6).

(Our soul, as soon as it enters into the new and never before trodden way of this life, directs its eyes toward the end of its highest good and therefore, whatever thing it sees that seems to have in itself some goodness, it believes to be that. And because its knowledge is at first imperfect, because it is neither expert nor instructed in doctrine, little goods seem great to it, and from those it first begins to desire. Whence we see that little ones desire most greatly an apple; and then, proceeding further, to desire a little bird; and then, further beyond, to desire a beautiful suit; and then a horse, and then a woman, and then modest wealth, then great, and then more. And this occurs because in none of these things does it find that which it goes searching for, and it believes that it will find that thing further on. By which one may see that one desirable object stands above another in the eyes of our soul in a way that resembles a pyramid, so that the least at first covers them all, and is as it were the tip of the final desirable thing, which is God, who is the foundation of all of them. So that, the more one proceeds from the tip toward the foundation, the more desirable things appear. And this is the reason that, in the process of acquiring what is desired, human desires grow greater.)

Given that there is always something else to desire ("e poi più"), and that the more one has the more one wants, the Monarch ought not to be the least afflicted by "cupidity," but the most. In the first passage cited, however, as in the parallel passage in *Convivio* (4:4:3–4), Dante seems to assume that "monarchy" is an office capable in and of itself of transforming the "will to power" into a "will to judgment" in the secular world. In so doing, he presumes that the person occupying that office, alone of human kind, will be free of the effects of the Fall of humanity, i.e., without a will tainted and weakened by sin, even though he will later make it clear that the universal effects of the Fall make imperial justice necessary in the first place (3.4.14–15).[34]

Dante's apparent ability to make such an assertion without falling immediately into contradiction likely depends upon the purely rational terms in which book 1 operates, a point stressed by the twice-repeated citation of Aristotle as *auctoritas* in support of his claim, rather than any of the possible scriptural, patristic, or scholastic theorists of human desire. These rational terms are at once human (human nature has just been defined in terms of a collective "possible intellect") and ahistorical (apparently valid in any time

---

[34] For a succinct account of Dante's understanding of sin and vice in the *DC*, see Durling and Martinez 2003: 8–10. Even if, as they argue, the Fall for Dante does not result inevitably in sinful behavior, the acquisition of a virtuous habit is a result of individual discipline, not the occupancy of the imperial office per se. The representation of a "desireless" Emperor, and a perfectible human community, in book 1 seem to contrast with the claim in 3.4.14–15 that the Empire as well as the Church serve as "remedia contra infirmitatem peccati" (Foster 1977: 240–2; Took 1990: 169–71). On the contested significance of the latter passages, see Vinay 1950: 216–19 nn, Maccarrone 1955: especially 39–42, 117 *et passim*; Nardi, e.g., 1921c, 1979: 450–2 nn; R. Kay 1998: 228 n. See also Chapter 7, section iii.

and every place), and they permit a temporary amnesia concerning the fundamental gap between divine perfection and the corrupted temporality of a post-Edenic world. But when, in book 2, the figure of the Empire is tested against the realities of history (the usurping violence it apparently used to gain sway over the world [2.1]) and the failings of individual Emperors (e.g., Constantine's abdication of his imperial office and division of the Empire [2.11.8; cf. 3.10; see n 47]), the flaws of the argument become potentially visible. They become even more evident in book 2, and especially in book 3, as the Empire is confronted with the competing claims of the City of God on earth, that is, the Church Militant, to hold dominion over the City of Man. And they are still further exposed by the re-introduction of theologically grounded articles of faith – including the universal fallenness of human nature, the inability of men to establish true internal and external justice without the gratuitous intervention of divine grace, and the supreme authority of God to which all human authorities are secondary. By book 3, then, the claims of book 1 can only be maintained by submitting them to radical modifications.

The obstacles Dante faces become evident in the very first chapter of book 2, when he turns from ideal rationality to historical realities. He begins the book with a recantatory confession that he once espoused the common opinion that the Roman Empire held its dominion illegitimately – that it was the product of a will to power usurping control over others through the exercise not of judgment but of brute force (2.1.2–3; cf. *CV* 4.4.8–9). This position, recognizably that of Augustine in *De Civitate Dei* (e.g., 1.Preface and 14.28, but *passim*) is incompatible with the one articulated in the first book.[35] Brute force, exercised extra-legally and hence personally, is the antithesis of judgment exercised *ex officio*. The desire for conquest and imperial domination is that with which Dante's Monarch must not be burdened, if he is to claim the right to judge all others legitimately.

Book 2, then, has a twofold mission. The first objective, which is advanced only tacitly, is to prove that the ideal monarchy sketched in

---

[35] On Dante's debts to and disagreements with Augustine's treatment of (Virgil's) Rome, see E. Gilson 1939: 201–5 *et passim*; Davis 1957: especially 45–55, Peterman 1973: 29–30; Mazzotta 1979: chapters 3–4 *et passim*. Here, Dante ironically reinforces his polemical stance by offering a positive list of Roman examplars of virtue (*MN* 2.5) deriving, as is well known, from a similar, but negatively weighted, list in Augustine's *CD* 5.8 (Davis 1957: 47; P. Shaw 1995: xxii–xxiii; Cassell 2004: 72–3; also *CV* 4.5). Augustine's position was largely reinforced by Orosius' *Adversus Paganos*, a primary source of Roman history in the Middle Ages (Davis 1957: 55–65). It was taken up by Florentine Guelf radicals, with whom Dante was linked before his exile (Scott 2004: 151). For other contemporary versions of this view, see Vinay 1950: 107–8 nn. Speculative discussions of how and when this shift in Dante's thinking took place are in Passerin d'Entrèves 1952: 26–30; Ricci 1966; De Matteis 1980; Scott (1996: 27–35, 1997).

book 1 has an actual historical existence, namely in the Roman Empire. The second objective, openly stated, is to prove that the Roman Empire legitimately claims an absolute authority over the world – and that this legitimacy has been established by authoritative judgment rather than by usurping violence. Like book 1, and book 3, book 2 also asserts its essentially rational character by immediately offering a "first principle" that will underpin Dante's syllogistic argumentation.[36] Nonetheless, as already seen, book 2 consistently moves away from deductive rational argument: first in the direction of historical evidence (the citation of examples illustrating Roman universality and disinterested, heroic justice), but then, and primarily, in that of arguments based on predicates of faith, i.e., rationally unprovable assumptions grounded in divine *auctoritas*.[37]

This tendency is first apparent with the claim that various miracles performed on behalf of the Roman Empire illustrate direct divine intervention in their affairs (2.4). It comes to fruition, however, in the long section (2.7–9) in which Dante argues that the process of the Roman world conquest can be understood as an adjudicatory duel, a formal contest or "litigium," through which God's will was expressed.[38] This argument is the linchpin of book 2, since it is the means by which a phenomenology of violence becomes the evidence for its contrary, the operation of divine will and justice through the Roman people. At the same time, it constitutes a striking return-with-a-difference to the defining categories of book 1. To put it most simply: the duel is conceived of as an alternative mode of justice, as the "court of last resort" when there is no one with the authority to adjudicate a dispute:

[ubi] *iudicium* humanum deficit, vel ignorantie tenebris involutum vel propter presidium *iudicis* non habere. (2.9.1; see also 2.9.3)

(wherever human judgment is unequal to the task, whether because it is wrapped in the darkness of ignorance or because no judge is available to preside.)

---

[36] 2.2.1; cf. 1.2.4; 3.2.1. For Dante's logical procedures in their thirteenth/fourteenth century context, see P. Shaw 1995: xviiii–xix; Cassell 2004: especially 23–33. Points where Dante stresses his use of such procedures are 1.11.8–10; 1.14.1–3; 3.4.4–5; 3.5.3–4; 3.7.3; 3.8.3–6; 3.12.4–5; 3.14.9–10. Cf. Chapter 2, n 27.

[37] Cf. 2.1.7–8, 2.2.4–8, 2.10.1, 4–5. Compare also 3.10.3, where Dante marks a shift back to arguments from reason, as against the arguments based "in divinis eloquiis," which have dominated the first part of the book.

[38] On the adjudicatory duel and its later historical transformations, see Lea 1868 (with documents); Bryson 1938; Bartlett 1986; Kiernan 1988; Cuomo 1994. Although his focus is on the sixteenth century, I have also been considerably helped by Muir 1993: especially 247–72. Dante's adaptation of the theme is treated by Davis 1988. See also Vinay 1950: 166–7 nn; R. Kay 1998: 164–5 nn; Cassell 2004: 76–8 and nn. The argument, of course, sounds as absurd to modern ears (Scott 2004: 154) as it did to Vernani (*DRM* book 2, par. 84–93).

The argument is that God acts through the duel to express a judgment by conferring victory on the party which is in the right, so that "et quod per duellum acquiritur, de iure acquiritur" (whatever is acquired through a duel is acquired by right; 2.9.1). It is hard to miss, however, that the judicial duel conflates the two basic, opposed terms of book I: where "iudicium" served to resolve "litigium," now "litigium" itself has become the vehicle of judgment – a judgment between two apparently equal entities (cf. 2.9.2).

The argument "from dueling" introduces at least three additional elements that seem to qualify or discredit the claims of book I. First of all, it implicitly limits the basic notions both that the Emperor is the supreme judge of human affairs and that such judgment is indispensable: if the duel works as Dante claims, it can replace imperial judgment and thus God assumes directly the role of supreme judge in matters earthly. Second, it takes for a premise that the duel is only adjudicatory if the parties involved submit themselves voluntarily and humbly to divine justice and not in a spirit of violent cupidinous contention (9.2, 4, 9) – leaving one to wonder what means of human judgment can determine whether this is or is not the case.

Finally, and most importantly, the mode of argument itself tends to vitiate Dante's claim to have proceeded on rational grounds, that is, on grounds that could be substantiated with available human resources. In chapter 7, Dante divides his way down through the increasingly obscure and irrational means by which God's judgment appears to human beings:

Ad bene quoque venandum veritatem quesiti scire oportet quod *divinum iudicium* in rebus quandoque hominibus est manifestum, quandoque occultum. Et manifestum potest esse *dupliciter*: ratione scilicet et fide. Nam quedam *iudicia Dei* sunt ad que *humana ratio* propriis pedibus pertingere potest. (1–2)

Quedam etiam *iudicia Dei* sunt, ad que etsi *humana ratio* ex propriis pertingere nequit, elevatur tamen ad illa cum adiutorio fidei eorum que in Sacris Licteris nobis dicta sunt . . . Nam hoc *ratio humana* per se iustum intueri non potest, fide tamen adiuta potest. (4–5)

Occultum vero est *iudicium Dei* ad quod *humana ratio* nec lege nature nec lege Scripture, sed *de gratia spetiali* quandoque pertingit; quod fit pluribus modis: quandoque simplici revelatione, quandoque revelatione disceptatione quadam mediante. Simplici revelatione *dupliciter*: aut sponte Dei, aut oratione impetrante; sponte Dei *dupliciter*: aut expresse, aut per signum; expresse, sicut revelatum fuit iudicium Samueli contra Saulem; per signum, sicut Pharaoni revelatum fuit per signa quod Deus iudicaverat de liberatione filiorum Israel . . . [omitted: illustration of "oratione impetrante"]. (7–8)

Disceptatione vero mediante *dupliciter*: aut sorte, *aut certamine; "certare" etenim ab eo quod est "certum facere" dictum est.* Sorte quidem *Dei iudicium* quandoque revelatur hominibus ut patet in substitutione Mathie in *Actibus Apostolorum.* Certamine vero dupliciter *Dei iudicium* aperitur: vel ex collisione virium sicut fit per duellum pugilum, qui duelliones etiam vocantur, vel ex contentione plurium ad aliquod signum prevalere conantium sicut fit per pugnam athletarum currentium ad bravium. (9)

(In order to get a secure grasp of the truth of our question it must be borne in mind that divine judgment in [human] affairs is sometimes revealed to men and sometimes it remains hidden. Now there are two ways in which it can be revealed, i.e., by reason and by faith. For there are some judgments of God which human reason can arrive at by its own unaided efforts . . . Then there are some judgments of God to which human reason . . . can . . . be raised with the help of faith in those things which are said to us in the [Holy] Scriptures [. . .]. For human reason cannot see this [that no one without faith can be saved] to be just by its own powers, but with the aid of faith it can [. . .] But that judgment of God is hidden which human reason arrives at neither through the law of nature, nor the law of the Scriptures, but occasionally through a special grace. This can happen in several ways, sometimes by [simple] revelation and sometimes by [a mediating arbitration]. There are two ways in which it can happen by [simple] revelation: either by a spontaneous act of God or by God in response to prayers. By a spontaneous act of God there are two ways: either openly or through a sign . . . openly, as when the judgment against Saul was revealed to Samuel; by a sign, as when what God willed regarding the liberation of the children of Israel was revealed to Pharaoh through a sign . . . [omitted: example of petitioning prayers]. There are two ways in which it can be revealed through a mediating arbitration: either by lot, or through a contest; for the word "certare" ["to decide something by a contest"] derives from "certum facere" "to compete" ["to make certain"]. God's judgment is sometimes revealed to men by lot, as in the substitution of Matthias in the *Acts of the Apostles.* God's judgment can be revealed by a contest in two ways: either by a clash of strength, as happens in a [duel] between two champions, who are called prize-fighters, or through competition among a number of people who vie with one another to reach an agreed goal, as happens in a race between athletes competing to reach the finishing line first.)

At the most obscure end of this ramifying process, divine judgment appears only in strenuous conflict, "certamen," which is divided into duels (between two parties) and athletic competitions (among many).

In the schematic thoroughness of his exposition, Dante is ostensibly reaffirming the totalizing and systematic rationality of his own discourse, in an evidently Scholastic mode, namely, the analytical process of *divisio* earlier employed in the *Vita Nova* as well as in *Convivio*'s commentaries.[39] Yet

---

[39] On *divisio*, see again Chapter 1, n 50. For *VN* and *CV*, see Chapter 4, sections ii–iii, and nn 4, 20, 22, as well as n 40 below.

the point being made so rationally is that reason is often reduced to help-less dependence on obscure signs that gesture toward the invisible, supra-rational "iudicium Dei." The successive, ramifying divisions of Dante's argument, far from making his case transparently rational, take readers further and further away from either the syllogistic proof they themselves can derive immediately from empirical evidence or from the direct revela-tion available in Scripture, into an area which is as remote from any direct insight into "divine judgment" as human reason can get. Moreover, the logic of division itself, the continual splitting into two and again into two, runs dynamically counter to the absolute priority of unity on which, again, book 1 rested.[40]

The ultimate consequence of this rational division, then, is the literal squaring off of two opposed "equals" in a contest that determines the subordination of one to the other. Dante specifically notes that "duel," the effective *terminus* of the process of division, derives etymologically from "duos" (two):

[Q]uam quidem collisionem [virium], quia primitus unius ad unum fuit ipsa inventa, 'duellum' appellamus. (2.9.2)

([W]e call this clash of strength [a "duel"] because originally it was devised as combat between [one man and another one].)

Recourse to the duel thus marks Dante's drive to a unitary imperial author-ity with a "duality" that is not only conceptual, but actually moves into the realm of corporeal violence, and that can only be justified by an appeal to supra-rational forces. The upshot of book 2, then, is to subordinate the autonomy of the highest human judicial authority to God's higher author-ity, in the process implicitly calling into question the "rational necessity" for the existence of such a human authority, introducing elements of violence,

---

[40] There is a particularly interesting parallel between this *divisio* and the one of "Donne ch'avete intelletto d'Amore" in *VN* 19. Both Durling and Martinez (1990: 55–69; also Durling 2001, 2003) and Stillinger (1992: 95–100) explore the fact, first noted by Spitzer 1937 (131–2), that the latter division presents a series of paired terms and in each case divides only the second and more sensual of the two. For Durling and Martinez this reflects the neo-platonic "procession and return" of creation, from unity to multiplicity, but also back again, by inviting readers to complete the division of the first parts for themselves (though unprovable, I suspect this reading is correct). For Stillinger, in keeping with Spitzer's terse suggestion, it implies that Dante's fascination with the sensuality of Beatrice competes with the spiritualizing impulse of the *canzone*. In *MN*, the underlying model is a descent into multiplicity and materiality which renders humanity's pursuit of direct knowledge of the divine more and more difficult. Thus, while the declared aim of the passage is to identify means to reascend to God's originating intention, the effect is to undercut the reader's belief that rational proof is available to support a direct linkage between the first *Auctor* and the legitimate authority of the Roman Empire. On this general question, see Copeland 1991: 214–19 who notes late medieval associations between *divisio textus* and the socio-linguistic division of Babel.

of division, and of irrationality (or supra-rationality) into that which was originally justified on the grounds of its essential peacefulness, unity, and reason.

The last two chapters of book 2 adduce a final argument for the divine authorization of Roman justice. They again take up the theme, already present in *Convivio* 4 (5.1–10) of the necessary role of the Empire in preparing the world for the birth of Christ, to which is here added its function in the punishment of human sins through the crucifixion. In relation to the preceding chapters, the aim of this argument is to reassert the need for imperial justice, now seen not apart from, but in subordinate harmony with, divine justice.[41] The final section of book 2 is prefaced by a digressive diatribe against those clergy who ostensibly defend the Christian faith by attacking the Empire, while despoiling and corrupting the very Church they claim to represent (10.1–3; cf. 9.20; 11.7). This attack anticipates the burden of book 3, which undertakes to defend the autonomy of imperial authority by arguing that it derives directly from God rather than through the mediation of the temporal Church. At this point the treatise moves from the historical past into the present moment of its author's life and simultaneously acknowledges its place in a contemporary polemic: the war of words between imperial and papal publicists (see n 6).

Despite Dante's significant personal stake in this controversy, he continues even at this late stage to minimize the historicity and personality of his topics by avoiding punctual references to any of the major individual protagonists or contemporary historical circumstances of the conflict, including his own minor part therein.[42] Nonetheless, as book 3 opens he does predict that this intervention will draw him personally into the center

---

[41] Particularly audacious is Dante's assertion (absent from *CV*) that the "punishment" of Christ had to be carried out by a legitimate human judge in order to constitute lawful retribution for Adam's original sin (2.11.4–5), when the role of Rome could as easily be explained with reference to another Augustinian doctrine – namely that good can be done, unwittingly, by evil men, if the divine will works through them (e.g., *CD* 11.17). It fails to address the common medieval claim that Pilate committed a horrendous crime in punishing an innocent, not to mention offering violence to God Himself. Finally, it blurs the distinction between divine and human justice. Presumably, the offense of Adam was against God, not against humankind (in fact, humankind is the "defendant" on whom justice is meted out by proxy) and it is hard to imagine the legal grounds for a human being or institution adjudicating a case in which God was one of the parties – if there is "no judgment among equals," *a fortiori* there is no judgment of superiors by inferiors. On the latter two points, see Vernani's critique of Dante's reasoning (*DRM* book 2, par. 99–114). Vernani is a partisan polemicist, true, but in this case his arguments seem cogent (Vinay 1950: 186 n; *pace* Nardi 1965c). For an equally partisan, though still useful, view of Vernani, see Cassell 2004: 45–9 *et passim*; cf. Took 1990: 167–9.

[42] See again nn 2, 8 on unsuccessful attempts to link *MN* to specific events. Dante's political *Eps.* and the *DC* provide a more direct window on to his engagement with these events. See also n 56; Chapter 1, n 75.

of that conflict: "forsitan alicuius indignationis in me causa erit" (it . . . will . . . perhaps be a cause of some [indignation] against me; 3.1.2).[43] Strikingly, Dante now explicitly describes his task in terms of an athletic contest or battle:

[A]ssumpta fiducia de verbis Danielis premissis, in quibus divina potentia clipeus defensorum vertitatis astruitur, iuxta monitionem Pauli fidei loricam induens . . . gignasium presens ingredior. (3.1.3; see also 3.3.11)

([H]aving taken heart from the words of Daniel cited above, in which the divine power is said to be a shield of the defenders of truth, and putting on "the breast plate of faith" as Paul exhorts us . . . I shall enter the present arena.)

That this language recalls the metaphor of adjudicatory dueling in book 2 is clear, and becomes clearer still when he adds that "pro salute veritatis in hoc libro *certamen* incipio" (I engage in *battle* in this book in the cause of truth; 3.3.18).[44]

The passages just cited continue into book 3 the thematics of "litigium" that has guided Dante's argument throughout, though now personalized, and changed in other ways as well. The point is made ostentatiously at the beginning of chapter 3:

In introitu ad questionem hanc notare oportet quod prime questionis veritas magis manifestanda fuit ad ignorantiam tollendam, quam ad tollendum *litigium*; sed que fuit secunde questionis, quasi equaliter ad ignorantiam et *litigium* se habebat: multa etenim ignoramus de quibus non *litigamus* . . . Huius quidem tertie questionis veritas tantum habet *litigium*; ut, quemadmodum in aliis ignorantia solet esse causa *litigii*, sic et hic *litigium* causa ignorantie sit magis. (3.3.3)

(By way of preamble it should be noted that the truth of the first question needed to be demonstrated more in order to eliminate ignorance than to resolve a [*conflict*]; but the truth of the second question addressed ignorance and [*conflict*] in almost equal measure, for there are many things we do not know about which we do not [enter into *conflict*] . . . But the truth concerning this third question is so fiercely [contested] that just as in other matters it is ignorance which gives rise to [conflict], so here it is rather the [conflict] which is the cause of ignorance.)

In other words, while the problem addressed in book 1 was one of dissipating ignorance rather than engaging in "litigium," while that in book 2 was equal

---

[43] The prediction was accurate, at least in the middle term, as can be seen from Vernani's fierce attack on the treatise (*DRM*), from its official proscription as heretical by Cardinal Poujet in 1329, and by its later inclusion on the Index of prohibited books. For fortunes of *MN* in the years after Dante's death, see Cassell 2004: 33–41

[44] Cassell 2004: 50 points to an early anticipation of the military–athletic imagery applied to Dante in 1.1.5, though in that instance he is stressing the *lack* of competition in this field of inquiry.

parts of both activities (3.3.1), the burden of book 3 is a purely "litigious" matter.

At this juncture, then, the fantasy of humanity guided by reason, which informed the treatise at its outset, is replaced by a vision of leaders dominated by blind passion who nonetheless believe firmly in their own rationality:

Hominibus nanque rationis intuitu voluntatem prevolantibus hoc sepe contingit: ut, male affecti, lumine rationis postposito, affectu quasi ceci trahantur et pertinaciter suam denegent cecitatem. (3.3.4–5)

(For it often happens that men who guide their will by the light of reason, should be swayed by misguided impulses, put the light of reason behind them and are dragged by passion like blind men, and yet obstinately deny their own blindness.)

It is remarkable how far Dante, and his readers, have come since book 1 and how careful he is to mark the conceptual and rhetorical distance traversed. This then is how the treatise unfolds: from the rationally based claim in book 1 that the Monarch is the supreme judge who resolves all human divisions and conflicts from atop an absolute hierarchy, to the argument from faith in book 2 that the Monarchy's legitimacy and supremacy were established by divisive conflict in which the Roman state was one of two contending parties, to the situation in book 3 where it becomes necessary for a third party to adjudicate "litigiously" between two claimants to supreme judicial authority on earth, the Papacy and the Empire. From the ideal resolution of "litigii" by a human judge, to "litigium" itself as an occulted form of divine judgment, to a "litigium" in which Dante himself is caught up as an interested party, the treatise moves further and further from a disinterested and impersonal human rationality that judges from above. The ideal, "ahistorical" world of reason gives way, on the one hand, before the darkened signs of historical reality – first in the distant past of imperial Rome, then in the contentious present of warring Popes and Emperors – and, on the other, before the recognition that the only true and final judge, God himself, stands entirely beyond history.

The historical irony that erodes the ideal position staked out in book 1 becomes increasingly evident throughout book 3. Dante ostensibly defends the function of the Emperor as autonomous and supreme judge against the historical claims of the Church. Yet in order to maintain imperial autonomy and supremacy he is constrained to invoke a higher authority still, God, who confers legitimacy that neither reason nor history can provide. But he is also led to argue that the Emperor does after all have an earthly peer, though not a superior, namely the Pope, who is supreme in his own sphere, that of the spirit. Moreover, while this argument temporarily frees the Emperor from the Pope's authority, it also reinstates the dilemma of "judging among equals" that was to have been resolved by the installation of a universal monarchy.

Thus, at a pivotal moment in this book we find Dante representing as his opponent's argument one that is uncannily similar to his own in book 1:[45]

Summunt etenim sibi principium de decimo *Prime Phylosophie* dicentes: omnia que sunt *unius generis* reducuntur ad *unum*, quod est mensura omnium que sub illo genere sunt; sed omnes homines sunt *unius generis*; ergo debent reduci *ad unum*, tanquam ad mensuram omnium eorum. Et cum summus Antistes et Imperator sint homines, si conclusio illa est vera, oportet quod reducantur *ad unum* hominem. Et cum Papa non sit reducendus ad alium, relinquitur quod Imperator cum omnibus aliis sit reducendus ad ipsum, tanquam ad mensuram et regulam. (3.11.1–2)

(Adopting a principle from the tenth book of [Aristotle's] *Metaphysics* they say: all things belonging to a single species are [to be] referred to one thing which is the [normative] measure for all things that belong to that species; but all men belong to [a single] species; therefore they are to be [referred] to one man as [the] common measure for [all of them]. And since the supreme Pontiff and the Emperor are men, if that conclusion is valid, [it is necessary to subordinate them] to a single man. And since the Pope [must not be referred to] any other man, it remains that the Emperor along with all other men [must be referred] to him, as to their measure and rule.)

If, however, neither Pope nor Emperor can be "reduced" under the other, as Dante goes on to maintain, the critical logical step of book 1 has been

---

[45] In book 3, Dante attributes this argument, the *reductio ad unum*, to Aristotle's *MP* 10.1 (1052b.18–1053a.20), but there has been much discussion as to what the proximate medieval source is, and, especially, who the "dicentes" are. See, *inter alii*, Maccarrone 1955: 91–7; Nardi 1960a: 163–72, 1979: 482 nn; R. Kay 1998: 278–9 nn; Cassell 2004: 301–2, 332–4 nn. In any event, even if arguments in the two books do not match exactly, the principle of *reductio ad unum* clearly lies at the heart of book 1 (see again n 29). Compare especially 1.15.2: "Propter quod in omni genere rerum illud est optimum quod est maxime unum, ut Phylosopho placet in hiis que *De simpliciter ente* [i.e., *MP*]. unde fit quod unum esse videtur esse radix eius est esse bonum, et multa esse eius quod est esse malum." While there is no agreement about which Aristotelian passage Dante refers to here, Nardi 1979: 358 n points convincingly to 10.2, the chapter immediately following the one cited in *MN* 3.11; see also R. Kay 1998: 80–1 nn. Vinay 1950: 259n; Passerin d'Entrèves (1952: 56); Maccarrone (1955: 94–6); P. Shaw (1995: xvii–xviii, xxxi–xxxii) all note the resemblance between the two arguments, though the latter two believe the contradiction to be only apparent (cf. E. Gilson 1939: 188–90). Even if one supplies a distinction between the two arguments "from unity" that Dante himself did not take the trouble to make, the objections remain that, on the one hand, no earthly means of resolving a dispute between Emperor and Pope are available, and, on the other, that God himself might be said to supply the unifying principle that apparently necessitated a universal monarchy in book 1. See again the discussion of *DVE* 1.16, where the unifying *vulgare illustre* is compared to God as the *simplicissima substantiarum* (Chapter 3, sections ii–iii, and n 18).

contradicted – the potential for "litigium" has been reintroduced – and is being enacted by Dante's litigious attempts to settle the question against papal and decretalist objections.[46]

At this point, Dante at last brings out into the open the traditional distinction between person and office, the doctrine of "corporate" authority known as "the king's two bodies."[47] This doctrine allows him to assert that as men the Pope and Emperor may be "unius generis," but that their offices are of distinctly different and incomparable kinds: the one supreme over the life of body and soul in this world, the other over the fate of the soul alone in the next. An unintended consequence of making this distinction, however, may be to remind the reader that Dante originally skipped over it in book 1, where person and office are effectively conflated: the office functions only if its human occupant is without *cupiditas*; the human occupant is without *cupiditas* only if he holds this office.

The doctrine of "separate but equal" authorities leads Dante directly to the closing argument in chapter 15 that human nature is intrinsically divided in two, that humanity is, as it were, a "horizon" between two domains, corruptible and incorruptible, and thus has not a single "end" but rather "duos fines" (two goals; 3.15.7; cf. 3.15.6)[48] – a terrestrial paradise of human intellect and virtue, and a celestial paradise accessible only through faith and grace. In the end, unity, the founding value of *Monarchia*, has been maintained only by division. What is more, as the case of Frederick and Aristotle in *Convivio* 4 (discussed in Chapter 2) should suggest, divisions

---

[46] This doctrine of "dualitas" was closely associated with Hugutio of Pisa and developed, ironically, by publicists for the French monarchy (e.g., John of Paris) in their struggle with Boniface VIII. See Cassell 2004: 13–17, 217–18 n 38, 274 n 162 (also n 6 above). Given earlier discussion, it is unsurprising that Dante does not use the term "dualitas," although Cassell 2004: 104 points to the "duos fines" of 3.15 as a displacement of the Hugutian theme. See also nn 14, 27, 48. For more on the influence of Hugutio's political writings on *MN*, see Maccarrone 1955: 8–9. For the possible influence of Hugutio's *MD* on the first chapters of *MN* 1, see Martina 1972. See also Chapter 2, section ii, and n 22.

[47] E.g., in 3.11.4 "aliud est esse hominem et aliud est esse Papam"; in 3.6, 7, especially 7.7–8: "Auctoritas principalis non est principis nisi ad usum, quia nullus princeps se ipsum auctorizare potest . . . manifestum est quod nullus princeps potest sibi substituere vicarium in omnibus equivalentem"; in 3.10.5: "nemini licet ea facere per offitium sibi deputatum que sunt contra illud offitium"; in 3.10.10: "omnis iurisdictio prior est suo iudice: iudex enim ad iurisdictionem ordinatur et non e converso . . ."; and so on. The last two come from Dante's discussion of the donation of Constantine, which rests heavily on the restrictions that the imperial office imposes on the man who occupies it. On Dante's treatment of the *donatio*, which he believed to be authentic, in *MN* 3.10 and *CV* 4.4 as well as in the *DC* (*Inf.* 19.106–17; *Purg.* 32.124–60; *Par.* 20.55–60), see Nardi 1942d, 1960a: 238–45, 1979: 241–69; Maccarrone 1955: 71–97; R. Kay 1998: 262–3 nn; Davis 1998; Cristaldi 1999; Scott 2004: 160–2.

[48] The "double finality" also plays a crucial role in the *ECG*, par. 15. See Ascoli 1997: 334–5.

of this kind are as habitual with Dante as assertions of the necessity for absolute, unifying authorities.

According to the terms deployed in *Monarchia* book 1, Dante has put himself and his discourse on the horns of a dilemma. The effective equality of Pope and Emperor leaves no room for a legitimate or authoritative human judgment between them ("par in parem non habet imperium"), and yet judgment there must be ("et ubique potest esse litigium, ibi debet esse iudicium"). In one sense, the solution is easy: only God – the "simplicissima substantiarum" of *De Vulgari Eloquentia* – the One whose "iudicium" is by definition inaccessible to human reason – can ground these two "separate but equal" authorities because he is "omnium spiritualium et temporalium gubernator" (governor of all spiritual and temporal things; 3.15.18). Yet God's judgment must be revealed somehow to humanity, and Dante's text must somehow establish that it is the privileged vehicle by which that revelation takes place. To put it another way, just as in *Convivio*, the little gap, or "aporia" in Etienne Gilson's phrase, that appears between two absolute authorities on earth, is inhabited by Dante's text, which becomes the space of an adjudication that, whatever its divine origins, is finally represented as taking place within the tainted confines of historical divisions and human conflicts. And with this we can begin to reflect on exactly how Dante sets about claiming that space as uniquely, and legitimately, his own.

IV. "A DANIEL COME TO JUDGMENT"

To this point two avenues for approaching Dante's own authority in *Monarchia* have presented themselves. First is the general rhetorical stance of the Dantean "I": the unapologetic use of the tools of Latin philosophical and theological culture; the bald, bold claims for the originality and importance of his subject; the dismissive attitude toward those who oppose his point of view. Second, as seen at the end of each of the previous two sections, is the possibility of reconstructing Dante's unarticulated authorial subject position as a logical entailment of *Monarchia*'s treatment of both institutional and "epistemological" authorities. Strikingly, these two avenues go in apparently opposite directions – toward a confident, fully "authorized" philosopher, on the one hand, and, on the other, toward a belated, unofficial, "unauthorized" pretender who is subject to any and all of the authorities he speaks about so knowingly. What I will now suggest, however, is that the treatise programmatically sets out to bridge the gap between these two aspects of the Dantean "I," building upon the acquisitions of both

Convivio and *De Vulgari Eloquentia* and, at the same time, paralleling, with a difference, the strategies of the *Commedia*.

The most explicit articulations of Dante's position in the treatise appear in the opening chapters of each of the three books, where he briefly appears *in propria persona*. In chapter 1 of book 1, he makes a claim for both the social utility and the radical novelty of the subject he is treating. In chapter 1 of book 2, he refers to a dramatic change of mind concerning the place of the Roman Empire in salvation history. Finally, as just seen, at the beginning of book 3 he places himself within the economy of a fierce "litigium" over the proper relationship between temporal and ecclesiastical authorities. Taken together, these moments are a reminder that Dante, ostensibly subject to both Emperor and Pope in the hierarchical and unitary logic of his own treatise and liable to judgment by both of them, has undertaken to judge their quarrel and to resolve it, despite fierce objections from opponents whom he specifically identifies with the Papacy (cf. 3.3.7; 3.3.18).

At first, it seems obvious what Dante's solution will be. In book 1 he makes it evident that (philosophical) reason is at least the equal to authority, and he continues throughout the treatise to identify himself with the "voice of reason," particularly by his repeated insistence that each book's argument will be grounded in a rational "first principle" (1.2.4; 2.2.1; 3.2.1) and by his numerous recourses to syllogistic logic (see n 36). Nonetheless, beginning in book 2, arguments from reason are partially displaced by those from history and, above all, from the faithful interpretation of God's hidden judgment. Moreover, the way in which the Monarch's function is defined in book 1 has implicit consequences for Dante's stance: he argues rationally that the realization of the "possible intellect," depends on the pacifying judicial presence of the Emperor, but by book 3 the peace of reason has given way to unresolved "litigation," into which Dante himself has been drawn.

The point can be usefully made with reference to a traditional question of Dante scholarship that has been focused on *Monarchia* and has been articulated in epistemological terms rather than in those of rhetoric and power politics at issue here, namely Dante's supposed debt to Averroes, the renowned Arabic commentator on Aristotle's *De Anima*, in the treatise.[49] Indeed, as already shown, in the abstract terms of book 1 Dante does

---

[49] See again n 27. It is worth considering that Averroes was known to Dante as "The Commentator" (*CV* 4.13.8). As commentator on Aristotle, Averroes is in the situation of the humble modern *lector*. But the (generalizing, reifying) epithet with which he is citing paradoxically marks him as an *auctor* "worthy of faith and obedience," like Aristotle, *The Philosopher*. The conflation of the two roles

align himself with reason in an impersonal and collective form indebted to Averroes' formulation, arguing that no individual human person can, alone, realize the race's intellectual potential (1.3.4–9, especially 4 and 8). By book 3, however, the author of *Monarchia* speaks for, or at least as, himself – in the guise of an individual historical person caught up in a "certamen," a "war of words."

Chapter 3 (especially n 33) argued, using Corti 1981 as a point of departure, that in *De Vulgari Eloquentia* Dante flirts with a sort of linguistic equivalent of Averroism: the speculative grammarian's notion of an ideal "faculty of grammar" that is present "everywhere and nowhere" among humans, as the transpersonal, transnational, transhistorical potential for creating and using language. In the end, however, the universal and abstract faculty of language production along with the idealized *vulgare illustre* is reduced to the latter's instantiation in the personal language of Dante himself. Just so in *Monarchia* Dante gradually emerges as a solitary "voice of reason." The oxymoronic displacement from a universal and impersonal potential to an individual instance – whether of *oratio* or of *ratio* – is thus a typically Dantean procedure. What is more, it is homologous with what I have argued throughout this study is Dante's relationship to *auctoritas*, a transpersonal and transhistorical quality that is gradually displaced onto the individual person of Dante Alighieri.[50]

Monarchia, then, does revisit, though in displaced form, Dante's struggle in both *Convivio* and *De Vulgari Eloquentia* to square his own personality and historical modernity with the impersonality and antiquity that traditionally characterize genuine *auctoritas*: a struggle enacted primarily through the categories of nobility (*nobilitas*) and human free will (*arbitrium* or *voluntas*). On the face of it, the later treatise is less focused on individual personhood than its two predecessors. As already shown it aims to depersonalize and dehistoricize the Empire, as well as the Papacy, and thus to confer on it both a legitimacy and authority that no single, willful individual can claim for himself.

The process is constant, though it assumes different forms in each of the three books. Book 1, in addition to grounding itself in the depersonalized

---

constitutes a particular kind of precedent for the phenomena described in Chapter 4 (cf. Chapter 2, n 29, on whether Aquinas can be considered an "auctor').

[50] See Chapter 2, n 31; Chapter 6, section ii. From this perspective, Dante's invocation of Averroes does not constitute a fixed doctrinal position, but rather is a dynamic move, a "negotiating position," allowing displacement of the universal understanding of the "possible intellect" into the domain of his own, individual authorship (cf. E. Gilson 1939: 171). This is a good instance of how Dante's rhetorical needs and desires shape the unfolding of his thought.

concept of the "possible intellect," argues that the imperial office empties its holder of all personal desires. In book 2, what appears to be usurping violence, and thus the product of an individual "will to power," is sublimated through the concept of the "judicial duel" into an impersonal instrument for determining the divine will. In book 3, the doctrine of the "king's two bodies," physical and corporate, is used to discredit the attempts of individual emperors and popes to substitute their wills for the impersonal limits of their offices.

Nevertheless, in each case Dante's argumentation is unable to leave behind completely the recalcitrant, willful, and potentially illegitimate individual. In book 1 the traces are quite faint: besides the implicit question concerning the relationship between the avowedly "original" and individual rationalism of Dante's treatise and the impersonal "possible intellect," there is a lingering suspicion that the Emperor's individual desires will not be so easily eradicated as one might hope. In book 2, the issues are much clearer, though they again lead us back to the problematic status of the human will. The Augustinian critique of Roman politics from which Dante declares his difference in chapter 1 is rooted in a theology of the fallen will. Moreover, his central argument regarding the adjudicatory duel not only depends upon an analogy between individual conflict and contests between whole peoples, but also requires, as a (presumably unverifiable) precondition for success, that the contestants enter into the arena with the proper, humble, "individual" intention to submit themselves to God's will. Finally, in book 3 all of the attempts to locate legitimacy and hence authority of judgment in a variety of transpersonal sources – rationality (unity is always preferable to multiplicity), antiquity (the Roman Empire predates the Church), law and office – prove inadequate, subject to an endlessly divisive "litigation" in which Dante personally, willfully, participates.

Perhaps Dante's anomalous role can be accounted for, and in some sense "institutionalized," by recourse to the earlier version of the division of imperial from papal authority: namely, the symbiosis posited in *Convivio* 4 between the Philosopher's intellectual competence, which guides the Emperor's rule, and the Emperor's rule, which enforces the truths revealed by the Philosopher. It could be argued that Dante, who in *Convivio* was struggling to claim a subordinate philosophical status for his vernacular poetry, in *Monarchia* asserts his rational authority directly, and posits it as a necessary supplement to both Emperor *and* Pope, replacing in *propria persona* the otherwise excluded figure of the Philosopher. One strong support for this argument is Dante's eventual declaration that the Emperor's rule is the implementation of philosophical reason:

Imperatore, . . . secundum phylosophica documenta genus humanum ad temporalem felicitatem dirigeret. (3.15.10; cf. 3.15.8)

(The Emperor [guides the human race] to temporal happiness in conformity with the teachings of philosophy.)

In this way he completes the argument of book 1 that successful imperial rule is the necessary precondition for the full realization of human intellectual potential.

In the process, however, Dante creates a hermeneutic circle – the Emperor must be guided by philosophical reason for philosophical reason to prosper – that renders problematic any such solution. The very idea that the unified temporal authority of the supreme judge can be subdivided into will and intellect, Emperor and Philosopher, also implicitly undermines the absolute hierarchical autonomy posited in book 1, since in *Convivio* this split is used by Dante to disqualify Frederick II's pretensions to philosophical *auctoritas* (see again Chapter 2, section iv and n 17 above). In any case, as observed earlier, by the end of book 3 the treatise itself has abandoned its claims to occupy the space of philosophical reason in any simple or untroubled way. The turn to faith, the grounding of imperial authority not in logical necessity, as in book 1, but in God's occult judgment, has made it plain that philosophy will take you, and Dante, just so far.

To put it bluntly, the position Dante inhabits as author of *Monarchia* is potentially a *usurpation* – of authority appropriated by an individual person without a defined *officium*, without a legitimating "corporate" existence.[51] Either that, or Dante's is an authority conferred from beyond history and beyond reason – a special authority sent down by God – just as Dante argues explicitly that the Pope and Emperor both derive their distinct authorities directly from on high. Book 3 contains broad hints that the latter is the role Dante envisions for himself in *Monarchia* and perhaps elsewhere as well, a role that allows for a divinely conferred and ad hoc authority that is not linked to a formal office. In chapter 6 of book 3, Dante confronts yet another of the Biblical texts ostensibly adduced by the Decretalists in support of papal authority over the Emperor:

---

[51] As becomes clearer in the *DC* (see Chapter 7, section iii), Dante may be operating on the assumption that in the absence of legitimate rule by either Emperor or Pope, he is not bound to subject himself to their strictures – but this is a tautological position, since it is through his own argumentation that he defines what the legitimate forms of imperial and papal rule are.

De lictera vero primi libri Regum assummunt etiam creationem et depositionem Saulis, et dicunt quod Saul rex intronizatus fuit et de trono depositus per Samuelem, qui vice Dei de precepto fungebatur, ut in Lictera patet. (3.6.1; see 1 Kings 10:1, 15: 23–28)

(Then from the [Scriptures] of the first book of Kings the creation and deposition of Saul, and they say that King Saul was placed on the throne and removed from it by Samuel, who was acting as God's vicar by his command, just as we read in [Scriptures].)

The claim is that Samuel, the prophet and judge, was acting like the Pope as God's "vicarius" – his "lieu-tenant" or "placeholder." Dante objects that Samuel instead functioned as "legatus spetialis ad hoc, sive nuntius portans mandatum Domini expressum" ([special ad hoc legate or a nuntius who conveys the express command of God]; 3.6.3).[52]

The distinction Dante makes between "vicar" and "nuncio" is as follows:[53]

[A]liud est esse *vicarium*, aliud est esse *nuntium* sive ministrum: sicut aliud est esse *doctorem*, aliud est esse *interpretem*. Nam *vicarius* est cui iurisdictio cum lege vel cum arbitrio commissa est; et ideo intra terminos iurisdictionis commisse de lege vel de arbitrio potest agere circa aliquid, quod dominus omnino ignorat. *Nuntius* autem non potest in quantum nuntius; sed quemadmodum malleus in sola virtute fabri operatur, sic et *nuntius* in solo arbitrio eius qui mictit illum. Non igitur sequitur, si Deus per nuntium Samuelem fecit hoc, quod *vicarius* Dei hoc facere possit. (3.6.4–6)

([I]t is one thing to be a *vicar*, quite another to be a messenger [*nuncio*] or minister; just as it is one thing to be a ["*doctor*"; father of the Church] and another to be an *interpreter*. For a *vicar* is a person to whom jurisdiction is entrusted within the terms of the law or at his own discretion; thus within the limits of the jurisdiction entrusted to him he can take action by applying the law or by using his own discretion in matters of which his [over]lord knows nothing. But a messenger [*nuncio*] *qua* messenger [has no power of this kind]; for just as a hammer functions only by virtue of the [maker] using it, so a messenger [*nuncio*] too is entirely dependent on the will of [the one] who sends him. It does not follow, then, that if God did that using Samuel as his messenger [*nuncio*], the vicar of God may do it.)

---

[52] Maccarone 1955: 58 and R. Kay 1998: 236–7 nn argue that notwithstanding frequent references to Samuel in medieval discussions of the participation of clergy in the coronation of secular rulers, this text was not used in by hierocrats in the way suggested by Dante, which might indicate that he had particular motives – perhaps those proposed here – in adducing it (*sed contra*, see Nardi 1960a: 160–4, 209–19). See also Vinay 1950: 226–7 nn and the characteristically virulent refutation of Vernani (*DRM* book 3, par. 16–31).

[53] For the Pope as "vicarius Christi" in medieval doctrine, see Maccarone 1952. For Dante's distinction, see Maccarone 1952: 166–75; Cassell 2004: 93–4 and nn 326, 335.

The argument is a powerful but also a subtle one. The vicar seems at first the stronger and more impersonally authoritative figure since he is allowed to operate autonomously in place of his Lord, if only within the confines of a specifically delimited mandate, a "jurisdiction." The nuncio, or *interpres*, on the other hand, has no autonomy at all, no mandate to exercise recurring authority.[54]

The sharp boundaries that Dante puts on the latter figure are confirmed by the parallelism he creates between the relationship of vicar and nuncio, on the one hand, and *doctor* and *interpres* on the other. This apparently limited analogy recalls, and also reinforces, his earlier critique of the authority usurped over the Bible, and over the Fathers or "doctores," by the Decretalists (3.3.11–16), to whom, we may logically infer, Dante then refers with the word "interpres" (cf. Cassell 2004: 322 n 294, 327 n 336). There, as seen earlier, Dante carefully sketches the dependence of authority on temporal priority, making the Decretalists secondary to the Councils and the Patristic "doctores," and both of them secondary in turn to the Scriptures themselves. In this line he himself implicitly stands as the belated modern interpreter of derivative interpreters – and hence with even less authority in these matters than they. This passage thus provides a window onto the fundamental dilemma that haunts Dante in writing the treatise.

Considering that the hierarchical relationship subordinating *interpres* to *doctor* is closely analogous to the normative configuration of *commentator* with respect to *auctor* (indeed, as noted below, *interpres* is another name for a commentator [n 55]), one may infer that this dilemma is not very different from that dramatized more overtly in the formal auto-exegesis of *Vita Nova* and *Convivio*. Thus it is worth asking whether it is possible to find a solution in this case comparable to the ones adopted in those texts, whereby Dante manages simultaneously to occupy the position of humble interpreter and that of author worthy of interpretation, partly through the device (also employed in *DVE*) of implying that his authority derives from an extra-historical, transcendent source, which in effect removes him from the temporal hierarchy of authorities.[55]

---

[54] Similarly, and appositely, Minnis 1984 notes that in some medieval accounts a prophet is not to be considered an *auctor* proper, but rather a *scriptor* or *compilator*, because he merely copies down what God tells him to say. See also nn 25, 58.

[55] See Copeland 1991: 33, 88–92 on the classical and medieval usage of *interpres* and *interpretatio*, which, on the one hand, imply a faithful transmission of the sense of an authoritative text, by translation or commentary, and, on the other, a more exalted form of mediation, as in this passage from Isidore, *Etym.* (10.123; interpolations are Copeland's): "Interpres, quod inter partes medius sit duarum linguarum, dum transferet. Sed et qui Deum [quem] interpretatur et hominum quibus divina indicat mysteria, interpres vocatur [quia inter eam quam transferet]."

That this may actually be the case appears when we pursue the *nuntius/interpres* analogy a little further. The definition of the *nuntius* contains elements that potentially broaden the power of a modern *interpres* like Dante immeasurably, if only he can prove that he has received the necessary, divine, mandate. As the case of Saul's deposition by Samuel suggests, the power exercised on any given occasion by the nuncio may be greater than that of the vicar. As also happens with the judicial duel, the *nuntius* bypasses authorities established by time and reason in governing offices to become an ad hoc vehicle for expressing the will and the judgment of God directly in a given instance. He might, indeed, be said to be blessed with that "gratia spetiale" which Dante earlier associated with the supra-rational revelation of the hidden "iudicium Dei" (2.7.7).

Not by coincidence, the previously cited passage concerning the possibility of discovering God's hidden will under historical circumstances when there is no final judicial authority that can stand above the fray also contains the first reference to Saul's deposition by Samuel:

The hidden judgment of God is sometimes attained by special grace [*gratia spetiali*] . . . which is sometimes made express by simple revelation according to the spontaneous will of God: such was the revelation of Samuel's judgment against Saul. (2.7.7–8)

This recurrent concern with a figure of the prophet-judge of the Old Testament seems remarkably appropriate in a treatise that defines politics in terms of *iudicium* and that pursues a legitimate means for intervening in a situation where *iudicium* has been systematically displaced by *litigium*. In other words, that Dante's recourse to the case of Samuel may figure his own attempt to reveal God's opposition to papal usurpation of temporal political authority.[56]

The strongest evidence that this is Dante's strategy appears at the very beginning of book 3, in the most striking and audacious moment of self-reference in the treatise:

Conclusit ora leonum, et non nocuerunt michi: quia coram eo *iustitia inventa est in me.* (3.1.1)

(He has closed up the jaws of the lion, and they will not harm me: because *he has found justice in me.*)

---

[56] As numerous scholars have attested, in the political *Eps.* Dante repeatedly assumes the voice of a Biblical prophet (e.g., Passerin d'Entrêves 1952: 37; Mineo 1968: 143–60; Sarolli 1963: 243–4, 1966b: 64–6; Hawkins 1993: 50–3; Scott 1996: 44–5; Pertile 1997b; Martinez n.d.).

These words, presented as the first-person narrator's description both of his divinely sponsored mission and the persecutions it brings upon him, are actually a quotation from the book of Daniel (6:22),[57] and they thus strongly imply a parallel between Dante and the Old Testament prophet who here speaks in the first person.[58] Moreover, the words immediately following those quoted, as Pézard has observed (1973: 72–3), are a parallel phrase directed at Daniel's sovereign, Nebuchadnezzar: "Sed et coram te, rex, delictum non feci" (but as regards you, o King, I committed no crime).[59] In other words, the passage also alludes to and apotropaically wards off the threat that Dante might be perceived as presuming against the very authorities whose roles he sets out to define throughout the treatise.

The biblical Daniel, like Samuel, is not only a prophet, but also a judge. More exactly, as the cited passage suggests, he is a prophet whose message *is iustitia* and who becomes the individual vehicle ("in me") of divine *iudicium*. Through an identification with Daniel, then, Dante comes to

[57] To be clear: Dante is not passing Daniel's words off as his own. He expects the reader to recognize the Biblical source from which they derive, and in some sense to take them as an epigraph. However, medieval texts did not mark quotations as such, and so a basic equivocation exists between direct and cited discourse, on which Dante plays here. For a more famous example of this phenomenon, see *Inf.* 3.1–9 ("Per me si va . . ."), where the equivocation is between the gate of Hell and Dante's poem (see Freccero 1983c). One might argue that the double and unstable identification of the "I" in this passage with Dante and with Daniel supports a Spitzerian account (1946; see Chapter 1, section iv) of a depersonalized first-person pronoun – but I would reply that, to the contrary, the deliberate manipulation of the "I" in this way is a distinguishing trait of "Dante." Note also that the Book of Daniel oscillates between first-person voices (Daniel's and Nebuchadnezzar's) and impersonal narration.

[58] Pézard (1973) argues, only in part persuasively, that in the latter cantos of *Purg.* Dante models his prophetic mission on that of Daniel, and that the notorious DXV prophecy derives from the Book of Daniel as well. Armour 1989: chapter 7 sees Daniel (including the apocryphal Apocalypse) together with John as primary sources of Dante's visionary experience in *Purg.* 29–33. Daniel, it is well known, is also the source of the allegory of the "veglio" of Crete in *Inf.* 14. Gorni 1990: 126–9 links Dante and Daniel through the motif of numerological prophecy (cf. *Par.* 29.133–5, citing Daniel 7:10). See also Mineo 1968: 176–8. Perhaps the earliest Dante critic to stress this parallel (for the *DC*) was Guido da Pisa 1974, Prologus (1): "Scribitur Danielis, quinto capitulo, quod cum Baltassar rex Babillonie sederet ad mensam, apparuit contra eum manus scribens in pariete: Mane, Thechel, Phares. Ista manus est noster novus poeta Dantes, qui scripsit, id est composuit, istam altissimam et subtilissimam Comediam." Hawkins 1999: 20–3 notes Dante's identification with Daniel in *MN* together with other human authors of the Bible (especially Isaiah and Paul, with both of whom Dante links himself in 3.1.3). On Dante and Paul, see also Chapter 7, nn 115, 127. In 3.1.4, Dante refers to God speaking through the mouth of David. For Dante/David parallels, see Chapter 7, section v, especially nn 113, 119, 152. On Dante as "scriba Dei" generally, see Chapter 2, n 88, which also specifically explores an analogy in *Convivio* 4.3.5 between Dante and Solomon (cf. 3.1.2). See also nn 25, 54, 56.

[59] Ascoli 2003: 358–9 discusses Dante's explicit citation of Daniel in *Par.* 4, and the related use made of Nebuchadnezzar by the author of the *ECG*, par. 28. On this connection see the brief remarks of Sarolli 1973b; also Hollander 2005. Cf. Boccassini 2003: 438–9.

embody the figure (dear to Milton as well) of the "one just man" who stands up against persecuting powers, supported by God alone. Shortly thereafter, in a passage cited above, he emphasizes the appropriateness of these words to his own situation:

> Having taken heart from the words of Daniel cited above, in which the divine power is said to be a shield of the defenders of truth, and putting on "the breast plate of faith" as Paul exhorts us . . . I shall enter the present arena. (3.1.3; see also 3.3.11)

Daniel, then, is also the vehicle by which the two principal categories of the *Monarchia*, justice (*iudicium*; *iustitia*) and conflict are transferred from the impersonal realm of world government to the individual figure of Dante Alighieri (cf. E. Gilson 1939: 181).

The parallels do not stop here. Like Daniel, the exiled Hebrew who serves at the pleasure of the Babylonian king, Nebuchadnezzar, Dante is an exile and subject to unpredictable, tyrannical powers; like Daniel he positions himself as privileged interpreter of those who hold power, recognizing that his prophetic critique exposes him to accusations of insubordination and to the threat of extreme violence. Thus, even as Dante in book 3 depicts himself entering into the *litigium* which potentially violates peace, disrupts justice, and banishes reason, he also places himself, ad hoc and implicitly, in the empty seat where imperial judgment belongs,[60] falling back, as he does time and again in his earlier works, on the direct, extrahistorical and potentially miraculous, conferral of authority upon individual persons by God himself.

Making God the ultimate source of all authority effects the absolute depersonalization and dehumanization that Dante implies he requires. Because God supersedes every earthly source of judgment and legitimacy, he may also sponsor the conferral of authority on persons and entities in no other way qualified to possess it. In *Convivio*, the conferral of nobility directly on the individual soul by God personalizes the concept by freeing it from the external constraints of lineage and wealth.[61] In *De Vulgari Eloquentia*, the analogy between the panther, that is, the "vulgare illustre," and God as the "simplicissima substantiarum" confers on the Italian vernacular an authority that its belated modernity and Babelic temporality would deny it. In *Monarchia*, finally, the casually mentioned figure of

---

[60] Cf. *Par.* 27.22–4, where Saint Peter cries out against his usurping successors: ". . . il luogo mio,/il luogo mio, il luogo mio, che vaca/nella presenza del Figliuolo di Dio" (see also Chapter 7, sections v–vi).

[61] Dante's apparent contradiction of this point in *MN* is treated in Chapter 6, section ii.

the *nuntius*, along with the deliberate assimilation of the treatise's author to the prophet-judge Daniel, furnishes the image of a divinely commissioned messenger capable of occupying the otherwise unauthorized, and highly personal, space of the "aporia dantesca" between two separate but equal, and equally impersonal, forms of *auctoritas*. Dante has turned the acquisitions of *Convivio* and *De Vulgari Eloquentia* into a successfully completed fusion of authority and personality that operates from well within the confines of the late medieval discourse of *auctoritas*.

CHAPTER 6

Palinode and history

I. HISTORICIZING THE PALINODE

The preceding chapter placed *Monarchia* within an internal history of Dante's evolving relationship to the "culture of authority," arguing that in its completeness, in the absence of any reference to its author's lack of conventional *auctoritas*, and in its deployment of normative language, formal structures, and analytical procedures, it enters more fully into Scholastic philosophical culture than the works that precede it chronologically. Rather than claiming that the treatise has "solved" the problems facing Dante in his pursuit of authority, however, I identified the strategic negotiations by which the "arguing I" at once elides and confronts the tenuousness of his position within the treatise, including the subtle shift – never fully acknowledged as such – from authorization by natural reason to authorization by divine commission.

This chapter will pursue further the question of the "internal" and "external" historicization of *Monarchia* by testing it against the critical paradigm of the recantatory "palinode" by which – so it is frequently argued – Dante establishes a hierarchical sequence within his own *oeuvre* and creates the impression of having overcome the constraints of personality and world historical circumstances. The aims of this discussion are principally four: (1) to offer a methodological critique of the use of this category for understanding the internal workings of Dante's career; (2) to propose an alternate understanding of Dante's use of the palinode which emphasizes its contingent – historical – character as provisional and incomplete rhetorical strategy; (3) to set up *Monarchia*'s treatment of Dantean authority as an illuminating alternative to the *Commedia* where the palinode is at its most effective in masking the unstable historicity of Dante's project; (4) to prepare the way for a reading of the *Commedia* "beyond the palinode."

Within the economy of Dante's literary self-referentiality, the term "palinode," literally a "singing again" or "recantation," describes a particular form of auto-exegetical revisionism – namely the explicit and/or allusive invocation and transformation of materials from prior Dantean texts within their successors, above all the *Commedia*'s critical evocation of Dante's earlier efforts. From the mid-twentieth century down through the present day, Dante criticism has time and again exposed its author's propensity for repeating, correcting, and even overtly contradicting himself from one work to the next at a number of different levels – of concept, of image, of narrative, of character, and so on.[1] The exemplary sequence leads from *Vita Nova*, with its focus on Dante's love for a human, if virtually inaccessible, woman, Beatrice; through the apparent turn in *Convivio* to an allegorical "donna gentile," who represents Dante's first mournful then joyful recourse to the consolation of philosophy; and on to the return of Beatrice in *Purgatorio* 30, where she is revealed as a *figura Christi* and mediator of Dante's salvation.

However one charts this progression, and the variants are numerous,[2] Dante clearly meant each text to be understood as a sequential advance, of maturation or ascent, on its predecessor(s). This is already the case in the relationship of *Vita Nova* to the previously composed, free-standing poems it surrounds with prose, transforming them from lyric moments similar to those found in Cavalcanti and Guinizzelli, and in the Occitan and "Sicilian" poets before them, into something quite different.[3] By recontextualizing separately written lyrics within the structure of narrative "ragioni" and critical "divisioni" it assigns new meaning to those poems individually, as the example of "A ciascun'alma presa" suggests (Chapter 4, section ii). For that matter, by the episode of the "donna

---

[1] As so often, Contini was there early, speaking of Dante's characteristic "degradare un'esperienza precedente, toglierle la sua finalità intrinsica, usufruirla come elemento dell'esperienza nuova" (1939: 5). For the wider literary history of the palinode, from its classical roots into the Italian and English Renaissances, see Phillippy 1995.

[2] The problem of the slippage from Beatrice 1 (*VN*) to the "donna gentile" or Lady Philosophy of *CV* to Beatrice 2 (*DC*) was the subject of an acrimonious debate between Luigi Pietrobono and Michele Barbi across the first half of the twentieth century. See, e.g., Pietrobono 1938; Barbi 1941. See also J. Shaw 1938; E. Gilson 1939: 86–98; Nardi 1942a: 2–7, 127–31 *et passim*, 1956: 2–14. More recently the question has been reviewed by Corti 1983: especially 146–55; Barolini 1984: 15–23; Fenzi 1986: 47–51; Vasoli 1988a: liii–lx; Trovato 1990a: 239–44, 1994; Carugati 1994; Dronke 1997; O. Holmes 2001; Scott 2004: 113–16. As Stillinger points out, the *VN* episode is rarely read on its own terms (1992: 103–17; see also Harrison 1988: 110–17)

[3] See again Chapter 4, n 11; also the polemical review of the editorial history of *Vita Nova* vis-à-vis the *Rime* in Barolini 2004. Cf. De Robertis 2002: vol. 2, pt. 2.

gentile" (chapters 35–38) and, especially, the promise of a future work to be dedicated to Beatrice (chapter 42), the book seems to anticipate its own later supercession.

More generally speaking, in the Italian context, and even to some extent in our own, speculative theories of chronology[4] and of belated textual revision[5] have been deployed to create a coherent and evolutionary interpretation of Dante's literary career and intellectual biography, usually with the *Commedia* as ideal telos.[6] These discussions, which were characteristically guided by a commitment to the primacy of Dante's thought, then found powerful and appropriate correction in Gianfranco Contini's examination of the evolution of the Dantean career primarily in terms of stylistic, rhetorical, and narratological considerations. Of particular importance is his seminal insistence on Dante's ceaseless linguistic experimentalism and the rhetorical deployment of the first-person voice, culminating in the pilgrim/poet tension that structures the *Commedia* (see again, Chapter 1, section v, especially n 74; Contini 1957).

The dominant American variant of this critical strategy emerged in the early 1970s in part through John Freccero's elegant reading, with its debt both to Contini and to Bloomian theories of literary revisionism, of "Casella's Song" in *Purgatorio* 2 as a poetic recantation of the consolatory Boethian poetics of *Convivio* (Freccero 1973; also Hollander 1975b, 1990).[7]

---

[4] E.g., Bruno Nardi's placement of *MN* in 1308: see Chapter 5, n 2 and section iii of this chapter. Another pertinent example is the debate over the order of composition between *DVE* and *CV* (see Chapter 3, n 8). The controversy over the authenticity of the so-called *ECG* has depended heavily on speculative chronologies, the most complicated example being Kelly 1989. On this latter topic, see also Chapter 1, n 75; n 30 below.

[5] E.g., Pietrobono's claim (1932), backed by Nardi 1942a (but cf. 1962), that Dante retrofitted the ending of *VN* to support his later rejection of *CV*'s philosophical stance. Useful critiques are in Marti 1965; Corti 1983: 146–55; Harrison 1988: 144–51; Stefanini 1991; Gorni 1996: xviii–xxi; cf. Stillinger 1992: 116–17. Pietrobono's conclusions may be largely discredited (but cf. n 7), though the problem he tried to resolve remains.

[6] Barolini 1984: 29 puts it aptly: "Dante's poetic career achieves such absolute retrospective coherence . . . that we are perhaps tempted to endow his earlier poetic shifts with too much teleological coherence." Or, from another angle, see Harrison 1988: ix who describes "the hermeneutic trap of Dantology. The trap is one Dante set himself by embedding within his works the hermeneutic guidelines for interpreting them" (see also his sweeping and cynical but still persuasive account of how Dante critics have troped Dante's critical quest for authority [182–3]).

[7] Scott 1990b (also 1995) offers a detailed critique of the palinodic hypothesis as applied to *Purg.* 2. He follows Foster's insistence on the peaceable coexistence of two very different perspectives within the Dantean *oeuvre* (Foster 1977). Scott denies the presence of the palinode even as a rhetorical strategy, something he is able to do by sticking entirely to philosophical argumentation, rather than attempting to account for the imposing evidence that the *DC* systematically changes and contradicts passages from *CV* and other texts (see n 10), though he does acknowledge this in passing later (2004: 140–1).

The structure of the palinode was congenial to Freccero, since in the domain of literary intertextuality it approximates the psychic and narrative structures of conversion that form the basis of his reading of the *Commedia*. In addition, Freccero's essay has the special virtue of suggesting that palinodic structure is potentially paradigmatic for many, if not all, forms of Dantean intertextuality and literary history. The same essay which shows how "Amor che nella mente mi ragiona" is reinterpreted and recanted as it is re-contextualized, also suggests a revision of important literary-philosophical precursors, notably Boethius, as well as of an earlier portion of the *Commedia, Inferno* 5 (Freccero 1973: especially 188–94). In other words, the pattern of repetition and recantation is fundamental, not only among the various Dantean texts, but also between Dante's texts and the several classical

---

Lino Pertile has also offered a substantial critique of the *CV/DC* palinode (1993). Though denying the existence of some of the "palinodic" references to *CV*, Pertile's principal arguments against *this* revisionary theory are two. First, he calls attention to the limited circulation of the *trattato* (see Chapter 2, n 11), including the absence of any proof that it was disseminated during Dante's lifetime, which he takes to be a result of a decision to withhold the text from public consumption. On this basis he sustains that a palinodic strategy makes no sense if one cannot presume one's readers are aware of the target precursor. Second, he insists that since Dante–pilgrim's journey takes place prior to the composition of *CV* (i.e., in 1300), the recitations of "Amor che nella mente" and "Voi che intendendo," often read as palinodic of *CV*, must refer to the life of the *canzoni* prior to their incorporation in the prosimetrum. The latter argument seems particularly weak. For one thing, the skepticism concerning readerly knowledge of *CV* that drives his first objection, could easily be applied to the assumption of a hypothetical reader's detailed chronological knowledge of Dante's lyric canon. More to the point, the person writing the "poema sacro" *does* know *CV*, having written it, and I am not convinced that the motive of realistic consistency is always primary in writing the *DC* (*pace* Auerbach; cf. Kleiner 1994). The first objection, however, is more substantial, though still arguable. To begin with, the number and consistency of reversals between the two texts is such that an explanation of some kind is required, particularly given Dante's consistent recourse to palinodic strategies throughout his career. My next objection is a variant of the one Pertile attributes to Hollander, i.e., that Dante is his own first and best reader. For me, this point is strongly reinforced by Dante's use of self-commentary to build authority (Chapter 4). But, Pertile might well reply: authority with or over whom, if *CV* is not a public text? Here my answer would diverge from Hollander's (must, in fact, because as Pertile 1996 points out Hollander has not addressed this point): Dante's "quest for authority" is in part outwardly directed toward readers, but in part toward what we might now call "the super-ego" or "doxa" or "cultural discourse" or "ideology," that is, toward a set of internalized cultural norms which present themselves as obstacles to Dante's ambitions (which also derive from cultural norms and tendencies). Finally, it must be noted that Pertile is not against the thesis of Dantean revisionism at all – rather, he is a revisionist of revisionism, since his alternative to the palinode directed against *CV* is an argument that the discourse on poetry in *Purg.* is systematically critical of the failed "stil nuovo" poetics of *VN* (and this positive argument is comparatively persuasive). So far from being a revisionist is he that he embraces the highly tendentious Pietrobono-Nardi thesis concerning the "finale" of *VN* (75 n 26; cf. n 5 above), for which there is just as much hard evidence as there is for the public circulation of *CV* during Dante's lifetime, i.e., none. See also Barański 1995: 17–20 for a plausible extension of Pertile's thesis, as well as the later exchange of Hollander (1996) and Pertile (1996).

and medieval *auctores* he imitates and cites,[8] as well as within individual texts.[9]

On the latter point, again, *Vita Nova* anticipates what is to come. By ordering the poems chronologically, it creates the impression that the modes of love represented successively through the "libro della memoria" are constantly revising and superseding earlier lyric experiences (n 3; Chapter 4, n 11). To elaborate: the *libello*'s individual lyrics and discrete episodes are organized, *Symposium*-like, as an upwardly hierarchical series (1) of objects of desire, real and feigned (the "donna-schermo," the "donna gentile" and Beatrice herself) and (2) of types of desire for Beatrice (love dependent on the "salute," love independent of the "salute," love independent of her living person). The revisionary relationships of chapters 24 and 25 to chapter 3, and of chapter 42 to the work as a whole have already been considered in another context (see Chapter 4, sections ii and iv, respectively), and they are illustrative here as well. The case of *Vita Nova* thus blurs any sharp distinction between "external" palinode – recantation of an earlier work – and "internal" palinode – recantation of an earlier part of the same work – in Dante's *oeuvre*. The importance of this point will appear in short order.

The basic argument of most recent intertextual work on the palinode and on precursor poets is as follows: Dante evokes his own earlier texts or those of others in a variety of ways (verbal or conceptual echo, generic modeling, narrative episode, dramatic representation), only to define a limit to their value as models, usually in the form of a critique of the doctrinal substance conveyed by their literary practice.[10] In this account, Dante again and

---

[8] The most comprehensive study of Dante's treatment of precursor and contemporary poets, including himself, in the *DC*, is Barolini 1984. For near-contemporary vernacular poets, see Contini's seminal essays (1957, 1965b), as well as Boyde 1971; Barolini 1984; Mazzotta 1979: especially 192–226; also Giunta 1998; Steinberg 1999, 2007; Gorni: 2001. For Dante's treatment of Arnaut Daniel see, e.g., Menocal 1991, Martinez 1991. For Guittone d'Arezzo see Chapter 4, nn 11, 17, 46. For Cavalcanti, see Jacoff 1977; Corti 1983: 3–37; Harrison 1988: especially 69–90; Fenzi 1999b; Antonelli 2001; Durling 2003; Ardizzone 2003 among many others (see Chapter 4, especially nn 35, 39, 40, 44, 47; Chapter 5, n 27). For Cino da Pistoia see Chapter 2, section vi and nn 89, 90. For the classical poets generally see Barolini 1984; the survey of Brownlee 1993; the essays collected in Iannucci 1993a. For Ovid, see Chapter 1, n 27. For Virgil: Chapter 1, section ii and n 17; Chapter 5, n 5; Chapter 7, section ii. For Statius see Martinez 1977, 1989, 1995a, 1997; Wetherbee 1984, 1988; Scott 2004: 251–4; Martelli 2004: 155–181; as well as Chapter 7, section ii and nn 11, 22, 31, 34–36. It is arguable both that Guittone d'Arezzo previewed the use of palinodic structure and that Dante's practice derives in part from his (Antonelli 1995; Picone 1995b; Borra 2000; O. Holmes 2000: chapter 3, especially 68–9). The desire to obscure such a debt might account for Dante's virulent attacks on Guittone in *DVE* 1.13.1, 2.6.8; *Purg.* 24.55–7, 26.121–6.

[9] Singleton 1965b; Hollander 1969. See also Iannucci 1981; Shoaf 1983: 21–100; Fido 1986, 1989; and Chapter 7, especially sections iii, v.

[10] On the palinodic echoing of *CV* in the *DC*, in addition to Freccero 1973 and Hollander 1975b, 1990, 1996, see Pietrobono 1938; Mazzeo 1960: 180–2; Nardi 1965a: 75–9; Ransom 1977; Barolini 1984:

again leads his readers to the same conclusion – namely, that the union of Christian theology and poetic representation sets his *Commedia* apart from practically everything else that has ever been written, with the unique – and even then at times not absolute – exception of the Bible itself.[11]

Furthermore, Dante's inscriptions of literary history can also be characterized as typological, that is, as conforming to the pattern of salvation history as defined in the Bible, where the Christ event becomes the vehicle for a complete reinterpretation of the significance of the Hebrew Bible as the Old Testament.[12] For that matter, one could argue that Auerbach's notion of *figura*, that is the clarifying – at times recantatory – recontextualization of historical events in the eschatological frame of the *Commedia*, is another way of describing this phenomenon.[13] An example of the convergence of literary palinode with historical *figura* is the case of Guido da Montefeltro – whose belated conversion is initially celebrated in *Convivio* (4.28.8), but then subverted in *Inferno* 27, where his ultimate damnation is revealed. Guido's sorry tale at once corrects an "error" in the earlier text and sets the historical record straight from the infallible perspective of eternity. As will be seen, the treatment of Emperor Frederick II and his family operates in a similar way. In other words, this structure is a means for re-presenting a series of teleologically shaped histories: Dante's internal creative biography, the literary history of his relations with other poets, as well as the political-social history of his time.[14] By deploying the palinode in tandem with his representations of "the state of souls after death" (*ECG* 8.24) and of his own journey through the Other World, Dante confers upon the great poem a typological and eschatological perspective, *as if* at the end of literary history, fulfilling and transcending those who have written before, including his own earlier incarnations.[15]

24–40, 57–84; Jacoff 1988; Fido 1989; also Chapter 1, section ii; Chapter 2, especially nn 10, 76, and 86. On the palinode of the "rime petrose," see Freccero 1972; Sturm-Maddox 1987; cf. n 14. For *DVE*, see Chapter 3, n 59; Chapter 7, section v.

[11] For Dante's intertextual relationship with the Bible, especially in the *DC*, see Moore 1896: 47–91; Battaglia Ricci 1983: especially 197–228, 1988; Barblan 1988; Kleinhenz 1986, 1990, 1997; Barański 1987, 1989a; Benfell 1995, 1997; Hawkins 1999; Scott 2004: 299–305; *et al.* See also Chapter 7, section v.

[12] See Mazzeo 1960: 175–80; Hollander 1969 (24–6 *et passim*); Mazzotta (1979: chapter 5). On typology in general, see De Lubac 1959–65. On Dante's relation to the typological tradition in broader terms see Auerbach 1944; Chydenius 1958; Charity 1966. Cf. Freccero 1993; Martinez 2000. See also Chapter 1, n 69; Chapter 4, section ii and n 40.

[13] Auerbach 1944, 1945. See also Chapter 1, section v.

[14] Barolini 1984 puts it succinctly: "All texts end with the *DC*, but none come out of it . . ." (285–6).

[15] This is to extend Auerbach's concept of the *DC*'s figural relationship to history, as well as Freccero's understanding of the narrative perspective of the *DC*: "The view from paradise is a spatial translation of what may be called a memory of universal history. The coherence of the poem may be grasped

Re-examining the Dantean palinode, then, means reconsidering both the rhetorical organization of Dante's texts and their character as both products and interpretations of history. Chapter 1 argued that by focusing on how history appears, in its particular contingencies and as a conceptual domain, within the economy of Dante's representations, Dante criticism has typically set aside the question of how an unfolding set of historical events and circumstances made Dante and his representations possible in the first place – how history implies, subsumes, and, as it were, transcends the Dantean *oeuvre*, just as much as the other way around. The aim here, however, is not so much to deny the existence of the palinode, as some critics have,[16] but rather to see it for what it is: a powerful rhetorical device, rather than an accurate record of Dante's intellectual–spiritual biography. It can then become a tool to historicize Dante's literary career, particularly its evolving relationship to traditional modes of authorship and authority. Understanding the palinode as rhetorical strategy means becoming aware that before one can identify the "historicity" of Dante's texts, one must recognize how elaborately those texts seek to conceal their subjection to history by apotropaic representations of it.

Indeed, what makes the question of the historicity of Dante and his texts so difficult to approach – over and above the intrinsic complexity of charting the lines of force from world to text and back again – is that the palinode is a rhetorical device – a figure of thought – designed specifically to anticipate and preclude this very question. Dante offers a comprehensive narrative spanning the length of the poem, whose continuities are signaled not only by the recurrence of common elements, but also, and just as importantly, by meaningful alterations in those elements and the relationship between them. Thus, unruly differences and contingencies of self and of history are at once acknowledged and contained by their placement within a hierarchical narrative order, where what comes above and last subsumes and interprets what comes below and before.

---

with a view to its totality, a view from the ending, just as the coherence of the poet's life could be grasped only in retrospect, from the perspective of totality in death. Clearly the same may be said of universal history, whose coherence may be perceived only from the perspective of eschatology . . ." (1966: 26). Cf. Mazzotta 1979: "The palinode constitutes the temporal ground which sustains the possibility of dramatizing history's renewal" (17). See also Chapter 1, section v.

16 E.g., Scott 1990b; see n 7. Durling and Martinez 1990, who stress throughout the importance of the *rime petrose* in the development of the "microcosmic poetics" of the *DC*, make the important point that by reading the minor works, in particular the *rime petrose*, exclusively through the filter of a presumed palinode in the *DC*, and not on "their own terms," significant interpretive opportunities are lost and a reductive image of Dante's development is reinforced (especially 2–6).

Against the fictive power of the palinode stands the factual power of historical event. One might indeed expect that the palinode would find its limits under extreme forms of historical pressure. The obvious example is the intervention of death – a death so sudden or disruptive that no room for the writing of a *retractio* remains. In Italian literary history, useful examples appear in the later cases of Poliziano's *Stanze* and Boiardo's *Orlando Innamorato*, one left unfinished after the assassination of its Medicean protagonist and patron, the other after the author's own demise. It is just such a death that Dante mimes and tropes, and apotropaically overcomes, as he looks back with palinodic perspective on his earlier works. Arguably, the motive engine for Dante's powerful recourse to the palinode in *Vita Nova* was the death of Beatrice (cf. Harrison 1988). It may not be too much to speculate that the untimely death of his sometime "primo amico," Guido Cavalcanti, gave him further impetus to seek the palinodic perspective par excellence, one coincident with "the state of souls after death," that is, the omniscient perspective of divine justice beyond individual lives and beyond history itself. Nonetheless one would still have to acknowledge Dante's luck in surviving long enough to close the *poema sacro* whose visionary and revisionary power depends to no little extent on its seamless totality.[17]

Death is not the only way in which history makes itself felt or resists authorial attempts to bring it under control by giving it a definite shape. Nonetheless, it would have taken something or someone quite extraordinary to resist incorporation and appropriation within the providentially poetic order of the *Commedia*; something, or someone, that was crucial in the most basic way to Dante's historical experience and to his project for interpreting it; something, or someone, that could neither be reduced to the mere effluvia of contingency nor exalted to a work of divine grace. Such elements, I submit, can be found in *Monarchia*, the one major treatise Dante actually completed, and which also constitutes, with a few of the epistles, his most direct literary attempt to influence the course of contemporary political history. Such elements may also be found in the person of a crucial historical figure, the Emperor Frederick II, whose powerful hold on Dante's poetic and political imagination is revealed by his recurrent appearances in the major post-exilic works.

---

[17] Boccaccio plays on this possibility in the story of Jacopo di Dante finding the last thirteen cantos of the *Par.* after his father's death, led to them by a dream vision (Boccaccio 1974: 484–6 [1st redaction; par. 183–9], 527–8 [2nd redaction; par. 121–7]).

II. PALINODE *MANQUÉ* IN *MONARCHIA*

In contextualizing and thus historicizing the Dantean palinode, two important points should be considered, both of which can be usefully illustrated by recourse to *Monarchia*. In the first place, the pattern of allusion and repetition-in-difference in Dante's *oeuvre* is not limited to the *Commedia* vis-à-vis the other texts: more and less explicit echoes also connect certain from among the so-called *opere minori* to others. Secondly, the palinode is only one of several forms of auto-exegesis deployed by Dante throughout his *oeuvre*, and, as seen in previous chapters, is by no means the only mode of problematic self-citation to be found there. In other words, once one moves beyond the encompassing shadow of the *Commedia*, it becomes more difficult to establish the hierarchical narrative and conceptual order that characterizes the *sacrato poema*'s definition of its relationship to the treatises. At the same time, it becomes correspondingly easier to interrogate the privilege that it usually enjoys in such discussions.

Seen in this light, even the passage from *Vita Nova* to *Convivio*, fundamental to most accounts of the palinode, becomes much harder to pin down. That *Convivio*'s love story is defined in relation to *Vita Nova*'s is obvious, particularly through the dramatization of a struggle between two different thoughts of love (2.2.1–5 *et passim*). However, Dante is careful to avoid stating that love of Lady Philosophy has actually displaced that of Beatrice who, he says, continues to dwell in his soul (*CV* 2.2.1; cf. 2.8.8). Moreover, as has often been noted, the stories told in the two works about the "donna gentile" are not easily reconciled with one another, and especially not with the hierarchical narrative chronology that a true palinode would establish. That the "donna gentile" is rejected in *Vita Nova* in favor of a return to Beatrice seems simply to contradict the allegorical reading of *Convivio* and is only recuperable into a palinodic narrative if it is taken as a prophetic, a-chronistic prolepsis of the *Commedia*'s supercession of the later treatise!

Finally, Dante gives an account of the *trapasso* from *Vita Nova* to *Convivio* as mapping the passage from one stage of life to another, from youth to maturity, which, although not entirely incompatible with the palinode, suggests a model of continuous "evolution" of the human subject over time, rather than a radical "conversion" from an old to a new self.[18] In other words, *Convivio*'s return to *Vita Nova* suggests palinodic rejection of erotic

---

[18] As observed in Chapter 2, n 13, this model is sufficiently important to Dante that he elaborates an allegorical version of it in book 4, normalizing it as a pattern for all humanity.

desire in favor of love of wisdom, yet works simultaneously to minimize and qualify the differences between them, leaving a substantial uncertainty and ambivalence that foregrounds the "subjective," historical, and rhetorical character of Dante's self-reflection. Hence, the prevalent interpretation of the relationship between the two works in palinodic terms is determined largely by the invocation of the "terminal" perspective of the *Commedia*, which apparently rejects *Convivio* as it turns back to Beatrice, and fulfills the promise of *Vita Nova*, chapter 42.[19]

This example also implicitly suggests how palinodic readings fetishize the rejected precursor text by assigning to it a single unequivocal meaning which is belied by its internal self-differences. An obvious instance is the typical failure of those who read *Convivio* from the palinodic perspective of the *Commedia* to note the several points at which Dante subordinates philosophical wisdom to divine truth.[20] As already suggested, in *Vita Nova*, as in each of the other three *opere minori* studied closely, there is a dynamic evolution, whereby the point of arrival contradicts and/or supersedes the point of departure. In other words, the operation of an "intra-textual" palinode, which involves the structured multiplication of perspectives within a given text, paradoxically qualifies the operation of the intertextual palinode, which reduces the prior text to a "moment" of reified meaning.

To this point I have argued that while the strategy of palinodic revisionism informs texts other than the *Commedia*, it does so in ways that considerably complicate our understanding of how Dante works. In other cases, however, apparent contradictions are present that cannot easily be resolved into a palinodic chronology and hierarchy, to the extent that any attempt to see the device at work at all seems captious. An obvious example, explored in Chapter 3, is the apparent disagreement between *Convivio* and *De Vulgari Eloquentia* over the relative nobility of grammar (i.e., Latin) and *volgare* (i.e., Italian), with the accompanying difference in language used by the treatises themselves. As noted, this *divario* reflects a split within Dante's project, as he then understood it, between the use of Latin, and authoritative Latin culture, as a model – even as a goal, – and the valorization of the vernacular as a vehicle of culture in its own right. More to the immediate point, the shift in attribution of "nobilità"/"nobilitas" from one language to the other is actually accompanied by a situationally determined shift in

---

[19] In the *DC* what appears in *CV* itself as ambivalence is reinterpreted as, instead, having been a flat rejection of the experience of *VN* and of Beatrice, which is now recuperated. The key passages are *Purg.* 30.115–41 and 33.85–90. See n 7 on the complications introduced into this schematic by Pertile 1993 and Barański 1995.

[20] As seen in Chapter 2, n 86, *CV* tends to qualify and question its own philosophical humanism.

what *nobility* is understood to be (cf. Chapter 3, section v, especially n 56), without any hierarchical order being established between them, and thus without any implication of recantation. In other words, *either* Dante adopts different and even opposed positions according to the contingent needs of a given argument (i.e., he is shamelessly rhetorical in his deployment of concepts), *or* his notion of dialectic allows for the determination of truth value according to specific context, following the Abelardian "sic et non," or both (cf. Chapter 5, n 27).

Another interesting instance of this latter phenomenon, at least from the point of view of this study, is the pattern of connections that link *Convivio*, book 4, to *Monarchia* (Chapter 5, especially section i and n 3). On the one hand, *Monarchia* picks up and develops several of Dante's claims about the Roman Empire in *Convivio* 4.3–5, including the necessity of a single, universal monarchy; the supreme role of the Emperor as guide of human will and as ultimate judge over human actions; the directly mandated assignment of Empire to the Roman people, and the privileged place of Rome in salvation history. Moreover, the evidence adduced concerning the providential nature of Roman history in *Monarchia* 2 reflects the same close reading of Virgil's *Aeneid* as the latter part of *Convivio* 4 and as the *Commedia* itself (Leo 1951; see again Chapter 5, n 6). On the other hand, at many points, including in its very first chapter, *Monarchia* can be read as "palinodically" assuming an overt philosophical authority for Dante that he had avoided attributing to himself in the earlier work (Chapter 5, section i, and n 12). In addition, *Monarchia* affirms imperial authority while *Convivio* is primarily concerned with delimiting it, while the later treatise's claims for Rome's place in salvation history are more audacious than those of the earlier work (Chapter 5, nn 3, 17, 41). *Monarchia*, then, at once evolves from and goes beyond *Convivio*, in a way that might read as a "typological" fulfillment, if not as including the radical type of break that characterizes a palinodic "conversion."

A more complex form of intertextual resemblance-in-difference between the two treatises also exists, involving one fundamental element of *Monarchia* that is entirely absent from *Convivio*, namely consideration of the relation between Empire and Church and the systematic liberation of imperial authority from direct subordination to the papacy. This change, in turn, seemingly entails the disappearance of the Philosopher, if not of philosophy, as the indispensable supplement to the Emperor's rule (Chapter 5, n 17). While *Monarchia* departs "thematically" from *Convivio* here, however, it is simultaneously reusing the latter's basic conceptual and argumentative strategy. Again, just as the Emperor and Philosopher are assigned specific and delimited areas of authoritative competence in *Convivio* (4.6.17–20), so in *Monarchia*, Emperor and Pope are set in complementary and inter-dependent relationship with each other (3.15.15).

Chapters 2 and 5 argued that this strategy – which Etienne Gilson called the "aporia dantesca" – for defining but also circumscribing absolute author-ity allows Dante in both *Convivio* and *Monarchia* to create a conceptual and rhetorical space for his own *auctoritas* to emerge. Now, instead, I want to emphasize how the transfer or displacement of a complex of concepts regarding imperial authority and an argumentative strategy concerning the separation and interdependence of institutional authorities works to create not only a continuity, but also a notable shift between the two treatises – one which cannot be adequately grasped in terms of the palinode. One might at first assume that by substituting the Pope for the Philosopher as the intellectual/spiritual Other of the Emperor, Dante has replaced reason with faith as the most important mode of human vision, thus following the typical pattern of palinodic recantation as deployed in the *Commedia*. Yet *Monarchia* does *not* do this, at least not overtly. The function of the Empire in both treatises is to fulfill the terrestrial *bonum* of rationality and justice (1.11 and 3.15; cf. Trovato 1988, 1990 a and b). Moreover, notwith-standing the treatise's increasing recognition of the obstacles, internal and external, to reason's understanding, and its hints concerning the possibility that Dante enjoys prophetic inspiration, *Monarchia* never explicitly surren-ders the perspective of rationality. Finally, and most obviously, the principal function of the argument concerning the separate but equal relationship of Pope and Emperor in book 3 is to limit rather than affirm papal authority, and so the spiritual domain is specifically *not* given absolute privilege over that of reason.

The disappearance, or, better, the sublimation, of the figure of the Philosopher between *Convivio* and *Monarchia* thus requires a different and non-palinodic explanation: namely, as suggested at the end of Chapter 5, that the Philosopher would be an obvious *terzo incomodo* in this context. Since the Emperor's judicial authority in the domain of natural reason is necessarily unitary and undivided, the re-assertion of the philosopher's intellectual authority as a necessary complement to it would compromise and vitiate it by dividing what is by definition indivisible, as well as intro-ducing an unbalancing asymmetry in the neat duality of book 3. The suspi-cion, then, is that this echoing of *Convivio* in *Monarchia* is not a deliberate revisionary evocation of an earlier text by a later one. Rather, it rehearses a conceptual and rhetorical strategy which had served Dante's turn in the past – one that unveils not the transcending emergence of new and stable meaning, but instead an essential rhetoricity subtending and potentially evacuating meaning. This is not to discount the seriousness of the politics articulated in *Monarchia* – I would argue that the very importance Dante attaches to them drives him to deploy an intrinsically flawed line of argument.

Support for this hypothesis comes at one key point where *Monarchia* flatly contradicts *Convivio*, on a topic that constitutes the very substance of book 4 of the earlier treatise, and that is also closely related to the issue that divides *Convivio* and *De Vulgari Eloquentia*. As seen in Chapter 2, *Convivio* systematically asserts that nobility is individual and divinely infused, not genealogical, racial, social, and/or economic in origin, attributing the opposing position to Frederick and his vulgar followers (4.canzone.21–40; 3.5–10). However, as also observed there, the opinion attributed to Frederick in *Convivio* can best be located in Aristotle's *Politics* (4.8.1294a.20–21), rather than in any of the Emperor's surviving writings. In *Monarchia*, by contrast, Dante adduces *as his own* the Aristotelian definition of nobility, now attributing it to its proper source: "est enim nobilitas virtus et divitie antique, iuxta Phylosophum in *Politicis*" (nobility is virtue and ancient wealth, as Aristotle says in the *Politics* [2.3.3–4]).

Discounting again the unpersuasive scholarly claims that Dante had not yet read the Aristotelian treatise when he wrote *Convivio* (Chapter 2, nn 56 and 58), this reference at the least exposes a disingenuous and strategically motivated line of argument in the earlier work. It does not, however, then place *Monarchia* in a position of palinodic superiority, since, as *Convivio* does reveal, the imperial/Aristotelian definition of nobility is at odds with the Christian notions of free will and of the autonomous value of the individual soul. Instead, I conjecture, the open use of the Aristotelian definition in *Monarchia* is dictated by a shift of conceptual domains and is equally strategic in nature.[21] In the domain of (Christian) ethics, which

---

[21] Scott sees "no change of heart" on the subject of nobility between *CV* and *MN* (2004: 152), while Cassell 2004 (67–9, 305 nn 123–125) does. The rhetorical situation is actually rather complex. Dante offers two definitions of individual nobility in the passage, with further subdivisions: "Quod quidem primo sic probatur: nobilissimo populo convenit omnibus aliis preferri; romanus populus fuit nobilissimus; ergo convenit ei omnibus aliis preferri. Assumpta ratione probatur: nam, cum honor sit premium virtutis et omnis prelatio sit honor, omnis prelatio virtutis est premium. Sed constat quod merito virtutis nobilitantur homines, virtutis videlicet proprie vel maiorum. Est enim nobilitas virtus et divitie antique, iuxta Phylosophum in *Politicis*; et iuxta Iuvenalem: 'nobilitas animi sola est atque unica virtus.' Que due sententie ad dua nobilitates dantur: propriam scilicet et maiorum. Ergo nobilibus ratione cause premium prelationis conveniens est." Dante here puts into play both definitions of nobility, his and "Frederick's," and tries to have it both ways. The need to include antiquity is obviously related to the fact that he is applying definitions of individual nobility to a collective and transhistorical corporate entity – and the connection of nobility to virtue seems forced when it is moved from the individual into the collective domain, just as the application of the category of the "duel" to a people does.

is the domain of *Convivio*, nobility must be individual. In the domain of politics, especially imperial politics, the need for institutional continuity – within the Roman people, and from one Emperor to the next – requires a social and transpersonal concept of nobility consonant with the doctrine of the "king's two bodies" that subtends much of *Monarchia*'s argumentation. For this reason, Dante adopts such a concept without hesitation, despite having demonstrated his awareness of the problems it presents from another perspective.

In short, the contradictions between *Convivio* and *Monarchia* do not become the basis of a hierarchically articulated palinode or establish Dante's transcendent authority over his material. Rather the parallel passages in the two texts are mutually subversive, in the limited sense that their juxtaposition reveals how *both* treatises have deliberately suppressed relevant conceptual steps for strategic (i.e., contingent rhetorical and historical), reasons. The relation between the treatises is thus based at least as much on convenient forgetfulness as it is on a confessional and recantatory remembering, and it points obliquely to the contingency and interestedness of the author's construction of his own intellectual history.

This idea finds further confirmation in looking at the single greatest change in the material concerning Empire that is passed on from *Convivio* to *Monarchia* – an alteration not by addition or revision, but rather by suppression, and thus infrequently remarked upon. In *Convivio*, the discourses concerning imperial authority and the role of the Roman *imperium*, as well as that regarding nobility, are inextricably linked to a dominant historical figure, Frederick II of Swabia. Frederick is designated by Dante as the "last emperor of the Romans" (4.3) since none of his German-born successors had been properly installed in office to that date. Nor had they made what Dante felt was the obligatory effort to take up their proper place in the center of Empire, Italy, as Frederick, virtually alone among the holy Roman emperors, had done.[22] *Monarchia*, however, is the only one of Dante's four major post-exilic writings in which there is no reference to Frederick, although the material linked to his name in *Convivio* is largely conserved, and although it is the one work where one would most expect to find him, given its exclusive focus on imperial politics.[23]

---

[22] For the historical Frederick, see again Chapter 2, n 55. See also the discussions of Dante's treatment of Frederick in *CV* and *DVE* in Chapters 2–3.

[23] Vallone 1965: 364–6 sees allusions to the writings of Frederick and especially Manfredi in *MN*. See also Imbach 1996: 97–128 *et passim* and Boccassini 2003, both of whom stress the importance of the Frederican precedent for Dante's assumption of the role of lay-philosopher in *CV* and *MN*.

In an important consideration of this key figure, Roger Dragonetti has argued that Dante's treatment of Frederick embodies the power of poetry to absorb and transform the raw materials of history through its representations (Dragonetti 1989). It would be folly to deny this point, which is applicable to materials concerning Frederick as they appear in *Convivio, De Vulgari Eloquentia*, and the *Commedia*. That Dante uses Frederick as a stalking horse for Aristotle in *Convivio* gives additional support to Dragonetti's thesis. However, I will now argue that the reverse is *also* true: that Frederick can be used as a means of understanding how history intrudes upon Dante, disrupting the narrative schemes by which he seeks to impose order on temporal contingency.

From either perspective, it is clear that at least from 1301 onwards, Frederick played a decisive role in Dante's historical imagination – in his politics, his linguistics and attendant poetics, and, above all, at the point of potential intersection between them, the place where power, knowledge, and imagination might meet and collaborate, offering Dante a point of insertion back into the ethical and political life from which his exile had excluded him. In *Convivio*, as just seen, Frederick's crucial place in any even minimally historicized understanding of the institution of Empire and the political circumstances of Italy in the thirteenth and early fourteenth centuries is plainly acknowledged. At the same time, Dante implicitly stages himself, via his poetry and commentary, as the philosopher who stands as necessary complement to the Emperor, embodied by Frederick.

De Vulgari Eloquentia makes the point even more plainly. Dante's account of the development of the illustrious Italian vernacular places its origins at the court of Frederick, as both a patron and a poet in his own right (1.12.1–4). Dante himself figures as the consummate and climactic voice of the *vulgare illustre*, the lineal descendant of the *scuola siciliana*. His later definition of the *vulgare illustre* as the language which could be spoken and written in the central royal court of Italy looks back to Frederick's court as an empirical model for what once was and perhaps will be again (1.18.2–5). Here he posits a complementary relationship between the poet guided by the "gratioso lumine rationis" (1.18.5) and his powerful patron.

Nor is the value Dante attributes to Frederick in *Convivio* and *De Vulgari Eloquentia* exclusively historical and political – he also confers on the emperor an ethical worth equivalent to his historical importance: Frederick and his son Manfred are praised to the skies in *De Vulgari Eloquentia*:

illustres heroes, Fredericus Cesar et benegenitus eius Manfredus, *nobilitatem* ac *rectitudinem* sue forme pandentes donec fortuna permisit humana secuti sunt, brutalia dedignantes. (1.12.4)

(those *illustrious* heroes, Frederick Caesar and his worthy [well-born] son, Manfred, knew how to reveal the *nobility and [rectitude]* that were in their hearts; and, as long as Fortune allowed, they [behaved with humanity], despising the bestial life.)

It is particularly noteworthy that Dante here assigns Frederick the three attributes which are most fundamental and laudable in the language of *Convivio* and *De Vulgari Eloquentia*: illustriousness, nobility, rectitude.[24] Nonetheless, there are egregious problems implicit in linking Dante's imperial and poetic hopes to the "last emperor." Even in the quoted passage, the qualifier "donec fortuna permisit," which allows for an eventual descent from humanity into bestiality, foreshadows the contingencies which remove Frederick from any possible idealization.

As Dragonetti observes, these problems emerge full-blown, and in a figural-palinodic mode, in the *Commedia*, beginning with Frederick's damnation as a faithless epicurean in *Inferno* 10, a canto which calls sharp attention to the Guelf/Ghibelline, Church/Empire conflicts that had originated around Frederick and that still ravaged Italy during Dante's youth. The process continues with the episode of Pier delle Vigne, the emperor's unfortunate chancellor, as well as a noted prose stylist and poet of the Sicilian school. There Frederick appears, at least in Pier's highly interested account, as a capricious and violent ruler whose whims jeopardize the fortunes and the lives of his faithful counselors (cf. Stephany 1982). Through a number of carefully structured parallels between Pier's circumstances and Dante's own, *Inferno* 13 deliberately jeopardizes his convivial fantasy of the poet-philosopher's symbiotic relationship with an imperial master, along with any remaining hopes of implementing a rationally grounded political program in history (see again Chapter 2, nn 41 and 43). This palinodic structure is further articulated in a series of increasingly displaced allusions to Frederick via his family members – notably Manfred, his son, in *Purgatorio* 3, and Constance, his mother, in *Paradiso* 3. In *Purgatorio* 24, as is well known, Dante establishes a fundamental rupture between his own *dolce stil nuovo* and the poetics of *Il Notaio* and the Sicilian lyricists of Frederick's court.[25]

---

[24] For "rectitudo," see *DVE* 2.2.8; for "illustres," see 1.15.7; 1.16.6; 1.17.1–7; for "nobilitas," see 1.1.4–5; 1.3.3; as well as *CV* throughout, especially book 4.
[25] See also Chapter 7, section ii, and nn 26–28, 84, 116, 122, 147.

While the *Commedia* apotropaically as well as palinodically invokes Frederick only to dismiss him, *Monarchia* is a different story. There, as already noted, no palinode is deployed – Frederick is simply excluded. But why make so much of an absence, given the notorious difficulty of arguments, as it were, ex nihilo and in absentia? Because, as suggested earlier, so much of the material elaborated in *Monarchia* first appeared in *Convivio*, tightly linked to Frederick II. Because, as Dante says in *Convivio* (4.3.6), historically Frederick was either the last or, more likely, the penultimate occupant of the office he is discussing in *Monarchia*,[26] and this is a work whose evident goal is to reinstate Empire and Emperor at the center of the historical world. Because, finally, Frederick's open warfare with a series of Popes is the most pressing historical evidence – along with Boniface's and Clement's various escapades – of the need to find a solution to the problem of imperial vs. ecclesiastical claims to power.

This last item also tells us *why* such an exclusion might have seemed especially necessary to Dante, over and above the generalized tendency to idealize and abstract the Empire discussed in Chapter 5: Frederick's historical existence, his empirical occupancy of the imperial throne, constitutes a virtual point-by-point refutation of Dante's definition of the Emperor's role in *Monarchia*. Rather than bringing unity, Frederick created divisions; rather than reconciling reason with faith, he was a reputed unbeliever and heretic; rather than submitting, with filial piety, to the spiritual authority of the Church, he contested it fiercely; and so on. His name by itself would be a reminder of the disruptions in the imperial line that severed the institution not only from its Roman origins, but even from the recent medieval past. The strain of recuperating the apparent violence and illegitimacy of the original Roman Empire is, as argued in the previous chapter, evident in the convoluted attempts of book 2 to show that Roman world domination is legal and even divinely sponsored. Frederick's presence in *Monarchia* would intensify the problem: he is too near in time; he is too obviously at odds with the rationalized fantasy of a *connubio* between Church and State. In other words, he is too messily "historical" to be confronted within the boundaries of the treatise.

---

[26] Of course, Henry VII is also excluded. The reasons for focusing on Frederick are that *CV* 4.3–6, where key ideas that will inform *MN* first appear centers on him and that his legacy thoroughly dominated Dante's political experience and imagination well into the first decade of the fourteenth century. One sign of Frederick's continuing hold on Dante's imagination comes in *Purg.* 16.117 (cf. Chapter 7, n 42). In another sense, Frederick is merely symptomatic of a range of compromising historical material excluded from the ideal vision of Empire in *MN*, including Henry's failure to live up to expectations. An analogous reading of the relationship of *Eps.* 5–7 to *MN* might also be possible.

It may well have been obvious from the outset why Frederick was excluded from *Monarchia*, and, for that matter, why Boniface, Clement and Henry VII are not mentioned either.[27] What I suspect was not obvious to start with, and what should be clearer now, is the relevance of this exclusion to an understanding of the palinode as a rhetorical-conceptual device for the textual inscription of history. Because the telos of the treatise is the transformation of the historical scene, Dante is simultaneously asserting the priority of the secular world and suppressing significant features of it. A palinode would not work in this text because the prior contingent elements that would otherwise be offered only to be retracted cannot be allowed to appear for even the fleeting moment necessary to recant them, cannot (*pace* Dragonetti) be fully textualized. These elements cannot be subjected to palinodic reversal because they are, at base, neither an unmitigated fiction nor a pure concept of Dante's – instead they are *history* – or rather they are the historical significance of Frederick as it has pressed itself upon Dante and expressed itself in his writings.

Not that I would or could claim, simply inverting Dragonetti, that history, in the person of Frederick II, makes itself felt in an unmediated and/or irresistible way. No doubt Dante could, like anyone else, ignore inconvenient historical facts, especially those a generation or two in the past, at his discretion. This case is based on two related points: (1) Dante's thought about language and politics in his post-exilic experience was shaped in relation to the historical figure of Frederick, in a way that points directly to *Monarchia* and makes his absence from it striking; (2) Dante usually prefers, both in the *Commedia* and elsewhere, to dominate and transform historical materials through his representations, if this is possible at all. Frederick is missing, in other words, because he is at the origin of Dante's political discourse and yet cannot be incorporated and recuperated within that discourse, at least not in *Monarchia*.

III. BEYOND THE PALINODE: BETWEEN *MONARCHIA* AND THE *COMMEDIA*

Perhaps this incapacity is not a problem. After all, as just suggested, Frederick *is* present, and *is* accommodated, within the framework of the *Commedia*. His placement in the circle of the heretics might serve, among other things, as a palinode with respect to both *Convivio* and *De Vulgari*

---

[27] Similarly, as pointed out in Chapter 5, Dante's own historical circumstances, though not his narrative "I," are excluded from the work.

Eloquentia, the contrast between the relatively positive depictions in those treatises and the discovery of his damnation paralleling the shift from Guido da Montefeltro as exemplar of wise old age to Guido da Montefeltro as human torch. Why not then simply locate *Monarchia* at an intermediate spot within the chronology of palinodic transcendence – after *Convivio* but before the *Commedia*? *Monarchia*'s inability to absorb and interpret the materials of history, including Frederick, might be remedied by the transhistorical, "figural" framework offered by the *poema sacro*, which also allows Dante openly to assume the prophetic role that he can only hint at for himself in *Monarchia*.

In defense of just such a thesis, as we have seen, Nardi argued that *Monarchia* was written around 1308, and that the treatise's commitment to rationalist argument and to an (Averroistic) separation between the natural and supernatural ends of human life marks it as a successor to *Convivio* and as forerunner to the *Commedia* (Chapter 5, n 27). The *Commedia*, in this account, then moved to heal the split between reason and faith, nature and grace, with the former now clearly subordinated to the latter,[28] and with the most risky of Averroistic propositions, the separation of the possible intellect and the mortality of the soul, clearly rejected (*Inf.* 10; *Purg.* 25.58– 67).[29] However, as observed repeatedly, Nardi's hypothesis about the dating of the treatise can no longer be sustained. Even apart from the manuscript evidence, the discussion earlier in this chapter suggests his line of argument is based primarily on internal and thus tautological grounds, the grounds of the palinode itself.[30]

---

[28] For the supposed overcoming of Dante's "Averroistic" phase with the *DC*, see Nardi 1921c: 255–75, 1930a: 297–302; 1940b: 237–45; 1960a: 83–120, 309–13; Passerin d'Entrèves 1952: 59–75, 109–10; cf. Mazzeo 1960: 163–6. A full examination of this question would begin with *CV* 4.21, where Dante gives his first account of how the "possible intellect" is infused into the individual soul (the phrase is used twice, in par. 5 and 7; see Scott 2004: 134–5). Whatever the sources of Dante's use of the term there and however he understands it in relation to Averroes and his thirteenth-century avatars (both issues are contested), two relevant points can be made. First, the argument in which the term figures is at the service of the affirmation of individual, differential nobility of soul, as against collective intellectual potential (see Chapter 2, section iv). Second, Dante at once qualifies and reinforces his rational account by invoking St Paul on the hidden mysteries of God's wisdom (4.21.6): qualifies because he stresses the failure of the intellect to arrive at the highest mysteries; reinforces because the mystery in question is how the human intellect is produced and can then be understood, intellectually ("a me medesimo pare maraviglia, come cotale produzione si può pur conchiudere e con lo intelletto vedere"). He then adds a specifically theological account to the philosophical one (4.21.11–12).

[29] *Par.* 2.49–148 palinodically corrects the treatment of lunar spots in *CV* 2.13.9, which had followed the teaching of Averroes (cf. *Par.* 3.3–4). See Chapter 3, n 4. This still leaves open for discussion Dante's placement of Siger of Brabant, who reasoned out "invidiosi veri," in *Par.* 10.136–8.

[30] See also Ascoli 2003 on how the force of interpretive desires guides debates around the dating, and authentication, of Dantean texts.

What then of the apparent difference in the treatment of the "possible intellect" in the two works? One tack, not to be lightly dismissed, is that Dante's use of the term does not in fact bring with it the heretical baggage associated with the Averroistic concept as deployed by, say, Siger of Brabant (E. Gilson 1939: especially 212–24). Coming at the question from another angle, the presentation of human intellect in collective rather than individual terms may well be seen as a tactical move to avoid a personalization of reason, which would compromise both the Emperor's authority and Dante's, rather than as a polemical adherence to radical Averroism (see again Chapter 2, n 31; Chapter 5, n 50).

While there are indeed numerous points of thematic and argumentative contact between *Monarchia*'s and *Commedia*'s equally extensive treatments of the two great institutions and the relations between them, there is no particular reason to assume from these that the treatise came before the poem.[31] In fact, as will be seen, one might easily argue for the reverse. Nardi's articulation of the *Monarchia* dating controversy in terms of a palinodic unfolding of Dante's career does suggest, how, at least heuristically, the treatise can be used to stage a confrontation between scholarly belief in a conceptually coherent, progressively directed evolution in Dante's writings (the impulse to find their "total coherence," discussed in Chapter 1, section v), on the one hand, and, on the other, "history," as the external determination of a given moment in the career by contingent circumstances and local desires.

To illustrate what is at stake, methodologically, I will look briefly at two points of contact between poem and treatise from the perspective of the "duel" between palinode and history. First is the treatment in *Monarchia* 3.4 of the Decretalists' allegorization of the "duo magna luminaria" (two great lights; 3.4.2) of Genesis 1: 16–18 in dubious support of the subordination of the "lunar" Empire to the "solar" papacy, which may be compared to *Purgatorio* 16 (106–12), where Dante puts a very different allegorization of the passage in the mouth of Marco Lombardo, who posits two separate but equal "suns" figuring the two great institutional

---

[31] As, e.g., Chiavacci-Leonardi 1977: 168–74 points out, the *DC* and *MN* undoubtedly share important theses. These include the parallelism between imperial and salvation history (e.g., *Inf.* 34; *Par.* 6–7); the complementary yet distinct functions of Pope and Emperor (e.g., *Purg.* 16); and so on. The *DC* takes a more overtly critical view of the recent history of the papacy (e.g., *Inf.* 19; *Purg.* 20 and 32; *Par.* 27), but there are hints at this in *MN* (e.g., 2.11.7, 3.3.18), which in any case focuses on an ideal, positive situation, the empirical absence of which is described in the *DC*. For a review of major scholarly comparisons of *DC*'s politics with *MN*'s to the date of her writing, see Ferrante 1984: 3–7. Like Maccarrone 1955, Mazzoni 1966a, Chiavacci-Leonardi 1977, and Scott 1996: 51 (also 1997), she sees the two as essentially compatible.

authorities.[32] Second are the parallel passages on human freedom just mentioned, which will be scrutinized to determine whether their relationship can be construed in palinodic terms and, if so, which text is recanting which.

In the case of the "two lights" imagery there is an obvious contrast between Dante's two treatments, which lends itself easily to a palinodic reading. The problem is, in what direction does the palinode run? In *Monarchia*, Dante's argument against the hierocratic interpretation of the passage is based on a perceived incompatibility between the letter of the Biblical text and the allegory that the Decretalists educe from it. The creation of the two lights occurred before the creation of humankind; therefore, the passage can have nothing to do with earthly governance of humanity, which in any case became necessary only after the Fall. In *Purgatorio*, instead, Dante not only has Marco Lombardo present an alternate allegorization of the passage, he further forces the letter of the Biblical text by turning the sun and moon into two suns ("due soli"; 107).

In pursuit of a palinode, one might argue that the passage in *Monarchia* supersedes the one in *Purgatorio* because it demonstrates a sophisticated and proto-modern understanding of the violence often done by allegory to the letter of the Bible.[33] However, one might then counter that this reading projects the historical directionality of Western hermeneutics onto Dante in a way that is based purely on structural analogy; that later in the same chapter of *Monarchia* Dante reverses field and gives, however grudgingly, his own allegorical version of the sun/moon opposition (3.4.17–22); and that, on the contrary, and has commonly been argued, the *Commedia* supersedes *Monarchia* here because it abandons a rationalist approach to Biblical signification for one based in a higher, spiritualized interpretation.

---

[32] On Dante's treatment of the "two lights" in *MN* and *DC* and in relation to the traditional uses of the image: E. Gilson 1939: 185–7, 222–3; Kantorowicz 1951; Passerin d'Entrèves 1952: 64–5; Maccarrone 1950, 1955: 27–56, 131; Nardi 1930a: 291–2, 1960a: 185–207; Ferrante 1984: 101–3; Lerner 1986: 220–1; Scott 1996: 154–7, 1997, 2004: 157–8; Cassell 2001, 2004: 86–90 and nn. My reading begins from Mazzotta 1979: 9. Scott shows the full range of Dante's use of this imagery, from a traditional reproduction of the hierocratic interpretation of the "two lights" in *Ep.* 5 to Emperor Henry VII as Christological sun in *Eps.* 6–7 (1996: 42–5; 1997: 94) to the divergent images in *MN* 3 and *Purg.* 16. He sees no shift in perspective accompanying the change in imagery between the latter two texts (2004: 158). See also Cassell's review of this material (2004: 86–93). Cf. Chapter 5, n 26.

[33] This point is made even more forcefully in a later chapter, 3.9, in which Dante refutes the Decretalists' interpretation of the "two swords" passage in Luke (22:38) with a detailed contextual reading of the whole episode. The chapter, however, more than offering programmatic advocacy for reading *ad litteram*, is an ad hoc exercise designed slyly to discredit the papacy by painting Peter, the first Pope, as a *literalist* who often mistook Christ's *figurative* words and erred by acting too hastily. See again Chapter 1, n 52; Chapter 5, n 26. On the place of the *sensus litteralis* in Dante's understanding of allegory see again Chapter 2, section v and nn; Chapter 4, section iii. On *MN* 3.9 generally, see, e.g., Vinay 1950: 238–47 nn; Maccarrone 1955: 67–71; Nardi 1960a: 235–8; Kay 1998: 252–61; Cassell 2004: 96–8 and nn.

Finally, and perhaps most importantly, the simplest hypothesis might be that the differences can be accounted for not palinodically but rhetorically, and that they are thus relatively independent of chronology. Dante uses related materials differently in different contexts based on generic considerations and divergent argumentative purposes.[34] In *Monarchia*, the point of the passage is to refute in detail the arguments of the Decretalists – not to mention the Pope and his representatives – from a rational or at least rationalizing perspective. In *Purgatorio*, no competing views are entertained and Marco simply offers a figurative précis of a truth about human institutions that is guaranteed *sub specie aeternitatis*. Additionally, *Monarchia* is directing its discourse toward an ideal *desideratum*, while the *Purgatorio* passage is focusing on the failure of that ideal in the present historical circumstances. In the end, the conceptual point is substantially the same: the Empire is, or should be, autonomous with respect to the Church.

A second, even more obvious, though less frequently analyzed case is that of the Dantean auto-citation in *Monarchia* 1.12.6 (see Chapter 5, n 2), previously mentioned only in connection with the dating of the treatise. Here is the passage in question:

. . . hec libertas [of the will and of judgment] sive principium hoc totius nostre libertatis est maximum donum humane nature a Deo collatum – sicut in Paradiso *Comedie* iam dixi.

(. . . this freedom or this [originating] principle of all our freedom is the greatest gift given by God to human nature, as I said in the *Paradiso* of the *Comedy*.)

The reference is to *Paradiso* 5, lines 19–24:

> Lo maggior don che Dio per sua larghezza
> fesse creando, e a la sua bontate
> più conformato, e quel ch'e' più apprezza,
> fu de la volontà la libertate;
> di che le creature intelligenti
> e tutte e sole, fuoro e son dotate.
>
> (19–24)

(The greatest gift that God, in his generosity, gave in creation – the most in keeping with his goodness, and the one he values the most – was the freedom of the will, with which intelligent creatures, all of them and only them, were and are endowed.)

In an earlier treatment of some of the materials presented in this chapter, I argued that the recall of *Paradiso* in *Monarchia*, whether part of the original

---

[34] Freccero 1961, refuting Nardi 1959, offers an example of this type of argument, alternative to the palinodic hypothesis, in discussing apparent contradictions between *Inf.* 34 and the *Q*.

text or a later authorial revision, might itself constitute a recantatory revision of the earlier work (Ascoli 1995: 176; cf. Scott 1990b: 272). Such a reading, if justified, would at once confirm Dante's propensity for modifying and/or recanting prior positions and undercut the scholarly tendency to make the *Commedia* the transcendent telos of recantatory narrative. Subsequent inspection of the two passages, however, has led me to a recantation of my own: far from contradicting one another, the two, when they are not in overt agreement, seem to complement rather than to qualify or subvert one another – and the rhetorical strategy of the *Monarchia* passage seems deliberately to emphasize this. This example of auto-citation presents a special challenge to a Dante critic more accustomed to finding the writer at odds with himself as he takes up comparable subjects from work to work.

The two texts, in fact, take a similar, and apparently orthodox, line on free will as the distinguishing gift of God to humanity. This similarity increases when we discover that the one apparent difference between the two excerpts given above, namely that *Paradiso* 5 refers to free will as a gift given to "creature intelligenti" "tutte e sole," that is, to both humans and angels, and to no other creatures, is matched in *Monarchia* by the argument leading up to the passage previously cited:

Propter quod sciendum quod principium primum nostre libertatis est libertas arbitrii . . . [U]t dicant liberum arbitrium esse liberum de voluntate iudicium . . . Et ideo dico quod iudicium medium est apprehensionis et appetitus: nam primo res apprehenditur, deinde apprehensa bona vel mala iudicatur, et ultimo iudicans prosequitur sive fugit. Si ergo iudicium moveat omnino appetitum et nullo modo preveniatur ab eo, liberum est; si vero ab appetitu quocunque modo preveniente iudicium moveatur, liberum esse non potest, quia non a se, sed ab alio captivum trahitur. Et hinc est quod bruta iudicium liberum habere non possunt, quia eorum iudicia semper ab appetitu preveniuntur. Et hinc etiam patere potest quod substantie intellectuales, quarum sunt inmutabiles voluntates, necnon anime separate bene hinc abeuntes, libertatem arbitrii ob inmutabilitatem voluntatis non amictunt, sed perfectissime atque potissime hoc retinent. (1.12.2–5)

([I]t must be borne in mind that the first principle of our freedom is free will . . . [F]ree will is free judgment in matters of volition . . . I say that judgment is the link between perception and appetition: for first a thing is perceived, then it is judged to be good or evil, and finally the person who judges pursues it or shuns it. Now if judgment controls desire completely and is in no way pre-empted by it, it is free; but if judgment is in any way at all pre-empted and thus controlled by desire, it cannot be free, because it does not act under its own power, but is dragged along in the power of something else. And that is why the lower animals cannot have free will, because their judgments are always pre-empted by desire. And from this it is also clear that [intellectual substances (i.e., angels)], whose wills are unchangeable, as well as human souls who leave this world of ours in a state of grace, do not lose free will on account of the fact that their wills are unchangeable; in fact they retain it in its most perfect and true form.)

In other words, while isolating the reference to *Paradiso* might lead to the idea that *Monarchia* takes a more specifically human and rationally human-istic view of free will, looking at the context as a whole shows instead that here too Dante has in mind this faculty's spiritual role in the achievement of eternal salvation for angels and humans alike.[35]

The continuing awareness of this further dimension of the problem leads Dante to a final assertion:

Hoc viso, iterum manifestum esse potest quod hec libertas sive principium hoc totius nostre libertatis est maximum donum humane nature a Deo collatum – sicut in Paradiso *Comedie* iam dixi – *quia per ipsum hic felicitamur ut homines, per ipsum alibi felicitamur ut dii.* (1.12.6)

(When this has been grasped, it can also be seen that this freedom or this [originating principle] of all our freedom is the greatest gift given by God to human nature – as I said in the *Paradiso* of the *Comedy* – *since by virtue of it we become happy here as men, by virtue of it we become happy elsewhere as gods.*)

Clearly, the first happiness is the one that primarily concerns Dante in this chapter and in *Monarchia* as a whole. However, he does specify that the second happiness, i.e., the blessed life, pertains to the "[intellectual substances (i.e., angels)], whose wills are unchangeable, as well as human souls who leave this world of ours in a state of grace" (cf. Chapter 4, nn 1, 14, 27).

Moreover, the distinction here between two different forms of human happiness is by no means *pro forma* or extrinsic to the concerns of the treatise: it clearly anticipates the crucial distinction at the end of book 3 between the two horizons of human existence – material and spiritual, temporal and eternal – and the two corresponding institutions, Empire and Papacy, that are charged, respectively, with offering guidance toward the one and the other.[36] It is no coincidence that the passage from *Paradiso* ends with a warning against the gratuitous making of vows – which specifically involve a *sacrifice* of the will and which are by definition actions in this life

---

[35] Note that the continuity between the argument in 1.12.2–5 and the citation in 1.12.6 – together with the conceptual parallel between the former and the cited passage in *Par.* 5 – offers further grounds for supposing that the citation was present "from the beginning," or at least that it was co-extensive with the final draft of the treatise.

[36] This passage, emphasizing individual will, counters the strong "Averroistic" reading of the "possible intellect" in *MN* 1 and also supports a reading of the "two ends" of humanity as complementary rather than opposed (see n 28; Chapter 5, n 27; also Took 1990: 169–73).

aimed at obtaining salvation in the next[37] – along with an exhortation to return to the fundamentals of Christian living:

> Siate, Cristiani, a muovervi più gravi:
> non siate come penna ad ogne vento,
> e non crediate ch'ogne acqua vi lavi.
>   avete il novo e 'l vecchio Testamento,
> e 'l pastor de la Chiesa che vi guida;
> questo vi basti a vostro salvamento.
>
> (5.73–78)

(O Christians, be slower to take action; don't be like a feather stirred by every breeze, and don't believe that any old water will wash your sins away. You have the New and the Old Testament, and the Pastor of the Church who guides you; let this suffice for your salvation.)

In other words, beginning from the root concept of free will, the passage in *Monarchia* focuses on the institutional guide concerned with directing the will in the temporal sphere, and the one in *Paradiso* emphasizes the same question in the eternal realm. At least in this regard, then, *Monarchia* and *Commedia* appear as two aspects of a single coherent project.

Whether or not the two texts and their two perspectives can finally be reconciled, it should be evident that here Dante has adopted yet another rhetorical strategy for relating his texts, one that attempts to harmonize apparently contradictory moments rather than creating a palinodic hierarchy among them. That does not mean, however, that Nardi was wrong to see a potential doctrinal fissure that separates *Monarchia* from the "poema sacro." Nor does it mean that one should ignore the recourse to palinodic strategies in the *Commedia*, which oppose its revelatory perspective to the philosophical rationalism of *Convivio*, an opposition that the "two horizons" thesis at once acknowledges and minimizes. Rather it suggests, once again, that Dante adopts different conceptual and rhetorical strategies to suit different circumstances and needs. In this particular case, I refer to the felt need to return to a philosophical-political perspective that one might assume – especially based on the deployment of the palinode in the *Commedia* – had been superseded once and for all, without at the same time implying that the *Commedia* itself had been in any way left behind.

From the perspective of this study, moreover, it is particularly significant that the two passages not only pose the problem of the relationship

---

[37] On vows and the will in the Heaven of the moon, see Mazzotta 1993a: chapter 2, especially 36–46. Cf. Ascoli 1994.

between Dantean works, but that they also do so around the key questions of the status of individual will (closely linked to the interpreting *iudicium* that it exercises), and of its complex relationship to the authority of transpersonal institutions. In *both* cases, what is stressed is the tension between the basic freedom of the will, on the one hand, and, on the other, its mutability in the face of historical circumstances, its frequent subjection to forces beyond its control. The *Paradiso* passage is specifically directed at the exemplary case of Piccarda de' Donati – her forcible removal from the convent life to which her vow had bound her – and it notes that the structure of the vow is that of choosing to surrender one's freedom of choice as a sacrifice to God (see Mazzotta 1993a: chapter 2). Though Dante, through Beatrice, begins by affirming the absolute character of the vow, his ultimate goal is to offer a (proto-Lutheran) warning against the making of vows, on the grounds that the contingent will of the individual may well not be able to live up to its commitment. The *Monarchia* passage implies that the human will is variably successful in actualizing its choices, depending on whether it is in harmony with its political-social surroundings or not (1.12.8–11; cf. *Purg.* 16, discussed in Chapter 7, section iii) – and it focuses on the paradoxical position of the monarch to whom all are subject, but who, for his part, is subject to all (1.12.12). Both passages, in other words, place the living individual within a historical flow that constitutively precludes the achievement of the transcendent "perspective of the end" that palinodic recantation aims to establish.

Finally, however, the auto-citational reference to *Paradiso* 5 in *Monarchia* 1.12 serves one other function, which, at least from the revisionist perspective of this study, might be thought of as more properly and simply "palinodic," or at least "progressive," though with respect not to the *Commedia* now, but rather to the earlier treatises. Earlier I asserted that as a whole *Monarchia* signals Dante's entrance into and embrace of a "depersonalized" Latin philosophical culture, as against the world of vernacular poetry with which he personally is so closely identified. But at this single, key, moment, Dante cites his own most ambitious vernacular, poetic work as a philosophical *auctoritas*, on a par with those of Aristotle, Cicero, Homer, Virgil, and the other classical *auctores*. Furthermore, he does this at the very point when he is both asserting the defining primacy of individual will and *iudicium*, and positing their potential for harmonious intersection with the institutional *auctoritas* of papacy and Empire, and thus with the ends of human existence as a whole. That he can so casually and convincingly do so, in a way to which he aspired, but had not yet arrived at, in *Convivio* and *De Vulgari Eloquentia*, is a sign that with the *Commedia* he felt he had, indeed, fully authorized himself, his language, and the discourse of poetry. But it is also a tactical device for affirming his authority and that of his work. The means by which that authorization is undertaken within confines of the *Commedia* itself will be the subject of the next chapter.

CHAPTER 7

The author of the Commedia

I. "IN DEATH HE WAS UNDIVIDED"

Near the beginning of this study, I wrote that what came after would constitute a protracted gloss on *Inferno* 1, line 85, Dante's address to the character "Virgil" (hereafter *Virgilio*) as "lo mio maestro e 'l mio autore." In retrospect, and from the perspective of this final chapter, those words, and indeed the *Commedia* itself as verbal object, constitute a gloss on, because they are in part a consequence of, the elaborate, uneven process of "self-authorization" described in the preceding six chapters, particularly as this unfolds in *Vita Nova, Convivio* and *De Vulgari Eloquentia*. What follows, then, will do triple duty. First, predictably, I offer it as a reading of some aspects of the *Commedia* "in the light of" the historical context(s) and methodological caveats developed around those works of Dante. From this angle, the *poema sacro* will figure as yet another example of Dante's long-term engagement with the figure of the *auctor* and the culture of *auctoritas*, although, inevitably, as *primus inter pares*. Secondly, viewed in another way, the *Commedia* serves simply as a means of verifying the significance that has been attributed to the "other" works, because it repeats, "corrects," and develops the issues with which they first grappled. Finally, looking beyond the "internal history" of the Dantean *oeuvre*, in whichever direction we might be reading it, this chapter suggests both how the *Commedia* positions itself in relation to the past and present it knows, or thinks it knows, and the future it imagines, of the "external" history, or rather, multiple, intersecting, histories, of authorship and authority in Western culture, and how we might, from our perspective, re-historicize that poem and the *oeuvre* it so deliberately subsumes.

Hints have emerged along the way as to what significance such a reversal of perspectival orientation might have. Chapter 2 suggested that, with Mazzotta, the meaning of the *autore* from *avieo* is better understood if we see the "ties that bind" it to the related metaphors of God as "Alfa e

O" of "quanta scrittura / . . . mi legge Amore" (all the writing that Love reads to me; *Par.* 26. 17–18) and the universe as a book ("volume") bound together by divine Love (*Par.* 33.86–7). However, I might better have said that the later work unfolds implications already available in the earlier. Whereas Chapter 1 suggested that *autore* as applied to the character *Virgilio* in *Inferno* 1 combines and thereby transforms the two etymologies of the word given in *Convivio* 4.6, it might better have said, as indeed was said in the chapter that followed, that the Dante of *Convivio* is already measuring and tacitly bridging the distance between them even as he first puts them into play, having already substantially transfigured the categories received from Hugutio.

It is not by chance that these two examples are taken from the last and the first cantos of the *Commedia* in which the word *autore* appears and that together they amount to an argument for re-viewing the now-classic formulation of Dante's presentation of himself and his *poema sacro* as articulated between *Virgilio*'s human, poetic, authorship and God's divine, theological authority. In fact, this chapter will proceed from a rereading of *Inferno* 1, through a re-consideration of Dante's definitive *sorpasso* of his *maestro e autore* in cantos 16 to 27 of *Purgatorio*, to a re-contextualization of the description of the Deity as "verace autore" (*Par.* 26.40) in the light of its place in the linguistic and thematic economy of the canto and larger episode of which it is a part. In the process, I will explore various specific formal and conceptual strategies deployed alongside the palinode to resolve such concerns and, more often than not, deliberately to conceal their genealogical ties to the "internal" and "external" histories recalled above.[1]

Even as the Dante of the *Commedia* is placed within rather than above the historical problems of *auctoritas* as both he (earlier) and his culture defined them, an accounting must be made of the fact that while each of the four works most closely studied to this point approaches the question of authority as a complex of problems (of language, mode, form, personality) for which only provisional and often mutually conflicting solutions can be located, in the *Commedia* those solutions, at least in appearance, are implemented fully and integrated seamlessly. There, the vernacular, in poetic form, is put without question to work in the service of the highest

---

[1] For instance, by limiting the words *autore* and *autoritade* to five uses in three cantos. As will become apparent, issues developed in other works specifically in terms of the language of *auctoritas* still appear prominently in the *DC*, though not identified as such. The motives behind this terminological shift will appear in sections iii and v. In contrast to *autore* is its running-mate *maestro* (Chapter 2, n 25), which is used one hundred and fourteen times in the poem, primarily in address to or description of *Virgilio* (ninety-nine), but occasionally with other applications, especially as a coy periphrasis to God as maker–artist of the edifice of *Inf.* (15.12; 31.85; cf. 11.104) and of *Purg.* (12.64).

and most comprehensive of subjects, though at the same time ranging freely through the full gamut of styles sanctioned (and kept separate) by classical rhetoric as by his own treatise on poetic language; classical *auctores* and an Italian *autore* converse harmoniously as potential equals, while the "bello stilo" of the latter is said to derive immediately from that of the former; poetry and philosophy mingle easily under the watchful eye of theology. There, Dante derives his journey and his poetic mission on a direct line from divine inspiration; he speaks constantly and unapologetically of himself in the first person; he assumes without equivocation a prophetic mantle that lifts him beyond even the great Latin and Greek poets to the level of Biblical authors, even to that of the New Testament authors of the Gospels, the Epistles, and the Apocalypse. All this notwithstanding, it should also be noted that even here – where the machinery of self-authorization runs with astounding comprehensiveness and efficiency – even here Dante never applies the words *autore* and *autorità* directly to himself.

At the heart of the matter in the *Commedia* as in each of the earlier works, is one basic problem. From the beginning, I have argued that, in Dante's explicit conceptualization, largely compatible with a generalized "medieval" view, *auctoritas* and individual personality are radically distinct from one another and that, at the same time, he aims work after work at reconciling the two qualities around and through multiple emanations of a textualized "io." It is thus worth briefly rehearsing the most important instances of this phenomenon, before turning to its manifestation in the *poema sacro*. In *Vita Nova*, the abstract discussion of the trope of personification reveals how Dante has consistently presented his own emotions in an objectified and impersonal form. The exemplary *auctoritas* of five classical poets, the same who will reappear in *Inferno* 4, is deployed to justify this use of the trope, but only in conjunction with the individual modern poet's attempt to demonstrate that he, personally, knows what he is doing in employing it. In *Convivio*, Dante's personal presence compromises the authority that his works had obtained when circulating independently of him – and the solution to this problem is to offer a first-person defense of himself and, subsequently, to define that *nobiltà* which goes hand-in-hand with *autorità*, and from which all virtue springs, as a specifically individual quality. In the same text, the impersonally presented definition of the poetic *autore* from *avieo* conceals Dante's singular first-person reference to himself as the one who binds the Italian language together "with rhythm and rhyme," so that it may obtain a permanence equivalent to that of Latin. In *De Vulgari Eloquentia* the worst-case scenario for the vernacular has each individual expressing himself "ad placitum" (1.3.3) and thus creating a language that he alone, like Nimrod, can understand, while the idealized *vulgare illustre* exists "everywhere and nowhere" and belongs to no particular place or person. Yet, in the end, the *vulgare illustre* is identified implicitly but surely with one person, the "friend of Cino," that is, Dante himself. In *Monarchia* an argument in favor of the absolute, depersonalized authority of the *officium* of the Emperor, as well as that of the Pontiff, is articulated by an individual *nuntius* or, indeed, prophet, whose status is contingently ad hoc, and specific to his person alone.

Chapter 4 showed that Dante's most consistent and elaborate strategy for confronting and resolving this tension is the deployment of a grammatical and formal division of the writing and written "io": between first-person plural and third-person singular Dantes in *De Vulgari Eloquentia*, between commenting reader and commented-upon author in both *Vita Nova* and *Convivio*. Each of the earlier works pursues its own distinctive combination of formal and thematic strategies to heal the divisions that Dante recurrently imposes upon himself in the quest to instantiate an authorial self "worthy of faith and obedience." Each, with the qualified exception of the final chapter of *Vita Nova*,[2] fails on its own terms. Each, however, also helps to clarify the nature of the problem to be solved, and each takes preliminary steps toward a solution, by arriving, near its conclusion, at a provisional abolition of the formal, psychic, linguistic, and/or temporal divisions that keep Dante, modern *lector* and *dicitore in rima*, subject of desire and victim of unjust exile, from coinciding with Dante, *autore* on-the-make.

Chapter 4 concluded with the claim that the most potent sign of the *Commedia* having overcome the principal obstacles between Dante and the authorial status he had earlier so ardently pursued is that it begins where the others end: with the disappearance of the formal and even grammatical divisions that fragment him into multiple Dantes (Chapter 4, section iv, and n 53). The hybrid structures of auto-commentary reify a distinction between "subjective" and "objective," present and past, versions of the person we call "Dante" (although he is never so named in any of those texts), which is correlated at various moments with the distinctions between Latin and Italian – prose and poetry – lyric, (biographical) narration, and analytical exposition. In the *Commedia*, the separation of the latter three modes has given way to a seamless fusion thereof, while the need to prop vernacular verse against prose and/or Latin has vanished without a lingering trace.

---

[2] The qualification, of course, is that success depends on the promise of a future writing that distantly resembles the *DC* (cf. Chapter 6, n 5), not only lying outside the text, but "oltre la spera che più larga gira," i.e., beyond the confines of history.

Most of all, in the place of the variously divided Dantes of the early works, we find what Contini has called the *poeta-personaggio* – a first-person "io" who narrates the journey through the three realms of the Christian afterlife of his own younger self, with whom he consistently identifies grammatically. These two aspects of the Dantean "io" can be separated for purposes of analysis (that is the point of Contini's formulation), but they are both presented as expressions of the personality of a single historical individual named Dante, who is, remarkably, called by that name, once and memorably, within the confines of the text (*Purg.* 30.55). Moreover, there is reciprocity and continuity between the two (cf. Battaglia Ricci 1983: 151–7; Gellrich 1985: 164), as is evident from the first lines of the poem:

> Nel mezzo del cammin di nostra vita
> *mi ritrovai* per una selva oscura,
> ché la diritta via era smarrita.
>   Ahi quanto a dire qual era è cosa dura
> esta selva selvaggia e aspra e forte
> che nel pensier rinova la paura!
>   Tant'è amara che poco è più morte;
> ma per trattar del ben *ch'io vi trovai,*
> dirò de l'altre cose *ch'i v'ho scorte.*
>
> (Inf. 1.1–9)

(In the middle of the journey of our life, I came to myself in a dark wood, for the straight way was lost. Ah, how hard a thing it is to say what that wood was, so savage and harsh and strong that the thought of it renews my fear! It is so bitter that death is little more so! But to treat of the good that I found there, I will tell of the other things I saw.)

What the "io" found then, the "io" speaks of now: the experience of the first-person Dante is the subject of the first-person Dante's poetry. The *poeta* makes the *personaggio* visible – authors him – but at the same time the journey of the *personaggio* provides not only the subject matter for the *poeta*, but also the story of how the individual called Dante became capable of writing the *Commedia*. The two share emotions (e.g., *Inf.* 1.3–6; 26.19–21); at times they are confused grammatically (e.g., *Inf.* 6.4–9); the *personaggio* is designated as an accomplished poet (*Inf.* 1.86–7; 4.97–105) on his way to bigger and better things. His encounters with the denizens of the other world explicitly furnish him with material for writing: whether in the form of the stories he is asked to retell by various sinners (e.g., Pier delle Vigne), of the prayers solicited by purgatorial penitents (e.g., Manfred), or of the prophetic missions with which he is charged by Beatrice,

Cacciaguida, and St. Peter himself. So much is well-known, from Contini, Freccero, and a few others (Chapter 1, section v).

From the perspective developed here, the *Commedia*'s successful healing of the divisions that separate "Dante" from himself in other works might have one of two meanings. First, it might betoken the newly felt possibility of simply appearing in the role of *autore* without the support of a justificatory self-commentary. Rather than treating himself as an author, he leaves it to others to do so and thus *de facto*, he becomes more like a normative medieval *auctor*. On the other hand, it might mean that Dante now feels free to appear without apology as a first-person character and author, free to assert the paradigmatic validity of his own experience for the moral and spiritual edification of others,[3] and, more importantly, fully and obviously in control of the meanings of his own text. It might mean, in other words, that he has assumed the guise of the modern, personalized, author. It is another of the special features of the *Commedia*, however, that these two, historically opposed, meanings, coexist without evident contrast.

How, again, is this possible, rhetorically? conceptually? "existentially"? The examples rehearsed above of how *Convivio* 4.6.1–5 prepares the way for the strategic use of the word *autore* in the *Commedia*, begins to give an idea – but it does not tells us why what was implicit there is explicit here. The *Commedia*'s systematic deployment of the palinode in its broadest sense, as a principle for creating narrative effects of teleology, which is already intermittently at work in the *prosimetra*, is crucial, but not sufficient in itself as explanation. What follows will describe some of the most fundamental self-authorizing mechanisms of the *Commedia*.

In the process we will see how the poem has consistently made it difficult for critics to situate the "author of the *Commedia*" as a "subject of history," including the history of Western authorship, or, perhaps better, has made it so *easy* for them *not* to do so. "The fiction is that it is not a fiction," said Charles Singleton, anachronistically, using language to describe the *Commedia* that he may well have drawn from Baldassare Castiglione's *Libro del Cortegiano*, the Renaissance work he so elegantly translated (cf. Ascoli 1991b: 191–2). More often than not, Dante criticism has concentrated on recounting the content of that "fiction" (in the sense of "imaginary creation"), rather than on exploring either its status as a "made object"

---

[3] As seen in Chapter 1, section iv, Freccero, following Spitzer 1946, argues that Dante is precisely not "modern" in his self-presentation, but follows the example of Augustine, who speaks of himself only "for the benefit of others" (in accordance with *CV* 1.2.14). For reasons suggested throughout this study, however, I believe that the Dantean "problematics of personality" cannot simply be reduced to the Augustinian paradigm.

(*fictio* in the sense Dante uses it in *DVE* 2.4; cf. Chapter 2, n 80), or how his making aimed so precisely at effacing itself, its own historicity, and its author's.[4]

II. WHEN "DANTE" MET "VIRGIL"

Virtually all recent accounts of Dante's "quest for authority" in the *Commedia* begin with the figure of Virgil, *Virgilio*, who accompanies Dante-*personaggio* through the first sixty-one cantos of the poem and who provides not only moral and rational guidance toward spiritual ends, but also a poetic model both to be imitated and to be surpassed (Chapter 1, n 17; Chapter 6, especially n 8). The treatment I offer will prove no exception to that general rule. What it *will* do, however, is re-describe the function of this character, the *autore*-function it might be called, in ways made possible, and desirable, by the questions asked and the problems raised in the preceding pages.

Many, and among the most influential, current interpretations of Dante's relationship to Virgil/*Virgilio* have dwelt on the tension between an overt deference to and admiration for the "altissimo poeta" (*Inf.* 4.80) on the part of Dante-*personaggio* and an implicit and allusive critique of the limitations of pagan culture from the theological perspective of Dante-*poeta*. More often than not, this approach draws on a practice of ironic intertextual allusion that functions with respect to a Virgilian precursor text (usually but not always *Aen.*), as palinodic references do to earlier Dantean works. Overall the results are persuasive – it is now hard to deny that Dante does effect these ideologically motivated transformations of Virgil's works – but they have long since ceased to yield new insight into how and why Dante does what he does in the *Commedia*. Rather, they simply reinforce, time and again, a straightforward "vertical" opposition between the rationally-based authority of pagan poetry and a Christian poetics, that of a *theologus-poeta*, poet-prophet, and/or *Scriba Dei*, whose ultimate grounding is in the mysteries of faith (Chapter 2, n 88).

One result of this procedure is that the narrative dramatizations of the Dantean "io's" transition from lost soul to inhabitant of "Eden regained," as from *personaggio* to *poeta* are curiously flattened out: at every point in

---

[4] As mentioned in Chapter 1, section v, most Dante critics would recognize, in principle and occasionally in practice, the "rhetoricity" and "historicity" of the *DC*. However, in making the illumination of the textual complex named "Dante" the primary goal of their scholarship and, within that complex, in making the composition of the *DC* particularly the first and final cause of the rest of the *oeuvre*, much of what the text potentially means is *de facto* excluded from consideration.

the *Commedia* (even in *Par.*, long after *Virgilio* has disappeared, though not traces of Virgilian texts), the same opposition is established, the same reversal of hierarchy takes place, the same (and in the end, rather unpleasant) dispatching of the father/rival is carried out. For this reason, among others, section iii rehearses a key stretch of Dante-*personaggio*'s itinerary under *Virgilio*'s supervision to suggest how complex and at times ambivalent is its sequential articulation, how closely the two strands of narrative (psychological–spiritual and poetic) are intertwined, and, of course, how intimately and problematically they are tied to the process of self-authorization. In other words, it is worth returning to the traditional question of *intra*-textual development of character, especially over the course of *Purgatorio*, that has not been seriously or at least systematically revisited since the seminal work of Singleton in the 1950s.[5]

There is a second way in which this method has obscured important aspects of the intratextual function of *Virgilio* in the *Commedia*, even as it illuminates others. In so heavily stressing the filiation of Dante's poetic authority with the historical Virgil's and in probing the pathos that accumulates around the character of *Virgilio* at once loved and eternally excluded from the presence of Love itself, the criticism frequently loses sight of the fact that the character's relationship to the historical person who wrote the *Eclogues* and *Georgics*, as well as the *Aeneid*, is in an important sense "arbitrary," that is, willfully imposed by the historical author named "Dante." Behind this imposition are purposes which include, but are by no means limited to, that of acknowledging and circumscribing creative debts to the cluster of texts bearing the name "Virgil" and the accreted interpretations that surround name and text alike in a complex that we have been calling the *auctor*. Among those purposes, as already seen, are those of re-negotiating, and first of all through the consummately strategic designation of *Virgilio* as "autore" in *Inferno* 1.85, the relationship between poetic style and rational understanding which had been a major preoccupation of "Dante" in *Convivio* (and elsewhere) and which up to this point had been articulated without direct reference to "Virgil." Furthermore, they include the use of this name to bring together the "epistemological" authority of philosophy with the institutional *auctoritas* of Empire, which in *Convivio* were explored in the juxtaposition of two other names, "Aristotile" and "Federico."

There is an apparent, though only apparent, conflict between the two problems with the critical treatment of the *Virgilio*/Virgil complex adduced

---

[5] A few scholars (e.g., Swing [Seung] 1962; Cogan 1999) attempt comprehensive accounts of the *DC*'s moral-spiritual architecture, but the "pilgrim's progress" plays a minor role in these studies.

here. On the one hand, I am arguing for a return to a "characterological" reading of *Virgilio* that temporarily brackets "his" tormented relationship to the historical Virgil; on the other, I seem to propose a version of the even more old-fashioned interpretation of the character *Virgilio* as an allegorical cipher, a figurative personification, for Poetry, for Reason and/or for Empire. Or rather, for the larger analytical category that Dante has used repeatedly to bring these categories, and others still, together, namely, Authority. Which will it be then: the *Commedia* as prototype of the realistic novel?[6] Or as "allegorical" in the schematic, mechanical sense used by Dante criticism before Auerbach and Singleton redefined it? Neither, of course. The point, instead, is that in the *Commedia* Dante uses the character *Virgilio* to synthesize and sublimate, to "naturalize," as it were, these abstract categories.[7] *Virgilio* does not "personify" Reason, or any of the other qualities listed, in the same way that Dante says he had figured *Amore* as a living person in *Vita Nova* 25 or as he says he figured *Filosofia* as a beautiful woman in "Voi che intendendo" and "Amor che nella mente." Rather, *Virgilio* functions, through the deliberate devices of Dante's representational art, to fuse those abstractions, those "accidents in a substance," with a "substance," or rather, in the shade, the verbal shadow, of what was or might have been a substantial person. But at the same time, following the logic of personification as it emerged in a reading of *Vita Nova*, he functions as a projection of Dante's own psychic reality.

Here, then, is one more reason why the localization in *Virgilio*/Virgil of the problem of authority and authorship by Dante criticism has concealed as much as it has revealed. We have already seen that scholars have failed to interrogate *Virgilio*'s designation as *autore* in its fusion of definitions and concerns first articulated in *Convivio* 4.6 and in its evocation of the highly problematic, late-medieval version of the "culture of authority." Most particularly, we can now see that the presence of *Virgilio* as speaking, acting character in the *Commedia*, in the terms of that culture and specifically in those of Dante's obsessive engagement with it, is an oxymoron: the long-dead, and hence thoroughly depersonalized, *auctor* emerges from the pages that contain his *auctoritates* and appears as if *alive and in person*.

In order to appreciate to what artistic lengths Dante goes both to create the representational effect of personal presence, and to mark the astonishment that he (as a character) feels and that he expected his late-medieval

---

[6] This is the position of Auerbach (especially 1944, 1945). See also Freccero's critical recasting (1975b) of Lukács's claim (1920: 68–70 *et passim*) that Dante's work represents a crucial turn in the passage from epic to novel. Cf. Ascoli 2005.

[7] For the concept of "naturalization," see again Chapter 4, n 70.

reader to feel as well, it is worth rehearsing briefly elements from the first
half of the first canto of the *Commedia*.[8] To begin with, a first-person voice
recalls that "I found myself (again)" in an obviously symbolic landscape of
wood, sea and mountain (cited above). Beginning in the fourth line this
"io" identifies himself as a poet who will write down in the present what
he experienced in that past moment of his existence, despite the very real
fear he will re-experience in memory by doing so. His account of the spir-
itual crisis that afflicted him, as Singleton in particular emphasized (1954:
especially 5–13; see also Barański 1987: 114–18), is written in the mode of
"personification allegory": wood, beasts, mountain, even his own feet, all are
actually figuratively externalized representations of an inner psychic reality.
Along with this referential mode goes an impression of estrangement and
isolation – Dante is a "stranger in a strange land": alien even to himself,
and profoundly alone.

Within sixty-one lines, he is joined by another character, first described
by the narrating "io" as "chi per lungo silenzio parea fioco" (63) and then
referred to by that voice as "costui" (64). Slowly an identity emerges: the
character who has become the narrator enters into dialogue with this hoarse
and shadowy figure:

> Quando vidi costui nel gran diserto,
> "*Miserere* di me," gridai a lui,
> "qual che tu sii, od ombra od omo certo!"
> (64–6)

(When I saw him in the great wilderness, "*Miserere* – on me!" I cried to him,
"whatever you may be, whether shade or true man!")

The figure replies, slowly revealing aspects of an historical identity: first,
that he was a man but is no more (because now dead); that he was from
Lombardy, specifically Mantua; that he was born in the time of Julius
Caesar and lived his life under the reign of the Emperor Augustus, before
the coming of Christ; finally, that he was a poet who sang the story of
Aeneas:

> Rispuosemi: "Non omo, omo già fui,
> e li parenti miei furon lombardi,
> mantoani per patrïa ambedui.
>   Nacqui *sub Iulio*, ancor che fosse tardi,
> e vissi a Roma sotto 'l buono Augusto

---

[8] Cf. Picone 1997a: 51–4 who similarly rereads this sequence in terms of the Dantean construction of
auctoritas, though with a significantly different emphasis.

> nel tempo de li dèi falsi e bugiardi.
> Poeta fui, e cantai di quel giusto
> figliuol d'Anchise che venne di Troia,
> poi che 'l superbo Ilïón fu combusto."
>
> (67–75)

(He replied: "Not a man, I was formerly a man, and my parents were both Lombards, Mantuans both by birth. I was born *sub Iulio*, though it was late, and I lived in Rome under the good Augustus in the time of the false and lying gods. I was a poet, and I sang of that just son of Anchises who came from Troy, when proud Ilion was destroyed by fire.)

The first-person singular narrator recounts how, based on these clues, the first-person character he once was is able to identify his shadowy interlocutor by name – "Or se' tu quel Virgilio e quella fonte/che spandi di parlar sì largo fiume?" (Now are you that Virgil, that fountain which spreads forth so broad a river of speech? [79–80]). Within another five lines the unnamed character has further identified the shade of Virgil as his *maestro e autore*, on the specific grounds that the reading of his interlocutor's poem, the *Aeneid*, has taught him the art of poetry.

In the short space between the opening of the poem and the encounter with *Virgilio*, momentous changes take place, both dramatically and in representational mode. The solitude of the first-person narrator is broken, and his estrangement relieved, by the appearance of *another person*, who clearly responds to the quintessentially human plea to "have pity on me." At the same time, again as Singleton stressed, the mode of reference shifts from personification allegory to a representational fiction which is "really" taking place, though it too may have additional allegorical meanings.[9] These two shifts are of a piece: the presence of *Virgilio* as an "other" breaks the narcissistic spell of personification allegory, according to which, at least in representational effect, there is nothing to be found in the world but projected and fragmentary images of the isolated self.[10] Not accidentally, this shift from alienated personifications to the mimesis of personal presence

---

[9] This does not mean I agree with Singleton 1954 and Hollander (especially 1969, 1976), that the two representational modes necessarily correspond to the "allegory according to the poets" and the "allegory according to the theologians." As suggested in Chapter 2, the poetic "bella menzogna" can be convincingly representational or not – in fact, the word "menzogna" would suggest that it *is* persuasive, since a lie by definition is a falsehood representing itself *as the truth*.

[10] Tambling 1992: 356–7 argues that Dante's conversations with the dead are expressions of a melancholic, Beniaminian *prosopopeia*. I respond, and I think (resuscitating the dead) Benjamin (1928) would too, that Dante's voyage in the Other World is a *denial* of death, and that the Baroque allegory of the *Trauerspiel* is, as it were, the residue of Dantean allegory, when all that remains is the *selva oscura*, "a land of unlikeness," gesturing toward the void. On Dante, melancholy, and Benjamin, see also Pinto 1994. On Dante and *mourning*, see Vickers 1989; Martinez 1997, 1998, 2003a.

morphs almost immediately from psychic crisis to poetic *bildungsroman*: *Virgilio*'s appearance holds out the hope that Dante-*personaggio* can be "saved from himself," not least because it seals the "io's" identification of himself as a poet, and thus as the forerunner of person writing the *Commedia*. Here, in other words, is a point where Dante evokes only to erase that formal and existential split between plural "Dantes" characteristic, even definitive, of the early works, and predicated on the problem of reconciling historical person with impersonal poetic authority. This move is made both plausible and possible by the fact that Dante is in – has as poet put himself as character in – the presence of a previously absent and impersonal *auctor*.

A final objection to the intertextual interpretation of the *Virgilio*/Virgil dyad, then, is that it misses what is "hidden in plain sight," namely that "their" most important contribution to Dante's appropriation of an authoritative role in the *Commedia* – from a position "nel mezzo del camin di nostra vita" – which he understands to be antithetical to such an appropriation, is already firmly in place by the end of *Inferno* 1 and remains constant and identical at every subsequent point throughout the text. This contribution comes in the form of two simple, yet in their effect cataclysmic, predicates of Dante's representation: that he will enter into a personal relationship with the *auctor*, Virgil, who has turned into a person, *Virgilio*, and that this relationship will unfold *sub specie aeternitatis*, in a world outside of and above historical contingency.

Without any of the strenuous argumentation or elaborate formal devices from the earlier works, and yet with their statements of and attempted solutions to the problem as his *conditio sine qua non*, Dante tacitly bridges the temporal, epistemological and ontological abyss that separated him and all modern, vernacular poets from the *auctoritas* of the ancients, and puts himself well down the road to traversing the even greater distance from the human authors of Scripture, not to mention the "verace autore," the inspiring Love who dictates within.

More specifically, a twofold process is dramatized, which effortlessly reconciles the ostensibly irreconcilable. On the one hand, by staging a direct encounter with his *maestro e autore*, Dante restores to Virgil/*Virgilio* the personal and historical dimension that as long dead *auctor* he had apparently transcended.[11] On the other, he confers upon himself something of

---

[11] Barkan 1986: 138–9 makes a similar point to other ends. Dante's resuscitation of Virgil has an important precedent in Fulgentius' fifth- or sixth-century commentary on the *Aen.* (translated in Fulgentius 1971), which takes the form of a colloquy with the dead poet, although direct knowledge of Fulgentius's texts by Dante has not been established (Pizzani 1971). Fulgentius too uses the device to locate Virgil as representative of pagan culture vis-à-vis Christianity, and plays the superiority of

the impersonal, supra-historical *auctoritas* that belongs to the medieval *Virgilius*.[12] The effect of leveling *is* partially masked by the rhetoric of deference that Dante-*poeta* puts into the mouth of Dante-*personaggio*. Nonetheless, the most profound cultural and historical differences between modern reader and ancient *auctor* are elided in the very moment that the two enter into amicable conversation, however hierarchically structured. Indeed, Dante suggests that his *reading* of Virgil led directly to his meta-morphosis into a *writer* who wins honor with his lovely style.[13] Dante-reader speaks to *Virgilio autore*; as a consequence, this Dante-reader can openly affirm his continuity with Dante-*poeta*.

The use of the word *onore* by which the *personaggio* indicates his prior success as a poet is especially telling, since it immediately follows upon the characterization of *Virgilio* as paradigm and paragon of poets ("delli altri poeti *onore* e lume") and then is insistently deployed with reference to the "bella scola" of classical *auctores* in *Inferno* 4.[14] Indeed, if the consequences of having "Dante" meet *Virgilio* are not clear from the start, they have become so by the latter canto, where Dante-*personaggio* is declared by Dante-*poeta* to have become "sesto tra cotanto senno" in the glorious band of classical poetic *auctores* – at once last and least and last and best.

What makes the later episode particularly significant, of course, is its rela-tionship to the parallel episode – Dante's first explicit foray into authority-building – in *Vita Nova* 25, where the same five classical poets (Virgil, Horace, Ovid, Lucan and Homer) appear in the form of *auctoritates*. As critic after critic has observed, where Dante earlier assimilated vernacular *dicitori d'amore* to the ancients on the single point of using figurative lan-guage, while sharply restricting their practice and prestige in other ways, here he has put himself alone of all the moderns on a footing of equal-ity with those same *auctores*. What has not, however, been observed, are two specific points of comparison that go along with the basic, palinodic, repetition-in-difference.

---

his religion off against the superior learning and poetic accomplishment of the Latin bard (Shapiro 1998: 92). Fulgentius uses "Virgil" to lend the weight of authorial intention to his interpretation of the *Aen.* However, he remains within the role of commentator and despite an initial invocation of the Muses does not use the device to move himself into the role of poetic *auctor* in his own right. On Fulgentius's reading of Virgil, see Comparetti 1872: 106–16; De Lubac 1959–65: 2.2.234–7; Pizzani 1971.

[12] On the medieval Virgil, see Comparetti 1872; Spargo 1934; De Lubac 1959–65: 2.2.233–62; Thompson 1974.

[13] As a corollary to this reading of the appearance of *Virgilio* as dramatizing the reemergence of a living speaking person as against an authoritative written text, I much prefer the reading of "fioco" (63) as "hoarse" rather than as visually "faint" (*pace* Hollander 1983a).

[14] *Inf.* 4.73, 74, 76, 80, 93, 100, 133. See, *inter alia*, Hollander 1968, 1969; Iannucci 1993b; Picone 1997a.

Chapter 25 begins by spelling out a problem concomitant with the use of the rhetorical figure of *prosopopeia* and ends with the imperative that the moderns "explain themselves." Together, *Inferno* 1 and 4 constitute a dramatic and deliberate contrast with both these positions. Rhetorically speaking, Dante has "personified the personifiers," given personal features and voices to what, instead, he knows perfectly well to be names designating literary texts, texts which are, in turn, composed of verbal figures of every kind.[15] At the same time, he has in effect reversed his practice in *Vita Nova* of writing biographical *ragioni* and analytical *divisioni*, which embodied and ostensibly satisfied the needs of moderns to make their intentions explicit, while no evidence was offered that the ancients did the same, or needed to do so. In *Inferno* 1 and 4, *Virgilio* provides considerable biographical detail and a *précis* of his greatest work,[16] and he and all his fellows of the poetic *bella scola* have their current situation (endless, infinite desire without any hope in the "nobile castello") ascribed to historical-biographical contingency, namely, having lived before the coming of Christ. The "Dante" who writes *Inferno*, instead, offers no explanation at all of his signifying practice in general. One comes, but only in *Purgatorio* 24, and even then initially as Dante-*personaggio*'s comment in relation to his practice in *Vita Nova* (see n 27), not *necessarily* as Dante-*poeta*'s account of what is going on in the *Commedia* (Pertile 1993, 1994), much less of the rhetorical device of bringing ancient authors back to life.[17]

Any number of studies have analyzed the dramatic specifics of Dante-*personaggio*'s first encounter with Virgil, and those of the two subsequent episodes with which it is rightly linked, *Inferno* 4 and the meeting of Dante and *Virgilio* with *Stazio* (the late classical poet, Statius) in *Purgatorio* 21–22, which effect his complete authorizing assimilation into the company of ancients (e.g., Picone 1997a: 60–5). These studies, however, have dwelt on the textual details of the episodes and their intertextual relationship to the classical texts that bear the names of the ancient *auctores* with

---

[15] On this score, recall the "meta-poetic" moment in *VN* 25 where Horace is cited citing Homer personifying his own poetic art as "the Muse" (Chapter 4, n 42; cf. nn 28, 157 below).

[16] The information provided may follow the standard *vita auctoris* of the *accessus*/commentary tradition, as Alessio and Villa 1984 argue, but, again, it makes a significant difference that it is *Virgilio* himself who presents the information rather than a belated commentator.

[17] Dante does drop a rather broad hint as to what is going on, however, by a second reprise of *VN*, when he has Francesca posit as substantial what is said to be "accident" and figure in chapter 25, namely *Amore* (Chapter 4, n 52; n 28 below) Curiously, while the debts of both cantos 4 and 5 to this chapter in the *libello* have been frequently observed, the relationship between the two allusions has not been noticed or glossed.

whom Dante consorts.[18] As already noted, they do not understand those episodes in relation to the intricacies of the Dantean discourse of authority. Nor, more immediately, do they record the simple fact that by putting himself in the personal presence of *auctores* Dante has already overcome the greatest obstacle to claiming a status comparable to theirs, or superior to it, precisely in virtue of the fact that the difference between them has been leveled expressly for his benefit by an omniscient and omnipotent Deity they did not recognize. These critics have, it is true, identified the basic pattern of chiasmus by which, even as Dante *personaggio* and/or *poeta* moves *Virgilio*/Virgil and company down toward his own status as living, fallible "subject of history," he moves himself up to their level. Indeed, as these critics have also shown repeatedly, he goes beyond them, as a specifically Christian poet who can achieve ontologically the eternal perfection of life which the classical *auctores* only possess textually, and then with qualifications. But what has not been discussed is the radical transformation that is thereby implicitly effected in the received historical discourse on authorship.

As should be clear from the previous chapter, Dante makes every effort to conceal that such a transformation has taken place or, rather, to deny that it has implications for anything but the unique case of himself and his *Commedia* – that it might redefine the "author function" in terms which could then become the basis for a historical *praxis* imitable by others. How is he able to get away with drastically revamping the canons of authority to suit his individual circumstances and writerly desires without visibly disturbing the "world picture" to which impersonal *auctoritas* was so fundamental? The answer – also simple, also presented as a *given* (by God's Grace, at that) – is that even as he personalizes, and thus in a sense historicizes, the ancient *auctores*, he simultaneously, and conversely, confers on himself a condition basic to medieval notions of *auctoritas*: namely, a comprehensive view of history grounded outside of history.[19] He accomplishes this feat by removing himself, literally, from the domain of temporal contingency

---

[18] For Dante's use of Statius generally, see Chapter 6, n 8.

[19] For an analogous example of how the historicity of *auctoritas* can be acknowledged and transcended see Stillinger 1992: 32, who suggests how the layout of the *sacra pagina* in Peter Lombard's Psalm commentary, which presents for simultaneous viewing the Biblical text and temporally successive strata of commentary, "spatializes" and thus figuratively dehistoricizes the hierarchical dissemination of authority over time. Cf. Chapter 1, n 8. In the first instance, however, my argument develops what I take to be Auerbach's fundamental point about the rhetorical consequences for the representation of human life "in this world" through the adoption of the perspective of "the life to come." On Auerbach, see also Chapter 1, section ii and v; Chapter 6, section i, and n 15; Ascoli 1991b: 190, 1991–1992.

and asserting as his own, from *Inferno* 3 forward, the perspective of an *altro mondo* beyond historical time and corporeal death,[20] from which he can draw less and then more and more directly on the supreme authority of the "verace autore." This fundamental strategy, presented in the guise of a divinely conferred experience, rather than as a set of representational choices, is what allows him to imagine a community of poets from different times and places entering directly into timeless conversation. Implicitly, it also permits him to transcend those personal and historical attributes that impede his access to authority. To repeat, for emphasis, the basic point: both of these features – the personalizing of the ancients and the depersonalizing, or rather, the de-historicizing of Dante himself – are presented as simple predicates of the poem. No one who reads the *Commedia* is unaware of them; at the same time, to my knowledge, no one, with the partial exception of Erich Auerbach, has considered how intimately they relate to the topic explored here.

If Dante has, for all intents and purposes, settled the question of his authority in the *Commedia* before ever posing it, why, in the end, does he never use the word *autore* of himself in the poem? Why does he continue to dwell on the full range of issues surrounding that word throughout the poem? An answer to the first question will have to wait until the final section of this chapter. To the second, there are plural *answers*, which the balance of this section will probe, and which will become clearer still in section iii. One response is that because the "solution" described hovers between the ontological and the rhetorical (i.e., again, "the fiction is that is not a fiction"), Dante still feels some of the compulsion, so present in the earlier works, to develop and defend it. Another is that while it may be immediately evident that Dante-*poeta* begins with a certain *autorità*, the nature of that authority is extensively elaborated over the course of the *Commedia*. In other words, Dante's acquisition of authority *is not only the condition of possibility for the writing of the poem; it is also integral to the subject matter of the poem.*

This last phrase could be interpreted to mean that the poem is truly "modern" in the sense that is primarily, self-consumingly, concerned with its own poeticity and "artifactuality." I do not intend it in that way, though

---

[20] This is not to say that the pilgrim does not experience time sequentially over the course of the poem, just that within the space of the *DC* he can imagine direct contact with the persons who populate the historical past that is of significance to him, as well as claiming mediated access to the divine gaze which sees all times and place at once. On the temporalities of the *DC* see Masciandaro 1976; Freccero 1983a: especially 270–1; Durling and Martinez 1990; Barolini 1992: especially 166–72; Cornish 2000b. For *VN* see Chapter 4, n 82. Cf. Ricoeur 1983.

I would certainly agree that Dante understood the basic proposition that unless authority is repeatedly *represented* it ceases to exist. It could also be taken to indicate a version of the thesis that Dante and his work operates a vertical shift from "poetic" to "theological" authorship (Barolini 1984: 268–9; also Hollander 1968: 144–5, 1969: 78; Brownlee 1990: 53). But although I have no doubt that the poem ultimately casts Dante in the role of *scriba Dei* referring to the dictates of the *"verace autore,"* I will argue that this approach has regularly occluded central aspects of the topic, notably the exploration of Dante's relationship to the institutional *auctoritas* of Church and Empire. What I refer to, instead, is a rather elaborate variant of the Contini–Freccero argument concerning the narrativity of the *Commedia*: namely that the authority Dante has conferred on himself at the outset is what allows him to proceed with an extended interpretation of the relationship of the individual in general and an individual in particular (himself) to the full gamut of authorities – epistemological, institutional, and, finally, the divine, where knowledge and power co-exist completely and comprehensively.

Before expanding on the contents of this last paragraph, I would like to offer yet another response to the question posed, in the form of a reading of the previously mentioned encounter of *Virgilio* and Dante with *Stazio* in *Purgatorio* cantos 21 and 22. I begin with a reformulation of accepted critical wisdom that this canto – with its celebration of the authoritative effects of Virgil/*Virgilio*'s texts on its later readers – definitionally circumscribes Virgilian *auctoritas* and prepares the symbolic *translatio auctoritatis* that takes place definitively at the end of *Purgatorio* 27.[21] I will go on to argue, however, that the episode entertains a residual counter-argument according to which the gap between the person who writes and the authoritative text written cannot ever be completely closed and thus the temporary detour beyond history fails to guarantee that the resultant text will escape the vicissitudes of (mis-)interpretation by future readers. In other words, the episode both reaffirms and interrogates the two predicates of Dantean *auctoritas* (personalization and de-historicization).

It is no secret that the meeting of Dante-*personaggio* and *Virgilio* with *Stazio*, the late classical poet who authored both the *Thebaid* and the incomplete *Achilleid*, in *Purgatorio* 21–22 has a special, complementary role with respect both to the first meeting between "Dante" and *Virgilio* and to the *nobile castello* episode, the latter of which is elaborately recalled in canto 22 (9–15, 97–114). The episode produces another version of the personal assimilation of Dante into the company of the ancients, distilled down from six

---

[21] See, for instance, Barolini 1984: 258–70; Martinez 1995a.

(or five plus one) to a Trinitarian three, in keeping both with *Stazio's* appearance as the risen Christ (betokening the successful completion of his salvific *imitatio Christi*) and with the inspirational poetics of "notation" that will be presented during the encounter with Bonagiunta in canto 24. Even more to the point, it specifically describes a meeting between the great poetic *auctor* and another of his readers, who declares that, as a result of reading *Aeneid*, book 3, and the fourth *Eclogue*, he not only became a poet (and, Dante's medieval audience understands, an *auctor*),[22] but also learned a decisive moral lesson (the viciousness of prodigality as the symmetrical opposite extreme of avarice) and was converted to Christianity (22.37–42, 64–6; cited below). The episode thus models the metamorphosis of *lector* into writer and, eventually, into *auctor*, albeit in a more traditional scheme that requires the passage of centuries. It also coordinates poetry, Virgil/*Virgilio's* poetry, with both classical moral philosophy (the Aristotelian golden mean ostentatiously adapted to the Christian scheme of seven deadly sins) and Christian theology, highlighting at this key transitional point the convergence of three principal modalities of *auctoritas* around a single figure – or rather two figures, *Virgilio* and Dante *personaggio-poeta*, with the mediation of a Christological third.

The episode, then, represents the point of nearest approach of *Virgilio*, and the texts bearing the name of Virgil, to a Christian poetics, and thus the maximum convergence between the classical *auctor* and his latter-day protégé, the Christian *autore*. At the same time, as critics have repeatedly noted, numerous features of the episode signal the gaping abyss that will ultimately separate *Virgilio* – doomed to return to his niche at the edge of Hell – from Dante-*personaggio*, assured of assumption into Paradise – and that will divide the obscurely prophetic texts of Virgil from the *poema sacro* of Dante-*poeta*. These features translate with surprising ease into the terms deployed above in describing the function of *Virgilio*/Virgil as "authority in person." As an example, consider *Stazio's* famous embrace *manqué* of his beloved *auctor*:

> Già s'inchinava ad abbracciar li piedi
> al mio dottor, ma el li disse: "Frate,
> non far, ché tu se' ombra e ombra vedi."
>   Ed ei surgendo: "Or puoi la quantitate
> comprender de l'amor ch'a te mi scalda,
> quand' io dismento nostra vanitate,
>   trattando l'ombre come cosa salda."
>
>   (*Purg.* 22.130–6)

---

[22] Dante cites *auctoritates* of Statius in *CV* 3.8.10, 11.16; 4.25.6–8.

(Already he was bending to embrace my teacher's feet, but he told him: "Brother, do not, for you are a shade, and a shade is what you see." And he, rising: "Now you can grasp the greatness of the love that burns in me toward you, when I forget our emptiness, treating shades like solid things.")

Where the dynamic unfolding of *Inferno* 1 emphasizes *Virgilio's presence* for Dante (notwithstanding his disclaimer: "non omo; omo già fui"), this episode instead points toward his evanescence, and indeed toward his impending disappearance from the poem altogether. As Dante-*personaggio's* full assumption of personal authority comes closer and closer, *Virgilio*/Virgil's fusion of personal presence with *auctoritas* begins to come undone.

Indeed, as Mazzotta has shown (1979: 221–4), the episode stresses – first implicitly then overtly – the gap between *Virgilio's* understanding of the texts bearing his name and the authoritative effects they have on their readers. Consider, to begin with, *Stazio's* description of his moral conversion away from prodigality after reading lines from the Polydorus episode of *Aeneid* 3 (56–7):

> "Or sappi ch'avarizia fu partita
> troppo da me, e questa dismisura
> migliaia di lunari hanno punita.
>   E se non fosse ch'io drizzai mia cura,
> quand' io intesi là dove tu chiame,
> crucciato quasi a l'umana natura:
>   'Per che non reggi tu, o sacra fame
> de l'oro, l'appetito de' mortali?,'
> voltando sentirei le giostre grame.
>   Allor m'accorsi che troppo aprir l'ali
> potean le mani a spendere, e pente'mi
> così di quel come de li altri mali."
>
> (*Purg.* 22.34–45)

("Know then that avarice was too distant from me, and thousands of months have punished this lack of measure. And had it not been that I straightened out my desires, when I understood the place where you cry out, almost angry at human nature: 'Why do you not, O holy hunger for gold, govern the appetite of mortals?' I would be turning about, feeling the grim jousts. Then I perceived that one's hands can open their wings too much in spending, and I repented of that as of my other vices.")

This passage has given rise to a famous interpretive *crux* based on its evident misreading of the Virgilian pre-text, which uses *sacer* in its other and opposite meaning of "unholy" in condemning the avarice of Polymnestor that led him to murder Priam's youngest son, Polydorus.[23] The question has been whether Dante-*poeta* misremembered or misconstrued the passage or whether he (and/or his character, *Stazio*) deliberately misread it to their own purposes. The answer, to me virtually certain, is the latter, given that in a passage immediately preceding the introduction of the risen *Stazio* into the poem, Dante refers specifically to Polymnestor as an exemplar not of prodigality but of avarice (20.115–17; see also Durling and Martinez 2003: 373–4).

The deliberate wrenching of Virgil's words to a meaning exactly opposite to that appropriate to the original context suggests a notion of medieval textuality very similar to the one described by Dagenais and Carruthers, among others (cf. Chapter 1, section iv), in which signification is out of the control of a text's author and in that of the *lector*, who discovers meanings that suit his own moral and spiritual needs and do not necessarily correspond to the writer's original intentions. This in turn suggests a contrast with the principle articulated in *Vita Nova* 25 that an author should be able to explain what he means. Not that Virgil/*Virgilio* did not intend the "original" meaning, just that his reader(s) (*Stazio*, but also Dante-*poeta*) did not feel constrained by that intention: no more, ironically, than many of Dante's subsequent readers felt constrained by what seem obvious hints at his intentions (e.g., the Polymnestor reference mentioned above).

This complicated staging of the *auctor*/*lector* dialectic is merely preliminary to the remarkable passage in which *Virgilio* queries *Stazio* about why his *Thebaid* shows no signs of his conversion to Christianity, and *Stazio* replies:

> . . . . . . "Tu prima m'inviasti
> verso Parnaso a ber ne le sue grotte,
> e prima appresso Dio m'alluminasti.
>   Facesti come quei che va di notte,
> che porta il lume dietro e sé non giova
> ma dopo sé fa le persone dotte,
>   quando dicesti: 'Secol si rinnova;
> torna giustizia e primo tempo umano,
> e progenie scende da ciel nova.'
>   Per te poeta fui, per te cristiano."
>   (22.64–73)

("You first directed my steps toward Parnassus to drink from its grottos, and first illuminated me concerning God. You did as one who walks at night, who carries the light behind him and does not help himself, but instructs the persons coming

---

[23] The controversy is summarized with extensive bibliography in Hollander 2003: 463–4. In particular, see Shoaf 1978; Martinez 1989.

after, when you said: 'The world renews itself; justice returns and the first human time, and a new offspring descends from heaven.' Because of you, I was a poet, because of you, a Christian.")

This is the point, indicated above, where poetic and spiritual authority are linked, if not completely conflated, and where *Virgilio*/Virgil seems most completely absorbed into salvation history. At the same time, it is also the point where a radical split appears between *Virgilio-personaggio* and the texts, the *auctoritates*, which bear the name of Virgil.

Crucial to this reading is the figure that *Stazio* uses to describe how without himself knowing, much less embracing Christ, "Virgil" could facilitate the redemptive conversion of others: "Facesti come quei che va di notte,/che porta il lume dietro e se non giova/ma dopo sé fa le persone dotte."[24] The image is mimetically preposterous: how can a person guide someone else when he can't see where he is going himself?[25] The very difficulty of the image points to a conflict between two referents which Dante-*poeta* had to this point systematically conflated in the name "Virgilio" ("or tu se quel Virgilio . . .") and which for analytical purposes are here separated into (1) the human person, author in the modern sense of a book; and (2) the book itself as *auctoritas* in the medieval sense. As book, "Virgil" lights the way to Christianity for readers; as person, he stumbles hopelessly about in the half-light of Limbo. In other words, Virgil's text expresses a meaning unknown to its author, one which he did not intend and one which must be found, even invented, by allegorizing readers (Mazzotta 1979: 220–2; see also Martinez 1995a: 158–61; Marchesi 2003). What began in *Inferno* 1 as the personalization of the *auctor* (authority with a human face) has led to a separation of the humanized and fallible writer, loveable though damned, from texts that bear his authoritative name, but do not express any meaning he intended. Rather, we infer, they have become the vehicles for expressing the divine Author's will and executing His purposes.

Stazio reflects a similar, though mirror-reversed, split between writer and text. Where Virgil is a pagan whose writing conveys Christian meanings, *Stazio* was a Christian whose texts deliberately failed to reveal their maker's inward acceptance of the highest spiritual truth. In point of fact, *Virgilio*

---

[24] Mazzotta 1979: 220–1 succinctly condenses the classical (Ennius; Cicero) and Biblical patristic (Paul; Augustine) analogues of the image. Despite the precedents, I would nonetheless argue that, in context, Dante's version emphasizes the disparity between the person and the text bearing the name "Virgil."

[25] Compare *CV* 1.11.3–4, in which Dante specifically mocks the figure of the "blind guide" and which concludes: ". . . *onde qualunque ora lo guidatore è cieco, conviene che esso e quello, anche cieco, ch'a lui s'appoggia, vegnano a mal fine. Però è scritto che ' l cieco al cieco farà guida, e così cadranno ambedue ne la fossa* " (1.11.3–4). The reference is to Matthew 15:14, also echoed in *Purg.* 18:18 (see section iii).

calls attention to this split just before *Stazio* describes the role of the fourth *Eclogue* in his conversion:

> "Or quando tu cantasti le crude armi
> de la doppia trestizia di Giocasta,"
> disse 'l cantor de' buccolici carmi,
>   "per quello che Clio teco lí tasta,
> non par che ti facesse ancor fedele
> la fede, sanza qual ben far non basta.
>   Se cosí è, qual sole o quai candele
> ti stenebraron sí, che tu drizzasti
> poscia di retro al pescator le vele?"
>   Ed elli a lui: "Tu prima m'inviasti
> verso Parnaso a ber ne le sue grotte,
> e prima appresso Dio m'alluminasti."
>
> (*Purg.* 22.55–66)

("When you sang the cruel warfare of the double sorrow of Jocasta," said the singer of the Bucolic songs, "from that which Clio [Muse of History] touches on with you there, it does not seem that you had yet been made faithful in the faith without which doing good is not enough. If this is so, which sun or which candles so removed the darkness from about you so that you then directed your sails behind the fisher of men?" And he to him: "You first directed my steps toward Parnassus to drink from its grottos, and first illuminated me concerning God.")

What remains unsaid but nonetheless evident at this point is that the third, largely silent, member of the party, Dante, is the only one of the three who is both a Christian and the writer of poetry which expresses meanings consonant with his spiritual identity.[26]

The point *is* made explicit just two cantos later, in Dante-*personaggio*'s summary of his poetics to Bonagiunta da Lucca:

> E io a lui: "I' mi son un che, quando
> Amor mi spira, noto, e a quel modo
> ch' e' ditta dentro, vo significando."
>
> (24.52–4)

(And I to him: "I am one who, when Love inspires me, I take note, and in that fashion which he dictates within, I go on signifying.")

Dante's poetry, unlike that which goes under the names of "Virgil" and "Statius," is an exact and conscious reflection of what divine Love, that is,

---

[26] This reading, rehearsed because of its necessary place in the larger argument, is already clearly articulated in Barolini 1984: 258–70, especially 270. See also Ferrante 1984: 237–9; Durling and Martinez 2003: 622, which also posits *Purg.* 24.52–4 as completing the sequence.

the Holy Spirit, the third person of the Trinity, communicates to him.[27] At this point, then, the *translatio auctoritatis* from the eternally divided *Virgilio*/Virgil dyad to the "integrated" Dante who is both *personaggio* and *poeta* is virtually complete, as is the transformation of the impersonal ancient *auctoritas* into a modern, individualized ("io mi son un . . .") writer who knowingly receives direct inspiration of the Holy Spirit.

This Love, the truth and source of all human loves, who already inspired Dante-*personaggio* to write the great *canzone* of *Vita Nova*, "Donne che avete intelletto d'amore" (24.51; cf. *VN* 19), is clearly set in opposition to the personified "accident" of Francesca (*Inf.* 5.100, 103, 106),[28] and before her of *Vita Nova* 25.[29] The passage, a poetics "bound together with rhythm and rhyme," illustrates perfectly the point made earlier concerning the integration in the *Commedia* of the different modes, and divided Dantes, of *Vita Nova*, at the same time as it highlights the coincidence of *personaggio* and *poeta*, ambiguously implying that the poetics of the *Commedia* is, or will be, no different than that of the earlier work. It momentarily erases the temporal difference that separates Dante-character in the *Commedia* from his human "maker." Here, as in "Le dolci rime d'amor ch'io solia," Dante's verse "explains itself." But here, unlike *Convivio*, Dante seems to

---

[27] See especially Mazzotta 1979: 197–207; Martinez 1983; also Hollander 1976: 116 and n; Freccero 1983b: 204. Pertile 1994 has reopened the long-standing question of whether the episode as a whole (24.49–63) deals with (a) Dante's poetics particularly or those of a school of poets headed by Guinizelli; (b) Dante's poetics in *VN* or those of the *DC*. Pertile's argument convinces insofar as he adduces a metaphorics of falconry to explain the key terms "nodo," "ritenne," and "penne," but not as it excludes the co-presence of other metaphorics, such as notarial transcription ("Il notaio"; "noto"; "dittator"; "ditta") and spiration. For me, his reading complements rather than supersedes those cited above. An episode from *Inf.* clearly evoked in *Purg.* 24 suggests that indeed notarial–scriptorial and falconry metaphors are being fused, with an added nautical element. Dante's notation of Love's dictates here recalls and supersedes the written "note" of his "comedìa" by which he swears in *Inf.* 16.127 and which are punningly echoed in the "figura" of Geryon "notando" (literally, swimming) in *Inf.* 16.131, 17.116 (Noakes 1988: 65–6; Ascoli 1987: 277–8). Geryon is painted with "nodi" (17.15), which clearly indicate rhetorical deceptions, not the falconer's jess, but is also compared to a falcon (17.127–9), not to mention a beaver (17.19), a skiff (17.22), a ship (17.100), an arrow (17.136). On Geryon as object and double of Dantean representation, see Ferrucci 1971; Hollander 1976: 76; Barolini 1984: 213 and n, 1992: 58–73; Ascoli 1989: 44. On *Purg.* 24, see also nn 26, 28, 86, 114, 116, 122, 147; Chapter 5, n 25.

[28] Cf. Chapter 4, n 52, on personification in *Inf.* 5. In addition to Francesca's three references to erotic "Amore" personified, Love is clearly identified as a person five other times (*Purg.* 24.53; 31.117; *Par.* 10.1, 26.18, 28.12), in each case referring specifically to the Paraclete or to Dante's divinely-inspired Love for Beatrice. Of particular interest in this context is *Virgilio*'s equivocal use of the word "Amore" in *Purg.* 22.10–12, referring to the reciprocity inspired when he learned of *Stazio*'s love for him: "Virgilio incominciò: 'Amore,/acceso di virtù, sempre altro accese,/pur che la fiamma sua paresse fore . . .'." *Virgilio*'s *innamoramento* distantly echoes Francesca's "a nullo amato amar perdona," with a moral qualifier, which, however, does not arrive at the divine Love of *Purg.* 24. Compare *Virgilio*'s exposition of misdirected love as the root cause of all of the sins in Purgatory (17.82–139).

[29] See Chapter 4, section ii, especially nn 36, 44, 47.

claim that the poem's significance is guaranteed *sub specie aeternitatis* by its second, transcendent, Author, in whom it originates, and to whom it ultimately refers.

I began with the claim that *Purgatorio* 21–22 (plus 24) amounts to the fulfillment of the promise of Dantean *autorità* implied by a personal encounter with *the* poetic *auctor*, Virgil/*Virgilio* in *Inferno* 1, which in turn was made possible by the fiction of Dante-*personaggio*'s removal from the world of history and the acquisition of a timeless, transcendent perspective. However, the promise is fulfilled only by the undoing of one of its predicates. By reintroducing the gap between the "person" *Virgilio* and the texts that bear his name and especially by the preposterous figure of the blind guide, Dante-*poeta* shows (again in the spirit of *VN* 25) that he knows the truth about his use of the character *Virgilio* to impersonate *auctoritas* and in that very gesture, which reveals him as the author in a modern sense of his *maestro e autore*, demonstrates his own controlling authorial mastery.

Does he in some way compromise the other predicate, the transcendence of history, as well? In a certain sense, and only by implication, yes. The meeting of *Virgilio*, *Stazio*, and Dante-*personaggio* is possible, as the initial encounter with *Virgilio* and then the other classical poets was, because it takes place beyond "the land of the living" and outside of historical time. Nonetheless, it unfolds so as to generate a multiplicity of histories, beginning with a history of the relationship between Roman culture and Christianity (Virgil is pre-Christian; Statius a product of the period when pagan and Christian cultures coexisted; Dante lives in a time of Christian dominance). More directly to the point, the scene generates a history and/or a historicization of authorship. From an author who clearly does not control the most important meaning of his text, we move to one who does exercise control over what he writes, but only in order to conceal what means the most to him, and then finally to one who says what he means and means what he says. Dante thus implicitly fashions a history that leads from impersonal *auctoritas* to personal, intentional authorship.[30]

On the one hand, the chronological ordering of this sequence constructs a history of authorship as progressive, indeed as "typological" (Chapter 6, n 12), making Dante the *telos* and *eschaton* who fulfills and escapes the limitations of contingency that enfold his precursors. On the other hand, if we look at the episode in terms of its own *synchronic* representation of

---

[30] See Chapter 4, sections ii–iii. Marchesi 2003 also reads *Purg.* 22 in terms of authorial intentionality, but takes *Stazio*'s mode of interpreting Virgil's texts as reflecting Dante's primary view of the matter in the *DC*, and thus a shift away from the intentionalist model of *VN* and *CV*. See also Franke 1996; Coassin 1996.

the three poets, and thus at *Virgilio, Stazio,* and Dante himself as concurrently available configurations of the relationship between writer and text, a typology of a different sort is generated. In this light, we see a neutral display of a range of possibilities concerning the search for an intersection between a writer's intentions and the meaning of his work – a connection which emerges as *possible* but not *necessary.* Paradoxically, this synchronic display of structural potentiality implies that authorship is a *contingent* phenomenon, which will express itself differently in accordance with multiple historically determined variables. This account radically *historicizes* authorship, even as it qualifies any teleological-typological history thereof.

If one adds to this the *ethos* of authorship carried over from *Vita Nova* (the author writes what he knows and knows what he writes), we can read the episode as articulating both Dante's understanding of the intrinsic historicity of authorship and his desire intentionally to control the threat to meaning, his intended meaning, that this poses. And while the representation generated by the convergence of this understanding and that desire may predicate the transcendence of history, it also previews a historicized will to historical authorship that looks very much like the "modern" transformation of the "author-function" considered in Chapter 1, section iii.

If we look at the episode instead from the point of view of *readership,* the historical dimension is even clearer. In the first instance, the static opposition between authors and readers, upon which the culture of authority is predicated, breaks down as readers dynamically transform themselves into authors through the act of reading itself ("per te poeta fui . . ."). Furthermore, as a corollary to the variable success of authors in making their individual intentions visible through their texts, we come to understand that those texts have histories independent of their authors – they are read in different ways in different times by different persons. As seen, this is explicitly true for Virgil. It is implicitly so for *Stazio,* since Dante's readers would likely have known that prior readings of the *Thebaid* and the *Achilleid* interpreted it as the product of a pagan, not a Christian, author.[31] The situation is apparently indeterminate for Dante, *personaggio-poeta,* since his case is not discussed during the episode, and since within the fictions of the poem no *Commedia* yet exists to be read or mis-read. Nonetheless, the subsequent example of Bonagiunta, who used to understand "Donne ch'avete" in one way and now learns to understand it as its author would wish, is suggestive that his work too fits the paradigm. This phenomenon

---

[31] See Paratore 1975 and Hollander 2003: 466 for summaries of the critical discussion of whether Dante did or did not have any source(s) for the conversion of Statius. Cf. Padoan 1959.

reinforces the *desire for* authorial control and promotes the fantasy of its actualization apotropaically, that is, in virtue of the threat it poses to the successful imposition of writerly will.

Finally, despite the fact that in cantos 21 and 22, and again in 24, attention to the individual writer's intention is coordinate with an imperative to disclose a transpersonal Truth, the *Stazio* episode seems surprisingly willing to contemplate the additional corollary of "modern" authorship, namely the power of the individual writerly will to reshape the raw materials of history through the imposition of narrative forms and rhetorical figures upon it. *Virgilio*'s status as literary device invented by Dante-*poeta* is indirectly unveiled by *Stazio*'s use of the catachrestic figure of the "blind guide" in describing Virgil's role in his conversion. Moreover, the tale of conversion by itself might suggest that the character *Stazio* too is a product of Dante's fictionalizing imagination, since, as just mentioned, it is nowhere to be found in the historical record available to Dante nor, as *Virgilio* helpfully points out, can it be deduced from reading the works of Statius, ironically placed under the sign of Clio, Muse of *History*. Of course, throughout the *Commedia* Dante makes frequent use of shockingly unexpected appearances (Guido da Montefeltro in Hell [canto 27]; his son in Purgatory [canto 5]; Cato, a suicide, in Purgatory [cantos 1–2]; Ripheus in the Heaven of Jupiter [canto 20]; and so on) to reinforce the rhetorical effect that his voyages in the world outside of history give him special access to hidden truths. But each time he does so, and especially here, he necessarily also invites the suspicion that he has invented these astounding "revelations" out of whole cloth.

The point is driven home by two curious features of Virgil's account of life in Limbo, in the continuation of the passage cited above:

> "Euripede v'è nosco e Antifonte,
> Simonide, Agatone, e altri piùe
> Greci che già di lauro ornar la fronte.
>   Quivi si veggion *de le genti tue*
> Antigone, Deifile e Argia,
> e Ismene sí trista come fue.
>   Védeisi quella che mostrò Langia;
> *èvvi la figlia di Tiresia*, e Teti,
> e con le suore sue Deïdamia."
>   (22.106–14)

("Euripides is there, and Antiphon, Simonides, Agathon, and other Greeks still who once decorated their brows with laurel. There are seen from among your people Antigone, Deipyle, and Argia, and Ismene, sad as she was. There is seen she who showed Langia; there is *the daughter of Tiresias*, and Thetis, and Deidamia, with her sisters.")

Consider first the reference to the "daughter of Tiresias," another notorious crux in Dante scholarship, since it apparently locates in Limbo that same Manto who appears in *Inferno* 20 as one of the damned diviners. This passage has been explained alternately as a mere lapse in Dante's otherwise seamless artistry, or as a deliberate artistic stratagem,[32] now most commonly understood to reinforce the subversion of Virgil's authority in *Inferno* 20, where *Virgilio* corrects his namesake's treatment of the founding of Mantua in the *Aeneid*.[33] The most prominent version of the latter position, Hollander's, sees the first Manto as "Virgilian" and bad, and the second as "Statian" and good (1980b: 209–12).

From my point of view, it does not really matter which interpretation – intentional contradiction or unintentional slip – is correct since in either case the passage, in its violation of the mimetic version of the law of non-contradiction, points to the constructedness, and in this sense the ficticity, of the poem. What permits the equivocation, or error, to occur at all is that Dante clearly, consciously or unconsciously as may be, distinguishes between at least two Mantos each of whom is specifically linked to a different classical poet and poem: in *Inferno* 20 to the *Aeneid*; in *Purgatorio* 22 to the *Thebaid*. To complicate matters, and to complicate Hollander's interpretation as well, in both cases Dante "contaminates" (in the technical rhetorical sense) the Manto of the one with the Manto of the other and turns them in directions different from those present in either classical text.[34] In other words, taken together the two passages point up the

[32] Hollander 2000: 343 cites Toynbee 1914: 421–2 to exemplify the first position, before reasserting the second, which he attributes to himself (1980b: 205–13) and R. Kay 1978. There have also been efforts, unconvincing, to prove that line 113 is textually corrupt (on the critical tradition see Padoan 1971; Hollander 1980b: 208–9 and nn).

[33] The point of this maneuver is to distinguish between false prophecy or divination and true prophecy. For some critics, Virgil's medieval reputation as a necromancer and source of divinatory revelation, through the *sortes Virgilianae* (Comparetti 1872; Spargo 1934), requires that he and his work be distinguished from the diviners, especially in light of the truly prophetic function later attributed to him (D'Ovidio 1901; cf. Hollander 1980b: 188–200). For more recent critics, it is a question of distinguishing Dante from Virgil, either to affirm the superiority of the former over the latter (Hollander), or to simultaneously entertain and apotropaically overcome the risk that Dante himself might be condemned as a false prophet (Barolini 1998a; cf. Mazzotta 1979: 80).

[34] The Manto of *Inf.* 20, whom Dante, through *Virgilio*, distinguishes from the Manto of Virgil in *Aen.* 10, is a virgin (82) and closely linked to her father and to Thebes (40–2, 60–1) as in the *Theb.* (thus far, Hollander and R. Kay), but the condemnation of her prophetic talents distinguishes her from both "pre-texts." The Manto of *Purg.* 22 seems to derive her identity from the piety toward her father shown in the *Theb.*, but her associations there with (false) prophecy are seemingly repressed, since she is now assigned to the circle of the virtuous pagans. In fact, the two Statian episodes,

specificity of the character "Manto" in the textual worlds of the two epic poets whose names have been assigned to Dantean characters, as well as revealing, intentionally or not, Dante's difference from both and, just as importantly, from himself as well.[35] We are left with the distinct impression that it would be impossible to ascertain exactly the relation of any one of these poetic figures to a possible historical original and with an example of Dante's ability to reinterpret received materials in more than one way, depending on the needs of his artistry.

This idea becomes almost explicit in an earlier line from the same passage, in which *Virgilio* introduces the sub-list of his fellow denizens of Limbo, into which Manto is then inserted, with the following qualifier: "there are seen from among *your* people . . .," i.e., she, and the others, are specifically designated as characters from *Stazio*/Statius' *Thebaid*. One could, of course, argue that since *Virgilio* identifies *Stazio*/Statius with Clio, Muse of History, that "his people" and the historical individuals they are based on are one and the same (R. Kay 1978). Still, the taint of ficticity hangs over them: because Manto has already figured in two alternative and mutually exclusive poetic accounts (Virgil's and *Virgilio*'s) and because *Stazio* has already revealed that his poem is capable of deceit by omission (since it fails to reflect his own true spiritual condition). If this is so, then *Virgilio* puts himself, as denizen of Limbo, on the same footing as "Statius' people." This in turn means, at the very least, that the line between history and fiction is being blurred, and, at the most, and in keeping with the earlier catachresis, that Dante is specifically emphasizing the fact, the fact of fiction, that Manto, *Stazio*, and *Virgilio* alike are his own rhetorical inventions – that they are "Dante's people." This furtive glimpse into the ficticity of the poem specifically unveils both its construction of a history in which Dante himself

---

Theb. 4.406–684 and 10.589–685, in which Manto appears bear closer scrutiny than they have had to date. In both of these, Manto participates in prophesying the outcome of the Theban civil war. In the first case, Tiresias and she together summon tormented souls from Avernus, recalling the horrific Erictho episode of Lucan's *Pharsalia* (with which Virgil/*Virgilio* is associated in *Inf.* 9; Quint 1975); in the second the goddess *Virtus* descends from heaven and assumes Manto's form to prophesy. Respectively, the episodes match up with the hellish divination of *Inf.* 20 and the use of an unwitting human agent (in this case, Virgil) to prophesy divine truth in *Purg.* 22. In the second case, the connection between Tiresias' blindness and the image of Virgil as "blind guide" becomes important. Similarly, Statius' principal reference to Clio, Muse of History – invoked in his regards in *Purg.* 22 – prefaces the incident of *Virtus*' assumption of the form of Manto (10.628–31). (The other reference to Clio is at 1.41, followed immediately [42] by an allusion to Tiresias.)

[35] To summarize a confusing situation: *Virgilio*'s version of Manto (Dante's first version) differs from Virgil's in denying her a role in the founding of Mantua (Virgil/*Virgilio*'s native city). *Stazio*'s version, which is also Dante's second version, differs from Dante's first version in its assessment of the character's moral standing (1st vs. 8th circles of Hell), as well as from the Statian original (see again n 34).

functions as teleological *terminus* and its appropriation of the power to assign specific meaning to historical lives by their placement in the economy of "rewards and punishments" in a world to come (Virgil's placement in Limbo; Manto's double appearance in the first and eighth circles; *Stazio*'s unexpected presence in Purgatory). In other words, it strikes at the very heart of the textual mechanisms by which Dante formulates and guarantees his privileged place as "authorized" poet of the *Commedia*.

The encounter of *Virgilio* and Dante with *Stazio*, then, at once constitutes Dante as author and reveals the rhetorical mechanisms by which this constitution is effected. In both ways it points to historically specific traits of the "modern" author: first it exemplifies the birth of authorial intention as full control of the writing subject over the text he writes; second, and precisely as an effect of the range of rhetorical and narratological options inherent in this concept of intentional authorship, it anticipates, without explicitly acknowledging, the imaginative autonomy of the textual world so generated (that is, it prefigures the emergence of the modern "author-God").

If it does these things, and especially the latter, it does them in a way that leaves us uncertain – as we are uncertain if Dante-*poeta* "knew what he was doing" when he introduced Manto for a second time – whether this particular textual event was produced by a conscious act of authorial intention or not.[36] We cannot determine if Dante unconsciously previews a form of authorship whose possible historical significance exceeds his purview, or if he intentionally explores the consequences of the intentional authorship he has systematically constructed. Is he to the impending future (let us call it Petrarch, for the sake of argument) as "his" *Virgilio* was to "his" *Stazio*? Or does he foresee in some way the uses – no doubt ideologically repellent to him – that would be made of the "author–function" as he (and others) had transformed it?

III. *VIRGILIO* CROWNS "DANTE"

The *Commedia* begins in the certainty that Dante-*personaggio* will learn from *Virgilio* what it takes to become an *autore*. On the one hand, then, the destiny of Dante as author at once traditionally authoritative and newly

---

[36] Here I may seem to contradict myself: the episode exemplifies authorial intention; it leaves us in doubt as to Dante's authorial intention – my point, however, is that the text's treatment of *Virgilio* and *Stazio* in 21–22 and then of Dante-*personaggio* in 24 clearly focuses on the question of authorial intentionality, while the Manto conundrum leaves us in doubt as to whether the empirical author, Dante, is in control of this particular textual feature.

personalized is sealed from the outset, in large measure by the simple presence of *Virgilio* as character. On the other hand, and despite the transhistorical fiction, the *translatio* of authority from *Virgilio* to Dante, the evolution from *personaggio* into "poeta," must still unfold – narratively, temporally – over the course of the poem.

From what was said in the preceding section concerning cantos 21–22 and 24, the core of a "meta-poetic" sequence that also includes the meetings with Guido Guinizelli and Arnaut Daniel in canto 26, it might appear that these constitute the pivotal moments in the "authorization" of Dante. And this has been, by and large, what one would gather from the criticism as well. What this section will argue, however, is that the cantos explicitly focused on poetry are part of a larger sequence, which is inaugurated in *Purgatorio* 16.[37] The sequence as a whole (as, indeed, the entire poem to this point) culminates with Dante-*personaggio*'s "coronation" by *Virgilio* at the end of 27, which ratifies the successful completion of his journey through Hell and Purgatory under *Virgilio*'s tutelage and his accession to a primordially sinless state expressed as an autonomous and sovereign subjectivity.

The coronation signals Dante's readiness to reenter the Earthly Paradise, lost to humanity at the Fall, and then to receive indoctrination in the mysteries of the earthly and heavenly paradises in the company of Beatrice-Revelation. It also signals the moment when the *personaggio* acquires, even as the *poeta* defines and deploys, a comprehensive new *autorità* uniting poetic and philosophical authorship around questions of imperial and papal authority, within an encompassing theological framework.[38] The significance of the episode in this respect has been largely overlooked, even if its force as ritual drama has not. On the one hand, this happens because it seemingly lacks the intertextual and meta-poetic pyrotechnics of episodes that *have* usually absorbed critical attention. On the other hand, it is a consequence of the prevailing poetry-theology paradigm in the scholarship, which largely ignores the degree to which poetic *autorità* had for Dante, at least since the time of his exile from Florence, consistently been intertwined with questions of moral philosophy and institutional government.

Once again "Virgil" is the starting point: not as a text cited and traduced by Dante-*poeta*, but rather as the ambulant *autore*-function, the fictive character who accompanies Dante-*personaggio* for over three-fifths of the

---

[37] For useful overviews of the strong political dimension of *Purg.* as a whole, see Ferrante 1984: especially chapter 4; Scott 1996.

[38] As will be seen below, on this score my analysis has something in common with the interpretations of Ferrante and Scott, while departing from the largely apolitical readings in the Singleton-Freccero line.

Commedia. Virgilio remains in company with Dante until some point just prior to the appearance of Beatrice in *Purgatorio* 30. The last the reader sees of *Virgilio* is his stupefied reaction to the pageant of the Church Militant in canto 29 (55–7), marking a complete inability to participate in the experience Dante will now undergo. Only one hundred and thirty-eight lines later does Dante suddenly become aware of his beloved guide's absence (30.42–57). If *Virgilio*'s departure from the poem is attenuated, however, the moment in which his mission of guiding Dante is completed could not be more clearly defined. It comes, as every reader of the *Commedia* knows, at the end of canto 27, after Dante has crossed the barrier of fire punishing the lustful, passing out of *Purgatorio* proper and arriving at the threshold of the terrestrial Paradise.

After the dream of Lia and Rachel, after a last night in company with his faithful guide, Dante receives these words, in which *Virgilio* announces that his duties as guide are fulfilled:

> Tratto t'ho qui con ingegno e con arte;
> lo tuo piacere omai prendi per duce;
> fuor se' de l'erte vie, fuor se' de l'arte.
>   Vedi lo sol che 'n fronte ti riluce;
> vedi l'erbette, i fiori e li arbuscelli
> che qui la terra sol da sé produce.
>   Mentre che vegnan lieti li occhi belli
> che, lagrimando, a te venir me fenno,
> seder ti puoi e puoi andar tra elli.
>   Non aspettar mio dir più né mio cenno;
> libero, dritto e sano è tuo arbitrio,
> e fallo fora non fare a suo senno;
>   per ch'io te sovra te corono e mitrio.
>
>   (130–40)

(I have brought you here with understanding and with art. Take henceforth your own pleasure for your guide. Forth you are from the steep ways, forth from the narrow. See the sun that shines on your brow, see the tender grass, the flowers, the shrubs, which here the earth of itself alone produces: till the beautiful eyes come rejoicing which weeping made me come to you, you may sit or go among them. No longer expect word or sign from me. Free, upright, and whole is your will, and it would be wrong not to act according to its [wisdom]; wherefore I crown and miter you over yourself.)

The passage focuses exclusively on *Virgilio*'s role as moral-intellectual guide, omitting explicit reference to his function as poetic model. Nonetheless, as will now be seen, it represents a key step in the dramatic reconciliation of personality and authority, and has profound implications for Dante's construction of himself as poetic *auctor*.

The doctrinal import of the passage is plain: Dante-*personaggio* has reached a stage of development in which the fallen will has been restored to its prelapsarian integrity, rendering him worthy of reentering the garden from which Adam and Eve were banished shortly after their creation (cf. Singleton 1958: 9–12, 39–56, 91). As a consequence, he no longer needs an earthly guide, not even one as illustrious as *Virgilio*/Virgil. He has achieved autonomous personhood in the terms that such a state was conceivable in the Christian Middle Ages: namely as complete freedom to act according to the dictates of one's own faculty of rationally informed choice.[39] This last point should also show how the passage relates to the issue at hand – Dante's coronation validates his assertion of an individualized first-person perspective throughout the *Commedia* (since the *poeta*, presumably, still bears the symbolic crown conferred by *Virgilio*) – he has found a way, *sub specie aeternitatis*, to reconcile individual personality with unfettered access to moral virtue and intellectual truth – to justify a departure from one set of cultural norms by recourse to another.

What we will now see is how this speech forms a nexus between the vertical axis of authority (poetic authority transformed into/subsumed by theological authority) that leads Dante from *Virgilio* up to God, on the one hand, and, on the other, the "horizontal" axis which pairs Empire and papacy, with the *aporia dantesca* mediating between them. The significance of the "coronation scene" can only be fully appreciated in narrative-thematic context: in the first instance as the culmination of a sequence of cantos beginning with *Purgatorio* 16, which both expounds the problem of the will and links it to the issue of the "two suns" of earthly institutional authority; in the second, as the necessary precondition for Beatrice's conferral of a poetic mission upon Dante in the final cantos of the second canticle.

---

[39] For Dante's understanding of "free will," especially in the *DC*, see Nardi 1940c; Swing 1962: 59–61 *et passim*; Boyde 1993: 193–214. This reading owes its greatest debt to Freccero on the role of the will in Dante-*personaggio*'s experience (1959; see also 1966; also nn 49, 68 below). To reduce a range of terms and distinctions to a basic idea sufficient to my purposes, for Dante the "will," when working correctly, consists of the direction of appetite according to rational judgment, and when working badly, of choices made in ignorance guided by appetite alone. The key is that Dante continually focuses attention on the individual will and its potential for freedom. In cosmic terms, this freedom is the freedom to love the one true good and to surrender any claims to absolute autonomy in a sacrifice of the will to God, referred by Marco Lombardo in the phrase "liberi soggiacete" (16.80) and expanded upon by Beatrice in *Par.* 5. For this reason, then, Dante will find himself once again in a subordinate position within a few cantos when Beatrice, as figure of divine Revelation and representative of the order of Grace, takes over from Virgil. Thus the freedom Dante acquires in *Purg.* 27 can by no means be confused with the notion of secularized selfhood often identified (not always accurately) with a burgeoning modernity.

The close relationship between will and authority has emerged at a num-
ber of points during this study. In both *Convivio* and *Monarchia*, authority
in one crucial acceptation is defined as dominion over the will of individual
human subjects. The *auctoritas* of the Emperor consists in the "reining in"
of human will through enforcement of the *ragione scritta*, law understood
as the practical implementation of reason (and as the pre-condition for
the fulfillment of human potential for rationality). The point, again, is
that ideally the willful subject, the individual person, should be subject to
an impersonal authority. Imperial rule may be exercised through an indi-
vidual, but that individual is constrained to operate within the prescribed
limits of his office and as such is even said to be "without desire," and
thus exempt from the erroneous choices characteristic of the fallen will and
post-lapsarian personhood. In relation to this imperative, then, Dante must
deploy the rhetorical-conceptual stratagems of the *aporia dantesca* and the
prophetic *nuntius* to construct, allusively and implicitly a perspective for
himself *qua* individual subject outside the grasp of Emperor, Philosopher,
and/or Pope.

Similarly, a reading of *De Vulgari Eloquentia*, showed that the Babelic
caprices of the individual will are the principal obstacle to the constitution
of an authoritative language and poetry, that the regulation of the will is the
subject matter of the highest – most authoritative – poetic style (2.2.6–7),
and that Dante's own will to authorship coincides with the constitution of
the *vulgare illustre* and of its finest expression, the tragic *canzone* (2.8.8; cf.
2.1.5–7). From this perspective, then, it is especially significant that, in the
final example treated in Chapter 6, Dante cites an *auctoritas* from his own
work on a question concerning the faculty of free will, and that the focus
of the relevant passages in both *Monarchia* 1.12 and *Paradiso* 5 is on the
historical contingencies that circumscribe the will as we attempt to exercise
it in this life.

All of these examples, though most obviously the first, are relevant to
the other passage from the *Commedia* discussed in Chapter 6, Marco Lom-
bardo's discourse in *Purgatorio* 16 on the "anima semplicetta," which begins
as an affirmation of free will, but ends by qualifying – making contingent –
the individual soul's freedom and submitting it to the guidance of the
twinned "solar" authorities of the Church and the Empire.[40] The vocabu-
lary of authority does not appear in canto 16, or for that matter anywhere

[40] Critics who have treated Marco include Ferrante 1984: 198–9, 228–31 and Scott 1996: 149–57, both
of whom insist upon the centrality of his discourse to the *DC*. See Singleton 1965a on *Purg.* 14–20
as the "center" of the poem and on the crucial place of will at the center of this center. See Swing
1962: 199–204, who positions *Purg.* 16 between *Inf.* 15 and *Par.* 8.

in the *Commedia* between *Inferno* 4 and *Paradiso* 26;[41] no special connec-
tion is made between the topics treated in Marco's discourse and Dante's
development either as *personaggio* or as *poeta*. Nonetheless, as the parallel
instances from the works just mentioned suggest, and as the "coronation
scene" will make plain, the nature of Dantean authorship and authority is
fundamentally at stake here.

Let us consider the scene in more detail. To Marco, who is purging the
sin of wrath in the blinding smoke of the third *girone*, Dante addresses
a question concerning the origins, whether celestial or terrestrial, of the
virtue-less "malizia" that pervades the world in his day (16.58–63). Marco
immediately understands that Dante is potentially calling into question
the existence of free will and, along with it, the divine justice by which
the denizens of Hell are damned and by which he, Marco, and others,
are constrained to the torments of purgation en route to the realm of the
blessed:

> . . . . "Frate,
> lo mondo è cieco, e tu vien ben da lui.
>   Voi che vivete ogne cagion recate
> pur suso al cielo, pur come se tutto
> movesse seco di necessitate.
>   Se cosí fosse, in voi fora distrutto
> libero arbitrio, e non fora giustizia
> per ben letizia, e per male aver lutto.
>   Lo cielo i vostri movimenti inizia;
> non dico tutti, ma, posto ch'i 'l dica,
> lume v'è dato a bene e a malizia,
>   e libero voler, che, se fatica
> ne le prime battaglie col ciel dura,
> poi vince tutto, se ben si notrica."
>
> (65–78)

("Brother, the world is blind, and you surely come from there. You who are alive
still refer every case up to the heavens, just as if they moved everything by neces-
sity. If that were so, free choice [will] would be destroyed in you, and it would
not be justice to have joy for good and mourning for evil. The heavens begin
your motions; I do not say all of them, but, supposing I say it, a light is given
you to know good and evil, and free will, which, if it lasts out the labor of
its first battles with the heavens, afterwards overcomes all things, if nourished
well.")

---

[41] That Dante would have understood the situation in those terms is, however, clear from *MN* where,
as Chapter 5 showed (see n 21), he uses them extensively.

Marco then amplifies this point by giving an account of the prototypical human subject, the "anima semplicetta" (simple soul), as it enters into and experiences the world, but in doing so he seemingly confuses the issue that he aims to clarify.

Specifically, he says of the typical human soul that its innocent yet ignorant will is not sufficient on its own to choose between good and evil objects of desire, but rather requires laws to constrain its choices and guidance to help it know which pleasures to follow and which not:

> "Esce di mano a lui [God] che la vagheggia
> prima che sia, a guisa di fanciulla
>   che piangendo e ridendo pargoleggia,
> salvo che, mossa da lieto fattore,
> volontieri torna a ciò che trastulla.
>   Di picciol bene in pria sente sapore;
> quivi s'inganna, e dietro ad esso corre,
> se guida o fren non torce suo amore.
>   Onde convenne legge per fren porre;
> convenne rege aver, che discernesse
> de la vera cittade almen la torre."
>
>   (85–96)

("From the hand of him who desires it before it exists, like a little girl who weeps and laughs childishly, the simple little soul comes forth, knowing nothing except that, set in motion by a happy Maker, it gladly turns to what amuses it. Of some lesser good it first tastes the flavor; there it is deceived and runs after it, if a guide or rein does not turn away its love. Therefore it was necessary to have a king who would discern the tower at least of the true city.")

The passage has evident connections to the theory, articulated in *Convivio* 4 (12.15–18), of the endless pursuit by human desire of the one true thing (God) through a world of deceptive appearances. And what follows has equally evident filiations with the definition of imperial authority as a necessary reining in of the "volontade umana" (4.9.10).

At this juncture Marco asserts that every human soul has need, while on earth, of two complementary guides, in a passage that bears indirectly on the guidance Dante is receiving from *Virgilio* and that was considered from another perspective in Chapter 6:

> "Soleva Roma, che 'l buon mondo feo,
> due soli aver, che l'una e l'altra strada
> facean vedere, e del mondo e di Deo.
>   L'un l'altro ha spento; ed è giunta la spada
> col pasturale, e l'un con l'altro insieme

> per viva forza mal convien che vada;
>   però che, giunti, l'un l'altro non teme . . ."
>
>   (106–12)

("Rome, which made the good world, used to have two suns that made visible the two paths, of the world and of God. One sun has extinguished the other, and the sword is joined to the shepherd's staff, and it is ill for those two to be violently forced together, for, joined, neither fears the other . . . ")

Here, as in *Monarchia*, Dante derives the need for imperial as well as papal rule from the problem of regulating unstable human desire. Here too he divides that rule into a temporal and a spiritual domain and requires a separation between them.

On the other hand, as the previous chapter began to show, there are also significant differences from *Monarchia*, for example in the treatment of the "duo magna luminaria."[42] More to the present point, this passage, like the *Commedia* in general, stresses the historical failure of the two temporal authorities to provide necessary guidance for the individual souls under their supervision. From this perspective, it is no accident that Frederick II – whose role as poster-boy for the disastrous history of Church–Empire relations and the significance of whose exclusion from the political treatise were highlighted earlier – is named for the last time in the poem immediately following the discourse on the "due soli":[43]

> "In sul paese ch'Adice e Po riga,
> solea valore e cortesia trovarsi,
> prima che Federigo avesse briga;
>   or può sicuramente indi passarsi
> per qualunque lasciasse, per vergogna,
> di ragionar coi buoni o d'appressarsi."
>
>   (16.115–20)

("In the land watered by the Adige and the Po valor and courtesy used to be found, before Frederick found opposition [or "had his troubles there"]; now anyone can pass through confidently who is ashamed to speak to the good or to draw near them.")

---

[42] For the "due soli" in relation to the "duo magna luminaria" of *MN*, see Chapter 6, section iii, especially n 32. It is not often (ever?) remarked that the phrase contains a pun, meaning also and cogently "two alone."

[43] Occasional questions have been raised about the identification of this "Federigo." I side with the vast majority opinion, on the grounds that: (a) Frederick II did have military problems in this area; (b) a reference to him in the context of the "two suns" debate is apt, as established in Chapter 6 (n 26).

The Emperor's name appears in reference to his troubles with the Church and the larger social consequences thereof, namely, their devastating effects on the social world of Marco's beloved Lombardy. Again: where in *Monarchia*, written from the interested perspective of a historical actor, Dante had avoided referring directly to contemporary historical realities, aiming instead to provide a theoretical justification for the "separate but equal" configuration of the two great earthly authorities, in the *Commedia*, adopting a position outside of the historical fray, he paradoxically assumes a special freedom to represent history and a special authority to interpret it.

The canto differs from *Monarchia* not only in detailing the historical scene in which institutional authorities operate, but also in theorizing the position of the individual subject within it, through the generalized character of the "anima semplicetta," a theorization which Dante avoided in the treatise by focusing on the collective "possible intellect." Taken together with the focus on the historical failure of the *due soli*, this fable of human subjectivity has important implications regarding Dante's own subject position within the economy of institutional authority in the temporal domain. Notably, although we must assume that Dante, like all living humans, is in need of and legally subject to both of the "suns," the situation described by Marco modifies the terms of that subjection. It is not only that Dante has once again opened up the intermediate space of the *aporia dantesca* for himself, by circumscribing both papal and imperial authority. Rather, by asserting, from the presumptively infallible (though not complete, as will become apparent) perspective of a redeemed denizen of the afterlife that the two authorities are not functioning properly – in the case of the Empire, not at all; in the case of the papacy, abusively only[44] – Dante implicitly questions the requirement that he submit himself to them. In other words, he makes an assertion of respect for the proper authorities in their ideal form an occasion for justifying his apparent disregard of them in their actual state.

By extension, the lack, or ineptitude, of these universally prescribed governors is in some measure responsible for placing Dante in the state of spiritual crisis in which he found himself at the beginning of the *Commedia*. The absence and/or failure of properly exercised *officia* occupied by appropriately impersonal (i.e., desireless) *vicari*, then, makes it necessary for Dante-*personaggio* to undergo the ministrations of a special guide

[44] According to St Peter, to whom Dante gives the final word on the subject, the papacy too is vacant in God's eyes: "Quelli [Boniface VIII] ch'usurpa in terra il luogo mio,/il luogo mio, il luogo mio che vaca/ne la presenza del Figliuol di Dio" (*Par.* 27.22–4).

mandated by grace, namely *Virgilio*,[45] who in this sense is structurally identical to the *nuntius* of *Monarchia*. His is an ad hoc mission divinely conferred, through a chain rising up from Beatrice to Lucia to Mary to, presumably, God himself (*Inf.* 2.94–108). Conversely, Dante-*poeta*'s mission as divine *nuntius* or prophet, as expressed here and elsewhere, will be to describe, deplore, and seek to remedy that failure – though only after he has himself moved more clearly beyond the need for their guidance or its equivalent is the *personaggio* given the charge that turns him into this new kind of *poeta*.

Canto 16 introduces two basic sets of terms: a discourse on free will, on the one hand, and, on the other, a discussion of the relation between institutional authorities and individual persons. Both prove crucial to understanding Dante's figuration of himself as *personaggio* and as *poeta*, as well as the eventual fusion of the two in a *personaggio–poeta*. These two sets of terms, and these two aspects of the Dantean "io," converge at the moment of *Virgilio*'s "coronation" of his erstwhile pupil. Before they do so, however, Dante will revisit the issue of free will and that of temporal authority separately and in significant ways to address unanswered questions raised by Marco's words.

In cantos 17 and 18, *Virgilio* addresses the issue of free will at far greater length than Marco, and independent from the question of institutional guidance that complicated the picture in canto 16. In these cantos, *Virgilio* correlates the structure of Purgatory with the nature of the sins it houses and justifies punitive atonement of the sinners.[46] In 17.91–139, he shows how all human actions, whether sinful or virtuous, are the products of misdirected love,[47] amplifying and conceptualizing Marco's description of the "anima semplicetta" whose desire for its maker leads it into erroneous passions.[48]

In the following canto *Virgilio* responds to another of Dante's queries by coordinating his account of the origins of sin in love with the problem of free will (18.10–75), to suggest why the individual soul can justly be held accountable in the afterlife for "ogne buono operare e 'l suo contrario" (every good action and its contrary; 18.15). His discourse culminates as follows:

[45] A related view is in Ferrante 1984: 77.

[46] See Mazzotta's discussion of cantos 16–18 in terms of the faculty of imagination (1993a: 116–34).

[47] See especially 103–5: "esser convene/amor sementa in voi d'ogne virtute/e d'ogne operazion che merta pena." The beginnings of the discussion of the nature of love actually come in canto 15.43–81.

[48] See especially 127–8: "ciascun confusamente un bene apprende/nel qual si queti l'animo, e disira."

"... innata v'è la virtù che consiglia
e de l'assenso de' tener la soglia.

    Quest'è 'l principio là onde si piglia
ragion di meritare in voi, secondo
che buoni e rei amori accoglie e viglia.

    Color che ragionando andaro al fondo,
s'accorser d'esta innata liberate;
però moralità lasciaro al mondo.

    Onde, poniam che di necessitate
surga ogne amor che dentro a voi s'accende,
di ritenerlo è in voi la podestate.

    La nobile virtù Beatrice intende
per lo libero arbitrio, e però guarda
che l'abbi a mente, s'a parlar ten prende."

                                                        (62–74)

("... innate in you is the power that gives counsel and must guard the threshold of
assent. This is the principle that accounts for the cause of merit in you, according
as it accepts or winnows good or evil loves. Those who reasoned things out to their
foundations recognized this innate liberty; thus they left morality to the world.
Therefore, supposing that every love kindled in you arises by necessity, in you is
the power to restrain it. This noble power Beatrice understands as free choice, and
therefore see that you remember it, if she speaks to you about it.")

As Singleton observed (1965a), *Virgilio* echoes Marco's initial insistence
that the evil of the world is attributable to the "libero voler" of human
individuals and that divine punishment and rewards for earthly deeds are
therefore justified (18.73 and 16.73).

Why does Dante repeat himself? The simple answer is that rather than
repeating he is elaborating, giving a philosophical underpinning to concepts
that Marco rehearsed rapidly and in "mythic" form, and at the same time
revealing their significance for the structure of Purgatory in particular and
the system of divine justice in the afterlife in general. The sequence might
thus be taken to reflect the typical Dantean procedure – structurally related
to the palinode, and at times coextensive with it – of returning repeatedly
to certain topics, each time adding greater specificity and clarity.

At the same time, however, *Virgilio's* discourse departs dramatically from
Marco's, in this case by subtraction rather than addition. Where Marco's
defense of free will morphed into the assertion of the essential role of
institutional guides in shaping the individual soul's exercise of its will in
the pursuit of what it desires, *Virgilio's* focus is resolutely individual, linking
its subject to *moralità*, as against politics. At first, this shift might simply

be a question of emphasis – an effort to redirect attention away from the historical community, and onto the ultimate destiny of individual souls, and of Dante in particular. I argue, however, both that it provides a necessary corrective to Marco and that it has a special relevance to Dante's individual itinerary in the *Commedia*, which takes place independent of the *due soli*.

Marco's discourse – despite its stated aim of rescuing the orthodox doctrine of free will and the system of divine justice that derives from it – significantly muddies the doctrinal waters when, in the end, it gives a final assignment of blame:

> "Ben puoi veder che la mala condotta
> è la cagion che 'l mondo ha fatto reo,
> e non natura che 'n voi sia corrotta . . ."
> (103–5)

("You can see clearly that bad government is the cause that has made the world wicked, and not nature corrupt in you.")

In trying to negotiate between the two alternative explanations of the world's corruption – the "libero arbitrio" of men and the "necessità" of heavenly influence – Marco chooses a *via di mezzo* that moves the terms of his discussion off the dogmatic high-ground. The stars cannot be blamed, since it would be unjust to punish men for faults not in their own control. Yet, on the other hand, rather than giving the "anima semplicetta" and thus humanity generally responsibility for its damnable loves, he makes culpable the failures of institutional guides, denying that "nature corrupt in you" can be held accountable. Marco thus substitutes a social determinism (the absence of the *due soli*) for an astrological one.

In other words, *Virgilio*'s return to the topic of free will is a necessary corrective to Marco's problematic defense, which simultaneously manages to deny the primacy of free will and, at the very same time and the opposite extreme, to negate the corrupting effects of the Fall on the human faculty of choice.[49] By omitting any reference to institutional guidance, *Virgilio* can maintain a steady focus on the responsibility of human beings for their own

---

[49] It is a fundamental tenet of Christian doctrine that the human will was wounded at the Fall by the sinful choice of Adam and Eve to ignore the divine prohibition. The direction of Dante's journey, as is well known, is initially determined by the "impediment" of his "lame" will (Freccero 1959; see also nn 39, 68), which only divine Grace can remove. To deny that human nature is "corrupt" seems to contradict this understanding. The apparent doctrinal problem is noted by Singleton in his commentary to *Purg.* (1970–76, vol. 2, pt. 2: 362, 365; but see also the moderating interpretation of Durling and Martinez in 2003: 271–2 and the less persuasive argument of Chiavacci-Leonardi 1991, vol. 2: 481–2 that "corrotta" refers to the effects of the stars initially addressed by Marco rather than to those of original sin). Cf. Chapter 5, n 34.

actions. He does not address the fallenness of the will, though in specifying that he can speak to the issue only from the perspective of reason and that Beatrice will further enlighten Dante on it from the perspective of faith, he undoubtedly alludes to the mysterious reconciliation of freedom and fallenness in the will as defined by Christian doctrine. Beatrice, as noted in Chapter 6, does return to the topic of the will, particularly in *Paradiso* 4 and 5, introducing a distinction between the absolute and contingent wills (4.64–114), followed by a discussion of the "sacrifice of the will" in vows (5.19–84), which contrasts the perfection of the will in the angels and the saints – that is, human beings who are already saved – with its imperfections as humans exercise it in this life.

That such a progressive, corrective, internally palinodic, process is at work is clearly marked in the language *Virgilio* uses in his *captatio* to Dante as he begins his answer:

> "Drizza," disse, "ver' me l'agute luci
> de lo 'ntelletto, fieti manifiesto,
>   l'error de' ciechi che si fanno duci."
>   (17–19)

("Direct," he said, "toward me the sharp eyes of your intellect, and I will make manifest to you the error of the blind who claim to lead.")

Virgilio picks up Marco's accusatory reference to the blindness of the world (and of Dante in particular), as well as the general question of intellectual leadership ("duci") the Lombard soul then addresses.[50] The words, however, also recall that Marco himself, along with the other wrathful, is punished by blindness, and thus he too can be seen as a "cieco" who makes himself into a "duce" for Dante. For that matter, they anticipate the paradoxical image of the "blind guide" applied three cantos later to *Virgilio* by *Stazio* (n 25). In other words, as *Virgilio* corrects Marco he also anticipates his own correction, as the double reference to Beatrice, at the beginning and the end of the speech on free will (18.47–48, 73–75), also indicates.

Thus far we remain well within the palinodic paradigm, now extended to include the internal dynamics of the *Commedia* itself, where vertical progress through the realms of the other world brings with it a continuous reframing of fundamental problems from new and higher perspectives (Singleton 1965b). What remains to be accounted for, however, is why

---

[50] That Marco is from Lombardy, like Virgil, may be another signal that the discourses are closely related. Virgil's Lombard origins, as has often been noted, are frequently stressed, from his very first appearance (*Inf.* 1.68–9), through the encounters with Guido da Montefeltro (*Inf.* 27.19–21) and Sordello (*Purg.* 6.71–75).

Dante risks double doctrinal confusion by introducing Marco's discourse in the first place, when he so clearly later indicates awareness of the problems with it. The point, then, is that the palinode of canto 18 is only partial: while it restores the proper ethical understanding of free will, it does not address the original cause of the confusion, namely the polemical insistence on the need for two institutional guides, properly configured in relation to one another and the human subjects under their supervision. Chapter 5 argued that the rationale for universal Empire in *Monarchia* 1 is conceptually undermined in books 2 and 3, without Dante either acknowledging the problem or altering his initial affirmation. The *Commedia*, despite its far more powerful formal and imaginative resources, is similarly unable either to give a stable doctrinal rationale for Dante's theory of the *due soli* or to renounce it: the palinode is once more revealed as the rhetorical tool of Dante's contingent historical interests.

One final point must be made about the sequencing of cantos 16, 17, and 18. In addition to a progressive treatment of general doctrinal issues – the political doctrine of the *due soli*, the moral doctrine of *libero arbitrio* – the sequence is also tracking the evolving subject position of Dante-*personaggio*. If Marco's discussion of the *due soli* both affirms their necessary temporal roles and suggests why it might be that Dante's own spiritual journey has proceeded without them, *Virgilio's* words then project a utopia of perfectly individualized and actualized free will. And though his account does not entirely square with the messy realities of the historical world, it does anticipate both the impending liberation of his pupil from all need for further guidance and the affirmation that "free, healthy, and straight is your will" (27.140). The double reference to Beatrice, then, not only puts epistemological limits on *Virgilio's* guidance, it also projects the conclusion of this part of Dante's journey, and the opening of the next.

Cantos 19 and 20 return to the question of institutional authorities,[51] extending the discussion of canto 16 to a consideration of the relationship of person to office, and this in two senses: first, as concerns the ratio between an office and the person who holds it at any given time; second, as concerns Dante's relationship as individual subject both to an authoritative office and to the person who occupies it. These cantos bring into sharp focus Dante's

---

[51] For considerations of these cantos as a pair, see the brief remarks of Ferrante 1984: 233–7 and the more extensive treatment of Scott 1996: 158–78. The emphasis of my analysis differs considerably from theirs.

new subject-position, in the light of his journey to this point and of the eschatological perspective it has conferred upon him.

Canto 16 suggests in a general way that the failure of the papacy comes from the substitution of individual desires of those who hold ecclesiastical office for the properly impersonal, other-directed, exercise of their duties (16.100–2). In cantos 19 and 20, however, the relationship between individual soul and institutional office is fully dramatized through encounters with one eminent figure from ecclesiastical history and one from the world of politics: a one-time pope – Ottobuono Fieschi, who reigned as Adriano V – in canto 19, and, in canto 20, Ugo Ciappetta (Hugh Capet), founder of the Capetian dynasty of French kings. Even as he focuses attention on the distinction between the office of the papacy and the persons who occupy it (Ottobuono, on the one hand, and Bonifazio VIII, on the other), Dante also puts a spotlight on his own location vis-à-vis these personifications (or impersonators) of *auctoritas* in a way that sheds particularly useful light on what comes later.

Both Ottobuono and Ugo are singled out as being guilty of avarice, the "antica lupa" (20.10; cf. 7–15), which hearkens back to the voracious "lupa" of *Inferno* 1 and which, like that symbolic beast, is at once a specific form of sin and another name for all the misguided human desires that direct attention down to earth rather than up to heaven (Chapter 5, n 32), the latter point reinforced by *Virgilio's* immediately preceding discourse on misdirected love as the root of all the sins atoned for in this realm. By their symmetrical placement in successive cantos, the two combine to illustrate the corruption brought into the world by the institutional failures delineated in canto 16. Ottobuono, though not himself culpable in Dante's eyes of betraying the Church's mission in the same way that Boniface VIII or Clement V are – as he says, he ruled for only a little more than a month – nonetheless illustrates its failures amply.

The one-time Pope's lust for possessions recalls *Inferno* 19 where the avarice-driven simony of pope after pope leads to Dante's first diatribe against the papacy's usurpation of the Empire's temporal wealth and power (88–117).[52] Furthermore, we learn that this man who declares in authoritative Latin that "scias quod ego fui successor Petri" (know that I was the successor of Peter; *Purg.* 19.99) became a true Christian only *after* his ascent into the papacy (16.103–8). From this ferociously ironic perspective,

---

[52] For the connections between cantos 19 of *Inf.* and *Purg.*, see Scott 1996: 163–6; Durling and Martinez 2003: 324–5.

perfectly in keeping with that of *Inferno* 19, as with *Purgatorio* 16, it seems quite possible that most of the hierarchy of the Church is occupied by unbelievers interested only in promoting and satisfying their own personal desires.

In canto 20, the focus shifts to *temporal* governance. Ugo is not an emperor; he was himself never even king of France. But the underlying point is that the French kingdom has assumed an unwarranted political independence from the universal Empire, further reflecting the corrupting effects brought on by the absence of a correct configuration among the *due soli*.[53] This episode (20.40–96), again building on *Inferno* 19 (especially 106–11), as well as various references earlier in *Purgatorio* (6.76–151; 7.88–136), prepares the allegorical union of the "puttana" (the papacy) with the "gigante" (King Philip IV "The Fair" of France, the latest and worst descendant of Hugo), the climax of the second canticle's representations of the evils that have beset the Church over the centuries (32.100–56; see nn 87–89).

The violence done to the proper ordering of ecclesiastical and politi-cal authorities is exemplified through Ugo's condemnation of the assault against the papacy, in the person of Boniface, by Philip's minions:

> Perché men paia il mal futuro e 'l fatto,
> veggio in Alagna intrar lo fiordiliso [the French royal emblem]
> e nel vicario suo Cristo esser catto.
>   Veggiolo un'altra volta esser deriso;
> veggio rinovellar l'aceto e 'l fiele,
> e tra vivi ladroni esser anciso.
>   Veggio il novo Pilato sí crudele
>
> (20.85–91)

("So that its future crimes and those already done may seem less, I see the fleur-de-lys enter Agnani, and in his vicar Christ taken prisoner. I see him mocked again, I see the vinegar and the wormwood renewed, I see him killed between living thieves. I see the new Pilate so cruel . . .")

In this deliberately scandalous vision, the violation of the papacy in the person of Boniface is nothing less than another crucifixion, an assault upon the earthly body of Christ.

Dante-*personaggio*'s encounter with Ugo aims to develop the reader's understanding of the relation of institutional authority to individual per-sons (cf. Scott 1996: 172–4). Ugo's condemnation of Phillip's attack on

---

[53] On Dante's reading of the Capetian dynasty in this canto, see Fenzi 2004; also Scott 1996: 168–77; Martinez 2003a: especially 303, 308–12.

Boniface does not depend on a positive evaluation of the latter's personal
qualities – his account supplements, but by no means reverses, the prophecy
of this pope's personal damnation in *Inferno* 19. Rather, it is the assault on
the Pope's second, institutional and official, body that is deplored. In other
words, Dante uses Ugo to call attention to the basic structure of institutional
authority, in which an impersonal function is represented by a historical,
and at times inadequate, person. The passage thus at once affirms the
authority of the papacy *qua* papacy and leaves intact the condemnation
of one occupant of it. At the same time it exemplifies how the seemingly
infinite human desire for wealth will often be the lever by which the Pope's,
or the King's, two bodies are pried apart.[54]

The same issue was explored in even more consequential detail in the
preceding encounter with Ottobuono. The erstwhile Pope's account of the
motive for his belated conversion also focuses attention on the problem of
relating person to office, extending it to include the difference between the
status of the individual office-holder in our world, and in the next:

> "Un mese e poco piú prova' io come
> pesa il gran manto a chi dal fango il guarda,
> che piuma sembran tutte le altre some.
> La mia conversione, omè!, fu tarda;
> ma, come fatto fui roman pastore,
> così scopersi la vita bugiarda.
> Vidi che lí non s'acquetava il core,
> né piú salir potiesi in quella vita;
> per che di questa in me s'accese amore.
> Fino a quel punto misera e partita
> da Dio anima fui, del tutto avara;
> or, come vedi, qui ne son punita.
> Quel ch'avarizia fa, qui si dichiara
> in purgazion de l'anime converse;
> e nulla pena il monte ha più amara.
> Sì come l'occhio nostro non s'aderse
> in alto, fisso a le cose terrene,
> cosí giustizia qui a terra il merse."
>
> (16.103–20)

("One month and a little more, I felt how the great mantle weighs on one who
keeps it from the mud, for all other burdens seem a feather. My conversion, alas!,
was late; but, when I became the Roman shepherd, then I discovered life to be

---

54 The latter point, evident from the context of the *girone* of avarice, is stressed by the reference to the
   "ladroni" among whom Boniface is crucified. (It is also possible to interpret these as the henchmen
   of Philip who carried out the attack – but the motif of theft, as against murder, suggests simony.)

deceptive. I saw that my heart was not quieted there, nor could I rise any higher in that life; thus was kindled in me the love of this one. Until that point I was a wretched soul separated from God, entirely greedy; now, as you see, I am punished for it here. What avarice does is shown here in the penance of the inverted souls, and the mountain has no pain more bitter. Since our eyes, fixed on earthly things, were not raised up, so here justice has sunk them to the earth.")

Ottobuono's speech emphasizes, on the one hand, the existential effects of the office on the individual who shoulders its impossible burden, metonymically designated by the papal "mantle."[55] On the other hand, it points up the dependence of the office upon the person occupying it to maintain its proper dignity, protecting it against the "fango" into which it too often falls.

The focal point of the passage is Ottobuono's description of his conversion, which he links causally to his entrance into the office. In one sense, this suggests the effect that the office can have on the person, positing a "growing together" of the two bodies. At the same time, the episode clearly implies that there is no necessary connection between an individual's personal faith and the occupancy of an office whose purpose is to guide all the Christian faithful.[56] We know that other popes, like Nicholas, Boniface, and Clement, did not convert on assuming the office; we know that Ottobuono was not a true Christian when he was priest and then a cardinal.

If one then compares Ottobuono's description of the effects his office had on him to *Monarchia*'s general theory of the transformation of the person who occupies the imperial seat, the split between the two bodies becomes even more pronounced. Just as in *Monarchia*, Dante argues that desire ends when one ascends to the highest imperial office, Ottobuono's avarice terminated only when he assumed the papacy. The reason given, however, is very different: in the treatise the claim is that desire for earthly things is truly stilled when one "has everything" in virtue of becoming Emperor; here, instead, the assumption of the highest office brings recognition that earthly desire *has no end*, and that one must look upward and beyond to a more suitable object of love – God. In other words, Ottobuono's story implicitly refutes the argument of *Monarchia* 1 (and *CV* 4), and with it the grounds upon which Dante founds his claim there for the Empire as legitimate font of earthly justice, as well as the notion of a necessary

---

[55] Cf. *Inf.* 19.69. There is probably also an ironic reference to the tonsured hypocrites – presumptively clerics – whose golden capes are lined with lead: "o etterno faticoso manto" (*Inf.* 23.67). Hypocrisy is structurally equivalent to the doubled person of the "King's Two Bodies," and is the endemic ill of those who fail to make personal actions correspond to authoritative roles.

[56] Note the structural analogy between the uncertain relationship of person to office here and the equally uncertain relationship of writer to text in *Purg.* 22 (see section ii).

conformity between personal desires and institutional position (*pace* Scott 1996: 168–9). Despite the implicit contradiction, the passage cannot really be seen as palinodic, and could not be so even if there were still grounds for thinking that the *Commedia* came after *Monarchia*: there is no accompanying renunciation of the treatise's governing fantasy of a universal monarchy ruled by a desireless monarch. Rather Ottobuono's words ultimately further a different, even opposite, rhetorical-conceptual purpose, namely that of strengthening Dante's claim on an "unofficial" and personalized authority, thus permitting him to reassert the necessity of Empire.

The end of the encounter reveals its grand implications for Dante's individual relation to the *due soli*. As Dante makes ready to depart, he bows down to Ottobuono:

> Io m'era inginocchiato e volea dire;
> ma com'io cominciai ed el s'accorse,
> solo ascoltando, del mio reverire,
>   "qual cagion," disse, "in giù ti torse?"
> E io a lui: "per vostra dignitate
> mia coscienza dritto mi rimorse."
>   "Drizza le gambe, levati su, frate!,"
> rispuose; "non errar: conservo sono
> teco e con li altri ad una podestate.
>   Se mai quel santo evangelico suono
> che dice 'Neque nubent' intendesti,
> ben puoi veder perch'io cosí ragiono."
>
> (19.127–38)

(I had knelt and wished to speak, but as I began, and he perceived, by hearing alone, my reverence, "What cause," he said, "has bent you down so?" And I to him: "Because of your dignity my conscience reproached me when I stood erect." "Straighten your legs, rise up, brother!" he replied; "do not err: I am a fellow-servant, with you and the others, of one Power. If you have ever heard that holy sound in the Gospel that says 'neque nubent,' you can see clearly why I speak thus.")

Dante's kneeling aims to acknowledge the papal dignity and authority of his interlocutor. What Ottobuono points out to him, however, is that he was entitled to be called Pope and treated with special reverence only while alive, and even then held no authority over those already in the next world.[57] He does this by means of an allusion to the episode in the Gospel

---

[57] On the other hand, as is often stressed by the purging sinners, any living person can make their penance shorter by praying for them. Martinez 1995a: 156 notes that the episode also anticipates *Virgilio*'s refusal of *Stazio*'s embrace in *Purg.* 21.

of Matthew (22:30) where Christ tells the Sadducees that there will be no marriage in heaven. As commentators have long known, this passage was regularly interpreted to mean that the sacramental offices of the Church, which mediate the Word of God for the living, were no longer necessary once a soul could experience God's justice and mercy directly.[58] The force of this episode is both greater and clearer in light of Dante's specification only three cantos earlier that the papacy and the Empire are constituted to provide, respectively, spiritual and moral guidance to human beings in this world. Denizens of the *next life* do not require such guidance, either because they are beyond its help (damned to Hell), or because they now possess both the intellectual illumination and purity of will to carry on without it (though not without the continuous support of God's Grace). Thus, they are no longer subject to the authority of either Pope or Emperor.

One purpose of this exchange is to reinforce Dante's claim of due piety toward the papacy, despite his recurrent criticisms of some of its individual occupants – and this is also an aim in the subsequent canto where Dante has Ugo condemn Philip's attack on Boniface. More significantly, however, it reveals that the experience of the afterlife puts the soul – and Dante-*personaggio* in particular – beyond an obligatory earthly subjection to the "two suns." It, he, acquires a perspective superior to that of the occupants of those offices, because it/he is no longer subject to the blind desires afflicting even the most illustrious of human beings. As Scott (1996: 181 and nn 9–10) observes, this point is closely related to one made more explicitly in *Monarchia*, as Dante explains why there was no need for the two institutional authorities prior to the Fall (see Nardi 1921c: 215–44; also Chapter 5, n 34):

Cum ista regimina [papacy and Empire] sint hominum directiva in quosdam fines [i.e., temporal and spiritual happiness: cf. *Monarchia* 3.15] . . . si homo stetisset in statu innocentie in quo a Deo factus est, talibus directivis non indiguisset: sunt ergo huiusmodi regimina remedia contra infirmitate peccati. (3.4.14)

(Furthermore, given that these two powers guide men toward certain ends, as we shall see presently, if man had remained in the state of innocence in which he was created by God, he would have had no need of such guidance; such powers are thus remedies for the infirmity of sin.)

We are now, at last, ready to turn to the moment when Dante-*personaggio* undergoes the "coronation" that ends his subjection to *Virgilio*'s guidance as he enters into that same "state of innocence in which [humanity] was

---

[58] For example in the fourteenth-century glosses of Jacopo della Lana, L'Ottimo Commento, Benvenuto da Imola and Francesco da Buti. Consulted electronically in the *DDP* database.

created by God." A first examination of the scene suggested that Dante's liberation from *Virgilio* consists in acquisition of a form of pre-fallen personhood that relieves him of the need for further guidance by his one-time "maestro e autore." The "limp" of the wounded will that necessitated *Virgilio's* initial intervention (see nn 49 and 68) has been cured, restored to its pre-fallen condition (27.131, 138), and is now in perfect harmony with the understanding of the intellect (139), which can interpret the light of the "sun that shines on your brow" (133), visible symbol of divinity. As the soil of the earthly paradise brings forth life "of itself alone" (135), Dante assumes autonomous control over his own thoughts and actions, though only within the sphere of nature.[59] What can be seen now, however, are the implications this event has for redefining Dante-*personaggio's* relationship to the "two suns" of earthly institutional authority and thus for preparing his transformation into the willful yet authoritative *poeta* who will write the *Commedia*.[60]

The need for *Virgilio's* guidance first arose, I have argued, at least in part because of the absence of a proper relationship between the "two suns." Thus, Dante's separation from *Virgilio* is equivalent to liberation from subjection not only to his *maestro e autore*, but also to the twinned guides of Empire and Papacy.[61] So far, this claim is based largely on logical inference: guides are needed for salvation; the prescribed institutional authorities are absent; Dante is given an ad hoc guide to take their place. Nonetheless, it also has a substantial textual basis, since the final lines of *Purgatorio* 27 not

[59] See Kantorowicz 1957: 491–5; Ferrante 1984: 243–4; Scott 1996: 52–4, 64–5, 181, 1997: 97–8. It is no contradiction that Dante returns to a child-like and dependent state when he enters into the presence of Beatrice in canto 30 (especially 40–5, 79–81), since her authority over him comes from her status as direct representative of the order of Grace and as figure of divine Revelation, and does not imply any subjection to earthly authorities. See Hollander 1976 (also 2003: 573) for a broad schematics of the successive guides and their functions.

[60] Ferrante 1984: 243–4 makes a related point, seconded by Scott 1996: 181–4 (also 1997: 97–8, 2004: 66–7), though neither refers to the larger sequence identified here. On one point I disagree strongly with Ferrante's analysis, which in this is echoed by Hollander's commentary (2003: 573), and, more cautiously, by Scott. She argues that Dante believed the "state of innocence" embodied in the Earthly Paradise to be recoverable by all human beings in this life and that Dante is here a tropological example for others. The passage in *MN* cited above (3.4.14), which is educed in support of the point, says nothing of the kind, however: it only insists that *because* humanity is fallen Empire and Papacy are necessary, not that there will be a "withering away of the state." *MN* does foresee a realization of the full *intellectual* potential of human kind, but only under the guidance of an Emperor who continues to "ride" the *volontà umana*, which presumably remains a problem. Dante is claiming for himself a state enjoyed only by Adam (and Eve) and decidedly *not* generalizable to the rest of humanity. In addition, *Virgilio* crowns Dante only "over himself," not others, and while this gives him special standing as *nunzio* or prophet, it does not make him a "surrogate emperor and pope" (*pace* Ferrante 1984: 243).

[61] Scott 1997: 98 also asserts that in the *DC*, especially *Purg.* 27, Virgil represents the successful union of philosophy with imperial authority proposed in *CV* 4. See again Chapter 5, n 5.

only echo the themes of free will and guidance articulated in cantos 16 and 18, but also allusively attach them to the questions of the impersonation of institutional authority raised in cantos 16, 19 and 20 (followed in cantos 21–22, as seen in section ii, by the interrogation of personhood and poetic authorship). The lines, in short, connect Marco's abstract discourse, and what follows from it, to Dante's graduation ceremony.

The connections are signaled in multiple ways. Near the beginning of the canto, *Virgilio* gets Dante to pass through the flames of the seventh and last *girone*. This will be *Virgilio*'s last act of guidance in Dante-*personaggio*'s journey, and a self-canceling one at that, since he fails to move Dante on his own; only the name of Beatrice, who is about to replace him, can do so (27.19–42). In describing his response to the "nome/che ne la mente sempre mi rampolla" (the name that burgeons always in my memory; 27.42), Dante describes himself as a "fanciul . . . vinto al pomo" (a little boy who is persuaded by an apple; 27.45), a phrase that harkens back to the "anima semplicetta" of Marco Lombardo's discourse who "a guisa di fanciulla / . . . piangendo e ridendo pargoleggia" (like a little girl who weeps and laughs childishly; 16.86–8) following after whatever object of desire presents itself first.

Moreover, the guidance that brings Dante to make the definitive passage out of Purgatory proper, and thus, symbolically, restores his will to its prelapsarian purity and autonomy, is doubly linked to twinned guides. The passage describing his crossing of the flames begins with a reminder that Dante now has two escorts, *Virgilio* and *Stazio* ("Volser verso me le buone scorte" [my good guides turned toward me]; 19). It ends with a success brought about by the combined force of *Virgilio* and Beatrice. In other words, a structural analogy exists between the complementary roles that the *due soli* should but do not take in guiding the "anima semplicetta" and the parallel functions that *Virgilio/Stazio* and then *Virgilio/*Beatrice take in leading Dante toward spiritual maturity.

The insistence on twinned guides continues as Dante, *Stazio*, and *Virgilio* rest on the steps during the night preceding the final passage out of Purgatory. The "buone scorte" are now described as twin shepherds protecting their charge:

> Quali si stanno ruminando manse
> le capre, state rapide e proterve
> sovra le cime avante che sien pranse,
>   tacite a l'ombra, mentre che 'l sol ferve,
> guardate dal pastor, che 'n su la verga
> poggiato s'è e lor di posa serve;

> e quale il mandrian che fori alberga,
> lungo il pecuglio suo queto pernotta,
> guardando perché fiera non lo sperga;
>   tali eravamo tutti e tre allotta,
> io come capra, ed ei come pastori,
> fasciati quinci e quindi d'alta grotta.
>
> (27.76–87)

(As the she-goats ruminate tamely, though they were swift and wild on the peaks before feeding, silent in the shade, while the sun burns, guarded by the shepherd who has leaned on his staff [crook] and allows them to rest; and as the cowherd who dwells in the field spends the night alongside his cattle, guarding them lest any wild beast disperse them; so were we three then, I like a she-goat, they like shepherds, enclosed on both sides by the high cliff).

The passage goes well out of its way to stress the pattern of doubling. Two types of guides are specified – shepherd and cowherd – and then in completing the simile Dante depicts himself as a one-man herd of she-goats guided by two shepherds,[62] an image whose violation of mimetic decorum (reversing the expected one shepherd–multiple sheep configuration) begs for an allegorical gloss that the *due soli* passage retrospectively provides.

It is not, however, only the twinning of the guides that connects this complex simile to the earlier canto, but also the doubled motif of pastoral care and ruminating beasts ("as the she-goats ruminate tamely . . . guarded by the shepherd"). The figuration of spiritual care as the tending of a flock – usually sheep – is Biblical (see especially John 10: 1–15), and of the twenty other uses of the word "pastor," and the related "pasturale" and "pasturare," in the *Commedia*, eighteen refer to priests and other ecclesiastical leaders, and of these, eleven to a pope or popes specifically.[63] Similarly, rumination is not only a traditional figure of contemplative and spiritual activity, but was directly connected to the Church's mission of spiritual guidance (Singleton 1970–76, vol. 2, pt. 2: 363–4). 16.98–9 is the only other place in the *Commedia* where the figures of the shepherd and of rumination appear together: "'l pastor che procede,/rugumar può, ma non ha l'unghie fesse" (the shepherd who shows the way may ruminate, but does not have cloven

---

[62] By gendering the goats female, presumably to further stress the submissiveness of his position, Dante also makes a connection to the similarly gendered "anima semplicetta."

[63] References to the pastoral mission of the papacy are at *Inf.* 19.83, 106; *Purg.*16.98, 110, 19.107; *Par.* 5.77, 6.17, 9.132, 15.144, 20.57, 27.55 (for this last, see n 100). Other references to ecclesiastical shepherding are at *Inf.* 20.68; *Purg.* 3.124, 18.126, 24.30; *Par.* 9.53, 11.131, 21.131. The other two references are to actual shepherds (though in one case to those who witnessed Christ's birth): *Inf.* 1.9.72; *Purg.* 20.140. For useful interpretations of the passage from another angle, see Sarolli 1966a: especially 404–5; Hollander 1980b: 183; Ferrante 1984: 112–14.

hooves; cf. 16.110). There the images indicate, building on the exegetical tradition surrounding Leviticus 11:3 (Maccarone 1950: 166–9), the necessary separation of the "ruminative" spiritual mission of the papacy from the temporal office of the Emperor, and the failure of current popes to observe it. Following the logic of these images, then, *Virgilio* and *Stazio* together provide successful, twinned, guidance to Dante where the Papacy and Empire have failed.[64]

Importantly, the simile in canto 27 transfers the function of rumination, of meditative activity, from the pastoral guide to the guided "she-goat," hinting that the dependent individual is on its way to spiritual independence, as almost immediately proves to be the case. Dante makes this transfer evident as he then applies the metaphor of rumination (the third and final use of the word in the poem) directly to himself in introducing the third and final dream of *Purgatorio*, that of Lia and Rachel:

> Sí ruminando e sí mirando in quelle [le stelle],
> mi prese il sonno; il sonno che sovente,
> anzi che 'l fatto sia, sa le novelle.
>
> (27.91–3)

(Thus ruminating and gazing at [those stars], sleep took me, sleep that often, before the event comes, knows the news [new things; what is to come].)

That the nature of this rumination is intellectual and/or spiritual is indicated by its object, the stars, which traditionally, and repeatedly for Dante, represent the point of transition between the sensory and intellectual/spiritual worlds (see sections vi–vii). The two figures of the dream, Lia and Rachel, indicate two aspects of Dante's own experience and, like the other dreams, both have a pivotal and "liminal" function – rehearsing what has recently passed and preparing a change to come.[65] Specifically, as is well known, they stand both here and in traditional medieval allegory for the active and contemplative lives: that is, for the domain of the will, on the

---

[64] Not that there is a one-to-one correspondence between *Virgilio* and *Stazio*, on the one hand, and Emperor and Pope, on the other, although the fact that one poet is identified with the Empire and the other with Christianity reinforces the parallel at a structural level. The logic at work here is not strictly rational, but rather directed toward the fulfillment of a textual desire – that of establishing Dante's independence from earthly authorities of all kinds (see also n 67).

[65] Barański 1989c (also 1986b), elaborating Hollander 1969 (136), highlights the retrospective character of all three dreams in *Purg.*, as well as of canto 27 in general (see also 1986b), complementing rather than contradicting the more traditional reading of them as prophetic. His reading of the last dream reinforces mine in that he attributes to it a "pivotal" function in the text, but our evidence is very different. On dreaming, and imagination, in Dante, see Boyde 1993: 119–39; on the imagination, Mazzotta 1993a: chapter 6.

one hand, and for that of purely speculative intellectual experience on the other (see, e.g., Durling and Martinez 2003: 469–70).

These two aspects of individual existence, as seen, are consistently linked by Dante to twinned authorities who are also guides, though not always to the same ones. In *Convivio*, it is the Emperor who guides the active life of the will, and the Philosopher who is "worthy of faith and obedience" in the intellectual realm. In *Monarchia*, the same structure pairs the Emperor, again linked to the will, with the Pope who regulates the "other horizon," of human life, the one that looks toward spiritual fulfillment in a world to come. Here, given that *Virgilio*'s guidance is about to be superseded, one might argue that Rachel stands for Dante's achievement of a fully rational existence together with the purified will represented by Lia. What is depicted in the dream would then be the achievement of perfection within the order of Nature, beyond which *Virgilio* himself, as he repeatedly tells Dante, is not able to go. On the other hand, since Lia and Rachel are Biblical figures traditionally allegorized in a spiritualized Christian version of the *vita activa/vita contemplativa* opposition (that of works and faith), and since the integration of these two lives attends Dante's admission into a prelapsarian state to which *Virgilio* does not have access, the dream suggests something closer to *Monarchia*'s version of the twinned guides.

The latter interpretation is further supported when (as is well known) it turns out that Lia and Rachel anticipate the arrival of the two female escorts who will assume responsibility for Dante in the Earthly Paradise. Lia, whose active function is figured by the gathering of flowers to make a garland (27.97–102), anticipates Matelda, who is also gathering flowers when Dante first encounters her (28.40–41). Beatrice, who informed us at the outset that she is Rachel's seatmate in the celestial rose (*Inf.* 2. 102), is further connected to her here, not least of all by the brilliant (yet somehow overlooked) pun by which Rachel sitting at her "miraglio" (27.105), figuring the speculative operations of contemplation, is echoed in the imaging of Beatrice-Revelation as metaphorical "am*miraglio*" who encourages others to "ben far" (30.58, 60), while she is the essence of goodness ("ben son, ben son Beatrice"; 30.73).[66]

---

[66] 27.103–3: "Per piacermi a lo specchio, qui m'addorno;/ma mia suora Rachel mai non si smaga/dal suo miraglio, e siede tutto giorno." For the Lia:Rachel::Matelda:Beatrice analogy, and its limitations, see Pacchioni 2001: especially 58–9; cf. Hollander 1969: 151–60; Armour 1979; Boyde 1993: 137–9. The metaphor of the "admiral" also evokes the typological prefiguration of the Church by Noah's Ark. This would give retrospective support for the notion that the guidance of the Church is at issue in the earlier sequence. See Pertile 1998: 74–84 for a different but potentially complementary interpretation.

Whatever one decides the exact referent of the two dream-women to be –
and it seems likely that Dante wanted to have it both ways[67] – it should
now be evident that, within the dramatic economy of canto 27, and of
the sequence beginning in canto 16, they prepare the shift from Dante as
sheepish "fanciullo" in need of guidance to fully mature, self-guided person.
Two external guides (here *Virgilio* and *Stazio*) are presented, and they are
immediately replaced by personifications of two internal faculties, a shift
whose significance is then revealed in *Virgilio's* final words, which we can
now revisit, distilled to the essentials:

"I have drawn you here with wit and with art. Your own pleasure take now as
leader . . . See the sun that shines on your brow . . . No longer await any word or
sign from me: free, upright, and whole is your will, and it would be a fault not to
act according to its intent [understanding]; Therefore you over yourself I crown
and miter." (130–1, 133, 139–42)

The passage is designed to complement the doctrinal burden of canto 16
and its subsequent elaborations. Where the "anima semplicetta" was only
confused and corrupted when it followed its own "piacere," Dante, not
unlike the Emperor of *Monarchia*, can make his desires his guide, because
they are properly directed. Moreover, the language *Virgilio* uses suggests
pointedly that Dante's newly purified "arbitrio" and "senno" can do the
work that Marco assigned to the papacy and the Empire. Notably, the
natural sun, figure of God, recalls but also replaces the two temporal "suns,"
which are no longer needed to mediate His truth.[68] "Arbitrio" and "senno,"
will and intellect, active and contemplative, are now joined in Dante. Last
of all, and decisively, *Virgilio* confers on Dante the authority over himself

---

[67] The dream does not lend itself to straightforward, one to one, allegorizing. Clearly Lia and Rachel
are related to the will-ethics-active life/intellect-metaphysics-contemplative life opposition internal
to human life on earth. Just as clearly, they anticipate the Empire/Papacy pairing of 27.142, and thus
the two goals of humankind, one in this world, one to be achieved only in the next. Finally, they
anticipate the coming opposition between perfected Nature-Matelda and Grace-Beatrice, which
applies to experiences available only beyond the confines of fallen history. Their meaning, thus, is
"over-determined" and available for different interpretations according to the textual angle from
which they are approached. I see this as related to the two, never explicitly reconciled, variants on the
aporia dantesca discussed, respectively, in Chapter 2 and Chapters 5–6 – the Emperor/Philosopher
pairing of *CV* and the Emperor/Pope pairing of *MN*. Cf. Chapter 5, n 17.

[68] As Freccero points out (1959; see also 1966), the need for Virgil's guidance first arises when Dante,
hampered by his wounded will (nn 39, 49), fails to "guide himself" by the aid of the symbolic
sun alone (*Inf.* 1.16–60, especially 17–18, 38, 60). *Purg.* 27 clearly refers back to that earlier failure,
revealing a Dante whose will is no longer fallen. The initial failure and the later reversal are then
recalled retrospectively in *Par.* 26 (55–63; cf. 118), which also systematically evokes the coronation
scene (sects. v–vi and especially nn 100, 101, 155). Recognizing that the *due soli* enter into this same
pattern, and that Marco Lombardo's discourse on the "anima semplicetta" constitutes a gloss on the
need for intellectual and spiritual guidance in this world, expands the range of meanings attributable
to the scene in *Inf.* 1. On recollections of *Inf.* 1 in *Purg.* 27 see also Barański 1986b: 231–4 and nn.

here and personally that the Monarch and the Pope held over him, and all human beings, in our world and institutionally, assigning him symbolically the crown of the one and the identifying miter of the other.[69]

Let me briefly review the process that leads up to this momentous change in Dante-*personaggio*'s status. Canto 16 at once reminds us of the necessary subjection of all living human beings to the twinned authorities of Empire and Papacy, but at the same time, by suggesting their present inefficacy, implicitly excuses Dante-*poeta*'s critical attitude toward them. The encounter with the former Adrian V then introduces the doctrinal point – illustrated by the biblical text "neque nubent" – that puts Dante-*personaggio* on an equal footing with Ottobuono Fieschi and makes clear that as long as he enjoys the perspective of "the world to come" he is not subject to the authority of the Pope, which pertains only to those who live in this world. Finally, as Dante-*personaggio* achieves the spiritual goal that he has pursued under *Virgilio*'s guidance from the beginning of the poem over sixty-one cantos, through both Hell and Purgatory, he receives – as what must be taken to be a permanent acquisition, which will remain with him once he returns to the "secular world" – autonomous status that frees him *sine die* not only from the need for *Virgilio*'s tutelage, but also from that of the two suns. In other words, the "coronation" ceremony potentially extends Dante's status as autonomous person, who has personal authority over himself, back into the domain of history. For that matter, as suggested earlier, since Dante's "freedom" to move about without a guide within the confines of the Other World will last for just two cantos, until – as *Virgilio* himself says – Beatrice arrives, the ceremony only really has sense if it is meant to cover the time after his return to earth (see n 59).

From the point of view of the fundamental opposition between personality and authority that continually structures Dante's understanding of himself as human subject and as poetic, philosophical and/or theological author, the implications of this symbolic crowning are great. The adoption of the perspective of the after-life, in the particular form that we have seen this take, allows Dante to reconcile the opposed terms *and in a way that remains embedded within the strictures of Christian doctrine*. Institutional

---

[69] For this reading of "corono e mitrio," see Ferrante 1984: 43, 243 *et passim*; Scott 1996: 180–1, 2004: 258, 180–1. Singleton (1958: 65–6, 90–1; 1970–76, vol. 2, pt. 2: 665) and Contini (1959) both asserted that the passage refers primarily to the Emperor alone (in fact, Pope and Emperor alike possessed both symbolic implements, on which see Armour 1989: 143–8). However, the internal evidence here educed to show the sequence from canto 16 to canto 27 seems conclusive. *Pace* Quondam 1970 and Consoli 1971, the point is not that *Virgilio* has or does not have the intrinsic authority to confer these offices on Dante, but that his actions acknowledge Dante-*personaggio*'s achievement of a moral state that frees him from the authority of both Pope and Emperor. See also Kantorowicz 1957: 491–5.

authority, like "the law," is a phenomenon of the post-lapsarian world, a supplement necessary to correct the fallen will and the darkened intellect (see again Nardi 1921c). The reacquisition of pre-fallen personhood, in a narrative temporality that projects its extension back into Dante's historical life, effaces the opposition: Dante "crowned and mitered" can overtly position himself beyond the grasp of imperial and, especially, papal authority, without denying that such authorities – properly configured – retain their preeminence in general within the world of history, where the prototypical "anima semplicetta" still desperately needs the guidance that they were designed to provide. The contrast with *Monarchia*, where an earthbound, exclusively rational perspective left him logically subordinate to both, unable to confront his own subject–position directly, is at once clear and instructive.[70]

Revising the schematics of authority first proposed in Chapter 2 and then reconfigured in Chapter 5 accordingly, it looks like this:

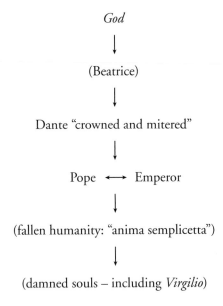

$$God$$
$$\downarrow$$
$$(Beatrice)$$
$$\downarrow$$
$$\text{Dante "crowned and mitered"}$$
$$\downarrow$$
$$\text{Pope} \longleftrightarrow \text{Emperor}$$
$$\downarrow$$
$$\text{(fallen humanity: "anima semplicetta")}$$
$$\downarrow$$
$$\text{(damned souls – including } Virgilio)$$

What this diagram, compared with earlier versions, suggests by omission, is that the investiture of Dante as "sovereign subject" does not directly address his poetic mission. To put it another way, what has been shown so far is

---

[70] This is a variant of Auerbach's argument concerning eschatological perspectivalism in the *DC*, its function as a means by which Dante more fully interprets, and indeed masters, the contingencies of the "secular world" (see again n 18).

how the ceremony liberates Dante-*personaggio* from moral, intellectual, and spiritual authorities which have been placed over him, but not how it helps to confer a poetic-prophetic authority that will allow him legitimately to address the crisis of authority that invests the temporal world, that is, how it transforms him from *personaggio* into *poeta*, not to say *auctor*. And yet, as will now appear, this is also the moment in which Dante-*personaggio* turns into Dante-*poeta*, or rather, in which it becomes most evident that the two Dantes are simultaneous, just as the apparently distinct questions of institutional authority (the two suns) and epistemological authority (poetic, philosophical, theological, as may be) turn out to be inseparable.

IV. A PERFECT POET

To begin with the obvious: despite the absence of any mention of poetry in the ceremony, *Virgilio* performs the coronation, that same *Virgilio* initially defined by Dante as his *maestro e autore* in poetic style.[71] The ritual gesture finally eliminates any moral and intellectual basis for hierarchical distinction between master and pupil. On this basis alone one might infer that if Virgil/*Virgilio* is Dante's "author" in the semi-anachronistic sense proposed in Chapter 1, his "work" is now complete and Dante is ready to assume the mantle of authorship himself. Moreover, the "meta-poetic" sequence, and especially cantos 21–22 and 24, had, as seen in section ii, prepared just such a conclusion to the *translatio auctoritatis* set in motion in *Inferno* 1.

The ostentatious linking of *Stazio*'s guidance to *Virgilio*'s in the second half of canto 27 not only serves as a relay to activate the "two suns" motif and all that goes with it, it also helps us to recall that as the teacher of *Stazio* before Dante, *Virgilio*'s lessons were not only in poetry, but also in ethics (the vice of prodigality) and spirituality ("per te poeta fui, per te cristiano"). In other words, as suggested earlier the sequence focused on the relationship of the individual soul to the institutional authorities (cantos 16–20) is inseparable from the "meta-poetic" sequence (cantos 21–26): canto 27 then represents the point where they most completely intersect. As the ethical–spiritual sequence reveals the intrinsically divided structure of institutional authority in the yoking of fallible, history-bound individual and impersonal, unchanging office, so the *Virgilio-Stazio* meeting focuses

---

[71] Picone 1987c sees the coronation as a poetic laureation, but omits the moral-institutional implications of the scene. More apt is Boyde's brief but compelling suggestion that the "ghirlanda" woven by Lia, the figure of the active, ethical life, is a specifically poetic ornament (1993: 313 n 54), which would anticipate both Dante's coronation and the poetic "corollario" of her döppelganger, Matelda (see nn 77–78).

on an analogous split between the individual person who writes and the textual *auctoritates* that bear his name. Again, the two classical poets represent different, complementary versions of that division: Virgil's poetry teaches moral and spiritual lessons he himself did not intend or benefit from; *Stazio* personally embodied the benefits of those lessons, but did not express them in his own poetry. Dante-*poeta*, under the dictation of divine Love, heals the split, and with it the need to imagine *auctoritas* as a transpersonal quality. Dante's coronation, then, signals not only his liberation from institutional authorities as he, personally, achieves the restoration of prelapsarian will and intellect, it also symbolically completes the fusion – heralded in *Purgatorio* 24 – of perfected moral-spiritual being with the ability to author a poetic text capable of expressing the truth about this new condition.

That the restoration of the pre-fallen will includes access to a new form of specifically poetic authorship is confirmed and reinforced in canto 28, as Dante enters the earthly paradise and begins to enjoy the benefits of his new status. Matelda, who assumes responsibility for Dante pending the arrival of Beatrice, describes Eden as the place given to the first humans as their home by God and after lost to them by their own sin, and then describes the natural perfection of the place in contrast to the fallen nature of the post-lapsarian world below. As a final "corollario," given unasked and "per grazia" (like Dante's unique journey itself!), she compares this place with the fables of the "golden age" of human innocence and perfect Justice recounted by the classical poets, especially Ovid (*Met.* 1.89–112):

> "Quelli che anticamente poetaro
> l'età dell'oro e suo stato felice,
> forse in Parnaso esto loco sognaro.
>   Qui fu innocente l'umana radice;
> qui primavera sempre e ogne frutto;
> nettare è questo di che ciascun dice."
>   (*Purg.* 28.139–44; cf. 31.139–45)

("Those who in ancient times wrote in their poetry of the age of gold and its happy state, perhaps in Parnassus dreamed of this place. Here the human root was innocent; here there is always spring and every fruit; this is the nectar of which each one tells.")

Since she has already told Dante what the place is and its nature, the purpose of the corollary is clearly that of re-establishing the "typological" link between classical culture and salvation history that was given special prominence in the *Virgilio–Stazio* encounter. Thus it evokes, in more general terms, the attribution to Virgil by *Stazio* of an unwitting prophecy of the redemptive Christ event which in fact made possible the return of Astraea, Justice, and with her the *true* golden age: paradise regained.

The list of qualities shared between the poetic dream of the ancients (innocence; eternal spring; nectar) and the "divina foresta" in which Dante now wanders points first to the new moral and spiritual state ritually acknowledged in the coronation. However, by doubly stressing the role of ancient poets in representing the "golden age" ("poetaro"; "in Parnaso") and by echoing *Purgatorio* 22, the passage also anticipates the new poetic representation of this place that Dante *poeta* will later provide – is providing, even as we read – grounded not in an evanescent dream, but rather in the *personaggio*'s unique empirical experience. The subsequent reaction of *Virgilio* and *Stazio*, specifically designated as "miei poeti" and expressing surprised recognition together with delighted complicity, further emphasizes the point:

> Io mi rivolsi 'n dietro allora tutto
> a' miei poeti, e vidi che con riso
> udito avëan l'ultimo costrutto"
>
> (145–7)

(I turned entirely around, back to my poets, then, and I saw that they had smiled hearing her last construction.)

We are still at a stage, however, where it might seem that while Eden, along with the inner state Dante has gained in order to achieve access to it, represents a new object of poetic representation, the status of poetry and of the poet remains constant (for example, "miei poeti" distantly recalls "mio autore," perhaps implying that the same "bello stilo" learned from Virgilio/ *Virgilio* will serve Dante's turn here as it has in the past). This, however, is distinctly not the case, as can be illustrated by a closer examination of the pivotal verse 141: "forse in Parnaso esto loco sognaro."

The received reading of the passage is that it parallels and amplifies the subordinate clause that preceded it, so that in the process of the poetizing "l'età d'oro" the ancients were dreamily anticipating a reality they did not/could not know – namely Eden. The principle clause is "Quelli [ancient poets] sognaro esto loco [Eden]" and although "l'età d'oro e suo stato felice" is part of a subordinate clause modifying "quelli" rather being linked directly to "esto loco," the connection between the two locales is easily inferred, especially given the list of shared attributes forthcoming in the next tercet. The element that both seems to seal the validity of this reading and, from my point of view, to generate an alternative to it, is the prepositional phrase "in Parnaso." Parnassus, of course, is the home of the Muses (and of Apollo, in his capacity as their father and God of poetry and music), and to place poets locatively "in Parnaso" is then taken to figure metonymically the writing of poetry under the Muses' tutelage. Despite the fact that, taken in this way, "in Parnaso" is redundant, saying the same thing as "poetaro," the traditional gloss must be given its due.

At the same time, however, the complex syntax of the passage is undoubtedly ambiguous, yielding a second and complementary interpretation that makes plain the effects of the "coronation" on Dante's standing as poet. Specifically, the words "in Parnaso" can also be construed as "in or through – by means of – the figure of Parnassus," with the resultant meaning that "perhaps the ancients poets who wrote about the age of gold dreamed of this place under the figure of Parnassus."[72] In this construction, Eden is not only the reality concealed in the myth of the "age of gold," it is also the Christian truth behind the myth of Mount Parnassus as the home of the Muses and scene of poetic inspiration: the earthly paradise is, in other words, the place in which poets and poetry, or, more accurately, a poet and his "poema sacro," achieve a perfected state (see also Pizzorno 1994).

Semantically and syntactically this latter reading is possible. The preposition "in" is used in similar ways elsewhere in the *Commedia*,[73] while the juxtaposition of "Parnaso" with "esto loco" suggests the structure of apposition, with the implication of equivalence. The curiously hesitant "forse," traditionally understood to apply to a "esto loco sognaro" can also be construed, based on its pivotal position in the tercet and its immediate proximity to our key prepositional phrase, as marking a separation from the previous two lines, constituting them as a single extended nominal clause and at the same time drawing attention to "in Parnaso" as possible predicate of "sognaro," rather than as adverb of metaphorical–mythical place. Thus

---

[72] A survey of commentaries in the *DDP* database reveals only one commentary from the eighteenth century on – Pietrobono's – which takes the line in this way. Curiously, several commentators from the first century after Dante's death saw an equation being made between Eden and Parnassus (Jacopo della Lana; Pietro Alighieri [1]; Francesco da Buti; Anonimo Fiorentino; Johannis de Serravalle). Among modern critics, Smarr 1987: xxviii briefly anticipates this reading, while others assume it *en passant*: Dragonetti 1968: 242–3; Hollander 1969: 156; Armour 1979: 22 n; Cioffi 2000b; Raffa 2000a: 75; Antonelli 2001: 297. See also Masciandaro 1991: 19, 203–4.

[73] E.g.: "Così s'osserva *in me* lo contrapasso" (*Inf.* 28.142); "falsificando sé *in altrui forma*" (*Inf.* 30.41); "io mi specchiai *in esso* qual io paio" (*Purg.* 9.96); "da che Dio *in te* vuol che traluca/tanto sua grazia, non ti sarò scarso" (*Purg.* 14.79–80); "*nel vicario suo* Cristo esser catto" (*Purg.* 20.87); "e 'l suo voler piacermi/significava *nel chiarir di fori*" (*Par.* 15.8–9); "per vedere *in Beatrice* il mio dovere" (*Par.* 18.17); "vedëa il tacer mio/*nel veder di colui* che tutto vede" (*Par.* 21.49–50).

construed, the words have a genealogical meaning similar to an English phrase such as "I see the mother in the daughter, the father in the son."[74]

Several contextual elements bolster this reading. The most obvious is the mountain-top setting of Dante's Eden,[75] which creates a resemblance with Mt. Parnassus.[76] Just as important is the immediately preceding mention of the divinely originating spring from which Eunoe and Lethe flow, and which provides an analogy to the Parnassian spring – Castalia, Aganippe, or Hippocrene, as may be – of poetic inspiration:

> "L'acqua che vedi non surge di vena
> che ristori vapor che gel converta,
> come fiume ch'acquista e perde lena;
>   ma esce di fontana salda e certa,
> che tanto dal voler di Dio riprende,
> quant' ella versa da due parti aperta.
>   Da questa parte con virtù discende
> che toglie altrui memoria del peccato;
> da l'altra d'ogne ben fatto la rende.
>   Quinci Letè; così da l'altro lato
> Eünoè si chiama, e non adopra
> se quinci e quindi pria non è gustato:
>   a tutti altri sapori esto è di sopra.
> E avvegna ch'assai possa esser sazia
> la sete tua perch' io più non ti scuopra,
>   darotti un corollario ancor per grazia."
>
>   (28.121–36)

("The water that you see does not rise from a vein that vapor condensed by cold restores, like a river that gains and loses fullness, but issues from a firm, sure fountain that takes from the will of God as much as it pours forth, opened in two directions. On this side it descends with the power to take away all memory of sin; on the other it gives back the memory of every good deed. Here it is called Lethe, as on the other side Eunoè, and it is not effective before it is tasted both on this

---

[74] The use of the technical word "costrutto" in line 147 might be taken as a hint to consider carefully the syntactical complexity and consequent semantic ambiguity of Matelda's "corollario." The reaction of "Dante's poets" with which it is associated could be produced by either of the two possible readings of the passage, but perhaps sits even better with the second, which emphasizes more strongly the *mestiere del poeta* (cf. Pizzorno 1994).

[75] This symbolic identification does not preclude the presence of other associations evoked by Dante's polysemous landscape, for example, that between Mt. Purgatory and Mt. Sinai described by C. Kaske 1971.

[76] Parnassus traditionally has two peaks. But Dante covers this at the beginning of *Par.* when he says that the first two canticles of the poem have been composed under the auspices of *one* "giogo" of the poetic mountain (that of the Muses), while the last will require the second peak, that of the father of the Muses, Apollo, i.e., God (1.16–18).

side and on that: this is a savor above all others. And while your thirst might be well satisfied though I should discover nothing more to you, I will give you still a corollary.")

The corollary that follows, as just seen, is the passage that links Eden with the poetry of the golden age and, I argue, with the figurative source of poetry itself.[77] Three cantos later, Dante again refers to Parnassus, in specific conjunction with the topos of drinking from the well-spring of poetry ("chi palido si fece sotto l'ombra di Parnaso, o bevve in sua cisterna"; [who[ever] has become so pale beneath the shadow of Parnassus or has drunk so deeply from its well; 31.140–1]), only shortly after Dante-*personaggio* has been immersed in Lethe by Matelda, and has, in fact, drunk of its waters (La bella donna ne le braccia aprissi;/abbracciommi la testa e mi sommerse/ove convenne ch'io l'acqua inghiottissi"; "The beautiful lady opened her arms, embraced my head, and submerged me, so that I had to swallow some of the water; 31.98–100). From this perspective, the many-faceted, much-interpreted, Matelda takes on the additional character of Muse-analogue.[78]

I am not arguing, however, that this alternate reading should take the place of the traditional one: there is no doubt either in terms of syntax or of literary historical precedent that the more usual interpretation is *also* "correct." Rather, the ambiguity seems deliberate and the two readings complementary: together they reflect the highly unusual, indeed virtually unprecedented, situation in which Dante-*poeta* has placed himself.[79] The

---

[77] The use of the word "corollary" implies logical entailment, reinforcing the idea that the essential moral-spiritual nature of the place has determinate consequences for its relationship to poets and poetry. Furthermore, as commentators on the passage have long recognized (e.g., Durling and Martinez 1996: 489), before being adapted to the vocabulary of philosophical logic, the Latin word *corollarium* meant "wreath" or "garland" and thus might be taken as a figure of poetic laureation, as well as an extension of, a corollary to, the coronation ceremony of canto 27. An additional possible link joining the rivers of forgetfulness and recollection to Parnassus: the latter's inhabitants, the Muses, are the daughters of Mnemosyne, Memory (see also nn 71, 78).

[78] Pietrobono, as recorded in the *DDP* database, makes this point; also Armour 1979: 22 and n 22, though his primary reading of her is as the Sophia of the Bible and of *CV*. The reference to Urania, Muse of Astronomy, and to Helicon, the poetic river that derives from the "Pierian spring" near the beginning of the following canto (29.37–42) adds indirect support. See Pizzorno 1994 for the suggestion that Matelda's movements may figure a poem, a *canzone*. Despite the political-institutional cast of my interpretation, I am not convinced by the traditional, topical reading of Matelda as the historical Matelda of Canossa (e.g., Nardi 1944b), revived by Ferrante (1984: 246–8) and, cautiously, by Scott (1996: 182–4). See also the more nuanced reading of Pertile 1998: 79–84. Compare Singleton's gloss of Matelda as Astraea, which relies heavily on the traditional reading of 28.139–44 (1958: 204–21). For the principal interpretive proposals, see Forti 1971; Armour 1979; Mazzaro 1992; Cioffi 2000a.

[79] Wlassics 1975: 8–34 highlights Dante's frequent uses of ambiguous syntactical constructions for specific semantic purposes.

pagan poets may have distinguished between the "age of gold" as object of representation and "Parnassus" as the condition of possibility for representing it poetically, but Eden is simultaneously the true "age of gold" – the place of perfected individual and social Justice – and the Christian reality behind the myth of Parnassus.

As seen earlier, the theme of Parnassus had been first explicitly introduced by *Stazio* in *Purgatorio* 22.64–6, a passage that prepares his declaration of a double indebtedness, as poet and as Christian, to Virgil, who will himself later recall the mountain of the Muses (104–5). As also seen, however, the underlying burden of the episode is that the split between poetry and inward spiritual experience, differently exemplified by *Stazio* and by *Virgilio*, will be healed by Dante.[80] The convergence of the moral "golden age" and the symbolic site of poetic inspiration in Eden, in this canto, is the final emblem of that healing.[81] The point is that what separates Christian Eden from classical Parnassus, further distinguishing Dante from Virgil/*Virgilio*, as well as from *Stazio qua* poet (since his poetizing days are long over by the time he reaches Eden), is that in it moral, intellectual, and artistic perfections are simultaneous, perhaps even identical: to know the good is to do good is to make the good, which is also the beautiful.[82]

Dante's coronation, then, not only gives him moral-intellectual authority over himself, but also makes this authority the direct gateway to a new source of poetic *autorità*, one which constitutes the typological fulfillment of the pagan locus of poetry par excellence. The crown *Virgilio* puts on Dante's head looks more and more like it also subsumes the poet's laurel, all the more so, since, as Dante points out in *Paradiso* 1.29, the laurel is used to crown "o cesare, o poeta," and Dante has just become "Caesar" unto himself. Even more importantly, it forecasts the poetic "cappello" he later imagines receiving at his baptismal font (*Par.* 25.7–9; see sect. vi).[83] In a very specific sense, then, the *auctoritas* of Dante-*poeta* derives directly

[80] In addition to *Stazio*'s citation of the fourth *Eclogue*, Canto 22 also contains a prominent reference to the Golden Age (148–53). On this topic, see Shoaf 1978; Mazzotta 1979: 225; Martinez 1989.

[81] A further corollary, this time mine, gracious or not, would be that unfallen Adam, for Dante the inventor of human language, was also the "first poet," a point potentially reinforced by the appearance of the first human being in *Par.* 26 (see section v and nn 155–56).

[82] This would be the definitive solution to the "bellezza"/"bontà" opposition played out in *CV*. See Chapter 2, section v, especially nn 64, 70, 80.

[83] For the debate over what the "cappello" refers to, see, e.g., Fumagalli 2002: 393–404. Deciding among the proposals – the laurel wreath; an academic's hat; a cardinal's – is difficult, in large part because in the examination suite, as in the coronation scene, Dante is undergoing multiple authorizations: as "poeta," as scholastic "baccialiere," as St Peter's designated mouthpiece in criticizing the hierarchy of the contemporary Church. Fumagalli stresses the connection to the coronation of Albertino Mussato and the Northern Italian humanists, noting the apparent recall of this passage in Dante's second eclogue (42–44) to Giovanni del Virgilio (Ascoli 2009; Chapter 1, n 75).

from the narrated experiences of Dante-*personaggio* – there is no longer any substantive distinction between them.

But there is more. What we have seen so far is that Dante-*personaggio* has redefined his subject position so as to transfer to himself the authority that the two "suns" have over him personally. This acquisition, in turn, has given him access to the true Parnassus, that is, to a poetic authority of which Virgil/*Virgilio* could only dream. What is also true, however, is that Dante's mission, *qua poeta*, then is shown to be none other than to describe the crisis of historical authorities defined by Marco Lombardo and to announce prophetically a divine remedy to it. In certain respects, this is old news by the time Dante and his readers get to Eden. Throughout *Inferno* and *Purgatorio*, the reader is treated to a series of denunciations, in a prophetic voice, of the failure of the two suns: Dante-*personaggio*'s violent outburst against the temporal wealth of the papacy and the donation of Constantine in *Inferno* 19.88–123; Dante-*poeta*'s diatribe against the failures of modern Monarchs to reclaim the "garden of the Empire" in *Purgatorio* 6.76–151; the "ventriloquized" remarks of Marco Lombardo in *Purgatorio* 16. The narrative priority of these moments, and others, with respect to the coronation scene, masks the fact that they are, according to the premises of the poem, written after the journey has been completed and thus, *a fortiori*, after the events related in *Purgatorio* 27. In other words, the poem plays continuously on the double temporality of Dante as character *in via* and Dante as poet who, like God, knows the whole story simultaneously.

That the coronation constitutes a decisive event in the spiritual existence of Dante, and that this is strictly coordinated with his access to a poetic-prophetic authority directed at the "due soli," is further confirmed when Beatrice gives Dante two commissions to write of what he has seen:

> . . . [I]n pro del mondo che mal vive,
> al carro tiene or li occhi, e quel che vedi,
> ritornato di là, fa che tu scrivi.
>
> (32.103–105)

([F]or the good of the world that lives ill, keep your eyes now on the chariot, and what you see, returning over there, be sure that you write.)

And then, most famously:

> Ed ella a me: "Da tema e da vergogna
> voglio che tu omai ti disviluppe,
> sí che non parli più *com'om che sogna*.
>   Sappi che 'l vaso che 'l serpente ruppe,
> fu e non è; ma chi n'ha colpa, creda

> che vendetta da Dio non teme suppe.
>   Non sarà tutto tempo sanza reda
> l'aguglia che lasciò le penne al carro
> per che divenne mostro e poscia preda;
>   ch'io veggio certamente, e però il narro,
> a darne tempo già stelle propinque,
> secure da ogni intoppo e d'ogne sbarro,
>   nel quale *un cinquecento diece e cinque,*
> *messo di Dio,* anciderà la fuia,
> con quel gigante che con lei delinque.
>   E forse che mia narrazione buia,
> qual Temi e Sfinge, men ti persuade,
> perch'a loro modo lo 'intelletto attuia;
>   ma tosto fier li fatti le Naiade,
> che solveranno questo enigma forte
> sanza danno *di pecore* o di biade.
>   *Tu nota; e sí come da me son porte,*
> *cosí queste parole segna a' vivi*
> *del viver ch'è un correre a la morte.*
>   (33.31–54)

(And she to me: from fear and shame I would have you disentangle yourself now, so that you speak no more like one who dreams. Know that the vessel the serpent broke was and is no more; but let him who is to blame believe that God's vengeance fears no sop. Not for all time without heir will the eagle be who left his feathers on the chariot, whereby it became a monster and then booty, for I see clearly, and therefore I relate it, stars already near, secure from all obstacle and all barrier, that will give us a time in which a five hundred ten and five, messenger of God, will slay the thieving woman and the giant that transgresses with her. And perhaps my narrative, dark like Themis and the Sphinx, persuades you less, because in their manner it blunts the intellect, but soon events will be the Naiads who will solve this hard enigma, without loss of sheep or grain. *Do you take note and just as they come from me write these words to those who live the life that is a race to death.*)

Both charges are specific to the visions and the words Dante-*personaggio* is immediately experiencing, rather than to the journey as a whole – but they are also the first references in the *Commedia* to a divine commission to write being delivered directly to the character Dante.[84] They should thus be read,

---

[84] Up to this point references to what Dante will write have primarily concerned the *personaggio*'s promises, and occasionally threats, to sinners and penitents that he will relate their conversations upon his return to the world of history. On the "investitura profetica" in *Purg.* 32–33, see Nardi 1942b: 336–9; Mineo 1968: 254–6; also Armour 1989: 215–6, 232 *et passim*; Scott 1996: 213, 2004: 302–5. Gorni aptly points to the connection between "tu nota" and "quando/Amor mi spira, noto" (*Purg.* 24.53), as well as between 33.53 and Revelation 22:10. Note also the allusive connection to 28.141 ("forse in Parnaso esto loco sognai") in "non parli più come uom che sogna" (also evocative of the dream of Lia), and to a pastoral metaphorics ("sanza danno di pecore"; cf. n 63).

in tandem with the later commissions of Dante's ancestor Cacciaguida (*Par.* 17.106–42), and of St. Peter (*Par.* 27.19–66), as the poem's most elaborate accounts of its author's poetic and prophetic mission.[85] They may also be taken as the equivalent, now explicit and particularized, of Dante's flirtation with the role of divine *nuntius* or *scriba Dei*, analogous to that of Daniel, in *Monarchia*.[86]

Both charges, moreover, pertain to the institution of the Church and focus on the problems created by the confusion between ecclesiastical and political authority, with a double focus on the absence of the legitimate Empire and the all-too-present interference of the illegitimate French monarchy. The first commission comes in the middle of the allegorical vision of the history of the Church Militant – immediately following Dante's witnessing of the pageant of the Church up to the time of the Crucifixion and Resurrection, and just preceding the vision of the seven catastrophes that have afflicted it between Christ's Ascension and Dante's own day.[87] Of these misfortunes the first and the third concern the Empire – first the early persecutions of the Church by pre-conversion Emperors, then the contamination of the Church with worldly wealth and power by the donation of Constantine (Chapter 5, n 47) – and the series concludes with the allegory of the whorish papacy first wooed and then battered by the French "giant," Philip the Fair.[88] If the first commission invites Dante to report on the past and present degradations of the Church, linked closely to the politicization of its mission, the second focuses on a prophecy of an obscure remedy to come, which specifically includes the return of an "heir" to the depredating imperial "eagle," a "cinquecento dieci e cinque" (DXV), who will now, apparently, participate in setting matters right.[89] In

[85] Nardi 1942b; Mineo 1968: 254–62; Hawkins 1997: 33–5; Scott 2004: 302–5.

[86] That Dante associates himself with a range of Biblical scribes, especially John, in *Purg.* 28–33, (especially 29 and 32) is no secret. See, e.g., Nardi 1942b; Sarolli 1963; Mineo 1968: 233–56; Pézard 1973; Hollander 1976; Battaglia Ricci 1983, 1988; Hawkins 1988; Barolini 1989b; Herzman 1992; Pertile 1998. For the Gospel of John and Revelation as models for Dante in *VN*, see, respectively, O. Holmes 2000: chapter 7 and Nolan 1970. For Dante's use of Biblical citation generally see Chapter 6, n 11. See also sections v–vi.

[87] The general thrust of the sequence is clear and relatively homologous versions appear in all major recent commentaries. See R. Kaske 1974, 1983 for an important, if idiosyncratic, elaboration of its meaning, as well as Scott 1996: chapter 10.

[88] The basic terms of the "puttana"/"gigante" allegory were established long ago. For a more detailed analysis of the episode's iconography, see Pertile 1998: 203–25.

[89] Whether the "eagle" will act by itself or in tandem with the second coming of Christ, whether it is the same thing as the "DXV," is not clear, but clarity on this point is also not essential for my claim here, namely that Dante is prophesying a remedy for the failures of the two suns (cf. Armour 1989: 241–50). For useful reviews of the principal proposed solutions to the DXV prophecy, see Mazzamuto 1970; Raffa 2000b. See also Scott 1996: chapter 10 for a recent political interpretation.

other words, the first charge substantiates Marco's discourse on the failings
of the "two suns" and the second foresees a divinely provided remedy.[90]
This, in turn, reveals how it is that Dante's "crowning and mitering" has
not only liberated him personally from the institutional authorities, but has
given him special, ad hoc, authority concerning them, as poetic-prophetic
nuntius of the divine will.

In short, Dante-*personaggio*'s experience with Beatrice in the earthly par-
adise renders explicit the authorizing effects of his investiture by *Virgilio*.
It shows as well the relevance of the "coronation" to the claims that Dante-
poeta makes for the legitimacy of his simultaneous reproduction and tran-
scendence of traditional canons of institutional and poetic authority in the
Commedia. So explicit is Beatrice in her first charge to Dante, that she
does not hesitate to preface it with a revelation of the previously implicit
consequences of the poem's narrative: even after Dante's return to earth he
will retain an autonomous status that only the reacquisition of a pre-fallen
state, and with it a predetermined guarantee of salvation, could give him:

> "Qui sarai tu poco tempo silvano;
> e sarai meco sanza fine cive
> di quella Roma onde Cristo è romano.
>   Però, in pro del mondo che mal vive,
> al carro tiene or li occhi, e quel che vedi,
> ritornato di là, fa che tu scrivi."
>
>   (32.100–105)

("Here you will be but briefly a dweller in the wood [forester], and with me, without
end, you will be a citizen of that Rome of which Christ is a Roman. Therefore, for
the good of the world that lives ill, keep your eyes now on the chariot, and what
you see, returning back there, be sure that you write.")

Note especially how Beatrice's phrasing suggests that there will be no inter-
ruption in Dante's dwelling in Eden prior to his final assumption into
Paradise after death, implying that she is referring not simply to his phys-
ical presence in the place itself, but rather to his inner possession of the
moral condition for which it stands.[91] Note also the causal link that she
establishes ("però") between this description of his newly acquired spiritual
state and the commission she gives him, duplicating their conjunction in
the coronation scene and its aftermath in canto 28.

---

[90] The phrase "in pro del mondo che mal vive" recalls the language of *Purg.* 16, where "mondo" appears
seven times (47, 58–9, 66, 81, 103–4, 106, 108), more than in any other canto. The two cantos are
also connected by references to the "celestial Rome" (16.95–6, cf. 106).

[91] In other words, as was implied at the beginning of canto 28, for Dante the "divina foresta" has
replaced the "selva oscura" as metaphor for his inner condition in this life (28.2).

Finally, the implications of this sequence in relation to Dante's discourse on authority throughout his career remain partially masked, and for relatively good reasons. First, although a reading of *Monarchia* suggests that Dante thinks of the "two suns" question as being concerned with the *auctoritas* both of those who hold the highest institutional offices and of one, like himself, who attempts to describe and/or prescribe the nature and modality of said offices, the language of authority is not overtly present at this point in the *Commedia*. Second, the freedom that Dante gains at the end of canto 27 in some sense immediately disappears as a new and more imposing guide, Beatrice, replaces the first, and Dante is cast immediately again in the role of subject – although not in such a way as to undo what his travels with *Virgilio* have done. The point, again, is that the autonomy Dante has just acquired applies to his relation to life in our world, while Beatrice's guidance pertains to the world he is currently occupying, the world beyond history.

Similarly, the significance of this narrative of authorization in the context of a history of Western authorship is even more thoroughly obscured. In one sense, the move that Dante makes in canto 27 is aimed at opening the doors to personal authorship – one predicated on the autonomy of the writing subject – that anticipates typical characterizations of the early modern author. On the other hand, precisely because Dante's experience is described in terms that are singular, if not completely unique, there is no way of imagining it as a template for writers in general: as far as the *Commedia* is concerned, Dante and only Dante can possess this form of *autorità*. To emphasize a different aspect of the same problem: only by removing himself – imaginatively, narratively – from the confines of history can Dante overcome the overwhelming limitations that historical circumstances seemingly impose on his writerly vocation. For this reason, as already suggested in a number of different ways, the *Commedia* can resolve the questions that other Dantean works raise but cannot answer, written as they are from historically-bounded perspectives. Nevertheless, it is also the reason why the other works are actually more reflective of Dante's historical position.

This is not to deny that the specially personalized author of the *Commedia* is an important indicator of historical trends, or that his rhetorical strategies would influence later writers coping with related problems of self-definition. Rather, it simply explains why those questions are so infrequently and incompletely raised in relation to a text whose systematic aim it is to remove itself and its author from subjection to the compromising flow of history, even as it looks back to name and to shape the world it seeks so ardently to leave behind.

V. "DI SÉ PARLANDO"

The second and final use of the word *autore* in the *Commedia* comes in *Paradiso* 26, along with the second and third of three mentions of *autorità/autoritade*. The scene is the eighth Heaven, that of the fixed stars, in the heavenly sign of the Gemini, at the boundary between time and eternity, the visible and the invisible heavens (Durling and Martinez 1990: 240–58; also Armour 1995: 410; Moevs 1995: 132–40). Dante, having been examined by Saints Peter and James on the theological virtues of Faith and Hope, now responds to the questioning of St. John (for Dante, author of the eponymous Gospel, three Epistles, and the book of Revelation) concerning the last and greatest virtue, divine Love, or *caritas*. Having already explained that God is the beginning and end of all he loves, Dante-*personaggio* goes on to answer John's query as to how his desire came to be so directed:

> E io: "Per filosofici argomenti
> e per *autorità* che quinci scende
> cotale amor convien che in me si 'mprenti:
>   ché 'l bene, in quanto ben, come s'intende,
> così accende amore, e tanto maggio
> quanto più di bontate in sé comprende.
>   Dunque a l'essenza ov' è tanto avvantaggio,
> che ciascun ben che fuor di lei si trova
> altro non è ch'un lume di suo raggio,
>   più che in altra convien che si mova
> la mente, amando, di ciascun che cerne
> il vero in che si fonda questa prova.
>   Tal vero a l'intelletto mïo sterne
> colui che mi dimostra il primo amore
> di tutte le sustanze sempiterne.
>   Sternel la voce del *verace autore*,
> che dice a Mоïsè, di sé parlando:
> 'Io ti farò vedere ogne valore.'
>   Sternilmi tu ancora, incominciando
> l'alto preconio che grida l'arcano
> di qui là giù sovra ogne altro bando."
>   E io udi': "Per intelletto umano
> e per *autoritadi* a lui concorde
> d'i tuoi amori a Dio guarda il sovrano."
>   (*Par.* 26.25–48)

(And I: "By philosophical arguments and by authority descending from here, that love is necessarily imprinted in me: for the good, in so far as it is good, as soon as it is known kindles love, and the greater, the more goodness it comprehends within itself. Therefore toward the Essence that so surpasses others that every good found outside it, is nothing but a ray of its light, more than toward anything else, the mind must move in love, in anyone who discerns the truth on which this proof is founded. This truth is set forth for my intellect by him who demonstrates the first love of all the sempiternal substances. The voice of the truthful [or true] Author sets it forth, who says to Moses, speaking of himself: 'I will make you see every Goodness.' You set it forth for me as well, beginning the high proclamation that cries out the secrets of this realm down there, beyond all other blazoning." And I heard: "According to human intellect and authorities agreeing with it, the highest of your loves keep turned toward God.")

The passage may be read as a faithful re-presentation of the epistemological hierarchy sketched by Aquinas (Chapter 2, n 32; cf. Hawkins 1992: 77 and n 13). Dante's two sources for understanding that God is both the most worthy object of love in himself and the source of what is loveable in all created things are (1) the "philosophical arguments" available to human reason, and (2) "authority which ascends from here above," namely the Old and New Testaments, specifically Exodus and either the Gospel of John or Revelation.[92]

Strikingly, the notion of human authority not directly sponsored by God, which Aquinas ranks as the least trustworthy mode of knowledge, is omitted entirely. The invocation of "colui che mi dimostra il primo amore," a thought variously attributed, but more often than not to Aristotle, might be taken as a partial contradiction of this claim, and a harkening back to invocations of "Il Filosofo" as *auctoritas* in *Convivio*. However, the insistence on rational proof convincing to the knowing subject ("mi dimostra") and the use of a pronoun ("colui") that could mean either a specific person or "(any)one who . . ." uses the potential of the human intellect for this purpose, works against such an interpretation (cf. Di Scipio 1995: 367–8 n).

In either case, the passage would seem to constitute yet another rejection of Virgil/*Virgilio*, who is mentioned by name later in the canto for only the second time in *Paradiso* (the other is in 17.19) and for the last time in the poem.[93] And in some sense it does, although in his two separate aspects,

---

92 The choices are John 1:1 and Revelation 1:8. Both look back to Genesis: John 1:1 with its reprise of "In the beginning" and Revelation 1:8 with the reference to God as "Alpha and Omega," then cited in line 17 (of which more anon). The latter choice seems stronger to me because of the subsequent citation and also of the reference to the *arcana Dei*, the hidden things revealed in the Apocalypse. Also obviously relevant is 1 John 4:8: "Deus caritas est" (cf. *VN* 24).

93 The name *Virgilio* appears juxtaposed with the word "volume" (26.119), which in his first appearance referred to the *Aen.* (*Inf.* 1.84) and now refers to the number of solar revolutions (years) between Adam's death and Christ's harrowing of Hell. As Hollander (1968: 144–5; 1969: 78–9) has shown this reference is part of a structured opposition between Virgil's book and God's (i.e., Creation as a whole: see *Par.* 33.86; also Chapter 2, n 87), mirroring the passage from human to divine *autore*. Other appearances of the word, all in *Par.*, are at 2.78, 12.122, 15.50, 19.113, 23.113, 26.119, 28.14. On 15.50, see Schnapp 1986: 146 and n 90.

as seen above, Virgil/*Virgilio* has been assimilated *both* to human reason at its most advanced, and as such a possible contender for "colui che . . ." (*Virgilio*), and to divinely-sponsored prophecy (the books, especially *Eclogue* 4, named "Virgil"). Thus, *Virgilio* is marked as deficient specifically in his capacity as *autore*, no longer an unchallenged font of truth "degno di fede e d'obedienza." And not just Virgil/*Virgilio*. According to the passage cited above, there is only one true and truthful Author, and while authority may be mediated by those to whom he delegates it, no one else – ancient or modern, pagan or Christian – can lay claim to the title. Or, rather, that title has ceased to mean what it meant when Dante applied it to his *maestro* in *Inferno* 1, which was already a dramatic step away from his earlier treatments. Specifically, an *auctor* in the traditional epistemological sense was understood *by definition* to be truthful and thus "verace autore" should be a redundancy. To the extent that "verace" has now become a necessary qualifier, it not only defines God as the One True Author, it also implies that a (human) *autore* not so qualified lacks constituent truthfulness – is a purveyor of linguistic constructs elaborated *ad placitum*, i.e., "made" fictions without any *necessary* relationship to the truth, except what the Truth itself, God, confers upon him/them.

Another way of putting this is that *Virgilio*, Dante, and all human authors are now reduced to the status of the *autore* from *avieo* in the purely formal, linguistic and/or stylistic, sense attributed to the word in *Convivio* 4.6 and *De Vulgari Eloquentia* 2. This transformation is marked, again, by the explicitation of the "divine analogy" subtending the "vowels of authority," first remarked by Mazzotta, in the juxtaposition of the designations of God as "Alfa e O" and as "verace autore." God is *the* veracious *autore* from *autentin* and he is also *the autore* from *avieo*. Thus in the upper reaches of the Heavens Dante is further away from explicitly *calling himself* an author than he was in *Convivio*, *De Vulgari Eloquentia* or *Epistle* 3, though his claims here as a writer, and specifically as a *poeta*, are indeed exalted.

I will return *modicum* to the question of the "vowels of authority" and the naming of divinity. For the moment, however, let us consider more closely the standing of the two human writers who *are* identified in the passage, namely Moïsè, who transcribed the words of God, "di sé parlando," and "tu," the pronoun conveying familiarity, used of Dante's examiner, St John, invoked either for referring to God as the "Word" or as "Alpha and Omega," or both (see n 92). Chapters 1 and 2 recalled the concept of the Bible's dual authorship – divine and human, divine through human – and foregrounded Minnis's thesis that the human authors of the Bible took on increasing importance during the thirteenth century. Chapters 4 and

5 began to suggest how Dante makes indirect use of the dual authorship model in works other than the *Commedia*, in order to justify his assumption of what would otherwise be, on his own terms, an unwarranted usurpation of authority.[94] It is in this light that the references to Moses and John, the human authors of *the* authoritative descriptions of the *origins* and *endings* of human history, need to be considered.

In order to do this, however, we also need to consider the larger context in which the divine authority mediated by the writings of the two "Scribes of God" is evoked. Dante's references to the words of Moses and John constitute the culminating moment in the three-canto (24–26) "final examination" process during which, like a "baccialier" formally examined in theology (by implication, at the University of Paris),[95] he answers questions of Saints Peter, James, and John concerning the three theological virtues. This process accomplishes a number of "authorization" functions simultaneously. For example, Dante, largely self-educated in Scholastic thought and, until very late in life it seems,[96] almost wholly external to the official university culture of his time,[97] arranges for the conferral of a degree,[98] as it were *honoris causae*, which at once places him within and lifts him far, far beyond the sanctioned forms and norms of philosophical-theological rationality.

In addition, the episode parallels and complements the earlier "coronation ceremony" (see n 68). If *Virgilio*'s authorizing gesture qualified Dante, *personaggio–poeta* in matters comprehensible by human reason, including the "mundane" institutional domains of both Empire and Church, this examination demonstrates his mastery of the three holy virtues which lead to transcendence of all things earthly. If the earlier scene was followed immediately by Dante's entrance into Eden, this one is succeeded by Dante's

---

[94] My concern with the "examination" episode overlaps significantly with Hawkins (1992), who also stresses its burden of "self-authorization," especially Dante's assimilation of himself to the human authors of the Bible. A number of differences between our approaches will be noted *ad loc.* Of these the most important is that while "authority" is the key term in Hawkins's own argument he does not examine or even refer to Dante's uses of the words *autore, autorità*, and *autoritade* and hence does not reflect on the extent to which the episode not only affirms Dante's authority, but also interrogates and transforms the concept, and indeed the signifying structure of the word itself. See also Benfell 1997.

[95] For the motif of the "bacciliere," see Moevs 1999: 70 and nn. Durling and Martinez 1990: especially 239–40 point to the earlier assimilation of Dante into the company of the leading Scholastic theologians (cantos 10–12), which also prepares his encounter with the Biblical *auctores* (240–2).

[96] The *Q* similarly staged Dante's "indoctrination" into the ranks of authorized Scholastic thinkers (see Chapter 2, n 27).

[97] On Dante's education, see again Chapter 2, section i and nn 4, 7, 23; Chapter 5, section i, and n 7.

[98] On the organization of the Scholastic curriculum, see again Marenbon 1987: 7–34. Cf. Chapter 2, section ii, and nn 27–28.

introduction to the first, and one of only two, denizens of that original home of humankind.[99] If the earlier scene led consequentially to the first major prophetic commission that authorized the writing of the *Commedia*, this one leads to the last. In the very next canto, St. Peter's tirade against the abusive occupancy of the papacy by "lupi rapaci" (27.40–66)[100] concludes with the demand that:

> "... [T]u, figliuol, che per lo mortal pondo
> ancor giù tornerai, apri la bocca,
> e non asconder quel ch'io non ascondo ..."
>
> (27.64–6)

([Y]ou, my son, who because of your mortal weight will go back down again, open your mouth and hide not what I do not hide.")

Indeed, St Peter's explicit commission is then strongly reinforced by Beatrice's obscure prophecy of divine vengeance (27.121–48), providing a further link to *Purgatorio* 32–33.[101] In other words, in cantos 24 to 26, Dante marks yet another passage from the role of student – *baccialiere* (24.46–51) or *discente* (25.64–6; cf. *Inf.* 11.104) – to a divinely sanctioned mission of teaching. In part this involves a redefinition of his target readership to the much more restricted audience of those able to follow the profound mysteries of Christian theology, the "arcano/di qui."[102] But it also puts a

---

[99] As Hawkins 1992: 91–2 stresses, Dante has his "Giovanni" ostentatiously dispel the widespread medieval legend, ambiguously encouraged by the coy references in John 21:22–23, that he had never died and was assumed "in body" into the Earthly Paradise (25.118–29). See Jacoff 1999 for detailed treatment of the legend(s). Hawkins focuses on the undoubted place of the incident in the episode's economy of self-authorization. For me, it has the additional function of emphasizing that Dante, *personaggio–poeta* is the only male human since Adam to have entered *in the body* into Eden. (I stress "male" partly because of the vexed question of who, or even what, Matelda is [cf. nn 66, 67, 71, 78, 154]).

[100] The "lupi rapaci" come from Matthew 7:15, where they are not described as "shepherds" but as "sheep," and designate "false prophets." Note the buried link to *Purg.* 27.76–87 (section iii and n 62) and the implied contrast between Popes as false prophets and Dante as true prophet commissioned by the archetype of Popes. See also Armour 1995: 414.

[101] Pertile 1991: 232–3 also suggests a link to Marco Lombardo. Although it comes just before Dante's transit from Saturn, the Heaven of Contemplation, into the Heaven of Fixed Stars, Beatrice's earlier promise of "... la vendetta/che tu vedrai innanzi che tu muoi" (22.14–15) is opening a sequence that her later invective closes. To complete the picture, this first prophecy introduces St. Benedict's lengthy screed against the corruption of monastic life (22.73–96), which anticipates Peter's attack on the papacy. Benedict and Peter represent the contemplative and active aspects of the Church's earthly mission, and thus recall the Rachel/Lia dyad of *Purg.* 27 (nn 65–67, 71).

[102] Dante narrows his audience to a highly talented few at the beginning of *Par.* 2, cautioning those in a metaphorical *picciolettta barca* (1) to turn back before they become lost. In canto 23, shortly after entering the sign of Gemini in the sphere of the fixed stars and before beginning the examination process, he recalls the image, now deflected back onto his poetic mission: "Ma chi pensasse il ponderoso tema/e l'omero mortal che se ne carca,/nol biasmerebbe se sott' esso trema:/non è

further seal on Beatrice's earlier charge to refer prophecies of retribution and reparation from above to the "mondo" at large.[103]

The process enacted here is far more elaborate than that of *Purgatorio* 27, with symbolic recognition conferred after (even during!) each of the three examinations. To begin with, as Brownlee (1984: 597–8; 1990: 50) emphasizes, after Dante responds satisfactorily to initial questioning on Faith by St Peter, the assembled souls sing an Italian translation of the "Te Deum Laudamus" (we praise you God), the original Latin version of which marked Dante's *admission* into Purgatory proper (*Purg.* 9.140). As Brownlee also notes, the force of the recall is heightened because in the earlier episode Dante had just passed muster before the angel who held the two keys of heaven in Peter's stead (1984: 598 and n). The song begins a pattern of praising Dante's success in the examination indirectly, through a celebration of the divine Grace that made it, and him, possible. Even more important, as will soon be seen, is the simple fact that this hymn constitutes the degree zero of a heavenly "stilo della . . . loda" (*VN* 26.4; cf. 18–19), that is, song as praise of God.

After then reciting his *credo* impeccably, Dante receives the following tribute directly from Peter:

> Come 'l segnor ch'ascolta quel che i piace,
> da indi abbraccia il servo, gratulando
> per la novella, tosto ch'el si tace;
>   così, benedicendomi cantando,
> *tre volte cinse* me, sì com' io tacqui,
> l'appostolico lume al cui comando
>   io avea detto: sì nel dir li piacqui!
>   (*Par.* 24.148–54)

(Like a lord who listens to what pleases him and then embraces his servant, thanking him for the news, as soon as he is silent: so, blessing me in his song when I fell silent, three times the apostolic light encircled me at whose command I had spoken, so greatly in my speech I pleased him!)

The triple circling, as Singleton notes, is a figurative coronation (1970–76, vol. 3, pt. 2: 397) and thus tacitly raises the "servant" to the "master's" level,

---

pareggio da picciola barca/quel che fendendo va l'ardita prora,/né da nocchier ch'a sé medesmo parca" (64–9). The purpose is not only to re-mark the "podoroso tema," but also to signal the importance of the upcoming episode for demonstrating that Dante is not a "sailing master" (guide; teacher) who "a sé medesmo parca."

[103] In a widely cited phrase, Getto 1966: 219 speaks of the examination scene as "il rito di un'investitura di carattere profetico."

a rhetorical move now more than familiar from *Convivio* and *De Vulgari Eloquentia*.[104]

This gesture makes the comparison with *Virgilio*'s "corono e mitrio" ineluctable, and all the more so since it actually contains a second, distinctly Virgilian, pre-text, alluding to the vain attempts of Aeneas to embrace the shades first of Creusa and then of Anchises (*Aen.* 2.793–4 and 6.700–2). These passages were earlier imitated by Dante in his own failed attempt to embrace Casella (*Purg.* 2.76–81) and in *Stazio*'s similarly empty effort to do reverence to *Virgilio* (21.130–6). The point is not only to show Dante's advance on himself and on *Stazio*, experientially, and on Virgil, poetically, at this advanced stage, but also to highlight the fact that the lack of bodies is no longer an indication of absence and loss, but rather of *presence* in the spirit (see n 99), to which Dante both as character and as poet has full access.

Finally, and most importantly, as Singleton notes (1970–76, vol. 3, pt. 2: 397), Peter's circling of Dante at the end of canto 24 repeats the identical gesture, then in relation to Beatrice, at canto's beginning (24.22–4). The repetition, which tracks Virgil's Creusa/Anchises sequence, implies a *translatio* of Beatrice's authority as guide in matters concerning revealed truth, and especially the Faith in which all such matters are rooted, to Dante: one might say that the examination covers the [im-]material she has "gone over" with him since their reunion.

Each of the next two examinations concludes with a choral celebration based on Biblical texts, the first from the Old Testament, the second appearing in both Old and New. The first, "sperent in te" (let them hope in you, o Lord; 25.98) retranslates into Latin the verse of Psalm 9:11 [10] by Dante attributed to David and cited at the beginning of his examination on Hope (25.73). As with "laudamo," the apparent interchangeability of Latin and Italian is one indication of Dante's success here, as is the fact that he himself "dictates" the song to be sung in his own honor (Brownlee 1984: 598–9). In addition to recapitulating the theme of the examination, the song does two other things that contribute to the authorization process. Affirming Dante's hopes, it reinforces Beatrice's declaration – obviating the need for the poet to praise himself directly – that her charge has better reason to hope than most of the Church Militant, because of the special Grace that has permitted his presence among the spirits of the Church Triumphant before death (25.49–56; Stephany 1995: 372). More speculatively, although the primary

---

[104] In the epistolary section of the *ECG*, the writer calling himself Dante performs a related maneuver in relation to his "friend," Lord Cangrande della Scala (Ascoli 1997: 319).

referent of "te" is clearly God, a secondary implication is that the members of the Church Militant now have even more reason to put their hopes in, or through, Dante himself, as *portavoce* of divine truth. Finally, the omitted subject of the verse, namely, "qui noverunt nomen tuum" (those who know your name), earlier translated as "coloro che sanno il nome tuo" (25.73), anticipates things to come in canto 26.

The first examination concluded with Peter's crowning gesture, his bene-diction, and an unspecified song; the second with a general chorus; the third with a chorus which now explicitly includes Beatrice's voice as well, as if to seal the culmination of her teaching:

> Sì com' io tacqui, un dolcissimo canto
> risonò per lo cielo, e la mia donna
> dicea con li altri: "Santo, santo, santo!"
> (*Par.* 26.67–9)

(When I fell silent, a most sweet singing resounded through the heaven, and my lady was singing with the others, "Holy, holy, holy!")

These words first appear in Isaiah 6:2–3 where the prophet sees the Seraphim gathered around the throne of God, chanting his praise.[105] They are then taken up in Revelation when "John," recalling the scene in Isaiah, puts them in the mouths of the four animals (4: 6–9; see Ezekiel 10: 4–14) also gathered around God's throne.[106] Here, as Brownlee has remarked (1984: 599–600), the transition to Italian is completed, incidentally suggesting the possibility of an unproblematic *translatio* from the Latin of the Vulgate into the more vulgar tongue and anticipating the dominant concern of the coming colloquy with Adam. From the detached rehearsal of the hopes of the living for salvation through God, the blessed now turn to their primary activity, namely His praise, which in this case too indirectly turns back onto Dante, since its object is the extraordinary example of divine Grace instanced by his performance in this examination particularly and in all three comprehensively.

I will come back to connect the praising of God, on the one hand, to, on, the other, the discourses on Love and language which, respectively, precede and follow, and to explore the significance of the sequence as a whole (Love, praise, language). Now, however, having established in general terms the

---

[105] As the angels specifically associated with Love, a recall of the Seraphim is appropriate here.
[106] The words "sanctus, sanctus, sanctus" also appear in the "Te Deum," creating an additional sym-metry between the first and last instances in which Dante's success is celebrated during the exam. See also Brownlee 1990: 50.

crescendo of authorizing gestures and symbols in cantos 24–26, it is time to pick up the deferred thread concerning the human authors of the Bible. The conflated citation of Isaiah and Revelation in "santo, santo, santo" is not simply a situationally and thematically appropriate Biblical *auctoritas*. Rather, it draws upon two first-person singular visionary accounts of Heaven itself. In other words, it represents, as it were, two precursors of Dante's own representations in this very segment of the *Commedia*: more if we recall that the four animals who chant God's praise represent the four evangelists.[107]

Dante then – and I am not the first (by a long shot), nor will I be the last to say this – builds a comparison between himself and various of the human authors of the Bible (in addition to Isaiah and John, in this episode alone Moses, David, Peter, and Paul can be added, and no doubt others as well), in a process that begins much earlier, and is particularly pronounced in the parallel episode of the Earthly Paradise.[108] The progress toward achieving effective parity with Biblical scribes made by the *personaggio–poeta* under Beatrice's tutelage can best be measured with reference to that earlier episode. Hawkins has cogently outlined the echoing contrasts between the two episodes. There Dante sees an allegorical pageant that contains figurative representations of the books of the Bible, derived (as noted above) from Revelation 4; here, he meets the authors of those books, their spiritual essence in any case, *in person*. There he compares his description of the four animals that figure the four Gospels to that in Ezekiel and John, and famously remarks that "John is with me," meaning that John's text agrees with what he saw (29.105); here "John is with him" *literally*. There he compares his visionary sleep to the sleep of the three favored apostles at the mountain-top transfiguration of Jesus, flanked by Moses and Elijah (32.73–82). Here he is interrogated personally by those three – Peter, James, John – now themselves transfigured by their passage into the next world.[109] In short, the "journey to authorship," which got off to such a conspicuous start when Dante entered *personally* into the

---

[107] The larger context of the passage, Revelation 4: 4–11, furnishes imagery from which Dante partially built his allegory of Biblical revelation in *Purg.* 29, especially 86–105.

[108] See, for instance, Nardi 1942b; Sarolli 1963; Mineo 1968; Battaglia Ricci 1983, 1988; Barblan 1988; Benfell 1997; Hawkins 1999: especially chapters 2–3. See also nn 86, 113, 115, as well as the discussion of Dante's identification with Solomon in Chapter 2, especially n 88, and with Daniel in Chapter 5, section iv. See also the essays of Jacoff 1988 on Dante and Jeremiah and Martinez (1997, 1998, 2003a, 2003b) on his use of Lamentations.

[109] On the Transfiguration in the *DC* generally and in *Par.* particularly, see Hawkins 1985; Schnapp 1986, 1988.

company of the poetic *auctor* par excellence, *Virgilio,* approaches zenith as his transhistorical fiction puts him *personally* in the company of Biblical scribes: "bella scola," indeed.

Not only is Dante is assimilating his work to the Bible, and himself to its human writers; in addition, as previously with *Virgilio,* he has here simultaneously staged and reconfigured the nature of a particular form of authorship in the process of appropriating it. In cantos 24 and 25 Dante's answers continually draw attention both to the referential status of Scripture in general, as authorial product of the third person of the Trinity, and to specific books of both Old and New Testaments written, or transcribed by individual human writers:

> . . . "Questa cara gioia
> sopra la quale ogne virtù si fonda,
>   onde ti venne?" E io: "La larga ploia
> de lo Spirito Santo, ch'è diffusa
> *in su le vecchie e 'n su le nuove cuoia,*
>   è silogismo che la m'ha conchiusa
> acutamente sì, che 'nverso d'ella
>   ogne dimostrazion mi pare ottusa."
> Io udi' poi: "*L'antica e la novella*
> *proposizion* che così ti conchiude,
>   perché l'hai tu *per divina favella?*"
> E io: "La prova che 'l ver mi dischiude,
> son l'opere seguite, a che natura
>   non scalda ferro mai né batte incude."
> Risposto fummi: "Dì, *chi t'assicura*
> *che quell' opere fosser? Quel medesmo*
>   *che vuol provarsi, non altri, il ti giura.*"
> "Se 'l mondo si rivolse al cristianesmo,"
> diss' io, "sanza miracoli, quest' uno
>   è tal, che li altri non sono il centesmo:
> ché tu intrasti povero e digiuno
> in campo, a seminar la buona pianta
>   che fu già vite e ora è fatta pruno."
>   (*Par.* 24.89–105)

("This precious jewel on which every other virtue is founded, whence did it come to you?" and I: "The plentiful rain of the Holy Spirit, diffused on both the old and the new parchments, is a syllogism that has concluded it for me so sharply that next to it every demonstration seems dulled." I heard then: "The old and the new propositions on which you base your conclusion, why do you hold them to be the speech of God?" And I: "The proof that discloses the truth to me is the resultant works, for which Nature never heats the iron nor pounds the anvil." I was answered: "Say, who assures you that those works took place? The very book you wish to prove, not someone else, swears it to you." "If the world turned to Christianity," said I, "without miracles, this one miracle is such that the others are not a hundredth of it: for you came into the field poor and hungry to sow the good plant, formerly a vine but now become a thornbush.")

As Barolini has pointed out, this argument stubbornly invokes the categories of philosophical rationality and just as stubbornly undoes them,[110] leaving them, as it were, trapped between empirical consequences (the conversion of "the world" to Christianity; the exemplary experience of Peter) and the invisible efflorescence of the Holy Spirit. And while this point is perfectly in keeping with Pauline doctrines concerning the "scandal" of Faith which defies and exceeds reason, it is important to note that the passage begins with divine inspiration and comes to rest on the biographical experience of one of the human authors of Scripture.[111]

From this point, Dante then moves on to an invocation of Biblical *auctoritates,* which oscillate between the typical "impersonal" citational practices and familiar, and even familial, address to the human author, or rather scribe, in person. This occurs during Dante's *credo* in canto 24:

> E io rispondo: "Io credo in uno Dio
> solo ed etterno, che tutto 'l ciel move,
> non moto, con amore e con disio;
>   e a tal creder non ho io pur *prove*
> *fisice e metafisice, ma dalmi*
> *anche la verità che quinci piove*
>   *per Moïsè, per profeti e per salmi,*
> *per l'Evangelio e per voi che scriveste*
> *poi che l'ardente Spirto vi fè almi;*
>   e credo in tre persone etterne, e queste
> credo una essenza sì una e sì trina,
> che soffera congiunto 'sono' ed 'este.'
>   *De la profonda condizion divina*
> *ch'io tocco mo, la mente mi sigilla*
> *più volte l'evangelica dottrina."*
>
>   (*Par.* 24.130–44)

(And I reply: "I believe in one God, sole and eternal, who moves all the heavens, unmoved, with love and with desire, and for this belief I have not only proofs

---

[110] Barolini 1992: 229–31; see also Noferi 1977: 39; Hawkins 1992: 93–4; Benfell 1997: 95–8; and, especially, Moevs 1999: 70–5.

[111] It is worth remembering that in *MN* (3.9), Dante also pays particular attention to Peter's personality, and its weaknesses, as it emerges in the Gospels (see again Chapter 6, n 33) and that he articulates the office/person problem most specifically in relation to a successor of Peter, Adriano/Ottobuono (section iii above).

physical and metaphysical, but that provided me by the truth that rains down from here through Moses, through prophets, and through psalms, through the Gospel and through all of you, who wrote when the burning Spirit made you nourishers. And I believe in three Persons eternal, and these I believe to be an Essence so one and so trine that it supports both *are* and *is*. About the profound nature of God on which I touch now, my mind is sealed numerous times by the teachings of the Gospels.")

Here, as in canto 26, Dante begins with reference to philosophical proofs ("physical and metaphysical"), before moving on to the invocation of Scripture, and especially of "*voi* che scriveste" under the influence of The Holy Spirit. Crucially, Dante then adds his own new "profonda condizion divina" as a "seal" on the "evangelica dottrina."

The process repeats in canto 25, now even more ostentatiously personalized:[112]

> "Da molte stelle [i.e., textual sources] mi vien questa luce;
> ma quei la distillò nel mio cor pria
> che fu *sommo cantor del sommo duce.*
>   'Sperino in te,' ne la sua tëodia
> dice, 'color che sanno il nome tuo':
> e chi nol sa, s'elli ha la fede mia?
>   *Tu mi stillasti, con lo stillar suo,*
> *ne la pistola poi; sì ch'io son pieno,*
> *e in altrui vostra pioggia repluo.*"
>
> (Par. 25.70–78)

("From many stars this light comes to me, but he who first distilled it in my heart was the highest singer of the highest Lord [i.e., David]. 'Let them hope in thee,' he says in his divine song, 'those who know thy name'; and who does not know it, if he has my faith? Along with his instilling, you instilled it in me by your epistle, so that I am full, and I in turn rain on others what you have rained on me.")

Again Dante moves from Old to New Testament, again his first reference is, "impersonally" to David, although with personal application to his own faith.[113] Again, his final address is *personally* to James, using the intimate "tu" and ends with the claim that he is exercising the same "distilling" function as his examiner, albeit at second hand (cf. Stephany 1995: 376).

---

[112] On the examination in *Par.* 25, see the very useful *lectura* of Stephany (1995), as well as Battaglia Ricci 1983: 229–36; Benfell 1997.

[113] On David as model for Dante-*poeta*, see Barolini 1984: 275–8; Hawkins 1992: especially 82–4; Benfell 1997: 92. For David as scribe of God's word, see *MN* 3.1.4; also n 119 and Chapter 5, n 25. See Stillinger 1992: 40–1, 66–9 for the Psalms (as glossed on the *sacra pagina*) as model for *VN*, and also as traditional examples of "songs of praise" (see nn 120, 122, 125). On the treatments of David as *auctor* in Trecento Biblical commentary, see Minnis 1984: 43–8, 88–93, 103–12.

The next passage then completes the stage-setting process for canto 26:

> E io: "*Le nove e le scritture antiche*
> pongon lo segno [of Hope's promise], ed esso lo mi addita,
> de l'anime che Dio s'ha fatte amiche.
> *Dice Isaia* che ciascuna vestita
> ne la sua terra fia di doppia vesta:
> e la sua terra è questa dolce vita;
> *e 'l tuo fratello assai vie più digesta,*
> *là dove tratta de le bianche stole,*
> *questa revelazion ci manifesta.*"
>
> (*Par.* 25.88–96)

(And I: "The new Scriptures and the old set forth the target for the souls whom God has made his friends, and that target points it out to me. Isaiah says that in the homeland each will be clothed in a double raiment: and the homeland is this sweet life; and your brother far more distinctly, where he treats of the white stoles, manifests this revelation to us.")

Once more the move is from Old to New, from third-person to second-person singular, specifically anticipating the central role of John in the following canto (along with the conflation of *auctoritates* of Isaiah and John in the chant "santo, santo, santo"), and recalling the reference to John in *Purgatorio* 29, as well as the scene of the Transfiguration evoked not so long thereafter.

We are now ready, at last, to return to the principal passage under consideration, *Paradiso* 26.37–48:

> "Tal vero a l'intelletto mïo sterne
> colui che mi dimostra il primo amore
> di tutte le sustanze sempiterne.
> Sternel la voce del *verace autore*,
> che dice a Moïsè, di sé parlando:
> 'Io ti farò vedere ogne valore.'
> Sternilmi tu ancora, incominciando
> l'alto preconio che grida l'arcano
> di qui là giù sovra ogne altro bando."
> E io udi': "Per intelletto umano
> e per *autoritadi* a lui concorde
> d'i tuoi amori a Dio guarda il sovrano."
>
> (see translation above)

The passage seemingly repeats a now-familiar pattern: moving from unnamed philosophical authority, to a third-person Old Testament scribe, to a second-person singular address of a New Testament figure. However, the careful prior establishment of that pattern highlights two important departures from it, both of which sharpen and clarify the distinction between human and divine "authors" of the Bible.

The first of these departures, of course, is the introduction of the words *autore* and *autorità* to describe the Scriptural texts cited and the Being in which they originate, a move which establishes the centrality of this conceptual complex to an understanding of the sequence as a whole. Let me illustrate this first by expanding a point first made near the beginning of this section. The last few paragraphs have repeated, with modifications of detail and emphasis, interpretive points made by Hawkins (1992). At this juncture, however, I need to register my disagreement with one crucial aspect of his argument, and thereby foreground the specific weight of my own: namely, that he refers several times without comment to the human writers of Scripture as *auctores*. In fact, however, this is exactly what Dante *does not* do and what he seems bent on making us understand *should not* be done. He ostentatiously avoids using *autore* in reference to John and the other Biblical writers, or of attributing the *autoritade* that "descends from here above" to them personally, assigning it uniquely to the "verace autore," God.

The point is actually prepared by the first citation of a scriptural *auctoritas* in the examination over *fede*:

> E seguitai: "Come 'l verace stilo
> ne scrisse, padre, del tuo caro frate
> che mise teco Roma nel buon filo,
>   fede è sustanza di cose sperate
> e argomento de le non parventi;
> e questa pare a me sua quiditate."
>   (24.61–6)

(And I continued: "As the truthful stylus has written for us, father, of your dear brother, who with you set Rome on the right path, faith is the substance of things hoped for and argument of those unseen, and this seems to me its quiddity.")

The locution "verace stilo," I submit, recalls the "bello stilo" of Virgil/ *Virgilio* as poetic *maestro e autore*, as well as the "dolce stil nuovo" of Dante himself (*Purg.* 24.57; also 24.62).[114] It is certainly intended to prepare us

---

[114] Latin "stylus" mean both "pen" and "style" (see e.g., Carruthers 1990: 219) and Dante was certainly aware of the common etymological root – in any case, at least according to the Petrocchi edition, he uses "stilo" to mean both. As for *verace*, the word appears fifteen times in the *DC*, twice in *Inf.*, five times in *Purg.*, seven in *Par.* Unsurprisingly, it was twice earlier applied to *Virgilio*, called "lo verace duce" (*Inf.* 16.62) and "quel verace padre" (*Purg.* 18.7). The shift in usage, which parallels the shift in the meaning of "autore," is first negatively marked by *Virgilio* himself in *Purg.* 21.16–18

to understand the specific gravity of "verace autore." The writer invoked, again in the most familiar manner, is Paul, ostentatiously absent from the scene and from the poem, and yet, as has long been known, the primary of Dante's many models among the human writers of Scripture.[115] However, it is not Paul who is "verace," but his stylus, which, we have to infer, follows the dictates of Divine Love, as Dante says his does in *Purgatorio* 24.52–4, rather than the independent intentions of the human writer.[116] As first argued above, at this point of maximum "authorization" Dante surrenders the possibility of calling himself *autore*, but takes John, Paul, and their scriptural peers with him.[117] He does find another title for himself, which they (mostly) cannot claim to share, and to which I will return in due course.

The second way that the passage in *Paradiso* 26 moves beyond those in the preceding cantos is in its characterization of the "verace autore" himself in much more specific and personal-personifying terms than, for example, those of the earlier reference to the inspiring "rain" of the Holy Spirit. Striking, on the one hand, is the immediacy of divine communication: God reveals himself not by writing but *viva voce* ("voce"; "dice"; "parlando") in words addressed directly to an individual interlocutor, words, to reinforce

---

in his *captatio* to *Stazio*: "Poi cominciò: 'Nel beato concilio/ti ponga in pace la verace corte/che me rilega ne l'etterno essilio.'" It was sealed in *Purg.* 30.7, when Dante-*poeta* uses the words "verace gente" to refer to the books of the Bible as they appear in the allegorical pageant of revelation (cf. 29.82–154). Like "verace stilo" this locution makes a deliberate feint toward attributing definitional truthfulness to the human authors of the Bible, but the "gente" in question are not the authors themselves but personified representations of the books that bear their names. In *Par.* most uses of the adjectives are applied directly to God (3.32; 11.84; 26.40, 106; 31.106) or that which derives directly from him (10.84; 24.44; 29.111; 30.98). The first use of the word in the poem is *Inf.* 1.12: "la verace via abbandonai." That "via," of course, is "the Way, the Truth, and the Light" of Christ (John 14:6). A connection to *Purg.* 24's metaphorics of notation and of "penne" is made earlier in *Par.* 24: "Di quella ch'io *notai* di più carezza/vi'io uscire un foco sí felice,/che nullo vi lasciò di più chiarezza" (19–21); "però salta la penna e non lo scrivo" (25). Note the emphasis here on Dante-*poeta's inability* to transcribe what Love shows to him. Cf. Pertile 1994, 2005. Also nn 27, 116.

[115] For Dante's use of and identification with St Paul and the writings that bear his name, see, first of all, Mazzeo 1958: 84–110, as well as Nardi 1942b: especially 285–7; Di Scipio 1980; Petrocchi 1988; Adinolfi 1988: 136–7; Jacoff and Stephany 1989: especially 61–4 and nn; Brownlee 1990: 46–7; Hawkins 1992: especially 305 n 6. The process began in earnest in *Inf.* 2, where Dante disingenuously declares "Io non Enea, io non Paulo sono" (32). See also n 127.

[116] Mazzotta 1979: 206 signals a parallel with Psalm 44:2 – "lingua mea calamus velociter scribentem"; cf. *VN* 19.2: "la lingua mia parlò quasi come per sé stessa mossa"; also *MN* 3.4.11, cited in Chapter 5, section ii, also n 25. The *DDP* database shows two modern critics: Campi (1888–93) and Fosca (2003–6) who cite the Psalm in glossing *Purg.* 24.52–4. Guido da Pisa (1974: Prologue, 4) cites the passage under the *accessus* heading of the "causam agentem" or "autorem" to describe Dante's authorship of the *DC* generally. See also Gorni 1981: especially 13–21. Cf. n 114.

[117] For a different reading of the phrase and of Dante's assimilation of himself to the human authors of the Bible, see Benfell 1997.

once again Brownlee's thesis, silently translated from (Hebrew into Greek into) Latin into "Dante's language," Italian. And this is in keeping with the context of personal revelation: God responds to Moses' specific request that He reveal Himself to him and him alone. This mountain-top revelation is a type of the Transfiguration (where Moses' presence alongside Christ enforces the parallelism without the need for much in the way of exegetical contortions) and in this way, but not only, is a model for Dante's imminent "tête-à-tête" with the Deity in *Paradiso* 33. And there is more: God is not only the originating "Alpha" of the *auctoritas*, He is also its "Omega," its subject matter: *He* is the "valore," the goodness – the worth – that *He* showed to Moses and that He is now in the process of showing to Dante.[118] God's first-person singular words about himself might remind us of *Convivio*'s rehearsal, observed in the breach, of the rhetorician's taboo against speaking about oneself. To the extent it does so, it further sharpens canto 26's reduction of the human authors of the Bible, not to mention Dante himself, to the role of "scriptores" in the service of the one Author for whom personal presence is no obstacle to the communication of truth, since He is Truth in person.

On the other hand, and in direct contrast with the first "hand," is a thickly layered rhetorical mediation of this written, human re-presentation of God's voiced self-presentation, which is not, in fact, itself a revelation of the divine nature, but a promise of a visual unveiling (of God's hindquarters! Exodus 33:23) to come. In theory, the "chain of custody" leads from a primordial event on Mount Sinai to Moses' text (Exodus) to Dante-*personaggio*'s experience to Dante-*poeta*'s recounting thereof, although in practice the sequence is reversed, with Dante-*poeta* transcribing his earlier self quoting Moses quoting God. When Dante represents God as "verace autore" "di sé parlando," then, the actual words presented are at three removes from God's immediate speech, and the last two removes involve the substitution

---

[118] As is well known the phrase translates Exodus 33:19 – "ego ostendam omne bonum tibi." For "bonum" in the *CV*, see Trovato 1990 a and b. The specific motive behind Dante's choice of "valore" will appear below. "Valore" has multiple meanings in the *Commedia*, but is used with increasing frequency to name God, particularly God the Father, as the poem progresses. See especially *Par.* 10.1–3: "Guardando nel suo Figlio con l'Amore/che l'uno el'altro etternalmente spira,/*lo primo e ineffabile Valore*" (also *Purg.* 11.4, 15.72; *Par.* 1.107, 33.81). There is an ironic recall of the symmetrical canto of *Inf.*, where Ulisse boasts of his "ardore/ . . . a divenir del mondo esperto/e de li vizii umani e del *valore*" (see also n 129). As Giacomo Poletto appears to have been the first to have noted (cited from *DDP* database; see also Valerio 2003: 90–1) the passage may well distantly echo Guido Cavalcanti's reply "per le rime" to "A ciascun' alma presa e gentil core" (*VN* 3; see Chapter 4), which begins "Vedeste al mio parere, onne *valore*" (Contini 1960, vol. 2: 544). In addition to yet another jab at his one-time first friend's insistence on Love's destructive powers, this recall supports the connections made below between God as Love in *Par.* 26 and the question of Love as initially posed in *VN*.

of Dante's words for the Deity's, creating an effect even more pronounced than the equivocal "sperent in te" of canto 25. In this light, it is hard to avoid an uneasy awareness that it is not only God who is "di sé parlando" here, but also Dante himself.[119]

Another useful way of posing this question is to inquire what it means that Dante (or for that matter Moses) is put in the position of representing God in the figure of a human being and using human language – in other words, of personifying Him – in the process using themselves and their words as the "image and likeness" in which that representation is grounded. This is a version of the problem initially posed in *Vita Nova* 25 and then rehearsed, with a difference, in Beatrice's discourse in *Paradiso* 4 on Scripture's "condescending" attribution of hands and feet to a transcendent God who entirely exceeds the human corporality that he both created and temporarily inhabited – inhabits still, in the mystery of the Eucharist (see Chapter 4, n 41).

In *Vita Nova* the problem was the poetic figuration of the "accident" of human desire as a walking, talking "substance." Now Love is a substance, the "first of substances" as Dante calls Him in *De Vulgari Eloquentia*, while the human body itself or, perhaps better, the human *voice*, is "accidental": in any case, the representation of Deity in human language and as a human body is just as clearly marked as both inadequate and deceptive in relation to the immaterial object which it represents, which it *embodies*, through the trope of *prosopopeia* and the related device of dramatic first-person speech (Chapter 4, especially n 50). Having finally arrived, near the conclusion of the *Commedia*, not just at the "truthful author," but at *the* one *true* author, who is also the Author of all that we call Truth – the *autore* who commands faith and obedience because he is both omniscient and omnipotent – Dante returns to the point from which he departed, before he could even bring himself to pronounce, or rather inscribe, the word, "author." The question again becomes this: is it God or is it Dante who is here "di sé parlando"?

This question, which has no definitive answer, is nonetheless perhaps better understood through a return to the founding "stylistic" conversion of *Vita Nova*: the shift from poetry which endlessly, indulgently described

---

[119] One might simply refer this to the Biblical topos of God speaking *through* the human *scriba* or *scriptor*, particularly David in the Psalms, as in *MN* 3.1.4: "quod timeam, cum Spiritus, Patri et Filio coecternus aiat per os David" (Psalm 111.7; cf. 109.1 and *MN* 3.4.11, cited in Chapter 5), but for the fact that all three cantos have put in the foreground the dynamics, and problematics, of Dante's extraordinary appropriation of such a role to himself. One might also argue that Dante's identification is with Moses, the original "ti" to whom God promises to show "omne bonum" – but then, what Dante-*personaggio* sees and hears, Dante-*poeta* writes, speaking at once of God and of himself.

the (destructive) effects of desire on the lover who writes, to a new "stilo della . . . loda,"[120] whose aim is to praise the other, or Other, whom one loves.[121] Indeed, the turn from praise of Beatrice to praise of God is already amply anticipated in the *libello*, for instance in chapter 24's claim that Beatrice can be *called* (i.e., named) *Amore*, because she resembles him/Him (par. 5 [Chapter 4, section ii, especially nn 36, 47]). The theme of praise, as has already been noted, runs through the whole of the examination suite.[122] From "te laudamo" to "santo, santo, santo," cantos 24–26 return again and again to the praise of Deity, occasioned by Dante-*personaggio*'s performance. Perhaps the most telling instance comes in canto 25, when Dante quotes David, "sommo cantor del sommo duce," on Hope:

> "'Sperino in te,' ne la sua tëodia
> dice [David], 'color che sanno il nome tuo':
> e chi nol sa, s'elli ha la fede mia?"
>
> (25.73–5)

("'Let them hope in thee,' he says in his divine song, 'those who know thy name'; and who does not know it, if he has my faith?")

The first key is the word "tëodia" – God-song – which might be taken precisely as designating the hymn as praise of the divine, even as it evokes David as author of Psalms (Barolini 1984: 277–9 and nn). The second, even more crucial, is the paradoxical second half of the verse: "color che sanno il nome tuo."[123] The paradox, of course, is that God *has no proper name*, because he cannot be adequately, properly, nominated in human language, much less understood by "color che sanno." As a consequence, the "divine names" are multiple, even infinite, as medieval theologians never tired of

---

[120] For the *stilo della loda* in *VN*, see Singleton 1949: chapter 4; De Robertis 1961: chapters 4–5; Stillinger 1992: 103–7; Fenzi 1999b: 19–23; cf. Martinez 1998. Tateo 1971: 42, 46–7 makes explicit what is implicit in Singleton, namely that the "loda" of Beatrice is closely analogous to praise of the ineffable Deity. See also nn 113, 122, 125.

[121] See Noferi 1977 for a brilliant meditation on the constitution of the Dantean self through the "appello al nome di Dio" (24), that is, to the divine "Altro," with specific reference to the story of the Edenic origins of language in *DVE* 1.4.4 (121–2). While she does not otherwise refer to the passages that concern me here, her perspective can be extended to them.

[122] Martinez 1983 explores how *Purg.* 24 deploys the intertwined issues of the *stilo della loda* and the naming of God. See also Moevs 2005: 89. The numerical coincidence between the purgatorial episode and the canto which introduces the examination suite reinforces the connection (see n 114).

[123] On the importance of this passage, see Hawkins 1992: 83–4, 86; Stephany 1995: 376–8. Note the by now more than predictable recall with a difference of Aristotle as "maestro di *color che sanno*" (*Inf.* 4.131), which intensifies the contrast between what the human intellect can comprehend rationally and that which lies entirely beyond its capacity. Compare the treatment of praising and naming in *CV* 3.11, where the object of praise is instead *Filosofia*, i.e., rational understanding personified.

repeating.[124] To name God in as many ways as possible is precisely the goal of the "stilo della . . . loda" *alla divina*.[125]

We have already had occasion to mention four different names assigned to God in canto 26, namely *Amore*, "santo, santo, santo" (the familiar rhetorical technique of naming God through the nominalization of His attributes), "Alfa e O," and "verace autore," and to suggest how the last of these serves as a point of reference and convergence for the other three. We can now turn to the last section of the canto, after the conclusion of the examination, when Dante encounters his "first parent," Adam, and satisfies his unspoken desire to learn about several aspects of the life of the original human, most memorably about what *language* he spoke. Although the criticism generally keeps the two halves of the canto well apart from one another,[126] this episode constitutes a final gloss on John's examination of Dante, and, indeed, a "window" on to Dante's constitution of himself as writer here and throughout both the *Commedia* and the rest of his *oeuvre*.

Dante's sight, which had momentarily been taken away by the brilliance of John's appearance,[127] is restored at the end of the examination on Love, marking in yet another way the new stage of "illumination" at which he has arrived (26.76–9).[128] That the first soul he then sees is Adam seals the parallel with *Purgatorio* 27–28: just as (re-)entrance into Adam's first home, Eden, is a consequence of and a reward for arriving at a perfection of the will and

---

[124] For Dante's use of various names of God (especially *virtù*, *amore*, and *segnore*), drawing on both pseudo-Dionysius and Aquinas, in the *rime petrose* and *VN*, see Durling and Martinez 1990: 138 n 6, 158 and n 42, 161–2 and nn 53, 54, 57; also Durling 2001. For the *DC*, see Mazzotta 1984: 192–3 on *Par.* 26; Martinez 1983 on *Purg.* 24; Barolini 1992: 231 on *Par.* 27.100–20. Among medieval authorities, begin with Pseudo-Dionysius, *De nominibus divinis* (in the Latin translation of Rabanus Maurus [*PL* 122.1111–72]); see also Isidore of Seville, *Etym.* 7.1 (Isidore 1911); Aquinas, *Summa Contra Gentiles* I.29–36 and *ST* 1 q. 13.

[125] The *stilo della loda* and with it *VN* are evoked in *Par.* 30, with a bridge formed between Dante's ultimate praise of Beatrice (16–18) and the praise of God by the Rose composed of the Church Triumphant (124–6) – a bridge anticipated in the first appearance of the word "loda" in the poem: "Beatrice, loda di Dio vera" (*Inf.* 2.103). A long scholarly tradition has documented echoes of *VN* in this canto. On the "stilo. . . de la loda," see also nn 113, 120, 122, 124.

[126] Critics tend either to be interested in the examination scene or, much more often, in the question of Adamic language, with its palinodic revision of *DVE* 1.4.4. In a fine *lectura* of the canto, Mengaldo, 1978b, points to some verbal and other symmetries between the two parts of the canto and in general to a shared focus on linguistic questions, but does not develop his analysis in the directions discussed here.

[127] Dante's blindness reinforces his assimilation to Paul (John says Beatrice "ha ne lo sguardo/la virtù ch'ebbe la man d'Anania," i.e., the apostle who cured Saul/Paul's blindness and completed his conversion [Act 9: 17–18]) and leads to a higher level of understanding (26.76–9); see Petrocchi 1988: 246–7. Cf. Virgil as "blind guide" and n 23.

[128] The scene simultaneously recalls Dante's emergence from the blinding fog of the *girone* of the wrathful at the beginning of *Purg.* 17, just after listening to Marco Lombardo and just before *Virgilio*'s discourse on misguided love (see section iii).

the intellect within the circumscribed possibilities of human nature – so the meeting with Adam is a first consequence of the successful completion of the examination process.[129] Much could be said about the function of the encounter in the economy of Dante's journey. Important here is the emphasis on the genesis and unfolding of historical time and individual human temporality, just at the point when the *personaggio* will leave the eighth heaven – which, together with that of the sun, most conspicuously marks the passage of time – for the timeless generator of time, the Primum Mobile, and thence to the eternal Empyrean.[130]

What specifically concerns me here is what concerns most critics who have studied this passage, namely Adam's response to Dante's unvoiced question about the language spoken in Eden. The passage is longer, by fifteen lines to thirteen, than his answers to the other three queries combined, and functions as a focal point for their concerns with temporality and historicity, channeled through the *questione della lingua*. As has often been noted, it re-proposes and reinterprets the issue of the status of "the vernacular" as the language universally spoken *first*, with it all its implications concerning Dante's own historicity and that of the tongue in which he poetizes, as articulated from *Vita Nova* 25 through *Convivio* and *De Vulgari Eloquentia*:

> "Tu vuogli udir quant' è che Dio mi puose
> ne l'eccelso giardino, ove costei
> a così lunga scala ti dispuose,
>   e quanto fu diletto a li occhi miei,
> e la propria cagion del gran disdegno,
> e l'idïoma ch'usai e che fei.
> . . . .
>   La lingua ch'io parlai fu tutta spenta
> innanzi che a l'ovra inconsummabile
> fosse la gente di Nembròt attenta:

---

[129] *Par.* 26, paired with 27, is the culmination of a structural-thematic sequence of parallel cantos in the successive canticles. The sequence begins with the fiery tongues of the false Counselors (*Inf.* 26–27) who abused the Holy Spirit, which John and the others "instill" and "distill." It then passes through the purifying flames which punish the lover–poets of *Purg.* 26–27. Adam's reference to the "trapassar del segno" as the cause of his and Eve's expulsion from Eden echoes Ulysses' hubristic transgression of the pillars of Hercules, which is explicitly recalled by Dante as he looks down from the Gemini at 27.82–3. See Fido 1986 for these parallels and additional bibliography, as well as Mazzotta 1979: 214–18; Valerio 2003; Cestaro 2003a. See also n 118.

[130] As Armour 1995: 418 observes, each of the four questions to which Adamo responds focuses on the historicity and temporality of the human condition: how fallen time began; how long Adam lived and how many years there have been in human history to date; how much time Adam spent in the Earthly Paradise; and, finally, how language is subject to time in the same way that human beings are.

ché nullo effetto mai razïonabile,
per lo piacere uman che rinovella
seguendo il cielo, sempre fu durabile.
    Opera naturale è ch'uom favella;
ma così o così, natura lascia
poi fare a voi secondo che v'abbella.
    Pria ch'i' scendessi a l'infernale ambascia,
I s'appellava in terra il sommo bene
onde vien la letizia che mi fascia;
    e *El* si chiamò poi: e ciò convene,
ché l'uso d'i mortali è come fronda
in ramo, che sen va e altra vene."

(26.109–14, 124–38)

("You wish to know how long ago God placed me in the high garden where she there readied you for so long a stairway, and how long it was a delight to my eyes, and the true reason for his great anger, and the language that I spoke and that I invented . . . . The language that I spoke was all extinct before Nimrod's people began the unfinishable work, for no rational effect, because of human preference, which changes following the heavens, has been everlasting. It is a natural operation that man speaks, but whether in this way or that, Nature allows you to do as it may please you. Before I descended to the oppression of Hell, the highest Good, whence comes the gladness that envelopes me, was called *I* on earth and later was called *El*. And that is necessary, for the usage of mortals is like a leaf on the branch, which departs and another comes.")

Scholars long ago pointed out the radically historical nature of human language as Dante has Adam describe it: his apparent attribution of the essential changeability of language to the Fall rather than, as in *De Vulgari Eloquentia* (1.7–8) to Babel; his consequent abandonment of the theory that Hebrew is the unaltered "language of Grace" spoken in Eden (1.4.4 and 6.5–6); the implicit yet staringly clear consequences of these two shifts for the *volgare/gramatica* hierarchy and/or opposition, now virtually eradicated (see Chapter 3, n 59).

A number of critics have then explored the implied corollaries of the discourse for Dante's own claims as writer. On the one hand, as Hawkins observes, the general historicization of language appears to be in tension with Dante's self-placement in the company of the human scribes of the Bible and his immanent access to the world beyond time (1992: 86). The paradox disappears, however, if one recognizes that his discourse on the *autoritade* of the Bible at canto's beginning is aimed at historicizing all human authorship, even the most traditionally "authoritative," and reducing the concept of the transpersonal, transhistorical *autore* to God and God

alone. Similarly, Dante's career-long struggle to remove the hierarchical sep-
aration between his vernacular language and the seeming permanence of
Latin, Hebrew, and other possible *gramatiche* finds a definitive solution
in this reduction of all language to the same status.[131] A corollary of this
point is that the power of a given language and of a given instance of
language use depends upon the individual person who uses and makes
a language, in keeping with Adam's first-person singular reference to the
"idioma che usai e che fei," and in distant parallel with Dante's treatment of
his relationship to the *volgare* in *Convivio* and in *De Vulgari* as described in
Chapter 3.[132]

Here too, and in perhaps the most obvious fashion in the entire *Comme-
dia*, what makes possible Dante's new perspective is his individual escape
from the confines of history. His individuality is marked, of course, by
the fact that the whole scene takes place not under but *in* his natal sign
of the Gemini,[133] where a scene unfolds that marks his experience off as
unparalleled in human history, except, perhaps, by the unnamed Paul and
except, though in reverse, by the first human being himself. Constitutively
associated with his sojourn in the Gemini are the framing glances back at a
world increasingly reduced to mere contingency in all its aspects. In canto
22, as he arrives in the sphere of the fixed stars he says:

> Col viso ritornai per tutte quante
> le sette spere, e vidi questo globo
> tal, ch'io sorrisi del suo vil sembiante.
> . . . .
>   L'aiuola che ci fa tanto feroci,
> volgendom' io con li etterni Gemelli,
> tutta m'apparve da' colli a le foci.
>
> (22.133–5, 151–3)

---

[131] A tempting analogy exists between this argument concerning the relative status of languages and
the argument advanced in *CV* that no family line is intrinsically nobler than another because *all
human beings descend from Adam* (4.15.3–4).

[132] Although counter-intuitive (we assume a thing must be made before it can be used), Robert
Hollander in personal correspondence suggested that Dante's order – uses and makes – is the
correct one: Adam used the language given to him by God – at least the name "I" and then made
the rest of his language, represented by the naming of animals. See also Imbach 1996: 209–10.
Clearly this question falls under the dispute between the prescriptive and speculative grammarians
discussed in Chapter 4. From my perspective, what is evoked is a process like that described by
Dante in *CV* in which a language is made *by use* (Dante's use of his beloved vernacular).

[133] Durling and Martinez 1990: 84–7, 91–6, 239–58 and nn offer the most comprehensive interpretation
of the significance of the Gemini for Dante both generally and in the specific case of *Par.* 22–27.
On Dante's astrology, see also R. Kay 1994; Cornish 2000b.

(With my sight I returned through every one of the seven spheres, and I saw this globe [the earth] to be such that I smiled at its base appearance . . . The little threshing floor that makes us so ferocious, as I was turning with the eternal Twins, appeared to me, all of it from the mountains to the river mouths.)

In canto 27, then, just after St. Peter's blistering attack on the failures of the Church and just before Beatrice's paired descriptions of the perfection of the Primum Mobile and the "cupidigia, che i mortali affonde," Dante's gaze returns below, to mark the passage of time, right before he leaves time behind:

> Da l'ora ch' io avea guardato prima
> i' vidi mosso me per tutto l'arco
> che fa dal mezzo al fine il primo clima;
>   sì ch'io vedea di là da Gade il varco
> folle d'Ulisse, e di qua presso il lito
> nel qual si fece Europa dolce carco.
>   E più mi fora discoverto il sito
> di questa *aiuola*; ma 'l sol procedea
> sotto i mie' piedi un segno e più partito.
>
>   (27.79–87)

(Since the hour when I had first looked, I saw that I had moved through all the arc that the first clime makes from its middle to its end, so that I saw beyond Gades the mad crossing of Ulysses and, nearer here, the shore where Europa made herself a sweet burden. And the site of this little threshing-floor would have been further discovered to me, but the sun below my feet was continuing a sign and more ahead.)

As seen in sections i and ii, that Dante-*poeta* has already "experienced" this perspective as *personaggio* makes possible the initial leveling and personalizing in his relationship with *Virgilio*. But it is also no accident that the perspective is given a cosmic "objective correlative" at the point when the authority, historicity, and *personality* of Dante and his language are most explicitly on display. Or that it coalesces around the meeting with Adam, who carefully reminds the reader that he (like Dante), has experienced Hell (Limbo) and Heaven, both the Earthly Paradise and the rigors of post-lapsarian history. Or, for that matter, as I will suggest in due course, that Dante uses a word, *aiuol[a]*, which appears nowhere else in the poem, to mark the episodes beginning and its end (22.151; 27.86).

I will come back shortly to the doubling that takes place between Adam and Dante, and how this moves beyond spiritual experience and the status of language in general to encompass the specificity of poetry and the poet.

Now, however, it is necessary to consider one more, previously undetected, link that ties together the end of canto 26 to its beginning and to a great deal more than that. Already in *De Vulgari Eloquentia* Dante had asserted that human language could only have begun with the word "God" – "El" in the Hebrew he then believed to be Adam's language – expressing the pure and complete joy of an unfallen creature in the presence of the source of all pleasure:

> Quid autem prius vox primi loquentis sonaverit, viro sane mentis in promptu esse non titubo ipsum fuisse quod "Deus" est, scilicet *El*, vel per modum interrogationis vel per modum responsionis. Absurdum atque rationi videtur orrificum ante Deum ab homine quicquam nominatum fuisse, cum ab ipso et in ipsum factus fuisset homo. Nam sicut post prevaricationem humani generis quilibet exordium sue locutionis incipit ab "heu," rationabile est quod ante qui fuit inciperet a gaudio; et cum nullum gaudium sit extra Deum, sed totum in Deo, et ipse Deus totus sit gaudium, consequens est quod primus loquens primo et ante omnia dixisset "Deus." (1.4.4)

(As to what was first pronounced by the voice of the first speaker, that will readily be apparent to anyone in their right mind, and I have no doubt that it was the name of God, or *El*, in the form either of a question or of an answer. It is manifestly absurd, and an offence against human reason, to think that anything should have been named by a human being before God, when he had been made human by Him and for Him. For if, since the disaster that befell the human race, the speech of every one of us has begun with "woe!," it is reasonable that he who existed before should have begun with a cry of joy; and, since there is no joy outside of God, but all joy is in God, and since God himself is joy itself, it follows that the first man to speak should first and before all have said "God.")

Although Adam's account of the origins and history of language revises *De Vulgari Eloquentia* significantly, it follows the treatise in this, that the two languages mentioned are each identified by the word they use to name God, "I" and only thereafter "El."[134]

---

[134] Discussion of these two names has focused on (1) the revision of *DVE*; (2) attempts to explain the source of the word "I" otherwise unattested as a name of the Judeo-Christian deity. On this last score, see the important discussion of Guerri 1907, who reviews a number of medievally sponsored possibilities before arguing that "I" stands for "One," i.e., designates God as unity and simplicity (69–70). See also Nardi 1921b: 190–5; Dragonetti 1961b; Mengaldo 1978b: 243–4; Barański 1989a: 113–14; Mazzocco 1993: 160–5, 176–9. Casagrande 1976, though ultimately unconvincing in his attempt to turn "I" into "Ia" does broach the theme of naming as praise. Hollander 1975a: 128–9 asserts that a linkage exists between "I" as a name of God in Adam's language and the apocopated form of the first person singular pronoun ("i" for *io*), in conjunction with arguing that Dante stages his vernacular as a return to Adamic language (a reading which seems to run contrary to Adam's basic point, that all human languages are the same in their mutability and transience). See also Martinez 1983: 46, 49 and Moevs 2005: 183.

In addition to following the path laid down in the treatise, the device is also consonant with the fundamental tendency in the three canto suite to praise God by naming Him, as with the proliferation of different names of God in the first part of canto 26: "santo, santo, santo," "Amore," "verace autore," and, most importantly "Alfa e O." Why is the last most important? Because, taken together, *Alfa, El, I* and *O* represent four of the five vowels,[135] the same vowels from which, Dante once claimed, the word *avieo* is composed, and which, as we have already seen, evoke not only a poetic-linguistic making-by-binding, but also the book of God's creation "legato con Amore, in un volume" (Chapter 2, section v, especially n 87; section i above). In other words, the thematics of authorship and authority, the problem of the historicity of language, the desire to name and praise God, are inextricably intertwined in and through the word *autore* from *avieo*, a name of God which is composed from other names of God, and which, in Dante's inaugural use, designated the authority of the human poet. In the same decade that Dante was writing the *Paradiso*, Albertino Mussato was deploying in defense of poetry the notion – attributed to a *locus classicus* in Aristotle – that the first theologians were poets, because they used ornamental language and, especially, *metaphorical substitutions* to designate and to celebrate divine mysteries not otherwise understandable.[136] Whether or not Dante was aware of Mussato's texts, or of the tradition they draw on, and there is precious little hard evidence to suggest that he was, he here constructs an analogous "poetics of the theologian," or *poetry-as-theology*.[137]

---

[135] Dante's "Alfa e O" instead of John's "Alpha e Omega" may be partly motivated by this stress on the vowels, and possibly also by desire for each of the vowels named to represent a different language (thus: Alfa, for Greek, and "O" for Dante's Italian, or Latin). On the other hand, as Nardi 1966b showed, this form of the phrase was common in medieval texts. Compare the use of "Alfa e O" in *ECG*, par. 33 [90], which also echoes the last line of *VN*. Sarolli 1963: 282–3 connects "avieo" and God as Alpha and Omega, but not in connection with *Par.* 26.

[136] For the "poetic theology" in the Trecento, see Curtius 1948: 214–27; Ronconi 1976; Trinkaus 1979: especially 88–105; Witt 1977, 2000; Greenfield 1981: chapters 3–8; Minnis 1984; Mesoniat 1984; Minnis *et al.* 1988; Ascoli 2009. For Mussato more specifically, see *Epistole Metriche* 1, 4, 7, 18 (in Mussato 2000); and the discussions of Galletti 1912; Vinay 1949; Dazzi 1964: 108–23; Billanovich 1996; Ronconi 1976: 20–46. Mussato's position was subsequently developed by such notables as Petrarch, Boccaccio, and Salutati. On this topic, see also Ascoli 2009 and Chapter 1, nn 5, 48.

[137] Mazzotta 1984: 192. For this topos applied in general to Dante, see Hollander 1976; cf. Tateo 1970b; Costa 1971; Ascoli 1997, especially 245 n 42, 250 n 78. Hollander sees Dante's approach as radically distinct from that of Mussato, Petrarch, *et al.*, insisting upon the designation "theologus–poeta" to distinguish it from the "poetic theology" topos. Although, as just seen, the examination suite climaxes Dante's approach to the ranks of human authors of the Bible, I am still not convinced that Dante claims to be writing an "allegory of theologians." If anything, the treatment of human writing and language in *Par.* 26 hints that the Biblical scribes are not so different from the poets, having no *proper* claim to the title of *autore*. On the traditional theological acceptance of the figurative-fictive elements of the Bible, see Chapter 2, n 75. Cf. Mazzotta 1979: 242–3; Minnis *et al.* 1988: especially

The claim I am making is based on the presence of four distinct "vowel-names" of God in close proximity to three uses of the word *autore* and derivatives. The primary element I have identified which has previously escaped scholarly attention is the symmetry that connects one pair of God's names, "Alfa e O," to another, "I" and "El."[138] This *prima facie* connection, which has never received any explanation at all, despite its evident demand for such, is reinforced by the fact that, as "I" and "El" are introduced in a specifically linguistic context, the formula "Alfa e O" is presented as part of a metaphor of (Biblical) writing and (Scholastic) reading: "Lo ben che fa contenta questa corte,/Alfa e O è di *quanta scrittura/mi legge Amore o lievemente o forte*" (16–18), with God as Love and as "verace autore" taking the place of the human "maestro."

The word "autore," together with four vowels, each represented as a name of God, in a context where the naming and praising of God is the central activity: this is sufficient to summon up the word "avieo" and all it has meant for Dante, from *Convivio* and *De Vulgari Eloquentia*, to *Inferno* 1.85. The fact that one vowel, "u," remains unaccounted for might, for example, be understood as a variant of the practice of omitting the vowels altogether from the Tetragrammaton, thus signaling the necessary incompleteness of even Dante's extraordinary adventure in naming the divine (cf. Chapter 2, section v). Nonetheless, it would still be convenient to find the fifth and last vowel, "u," written as "v," and it is indeed there for the finding in *Paradiso* 26. In particular, the canto *does* contain several phrases prominently featuring "v" that designate the Deity: "il *vero* in che si fonda questa prova" (26.36; repeated at 37), "*verace* autore" (40), "*verace* speglio" (106), "prima *virtù*" (84) and "*valore*" (42),[139] of which four are tightly clustered around "autore." In the same vein, the tercet in which God is named as "verace autore" highlights words that begin with "v" ("voce," "verace," "vedere," "valore"), while, crucially, "autore" is in rhyme with "valore," emphasizing

---

209–12; Pinto 1994: 122–44. For Dante's possible knowledge of Mussato, see Martellotti 1971; as well as Dazzi 1964; Raimondi 1966; Pastore Stocchi 1966; Ascoli 2009; Hollander 2007: note to *Purg.* 11.29–30.

138 Note that Dante's "maestro," the one who teaches by means of a *lectio* (Chapter 2, especially n 28), is not a human being but God as Love. Dragonetti 1961b, in his discussion of *CV* 4.3–5, signals a connection between "I" and "Alfa e O" in relation to "avieo," but does not include "El" and does not elaborate an interpretation of canto 26. As noted in Chapter 2, his interpretation of *avieo* differs substantially from mine. Developing Guerri 1907, Mazzocco 1993: 178–9 connects 'I' and 'El' to *avieo*, but not to "Alfa e O" or "autore."

139 To be sure, God is given other names still in the canto that do not fit the vocalic paradigm (but do reinforce the sense that this episode is particularly given over to naming divinity): e.g., "Lo ben che fa contenta questa corte" (26.16); "essenza" (26.31); "l'ortolano etterno" (26.65).

pointedly a connection between these two divine names.[140] As seen earlier (n 118), Dante makes a point of translating the Vulgate's "bonum" as "valore," perhaps for the specific purpose of highlighting the significance of "v"/"u" in the orgy of naming and praising God that is *Paradiso* 26. To complete this argument, we should once again note that, according to Dante-*personaggio*, God, the truthful Author, uses the phrase "ogni valore," "di sé parlando," i.e., to name Himself, giving it pride of place in the canto and making it the favored candidate to round out the "vowels of authority."

At the same time, there is an apparently opposite route one might take to explain the absence of "u"/"v." The letter "v" represents the number "5" in the Roman numbering system, an important point, given that "v" is the fifth and last of the vowels. Both Latin "vir" and Italian "uomo" begin with it, which accentuates the fact that in medieval symbology "5" represents human perfection and is so used by Dante at several points throughout the *Commedia*.[141] Dante, however, also uses this letter to emphasize the supreme imperfection of humanity, its pride, in the acrostic "VOM" of *Purgatorio* 12 (12–69).[142] "V," in other words, can name the highest attributes of divinity and the lowest depths of humanity, and, perhaps, also the encounter between the divine and the human. This is suggested in the two great, symmetrical prophecies of a Christological redeemer to come, the Veltro (*Inf.* 1.101) and the 515 (*Purg.* 33.43), transnumerated as DXV, both of which prominently feature our vagrant letter/number. One might then conclude that in the context of *Paradiso* 26 "v" figures both the

---

[140] My thanks to Ron Martinez for suggesting these last two points to me in support of my general argument. It is often observed that "Cristo" in the *DC* appears in rhyme only with itself. This rhyme sequence, which contains three names of God, Amore/autore/valore, might be thought of as a variant of that rule – the same is true of *Purg.* 11.2, 4, 6, where the rhyme is "amore," "valore," "vapore."

[141] See, e.g., the series of references in the Heavens of Mars (the fifth heaven) and Jupiter (*Par.* 15.57; 16.37, 48, 72; 18.28, 88, 93; 20.43, 69, 100; cf. Raffa 1992). On Dante's uses of the number five to indicate perfected humanity (e.g., in Ripheus and Solomon: *Par.* 10.109, 13.48, 20.69), see Sarolli 1971 (191–2 n 1, 270–2, 294–5 and nn), who situates them firmly within medieval numerological discourse, particularly the Victorine association of "five" with the human microcosm. Since in that discourse Adam and Christ are the only perfect "fives," *Adamo* himself might be taken to be the missing "V." Pézard 1967: especially 258–9 argues that the "legame" formed by the five vowels of authority in *CV* 4.6.3–5 can be represented as the five-point figure known as the "knot of Solomon," then confirmed by 4.7.13–15, where the pentangle is used to represent the highest intellectual faculty of humanity. While I remain skeptical, acceptance of Pézard's interpretation would only reinforce the point made here. Moevs 2005: 134–40 focuses attention on *Par.* 27.115–20 where Beatrice explains how the Primum Mobile gives the measure to time without itself being subject to temporal measurement: "come dieci da mezzo e da quinto" (like ten by two and five).

[142] On this negative side, see also the identification by John of Garland of "u" with the lowest and heaviest of the four elements, earth, cited in Chapter 2, n 63.

resemblance and the abyssal difference between the human author, Dante, and the divine *Autore*.

Such a tension might be represented by a striking textual feature of the Heaven of the fixed stars, one noted in passing a little while ago: namely that the episode is framed by two uses of a word, "aiuol[a]" to designate the insignificance of earthly existence in comparison to life eternal in the presence of God.[143] That word, I submit, bears an uncanny aural resemblance to the word "avieo."[144] The force of that resemblance becomes apparent *if* one accepts the contention that the word "avieo," broken up into its constituent vowels, stands behind the phrase "verace autore," which is the pivot around which canto 26 as a whole turns, which canto is the culmination of the examination suite, which is the focal point of Dante's sojourn in the fixed stars, which is the climax of his journey through the created universe and the dominion of time. On that complex, yet I believe justified, assumption, the further effect of the framing use of "aiuol[a]" is to polarize the distinction between the possible uses of "avieo" to designate: (1) the True Author who binds all history together in a single volume: (2) the human poet, Dante, who is subject to the desires and blindness of the fallen historical world and who may only speak of God through the proliferation of improper names.

Let us return then, one last time, to the meaning assumed by *autore* as Dante uses it in canto 26, *Paradiso*. First, the phrase "verace autore"

---

[143] The scholarship is unanimous in referring "aiuol" back to *MN* 3.15.11 ("areola ista mortalium") and *Ep.* 7.4 ("angustissima area mundi"). Most then refer all three locutions back to Boethius' *Cons.* 2.prose.7.5: "angustissima inhabitandi hominibus area relinquetur." Debate, however, surrounds the precise meaning of the word: is it simply "a tiny little space" (areola)? or a metaphorical "threshing floor"? The latter position is more common, the former strongly advanced in a recent note by Scott (2003). For these purposes, it is a matter indifferent which is correct, since what counts is the phonic transformation of "area" into "aiuola," a word which is, to date, unattested before Dante (though it recognizably derives from a word which is, "aia"). From the point of view of sense, I prefer "aiuola," because it suggests a Biblical winnowing (Matthew 3:11–12; see Swing 1962: 359 and Freccero 1970: 217–18), and thus attributes a positive function to earthly life, even as the limitations of that life come most starkly into view. This would be in keeping with the politicized uses of the word in both *MN* and *Ep.* 7. Moreover, to the extent that Scott's reading precludes multiple sources (e.g., in addition to *Cons.*, Virgil's *Georgics* 1.178–81) and overlapping metaphorics, I object to it on methodological grounds (see also n 27). Finally, the larger context of the Boethian passage (2.pr.7.12–19) is a sharp critique of the pursuit of earthly glory, of a famous name, which is the acknowledged source for much of Oderisi da Gubbio's similar critique in the *girone* of pride (*Purg.* 11.82–117, especially 91–3, 100–8), and which, it is widely agreed, constitutes one of the most egregious instances of Dante's simultaneous expression of humility and of pride concerning his poetic talents. Among many possible, see the wonderfully rich reading of *Purg.* 11 in Marks 1992, including connections to the colloquy with *Adamo* in *Par.* 26.

[144] Here again we seem to be missing one letter, in this case "e," although in my argument "e" is in any case represented by the word "El," which *does* appear in *aiuol*, aurally.

"binds together" the canto: tying the discourse on Love to the discourse on language, the representation of God to the construction of Dante as *scriba Dei*. Second, we see that, although there is no doubt that God fulfills the role of the *autore* from *autentin* – worthy of faith because of his omniscience and obedience because of his omnipotence – Dante's use of the word here derives primarily from that strange digression concerning the human poetic *autore* from *avieo* that he presented and then dismissed as irrelevant in *Convivio* 4.6. Moreover, we can see that if Dante explicitly denies himself, and all others, the title of *autore*, he claims for himself, and for himself virtually alone, an understanding of what that word means: the "name of names" that simultaneously reflects the radical contingency of human languages (each with its own name for Deity) and designates the totality of Being behind contingency (phonic differences nonetheless speak to and of an entity which is one and the same).

Finally, even in denying the name of "author" to himself, Dante reclaims it, through what turns out to be a systematic rhetorical confusion between his words and thoughts and those of the "verace autore." Earlier, I noted that praise of Dante's success during the examination takes the form of praise of God, and in particular suggested that when the saints sing "sperent in te," they are put in the position of quoting Dante, David, and God simultaneously and of hinting that while the "te" in question refers primarily to the Deity, it is secondarily Dante as His *portavoce*. Even more pointedly, as we have seen, God's quoted words of himself, in his capacity of "verace autore," "io ti farò vedere ogni valore," might be said to apply as well to Dante in his comprehensive review of the divine names, and his synthesis of them in the word "autore" itself. It is in this connection, then, that Hollander's insistence on a tacit equation between the Adamic "I" ("i" for "io"; 26.133) with the original name of God, also "I" (26.134) makes sense (see again n 134): not as an alternative to my reading of the passage in terms of the "vowels of authority," but as a corollary intrinsic to it.

Late in canto 26 we come upon a phrase, already mentioned in passing, that at once glosses and confirms this "mirror effect" between Dante and his Maker. When Dante meets *Adamo*, he confirms his understanding that in the blessed life, the need for language, predicated (according to *DVE*) on the reciprocal opacity of human minds to one another, and the multiple desires that reduce humanity to Babelic individuality, have vanished, because the saints possess direct access to the divine mind, in which all times, places, and persons are simultaneously present and transparently intelligible:

E cominciai: "O pomo che maturo
solo prodotto fosti, o padre antico
a cui ciascuna sposa è figlia e nuro,
    divoto quanto posso a te supplìco
perché mi parli: tu vedi mia voglia,
e per udirti tosto non la dico."
    Talvolta un animal coverto broglia,
sì che l'affetto convien che si paia
per lo seguir che face a lui la 'nvoglia;
    e similmente l'anima primaia
mi facea trasparer per la coverta
quant' ella a compiacermi venìa gaia.
    Indi spirò: "Sanz' essermi proferta
da te, *la voglia tua discerno meglio*
che tu qualunque cosa t'è più certa;
    perch' io la veggio nel verace speglio
che fa di sé pareglio a l'altre cose,
e nulla face lui di sé pareglio."

(91–108)

(And I began: "O fruit uniquely born mature, o ancient father to whom each bride is daughter and daughter-in-law, as devoutly as I can I supplicate you to speak with me: you see my wish, and to hear you sooner I do not tell it." Sometimes a hidden animal stirs in such a way that its affect appears as its covering follows it: similarly the first-made soul made me see through its wrapping how gaily it came to please me. Then it breathed: "Without its being expressed by you, I discern your desire better than you do whatever is most sure to you, for I see it in the truthful Mirror that makes itself like other things, but other things cannot make him like them.")

The passage, by recalling the fact of supra-linguistic communication fundamental to the eternal realm, already anticipates the temporality and instability that Adam will shortly attribute to human language in general, and to the naming of God, Dante's naming of God, in particular. In the very same moment, of course, the passage is claiming for Dante local access to the mind of God, the "verace speglio" in which all things appear as they truly are, as, indeed they themselves, and specifically Dante himself, cannot know of their own accord.

What interests me most, of course, is the echoing – mirroring if you will – of the phrase "verace autore," and before that, "verace stilo" (24.61; also 24.44: "verace fede"), in the phrase "verace speglio."[145] If the whole

---

[145] On the mirror imagery of *Par.* and the traditions behind it – especially the opposition between creation as mirror and Creator as mirror (specifically 26.106, as well as 2.94–105, 33.115–32, etc.)

of the canto, the episode, the canticle, and the *Commedia* is aimed at the subordination of the creation to its Creator, and of Dante's self-absorbed fear and alienation to the self-effacing praise of God, in the end the tables are turned back around: God becomes the "true mirror" in which Dante's inner self is wholly and truly reflected. If in one sense, Dante, like all humans, is God's "image and likeness" seen "per speculum in enigmate," in a more profound sense, we now learn, God is the one true mirror, in whom Dante, and all of reality, is perfectly represented, an image that will return in the final vision of canto 33 (115–32).

I do not think it is stretching a point to say that this is the ultimate enactment of Dante's express desire to "explain himself" in *Vita Nova* 25: access to the "verace speglio" makes plain his inner intentions both to himself and to his readers – the substance of the *Commedia* is thus coextensively a hymn of praise to God and a totalizing dramatization of the inner life of Dante Alighieri. Nor is it an exaggeration to claim that this passage constitutes the best textual-historical defense available (better, I would argue, than his own recourse to the notion of "figura") for Auerbach's thesis concerning Dantean *mimesis*: the fact that God, the author of all things, offers Himself as a comprehensive mirror of reality, is what guarantees the mimetic truth of Dante's poem. Thus it is, I believe, that Dante can at once anticipate the modern "author-God" – whose dual task is the novelistic representation of "the real" and the lyric representation of his own inner world – and remain firmly, doctrinally, within a paradigm that subordinates earthly reality and psychic experience to an ineffable and transcendent Being. Thus it is that he can take the medieval concepts of *auctor* and *auctoritas* to their ideal extremes and at the same time put himself at the threshold of modern authorship.[146]

– see James Miller 1977, who connects it to both the topos of the "book of creation" (Chapter 2, n 87) and Dante's own poetic representations in *Par.* (see also Colish 1983). Miller also points out that the "speglio" of God's mind is also the source of prophetic knowledge. De Marchi 2002: 378 briefly notes the connection between "verace stilo" and "verace autore," but not the third term. *Speglio* appears two other times in the *DC*: in the cryptic allegory of the "veglio" of Crete (*Inf.* 14.103, 105) and in Dante's encounter with Cacciaguida in *Par.* 15. The latter is more immediately relevant to the present context (though note the echo of "veglio" at line 64), since Cacciaguida anticipates Adam's role as Dante's primordial ancestor, and since the passage introduces the concept central to this discussion: "Tu credi che a me tuo pensier mei/da quel ch'è primo, così come raia/da l'un, se si conosce, il cinque e 'l sei;/e però ch'io mi sia e perch' io paia/più gaudïoso a te, non mi domandi,/che alcun altro in questa turba gaia/*Tu credi 'l vero; ché i minori e' grandi/di questa vita miran ne lo speglio/in che, prima che pensi, il pensier pandi;/ma perché 'l sacro amore in che io veglio/con perpetüa vista e che m'asseta/di dolce disïar, s'adempia meglio,/*la voce tua sicura, balda e lieta/suoni 'l disio,/a che la mia risposta è già decreta!" (15.55–69).

[146] Although the thought is slightly different, I would compare this reading to that of Battaglia Ricci. Summing up her findings on the "contamination" of literary with Biblical language in the *DC*,

VI. *THE PERFECT POET*

In the end, then, Dante never does take the final step to assign himself
the name of author, although the word remains at the very heart of his
self-construction as writer and although he discovers himself reflected in
the "verace speglio" who is also the "verace autore" and who moves his
"verace stilo" much as He moved that of Dante's döppelganger, Paul. As I
have repeatedly hinted, however, Dante does assign himself a title in this
part of the poem which seems calculated to replace, or to stand in for, that
of *autore*.[147] The title, of course, is *poeta* and it accompanies the re-dubbing
of his *Commedia* as a "poema sacro":

> Se mai continga che 'l *poema sacro*
> al quale ha posto mano e cielo e terra,
> sì che m'ha fatto per molti anni macro,
>   vinca la crudeltà che fuor mi serra
> del bello ovile ov' io dormi' agnello,
> nimico ai lupi che li danno guerra;
>   con altra voce omai, con altro vello
> *ritornerò poeta*, e in sul fonte
> del mio battesmo prenderò 'l cappello;
>   però che ne la fede, che fa conte
> l'anime a Dio, quivi intra' io, e poi
> Pietro per lei sì mi girò la fronte.
>
> (*Par.* 25.1–12)

(If it ever happens that the sacred poem, to which both Heaven and earth have set
their hand, so that for many years it has made me lean, may overcome the cruelty
that locks me out of the lovely sheepfold where I slept as a lamb, an enemy of the
wolves that make war on it, with another voice by then, with other fleece I shall
return as poet, and at the font of my baptism I shall accept the wreath: for there
I entered the faith that makes souls known to God, and later Peter so circled my
brow because of it.)

she says: "Proprio in questa contaminazione di materiali letterari e non [i.e., Biblical texts], cui è
affidata la funzione di resemantizzare in senso cristiano il topos letterario, si può . . . riconoscere
il segno e la marca della re-invenzione e ri-semantizzazione in senso sacrale del poema allegorico;
ma in essa si può riconoscere, anche, il contrario, il segno e la marca della 'letterarizzazione' di un
libro sacrale" (1988: 321).

147 Other terms used of Dante, by myself among others, are "prophet" and "scribe" (see Chapter 2,
n 88). However, while there is no doubt that Dante assimilates himself to the prophetic voices of the
Old and New Testaments it is important to remember that he uses the word "profeta" and relatives
only four times in the *DC* – three times in *Par.* 12 (60, 136, 141) culminating in the reference to
Siger; once in *Par.* 24 (136). Nor does he regularly use the word *vates*, by which poetry and prophecy
are traditionally linked (see Chapter 2, n 23). The activity of "scribe" is implied by the image of
Dante noting down the dictates of Love in *Purg.* 24 (see section ii and nn 27, 114); the word itself is
used only once, and applied specifically to Dante and his poem "quella materia ond'io sono fatto
scriba" (*Par.* 10.27).

Within the larger verbal economy of the *Commedia* the word *poeta* functions in tandem with the word *autore* and until this very late date, in subordinate relation to it.[148] As noun, the word first appears in *Virgilio's* self-description, shortly before Dante refers to him as *maestro e autore*. Unlike *autore*, however, it is a constant presence throughout the poem. It is applied twenty-one more times to Virgil, once to his peer, Homer, twice to poets in general, once to *Stazio* by himself (22.73), and three times to *Virgilio* and *Stazio* together ("i miei poeti"). Finally, it is used once, and once only, by Dante of himself,[149] with the obvious teleological-typological implication: as *autore*, *Virgilio* is superseded by God; as *poeta*, he is succeeded by Dante, who simultaneously adapts Macrobius' description of the *Aeneid* as "sacrum poema" to his own work, with the residual knowledge that "sacro" might mean one thing when used by or of Virgil and quite another when applied to this poet and poem.[150]

Just prior to the moment when Dante finally refuses to assign himself (or even the Biblical scribes) joint *"auctor*-hood" with the "verace autore," in canto 25 he explicitly posits dual heavenly and human "hands" in the writing of the "poema sacro." In his treatment of *autore*, Dante had effectively denied himself the possibility either of using the word in the sense it was first applied to *Virgilio* (because now inadequate to him) or in the sense it is applied to God (because *he* is inadequate to *it*). *Poeta*, however, seems to permit Dante to link himself to both. Why is it, however, that he feels that he can claim the status of *poeta*, but not that of *autore*?

One possible answer is that, as the division of labor between *Virgilio* and Dante in the "prologue scene" suggests, *poeta* is a word that one can apply to

---

[148] On the semantic field surrounding "poeta" and "poetare" in the Duecento and in Dante see the *tour-de-force* study of Stoffi-Mühlethaler 1986, as well as Schiaffini 1958. Also Chapter 1, n 5; Chapter 2, section i and nn 2, 23. Unlike *au[c]tor*, *poeta* could be used of moderns as attested for example by the proliferation of various handbooks on the writing of poetry in the thirteenth and fourteenth centuries (Geoffrey of Vinsauf; John of Garland; Matthew of Vendôme *et al.*).

[149] For Dante's use of the word "poeta" in the *Commedia*, see Barolini 1984: 264–73; Brownlee 1984: 602–9 and nn. *Par.* 1.29 anticipates 25.8, but refers only indirectly to Dante. Hollander 1969: 221 asserts that Dante is "the first vernacular poet to call himself 'poeta'" (see also Brownlee 1984: 605 n 17; Barański 1986a: 51–2). Brownlee also points out that the use of *poeta* in *Par.* 25 is the numerologically significant thirtieth in the poem (608). Things change slightly if one considers as well the verb "poetare," which appears six times, twice of ancient poets (*Inf.* 25.99, *Purg.* 28.139), twice of *Stazio* (*Purg.* 21.98, 22.89), and twice of Dante (*Purg.* 22.129, *Par.* 30.32), though again Dante's direct links to the activity of "poetizing" emerge later (cf. Barolini 1984: 264, 273). For "poeta" in *VN* see Chapter 2, section i and n 2; Chapter 4, section ii. For *CV* see Chapter 2, especially sect v and n 65; Chapter 3, section i; Chapter 4, section iii; For *Ep.*3, Chapter 2, section vi. For *DVE*, Chapter 2, section v and nn 80, 94; Chapter 3, section iv and nn 19, 49, 52, 55.

[150] On Macrobius' use of "sacri poematis" in reference to the *Aen.* (*Saturnalia* 1.24.13; cf. 3.1–12, for a discussion of Virgil's representation of sacred things, religion, and the gods), see Schiaffini 1953: 53; Mazzotta 1979: 143–4 and nn; Barolini 1984: 274; Fumagalli 2002: 402–3.

oneself personally, while *autore* must be conferred retrospectively by readers. Notwithstanding the implicit critique of the use of the word in reference to human writers carried out over the course of the examination suite, it seems likely, as suggested at the very beginning of this study, that Dante fully expected this poem to earn him the treatment, and the appellation, used of the classical and Biblical writers, as indeed it did in commentary after commentary over the course of the fourteenth century.

The text, however, points in a different direction. Despite the writerly collaboration with heaven, the *poeta* described at the beginning of canto 25 seems "human, all too human." Dante's coronation with the poetic *cappello* is posited as radically contingent, subject to the constraints of history – and it is deliberately set in contrast with the heavenly coronation just carried out by St Peter. It is linked specifically to the distinctive arc of his individual existence – his birth and baptism, his exile, his old age ("con altra voce omai, con altro vello") – and, by implication, to his impending death.[151] Notwithstanding its transhistorical matter, the writing of the poem has taken years, and has exacted a physical toll from its composer ("m'ha fatto per molti anni macro"). In certain respects, then, this usage, taken in conjunction with the redefinition of *autore* in the next canto, anticipates Petrarch's "modern" conception of the specialized, yet radically temporal, mission of the poet, which, most would agree, yields eventually to the notion of literature as an autonomous domain of human activity. Another way of putting it would be that while the word *autore* from *avieo* is being transferred from the human poet to God, the specialized writerly functions assigned to poetic *avientes* in *Convivio* 4.6 remain under the rubric *poeta* itself.

This does not mean, needless to say, that to be a *poeta* is an inferior occupation. On the contrary, over the course of the *Commedia*, and indeed, over the course of Dante's career, the word has accrued significance in such a way as to make Dante *qua poeta* a virtual *hapax* – a figure unique in the history of human writing, or rather, a figure with a single, extraordinary, peer. If in *Vita Nova*, the vernacular *dicitore d'amore* or *poeta* is ostensibly restricted to love as a subject, in the *Commedia* "Love makes the world go round," not to mention the stars, and every thing that *is*. If *poete* in the *libello* are those with a special license to use fictively figurative language, here, as *Paradiso* 4 so carefully explains, and as canto 26 illustrates, any language used of God, by poets or by "theologians," necessarily "condescends" to

---

[151] I do not mean to suggest, of course, that Sarolli 1966a, Mineo 1968: 262–72, and others are wrong to point to the prophetic resonance of these verses.

the use of *prosopopeia* (see Chapter 4, n 41). If in *De Vulgari Eloquentia* the poet produces artifacts "fictio rethorica musicaque poita" (Chapter 2, nn 82, 84), in the *Commedia* he no doubt still makes use of the full arsenal of rhetorical and musical artistry, but he (Dante) is also the one who can say: "I' mi son un che, quando/Amor mi spira, noto, e a quel modo/ch'e' ditta dentro vo significando" (*Purg.* 24.52–4). And if in *Convivio* the poet is the one who binds together words into "rhythm and rhyme," in the *Commedia* he does this, but in doing so he also represents, and mimes, God's poem, Creation itself, and in the end assumes the privilege of naming God Himself.[152]

Finally, if in *De Vulgari Eloquentia* the definition of an illustrious vernacular language finds its culmination, and its model, in the *constructio* of the *canzoni*, and if in *Convivio* the binding of poetry together implicitly constitutes the making of a language, in cantos 25 and 26 of *Paradiso* the imagined coronation of Dante as the *poeta* he already is prepares, and finds its crucial gloss in, the discourse of Adam on the first language ever made, the language of unfallen humankind, where God was known as "I." Paradoxically, what first makes the link between the two moments apparent, beyond Dante's fundamental propensity for understanding the making of language and the making of poetry as inextricably intertwined, is the theme of radical human contingency: the marked contingency of Dante's poetic career, the contingency of "l'uso d'i mortali" in the making and remaking of language which is "come fronda/in ramo, che sen va e altra vene,"[153] the contingency of "l'aiuol che ci fa tanto feroce" that brackets

---

[152] For that matter, a change has clearly taken place from the beginning of the poem to its end. *Poeta* referred by *Virgilio* to himself is one thing, *poeta* used by Dante of himself, obviously, quite another. The change is further marked, as Barolini in particular has shown, by the poem's tendency to rename itself. Having in the title and twice in the course of *Inf.* referred to the work as a *comedía*, he now claims it goes beyond the experience of any "comedian" or "tragedian" (30.22–4) and calls it a "sacrato poema" and "poema sacro," names which, beyond their associations with Macrobius's Virgil, have much in common with the "tëodia" attributed to David at 25.72. See also Battaglia Ricci 1983: 46–8, 54–5, 115–18, *et passim*. On this basis I would take Barański's "big tent" definition of Dante's re-vision of medieval comic style and genre (1991 a and b) one, self-consuming, step further, to argue that from the perspective of *Par.* it becomes clear that this poem, like the God it attempts to represent, does not have one *proper* name at all.

[153] The motif of the "fronda" spans the whole of canto 26. In his discourse concerning his love of Creation in proportion to its Creator, Dante says "Le fronde onde s'infronda tutto l'orto/de l'ortolano etterno, am' io cotanto/quanto da lui a lor di bene è porto" (64–6). As he prepares to speak to Adam after the examination concludes he compares himself to a bow bending in the wind: "Come la fronda che flette la cima/nel transito del vento, e poi si leva/per la propria virtù che la soblima,/fec' io in tanto in quant' ella diceva,/stupendo, e poi mi rifece sicuro/un disio di parlare ond' io ardeva" (85–90; note the evident recollection of Ulysses' fiery speech to *Virgilio* and Dante in the corresponding lines of *Inf.* 26 [again, 85–90]). The sequence, obviously, culminates with Adam's figuration of human linguistic usage as "come fronda." (cf. *Par.* 23.1, 24.117 [Di Scipio 1995:

and defines the poet and his language in the Heaven of the fixed stars, in the sign of Gemini under which he was born into "the life which is a race to death."

Once it is established, however, an underlying motive for the yoking of Dante *poeta* and Adam as "user and maker" ("l'idïoma ch'usai e che fei") of language can be discerned: it recalls, it explicates, and it confirms the identification between Dante *personaggio–poeta* as he reenters Eden and the only other human male to have dwelt there "in the body,"[154] that is, Adam.[155] If, as I argued earlier, to achieve the state of unfallen moral-intellectual perfection native to the earthly paradise is, as a necessary corollary, simultaneously to achieve perfection as a poet, then a further corollary would be that Adam himself must have been, at least *in potentia*, a *poeta*, and Dante's one and only peer.[156] And for that claim to make sense, one must be able to argue that the beginnings of language with Adam and the ends of Dante's

362], 27.119). The image evokes the mutability and mortality of creation and specifically connects to the "legno" and the "pomo" which were the occasion if not the cause of humanity's fall (Moevs 2005: 100–2). It binds the discourse in the first half of the canto on the "verace autore" who both is and speaks of Love to the discourse on human language which endlessly names and renames that Love in its second half. And it links Dante even more closely to Adam. Finally, notice the phrase "la propria virtù," suggesting the act of specific ("propria") individual will by which Dante raises himself up to communicate with his "first parent," and thus acting as a counter-weight to the sense of contingency and fallenness of the "fronda." This phrase resonates deliberately with the naming of the creator-God as "la prima virtù" only three lines earlier (84). On the vegetational thematics of this canto, see also Dragonetti 1968: 347–57; Stierle 2002: 410, 416; Cestaro 2003a: 163–5, cf. 105. On *virtù* as a name of God used by Dante, see also Durling and Martinez 1990: 158 and n 42.

154 Dante scrupulously avoids the idea that a woman could be either a linguistic innovator or a poet. In *DVE*, as is well known, he is prepared to rewrite the Bible in order to avoid attributing the origins of human speech to Eve, because it would be "inconvenienter" (indecorous, unseemly) to have woman speak before man (1.4.3). More complex is the case of Matelda in Eden. It seems to me, however, that part of the explanation for the mystery surrounding her identity is that Dante does not wish to historicize or motivate her presence (as he does instead with her counterpart, Cato) because it would complicate the parallel he is structuring between himself and Adam. See section iv and nn 71, 78 for the suggestion that she does function in some sense as poetic Muse.

155 See above for a number of the ways in which the meeting with Adam recalls Dante's entrance into Eden. Of particular significance in consolidating the identity between the two is Adam's fourth and final answer, in response to Dante's unspoken query as to how long Adam dwelt in Eden before the fall: "Nel monte che si leva più da l'onda,/fu' io, con vita pura e disonesta,/da la prim' ora a quella che seconda,/come 'l sol muta quadra, l'ora sesta" (139–42; cf. Hill 1982). Thus Adam dwelt in Eden from dawn until the hour just following noon, while Dante arrives in Eden just after dawn (*Purg.* 27.109–17) and leaves it precisely at noon (*Purg.* 33.103–4; *Par.* 1.43–5; see Pézard 1940: 83–6, especially n 4; also Armour 1979: 24; Brownlee 1990: 54). It may be a sign of deference that Dante's stay in Eden corresponds so closely to Adam's, but lasts just a little less – or it may be that the Adamic surplus is accounted for by the "vita . . . disonesta" after the Fall, but prior to the expulsion. In any case, a desire to emphasize the symmetry between the two would explain the emphatic terminal placement of Adam's response to the question of how long he stayed in Eden, as well as for Dante's curiosity about the matter.

156 This point elaborates a concise intuition of Mazzotta 1979: 218 (see also Dragonetti 1968: 373; Brownlee 1990: 51).

poetry are substantially identical. And so I have: Dante who names and praises, praises in naming, God is like Adam who first gave God a name, and so invented the first language.[157]

In closing, let us return once more, and briefly, to the fundamental problem of historicizing the conception of authorship and authority advanced and dramatized in the *Commedia*. In defining both language and poetry in terms of a radical contingency that yields, provisionally and temporarily, to the fabrications of individual human talents, Dante no doubt anticipates the humanized, historicized author traditionally associated with Petrarch and a dawning age of increasingly secular culture.[158] He thus reinforces the redefinition of the human *autore* to deprive "him" of "his" traditional medieval role as impersonal conveyor of timeless truth. At the same time, by stressing the virtually unique character of his poetic mission and gifts (after all, Adam's verbal *oeuvre*, the language of "I," has left no trace in the historical record), and its dependence on a virtually unprecedented infusion of Grace, Dante shoots past the now-obvious historical implications of his program (human authorship is personal and individual *in general*) to insinuate that he and he alone impersonates, or ever could, this new figuration of the poetic author.

---

[157] Cf. Corti 1983, especially the section entitled "Il *Paradiso Terrestre* della poesia" (70–6). Corti's focus is on *DVE* and, allusively, *Purg.* 24. The intertwining of language and poetry is emphasized by the well-known fact that Adam's description of the mutability of human language derives from lines 60–3, 70–2 of the *AP* of Horace, a passage whose hold on Dante's poetic-linguistic imagination is of long duration (see also *CV* 1.5.9, 2.13.10; *DVE* 1.9.6–10). Cf. Martinez 1995a: 154. See also Chapter 3, n 4; cf. n 15 above; Chapter 4, n 42. On possible links to the motif of the laurel branch in *Par.*, see Durling and Martinez 1990: 433 n 159.

[158] See Chapter 1, section iv. Also Ascoli 1991a, 2009.

Works consulted

I. PRIMARY SOURCES (N.B. EXCLUDED ARE TEXTS CITED ONCE BY AUTHOR, TITLE, AND/OR STANDARD NUMBERING SYSTEMS WITHOUT DIRECT QUOTATION)

Dante Alighieri. 1965. *Monarchia*. Ed. Pier Giorgio Ricci. Vol. 5 in *Le opere di Dante Alighieri*. Edizione nazionale a cura della Società dantesca italiana. Verona: Mondadori.

——— 1979a. *Epistole*. Eds. Arsenio Frugoni and Giorgio Brugnoli. In Dante Alighieri. *Opere minori*, vol. 2. Eds. Pier Vincenzo Mengaldo *et al*. Milan and Naples: Ricciardi.

——— 1979b. "Le Egloghe." Ed. Enzo Cecchini. In Dante Alighieri. *Opere minori*, vol. 2. Eds. Pier Vincenzo Mengaldo, *et al*. Milan and Naples: Ricciardi, 1979.

——— 1980. *Le Egloghe*. Eds. and trans. Giorgio Brugnoli and Riccardo Scarcia. Milan and Naples: Ricciardi.

——— 1988. *Opere minori*, vol. 1, part 2. Eds. Cesare Vasoli and Domenico De Robertis. Milan and Naples: Ricciardi.

——— 1996. *Vita nova*. Ed. Guglielmo Gorni. Turin: Einaudi.

Thomas Aquinas. 1951. *In Libros Politicorum Aristotelis Expositio*. Ed. R. M. Spiazzi. Rome: Marietti.

——— 1961–1967. *Summa contra Gentiles*. Eds. Ceslai Pera, D. Petro Marc, and D. Petro Caramello. 3 vols. Turin [Augustae Taurinorum]: Marietti.

Aristotle. 1941. *Nicomachean Ethics*. In *The Basic Works of Aristotle*. Ed. and trans. Richard McKeon. New York: Random House.

Giovanni Boccaccio. 1974. *Trattatello in laude di Dante*. Ed. Pier Giorgio Ricci. Vol. 3 in *Tutte le opere di Giovanni Boccaccio*. Ed. Vittore Branca. Verona: Mondadori.

Bonaventure. 1934–1964. *Opera Theologica Selecta*. 5 vols. Ed. L. M. Bello. Florence: Quaracchi.

William E. Burgwinkle, trans. 1990. *Razos and Troubadour Songs*. Volume 71, series B, in the Garland Library of Medieval Literature. New York: Garland.

Egidio Colonna. 1967. *De Regimine Principum Libri III*. Aalen: Scientia Verlag.

Gianfranco Contini, ed. 1960. *Poeti del Duecento*. 2 vols. Milan and Naples: Ricciardi.

Dino del Garbo. 1999. In Fenzi 1999a. Genoa: Il Melangolo. Pp. 86–174.

Margaret Egan, ed. and trans. 1985. *Les vies des troubadours*. Paris: Union Générale d'Éditions.

Fulgentius. 1971. *Fulgentius the Mythographer*. Trans. and introd. Leslie George Whitbread. Columbus: Ohio State University Press.

Guido da Pisa. 1974. *Expositiones et Glose super Comediam Dantis*. Ed. Vincenzo Cioffari. Albany, NY: State University of New York Press.

Guillielmus Brito. 1975. *Summa Britonis sive Guillelmi Britonis Expositiones Vocabularum*. Eds. B. A. Daly and L. W. Daly. Padua: Antenore.

R. B. C. Huygens, ed. 1970. *Accessus ad Auctores*. Leiden: Brill.

John Henry Marshall, ed. 1972. *The 'Razos de Trobar' of Raimon Vidal and Associated Texts*. London: Oxford University Press.

Albertino Mussato. 2000. *Écérinide; Épitres Métriques sur la Poésie; Songe*. Ed. and trans. Jean-Frédéric Chevalier. Paris: Les Belles Lettres.

Ovid. 1993. *Tristezze [Tristia]*. Ed. and trans. Francesca Lechi. Milan: BUR.

Giambattista Vico. 1977. *La scienza nuova*. Ed. Paolo Rossi. Milan: BUR.

Giovanni Villani. 2002. *Nuova cronica*. In *Giovanni Villani*. Ed. Giulio Cura Curà. Rome: Istituto Poligrafico e Zecca dello Stato.

Virgil. 1999. *Eclogues. Georgics. Aeneid I–VI*. Rev. edn. by G. P. Goold. Trans. H. Rushton Fairclough. Volume 63 of The Loeb Classical Library. Cambridge, MA: Harvard University Press. First published 1916.

Philip Wicksteed and Edmund Gardner. 1902. *Dante and Giovanni del Virgilio: Including a Critical Edition of Dante's 'Ecloghae Latinae' and of the Poetic Remains of Giovanni del Virgilio*. Westminster: Constable.

2. SECONDARY SOURCES

M. H. Abrams. 1953. *The Mirror and the Lamp*. New York: Oxford University Press.

1971. *Natural Supernaturalism; Tradition and Revolution in Romantic Literature*. New York: Norton.

David Abulafia. 1988. *Frederick II: A Medieval Emperor*. London and New York: Allen Lane, Penguin.

Marco Adinolfi. 1988. "I personaggi neotestamentari nella *Divina Commedia*." In Barblan, ed. 1988. Pp. 125–41.

John Ahern. 1982. "Binding the Book: Hermeneutics and Manuscript Production in *Paradiso 33*." *PMLA* 97: 800–9.

1990. "The Reader on the Piazza: Verbal Duels in Dante's *Vita Nuova*." *Texas Studies in Language and Literature* 32: 18–39.

1992. "The New Life of the Book: The Implied Reader of the *Vita Nuova*." *Dante Studies* 110: 1–16.

2003. "What Did the First Copies of the *Comedy* Look Like?" In Barolini and Storey, eds. 2003. Pp. 1–15.

Gian Carlo Alessio. 1984. "La grammatica speculativa e Dante." *Letture classensi* 13: 69–88.

1995. "A Few Remarks on the *Vulgare Illustre*." *Dante Studies* 113: 57–67.

Gian Carlo Alessio and Claudia Villa. 1984. "Per *Inferno* 1.67–87." In Iannucci, ed. 1993a. Pp. 41–64. Earlier version in *Vestigia: Studi in onore di Giuseppe Billanovich*, vol. 1. Rome: Edizione di Storia e Letteratura, 1984. Pp. 1–21.

Judson Allen. 1982. *The Ethical Poetics of the Later Middle Ages.* Toronto: University of Toronto Press.

Laurel Amtower. 2000. *Engaging Words: The Culture of Reading in the Later Middle Ages.* New York: Palgrave.

Roberto Antonelli. 1995. "Subsistant igitur ignorantie sectatores." In Picone, ed. 1995a. Pp. 337–50.

2001. "Cavalcanti e Dante: Al di qua del *Paradiso.*" In Picone, ed. 2001. Pp. 289–302.

and Simonetta Bianchini. 1983. "Dal *clericus* al *poeta.*" In *Letteratura Italiana. Vol. 2: Produzione e Consumo.* Ed. Alberto Asor Rosa. Turin: Einaudi.

Maria Luisa Ardizzone. 2002. *Guido Cavalcanti. The Other Middle Ages.* Toronto: University of Toronto Press.

ed. 2003. *Guido Cavalcanti tra i suoi lettori.* Florence: Cadmo.

Hannah Arendt. 1958. "What is Authority?" *Between Past and Present; Eight Exercises in Political Thought.* Enlarged edn. New York: Viking, 1968. First published 1958. Pp. 91–141.

Peter Armour. 1979. "Matelda in Eden: The Teacher and the Apple." *Italian Studies* 34: 2–27.

1989. *Dante's Griffin and the History of the World.* Oxford: Clarendon Press.

1995. "*Paradiso* XXVII." In *Dante's 'Divine Comedy'; Introductory Readings III: 'Paradiso.'* Special issue of *Lectura Dantis* 16–17: 402–23.

Albert Russell Ascoli. 1987. *Ariosto's Bitter Harmony: Crisis and Evasion in the Italian Renaissance.* Princeton: Princeton University Press.

1989. "The Vowels of Authority (Dante's *Convivio* IV.vi. 3–4)." In Brownlee and Stephens, eds. 1989a. Pp. 23–46.

1991a. "Petrarch's Middle Age: Memory, Imagination, History, and the 'Ascent of Mt. Ventoux.'" *Stanford Italian Review* 10: 5–43.

1991b. "'Neminem ante nos': Historicity and Authority in the *De vulgari eloquentia.*" *Annali d'Italianistica* 8: 186–231.

1991–2. "Boccaccio's Auerbach: Holding the Mirror up to *Mimesis.*" *Studi sul Boccaccio* 20: 377–97.

1993. "The Unfinished Author: Dante's Rhetoric of Authority in *Convivio* and *De Vulgari Eloquentia.*" In Jacoff, ed. 1993. Pp. 45–66.

1994. "Liberating the Tomb: Difference and Death in *Gerusalemme Liberata.*" *Annali d'Italianistica* 12: 159–80.

1995. "Palinode and History in the Oeuvre of Dante." In Cachey, ed. 1995. Pp. 155–86.

1997. "Access to Authority: Dante in the *Epistle to Cangrande.*" In Barański, ed. 1997c. Pp. 309–52.

1999. Review of Gregory Stone. *The Ethics of Nature in the Middle Ages: On Boccaccio's Poetaphysics.* In *The Medieval Review* (electronic journal: www.hti.umich.edu/t/tmr/). June 11, 1999.

2000a. "Authority." In *DE*. Pp. 72–5.

2000b. "Epistle to Cangrande." In *DE*. Pp. 348–52.

2003. "Dante after Dante." In Barolini and Storey, eds. 2003. Pp. 349–68.

2005. "Introduction." In Sergio Zatti. *The Quest for Epic*. University of Toronto Press. Pp. 1–12.

2009. "Blinding the Cyclops: Petrarch after Dante." In *Dante and Petrarch*. Eds. Theodore Cachey and Zygmunt Barański. Notre Dame, IN: University of Notre Dame Press.

2010. "Dante and Allegory." In *The Cambridge Companion to Allegory*. Eds. Rita Copeland and Peter Struck. Cambridge: Cambridge University Press, forthcoming.

Erich Auerbach. 1929. *Dante, Poet of the Secular World*. Trans. R. Mannheim. Chicago: Chicago University Press, 1961. First published in German 1929.

1941. "Sermo Humilis." In *idem*. 1958. Pp. 27–66.

1944. "Figura." In *idem*. *Scenes from the Drama of European Literature: Six Essays*. New York: Meridian Books, 1959. First published 1944. Pp. 11–76.

1945. *Mimesis; The Representation of Reality in Western Literature*. Trans. W. R. Trask. Princeton: Princeton University Press, 1953. First published 1945.

1954. "Dante's Addresses to the Reader." *Romance Philology* 7: 268–78.

1958. *Literary Language and its Public in Late Latin Antiquity and the Middle Ages*. Trans. Ralph Mannheim. Princeton: Princeton University Press, 1965. First published in German 1958.

Marcello Aurigemma. 1965. "Il giudizio degli antesignani dell'umanesimo e degli umanisti sul valore e sulle caratteristiche della 'latinitas' di Dante." In *Dante e Roma*. 1965. Pp. 153–87.

D'Arco Silvio Avalle. 1961. *La letteratura medievale in lingua d'oc nella sua tradizione manoscritta*. Turin: Einaudi.

Luca Azzetta. 2003. "Le chiose alla *Commedia* di Andrea Lancia, L'*Epistola a Cangrande* e altre questioni dantesche." *L'Alighieri* 44 [n.s. 21]: 5–73.

Zygmunt Barański. 1986a. "I trionfi del volgare: Dante e il plurilinguismo." In *idem*. 1996. First published 1986. Pp. 41–78.

1986b. "Funzioni strutturali della retrospezione nella *Commedia*: L'esempio del canto XXVII del *Purgatorio*." In *idem*. 1996. First published 1986. Pp. 221–54.

1987. "I segni della Bibbia: I. La lezione esegetica di *Inferno* I." In *idem*. 2000. First published 1987. Pp. 41–76.

1989a. "La linguistica scritturale di Dante." In *idem*. 1996. First published 1989. Pp. 79–128.

1989b. "L'(anti)-retorica di Dante: Note sullo sperimentalismo e sulla poetica della *Commedia*." In *idem*. 1996. First published 1989. Pp. 15–40.

1989c. "Il carattere riflessivo dei tre sogni purgatoriali." In *idem*. 1996. First published 1989. Pp. 255–80.

1991a. "*Comedía*. Notes on Dante, the *Epistle to Can Grande*, and Medieval Comedy." *Lectura Dantis* 8: 26–55.

1991b. "'Primo tra cotanto senno': Dante and the Latin Comic Tradition." *Italian Studies* 26: 1–36.

1994a. "La vocazione enciclopedica." In *idem*. 2000. First published 1994 as "Dante fra 'sperimentalismo' e 'enciclopedismo.'" Pp. 77–102.

1994b. "*L'iter* ideologico di Dante." In *idem*. 2000. First published 1994 as "Dante commentatore e commentato: riflessioni sullo studio dell'iter ideologico di Dante." Pp. 9–39.

1995 [1996]. "The 'New Life' of 'Comedy': The *Commedia* and the *Vita Nuova*." *Dante Studies* 113: 1–30.

1996. *'Sole nuovo, luce nuova': Saggi sul rinnovamento culturale in Dante*. Turin: Edizioni Scriptorium.

1997a. "Dante and Medieval Poetics." In Iannucci, ed. 1997. Pp. 3–22.

1997b. "I segni della creazione: Il mistero della *Questio de aqua et terra*. In *idem*. 2000. First published 1997. Pp. 199–219.

ed. 1997c. *Seminario dantesco internazionale/International Dante Seminar I*. Florence: Le Lettere.

1999. "Notes on Dante and the Myth of Orpheus." In Picone and Crivelli, eds. 1999. Pp. 133–54.

2000. *Dante e i segni: Saggi per una storia intellettuale di Dante Alighieri*. Naples: Liguori.

2001. *"Chiosar con altro testo": Leggere Dante nel Trecento*. Fiesole: Cadmo.

2005a. "Dante Alighieri: Experimentation and (Self-)Exegesis." In Minnis and Johnson eds. 2005. Pp. 561–82.

2005b. "The *Epistle to Cangrande*." In Minnis and Johnson eds. 2005. Pp. 583–9.

Zygmunt Barański and Patrick Boyde, eds. 1997. *The 'Fiore' in Context: Dante, France, Tuscany*. Notre Dame, IN: University of Notre Dame Press.

Michele Barbi. 1890. *Dante nel Cinquecento*. Rome: Polla, 1975. First published 1890.

1941. "Razionalismo e misticismo in Dante." In *idem*. *Problemi di critica dantesca (seconda serie)*. Florence: Sansoni. Pp. 3–86.

1964. "Introduzione." In Dante Alighieri. *Il Convivio*. 2 vols. Eds. G. Busnelli and G. Vandelli, introd. by Michele Barbi, appen. A. Quaglio. Florence: Le Monnier, 2nd edn.

Giovanni Barblan, ed. 1988. *Dante e la Bibbia*. Florence: Olschki.

Leonard Barkan. 1986. *The Gods Made Flesh: Metamorphosis and the Pursuit of Paganism*. New Haven: Yale University Press.

1991. *Transuming Passion: Ganymede and the Erotics of Humanism*. Stanford, CA: Stanford University Press.

Teodolinda Barolini. 1984. *Dante's Poets: Textuality and Truth in the "Comedy."* Princeton: Princeton University Press.

1989a. "Detheologizing Dante: For a 'New Formalism' in Dante Studies." *Quaderni d'Italianistica* 10: 35–53.

1989b. "Archne, Argus, and St. John: Transgressive Art in Dante and Ovid." *Mediaevalia* 13: 207–26.

1992. *The Undivine Comedy: Detheologizing Dante*. Princeton: Princeton University Press.

1994. "'Cominciandomi dal principio infino a la fine' (*Vita Nuova* XXIII.15): Forging Anti-Narrative in the *Vita Nuova*." In Moleta, ed. 1994. Pp. 119–40.

1997. "Guittone's *Ora parrà*, Dante's *Doglia mi reca*, and the *Commedia*'s Anatomy of Desire." In Barański, ed. 1997c. Pp. 3–23.

1998a. "Canto XX: True and False See-ers." In *Lectura Dantis: Inferno*. Eds. Allen Mandelbaum, Anthony Oldcorn, and Charles Ross. Berkeley: University of California Press. Pp. 275–86.

1998b. "Dante and Cavalcanti (On Making Distinctions in Matters of Love): *Inferno V* in its Lyric Context." *Dante Studies* 116: 31–63.

2000a. "Dante and Francesca da Rimini: Realpolitik, Romance, Gender." *Speculum* 75: 1–28.

2000b. "Medieval Multiculturalism and Dante's Theology of Hell." In *The Craft and the Fury: Essays in Memory of Glauco Cambon*. Ed. Joseph Francese. *Italiana* 9: 82–102.

2003. "Beyond (Courtly) Dualism: Thinking about Gender in Dante's Lyrics." In Barolini and Storey, eds. 2003. Pp. 65–89.

2004. "Editing Dante's *Rime* and Italian Cultural History: Dante, Boccaccio Petrarca . . . Barbi, Contini, Foster-Boyde, De Robertis." *Lettere italiane* 61: 509–42.

and Wayne Storey, eds. 2003. *Dante for the New Millennium*. New York: Fordham University Press.

Roland Barthes. 1957. *Mythologies*. Paris: Seuil.

1968. "The Death of the Author." In *Image, Music, Text*. Trans. S. Heath. New York: Hill and Wang, 1977. First published in French, 1968. Pp. 142–8.

Robert Bartlett. 1986. *Trial by Fire and Water: The Medieval Judicial Ordeal*. Oxford: Clarendon Press.

Lucia Battaglia Ricci. 1983. *Dante e la tradizione letteraria medievale*. Pisa: Giardini.

1988. "Struttura sacra e 'sacrato poema.'" In Barblan, ed. 1988. Pp. 295–321.

Carlo Battisti. 1955–56. "Le egloghe dantesche." *Studi danteschi* 33: 61–111.

Carla Benedetti. 1999. *L'ombra lunga dell'autore: Indagine su una figura cancellata*. Milan: Feltrinelli.

V. Stanley Benfell. 1992. "Nimrod, the Ascent to Heaven, and Dante's 'ovra inconsummabile.'" *Dante Studies* 110: 77–94.

1995. "Prophetic Madness: The Bible in *Inferno* XIX." *MLN* 110: 145–63.

1997. "Biblical Truth in the Examination Cantos of Dante's *Paradiso*." *Dante Studies* 115: 89–110.

Walter Benjamin. 1928. *The Origin of German Tragic Drama*. Trans. John Osborne. London: NLB, 1977. First published in German 1928.

Robert Benson and Giles Constable, eds. 1982. *Renaissance and Renewal in the Twelfth Century*. Cambridge, MA: Harvard University Press.

Aldo S. Bernardo and Anthony L. Pellegrini, eds. 1983. *Dante, Petrarch, Boccaccio: Studies in the Italian Trecento in Honor of Charles S. Singleton*. Binghamton, NY: MRTS.

Enrico Berti. 1973. "Politica." In *ED*, vol. 4. 1973. Pp. 585–7.

Luca Bianchi. 1994. "'Aristotele fu un uomo e poté errare': Sulle origini della critica al principio d'autorità." In *idem*, ed. *Filosofia e teologia nel Trecento: Studi in ricordo di Eugenio Randi*. Louvain-la-Neuve: FIDEM. Pp. 509–33.

Giuseppe Billanovich. 1961. "Tra Dante e Petrarca." *Italia mediaevale e umanistica* 4: 201–21.

1994. "L'altro stil nuovo: Da Dante teologo a Petrarca filologo." *Studi petrarcheschi* 9: 1–99.

1996. *Petrarca e il primo umanesimo*. Padua: Edizioni Antenore.

R. Howard Bloch. 1983. *Etymologies and Genealogies: A Literary Anthropology of the French Middle Ages*. Chicago: University of Chicago Press.

2003. *The Anonymous Marie de France*. University of Chicago Press.

Hans Blumenberg. 1966. *The Legitimacy of the Modern Age*. Trans. Robert M. Wallace. Cambridge, MA: MIT Press, 1983. First published in German 1966.

Daniela Boccassini. 2003. *Il volo della mente. Falconeria e Sofia nel mondo mediterraneo: Islam, Federico II, Dante*. Ravenna: Longo.

Pietro Boitani. 2003. "Moby-Dante?" In Barolini and Storey, eds. 2003. Pp. 435–50.

Corrado Bologna. 2002. "Canto XXX." In Güntert and Picone eds., 2002. Pp. 457–72.

Lina Bolzoni. 1995. *La stanza della memoria*. Turin: Einaudi.

Antonio Borra. 2000. *Guittone d'Arezzo e le maschere del poeta*. Ravenna: Longo.

Arno Borst. 1957–1963. *Der Turmbau von Babel: Geschichte der Meinungen über Ursprung und Vielfalt der Sprachen und Volker*. 4 vols. Stuttgart: Hiersemann.

John Boswell. 1994. "Dante and the Sodomites." *Dante Studies* 112: 63–76.

Steven Botterill. 1992. "Not of this World: Spiritual and Temporal Powers in Dante and Bernard of Clairvaux." *Lectura Dantis* 10: 8–21.

1994. "'Però che la divisione non si fa se non per aprire la sentenzia de la cosa divisa' (*Vita Nuova* 14, 13): The *Vita Nuova* as Commentary." In Moleta, ed. 1994. Pp. 61–76.

1996a. "Introduction." In Dante Alighieri. *De Vulgari Eloquentia*. Ed. and trans. Steven Botterill. Cambridge: Cambridge University Press. Pp. ix–xxvi.

1996b. "The Trecento: Minor Writers." In Brand and Pertile, eds. 1996. Pp. 108–27.

1997. "Dante and the Authority of Poetic Language." In Iannucci, ed. 1997. Pp. 167–80.

2005. "The Trecento Commentaries on Dante's *Commedia*." In Minnis and Johnson, eds. 2005. Pp. 590–611.

Pierre Bourdieu. 1992. *The Rules of Art: Genesis and Structure of a Literary Field*. Trans. Susan Emanuel. Stanford, CA: Stanford University Press. First published in French 1992.

1994. *Practical Reason: On the Theory of Action*. Stanford, CA: Stanford University Press, 1998. First published in French 1994.

William Bowsky. 1960. *Henry VII in Italy: The Conflict of Empire and City-State, 1310–13*. Lincoln, NB: University of Nebraska Press.

Patrick Boyde. 1971. *Dante's Style in his Lyric Poetry*. Cambridge: Cambridge University Press.

1993. *Passion and Perception in Dante's 'Commedia.'* Cambridge: Cambridge University Press.

Vittore Branca. 1967. "Poetica del rinnovamento e tradizione agiografica nella *Vita nuova*." In *Studi in onore di Italo Siciliano*. Florence: Olschki. Pp. 123–48.

and Giorgio Padoan, eds. 1966. *Dante e la cultura veneta; atti del convegno studi organizzato dalla Fondazione Cini*. Volume 21 in *Civiltà Veneziana*. Florence: Olschki.

Peter Brand and Lino Pertile, eds. 1996. *Cambridge History of Italian Literature*. Cambridge: Cambridge University Press.

Kevin Brownlee. 1984. "Why the Angels Speak Italian: Dante as Vernacular *Poeta* in *Par.* XXV." *Poetics Today* 5: 597–610.

1986. "Ovid's Semele and Dante's Metamorphosis: *Paradiso* XXI-XXIII." *MLN* 101: 67–82.

1990. "*Paradiso* XXVI." *Lectura Dantis* 6: 46–59.

1993. "Dante and the Classical Poets." In Jacoff, ed. 1993. Pp. 100–19.

1997. "The Practice of Cultural Authority: Italian Responses to French Cultural Dominance in *Il Tesoretto*, *Il Fiore*, and the *Commedia*." *Forum for Modern Language Studies* 33: 258–69.

and Walter Stephens, eds. 1989a. *Discourses of Authority in Medieval and Renaissance Literature*. Hanover, NH: University Press of New England.

and Walter Stephens. 1989b. "Introduction." In Brownlee and Stephens, eds. 1989a. Pp. 1–19.

Giorgio Brugnoli. 1965. "Il latino di Dante." In *Dante e Roma*. 1965. Pp. 51–71.

1998. *Studi danteschi, Vol. 1, "Per suo richiamo."* Pisa: Edizioni ETS.

Giorgio Brugnoli and Arsenio Frugoni. 1979. "Introduzione" and "Note." In Alighieri 1979a.

Francesco Bruni. 2003. *La città divisa: Le parti e il bene comune da Dante a Guicciardini*. Bologna: Il Mulino.

Frederick Robert Bryson. 1938. *The Sixteenth Century Italian Duel: A Study in Renaissance Social History*. Chicago: University of Chicago Press.

Jacob Burckhardt. 1869. *The Civilization of the Renaissance in Italy*. Trans. S. G. C. Middlemore. 2 vols. New York: Harper Colophon, 1929, repr. 1958. First published in German 1869.

Kenneth Burke. 1970. *The Rhetoric of Religion*. Berkeley: University of California Press.

G. L. Bursill-Hall. 1971. *Speculative Grammars in the Middle Ages. The Doctrine of 'Partes Orationis' of the Modistae*. The Hague: Mouton.

G. Busnelli and G. Vandelli. 1964. "Notes." In Dante Alighieri. *Il Convivio*. 2 vols. Eds. G. Busnelli and G. Vandelli, introd. by Michele Barbi, appen. A. Quaglio. Florence: Le Monnier, 2nd edn. 1st edn. 1934–1937.

Theodore Cachey, ed. 1995. *Dante Now: Current Trends in Dante Studies*. South Bend, IN: University of Notre Dame Press.

Glauco Cambon. 1966. "Dante and the Drama of Language." In *Dante's Craft: Studies in Language and Style.* Minneapolis: University of Minnesota Press, 1969. First published 1966. Pp. 23–45.

Mary J. Carruthers. 1990. *The Book of Memory: A Study of Memory in Medieval Culture.* Cambridge: Cambridge University Press.

Giuliana Carugati. 1994. "Retorica amorosa e verità in Dante: Il *De Causis* e l'idea della donna nel *Convivio.*" *Dante Studies* 112: 161–76.

Gino Casagrande. 1976. "'I s'appellava in terra il sommo bene' (*Par.* XXVI.134)." *Aevum* 50: 249–73.

Santa Casciani and Christopher Kleinhenz. 2000. "Introduction to *The Fiore.*" In '*The Fiore' and the 'Detto d'Amore.'* Eds. S. Casciani and C. Kleinhenz. Notre Dame, IN: University of Notre Dame Press. Pp. 3–31.

Anthony Cascardi. 1992. *The Subject of Modernity.* Cambridge: Cambridge University Press.

Anthony Cassell. 1984. *Dante's Fearful Art of Justice.* Toronto: University of Toronto Press.

　2001. "'Luna est Ecclesia': Dante and the 'Two Great Lights.'" *Dante Studies* 119: 1–26.

　2004. *The 'Monarchia' Controversy.* Washington, D.C.: The Catholic University of America Press.

Dino Castaldo. 1982. "L'etica del primoloquium di Adamo nel *De vulgari eloquentia.*" *Italica* 59: 3–15.

Adriana Cavarero and Franco Restaino, eds. 1999. *Le filosofie femministe.* Turin: Paravia.

Enzo Cecchini. 2004. "Introduzione." In Uguccione da Pisa. *Derivationes*: 2 vols. Ed. E. Cecchini. Florence: SISMEL. Vol. 1. Pp. xxi–xxviii.

Dino Cervigni and Edward Vasta. 1995. "Introduction." In Dante Alighieri. *Vita Nuova.* Eds., trans., introd. Dino Cervigni and Edward Vasta. Notre Dame, IN: The University of Notre Dame Press. Pp. 1–44.

Gary Cestaro. 1991a. "Irony of the Narrator in the *De Vulgari Eloquentia.*" *Italian Culture* 9: 15–27.

　1991b. "'. . . Quanquam Sarnum biberimus ante dentes . . .': The Primal Scene of Suckling in Dante's *De vulgari eloquentia.*" *Dante Studies* 109 (1991) 119–47.

　1997. "Dante, Boncompagno da Signa, Eberhard the German, and the Rhetoric of the Maternal Body." In *The Rhetoric Canon.* Ed. Brenda Deen Schildgen. Detroit, MI: Wayne State University Press. Pp. 175–97.

　2003a. *Dante and the Grammar of the Nursing Body.* Notre Dame: University of Notre Dame Press.

　2003b. "Queering Nature, Queering Gender: Dante and Sodomy." In Barolini and Storey, eds. 2003. Pp. 90–103.

A. C. Charity. 1966. *Events and their Afterlife: The Dialectics of Christian Typology in the Bible and in Dante.* Cambridge: Cambridge University Press.

Roger Chartier. 1992. *The Order of Books.* Trans. Lydia G. Cochrane. Stanford, CA: Stanford University Press, 1994. First published in French 1992.

M. D. Chenu. 1925. "Maitre Thomas est-il une 'autorité?'" *Revue Thomiste* 30: 187–94.

1927. "Auctor, Actor, Autor." *Bulletin du Cange: Archivium Latinitas Medii Aevi* 3: 81–6.

1950. *Toward Understanding St. Thomas.* Trans. A. M. Landry and D. Hughes. Chicago: Henry Regnery, 1964. First published in French 1950.

Paolo Cherchi and Antonio Mastrobuono, eds. 1988. *Lectura Dantis Newberryana, Volume 1.* Evanston: Northwestern University Press.

James Thomas Chiampi. 1981. *Shadowy Prefaces: Conversion and Writing in the "Divine Comedy."* L'interprete, 24. Ravenna: Longo.

Marguerite Mills Chiarenza. 1980. "Falsity and Fiction in the 'Allegory of the Poets.'" *Quaderni d'Italianistica* 1: 80–86.

1983. "Time and Eternity in the Myths of *Paradiso* XVII." In Bernardo and Pellegrini, eds. 1983. Pp. 133–50.

Anna Chiavacci-Leonardi. 1977. "La *Monarchia* di Dante alla luce della *Commedia.*" *Studi Medievali*, 3rd series, 8.2: 147–83

1991. "Note." In Dante Alighieri. *Commedia.* 3 vols. Ed. Anna Chiavacci-Leonardi. Milan: Mondadori.

Johan Chydenius. 1958. *The Typological Problem in Dante: A Study in the History of Medieval Ideas.* Helsingfors: Academic Book Store.

Caron Cioffi. 1994. "The Anxieties of Ovidian Influence: Theft in *Inferno* XXIV and XXV." *Dante Studies* 112: 77–100.

2000a. "Matelda." In *DE*. Pp. 599–602.

2000b. "Parnassus." In *DE*. Pp. 678–9.

Diskin Clay. 1999. "The Metamorphosis of Ovid in Dante's *Commedia.*" In Picone and Crivelli, eds. 1999. Pp. 69–85.

Flavia Coassin. 1996. "'A te convien tenere altro viaggio': Il problema dell' *auctoritas* e il genere della *Commedia.*" *Quaderni d'Italianistica* 17: 5–32.

Marc Cogan. 1999. *The Design in the Wax.* Notre Dame, IN: University of Notre Dame Press.

Marcia Colish. 1983. *The Mirror of Language: A Study in the Medieval Theory of Knowledge.* Rev. edn. Lincoln: University of Nebraska Press. Pp. 152–220.

Domenico Comparetti. 1872. *Virgil in the Middle Ages.* Trans. E. F. M. Benecke. Princeton: Princeton University Press, 1997. Rpt. of 1885 translation. First published in Italian 1872.

Domenico Consoli. 1971. "Mitriare." *ED*, vol. 3. P. 979.

1973. "Nobiltà e nobile." *ED*, vol. 4. Pp. 58–62.

Gianfranco Contini. 1939. "Introduzione alle *Rime* di Dante." In Contini. 1976. First published 1939. Pp. 3–20.

1957. "Dante come personaggio-poeta della *Commedia.*" In Contini. 1976. First published 1957. Pp. 33–62.

1959. "Alcuni appunti su *Purgatorio* XXVII." In Contini. 1976. First published 1959. Pp. 170–90.

1964. "Preliminari sulla lingua del Petrarca." In Francesco Petrarca. *Canzoniere.* Ed. and introd. Gianfranco Contini. Turin: Einaudi. Pp. vii–xxxv.

1965a. "Filologia e esegesi dantesca." In Contini. 1976. First published 1965. Pp. 113–42.

1965b. "Un'interpretazione di Dante." In Contini. 1976. First published 1965. Pp. 69–112.

1965c. "La questione del *Fiore*." *Cultura e Scuola* 13/14: 768–73.

1968. "Cavalcanti in Dante." In Contini. 1976. First published 1968. Pp. 143–57.

1973. "Un nodo della cultura medievale: La serie *Roman de la Rose-Fiore-Divina Commedia*." In Contini. 1976. First published 1973. Pp. 245–83.

1976. *Un'idea di Dante*. Turin: Einaudi.

Rita Copeland. 1991. *Rhetoric, Hermeneutics and Translation in the Middle Ages*. Cambridge: Cambridge University Press.

Rita Copeland and Stephen Melville. 1991. "Allegory and Allegoresis, Rhetoric and Hermeneutics." *Exemplaria* 3.1: 157–87.

Alison Cornish. 1999. "I miti biblici: La sapienza di Salomone e le arti magiche." In Picone and Crivelli, eds. 1999. Pp. 391–403.

2000a. "A Lady Asks: The Gender of Vulgarization in Late Medieval Italy." *PMLA* 115: 164–80.

2000b. *Reading Dante's Stars*. New Haven: Yale University Press.

2003. "Vulgarizing Science: Vernacular Translation of Natural Philosophy." In Barolini and Storey, eds. Pp. 169–82.

Maria Corti. 1959. "Le fonti del *Fiore di virtù* e la teoria della nobiltà nel Duecento." *Giornale storico della letteratura italiana* 136: 1–82.

1978. "Dante e la Torre di Babele: Una nuova *allegoria in factis*." In *eadem. Il viaggio testuale: Le ideologie e le strutture semiotiche*. Turin: Einaudi. Pp. 243–56.

1981. *Dante a un nuovo crocevia*. Florence: Libreria Commissionaria Sansoni.

1983. *La felicità mentale: Nuove prospettive per Cavalcanti e Dante*. Turin: Einaudi.

1993. *Percorsi dell'invenzione: Il linguaggio poetico e Dante*. Turin: Einaudi.

Dennis Costa. 1971. "Dante as Poet-Theologian." *Dante Studies* 89: 61–72.

Sergio Cristaldi. 1994. *La 'Vita nuova' e la restituzione del narrare*. Messina: Rubbettino Editore.

1999. "Dante, il profetismo goachimita e la donazione di Costantino." *Letture classensi* 29: 7–65.

Jonathan Culler. 1975. *Structuralist Poetics: Structuralism, Linguistics, and the Study of Literature*. Ithaca, NY: Cornell University Press.

1981. "Apostrophe." In *idem. The Pursuit of Signs: Semiotics, Literature, Deconstruction*. Ithaca, NY: Cornell University Press. Pp. 135–54.

Franco Cuomo. 1994. *Nel nome di Dio: Roghi, duelli, e altre ordalie nell'Occidente medievale cristiano*. Rome: Newton Compton.

Ernst R. Curtius. 1948. *European Literature in the Latin Middle Ages*. Trans. W. R. Trask. Princeton: Princeton University Press, 1953. First published in German 1948.

John Dagenais. 1994. *The Ethics of Reading in Manuscript Culture: Glossing the 'Libro de buen amor.'* Princeton, NJ: Princeton University Press.

Antonio D'Andrea. 1982. "La struttura della *Vita nuova*: Le divisioni delle rime." In *idem. Il nome della storia: Studi e ricerche di storia e letteratura*. Naples: Liguori. Pp. 25–58.

1987. "'L'allegoria dei poeti'; nota a *Convivio* II.i." In Picone, ed. 1987b. Pp. 71–8.

Dante e Bologna nei tempi di Dante. 1967. Ed. Facoltà di Lettere e Filosofia dell'Università di Bologna. Bologna: Commissione per i Testi di Lingua.

Dante e Roma: Atti del Convegno di Studi, Roma, 8–10 aprile, 1965. 1965. Florence: Le Monnier.

The Dante Encyclopedia (hereafter *DE*). 2000. Richard Lansing, ed. New York: Garland.

Charles T. Davis. 1957. *Dante and the Idea of Rome*. Oxford: Clarendon Press.

1965. "Education in Dante's Florence." In *idem*. 1984a. First published 1965. Pp. 137–65.

1967. "Brunetto Latini and Dante." In *idem*. 1984a. First published 1967. Pp. 166–97.

1975. "Dante's Vision of History." In *idem*. 1984a. First published 1975. Pp. 23–41.

1980. "Poverty and Eschatology in the *Commedia*." In *idem*. 1984a. First published 1980. Pp. 42–70.

1984a. *Dante's Italy and Other Essays*. Philadelphia: University of Pennsylvania Press.

1984b. "Dante's Italy." In *idem*. 1984a. Pp. 1–22.

1988. "Dante, Machiavelli, and Rome." *Dante Studies* 106: 43–60.

1993. "Dante and Empire." In Jacoff, ed. 1993. Pp. 67–79.

1998. "Canto XIX: Simoniacs." In *Lectura Dantis: Inferno*. Eds. Allen Mandelbaum, Anthony Oldcorn, and Charles Ross. Berkeley: University of California Press. Pp. 262–74.

Manlio Dazzi. 1964. *Il Mussato preumanista (1261–1329): L'ambiente e l'opera*. Vicenza: Neri Pozza.

Margherita De Bonfils-Templer. 1983. "La donna gentile del *Convivio* e il boeziano mito d'Orfeo." *Dante Studies* 101: 123–44.

1990. "Le due *ineffabilità* del *Convivio*." *Dante Studies* 108: 67–78.

Lawrence de Looze. 1997. *Pseudo-Autobiography in the Fourteenth Century: Juan Ruiz, Guillaume de Machaut, Jean Froissart, and Geoffrey Chaucer*. Gainesville, FL: University of Florida Press.

C. F. R. De Hamel. 1984. *Glossed Books of the Bible and the Origins of the Paris Book Trade*. Woodbridge, UK: D.S. Brewer.

Henri De Lubac. 1959–65. *Exégèse médiévale: Les quatre senses de l'écriture*. 2 vols. Paris: Aubier.

Paul De Man. 1971. "Criticism and Crisis." In *idem. Blindness and Insight: Essays in the Rhetoric of Contemporary Criticism*. Introd. Wlad Godzich. 2nd edn, rev. Minneapolis: University of Minnesota Press, 1983. 1st edn. 1971. Pp. 3–19.

1984. "Autobiography as De-Facement." In *idem. The Rhetoric of Romanticism*. New York: Columbia University Press. Pp. 67–82.

Pietro De Marchi. 2002. "Canto XXIV." In Güntert and Picone, eds. 2002. Pp. 373–90.

Maria C. De Matteis. 1970. "Aristotile." In *ED*, vol. 1. Pp. 372–7.

    1980. "Il mito dell'impero romano in Dante: A proposito di *Monarchia* II.i." *Letture classensi* 10: 247–56.

Domenico De Robertis. 1961. *Il libro della 'Vita nuova.'* Florence: Sansoni. 2nd enlarged edn. Pp. 5–173. These pages first appeared in 1st edn. 1961.

    1970. *Il libro della 'Vita nuova.'* Florence: Sansoni. 2nd enlarged edn. Pp. 177–278. [N.B., these pages added to 2nd edn; pagination otherwise the same].

    1973. "La prima vocazione di Dante." In *idem.* 2001. First published 1973. Pp. 3–29.

    1981. "La forma dell'evento: Una (quasi) datazione dantesca." In *idem.* 2001. First published 1981. Pp. 91–102.

    1984. "Introduzione" and "Note." In Dante Alighieri. *Opere minori*, vol. 1, pt. 1, pt. Eds. Domenico De Robertis and Gianfranco Contini. Milan and Naples: Ricciardi.

    1986. "Cavalcanti e la Bibbia." In *idem.* 2001. First published 1986. Pp. 31–9.

    1988. "Note." In Alighieri 1988.

    2001. *Dal primo all'ultimo Dante.* Florence: Le Lettere.

    2002. *Introduzione.* Vol. 2, pts. 1 and 2. In Dante Alighieri. *Rime.* 3 vols. Introd. and ed. Domenico De Robertis. Florence: Le Lettere.

Jacques Derrida. 1967. *Of Grammatology.* Trans. G. C. Spivak. Baltimore, MD: Johns Hopkins University Press, 1976. First published in French 1967.

    1974. *Glas.* Trans. P. Leavey, Jr. and Richard Rand. Lincoln, NB: University of Nebraska Press. 1986. First published in French 1974.

    1978. *Writing and Difference.* Trans. Alan Bass. Chicago: University of Chicago Press.

Francesco Di Capua. 1945. *Insegnamenti retorici medievali e dottrine estetiche moderne nel "De vulgari eloquentia" di Dante.* Naples: Loffredo.

Giuseppe Di Scipio. 1980. *The Presence of Pauline Thought in the Works of Dante.* Lewiston, NY: Mellen Press.

    1995. "*Paradiso* XXIV." In *Dante's 'Divine Comedy'; Introductory Readings III: 'Paradiso.'* Special issue of *Lectura Dantis* 16–17: 352–70.

Giuseppe Di Scipio and Aldo Scaglione, eds. 1988. *The "Divine Comedy" and the Encyclopedia of the Arts.* Amsterdam: John Benjamins.

Carlo Dionisotti. 1965. "Dante nel Quattrocento." In *Atti del Congresso Internazionale di Studi Danteschi.* 1965. Pp. 333–78.

    1967. *Geografia e storia della letteratura italiana.* Turin: Einaudi.

Francesco D'Ovidio. 1876. "Sul trattato *De vulgari eloquentia* di Dante Alighieri." *Archivio Glottologico Italiano* 2: 59–110.

    1901. *Studii sulla Divina Commedia.* Milan and Palermo: Sandron.

    1931. "Dante e la filosofia del linguaggio." In *idem. Studii sulla Divina Commedia, vol 1.* Naples: Guida. First published 1892. Pp. 291–325.

Roger Dragonetti. 1961a. *Aux frontières du langage poétique.* Volume 9 in *Romanica Gandensia.* Ghent: Romanica Gandensia.

    1961b. "Le sens du cercle et de le poète: Commentaire grammaticale d'un passage du *Convivio* (IV.vi.3–6)." In *idem.* 1961a. Pp. 78–92.

1961c. "La conception du langage poétique dans le 'De vulgari eloquentia' de Dante." In *idem.* 1961a. Pp. 9–77.

1968. *Pèlerin de la sainte Face.* Volume II in *Romanica Gandensia* 9. Ghent: Romanica Gandensia.

1989. "Dante and Frederick II: The Poetry of History." *Exemplaria* 1: 1–15.

Peter Dronke. 1970. *Poetic Individuality in the Middle Ages.* Oxford: Clarendon Press.

1986. *Dante and the Medieval Latin Traditions.* Cambridge: Cambridge University Press.

1994. *Verse with Prose from Petronius to Dante: The Art and Scope of the Mixed Form.* Cambridge, MA: Harvard University Press.

1997. *Dante's Second Love: The Originality and the Contexts of the 'Convivio.'* Leeds: The Society for Italian Studies.

Kevin Dunn. 1994. *Pretexts of Authority: The Rhetoric of Authorship in the Renaissance Preface.* Stanford, CA: Stanford University Press.

Robert M. Durling. 1965. *The Figure of the Poet in Renaissance Epic.* Cambridge, MA: Harvard University Press.

1992. "The Audience(s) of the *De Vulgari Eloquentia* and the *Petrose*." *Dante Studies* 110: 25–36.

2001. "'Mio figlio ov'è?' (*Inferno* X, 60)." In Picone, ed. 2001. Pp. 303–29.

2003. "Guido Cavalcanti in the *Vita Nuova*." In Ardizzone, ed. 2003. Pp. 177–85.

Robert M. Durling and Ronald L. Martinez. 1990. *Time and the Crystal: Studies in Dante's "Rime Petrose."* Berkeley: University of California Press.

1996. "Introduction" and "Notes." In Dante Alighieri. *Inferno.* Volume 1 of *The Divine Comedy of Dante Alighieri.* 3 vols. Ed. and trans. Robert M. Durling; comm. Robert M. Durling and Ronald L. Martinez; illus. Robert Turner. New York: Oxford University Press, 1996.

2003. "Introduction" and "Notes." In Dante Alighieri. *Purgatorio.* Volume 2 of *The Divine Comedy of Dante Alighieri,* 3 vols. Ed. and trans. Robert M. Durling; comm. Robert M. Durling and Ronald L. Martinez; illus. Robert Turner. New York: Oxford University Press.

Terry Eagleton. 1990. *The Ideology of the Aesthetic.* Oxford: Blackwell.

1991. *Ideology.* London: Verso.

Umberto Eco. 1985. "*L'Epistola* XIII, l'allegorismo medievale, il simbolismo moderno." In *idem. Sugli specchi e altri saggi.* Milan: Bompiani. Pp. 215–41.

Elizabeth Eisenstein. 1979. *The Printing Press as an Agent of Change: Communications and Cultural Transformations in Early Modern Europe.* Cambridge: Cambridge University Press.

Norbert Elias. 1939. *The Civilizing Process.* Trans. Edmund Jephcott. Oxford: Blackwell, 1994. First published in German 1939.

Enciclopedia dantesca (hereafter *ED*). 1970–78. 6 vols. Dir. Umberto Bosco. Rome: Istituto dell'Enciclopedia Italiana.

Ercole, Francesco. 1927–1928. *Il pensiero politico di Dante.* Milan: Alpes.

A. Ewert. 1940. "Dante's Theory of Language." *Modern Language Review* 35: 355–66.

Enrico Fenzi. 1986. "Introduzione al *Convivio*." In Dante Alighieri. *Opere minori*. Vol. 2. Eds. F. Chiappelli, *et al.* Turin: UTET. Pp. 11–57

ed. 1999a. *La canzone d'amore di Guido Cavalcanti e i suoi commenti antichi*. Genoa: Il Melangolo.

1999b. "Conflitto di idee e implicazioni polemiche tra Dante e Cavalcanti." In *idem*. 1999a. Pp. 19–70.

2004. "Tra religione e politica: Dante, il 'mal di Francia,' e le 'sacrate ossa' del esecrato San Luigi." *Studi danteschi* 79: 23–117.

Margaret Ferguson. 1975. "Saint Augustine's Region of Unlikeness: The Crossing of Exile and Language." *Georgia Review* 29: 842–64.

2003. *Dido's Daughters: Literacy, Gender, and Empire in Early Modern England and France*. Chicago: University of Chicago Press.

Francis Fergusson. 1953. *Dante's Drama of the Mind*. Princeton, NJ: Princeton University Press.

Joan M. Ferrante. 1975. *Woman as Image in Medieval Literature from the Twelfth Century to Dante*. New York: Columbia University Press.

1984. *The Political Vision of the "Divine Comedy."* Princeton, NJ: Princeton University Press.

Franco Ferrucci. 1971. "Comedìa." *Yearbook of Italian Studies*. 1: 29–52.

2001. "Plenilunio sulla selva: Il *Convivio*, le *Petrose*, la *Commedia*. *Dante Studies* 119: 67–102.

2002. "Allegoria come auto-investitura: Osservazioni sul *Convivio* di Dante." In *Sylva: Studi in onore di Nino Borsellino*. Ed. Giorgio Patrizi. Rome: Bulzoni. Pp. 81–96.

Franco Fido. 1986. "Writing like God, or Better? – Symmetries in Dante's 26th and 27th Cantos." *Italica* 63: 250–64.

1989. "Dall'Antepurgatorio al Paradiso terrestre: Il tempo ritrovato di Dante." *Letture classensi* 9: 65–78.

Joel Fineman. 1986. *Shakespeare's Perjured Eye: The Invention of Poetic Subjectivity in the Sonnets*. Berkeley: University of California Press.

Stanley Fish. 1972. *Self-Consuming Artifacts: The Experience of Seventeenth-Century Literature*. Berkeley: University of California Press.

Gianfranco Folena, ed. 1994. *L'autocommento*. Padua: Esedra.

Fiorenzo Forti. 1971. "Matelda." In *ED*, vol. 3. Pp. 834–40.

Kenelm Foster. 1977. *The Two Dantes and Other Studies*. London: Darton, Longman, and Todd.

Michel Foucault. 1966. *The Order of Things: An Archaeology of the Human Sciences*. New York: Vintage, 1970. First published in French 1966.

1968. "What is an Author?" In *idem*. 1977. Pp. 113–38.

1970. "Nietzsche, Genealogy, History." In *idem*. 1977. Pp. 139–64.

1977. *Language, Counter-Memory, Practice: Selected Essays and Interviews*. Trans. Donald F. Bouchard and Sherry Simon. Ithaca: Cornell University Press. First published in French 1968.

William Franke. 1996. *Dante's Interpretive Journey*. Chicago: University of Chicago Press.

John Freccero. 1959. "Dante's 'Firm Foot' and the Journey without a Guide." In *idem*. 1986. First published 1959. Pp. 29–54.

1961. "Satan's Fall and the *Quaestio de Aqua et Terra*." *Italica* 38: 99–115.

1966. "Dante's Prologue Scene." In *idem*. 1986. First published 1966. Pp. 1–28.

1970. "Introduction to *Paradiso*." In *idem*. 1986. First published 1970. Pp. 209–20.

1972. "Medusa: The Letter and the Spirit." In *idem*. 1986. First published 1972. Pp. 119–35.

1973. "Casella's Song (*Purg*. II.112)." In *idem*. 1986. First published 1973. Pp. 186–94.

1975a. "The Fig Tree and the Laurel: Petrarch's Poetics." *Diacritics* 5: 34–40.

1975b. "Dante's Ulysses: From Epic to Novel." In *idem*. 1986. First published 1975. Pp. 136–51.

1983a. "The Significance of *Terza Rima*." In *idem*. 1986. First published 1983. Pp. 259–71.

1983b. "Manfred's Wounds and the Poetics of *Purgatorio*." In *idem*. 1986. First published 1983. Pp. 195–208.

1983c. "Infernal Irony: The Gates of Hell." In *idem*. 1986. Pp. 93–109. First published 1983.

1986. *Dante: The Poetics of Conversion*. Cambridge, MA: Harvard University Press.

1993. "Introduction to the *Inferno*." In Jacoff, ed. 1993. Pp. 172–91.

John B. Friedman. 1970. *Orpheus in the Middle Ages*. Syracuse: Syracuse University Press, 2000. First published 1970.

1981. *The Monstrous Races in Medieval Art and Thought*. Cambridge, MA: Harvard University Press.

Northrop Frye. 1957. *The Anatomy of Criticism*. Princeton, NJ: Princeton University Press.

1976. *The Secular Scripture: A Study of the Structure of Romance*. Cambridge, MA: Harvard University Press.

Eduardo Fumagalli. 2002. "Canto XXV." In Güntert and Picone, eds. 2002. Pp. 391–404.

Alfredo Galletti. 1912. "La ragione poetica di Albertino Mussato e i poeti teologi." In *Scritti varii di erudizione e di critica in onore di Rodolfo Renier (con xx tavole fuori testo)*. Turin: Fratelli Bocca. Pp. 331–59.

Eugenio Garin. 1952. *L'umanesimo italiano*. Bari: Laterza.

Jesse M. Gellrich. 1985. *The Idea of the Book in the Middle Ages*. Ithaca, NY: Cornell University Press.

Giovanni Getto. 1966. "Il canto della fede." *Letture classensi* 1: 83–108.

Pompeo Giannantonio. 1969. *Dante e l'allegorismo*. Florence: Olschki.

Allen Gilbert. 1928. "Had Dante read the *Politics* of Aristotle?" *PMLA* 43: 606–13.

Etienne Gilson. 1938. *Reason and Revelation in the Middle Ages*. New York: Scribner's.

1939. *Dante and Philosophy*. Trans. D. Moore. New York: Harper and Row, 1963, rept. of 1949 edition. First published in French 1939.

Simon Gilson. 2005. *Dante and Renaissance Florence*. Cambridge: Cambridge University Press.

Claudio Giunta. 1998. *La poesia italiana nell'età di Dante. La linea Bonagiunta-Guinizelli.* Bologna: Il Mulino.

2002. *Versi a un destinatario: Saggio sulla poesia italiana del Medioevo*. Bologna: Il Mulino.

Guglielmo Gorni. 1981. *Il nodo della lingua e il verbo d'Amore*. Florence: Olschki.

1990. *Lettera, Nome, Numero: L'ordine delle cose in Dante*. Bologna: Il Mulino.

1995. "'Paragrafi' e titolo della *Vita nova*." *Studi di filologia italiana* 53: 203–22.

1996. "La *Vita nova* nell'opera di Dante," "Saggio di lettura," "Le 'divisioni' della *Vita Nova*." In Alighieri. 1996. Pp. ix–xlviii, 241–86.

2001. *Dante prima della 'Commedia.'* Fiesole: Cadmo.

Marie-Odile Goulet-Cazé, ed. 2000. *Le commentaire entre tradition et innovations*. Paris: Vrin.

Manuele Gragnolati. 2005. *Experiencing the Afterlife: Soul and Body in Dante and Medieval Culture*. Notre Dame, IN: Notre Dame University Press.

Cecil Grayson. 1963. "Dante e la prosa volgare." In Grayson. 1972a. First published 1963. Pp. 32–60.

1965. "'Nobilior est vulgaris': Latino e volgare nel pensiero di Dante." In Grayson. 1972a. First published 1965. Pp. 1–31.

1972a. *Cinque Saggi su Dante*. Bologna: Patron.

1972b. "Poetica e poesia di Dante." In Grayson. 1972a. Pp. 61–87.

Richard H. Green. 1957. "Dante's 'Allegory of Poets' and the Medieval Theory of Poetic Fiction." *Comparative Literature* 9: 118–28.

Stephen Greenblatt. 1980. *Renaissance Self-Fashioning: From More to Shakespeare*. Chicago: University of Chicago Press.

1988. *Shakespearean Negotiations: The Circulation of Social Energy in Renaissance England*. Berkeley: University of California Press.

2004. *Will in the World*. New York: Norton.

Jody Greene. 2005. *The Trouble with Ownership: Literary Property and Authorial Liability in England, 1660–1730*. Philadelphia: University of Pennsylvania Press.

Thomas M. Greene. 1982a. *The Light in Troy: Imitation and Discovery in Renaissance Poetry*. New Haven: Yale University Press.

1982b. "Petrarch Viator: The Displacements of Heroism." In *idem. The Vulnerable Text: Essays on Renaissance Literature*. New York: Columbia University Press, 1986. First published 1982.

Concetta Carestia Greenfield. 1981. *Humanist and Scholastic Poetics, 1250–1500*. Lewisburg, PA: Bucknell University Press.

Tullio Gregory. "Intenzione." In *ED*, vol. 3. Pp. 480–2.

Elizabeth Grosz. 1995. "Sexual Signatures: Feminism after the Death of the Author." In *eadem. Space, Time, and Perversion: Essays on the Politics of Bodies*. New York: Routledge. Pp. 9–24.

Domenico Guerri. 1907. "Il nome adamitico di Dante." In *idem. Scritti danteschi e d'altra letteratura antica.* Ed. Antonio Lanza, introd. Geno Pampaloni. Rome: De Rubeis, 1990. First published 1907. Pp. 57–73.

Georges Güntert and Michelangelo Picone, eds. 2002. *Lectura Dantis Turicensis. Paradiso.* Florence: Cesati.

Marziano Guglielminetti. 1977. "Dante e il recupero del 'parlar di sé medesimo.'" In *idem. Memoria e scrittura: l'autobiografia da Dante a Cellini.* Turin: Einaudi. Pp. 43–100.

John Guillory. 1983. *Poetic Authority: Spenser, Milton and Literary History.* New York: Columbia University Press.

1993. *Cultural Capital: The Problem of Literary Canon Formation.* Chicago: University of Chicago Press.

Peter Hainsworth. 1988. "Cavalcanti in the *Vita Nuova.*" *Modern Language Review* 83: 586–90.

Richard Halpern. 1991. *The Poetics of Primitive Accumulation.* Ithaca, NY: Cornell University Press.

Robert Hanning. 1977. *The Individual in Twelfth-Century Romance.* New Haven, CT: Yale University Press.

Giosué Harari, ed. 1979. *Textual Strategies: Perspectives in Post-Structuralist Criticism.* Ithaca, NY: Cornell University Press.

Robert P. Harrison. 1988. *The Body of Beatrice.* Baltimore, MD: The Johns Hopkins University Press.

Charles Homer Haskins. 1955. *The Renaissance of the Twelfth Century.* Cambridge, MA: Harvard University Press, 1976. First published 1955.

Nick Havely. 1998. *Dante's Modern Afterlife: Reception and Response from Blake to Heaney.* New York: St. Martin's.

2004. *Dante and the Franciscans: Poverty and the Papacy in the 'Commedia.'* Cambridge: Cambridge University Press

Peter Hawkins. 1985. "Transfiguring the Text: Ovid, Scripture, and the Dynamics of Allusion." In *idem.* 1999. First published 1985. Pp. 180–93.

1988. "John is with Me." In *idem.* 1999. First published 1988. Pp. 54–71.

1992. "Self-Authenticating Artifact." In *idem.* 1999. First published 1992. Pp. 72–95.

1993. "Old and New Parchments." In *idem.* 1999. First published 1993. Pp. 36–53.

1997. "The Scriptural Self." In *idem.* 1999. First published 1997. Pp. 20–35.

1999. *Dante's Testaments: Essays in Scriptural Imagination.* Stanford, CA: Stanford University Press.

and Rachel Jacoff. 2003. "Still Here: Dante after Modernism." In Barolini and Storey, eds. 2003. Pp. 451–64.

Richard Helgerson. 1983. *Self-Crowned Laureates: Spenser, Johnson, Milton and the Literary System.* Berkeley: University of California Press.

Ronald Herzman. 1992. "Dante and the Apocalypse." In *The Apocalypse in the Middle Ages.* Eds. R. Emmerson and B. McGinn. Ithaca, NY: Cornell University Press. Pp. 398–413.

Ralph Hexter. 1986. *Ovid and Medieval Schooling: Studies in Medieval School Commentaries on Ovid's "Ars Amatoria," "Epistulae ex Ponte," and "Epistulae Heroidum."* Munich: Arbeo-Gesellschaft.

Thomas Hill. 1982. "Adam's Noon: *Paradiso* XXVI.139–142." *Dante Studies* 100: 93–7.

Robert Hollander. 1968. "Dante's Use of *Aeneid* I in *Inferno* I and II." *Comparative Literature* 20: 142–56. Now in *idem.* 1983d. Pp. 117–54.

1969. *Allegory in Dante's "Commedia."* Princeton, NJ: Princeton University Press.

1974. "*Vita Nuova*: Dante's Perceptions of Beatrice." In *idem.* 1980a. First published 1974. Pp. 11–30.

1975a. "Babytalk in Dante's *Commedia*." In *idem.* 1980a. First published 1975. Pp. 115–29.

1975b. "*Purgatorio* II: Cato's Rebuke and Dante's 'Scoglio.'" In *idem.* 1980a. First published 1975. Pp. 91–105.

1976. "Dante as Theologus-Poeta." In *idem.* 1980a. First published 1976. Pp. 39–89.

1977. "The Validity of Boccaccio's Self-Exegesis in His *Teseida*." *Medievalia e Humanistica* n.s. 8: 163–83.

1980a. *Studies in Dante.* Ravenna: Longo.

1980b. "The Tragedy of Divination." In *idem.* 1980a. Pp. 131–218

1983a. "*Inferno* 1.63: 'Chi per lungo silenzio parea fioco' e la tradizione esegetica." In *idem.* 1983d. Pp. 23–79.

1983b. "Tragedia nella *Commedia*." In *idem.* 1983d. Pp. 117–54.

1983c. "Travisamenti danteschi dell'*Eneide*." In *idem.* 1983d. Pp. 81–115.

1983d. *Il Virgilio dantesco: Tragedia nella "Commedia."* Florence: Olschki.

1988. "*Paradiso* XXX." *Studi danteschi* 60: 1–33.

1990. "*Purgatorio* II: The New Song and the Old." *Lectura Dantis* 6: 28–45.

1992. "Dante and Cino da Pistoia." *Dante Studies* 110: 201–31.

1993. "Dante and His Commentators." In Jacoff, ed. 1993. Pp. 226–36.

1996. "Dante's Deployment of *Convivio* in the *Comedy*." *Electronic Bulletin of the Dante Society of America [EBDSA]* (www.princeton.edu/~dante/ebdsa/), October 7, 1996.

2000. "Commentary." In Dante Alighieri. *Inferno.* Trans. Robert Hollander and Jean Hollander; introd. and comm. Robert Hollander. New York: Doubleday.

2003. "Commentary." In Dante Alighieri. *Purgatorio.* Trans. Robert Hollander and Jean Hollander; introd. and comm. Robert Hollander. New York: Doubleday.

2005. "*Paradiso* 4.14: Dante as Nebuchadnezzar?" *Electronic Bulletin of the Dante Society of America [EBDSA]* (www.princeton.edu/~dante/ebdsa/), May 17, 2005.

2007. "Commentary." In Dante Alighieri. *Paradiso.* Trans. Robert Hollander and Jean Hollander; introd. and comm. by Robert Hollander. New York: Doubleday.

George Holmes. 1986. *Florence, Rome, and the Origins of the Renaissance.* Oxford: Clarendon Press.

Olivia Holmes. 2000. *Assembling the Lyric Self: Authorship from Troubadour Song to Italian Poetry Book*. Minneapolis, MN: University of Minnesota Press.

2001. "Dante's Two Beloveds: Ethics as Erotic Choice." *Annali d'Italianistica* 19: 25–51.

Forthcoming. *Dante's Two Beloveds: Ethics as Erotic Choice*. New Haven: Yale University Press.

Bruce W. Holsinger. 1996. "The Homoerotic Subject of the *Divine Comedy*." In *Premodern Sexualities*. Eds. Carla Freccero and Louise Fradenburg. New York: Routledge. Pp. 243–74.

David Hult. 1986. *Self-Fulfilling Prophecies: Readership and Authority in the First 'Roman de la Rose.'* Cambridge: Cambridge University Press.

1989. "Author/Narrator/Speaker: The Voice of Authority in Chrétien's *Charrete*." In Brownlee and Stephens, eds. 1989a. Pp. 76–96.

R. W. Hunt. 1948. "The Introductions to the *Artes* in the Twelfth Century." In *The History of Grammar in the Middle Ages: Collected Papers*. Ed. G. L. Bursill-Hall. Amsterdam: Benjamins, 1980. First published 1948. Pp. 117–44.

Silvia Huot. 1987. *From Song to Book: The Poetics of Writing in Old French Lyric and Lyrical Narrative Poetry*. Ithaca, NY: Cornell University Press.

ed. 1993. *The 'Romance of the Rose' and its Medieval Readers: Interpretation, Reception, Manuscript Transmission*. Cambridge: Cambridge University Press.

J. K. Hyde. 1973. *Society and Politics in Medieval Italy: The Evolution of the Civil Life, 1000–1350*. New York: St. Martin's.

Amilcare Iannucci. 1973. "Dante's Theories of Genres and the *Divine Comedy*." *Dante Studies* 91: 1–25.

1981. "Autoesegesi dantesca: La tecnica dell'episodio parallelo (*Inferno* 15-*Purgatorio* 11)." In *idem. Forma ed evento nella "Divina Commedia"*. Rome: Bulzoni, 1984. First published 1981. Pp. 83–114.

ed. and introd. 1993a. *Dante e la 'bella scola' della poesia: Autorità e sfida poetica*. Ravenna: Longo.

1993b. "Dante e la 'bella scola' della poesia (*Inferno* 4.64–105)." In *idem* ed. and introd. 1993a. Pp. 19–37.

ed. 1997. *Dante: Contemporary Perspectives*. Toronto: University of Toronto Press.

Ruedi Imbach. 1996. *Dante, la philosophie et les laïcs*. Paris: Éditions du Cerf.

Alfred Ivry. 1998. "Averroes." In *Medieval Philosophy*. Ed. John Marenbon. London: Routledge. Pp. 49–64.

Rachel Jacoff. 1977. "The Poetry of Guido Cavalcanti." Diss. Yale University. Abstract in DAI 39 (1978): 1620A–1621A.

1980. "The Post-Palinodic Smile: *Paradiso* VIII and IX." *Dante Studies* 98: 111–22.

1986. "Introduction." In Freccero. 1986. Pp. ix–xvi.

1987. "Models of Literary Influence in the *Commedia*." In *Medieval Texts and Contemporary Readers*. Eds. L. Finke and M. Shichtman. Ithaca, NY: Cornell University Press. Pp. 158–76.

1988. "Dante, Geremia e la problematica profetica." In Barblan, ed. 1988. Pp. 113–23.

ed. 1993. *The Cambridge Companion to Dante*. Cambridge: Cambridge University Press.

1999. "Dante and the Legend(s) of St. John." *Dante Studies* 117: 45–58.

Rachel Jacoff and Jeffrey T. Schnapp, eds. 1991. *The Poetics of Allusion: Virgil and Ovid in Dante's "Commedia."* Stanford: Stanford University Press.

Rachel Jacoff and William Stephany. 1989. *Inferno 2*. Philadelphia: University of Pennsylvania Press.

Hans Robert Jauss. 1982. *Toward an Aesthetic of Reception*. Trans. Timothy Bahti. introd. Paul de Man. Minneapolis, MN: University of Minnesota Press.

1979. "The Alterity and Modernity of Medieval Literature." *New Literary History* 10: 181–229.

Luis Jenaro-MacLennan. 1960. "Autocomentario en Dante y comentarismo latino." *Vox Romanica* 19: 82–123.

1974. *The Trecento Commentaries on the "Divina Commedia" and the "Epistle to Cangrande."* Oxford: Clarendon Press.

Victoria Kahn. 1983. *Rhetoric, Prudence and Skepticism in the Renaissance*. Ithaca: Cornell University Press.

Peggy Kamuf. 1988. *Signature Pieces: On the Institution of Authorship*. Ithaca: Cornell University Press.

Ernst Kantorowicz. 1931. *Frederick the Second, 1194–1250*. New York: Richard Smith.

1951. "Dante's Two Suns." *University of California Studies in Semitic Philology*. 11: 217–31.

1957. *The King's Two Bodies: A Study in Medieval Political Theology*. Princeton, NJ: Princeton University Press.

Carol Kaske. 1971. "Mt. Sinai and Dante's Purgatory." *Dante Studies* 89: 1–18.

Robert Kaske. 1974. "Dante's *Purgatorio* XXXII and XXXIII: A Survey of Christian History." *University of Toronto Quarterly* 43: 193–214.

1983. "The Seven *Status Ecclesiae* in *Purgatorio* XXXII and XXXIII." In Bernardo and Pellegrini, eds. 1983. Pp. 89–113.

Richard Kay. 1978. "Dante's Double Damnation of Manto." *Res Publica litterarum* 1: 113–28.

1992. "The Intended Readers of Dante's *Monarchia*." *Dante Studies* 110: 57–76.

1994. *Dante's Christian Astrology*. Philadelphia: University of Pennsylvania Press.

1998. "Introduction" and "Commentary." In Dante Alighieri. *Dante's 'Monarchia.'* Trans. and comm. Richard Kay. Toronto: Pontifical Institute of Medieval Studies.

Sarah Kay. 1990. *Subjectivity in Troubadour Poetry*. Cambridge: Cambridge University Press.

E. Kegel-Brinkgreve. 1990. *The Echoing Woods: Bucolic and Pastoral from Theocritus to Wordsworth*. Amsterdam: I.C. Gieben.

Henry Ansgar Kelly. 1989. *Tragedy and Comedy from Dante to Pseudo-Dante*. Berkeley: University of California Press.

Frank Kermode. 1967. *The Sense of an Ending*. New York: Oxford University Press.

V. G. Kiernan. 1988. *The Duel in European History: Honour and the Reign of the Aristocracy*. New York: Oxford University Press.

John Kleiner. 1994. *Mismapping the Underworld: Daring and Error in Dante's "Comedy."* Stanford, CA: Stanford University Press.

Christopher Kleinhenz. 1974. "Dante's Towering Giants: *Inferno* 31." *Romance Philology* 27: 269–85.

    1986. "Dante and the Bible: Intertextual Approaches to the *Divine Comedy*." *Italica* 63: 25–36.

    1990. "The Poetics of Citation: Dante's *Divina Commedia* and the Bible." *Annali d'Italianistica* 8: 346–59.

    1997. "Dante and the Bible: Biblical Citation in *the Divine Comedy*." In Iannucci, ed. 1997. Pp. 74–93.

    2000. "Cino da Pistoia." In *DE*. Pp. 170–1.

Konrad Krautter. 1983. *Die Renaissance der Bukolik in der lateinischen Literatur des 14. Jahrhunderts: Von Dante bis Petrarca*. Theorie und Geschichte der Literatur und der Schönen Künste, Texte und Abhandlungen 65. Munich: Fink.

Richard Lansing. 1992. "Dante's Intended Audience in the *Convivio*." *Dante Studies* 110: 17–24.

Bruno Latour. 1993. *We Have Never Been Modern*. Trans. Catherine Porter. Cambridge, MA: Harvard University Press.

Henry Charles Lea. 1868. *The Duel and the Oath*. Ed. Edward Peters. Additional documents trans. Arthur C. Howland. Philadelphia: University of Pennsylvania Press, 1974. Lea's text first published 1868.

Ulrich Leo. 1951. "The Unfinished *Convivio* and Dante's Rereading of the *Aeneid*." *Medieval Studies* 13: 41–64.

Seth Lerer. 1985. *Boethius and Dialogue: Literary Method in the Consolation of Philosophy*. Princeton, NJ: Princeton University Press.

    1993. *Chaucer and his Readers: Imagining the Author in Late-Medieval England*. Princeton: Princeton University Press.

Robert Lerner. 1986. "Petrarch's Coolness toward Dante." In *Intellectuals and Writers in Fourteenth Century Europe*. Eds. P. Boitani and A. Torti. Cambridge: D. S. Brewer. Pp. 204–25.

Jessica Levenstein. 2003. "The Re-Formation of Marsyas in *Paradiso* 1." In Barolini and Storey eds. 2003. Pp. 408–21.

Stanley Levers. 2002. "The Image of Authorship in the Final Chapter of the *Vita Nuova*." *Italian Studies* 18: 5–19.

C. S. Lewis. 1936. *The Allegory of Love: A Study in Medieval Tradition*. Oxford: Clarendon Press.

Lawrence Lipking. 1981. *The Life of the Poet: Beginning and Ending Poetic Careers*. Chicago: University of Chicago Press.

Massimo Lollini. 2001. *Il vuoto della forma: Scrittura, testimonianza, e verità*. Genoa: Marietti.

Elena Lombardi. 2000. "Syntax of Poetry: Language and Desire in the Middle Ages." Diss. New York University. Abstract in DAI 61 (2000): 1394A.

Dennis Looney. 2004. "Spencer Williams and Dante: An African-American Filmmaker at the Gates of Hell." In *Dante, Cinema, and Television*. Ed. Amilcare Iannucci. Toronto: University of Toronto Press. Pp. 129–44.

Joseph Lowenstein. 2002. *The Author's Due: Printing and the Prehistory of the Copyright*. Chicago: University of Chicago Press.

Gyorgy Lukacs. 1920. *Theory of the Novel*. Trans. Anna Bostock. Cambridge, MA: MIT Press, 1971. First published in German 1920.

Joseph Luzzi. 1998. "Literary History and Individuality in the *De Vulgari Eloquentia*." *Dante Studies* 116: 161–88.

Michele Maccarrone. 1950. "La teoria ierocratica e il canto XVI del *Purgatorio*." *Rivista di storia della chiesa* 4: 359–98.

    1951. "Teologia e diritto canonico nella *Monarchia* III, 3." *Rivista di storia della chiesa* 5: 7–42.

    1952. '*Vicarius Christi*': *Storia del titolo papale*. Rome: Facultas Theologica Pontificii Anthenaei Lateranensis.

    1954. "*Potestas directa* e *potestas indirecta* nei teologi del XII e XIII secolo." In *Sacerdozio e regno da Gregorio VII a Bonifacio VIII. Miscellanea Historiae Pontificiae 18*. Rome: Pontificia Università Gregoriana. Pp. 27–47.

    1955. "Il terzo libro della *Monarchia*." *Studi danteschi* 33: 5–142.

Enrico Malato. 1997. *Dante e Guido Cavalcanti. Il dissidio per la 'Vita nuova' e il 'disdegno' di Guido*. Rome: Salerno.

Alessandro Manzoni. 1868. "Lettera intorno al libro *De vulgari eloquio* di Dante Alighieri." In *idem. Scritti linguistici editi*. Eds. Angelo Stella and Maurizio Vitale. Vol. 19 of *Edizione nazionale e europea delle opere di Alessandro Manzoni*. Milan: Centro Nazionale di Studi Manzoniani, 2000. First published 1868. Pp. 105–20.

Simone Marchesi. 2003. "'Intentio auctoris' tra *Purgatorio* XXII e *Convivio*." In *Leggere Dante*. Ed. Lucia Battaglia Ricci. Ravenna: Longo. Pp. 57–72.

John Marenbon. 1987. *Later Medieval Philosophy (1150–1350): An Introduction*. New York: Routledge.

Aristide Marigo. 1948. "Introduzione." In Dante Alighieri. *De vulgari eloquentia*. Ed. Aristide Marigo, Append. Pier Giorgio Ricci. Florence: Le Monnier, 1968. 3rd edn. 1st edn. 1948. Pp. xv–clvi.

Herbert Marks. 1992. "Hollowed Names: *Vox* and *Vanitas* in *Purgatorio*." *Dante Studies* 110: 135–78.

Guido Martellotti. 1970. "Egloghe." In *ED*, vol. 2. Pp. 644–6.

    1983. *Dante e Boccaccio e altri scrittori dall'Umanesimo al Romanticismo*. Florence: Olschki.

    1971. "Mussato." In *ED*, vol. 3. Pp. 1066–8.

Maria Luisa Meneghetti. 1992. *Il pubblico dei trovatori: La ricezione della poesia cortese fino al XIV secolo*. Turin: Einaudi. 2nd edn. 1st edn. 1984.

Mario Martelli. 2004. "*Purgatorio* XXII." *Studi danteschi* 69: 119–83.

Mario Marti. 1965. "Vita e morte della presunta doppia redazione della *Vita nuova*." *Rivista di cultura classica e medievale* 7: 657–69.

    1970. "Cino da Pistoia." *ED*, vol. 2. Pp. 6–9.

1991. " '. . . 'l'una appresso de l'altra maraviglia' (Dante, *Vita Nuova*, XXIII)." *Giornale storico della letteratura italiana* 168: 481–503.

Antonio Martina. 1972. "Uguccione nel proemio della *Monarchia* di Dante." *L'Alighieri* 13: 69–74.

Lauro Martines. 1979. *Power and Imagination: City-States in Renaissance Italy.* Baltimore, MD: Johns Hopkins University Press, 1988. 2nd edn. 1st edn. 1979.

Ronald L. Martinez. 1977. "Dante, Statius, and the Earthly City." Diss. University of California at Santa Cruz. Abstract in DAI 38 (1978): 6707A.

1983. "The Pilgrim's Answer to Bonagiunta and the Poetics of the Spirit." *Stanford Italian Review* 4: 37–63.

1989. "La 'sacra fame dell'oro' (*Purgatorio* 22.41) tra Virgilio e Stazio: Dal testo all'interpretazione." *Lettura classensi* 18: 177–93.

1991. "Dante Embarks Arnaut." *NEMLA Italian Studies* 15: 5–28.

1995a. "Dante and the Two Canons: Statius in Virgil's Footsteps (*Purgatorio* 21–30)." *Comparative Literature Studies* 32: 151–75.

1995b. "'Nasce il Nilo': Justice, Wisdom, and Dante's *Canzone* 'Tre donne intorno al cor mi son venute.'" In Cachey, ed. 1995. Pp. 15–53.

1997. "Lament and Lamentations in *Purgatorio* and the Case of Dante's Statius." *Dante Studies* 115: 45–88.

1998. "Mourning Beatrice: The Rhetoric of Threnody in the *Vita Nuova*." *Modern Language Notes* 113: 1–29.

2000. "Allegory." In *DE*. Pp. 24–34.

2003a. "Dante's Jeremiads: The Fall of Jerusalem and the Burden of the New Pharisees, the Capetians, and Florence." In Barolini and Storey, eds. 2003. Pp. 301–19.

2003b. "Cavalcanti 'Man of Sorrows' and Dante." In Ardizzone, ed. 2003. Florence: Cadmo. Pp. 187–212.

N.d. "The Political Epistles: Imperial Receptions and the Voice of the Prophet." Unpublished manuscript.

Franco Masciandaro. 1976. *La problematica del tempo nella "Commedia."* Ravenna: Longo.

1991. *Dante as Dramatist: The Myth of the Earthly Paradise and Tragic Vision in the "Divine Comedy."* Philadelphia: University of Pennsylvania Press.

Antonio Mastrobuono. 1979. *Essays on Dante's Philosophy of History.* Florence: Olschki.

Pietro Mazzamuto. 1970. "Cinquecento dieci e cinque." In *ED*, vol. 2. Pp. 10–14.

Jerome Mazzaro. 1981. *The Figure of Dante: An Essay on the "Vita Nuova."* Princeton: Princeton University Press.

1992. "The Vernal Paradox: Dante's Matelda." *Dante Studies* 110: 107–20.

Joseph Mazzeo. 1958. *Structure and Thought in the "Paradiso."* Ithaca, NY: Cornell University Press.

1960. *Medieval Cultural Tradition in Dante's "Comedy."* Ithaca, NY: Cornell University Press.

Angelo Mazzocco. 1993. *Linguistic Theories in Dante and in the Humanists: Studies of Language and Intellectual History in Late Medieval and Early Renaissance Italy*. Leiden: Brill.

Francesco Mazzoni. 1951. "Per la storia della critica dantesca. I. Jacopo Alighieri e Graziolo Bambaglioli (1322–1324)." *Studi danteschi* 30: 157–202.

——— 1955. "L'Epistola a Cangrande." *Rendiconti della Accademia Nazionale dei Lincei. Classe di scienze morali, storiche e filologiche*, ser. 8, 10: 157–98.

——— 1957. "La *Questio de aqua et terra*." *Studi danteschi* 34: 163–204.

——— 1958. "Guido da Pisa interprete di Dante e la sua fortuna presso il Boccaccio." *Studi danteschi* 35: 157–98.

——— 1962. "Il punto sulla *Questio de aqua et terra*." *Studi danteschi* 39: 39–84.

——— 1963. "Pietro Alighieri interprete di Dante." *Studi danteschi* 40: 279–360.

——— 1966a. "Teoresi e prassi in Dante politico." In Dante Alighieri. *Monarchia. Epistole politiche*. Turin: ERI.

——— 1966b. "Le *Epistole* di Dante." In *Conferenze aretine*. Arezzo: Società Dantesca Casentinese. Pp. 47–100.

——— 1976–1978. "Giovanni Boccaccio fra Dante e Petrarca." *Atti e Memorie dell'Accademia Petrarca di lettere, arte e scienze di Arezzo* 42: 15–42.

——— 1979. "Introduzione alla *Questio de aqua et terra*." In Dante Alighieri. *Opere minori*, vol. 2. Eds. P. V. Mengaldo *et al.* Milan and Naples: Ricciardi.

Giuseppe Mazzotta. 1979. *Dante, Poet of the Desert*. Princeton, NJ: Princeton University Press.

——— 1983. "The Language of Poetry in the *Vita nuova*." *Rivista di studi italiani* 1: 3–14.

——— 1984. "Theology and Exile." In *idem*. 1993a. First published 1984. Pp. 174–96.

——— 1986. "The Light of Venus." In *idem*. 1993a. First published 1986. Pp. 56–74.

——— 1993a. *Dante's Vision and the Circle of Knowledge*. Princeton, NJ: Princeton University Press.

——— 1993b. *The Worlds of Petrarch*. Durham, NC: Duke University Press.

——— 1999. *The New Map of the World: The Poetic Philosophy of Giambattista Vico*. Princeton, NJ: Princeton University Press.

——— 2001. "L'esilio da Firenze: Il *De vulgari eloquentia* e il cerchio della frode." In Picone, ed. 2001. Pp. 233–47.

Stuart Y. McDougal, ed. 1985. *Dante among the Moderns*. Chapel Hill, NC: University of North Carolina Press.

Maria Luisa Meneghetti. 1997. *Le origini delle letterature medievali romanze*. Bari and Rome: Laterza.

Pier Vincenzo Mengaldo. 1970a. "Avieo." In *ED*, vol. 1. Pp. 82–3.

——— 1970b. "*De vulgari eloquentia*." In *ED*, vol. 2. 1970. Pp. 399–415.

——— 1978a. *Linguistica e retorica di Dante*. Pisa: Nistri-Lischi.

——— 1978b. "Appunti sul canto XXVI del *Paradiso*." In *idem*. 1978a. Pp. 223–46.

——— 1979. "Introduzione" and "Note" to *De vulgari eloquentia*. In Dante Alighieri. *Opere minori*, vol. 2. Eds. Pier Vincenzo Mengaldo *et al.* Milan and Naples: Ricciardi.

Maria Rosa Menocal. 1987. *The Arabic Role in Medieval Literary History.* Philadelphia: University of Pennsylvania Press.

1991. *Writing in Dante's Cult of Truth from Borges to Boccaccio.* Durham, NC: Duke University Press.

1994. *Shards of Love: Exile and the Origins of the Lyric.* Durham, NC: Duke University Press.

Claudio Mesoniat. 1984. *Poetica theologia: La 'Lucula noctis' di Giovanni Dominici e le dispute letterarie tra '300 e '400.* Rome: Edizioni di Storia e Letteratura.

Jacqueline Miller. 1986. *Poetic License.* New York: Oxford University Press.

James Miller. 1977. "Three Mirrors of Dante's *Paradiso.*" *University of Toronto Quarterly* 46: 263–79.

Maureen Miller. 2005. *Power and the Holy in the Age of the Investiture Conflict: A Brief History with Documents.* Boston: St. Martin's.

Niccolò Mineo. 1968. *Profetismo e apocalittica in Dante. Strutture e temi profetico-apocalittici in Dante: Dalla "Vita nuova" alla "Divina Commedia."* Catania: Università di Catania, Facoltà di lettere e filosofia.

2000. "Il 'commento' come forma della narrazione nella *Divina Commedia.*" *Letture classensi* 29: 131–41.

Alastair J. Minnis. 1984. *Medieval Theory of Authorship: Scholastic Literary Attitudes in the Later Middle Ages.* Philadelphia: University of Pennsylvania Press, 1988, 2nd edn. 1st edn. 1984.

1990. "*Amor* and *Auctoritas* in the Self-Commentary of Dante and Francesco da Barberino." *Poetica* [Tokyo] 32: 25–42.

1991. "*De Vulgari Auctoritate*: Chaucer, Gower, and the Men of Great Authority." In *Chaucer and Gower: Difference, Mutuality and Exchange.* Ed. R. F. Yeager. Victoria, B.C.: English Literary Studies. Pp. 36–74.

2001. *Magister Amoris: The 'Roman de la Rose' and Vernacular Hermeneutics.* New York: Oxford University Press.

and A. B. Scott, with David Wallace, eds. 1988. *Medieval Literary Theory and Criticism, c. 1100–c.1375: The Commentary Tradition.* Oxford: Clarendon Press.

and Ian Johnson, eds. 2005. *The Cambridge History of Literary Criticism; Vol. 2: The Middle Ages.* Cambridge: Cambridge University Press.

Christian Moevs. 1999. "Miraculous Syllogisms: Clocks, Faith, and Reason in *Paradiso* 10 and 24." *Dante Studies* 117: 59–84.

2005. *The Metaphysics of Dante's 'Comedy.'* Oxford: Oxford University Press.

Vincent Moleta. 1978. "The *Vita Nuova* as Lyric Narrative." *Forum Italicum* 12: 369–90.

ed. 1994. *'La gloriosa donna de la mente': A Commentary on the 'Vita Nuova.'* Florence: Olschki.

Louis Adrian Montrose. 1986a. "The Elizabethan Subject and the Spenserian Text." In Parker and Quint, eds. 1986. Pp. 303–40.

1986b. "Renaissance Literary Studies and the Subject of History." *ELR* 16: 5–12.

Edward Moore. 1896. *Studies in Dante, First Series.* Oxford: Clarendon Press.

Colin Morris. 1972. *The Discovery of the Individual, 1050–1200.* London: SPCR.

Edward Muir. 1993. *Mad Blood Stirring: Vendetta and Factions in Friuli during the Renaissance*. Baltimore, MD: Johns Hopkins University Press.

John M. Najemy. 1982. *Corporatism and Consensus in Florentine Electoral Politics, 1280–1400*. Chapel Hill, NC: University of North Carolina Press.

1993. "Dante and Florence." In Jacoff, ed. 1993. Pp. 80–99.

Bruno Nardi. 1917. "La dottrina delle macchie lunari nel secondo canto del *Paradiso*." In *idem*. 1967. First published 1917. Pp. 3–39.

1921a. "La conoscenza umana." In *idem*. 1985. First published 1921. Pp. 135–72.

1921b. "Il linguaggio." In *idem*. 1985. First published 1921. Pp. 173–95.

1921c. "Il concetto dell'impero nello svolgimento del pensiero dantesco." In *idem*. 1967. First published 1921. Pp. 215–75.

1922. "Raffronti fra alcuni luoghi di Alberto Magno e di Dante." In *idem*. 1967. First published 1922. Pp. 63–72.

1923. "Il tomismo di Dante e il P. Busnelli, S. J." In *idem*. 1967. First published 1923. Pp. 341–80.

1930a. "Tre pretese fasi del pensiero politico di Dante." In *idem*. 1967. Pp. 276–310.

1930b. "L'arco della vita (nota illustrativa al *Convivio*)." In *idem*. 1967. First published 1930. Pp. 110–38.

1938. "'Se la prima materia de li elementi era da Dio intesa." In *idem*. 1985. First published 1938. Pp. 197–206.

1940a. "Averroismo del 'primo amico' di Dante." In *idem*. 1985. First published 1940. Pp. 81–107.

1940b. "Dante e la filosofia." In *idem*. 1944a. First published 1940. Pp. 209–45.

1940c. "Il libero arbitrio e la storiella dell'asino di Buridano." In *idem*. 1944a. First published 1940. Pp. 287–303.

1942a. "Dalla prima alla seconda *Vita nuova*." In *idem*. 1944a. First published 1942. Pp. 3–20.

1942b. "Dante Profeta." In *idem*. 1985. First published 1942. Pp. 265–326.

1942c. "La filosofia d'amore nei rimatori italiani del Duecento e in Dante." In *idem*. 1985. First published 1942. Pp. 9–79.

1942d. "La *donatio constantini* e Dante." In *idem*. 1944a. First published 1942. Pp. 109–59.

1944a. *Nel mondo di Dante*. Rome: Edizioni di Storia e Letteratura.

1944b. "Chi e che cosa è Matelda?" In *idem*. 1944a. Pp. 275–84.

1956. "Le rime filosofiche e il *Convivio* nello sviluppo dell' arte e del pensiero di Dante." In *idem*. 1960a. Pp. 1–36.

1959. La caduta di Lucifero e l'autenticità della *Questio de aqua et terra*. Turin: Società Editrice Internazionale.

1960a. *Dal "Convivio" alla "Commedia."* Fasc. 35–9 in the series *Studi storici*. Rome: Istituto Storico Italiano.

1960b. *Il punto sull'Epistola*. Florence: Le Monnier.

1961. "Osservazioni sul medievale 'accessus ad auctores' in rapporto all' *Epistola a Can Grande*." In *idem*. 1966a. First published 1961. Pp. 268–305.

1962. "Dante e Guido Cavalcanti." *Giornale storico della letteratura italiana* 139: 481–512.

1965a. "Filosofia e teologia ai tempi di Dante." In *idem*. 1966a. First published 1965. Pp. 3–109.

1965b. "Tre momenti dell'incontro di Dante con Virgilio." In *idem*. 1966a. First published 1965. Pp. 222–37.

1965c. "Di un'aspra critica di Fra Guido Vernani a Dante." In *idem*. 1966a. First published 1965. Pp. 377–85.

1966a. *Saggi e note di filosofia dantesca*. Milan and Naples: Ricciardi.

1966b. "Tre brevi note alla *Commedia*.'" In *idem*. 1966a. Pp. 309–20.

1967. *Saggi di filosofia dantesca*. Florence: La Nuova Italia, 1967, 2nd edn. 1st edn. 1930.

1979. "Introduzione" and "Note" to *Monarchia*. In Dante Alighieri. *Opere minori*, vol. 2. Eds. Pier Vincenzo Mengaldo *et al*. Milan and Naples: Ricciardi.

1985. *Dante e la cultura medievale*. Paolo Mazzantini. Bari: La Terza, new edn. 1st edn. 1942.

Paola Nasti. 1998. "La memoria del *Canticum* e la *Vita nuova:* Una nota preliminare." *The Italianist* 18: 14–27.

Giovanni Nencioni. 1967. "Dante e la retorica." In *Dante e Bologna*. 1967. Pp. 91–112.

Barbara Newman. 1995. *From Virile Woman to Woman-Christ: Studies in Medieval Religion and Literature*. Philadelphia: University of Pennsylvania Press.

Susan Noakes. 1988. *Timely Reading: Between Exegesis and Interpretation*. Ithaca, NY: Cornell University Press.

1990. "Hermeneutics, Politics, and Civic Ideology in the *Vita Nuova*: Thoughts Preliminary to an Interpretation." *Texas Studies in Language and Literature*, 32: 18–39.

2001. "Dante e lo sviluppo delle istituzioni bancarie a Firenze: 'I subiti guadagni'." In Picone, ed. 2001. Pp. 249–61.

2003. "Virility, Nobility, and Banking: The Crossing of Discourses in the *Tenzone* with Forese." In Barolini and Storey, eds. 2003. Pp. 241–58.

Adriana Noferi. 1977. "Dante: La parola dell'altro e l'altro della parola." In *eadem*. 1998. First published 1977. Pp. 11–51.

1982–3. "Rilettura della *Vita nuova*." In *eadem*. *Riletture dantesche*. Rome: Bulzoni, 1998. First published 1982–3. Pp. 53–89.

Barbara Nolan. 1970. "The *Vita Nuova*: Dante's Book of Revelation." *Dante Studies* 88: 51–77.

Glending Olson. 1982. *Literature as Recreation in the Later Middle Ages*. Ithaca, NY: Cornell University Press.

Walter Ong. 1971. "Latin Language Study as a Renaissance Puberty Rite." In *idem*. *Rhetoric, Romance, and Technology: Studies in the Interaction of Expression and Culture*. Ithaca, NY: Cornell University Press. Pp.113–41.

Paola Pacchioni. 2001. "Lia e Rachele, Matelda e Beatrice." *L'Alighieri* 18: 47–74.

Giorgio Padoan. 1959. "Teseo *figura redemptoris* e il cristianesimo di Stazio." In *idem. Il pio Enea, l'empio Ulisse*. Ravenna: Longo, 1977. First published 1959. Pp. 125–50.

1966. "Cause, strutture e significato del *De situ et figura aque et terre*." In Branca and Padoan, eds. 1966. Pp. 347–66.

1967. "Note." In Dante Alighieri. *La Divina Commedia*. Ed. Giorgio Padoan. Vol. IX of *Le Opere di Dante*. Eds. Vittore Branca, Francesco Maggini and Bruno Nardi. Florence: Le Monnier.

1971. "Manto." *ED*, vol. 3. Pp. 810–11.

1973. "Orfeo." In *ED*, vol. 4. P. 192.

Ileana Pagani. 1982. *La teoria linguistica di Dante*. Naples: Liguori.

Antonio Pagliaro. 1962. "I 'primissima signa' nella dottrina linguistica di Dante." In *idem. Nuovi saggi di critica semantica*. Messina and Florence: G. D'Anna, 2nd edn., 1962. 1st edn., 1956. Pp. 215–46.

Maurizio Palma di Cesnola. 1995. *Semiotica dantesca: Profetismo e diacronia*. Ravenna: Longo.

Pantaleo Palmieri and Carlo Paolazzi, eds. 1991. *Benvenuto da Imola: Lettore degli antichi e dei moderni*. Ravenna: Longo.

Erwin Panofsky. 1957. *Gothic Architecture and Scholasticism*. Cleveland and New York: Meridian Books.

Carlo Paolazzi. 1994. *La 'Vita nuova': Legenda sacra e historia poetica*. Milan: Vita e Pensiero.

1998. *La maniera mutata: Il 'dolce stil nuovo' tra Scrittura e 'Ars poetica.'* Milan: Vita e Pensiero.

Gioacchino Papparelli. 1960. "*Fictio*: La definizione dantesca della poesia." *Filologia romanza* 7: 1–83.

Ettore Paratore. 1968. "Il latino di Dante." In *idem. Tradizione e struttura in Dante*. Florence: Sansoni. Pp. 136–53.

1975. "Stazio." In *ED*, vol. 5. Pp. 419–25.

Deborah Parker. 1993. *Commentary and Ideology: Dante in the Renaissance*. Durham, NC: Duke University Press.

1997. "Interpreting the Commentary Tradition of the *Comedy*." In Iannucci, ed. 1997. Pp. 240–58.

2000. (Untitled review). *Renaissance Quarterly*. 53.1: 239–42.

Patricia Parker and David Quint, eds. 1986. *Literary Theory/Renaissance Texts*. Baltimore, MD: Johns Hopkins University Press.

Alessandro Passerin d'Entrêves. 1952. *Dante as a Political Thinker*. Oxford: Clarendon Press.

Manlio Pastore Stocchi. 1966. "Dante, Mussato, e la tragedia." In Branca and Padoan, eds. 1966. Pp. 251–62.

1970. "Epistole." In *ED*, vol. 2. Pp. 703–10.

Lee Patterson. 1990. "On the Margin: Postmodernism, Ironic History, and Medieval Studies." *Speculum* 65: 87–108.

Jean Pepin. 1970. *Dante e la tradition de l'allegorie*. Paris: Vrin.

1999. "La théorie dantesque de l'allégorie, entre le *Convivio* et la *Lettera a Cangrande*." In Picone and Crivelli, eds. 1999. Pp. 51–68.

Lino Pertile. 1991. "Pella bianca, pella nera." In *idem*. 2005. First published 1991. Pp. 213–34.

1993. "Dante's *Comedy* Beyond the *Stil Nuovo*." *Lectura Dantis* 13: 47–77.

1994. "Il nodo di Bonagiunta." In *idem*. 2005. First published 1994. Pp. 85–113.

1996. "Lettera aperta a Robert Hollander sui rapporti tra *Commedia* e *Convivio*." *Electronic Bulletin of the Dante Society of America [EBDSA]* (www.princeton.edu/~dante/ebdsa/), October 8, 1996.

1997a. "La puttana e il gigante (*Purgatorio* XXXII, 148–60)." In Barański, ed. 1997c. Pp. 243–72.

1997b. "Dante Looks Forward and Back: Political Allegory in the *Epistles*." *Dante Studies* 115: 1–17.

1998. *La puttana e il gigante: Dal Cantico dei Cantici al Paradiso Terrestre di Dante*. Ravenna: Longo.

Larry Peterman. 1973. "Dante's *Monarchia* and Aristotle's Political Thought." *Studies in Medieval and Renaissance History* 10: 3–40.

Edward Peters. 1995. "The Shadowy, Violent Perimeter: Dante Enters Florentine Political Life." *Dante Studies* 113: 69–87.

Giorgio Petrocchi. 1988. "San Paolo in Dante." In Barblan, ed. 1988. Pp. 235–48.

Armando Petrucci. 1979. *Libri, scrittura e pubblico nel Rinascimento*. Bari: Laterza.

1995. *Writers and Readers in Medieval Italy: Studies in the History of Written Culture*. Trans. Charles Radding. New Haven, CT: Yale University Press.

André Pézard. 1940. *Le 'Convivio' de Dante: Sa lettre, son esprit*. Paris: Les belles lettres.

1958. "Le chant des géants." *Bulletin de la Société d'Études Dantesques* 7: 53–72.

1967. *La rotta gonna: Glose et corrections aux textes mineurs de Dante. Vol. 1: 'Vita Nuova,' Rime, 'Convivio.'* Paris: Didier.

1973. "Daniel et Dante ou les vengeances de Dieu." *Studi danteschi* 50: 1–96.

Patricia Phillippy. 1995. *Love's Remedies: Recantation and Renaissance Lyric Poetry*. Lewisburg, PA: Bucknell University Press.

Michelangelo Picone. 1977a. "Strutture poetiche e strutture prosastiche nella *Vita nuova*." *MLN* 92: 117–29.

1977b. "Modelli e struttura nella *Vita nuova*." *Studi e problemi di critica testuale* 15: 50–61.

1979. *'Vita nuova' e tradizione romanza*. Padua: Liviana.

1987a. "La *Vita nuova* fra autobiografia e tipologia." In *idem* ed. 1987b. Pp. 59–69.

ed. 1987b. *Dante e le forme dell'allegoresi*. Ravenna: Longo.

1987c. "*Purgatorio* 27: Passaggio rituale e *translatio* poetica." *Medioevo romanzo* 12: 389–402.

1993. "L'Ovidio di Dante." In Iannucci, ed. 1993a. Pp. 107–44.

ed. 1994. *L'Enciclopedismo medievale*. Ravenna: Longo.

ed. 1995a. *Guittone D'Arezzo nel settimo centenario della morte: Atti del Convegno internazionale di Arezzo, 22–24 aprile 1994*. Florence: Cesati.

1995b. "Guittone e i due tempi del 'canzoniere.'" In *idem* ed., 1995a. Pp. 73–88.

1995c. "Songbook and Lyric Genres in the *Vita Nuova*." In *"Libri poetarum in quattuor species dividuntur": Essays on Dante and "Genre."* Ed. Zygmunt Barański. (Supplement to *The Italianist* 15). Pp. 158–70.

1997a. "Dante and the Classics." In Iannucci, ed. 1997. Pp. 51–73.

1997b. "Dante Rimatore." In Barański, ed. 1997c. Pp. 41–57.

1999. "Dante e i miti." In Picone and Crivelli, eds. 1999. Pp. 21–32.

ed. 2001. *Dante: Da Firenze all'aldilà. Atti del terzo seminaro dantesco internazionale (Firenze 9–11 giugno 2000).* Florence: Cesati.

2003a. *Percorsi della lirica duecentesca.* Florence: Cadmo.

2003b. "Ovid and the *Exul Inmeritus*." In Barolini and Storey, eds. 2003. Pp. 289–307.

and Tatiana Crivelli, eds. 1999. *Dante, mito e poesia: Atti del secondo seminario dantesco internazionale, Monte Verità, Ascona, 23–27 giugno 1997.* Florence: Cesati.

Luigi Pietrobono. 1932. "Il rifacimento della *Vita nuova* e le due fasi del pensiero dantesco." In *idem. Saggi danteschi.* Turin: Nuova Biblioteca Italiana, 1954. First published 1932. Pp. 25–98.

1938. "Filosofia e teologia nel *Convivio* e nella *Commedia*." *Giornale dantesco* 41: 13–71.

David L. Pike. 1997. *Passage through Hell: Modernist Descents, Medieval Underworlds.* Ithaca, NY: Cornell University Press.

Raffaele Pinto. 1994. *Dante e le origini della cultura letteraria moderna.* Paris: Champion.

Ralph Pite. 1994. *The Circle of Our Vision: Dante's Presence in English Romantic Poetry.* Oxford: Clarendon Press.

Ubaldo Pizzani. 1971. "Fulgenzio." In *ED*, vol. 3. Pp. 71–2.

Patrizia Grimaldi Pizzorno. 1994. "Matelda's Dance and the Smile of the Poets." *Dante Studies* 112: 115–32.

J. G. A. Pocock. 1975. *The Machiavellian Moment: Florentine Political Thought and the Atlantic Republican Tradition.* Princeton, NJ: Princeton University Press.

Elizabeth Wilson Poe. 1984. *From Poetry to Prose in Old Provençal: The Emergence of the "Vidas," the "Razos," and the "Razos de Trobar."* Birmingham, AL: Summa.

Joy Hambuechen Potter. 1990. "Beatrice, Dead or Alive: Love in the *Vita Nuova*." *Texas Studies in Language and Literature* 32: 60–84.

Regina Psaki. 1996. "The Sexualized Body in Dante and the Medieval Context." *Annali della storia dell'esegesi* 13: 539–50.

2003. "Love for Beatrice: Transcending Contradiction in the *Paradiso*." In Barolini and Storey, eds. 2003. Pp. 115–30.

Antonio Enzo Quaglio. 1964. "Prima fortuna della glossa garbiana a 'Donna me prega' del Cavalcanti." *Giornale storico della letteratura italiana* 141: 336–68.

Edwin Quain. 1945. "The Medieval *Accessus ad Auctores*." *Traditio* 3: 215–64.

David Quint. 1975. "Epic Tradition and *Inferno* IX." *Dante Studies* 93: 201–7.

1983. *Origin and Originality in Renaissance Literature: Versions of the Source.* New Haven, CT: Yale University Press.

1986. "Introduction." In Parker and Quint, eds. 1986. Pp. 1–19.

Amedeo Quondam. 1970. "Corona." *ED*, vol. 2. Pp. 212–13.

Jean-Michel Rabaté. 1985. "A Portrait of the Artist as a Bogeyman." *Oxford Literary Review* 7: 62–90.

Guy Raffa. 1992. "Enigmatic 56's: Cicero's Scipio and Dante's Cacciaguida." *Dante Studies* 110: 121–34.

1996. "Dante's Mocking Pastoral Muse." *Dante Studies* 114: 271–91.

2000a. *Divine Dialectic: Dante's Incarnational Poetry.* Toronto: University of Toronto Press.

2000b. "Five Hundred Ten and Five." In *DE*. Pp. 380–2.

Ezio Raimondi. 1966. "Dante e il mondo ezzeliniano." In Branca and Padoan, eds. 1966. Pp. 52–69.

1967. "Una città nell'*Inferno* dantesco." In *idem. Metafora e storia: Studi su Dante e Petrarca.* Turin: Einaudi. First published 1967. Pp. 39–64.

Pio Rajna. 1890. "Lo schema della *Vita nuova.*" *Biblioteca delle scuole italiane* 2: 161–4.

1902. "Per le divisioni della *Vita nuova.*" *Strenna dantesca* 1: 111–14.

1921. "Il trattato *De vulgari eloquentia.*" In *Dante: Le vite, le opere, le grandi città dantesche, Dante e l'Europa.* Eds. G. Alimi *et al.* Milan: Treves. Pp. 77–86.

Daniel J. Ransom. 1977. "*Panis Angelorum*: A Palinode in the *Paradiso.*" *Dante Studies* 95: 81–94.

Giovanni Reggio. 1969. *Le egloghe di Dante.* Florence: Olschki.

Timothy J. Reiss. 1992. *The Meaning of Literature.* Ithaca, NY: Cornell University Press.

Pier Giorgio Ricci. 1965a. "Introduzione." In Dante Alighieri. *Monarchia.* Ed. Pier Giorgio Ricci. Vol. 5 in *Le opere di Dante Alighieri.* Edizione nazionale a cura della Società dantesca italiana. Verona: Mondadori.

1965b. "Dante e l'impero di Roma." In *Dante e Roma.* 1965. Pp. 137–49.

1966. "L'ultima fase del pensiero politico di Dante e Cangrande Vicario imperiale." In Branca and Padoan, eds. 1966. Pp. 367–72.

1971. "Monarchia." In *ED*, vol. 3: 993–1004.

Paul Ricoeur. 1983. *Time and Narrative.* Trans. Kathleen McLaughlin and David Pellauer. Chicago: University of Chicago Press, 1984. First published in French, 1983.

Silvia Rizzo. 1990. "Petrarca, il latino e il volgare." *Quaderni petrarcheschi* 7: 7–40.

Stefano Rizzo. 1969. "Il *De vulgari eloquentia* e l'unità del pensiero linguistico di Dante." *Dante Studies* 87: 69–88.

Giorgio Ronconi. 1976. *Le origini delle dispute umanistiche sulla poesia (Mussato e Petrarca).* Rome: Bulzoni.

Albert Rossi. 1985. "*Miro gurge* (*Par.* 30.68): Virgilian Language and Textual Pattern in the River of Light." *Dante Studies* 103: 79–102.

Sherry Roush. 2002. *Hermes' Lyre: Italian Poetic Self-Commentary from Dante to Tommaso Campanella.* Toronto: University of Toronto Press.

Vittorio Russo. 1977. "La *Monarchia* di Dante (tra utopia e progretto)." *Letture classensi* 7: 51–89.

1994. "'Voi che intendendo' e 'Amor che ne la mente': La diffrazione dei significati secondo l'autocommento del *Convivio*." In Folena, ed. 1994. Pp. 11–19.

Paul Saenger. 1997. *Space between Words: The Origins of Silent Reading*. Stanford, CA: Stanford University Press.

Edward Said. 1975. *Beginnings: Intention and Method*. Baltimore, MD: Johns Hopkins University Press.

Bruno Sandkühler. 1967. *Die frühen Dantekommentare und ihr Verhältnis zur mitteralterlichen Kommentartradition*. Munich: Münchner romanistiche Arbeiten.

Gian Roberto Sarolli. 1963. "Dante *scriba Dei*: Storia e simbolo." In *idem*. 1971. First published 1963. Pp. 189–336.

1966a. "Dante's *Katabasis* and Mission." In *idem*. 1971. First published 1966. Pp. 381–419.

1966b. "Autoesegesi dantesca e tradizione esegetica medievale." In *idem*. 1971. First published 1966. Pp. 1–39.

1971. *Prolegomena alla "Divina Commedia."* Florence: Olschki.

1973a. "Salomone." In *ED*, vol. 4. Pp. 1079–83.

1973b. "Nabucodnosor." In *ED*, vol. 4: 1.

Aldo Scaglione. 1988. "Dante and the Ars Grammatica." In Di Scipio and Scaglione, eds. 1988. Pp. 27–42.

Alfredo Schiaffini. 1953. "A proposito dello stile 'comico' di Dante." In *idem*. *Momenti di storia della lingua italiana*. Rome: Edizioni Studium. Pp. 43–56.

1958. "*Poesis* e *poeta* in Dante." In *Studi filologici e litteraria in honorem Leo Spitzer*. Ed. Anna Hatcher Granville. Bern: Franke. Pp. 379–89.

Brenda Schildgen. 2002. *Dante and the Orient*. Urbana, IL: University of Illinois Press.

Giancarlo Schizzerotto. 1976. "Uguccione." In *ED*, vol. 5. Pp. 800–2.

Jeffrey Schnapp. 1986. *The Transfiguration of History at the Center of Dante's "Paradise*. Princeton, NJ: Princeton University Press.

1988. "Trasfigurazione e metamorfosi nel *Paradiso*." In Barblan, ed. 1988. Pp. 273–92.

1989a. "Dante's Sexual Solecisms: Gender and Genre in the *Commedia*." *Romanic Review* 79: 143–63.

1991–2. "Un commento all'autocommento nel *Teseida*." *Studi sul Boccaccio* 20: 185–203.

John A. Scott. 1973. "Dante's Allegory." *Romance Philology* 26 (1973) 558–91.

1977. "*Paradiso* 30." In *Dante Commentaries*. Ed. David Nolan. Totowa, NJ: Rowman and Littlefield. Pp. 159–80.

1990a. "Dante and Philosophy." *Annali d'Italianistica* 8: 258–77.

1990b. "Dante's Allegory of the Theologians." In *The Shared Horizon*. Ed. Tom O'Neill. Dublin: Irish Academic Press. Pp. 27–40.

1995. "The Unfinished *Convivio* as a Pathway to the *Commedia*." *Dante Studies* 113: 31–56.

1996. *Dante's Political Purgatory*. Philadelphia: University of Pennsylvania Press.

1997. "Il mito dell'imperatore negli scritti danteschi." In Picone and Crivelli, eds. 1997. Pp. 89–105.

2003. *"Paradiso* 22.151: 'L'aiuola che ci fa tanto feroci': Philology and Hermeneutics." *Electronic Bulletin of the Dante Society of America [EBDSA]* (www.princeton.edu/~dante/ebdsa/), April 29, 2003.

2004. *Understanding Dante.* Notre Dame, IN: University of Notre Dame Press.

Cesare Segre. 1963a. "Il *Convivio* di Dante Alighieri." In *idem. Lingua, stile e società.* Milan: Feltrinelli, 1973. First published 1963. Pp. 227–70.

1963b. "Volgarizzamenti del Due e Trecento." In *idem. Lingua, stile e società.* Milan: Feltrinelli. Pp. 49–78.

Marianne Shapiro. 1986. "On the Role of Rhetoric in the *Convivio.*" *Romance Philology* 4: 38–64.

1990. *"De vulgari eloquentia": Dante's Book of Exile.* Lincoln, NB: University of Nebraska Press.

1998. *Dante and the Knot of Body and Soul.* New York: St. Martin's.

James Eustace Shaw. 1938. *The Lady 'Philosophy' in the 'Convivio.'* Cambridge, MA: The Dante Society of America.

Prudence Shaw [James]. 1981. "Sul testo della *Monarchia.*" *Studi danteschi* 53: 181–217.

1995. "Introduction." In Dante Alighieri. *Monarchia.* Ed. and trans. Prudence Shaw. Cambridge: Cambridge University Press. 1995. Pp. xiii–xlvi.

2005. [Critical apparatus]. In Dante Alighieri. *Monarchia.* Digital Edition. Ed. Prudence Shaw. Birmingham, UK: Scholarly Digital Editions; Florence: Società Dantesca Italiana.

R. A. Shoaf. 1996. "'Auri sacra fames' and the Age of Gold (*Purg.* XXII, 40–41 and 148–150." *Dante Studies* 96: 195–9.

1983. *Dante, Chaucer, and the Currency of the Word.* Norman, OK: Pilgrim Books.

1988. "The Crisis of Convention in Cocytus: Allegory and History." In J. Stephen Russell, ed. *Allegoresis: The Craft of Allegory in Medieval Literature.* New York: Garland. Pp. 157–69.

Maria Simonelli. 1966. "Il tema della nobiltà in Andrea Capellano e in Dante." *Dante Studies* 84: 51–64.

1970. "*Convivio.*" In *ED*, vol. 1. 1970. Pp. 192–204.

Charles S. Singleton. "*Vita Nuova* XII: Love's Obscure Words." *Romanic Review* 36: 89–102.

1946. "Latin in the *Vita Nuova.*" *Modern Language Notes* 30: 108–12.

1949. *An Essay on the 'Vita Nuova.'* Baltimore, MD: Johns Hopkins University Press, Rpt. 1977.

1954. *Dante Studies 1: Elements of Structure.* Cambridge, MA: Harvard University Press.

1958. *Dante Studies 2: Journey to Beatrice.* Cambridge, MA: Harvard University Press.

1965a. "The Poet's Number at the Center." *MLN* 80: 1–10.

1965b. "The Vistas in Retrospect." MLN 81 (1966): 55–80. First published 1965.

1970–76. "Commentary." In Dante Alighieri. *The Divine Comedy.* 3 vols. Trans. and comm. Charles S. Singleton. Princeton, NJ: Princeton University Press.

Quentin Skinner. 1978. *The Foundations of Modern Political Thought, Vol. 1.* Cambridge: Cambridge University Press,

Beryl Smalley. 1952. *The Study of the Bible in the Middle Ages.* Oxford: Blackwell.

Janet L. Smarr. 1986. *Boccaccio and Fiammetta: The Narrator as Lover.* Urbana, IL: University of Illinois Press.

1987. "Introduction." In Giovanni Boccaccio. *Eclogues.* Ed. and trans. Janet Levarie Smarr. New York: Garland. Pp. viii.–lxx.

1991. "Poets of Love and Exile." In Sowell, ed. 1991. Pp. 137–51.

Madison Sowell, ed. 1991. *Dante and Ovid: Essays in Intertextuality.* Binghamton, NY: MRTS.

John Webster Spargo. 1934. *Virgil the Necromancer: Studies in Virgilian Legends.* Cambridge, MA: Harvard University Press.

Ceslas Spicq. 1944. *Esquisse d'une histoire de l'exégèse latine au moyen age.* Paris: Vrin.

Gayatri Spivak. 1981. "Finding Feminist Readings: Dante–Yeats." In *American Critics in the Poststructuralist Age.* Ed. Ira Konigsberg. Ann Arbor, MI: University of Michigan Press. Pp. 42–65.

Leo Spitzer. 1937. "Osservazioni sulla *Vita nuova* di Dante." Trans. Herta Ament. In *idem. Studi italiani.* Milan: Vita e Pensiero, 1976. First published in German 1937. Pp. 95–146.

1946. "Note on the Poetic and Empirical 'I' in Medieval Authors." *Traditio* 4: 414–22. Also in *idem.* 1959. Pp. 100–12.

1955. "The Addresses to the Reader in the *Commedia.*" In *idem.* 1959. First published 1955. Pp. 574–95.

1959. *Romanische Literaturstudien, 1936–56.* Tübingen: Niemeyer.

1963. *Classical and Christian Ideas of World Harmony; Prolegomena to an Interpretation of the Word "Stimmung."* Ed. Anna Granville Hatcher, introd. René Wellek. Baltimore, MD: Johns Hopkins University Press.

Giorgio Stabile. 1970. "Autore"; "Autorità." In *ED*, vol. 1. Pp. 454–60.

Ruggiero Stefanini. 1991. "*Purgatorio* XXX." *Lectura Dantis* 9: 90–104.

Henry Justin Steinberg. 1999. "The Magnates, the Popolo, and the Lyric: Anthologies of Poetry in Italy from the *Memoriali Bolognesi* to Dante." Diss. University of Minnesota, Twin Cities. Abstract in DAI 60 (2000): 4004A.

2000. "Merchant Bookkeeping and Lyric Anthologizing: Codicological Aspects of Vaticano 3793." *Scrittura e civiltà* 24: 271–88.

2007. *Accounting for Dante: Urban Readers and Writers in Late Medieval Italy.* Notre Dame, IN: University of Notre Dame Press.

William Stephany. 1982. "Pier della Vigna's Self-Fulfilling Prophecies: The 'Eulogy' of Frederick II and *Inferno* 13." *Traditio* 38: 193–212.

1995. "*Paradiso* XXV." In *Dante's 'Divine Comedy'; Introductory Readings III: 'Paradiso.'* Special issue of *Lectura Dantis* 16–17: 371–88.

Karlheinz Stierle. "Canto XXVI." In Güntert and Picone, eds. 2002. Pp. 405–18.

Thomas Clifford Stillinger. 1992. *The Song of Troilus: Lyric Authority in the Medieval Book*. Philadelphia: University of Pennsylvania Press.

Brian Stock. 1996. *Augustine the Reader: Meditation, Self-Knowledge, and the Ethics of Interpretation*. Cambridge, MA: Harvard University Press.

2001. *After Augustine: The Meditative Reader and the Text*. Philadelphia: University of Pennsylvania Press.

Barbara Bargagli Stoffi-Muhlethaler. 1986. "'Poeta,' 'poetare' e sinonimi. Studio semantico su Dante e la poesia duecentesca." *Studi di lessicografia italiana* 8: 5–299.

Gregory Stone. 1994a. "Dante's Averroistic Hermeneutics (On 'Meaning' in the *Vita Nuova*)." *Dante Studies* 112: 133–59.

1994b. *The Death of the Troubadour: The Late Medieval Resistance to the Renaissance*. Philadelphia: University of Pennsylvania Press.

1998. *The Ethics of Nature in the Middle Ages: On Boccaccio's Poetaphysics*. New York: St. Martin's Press.

H. Wayne Storey. 1993. *Transcription and Visual Poetics in the Early Italian Lyric*. New York: Garland.

Sara Sturm-Maddox. 1987. "The *Rime Petrose* and the Purgatorial Palinode." *Studies in Philology* 84: 119–31.

Francesco Suitner. 1999. *Iacopone da Todi: Poesia, mistica, rivolta nell'Italia del Medioevo*. Rome: Donzelli.

T. K. Swing [Seung]. 1962. *The Fragile Leaves of the Sybil: Dante's Master Plan*. Westminster, MD: The Newman Press.

Jeremy Tambling. 1988. *Dante and Difference: Writing in the "Commedia."* Cambridge: Cambridge University Press.

1992. "Dante and Benjamin: Melancholy and Allegory." *Exemplaria* 4: 343–63.

G. Tanturli. 1993. "Guido Cavalcanti contro Dante." In *Le tradizioni del testo*. Eds. F. Gavazzeni and G. Gorni. Milan and Naples: Ricciardi. Pp. 3–13.

Francesco Tateo. 1970a. "Boezio." In *ED*, vol. 1. Pp. 654–58.

1970b. "'Aprire per prosa.' Le premesse critiche della poetica dantesca." In *idem*. 1972. First published 1970. Pp. 53–75.

1971. "La 'nuova materia' e la svolta critica della *Vita nuova*." In *idem*. 1972. First published 1971. Pp. 29–50.

1972. *Questioni di poetica dantesca*. Bari: Adriatico.

Mirko Tavoni. 1984. "*Vita nuova* XXV.3, e altri appunti di linguistica dantesca." *Rivista di letteratura italiana* 2: 9–52.

Charles Taylor. 1989. *Sources of the Self: The Making of the Modern Identity*. Cambridge, MA: Harvard University Press.

David Thompson. 1974. *Dante's Epic Journeys*. Baltimore, MD: Johns Hopkins University Press.

Brian Tierney. 1964. *The Crisis of Church and State, 1050–1300*. Englewood Cliffs, NJ: Prentice Hall.

1972. *Origins of Papal Infallibility, 1150–1350*. Leiden: Brill.

John Took. 1990. *Dante, Lyric Poet and Philosopher: An Introduction to the Minor Works*. Oxford: Clarendon Press.

Paget Toynbee. 1902. *Dante Studies and Researches*. London: Methuen.
    1914. *Concise Dante Dictionary of Proper Names and Notable Matters in the Works of Dante*. Oxford: Clarendon Press.

Charles Trinkaus. 1979. *The Poet as Philosopher: Petrarch and the Formation of Renaissance Consciousness*. New Haven, CT: Yale University Press.

Mario Trovato. 1976. "Il primo trattato del *Convivio* visto alla luce dell'*accessus ad auctores*." *Misure critiche* 6: 5–14.
    1988. "Dante and the Tradition of the Two Beatitudes." In Cherchi and Mastrobuono, eds. 1988. Pp. 19–36.
    1990a. "Dante's Poetics of Good: From Phenomenology to Integral Realism." *Annali d'Italianistica* 8: 231–56.
    1990b. "Dante's Stand against 'l'errore de l'umana bontade': *Bonum*, Nobility and the Rational Soul in the Fourth Treatise of the *Convivio*." *Dante Studies* 108: 79–96.
    1994. "The True 'Donna Gentile' as Opposed to the Apocalyptic Whore." *Dante Studies* 112: 177–227.

Walter Ullman. 1966. *The Individual and Society in the Middle Ages*. Baltimore, MD: The Johns Hopkins University Press.

Jonathan Usher. 1996. "Origins and Duecento." In Brand and Pertile, eds. 1996. Pp. 3–36.

Sebastiano Valerio. 2003. "Lingua, retorica, e poetica nel canto XXVI del *Paradiso*." *L'Alighieri* 44 [n.s. 23]: 83–104.

Alessandro Vettori. 2004. *Poets of Divine Love: Franciscan Mystical Poetry of the Thirteenth Century*. Toronto: University of Toronto Press.

Aldo Vallone. 1963. *La prosa della 'Vita nuova.'* Florence: Le Monnier.
    1965. "La componente federiciana della cultura dantesca." In *Dante e Roma*. 1965. Pp. 347–69.
    1981. *Storia della critica dantesca dal XIV al XX secolo*. 2 vols. Padua: Vallardi.

Thomas Curtis Van Cleve. 1972. *The Emperor Frederick II of Hohenstaufen: Immutator Mundi*. Oxford: Clarendon Press.

Luigi Vanossi. 1979. *Dante e il 'Roman de la Rose': Saggio su 'Il Fiore.'* Florence: Olschki.

Augusto Vasino, Pier Vincenzo Mengaldo, and Firenzo Forti. 1970. "Bologna." In *ED*, vol. 1. Pp. 660–7.

Cesare Vasoli. 1970. "Averroes." In *ED*, vol. 1. Pp. 473–9.
    1979. "Filosofia e Politica in Dante: Fra *Convivio* e *Monarchia*." *Letture classensi* 9: 11–38.
    1983. "Dante e l'immagine enciclopedica del mondo nel *Convivio*." In *'Imago Mundi': La conoscenza scientifica nel pensiero basso medioevale*. Todi: Accademia Tudertina. Pp. 37–73.
    1988a. "Introduzione" and "Note." In Alighieri, 1988.

1988b. "La Bibbia nel *Convivio* e nella *Monarchia*." In Barblan, ed. 1988. Pp. 19–39.

Donald Verene. 1989. In Brownlee and Stephens, eds. 1989a. Pp. 47–59.

Nancy J. Vickers. 1989. "Widowed Words: Dante, Petrarch, and the Metaphors of Mourning." In Brownlee and Stephens, eds. 1989a. Pp. 97–108.

Gustavo Vinay. 1949. "Studi sul Mussato I: Il Mussato e l'estetica medievale." *Giornale storico della letteratura italiana*, 126: 113–59.

1950. "Introduzione" and "Commentario." In Dante Alighieri. *Monarchia*. Ed. and comm. Gustavo Vinay. Florence: Sansoni, 1950.

1959. "Ricerche sul *De vulgari eloquentia*." *Giornale storico della letteratura italiana* 136: 236–74, 367–88.

1962. *Interpretazione della 'Monarchia' di Dante*. Florence: Le Monnier.

Paul Vlajcic. 1995. "Dante's Pastorals: The *Auctor* as Exile." Unpublished seminar paper. Newberry Library Seminar: "From *Auctor* to Author." Fall 1995.

Daniel Waley. 1969. *The Italian City-Republics*. 3rd edn. London and New York: Longman, 1988. 1st edn 1969.

Wendy Wall. 1993. *The Imprint of Gender: Authorship and Publication in the English Renaissance*. Ithaca, NY: Cornell University Press.

David Wallace. 2003. "Dante in England." In Barolini and Storey, eds. 2003. Pp. 422–34.

Robert Weimann. 1996. *Authority and Representation in Early Modern Discourse*. Ed. David Hillman. Baltimore, MD: The Johns Hopkins University Press.

Roberto Weiss. 1942. "Links between the *Convivio* and the *De Vulgari Eloquentia*." *Modern Language Review* 37: 156–68.

1969. *The Renaissance Discovery of Classical Antiquity*. Oxford: Blackwell.

Warman Welliver. 1981. *Dante in Hell: The "De Vulgari Eloquentia."* L'interprete, 21. Ravenna: Longo.

Winthrop Wetherbee. 1972. *Platonism and Poetry in the Twelfth Century*. Princeton, NJ: Princeton University Press.

1984. "'Per te poeta fui, per te cristiano': Dante, Statius, and the Narrator of Chaucer's *Troilus*." In *Vernacular Poetics in the Middle Ages*. Ed. Lois Ebin. Vol. 16 in the series *Studies in Medieval Culture*. Kalamazoo, MI: Medieval Institute Publications. Pp. 153–76.

1988. "Dante and the *Thebaid* of Statius." In Cherchi and Mastrobuono, eds. 1988. Pp. 71–92.

J. H. Whitfield. 1949. *Dante and Virgil*. Oxford: Blackwell.

Jon Whitman. 1987. *Allegory: The Dynamics of an Ancient and Medieval Technique*. Oxford: Clarendon Press.

W. K. Wimsatt and Monroe Beardsley. 1946. "The Intentional Fallacy." In *eidem. The Verbal Icon: Studies in the Meaning of Poetry*. Lexington, KY: University of Kentucky Press, 1954. First published 1946. Pp. 1–23.

Ronald Witt. 1977. "Coluccio Salutati and the Conception of the *Poeta Theologus* in the Fourteenth Century." *Renaissance Quarterly* 30: 539–63.

2000. *"In the Footsteps of the Ancients": The Origins of Humanism from Lovato to Bruni.* Volume 74 in *Studies in Medieval and Reformation Thought.* Ed. Heiko A. Oberman. Leiden: Brill.

Tibor Wlassics. 1975. *Dante narratore: saggi sullo stile della "Commedia."* Florence: Olschki.

Frances Yates. 1966. *The Book of Memory.* Chicago: University of Chicago Press.

Donna Yowell. 1986. "Ugolino's 'Bestial Segno': The *De Vulgari Eloquentia* in *Inferno* XXXII–XXXIII." *Dante Studies* 104: 121–44.

Slavoj Zizek. 1989. *The Sublime Object of Ideology.* London and New York: Verso.

ed. 1994. *Mapping Ideology.* London and New York: Verso.

Paul Zumthor. 1972. *Essai de poétique médiévale.* Paris: Seuil.

1973. "Autobiographie au Moyen Age?" In *idem. Langue, texte, énigme.* Paris: Seuil, 1975. First published 1973. Pp. 165–80.

1980. *Speaking of the Middle Ages.* Lincoln, NB: University of Nebraska Press, 1986. First published in French 1980.

Index of proper names and works cited

(N.B., Dante Alighieri is not included in the index, while his works are cited individually in alphabetical order. When the author is known, the work is cited under the author's name. When the work is anonymous, it is cited by title. Name and works cited in notes are indexed only when discussed.)